Risk Management in Sport

Risk Management in Sport

Issues and Strategies

Third Edition

Edited by
Herb Appenzeller

CAROLINA ACADEMIC PRESS
Durham, North Carolina

Library of Congress Cataloging-in-Publication Data

Appenzeller, Herb.
  Risk management in sport : issues and strategies / Herb Appenzeller. -- 3rd ed.
    p. cm.
  Rev. ed. of: Managing sport and risk management strategies. c2003.
  Includes bibliographical references and index.
  ISBN 978-1-61163-107-4 (alk. paper)
  1. School sports--United States--Management. 2. Risk management--United States.
  I. Appenzeller, Herb. Managing sport and risk management strategies. II. Title.
  GV346.A67 2012
  796.068--dc23
                          2012019057

Carolina Academic Press
700 Kent Street
Durham, North Carolina 27701
Telephone (919) 489-7486
Fax (919) 493-5668
www.cap-press.com

Printed in the United States of America

Dedication

To: Our contributing authors who during this important project, I could never have asked for better partners who shared their experience and expertise with unusual enthusiasm and

To: Ann Terrill Appenzeller who through her efforts, I have been able to complete this task. Her valuable suggestions, patience, encouragement, and helpful insights made this book a reality. Ann became the 33th author of the book.

With admiration and appreciation to all 33 authors.
Herb Appenzeller

Contents

Preface

Sport-related lawsuits continue to escalate in the 21st century. Pressure in the multi-billion dollar sport industry has increased against all who are engaged in the operation of sport. Risk management, long a vital part of business, medical and insurance industries, has become a valuable addition to law and sport in the sport industry. It is obvious that risk management has a vital role in combating the flood of lawsuits that confront all organizations associated with sport on every level. It seems that any adverse decision against an athlete or sport organization results in a costly lawsuit or the threat of a lawsuit. Risk management attempts to curb this trend by providing policies, procedures, safety audits, risk assessments and emergency action plans. Risk management for sport is not easy to define because it deals with complex issues. Herb Appenzeller, a pioneer in sport law and risk management, defines sport risk management as follows:

> Sport risk management is a process that develops a comprehensive risk management plan to eliminate or minimize loss exposure for injuries to participants and spectators and avoid financial loss. Sport risk management strategies need constant reevaluation, compliance with legal duties, and the responsibilities to create a safe environment (*Successful Sport Management* 2008).

John T. Wolohan, professor of sports law, Syracuse University writes in *Athletic Business* that,

> One of the most important tasks is to control or limit an organizations exposure to financial risk — either by insurance or by taking corrective measures that mitigate risks. While there are many ways to reduce an organization's exposure, one of the best is to develop a risk management plan.

He adds:

> In developing an effective risk management plan — which can include everything from the frequency and type of maintenance required on equipment to proper emergency procedures and training for personnel — it is essential that sports and recreation administrators try to identify any and all risks that may be associated with an activity. As a result, one of the first steps is to conduct a risk audit during which administrators walk around the facility and inspect for potential dangers. Inspection of all equipment for wear and tear is important, since the facility is liable for injuries suffered on defective and broken equipment that it knows, or should have known, poses a danger to users.

Wolohan concludes with important advice to all responsible for a safe sports environment:

> It is not enough, however, to conduct only a single or annual audit. For a risk management plan to be effective, it is essential that the plan incorporate a regular, systematic, inspection program that includes a written record of the inspection, including who conducted the audit, the date, any defects found, and any remedies taken to correct them (*Athletic Business* 2010).

Todd Seidler, a risk management expert and director of the sport administration program at the University of New Mexico, emphasizes the need for risk management plans, but cautions those who use such plans when he writes: "Every risk management plan is unique and must be designed specifically for each organization and activity" (Seidler, 2011). Seidler advises personnel responsible for administering the sport program: "not to merely copy other risk management plans when developing a plan for their venue or organization." Later in this book, he suggests that established plans can serve as a guide for a plan, but suggests a specific one for each individual venue or sport organization—not one copied.

Ann Franke, a risk management specialist, writes: "By being prepared and implementing a risk management plan, it is important to make certain that nothing is left to chance" (Franke, 2006).

Scott Clark, Risk Benefits Officer, Miami-Dade County School Board said: "Too often the organizations, which have delegated risk management to middle management positions, are looking to solve their strategic risk management issues with outside consultants." He advises risk managers to get the tools from the Risk and Insurance Management Society (RIMS) and make resources available to the risk managers within the organization (*Risk Central*, 2011).

The purpose of this book is to enable sport administrators to develop risk management plans and procedures, thereby making the sport industry safer. The book provides valuable resource material that, while not an exhaustive list of contracts, forms, laws and risk review guidelines and other important information, can be an effective guide on practical and useful information. The material can be adapted and modified to meet the needs of sport at every level.

In conclusion, Ronald Baron, a risk management pioneer, who started the Center for Sport Law and Risk Management in the early 1970s, said: "Risk management helps those who direct a sports program comply with their legal liabilities, provide safe programs, and enable sports personnel to defend themselves and their programs in the event of a lawsuit" (*Risk Management in Sport*, 2004).

Acknowledgments

Risk management in sport has become a vital factor in promoting safety for all who participate at every level of sport. It is important, even crucial, that resources for risk management are available to set policies and procedures for sport organizations and administrators.

Thirty-two authors with expertise and experience in risk management have contributed to the Third Edition of *Risk Management in Sport: Issues and Strategies*. The list of sport risk management authors reads like a "Who's Who" of sport safety. I am indebted to these experts who so willingly shared their knowledge and practical experience to set guidelines for all who are associated with sport. It is true that no one is immune from litigation; it has escalated beyond belief. As the editor I am grateful for such support for a resource for sport risk management.

Appreciation is due to the following people and sport organizations who also made this important book a reality:

- Linda Lacy and Keith Sipe, publishers of Carolina Academic Press, who have promoted a series of books dealing with sport management, sport risk management and other publications dealing with sport. Their vision as pioneers of sport safety has been a source of encouragement to many authors in a field of study that needs attention.

- Ann Terrill Appenzeller for her outstanding effort in every phase and detail of the book. Her knowledge of the legal aspects of sport and risk management greatly enhanced the preparation of the book.

- Todd Seidler, Director of Sport Management at the University of New Mexico, for his constant assistance in the development of the book. His understanding of the law and risk management has improved the book and his spirit of cooperation and friendship is invaluable.

- Ronald L. Baron, Co-Editor of *From The Gym To The Jury* newsletter who invited me to join him as a consultant with the Center for Sport Law and Risk Management. This enabled me to join him in conducting risk assessments nationwide. He is a valued colleague and friend.

- David Harlowe, Director of the Sport Management Group, for his expertise and dedication to sport safety and risk management.

- Thomas Appenzeller, my son, who has contributed so much to the welfare and safety in sport. His practical background and mission to teach sport safety has been outstanding. His research has contributed to improving all aspects of sport and his dedication to promote safety for all who participate in sport has been important to everyone associated with sport.

- Substantial portions of Chapter 1 and Chapter 20 from J.D. Hawkins, *The Practical Delivery of Sport Medicine Services: A Conceptual Approach*, PRC Publishing, Canton, Ohio, 1993. Such excerpts were reprinted with permission, all other rights reserved. Copyright, 1993, PRC Publishing, Inc., Canton, Ohio.

- *American College of Sport Medicine, Resource Manual for Guidelines for Exercise Testing and Prescription.* Philadelphia, Lea and Febiger, 1988. Reprinted with permission for use in J.D. Hawkins's chapter on "Emergency Preparedness."

Part I

Introduction

*The law expects sport administrators to develop risk management plans
and policies to ensure a safe environment for all who participate in sport.*

Herb Appenzeller

Chapter 1

Risk Management in Sport

The most important task for sport administrators may also be the most overlooked: legal management that includes the implementation of risk management strategies.

Herb Appenzeller

In the 21st century, diverse issues that lead to litigation continue to plague the sport industry. The troublesome issues of the 1980s and 1990s continue to end up in court. Today the issues are no longer just contract disputes or allegations of negligence. There is a trend toward more diverse issues that have tremendous impact on the sport industry.

Sport litigation involves athletes, administrators, athletic trainers, coaches, equipment manufacturers, officials, operators of facilities, physicians and even the unsuspecting spectator. Litigation involves everyone from youth sport to professional sport. It seems that no one is immune from litigation today.

Risk management in the sport industry has become a vital companion of sport law. For years risk management has been emphasized in the medical profession, and the insurance and business professions. With the unprecedented increase in litigation in the sport industry, risk management is extremely important to protect sport participants from injury and sport organizations, on every level, from expensive and damaging lawsuits. Everyone associated with sport is subject to litigation and claims of negligence that have led to injuries that could have been avoided.

Diversity of Lawsuits

A look at a few captions of cases reported in *From The Gym To The Jury,* a sport law newsletter, indicates the diversity of today's lawsuits and enormous awards:

- University Settles with Former Coach for $9 Million on Title IX Violation
- High School Baseball Players File $365,000 Suit Against School District
- Chaperone Ordered to Pay $700,000 for Lack of Supervision
- Ousted Athletic Director Gets $567,000 Settlement on Hazing Case
- Quadriplegic Awarded $11.3 million for Weightlifting Accident
- Teen Struck by Baseball in Batting Cage Awarded $1.15 Million
- Dive in Shallow Water Leads to $76.6 Million in Damages
- Teen Gets Nine Month Sentence for Hazing

- Paralyzed Wrestler Settles For $15 Million
- Dodgeball Head Injury Settled for $96 Million
- Parents Sue Basketball Camp for $2.5 Million

The suits are diverse and the awards have skyrocketed in the past few years. No one is certain how much awards will continue to escalate.

Sport Publications: A Response to Sport Litigation

The now Sport and Recreation Law Organization (SRLA), an organization of legal scholars and practitioners of law, compiled a list of legal publications in the field of sports (SSLASPA 1995). SSLASPA listed only five sport and law texts published in the 1970s. These texts included *From The Gym To The Jury* (H. Appenzeller 1970); *Athletics and the Law* (H. Appenzeller 1975); *Professional Sports and the Law* (L. Sobel 1977); *Physical Education and the Law* (H. Appenzeller 1978); and *The Law of Sports* (J. Weistart and C. Lowell 1979). These books were published in response to litigation in sport begun in the 1960s. In the 1980s, when the number of lawsuits increased dramatically, publications related to sport and law increased to 43. In the 1990s, 38 texts were added to the profession. By 1995, the list of authors had grown from four in the 1970s to 117 who produced 89 texts. Statistics by SSLASPA reported that by 1995 there were a total of seven journals of sport law, 22 sport law newsletters, 12 professional periodicals and 18 videos on a variety of sport law issues. In my opinion, the growth of sport and law publications was an attempt to meet the escalating litigation. It was and is today a desire to meet the needs of those associated with sport by reducing injuries and subsequent lawsuits against all who participate in the sport industry. In 2012 a majority of presentations at the SRLA Conference dealt with risk management issues. In addition to the presentations, a large number of recent books published deal with risk management.

The Rise of Sport Management

After I wrote *From the Gym To The Jury* in 1970, I was overwhelmed with the number of requests to speak on tort liability in sport across the United States. Liability in sport became a "hot topic" in the 1970s and on occasion the term "risk management" would surface. Risk management has been associated with business, and especially the insurance industry, for many years. Loss control, exposure to loss, pre- and post-loss objectives, risk management strategies, and risk management techniques were common terms in both the business and insurance industries prior to the 1970s. In the mid-1970s and especially in the 1980s and the 1990s, risk management became a familiar expression of a program designed to meet the sport litigation crisis head-on. As we enter the 21st century, risk management will become a companion to the sport industry in its attempt to reduce losses and exposures and increase the desire to make the sport industry safer.

Center for Sports Law and Risk Management

In 1987, I joined Ronald Baron and The Center For Sports Law and Risk Management (Center) as a special consultant. After 40 years of involvement in sport as a coach, athletic administrator, professor and director of sport management, I then had an opportunity to actively put into practice risk management strategies. This valuable opportunity to conduct risk reviews at all levels of sport gave me the insight into the problems confronting all who are involved with sport at every level. I now realize the importance of risk management on a firsthand basis. The Center conducted risk reviews across the United States for elementary and secondary schools, colleges and universities, professional sports venues and municipalities. These clients have similar problems. Here are some of the examples we have seen over the years:

- Exit doors locked in sports arenas while events are in progress.
- A lack of policy dealing with potential catastrophic events such as a fire, tornado, earthquake or bomb threat.
- An absence of proper signs in swimming pools, weight rooms, playing fields, racquetball courts, bleachers and other areas.
- A lack of informed consent agreements for participants in many schools.
- A lack of emergency medical response plans for participants and spectators at sports events.
- Accident and injury reports worded in such a way that they cause problems in litigation.
- People with disabilities denied access to facilities, in violation of federal law.
- A lack of expulsion policy for unruly spectators. Ushers, not security personnel, often mistreat spectators.
- Open drains and irrigation heads on playing fields.
- Participants playing on overlapping fields in sports such as softball, soccer, football, baseball and track.
- Areas where water and electricity mix that lack ground fault interrupters (GFIs).
- Inspection of facilities and equipment is often overlooked and not documented.
- Schools often lease facilities without requiring a certificate of insurance from the lessee. In many cases, the lessee is not required to indemnify the lessor in a facility use agreement.
- Insurance contracts often contain exclusions regarding sporting events, resulting in the facility or program having inadequate coverage.
- Glass doors and windows located under or near goals.
- Lack of due process procedures.

These are just a few situations observed during risk reviews that can plague a sport administrator. A risk management program is necessary as well as essential in today's litigious society (Appenzeller and Baron 2011).

Importance of Risk Management

Risks are inherent in sport and even the safest programs can never avoid accidents and injuries. The fact that an injury occurs does not mean that someone is liable. The law does expect, however, that sport administrators develop risk management and loss control programs to ensure a safe environment for all who participate in sport. Risk management has become a crucial part of the overall sport program. It is as important as budgeting, scheduling, insurance coverage, eligibility, equipment and facility management, contracts and other duties.

A problem in the past has been the low priority assigned risk management. For example, a facility manager admitted that if she implemented a risk management plan for her facility, her insurance premiums would be significantly reduced. She said she recognized that risk management is a good idea, but that she would not spend money to save money. Her response is typical of others in the sport industry who understand the need and value of risk management, but put it off, thereby exposing their sport program to losses.

Today insurance costs have skyrocketed, if insurance can even be purchased. Insurance companies are beginning to reward sport programs with an active risk management program by reducing premiums or agreeing to furnish insurance previously denied to some programs. The legislature of a state in the northeastern United States passed legislation providing a ten percent reduction of premiums for one year when a college or university organized a campus-wide risk management committee. This amounted to a savings of $35,000. Risk management should be a vital part of the 21st century and sport industry. Its benefits are many and its goals attainable in reducing injuries and losses.

Ronald Baron, Executive Director of The Center For Sports Law and Risk Management, sums up the importance of risk management when he writes:

> Risk management should help those who direct the sports program comply with their legal duties, provide safe programs and enable sport personnel to defend themselves and their programs in the event of a lawsuit (Baron 2004).

In the following chapters, 32 professionals in sport law and risk management discuss current issues in sport, and risk management strategies designed to make sport safer as we enter the 21st century.

References

Appenzeller, H.T. and T. Appenzeller. 1980. *Sports and the Courts*. Charlottesville, VA: The Michie Co.

Appenzeller, H.T. 2004, 2nd Edition. *Managing Sports and Risk Management Strategies*. Durham, NC: Carolina Academic Press.

Appenzeller, H.T. and R. Baron. 2004. *From The Gym To The Jury*. Greensboro, NC: The Center For Sports Law and Risk Management.

Baron, R. 2004. *Risk Management Manual*. Dallas, TX: The Center For Sports Law and Risk Management.

Chapter 2

The Legal System

The legal system can scare anyone who is not familiar with the ins and outs of the law.

Gil B. Fried

If one asked what the term "law" means, one would probably receive a different answer from each person asked. Law implies a multitude of definitions and concepts. Law is abstract, living, constantly changing, and evolving. Laws could be firm or flexible. At the same time, laws provide predictability, accountability, justice, protection, and even compassion. Law consists of the entire conglomeration of rules, values, and principles that govern daily conduct and can be enforced by either the government or individual citizens through courts. Thus, it is hard to give an exact definition for what is the law. Part of the problem is that laws were meant to change and reflect changes in society. Even if there were no written laws, society would establish moral, ethical, and natural laws to protect individual citizens from one another. That is why some of the earliest writing in recorded history, such as the Hammurabi Code, are laws designed to guide society.

There are three points that need to be addressed prior to analyzing the intricacies of the legal system. The first point is that plaintiffs and their attorneys sue everyone remotely involved in an incident if there is any possibility of liability or monetary recovery. Many individuals claim that this practice is destroying the American legal system. Most people also blame attorneys for this occurrence. While attorneys might be part of the problem, especially sleazy lawyers, they are not the only responsible party. In most cases the problem starts with a party who wants to sue and thinks they will make a fortune if they win a case. This party is called a plaintiff. Some plaintiffs have legitimate concerns while others might try to take advantage of the system. In the current legal system, plaintiff attorneys (especially in personal injury cases) have to sue all potential parties or they might be sued for malpractice. An attorney could be liable for malpractice if they could have recovered from a party, but failed to sue that party. Thus, to avoid being sued themselves, attorneys are forced to make sure all possible parties are sued. Thus, if a case against a certain party might appear to be remote, the reason why that party is being sued is probably due to the fact that an attorney was being thorough.

The second point is that individuals often confuse the law with justice. The law normally provides for one specific interpretation. Justice, however, does not necessarily mean the same thing to all people. Justice varies based on one's education, upbringing, social class, and related factors. Thus, while the law protects one's freedom of speech, many people might not think justice is served by letting a hate group demonstrate on public property. However, our society has determined that laws are often required to protect certain rights/views or people that the rest of society might not cherish or approve.

The third point is that there is a constitutional right to be an idiot and people exercise that right on a daily basis. This means that the law allows people to do stupid things. It is not against the law for someone to cross the street while walking on their hands. This is definitely not a smart activity, but the law does not prohibit such activity and if someone walked across the street on their hands it might cause accidents or other disturbances that might cause others to violate the law.

Types of Laws

Two primary areas of law will be discussed in this text: **common law** and **statutory law.** Since laws passed by legislative bodies (statutory laws) can never cover all potential circumstances, conditions, or occasions, common law can be used to provide specific guidance for interpreting the laws. Common law refers to cases that have been resolved by various courts over the years. The decisions of numerous courts over hundreds of years are combined to form our common law system. Some of the oldest laws still followed today revolved around the sale of land and were adopted by courts over 700 years ago. For example, numerous principles concerning the liability of an individual who failed to live up to a certain standard of conduct have been developed over the past five centuries. These cases comprise common law and provide precedence for future cases involving the same or similar facts. **Precedence** serves to create boundaries by which future cases can be decided. Once a case becomes precedence, all future analysis of the same or similar facts in that jurisdiction will rely upon the prior decision. Subsequent courts cannot ignore or overturn the prior decision unless a legislative body changes the underlying law upon which the decision was based or a higher court overturns the decision. Thus, when the United States Supreme Court concluded that Major League Baseball was exempt from antitrust laws, such a conclusion became precedence (Federal Baseball, 1922). Since there is no higher court than the Supreme Court, and the Supreme Court does not want to overturn this decision, the only way baseball can lose its antitrust exemption would be if the United States Congress changed the antitrust laws to specifically cover baseball.

Statutory laws are laws originating from and passed by legislative bodies. Statutory laws are adopted by all forms of government, including national, state, municipal, county, and city government entities. These laws are only valid for the area governed by the government entity and can cover such topics as zoning, advertising, taxes, or building a sport facility. An example of a statutory law impacting the sport world might be a noise ordinance that prevents a stadium from hosting a concert after a game because the municipality does not want any amplified noise after 10:00 at night. Statutory laws and constitutional laws are analogous in that both types of laws are adopted or changed by a voting system and form the framework of laws which guide our everyday actions. **Constitutional law** refers to laws embodied in the United States Constitution. In addition, each state has its own constitution. An example of constitutional law in sports involves prayer in a locker room. While most athletes are familiar with pre-game prayers, the Constitution prohibits states from endorsing any religion. Thus, if a public high school coach required players to pray before a game, the coach would be violating the constitutionally required separation of church and state. Many commentators call this a wall separating church and state. However, the wall is not a solid wall. The Supreme Court has interpreted this wall of separation to include the highest level of protection for children, while allowing a lower wall for adults who will presumably be less influenced or impacted by the state (government) engaging in a religious type of action. Thus, because adults are less impressionable, there are often prayer sessions starting a legislative session (Marsh, 1983).

The last area of law covered is administrative laws. **Administrative laws** refer to laws, rules, and regulations that are developed, adopted, and enforced by government units responsible for managing specific government agencies. While administrative laws are not as widely applied as statutory or common law, they still affect a variety of sports issues. Large portions of the economy are governed by federal administrative agencies. The regulations adopted by national administrative agencies such as the National Labor Relations Board (NLRB) or the Occupational Safety and Health Administration (OSHA) have the force of law. Besides federal agencies, state administrative agencies have jurisdiction over issues within their state such as workers' compensation, health laws, or local business practices. An example of an administrative law issue in sports can be seen in special taxes levied by some cities (Philadelphia and Pittsburgh as two examples) on professional athletes. Taxing bodies develop the tax rate, judge possible violations, and enforce collections.

The Court System

A court is a tribunal established by governments to hear certain cases and administer justice. Courts exist at various levels in both state and federal court systems. There are three primary court systems; state, federal, and administrative (administrative law courts are not seen frequently in sport cases and will not be discussed in this chapter). Legal authority, procedures, and the types of disputes heard are different in each court system.

State court systems traditionally consist of general or superior jurisdiction courts which are referred to by various names in different states. They are commonly called circuit courts, district courts, superior courts, or courts of common pleas. These courts are the initial trial court where the facts are judged by a jury and/or a judge. The jury/judge will analyze the facts and apply the law to the facts.

If a party to a suit does not feel the law was properly applied, he or she could appeal the case to an appellate court. An appeal is the process by which a party to a suit can challenge the legal decision rendered by a court. The appeals process is designed to guarantee that the court cannot exercise unchecked or abusive power. If the appellate court's decision is also disputed, the litigant can file another appeal to the state's supreme court. State supreme court decisions are final unless the decision involves an issue regarding the federal Constitution, laws, or treaties. Appellate courts and the state supreme court can only review issues of law. They cannot review the facts or re-analyze evidence. Lower courts hear most cases while appellate courts hear fewer cases and only a small number of cases reach the highest appellate court.

Highest Appellate Court
(Supreme Court)
_____

Appellate Court
_____

Trial Court
_____

Most cases are brought to state courts. However, if a dispute involves over $75,000, citizens of different states, or a question involving the Constitution or a federal law, the case would be brought in **federal court** (28 U.S.C. § 1332). Federal courts also hear patent, tax, copyright, maritime, and bankruptcy matters. If a party determines that the federal court misapplied the law, the party can petition a federal court of appeals. The United States is divided into 94 judicial districts, and there are 13 federal courts of appeals. The last resort for any party is to request that the Supreme Court review a case. The process of applying for review by the Supreme Court involves filing *a writ of certiorari. A writ of certiorari* is sent from the Supreme Court to a lower level court when at least four of the nine Supreme Court Justices vote to hear the case. The writ requires the lower court to turn the case over to the Supreme Court. The Supreme Court is often petitioned when there is a conflict between various decisions reached in judicial district courts or appellate courts. In some cases of national emergency the Supreme Court can intervene from the beginning to prevent conflict. Such intervention occurred in the election dispute between President George Bush and challenger Al Gore (Bush, 2001).

Typically, courts are distinguished by the types of cases they can hear. **Criminal courts** only resolve criminal matters in which the people, represented by a public prosecutor, bring charges against individuals who violate the law through the commission of a misdemeanor or felony. Cases between individuals, corporations, business entities, organizations, and government units involving non-criminal matters are resolved primarily in **civil courts**. The O.J. Simpson murder cases provide an excellent distinction between criminal and civil courts. Simpson was first tried by the State of California for allegedly harming state citizens. The criminal case resulted in a not guilty verdict. The double jeopardy rule prohibited Simpson from ever being tried again on the same charges in a criminal case. However, Simpson was subsequently sued by the victims' families in civil court. The criminal court decision has no bearing on the civil court case because a different burden of proof is required by the two courts. In order to convict someone in criminal court, the prosecutors must prove the accused committed the crime beyond a reasonable doubt. On the other hand, a person suing in civil court only has to prove by a preponderance of the evidence that the other side is the guilty party.

Jurisdiction

When a dispute arises involving either the application of a statute, a question of common law, or an individual's rights, the dispute is traditionally resolved through an appropriate **court** system. The court that has the right to hear a case has that right since it exercises jurisdiction over the matter. Courts can only hear a case if they have **jurisdiction** over the people involved or if the issue involved in the case occurred or is located within the court's jurisdiction. If a court does not have jurisdiction, then the court cannot hear the case. Most jurisdiction issues are simple to decide. However, more complex cases often involved more complex jurisdictional issues.

A **state court** has jurisdiction (authority) to hear a case if the case involves an event or activity which occurred within the state. A state court has personal jurisdiction if a disputant lives in that state or has significant contacts within the state. Typical cases brought in state court include breach of contract claims, personal injury suits, and suits involving real estate located in the state. If a high school athlete is injured during a practice they would most likely file their claim in state court if they were suing their coach and school. The issue becomes more complex if they sue an equipment manufacturer from another state.

Jurisdiction can be obtained by a court having jurisdiction over a person/company or the subject matter of the dispute. Thus, Federal Courts have subject matter jurisdiction over a case if the case involves federal issues such as interpreting federal statutes, federal crimes, and the Federal Constitution. Subject matter jurisdiction can also arise if the amount in controversy is over $75,000 and the disputing parties are located in different states. Using our injured high school athlete example, assume the school is in New York, the athlete lives in New York, and the injury occurred in New York. Even if the expected damages are over $100,000, courts in New York would have both personal jurisdiction over the litigants and subject matter jurisdiction based on the incident occurring in its state. However, if the athlete claims the injury was also caused by equipment manufactured in New Jersey, then jurisdiction changes. To avoid favoritism (one state's court ruling against people/companies form another state just because they are based elsewhere), the federal courts would be asked to hear the case since the dispute involves more than $75,000 and litigants are from two different states. Sometimes jurisdiction is easy to establish but other times it might be established by contracts or based on which law the plaintiff decides to sue under. Thus, when a discrimination claim arises, for example, a plaintiff can sometimes sue under a stricter state law or might decide to suc in a federal court under a federal anti-discrimination law.

The Legal System in Action

Detailed rules specify the how, when, and where questions associated with bringing about a lawsuit. These rules differ in each court and are often very complex. An example provides the best method of discussing the structure and processes involved in a lawsuit. The following is a fictitious example of such a case. Sarah Jones was a high school student and interscholastic basketball star in Houston, Texas. While playing in a sanctioned interscholastic event, Jones attempted to slam dunk the ball, but slipped on a water puddle. Jones tore her knee ligaments. She accumulated over $10,000 in medical bills, missed the remainder of the basketball season, lost $4,000 from not being able to work, and missed her chance to possibly receive a basketball scholarship from the University of Houston.

After Jones left the hospital, her father set up an interview with a lawyer to discuss their legal options. The lawyer was Ruth Smith, a young lawyer fresh out of law school. Smith asked numerous questions and discovered from Mr. Jones that he heard one official tell a coach immediately after the accident that the school had failed to sweep the floor prior to the match and the roof had been leaking for over two months. Utilizing her legal prowess, Smith thought she had a great negligence case and accepted the Jones as clients.

Smith initially performed research and discovered that the likely parties that should be sued included the school, the school district, the officials, the athletic director, the coach, and the high school athletic association. Jones, who brought the suit to recover her damages, was called the **plaintiff** while all parties being sued were called **defendants**. Jones and all the defendants lived or operated in Texas. Because there was no federal question, or litigants from different states, Smith's only option was to bring the suit in a Texas state court. Based on the medical expenses and potential future damages, Smith had to bring the case in a specific court with proper jurisdiction.

Smith remembered that special rules applied whenever a governmental entity is sued. Thus, after some initial research, Smith filed a **governmental claim** against the school district. Smith filed the claim specifically to avoid a statute of limitations issue. The **statute**

of limitation required the suit to be filed within a certain time period, or Jones would have been forever barred from filing suit. Each state has their own rules concerning filing a claim against the state. These governmental claim rules are designed to provide the state with notice it might be sued. Some states require the filing of a claim while others allow a party just to name the state in a lawsuit.

Smith prepared a **complaint** which described key facts available to Jones and provided enough information for the opposing side to know why they were being sued. A complaint indicates the title of the case, identifies all the parties, designates in which court the case is being filed, and tells the story of the dispute in a specified legal form. Smith had a specified amount of time within which she had to serve the defendants with a copy of the complaint that she had already filed with the chosen court. Smith was required to personally serve each defendant with the complaint. Some states allow a party to mail a complaint or to serve the complaint through a sheriff.

Within a specified time after receiving the complaint, the defendants filed an **answer** indicating why they were not liable for Jones' injuries. Along with their answer, the defendants served Jones (through her attorney) with several discovery requests. **Discovery** was used as a means to find out what Jones knew about the incident and her damages. Discovery is the process used to discover information about the opposing parties in a suit. Answers have to be given under oath or the penalty of perjury. Discovery tools could have included a request to inspect the gym, an independent medical examination of Jones, and possibly an independent psychological evaluation if Jones was claiming severe or extreme emotional distress.

The discovery requests included a request to produce all relevant documents in Jones' possession, such as medical bills, a request to admit certain facts such as admitting she did not miss any work or she did not receive lower grades as a result of the injury ("Request for Admissions"), specific questions such as her age, her address, or if she has a driver's license (called interrogatories), and a request to take Jones' deposition. Smith responded by serving similar discovery requests on all the defendants. Jones was required to attend a **deposition** where she had to answer numerous questions, under oath, asked by the defendants' attorneys. Smith had the right to request the same types of discovery from the defendants.

After several months of discovery, the defendants filed a **motion for summary judgment**. Summary judgment motions are brought when a party concludes that as a matter of law the undisputed facts are in their favor and they should win without having to go to trial. These motions are solely based on applicable case law and the facts uncovered through the discovery process. Summary judgment is one of several possible pre-trial motions. Other such motions include a demurrer, motion to sever, motion to strike, motion to remove for lack of subject matter jurisdiction and other motions which attack the complaint or require the production of requested discovery material. Such motions are brought when, as a matter of law, one party is or should be required to alter its case. For example, an injured high school athlete might have suffered a great injury, but due to governmental immunity bestowed on the high school principal, the principal could bring a summary judgment motion to be dismissed from the case as a matter of law.

Through summary judgment the judge determined that there were still issues of fact that were in dispute and as such, the judge denied defendants' summary judgment motion. The parties tried to settle the case, but when they were unable to reach a mutually acceptable settlement, they started preparing for trial. Both sides obtained witnesses on their own behalf. The court chose a trial date which was approximately two years after Jones was first injured.

Smith thought the facts favored her client. Her client made a good witness. Thus, Jones demanded a trial by **jury**. The plaintiff in a civil case always has the choice of whether or not he/she wants a jury. The twelve member jury was required to decide who was telling the truth and ultimately what the facts were. Each side prepared trial memoranda explaining its case and provided the memorandum to the judge. After resolving some disputes concerning what evidence would be allowed at trial, the judge allowed the parties to pick a jury. Utilizing a process called **voice dire**, each side interviewed prospective jurors and had the right to dismiss all biased jurors or a limited number of jurors that they just did not want. The size and role of a jury vary in different states. Some juries only examine facts or certain components of a case while other juries are responsible for analyzing all facts and determining damages.

Smith provided an eloquent **opening statement** which Perry Mason would have envied. The defendants also had a strong opening statement on their own behalf. The trial proceeded with Smith calling Sarah as the first witness. The plaintiff always presents his/her case first in civil cases. After answering all the questions asked by Smith, Jones was **cross-examined** by defendants' attorneys who were attempting to refute Jones' testimony or highlight any inconsistencies. Jones' father was a **fact witness** because he had specific facts concerning the accident and injuries. Both sides also acquired the services of **expert witnesses** to testify about the standard of care for schools, doctors to testify about Jones' injuries, and several high school basketball coaches. The trial continued with each side presenting its witnesses and the other side having the opportunity to cross-examine each witness. Documentary evidence was also introduced by each side. Throughout the trial, each side repeatedly made **objections** to certain questions or the introduction of some evidence. The judge was forced to determine, as a matter of law, which side was correct and which questions or evidence were legally allowable.

Each side concluded its questioning and then made its final **closing statement**. The closing statements provided a summary of the facts and law espoused by each side during the trial. The jury was given specific instructions by the judge concerning the law and how the jury was to apply the facts to the law. Based on the evidence presented, the jury returned a verdict in Jones' favor. The jury awarded Jones $14,000 for **actual lost damages** (medical expenses and lost wages) and $20,000 for **pain and suffering**. The lost scholarship was too speculative, thus, the jury was barred from awarding damages for that loss. Damages can only be awarded for definite amounts except when it comes to pain and suffering, where a jury can award an amount based on what they feel is appropriate.

The defendants were not happy with the jury's conclusion. The defendants' attorneys knew they could not challenge the jury's evidentiary conclusion, but felt the judge gave the jury an incorrect instruction concerning the school's duty to Jones. The judge could have overturned the jury's decision if the judge felt it was not supported by law or the facts. However, the judge affirmed the jury's decision. Defendants filed a **notice of appeal** which is the first step in the appeals process. Each side was required to submit a "brief" that outlined its legal analysis and then argue its case in front of three appellate judges. The appellate court, after carefully reviewing the lower court's actions, determined that the lower court made a **procedural mistake** in using an incorrect jury instruction. Therefore, the appellate court **remanded** (sent back) the case to the lower court to retry the case using the correct instruction. The number of judges hearing an appeal varies in different courts. Some appellate courts have as little as three judges while some appellate courts can have over nine judges listening to and analyzing a case. An appellate court can remand a case, uphold the lower court's decision, or overturn the lower court's decision.

Before the new trial began, the sides reached a **settlement** in which the school paid Jones $18,000. By the time Jones finally settled the case, she was in college and three years had elapsed since she brought the suit. The appellate court's reasoning was published in the state's official case registry and became precedence for any future cases dealing with the appropriate jury instruction to give concerning a school's duty to its students. However, from reading the published appellate court's decision, a reader would not know that the case was settled once it was remanded to the lower court. The appellate court report only indicated that it was remanding the case to be retried. Rarely does one discover what happens to cases because lower court decisions are not officially published. Furthermore, most cases are settled and the settlement terms are often confidential. While Jones' fictitious case went to trial, it is estimated that less than five percent of all cases filed ever reach a trial. Most cases are either dismissed prior to trial, settled, or defeated through summary judgment or other defensive maneuvers.

Only state appellate and state supreme court cases are officially published. All federal cases are published. Cases are commonly found in the following reporters: Federal District Court cases can be found in Federal Supplement volumes (cases are cited using the initials "F. Supp."); Federal Appellate cases can be found in the Federal Reporter ("F." or "F.2d" which is the second volume of Federal Reporters); U.S. Supreme Court cases can be found in three different reporters: United States Supreme Court Reports ("U.S."), Supreme Court Reporter ("S. Ct."), and Supreme Court Reports, Lawyer's Edition ("L. Ed."). Nine different reporters exist for various state courts or regional groupings of courts. These cases are found in the following reporters: Atlantic Reporter ("A." or "A. 2d"); Northeastern Reporter ("N.E." or "N.E. 2d."); Northwestern Reporter ("N.W." or "N.W. 2d."); Pacific Reporter ("P." or "P. 2d."); Southeastern Reporter ("S.E." or "S.E. 2d."); Southern Reporter ("So." or "So. 2d."); Southwestern Reporter ("S.W." or "S.W. 2d."); New York Supplement ("N.Y.S."); or California Reporter ("Cal.Rptr.").

In My Opinion

The legal system can scare anyone who is not familiar with the ins and outs of the law. Laws from a variety of sources, including statutory and common law, civil and criminal law, and federal and state law, form a complex patchwork of legal rights, obligations, and standards. The fundamental components discussed in this chapter will be seen in the chapters throughout this book. If a court of appeals is deciding whether or not to overturn a summary judgment decision reached by the trial court, you will now know how the case moved procedurally from obtaining all the undisputed facts to the legal standard that is being challenged on appeal. This chapter should serve as your road map to the legal system.

References

28 U.S.C. § 1332

Anderson, Ronald, Ivan Fox, and David Twomey. 1984. *Business Law.* 12th Edition. Cincinnati, OH: South-Western Publishing Co.

Coughlin, George Gordon. 1983. *Your Introduction To Law,* 4th Edition. New York: Barnes & Noble Books.

Federal Baseball Club v. National League, 259 U.S. 200 (1922).

George W. Bush, et al. v. Albert Gore, Jr., et al., 531 U.S. 98, 121 S. Ct. 525 (2001).

Marsh v. Chambers, 463 U.S. 783 (1983).

Chapter 3

Glossary of Legal Words and Phrases

Risk Management is one of the specialties within the field of management; a decision and management process.

Terrill Johnson Harris

Abrogate: To annul or repeal a law or an order.

Action: A lawsuit or case which one party brings against another in court.

Act of God: An event caused by nature; an act that is unforeseeable due to forces of nature.

Affirm: To concur with and ratify a decision by a lower court.

Appellant: The party who initiates an appeal to an appellate court.

Appellate Court: A court which reviews trials and decisions of lower courts for errors, as distinguished from a trial court where the case is originally filed and decided.

Appellee: The party against whom the appeal is taken; the party on the other side from the appellant.

Assumption of Risk Doctrine: If a person voluntarily places himself in a situation which he knows is dangerous, he consents to or assumes the risk of injury and may be barred from any recovery if he is injured.

Attractive Nuisance Doctrine: In many states, a property owner is liable for injuries to children on the owner's property when the owner knowingly leaves a dangerous instrumentality or creates a dangerous condition in a place apt to be frequented by children who do not realize their peril and are injured. The owner has to take reasonable precautions to prevent injuries to children who the owner knows will frequent the location or who may be attracted to the location by the dangerous condition or instrumentality.

Basis of Appeal: No appellate court will review the decision of a lower court unless the appeal is founded on errors in the former proceedings.

Certiorari: (Latin, "to be informed of"); an order of a higher court to a lower court to transfer the record of a case for review.

Charitable Immunity: The freedom of a charitable institution, such as a hospital, from being held liable for certain actions rendered in pursuit of its charitable undertaking.

Civil Law: Laws established to deal with private rights and remedies, as distinguished from criminal laws.

Class Action: A lawsuit brought on behalf of a large group of persons with similar claims against the same defendant; a few people may sue as representatives of the entire class.

Common Law: The body of law and jurisprudence which was originated, developed, and formulated in England prior to the time of the Colonial settlements in North America and which has become the law in most of the United States, except where it has been abrogated by statutes. In a large measure, the common law established the rules and regulations under which we live.

Complaint: A plaintiff's first formal pleading; a concise and plain statement of the facts on which the plaintiff bases the action. The complaint is followed by defendant's answer.

Comparative Negligence: In most states, the plaintiff's own negligence does not necessarily defeat the right of recovery. Negligence is measured in terms of each person's degree of fault. Even if the plaintiff is negligent, the plaintiff's damages can be reduced by the percentage the plaintiff was at fault. The principle applies differently in each state. In some states, the contributory negligence of the plaintiff will defeat his right to recover except where his negligence was slight compared to that of the defendant. Some states follow the comparative negligence rule only in specific situations, as in the case of employee against employer or certain types of hazardous employment.

Contributory Negligence: In a few states, any negligence, however slight, on the part of the plaintiff will bar the plaintiff's right to recover from the defendant, even if the defendant was negligent.

Criminal Law: The law dealing with offenses against the people and preventing harm to society; it declares which actions are crimes and sets the punishment for such actions.

Defendant: In a civil case, the person or corporation defending against or denying a claim; the person against whom relief is sought. In a criminal case, the person against whom a criminal charge is brought.

Enjoin: To require or direct a person or institution to do a particular act or refrain from doing a particular act.

Felony: A felony is any criminal offense for which the penalty may be death or imprisonment; each state's laws determine whether a crime is a felony or misdemeanor.

Foreseeability: The ability to anticipate or predict in advance; used in the context of a negligence action, a person is responsible for the foreseeable harm caused by his negligent actions, regardless of how the harm actually occurred.

Governmental Immunity: Also called sovereign immunity; an individual or institution cannot sue the government for negligence or certain other torts, unless the government consents to be sued or waives its immunity.

Guest Statute: A statute providing that a driver cannot be liable to a plaintiff "guest" unless the "guest" can prove either gross negligence or intoxication on the part of the defendant driver. To overcome the protection given to a driver by the statute, the "guest" must show: (a) that he was not a "guest" at all but a paying passenger; or (b) that the driver was intoxicated; or (c) that the driver was grossly negligent; or (d) that he did not acquiesce in the driver's reckless conduct or realize that the driver was drunk.

In Loco Parentis: (Latin, "in the place of a parent"); someone who stands in the place of a parent and is charged with the same rights, duties, and responsibilities.

Injunction: An order of the court requiring a party or institution to cease taking certain actions which are alleged to be harmful or to take certain actions to alleviate harm to others. A temporary injunction is an injunction issued for a set period of time and will expire after such period of time. A permanent injunction is an injunction which will stay in effect indefinitely from the date it is entered.

Invitee: One who goes upon the premises of another for business purposes, such as a customer in a store or a spectator to a game. Persons entering the premises of another fall into three general classes: (a) invitees, (b) licensees, and (c) trespassers. The owner of the premises must exercise ordinary care to make the premises safe for invitees, but has a lesser duty of care to licensees and trespassers.

Judgment: In legal sense, the official decision of a court.

Last Clear Chance Doctrine: The person who has the last clear opportunity of avoiding an accident, notwithstanding the negligence of the other party, may be held responsible for the accident. In terms of automobile law, if the driver having the right of way could have avoided an accident but does not do so, he may be held liable regardless of the negligence of the other person. The law does not recognize an indifference to the right of others. In these circumstances, the doctrine of contributory negligence has no place.

Liability: In a legal sense, the responsibility for an action; in civil cases, most often expressed in terms of fault with an accompanying responsibility to pay money damages to an injured party.

Licensee: One allowed to go on the premises of another for his own interest. In many states, the owner owes a licensee a duty of ordinary or reasonable care. Persons have been regarded as licensees when entering another's premises to visit employees of the owner, to transact business with them where the owner has no interest, to sell goods to tenants or employees, or to pursue a child who has run onto the premises.

Litigation: The filing and trial of a lawsuit between two or more parties for the purpose of enforcing an alleged right or recovering money damages for a breach of duty.

Misdemeanor: Any offense less serious than a felony and for which the penalty is normally a fine or imprisonment for less than one year.

Moot: An undecided point not settled by the court but concerning some matter which has, as a practical matter, already been decided by the happening of an event prior to the court's determination.

Negligence: The failure to use reasonable care under the circumstances, contrary to the conduct of a reasonable person. There are many types of negligence: concurrent—where two or more persons acting independently are negligent; gross—an intentional lack or failure to perform a legal duty; per se—negligence in violation of a statute; wanton—used as a partner with gross negligence and emphasizing reckless indifference to the consequences of one's act or omission.

Nuisance: Anything which reasonably interferes with enjoyment of life or property to the detriment of another.

Plaintiff: A person who brings a civil action against another person or institution.

Precedent: A decision of a court that must be followed in identical or similar cases arising at a later time. For example, the lower courts must follow the precedent set by the appellate courts.

Prima Facie: (Latin, "at first sight"); a fact presumed to be true unless disproved by contrary evidence.

Proximate Cause: The primary cause of an injury and without which the injury would not have happened.

Reasonable Person: A non-existent being whose standard of conduct decides negligence suits.

Remand: Action by a higher court to send a matter back to the lower court from which it came, with directions as to what must be done in the lower court.

Res Ipsa Loquitur: (Latin, "the thing speaks for itself"); a presumption of negligence arising when an injury that ordinarily would not happen in the absence of negligence occurs; proof that the instrumentality which caused the injury was under the exclusive control of the negligent party is required.

Respondeat Superior Doctrine: (Latin, "let the master answer"); a master or employer may be held liable for the wrongful acts of his servant or employee if the servant or employee is acting within the legitimate scope of his employment.

Risk Management: One of the specialities within the field of management; a decision and management process.

Statute: An act of the Legislature; refers to the laws passed by Congress and the state legislatures, as distinguished from judicial decisions.

Statute of Limitation: A statute placing a time limit or deadline for filing a lawsuit; a specified period of time after a person is injured or the right to sue has accrued. For example, the time limit for filing negligence suits in many states is three years after the date of the accident. After the limitations period has expired, the injured party is barred from bringing an action.

Summary Judgment: A judgment entered by a court without a trial because there is no genuine dispute about the facts; judgment is entered as a matter of law as applied to undisputed facts.

Tort: A wrongful act or a violation of a legal duty for which a civil action for damages may be brought; there must be a legal duty to the person harmed, a breach of that duty, and damage to the person harmed as the usual or proximate result of the breach of duty.

Vis Major: Act of God.

Part II

Tort Liability Issues

Anyone who engages in sport activities faces exposure to injuries and the possibility of losses regarding property, income through liability to others and life and health.

George Head and Stephen Horn, II
Essentials of Risk Management, Vol. 1

Chapter 4

Warnings, Waivers and Informed Consent

Risk warning and informed consent is one of the most critical aspects of sport risk management.

Richard T. Ball

There are many traditions in athletic administration for which it would be difficult to trace the historical basis. One of these is the requirement of participants and the parents of minors signing a form which constitutes consent to participation and includes language which acknowledges and accepts a certain degree of risk attendant to participation.

In recent years two legal phenomena have combined with this tradition to create a very challenging situation for athletic administrators. The first was the attempt to stem the rising tide of litigation against sport programs by having participants and parents execute documents which purported to *release* or to *waive* their right to sue the sport program from any liability for injuries arising from participation. The second was transference of the legal doctrine of *informed consent* from the practice of medicine to the sport arena. The result is one of the most complex legal issues facing sport programs today.

Duty to Warn of Risk

Legal duties develop a number of ways. Some are created by constitutional or statutory provision and others by administrative regulation, but the most common source is judicial edict. In negligence suits, the determination of whether the defendant owed a *legal duty* to the plaintiff is decided by the court. The criteria for answering this question were eloquently set forth by one court as follows:

> In the decision whether or not there is a duty, many factors interplay: The hand of history, our ideas of morals and justice, the convenience of administration of the rule, and our social ideas as to where the loss should fall. In the end the court will decide whether there is a duty on the basis of the mores of the community, always keeping in mind the fact that we endeavor to make a rule in each case that will be practical and in keeping with the general understanding of mankind (*Kleinknecht v. Gettysburg College* 1993).

A difficulty created by the judicial approach is that the pronouncement of legal duty is always retrospective. Until injury occurs, suit is filed and the court is asked to rule on the question, the parties have no way of being certain whether a duty exists. The *Kleinknecht* case, wherein the small Pennsylvania college attempted to rely on the assertion that it owed no duty to the plaintiff in this matter, the court decided otherwise. Sport programs must, therefore, do their best to anticipate the "ideas of morals and justice..., social ideas as to where the loss should fall ... (and) the mores of the community" in determining their responsibilities related to risk warning. It also behooves them to adopt a conservative approach in deciding "the convenience of administration of the rule ... (and what) will be practical and in keeping with the general understanding of mankind."

In school and youth programs, participation is usually encouraged on the basis that it will improve children's lives and enhance their education. In terms of legal duty, the controlling question is the propriety of inviting children to engage in such activities, and asking their parents to consent to participation, without making them aware of all potential ramifications. Most collegiate and elite amateur athletes are aggressively recruited, and even at the professional level participation is a *choice* which must be carefully weighed. One consideration is the risk involved, and, as discussed below, there can be serious legal consequences for failing to provide the information necessary to make that decision.

Injury Prevention

Risk warning is essential to reducing injury risk. Athletes are key participants in the prevention process but must possess the appropriate knowledge for doing so. Warning of the risk of injuries, particularly the most serious types, lays the foundation for teaching athletes how to prevent unnecessary harm.

The importance of risk warning is borne out in the history of catastrophic football injuries over past three decades. In the mid-1970s, it was determined that the technique of head-first contact in football was the principal cause of quadriplegia in the game. This was based in part upon data collected by the National Football Head and Neck Injury Registry, which indicated the occurrence of 99 cases of permanent quadriplegia during the period from 1971–75, a rate of nearly 20 cases per year (Torg 1982). A rule change, outlawing such behavior at the high school and collegiate level, was accompanied by a massive educational campaign, including locker room posters, warning stickers on helmets and educational videos designed to make coaches and athletes aware of these risks.

Evidence of the value and impact of this approach is found in the Annual Survey Of Catastropic Football Injuries, published by the National Center for Catastropic Sports Injury Research. The 2010 report, for example, states that during the 34 year period following implementation of the rule change, the annual rate of quadriplegia has been only 9.2 per year, and over the past 20 years the rate has been just 6.7 per year (Mueller & Cantu 2011), a reduction of 2/3 as compared with the 5-year period prior to the rule change and educational campaign. It should also be noted that the number of football players has increased significantly since the early 1970's.

The phenomenon of catastrophic injury, and the need to warn of the risk thereof, is not unique to football. Spring sports are commonly considered to be relatively safe, yet over the period from 1983–2010 they have produced an average of nearly 4 catastrophic injuries per year in the high school setting alone (NCCSIR Tables 2010). In baseball/softball, the primary culprits are headfirst sliding and failure to wear protective helmets at critical times. In track and field the major problem is the pole vault, where most injuries occur when the athlete misses or bounces out of the pit and strikes a hard object or surface. These, too, are risks which can be dramatically reduced by proper attention being paid by coaches and athletes to hazardous circumstances or behaviors (Mueller, Cantu and VanCamp 1996).

Perhaps the most dramatic example is cheerleading, which produced more than 4 catastrophic injuries per year from 1982–2010. Half of these occurred in college sport where the number of participants is only a fraction of their high school counterpart. At both levels, the rate of injury per 100,000 participants *exceeds the rate in football.* The primary cause is pyramid stunts, followed by situations where one participant is tossed into the air (Mueller, Cantu and VanCamp 1996).

Another concern is the persistence of "indirect" catastrophic injuries, defined by NCCSIR as those caused by systemic failure brought on by exertion during activity. Since 1982 these injuries have averaged 15.25 per year in all sport combined, the majority due to cardiac arrest but with an alarming number caused by heat illness. While the raw numbers in high school are greater, the rate of these indirect injuries per 100,000 participants is dramatically higher in college, where the availability of sport medicine support is significantly greater. The means for eliminating heat illness in sport have been known for decades and many cardiac risks can be alleviated by better reporting of individual and family medical history during preparticipation screening, immediate reporting of new symptoms and referral to appropriate care.

In all these examples, *athletes and the parents of minor athletes play a critical role,* far superior to that of coaches or health care providers. Without proper understanding and appreciation of the risks, however, athletes and their parents cannot fulfill this responsibility.

Risk vs. Benefit

This is not to recommend placing undue emphasis on the dangers of sport. The risks must be balanced against the benefits of sport and compared to the risks of everyday life. It is also important to provide *accurate information* about risk.

From studies conducted by the National Athletic Trainers Association, Inc. (NATA), at least 75 percent of sport injuries are minor (interfere with participation one week or less) and no more than 12 percent can be categorized as serious (interfere with participation more than three weeks). The catastrophic injury data compiled by NCCSIR must be viewed in the light of 5.5 million high school participants and another 280,000 collegiate participants each year. In any randomly selected population of U.S. teenagers and young adults, it is likely that the annual number of catastrophic injuries and illnesses unrelated to sport in a given year would be dramatically greater than those occurring during sport activity.

For example, a report released in March 1996 by Johns Hopkins School of Public Health Injury Prevention Center indicates that for males aged 15–19 the combined annual homicide and suicide rate is 8.31 per 100,000 in population (*The Arizona Republic* 1996). A report released by the Centers for Disease Control in December 1996 revealed that in 1995, teenaged drivers were involved in 7,993 fatal automobile crashes, bringing the total of such events to 68,206 for the previous eight years.

The fact that sport is safe when compared to everyday life activities and that athletes comprise a very healthy population, however, must not dull our senses with regard to risk warning. The goal is to make athletes aware of the *realities* of risk and then motivate them to take appropriate measures to reduce their own injury potential.

Informed Consent

In medicine, the concept of informed consent was created by the courts in lawsuits arising from treatments with bad results but in which there was no evidence of wrongdoing on the part of the health care providers. The underlying legal theory is based on the principle that human beings of adult years and sound mind have the right to determine what is done to their bodies. Although consent to treatment had been standard practice in medicine for many years, in giving birth to this new legal theory the courts said that doctors must provide patients with sufficient information to permit the *patient* to make an informed decision whether to submit to a particular treatment. The information must include the nature of the illness or injury, the nature of the proposed treatment, the risks involved in the treatment, the prospects of success, the risks of failing to undergo any treatment at all, and the availability of and risks involved in alternative treatments (*Hiddings v. Williams* 1991). If the patient experiences an unexpectedly bad outcome without having been provided all that information, the health care provider becomes responsible for any resulting injury *regardless of any negligence* in caring for the patient.

Application to Sport

While it is difficult to determine the origin of the practice of requiring athletes and parents to sign "consent" forms as a condition of participation, it is likely that little thought has been given to the legal implications of the process. Technically, this document constitutes an agreement between the signer(s) and the sport program. In the instance of "minors" the parents are agreeing to *allow* their children to engage in an activity which involves unusual risks. Adult athletes are agreeing to submit themselves to the circumstances of participation with the attendant risks.

With this long-standing tradition of consent for sport participation, it was predictable that the courts would expand the concept of *informed consent* to the athletic arena. As in the medical context, the athletes and the parents of minors must understand and appreciate the *full* ramifications of their consent, or it is not valid.

The landmark case was decided in Seattle, Washington, in 1981 (*Thompson v. Seattle Unified School District*). A running back on a high school sophomore football team lowered his head to gain extra yardage, rammed an opponent with the top of his helmet and was immediately rendered quadriplegic. Although the plaintiff had been taught not to use his helmet in blocking and tackling, this was a common technique for running backs and he had never been warned against it. His mother testified that, while she had a general understanding (based upon common sense, not any effort by the school district) that there was risk of serious injury in football, she never appreciated the possibility of such a severe outcome *particularly when there had been no rule violation*. The judge allowed and the jury accepted this theory of failure to warn, and the result was a verdict in the amount of $6.3 million (Ball 1981).

When the allegation is negligence, the plaintiff has to prove that the defendant violated the standard of care *and* that the negligent conduct caused the injury. Both requirements create a substantial challenge for plaintiffs in most cases. In failure to warn cases, however, the plaintiff is essentially saying "I could have controlled my (or my child's) own destiny. If you had made me aware of the risks I would have decided that I (or my child) would not participate, or would have changed behavior to remove the risk. Without participation or the dangerous behavior *there would have been no injury.* Thus your conduct caused the injury."

Unless there has been a conscientious effort to warn and obtain informed consent, it is extremely difficult to defend against this claim. The option of arguing to the jury that the plaintiff is not being truthful about steps that would have been taken if adequate warnings had been provided is a very risky defense strategy.

While the Seattle case was settled pending appeal and no formal opinion was ever published, news of the verdict spread rapidly through the national sport community. This marked the beginning of a wide range of efforts by sport programs to provide comprehensive risk warnings and obtain informed consent.

Alternatives to Accepting Risk

Just as with patients in the medical setting, athletes must be made aware of risk *and* informed of their alternatives. In sport there are two aspects to the latter requirement.

Unlike medical treatment, participation in sport is always optional. Upon becoming fully aware of the risks, an athlete or parent may choose another sport which poses fewer hazards, or select a form of recreation which has no risk. Anyone experienced in athletic administration knows, however, that the decision not to participate is seldom made. Even when athletes are confronted with known circumstances which might preclude participation, such as a cardiac condition or loss of a paired organ, they typically press for the right to participate over the objections of administrators and sport medicine professionals.

Therein lies the importance of presenting options and of the foregoing discussion about preventing injury through risk warning. Another alternative to *accepting* the risk is to take an active role in *reducing* the risk. With full appreciation of the risk and appropriate education about prevention, athletes and parents are in a position to choose that alternative. Thus, the issues of "risk warning" and "informed consent" are interrelated. Unless athletes and parents are advised of the risk of injury in their chosen sport, and fully understand that risk, they have not given legally effective consent to participation. For that reason it is essential to integrate warning and informed consent into one process.

Binding Contract

For adult athletes and parents of minors, the consent document constitutes a binding agreement if it meets traditional legal requirements for contracts. This means that both parties must 1) understand the terms of the agreement and 2) intend to be bound by the agreement. Most *minor athletes* cannot be legally held to their agreements regardless of whether they meet those requirements. It is therefore foolhardy to believe that their written consent relieves the school of responsibility in absence of informed consent by a parent.

It is still important, however, to have minor athletes participate in the risk warning process. In addition to the educational component and contribution to injury prevention, once they become adults these athletes have the right to initiate litigation for injuries sustained when they were minors. Regardless of the validity of their parent's consent, athletes can claim that *they* did not understand and appreciate the risk, and that if they had they would have decided not to participate or would have engaged in different behavior.

In litigation based upon that theory, former teammates typically become the most critical witnesses. In reality, even at very young ages, athletes can be made to understand and appreciate the potential for injury in athletics. If a conscientious effort has been made to assure that all athletes possess that understanding, and the plaintiff's involvement in that process can be documented, fellow athletes can be called to testify that they understood the risks *and* knew how to reduce them based upon the warning process. This provides powerful evidence for defending against a claim of failure to warn. While this may seem an unlikely scenario, it has been the basis of a successful defense in numerous sport injury lawsuits. Conversely, the testimony of former teammates that they were *not* told of the risks will be powerful evidence for the *plaintiff.*

Standard of Care

If the court decides that there was a legal duty to warn an injured athlete of the risk of injury, the jury will be told to determine whether the duty was breached. A critical question in that process is whether the sport program met the *standard of care* in fulfilling this legal duty. A number of factors may bear upon that decision.

The National Interscholastic Athletic Administrators Association (NIAAA), the largest organization of high school athletic directors, publishes a periodical entitled *Interscholastic Athletic Administrator* (IAA). An article written by the NIAAA Publications Committee in the Fall 1996 issue sets forth various "criteria developed for legal duties of athletic coaches and administrators." Two of these standards, under the heading "Provide Sport-Specific Warnings," state:

> 1. Under circumstances which assure understanding and appreciation of the information (preferably mandatory preseason meetings), provide athletes and parents with facts concerning general risk related to sport participation, e.g. nature and frequency of common injury occurrence and the potential catastrophic risks including head and neck injury, cardiac arrest, heat illness, substance abuse, nutritional disorders and the transmission of blood-borne pathogens. In addition, sport-specific risks should be discussed pertaining to the athlete's chosen activity including the types of common injury and the manner in which catastrophic injuries manifest themselves in that sport....
>
> 2. Require athletes and parents to certify in writing their understanding and appreciation of the information provided relating to safety standards, risks and preventive measures under circumstances which ensure that they are providing informed consent to participation (*Interscholastic Athletic Administrator* 1996).

This is strong evidence of the standard of care in U.S. high schools, and can also be used in lawsuits against other types of sport programs, including the collegiate level.

A number of lawsuits have held that athletes are entitled to compensation when team organizations and sport medicine providers fail to inform them of the risk of participation in their physical circumstances. Perhaps the most widely publicized of these cases was initiated by a professional football player who had suffered three serious knee injuries for which he received treatment and rehabilitation. His treatment included injections of corticosteroids which enabled him to continue to play. When he later became significantly disabled due to degeneration of his knees, he claimed the team had withheld information which was vital to his decision to continue to participate. The court ruled that he was entitled to full disclosure of information about his condition and the risk of continued participation (*Krueger v. San Francisco Forty-Niners* 1981). While it was settled without a trial, the suit filed by the family of collegiate basketball player Hank Gathers also included claims of failure to adequately warn and of conduct by his coach which was designed to diminish the effect of the warnings he was given. In fact, *even though he was an adult,* his mother claimed that she should have been informed of his condition and the potential ramifications of his continued participation in basketball (Herbert 1990).

The fact that these cases involved athletes with pre-existing conditions does not diminish their applicability to *all* athletes. Sport programs have the same responsibility to make healthy athletes aware of the potential for injury as to advise injured athletes with pre-existing conditions about the risks of continued participation.

Legal Expectations

Satisfying legal requirements for "informed consent" is not difficult. There are, however, certain essential steps to assuring successful achievement of the process. Considering the current standard of care discussed above, those working in athletic programs need to understand legal requirements for risk warning and informed consent.

Implementing appropriate methods helps assure that the consent to participation is given voluntarily and with full knowledge, thus making that agreement legally binding. It also emphasizes the responsibility of athletes and parents in accepting that risk and assuming their role in preventing injury.

Ineffective Approaches

While informed consent has become a widely recognized concept in athletics, the approach of most programs in fulfilling their responsibility is inadequate to meet legal expectations. This is not an instance where "something is better than nothing."

The consent form is frequently drafted by lawyers attempting to "legally" bind the signer. That typically leads to a document filled with stilted and confusing legal language which is difficult for even the most sophisticated reader to understand. An example of the danger of this approach arose in a Wisconsin case brought by an injured skier against the operator of a ski facility where he sustained an injury. The defendant moved for dismissal of the case based upon a comprehensive risk warning and release document which the plaintiff (and all other users of the facility) had been required to sign. In finding that the document did not relieve the defendant of liability, the court noted that the form contained 376 words in fine print, and included a 176-word sentence. The court held that the document was "not sufficiently clear, unambiguous or unmistakeable to release (the ski facility) from the alleged negligence in this case (*Cass v. American Home Assurance Company and Granite Risk Corporation* 2005).

In the case of minors, consent forms are too-often mailed or sent home with the student, along with a number of other documents to be signed by the parents before the child can participate. Another common error is to incorporate the "warning/consent" language into a comprehensive document which addresses a variety of issues, e.g. authorization for medical treatment, health insurance coverage requirements. Such a warning message does not have the necessary effect upon even those who read the document—and many parents do not carefully read such items before signing them.

Even when the risk warning is set forth in a separate document, there is simply no way to completely and properly characterize the risk of sport participation in written material, no matter how carefully worded. Beyond that, a significant percentage of our adult population is functionally illiterate in English. These concerns, combined with the risk of not knowing who really signed a document sent home to the parents, makes this method very ineffective.

Appropriate Methods

The most critical step is to adopt *administrative policies and procedures* from which no one is allowed to vary. These must be detailed in writing, distributed to all personnel and carry the weight of an organizational mandate. It is also wise to provide copies to athletes and parents of minors.

Universal application is essential. Though rare, as noted above catastrophic events are possible in any sport and the failure to require implementation of this approach for every team at every level is foolhardy. Whether talking about loss of vision due to impact from a badminton shuttlecock or tennis ball, heat illness or being struck by lightning while running cross country or suffering a spinal cord injury in football or wrestling, the athletes and parents all deserve the same quality of information about risk.

This concept will succeed only with *total staff commitment*. It must be accepted and applied by all sport personnel. Risk warning efforts can be sabotaged by athletic administrators or coaches who question or even ridicule the process, or apologize to athletes and parents for "wasting" their time with this exercise. Such minimizing behavior can be devastating in litigation. Not only does it diminish the informed consent defense, but could actually cause injury by encouraging athletes or parents to disregard precautionary measures.

Coaches' commitment can only be assured by properly educating them about the risk of injury and their role in prevention. They must then participate in the warning process by attending the informed consent meeting, emphasizing the importance of this information in their communications with athletes and parents, using it as a teaching tool with athletes, and reinforcing it throughout the season. They must also avoid sending conflicting messages which suggest that warnings should not be taken seriously or that "good" athletes disregard risk in favor of more aggressive performance.

Mandatory Preseason Meetings

To assure reasonable compliance with legal requirements for informed consent, athletes and parents must receive the information and sign the acknowledgment forms before participation begins. The ideal approach is a group setting which provides opportunity for athletes and parents of minors to receive input from key personnel, including administrators, coaches, sport medicine providers and equipment managers; have their questions answered; and fully understand the warning information. Since most athletes and parents are willing to accept sport risk even when it is explained in explicit terms, for those who may be uncertain the group process helps reinforce the perception that the risk is worth the benefits derived and that, even with the remote possibility of a catastrophic event, participation is preferable to fearful avoidance. Reported instances of parent or athlete refusal to give consent under these circumstances are more rare than catastrophic injuries. Most importantly, those who refuse consent are the ones who would have been most likely to vigorously pursue litigation if their child had been injured.

Sport Specific Information

It is important to provide specific information about the risks involved in the particular sport the athlete is considering. This includes not only the sport itself but:

1. Climate and other environmental circumstances;

2. Gender-specific issues;

3. The age and skill level of the athletes; and

4. Any particular circumstances unique to the community.

Figure 1. Soccer

Risks	Prevention
1. Head Injury (Head to head contact, high kicks, ball impacts, impact with goal)	1. Proper Technique Compliance with Rules Avoid Overly Aggressive Play Competition Between Players of Equivalent Skill and Maturity Report Minor Injury and Follow Medical Advice
2. Spinal Cord Injury (Head down collision with another player, goal, or the ground)	2. Avoid Overly Aggressive Play Compliance with Rules Proper Technique
3. Heat Illness (Minor to severe, including permanent brain injury or death due to dehydration and over-exertion in hot/humid conditions)	3. Proper Hydration Before and During Season Proper Nutrition Proper Conditioning and Acclimatization Proper Training Routine Procedures for Water Consumption During Competition
4. Orthopedic Injury (Fractures, sprains and dislocations, muscle strains)	4. Proper Conditioning and Strength Training Proper Training Routine Proper Technique Proper Equipment (Shin guards & shoes) Report Minor Injury & Follow Medical Advice

Taken from *Sport RISK: YOU Be The JUDGE Instructional Guide*. 1995. Phoenix, AZ: The BASIC Foundation.

The ideal method is sport-by-sport (or even team-by-team) meetings, but many find this to be administratively unworkable. It is acceptable to have multi-sport meetings before the fall, winter and spring sport seasons. These meetings should include a general session in which information relative to every sport and team is presented to the entire group, and then separate breakout sessions to discuss issues pertaining to each sport and level of play. Sport-specific handouts discussing both risk and prevention are an excellent way to reinforce the message (Figure 1).

Consent forms should be filled out and signed by the athletes and parents before leaving this meeting. Forms containing numerous blanks to be completed by the signers assure they have read and understood the information (Figure 2).

Figure 2. Athlete's Risk Acknowledgment and Consent to Participation*

NOTE: THE ATHLETE MUST PERSONALLY FILL IN ALL BLANKS. PRINT CLEARLY.

Name: _____ Date of Birth: _____

I wish to participate in the sport of _____ in the _____ sports
(School/Organization Name)
program during the _____ season. I realize that there are risks involved in my participation
(Year)
and attended a group meeting on _____ where these risks were discussed and explained.
(Date)
The meeting was run by _____. We watched the video _____,
(Name — Meeting Monitor)   (Title)
listened to presentations by administrators, coaches, and sports medicine experts and had all

our questions answered. I understand that the risks include a full range of injuries, from minor

to severe. I recognize the possibility that I might die, become paralyzed, or suffer brain damage

or other serious, permanent injury as a result of my participation in this sports program. I

realize that neither the protective equipment and padding used in the sport, the safety rules

and procedures of the sport, the coaching instruction I receive nor the sports medicine care I

am provided will guarantee my safety or prevent all injuries I might sustain. I agree to accept

these risks as a condition of my participation.

   ** I also realize that my _____ creates an additional risk for me, and I
(Pre-existing Condition)
discussed these risks with the athletic director, my coach(es), and the sports medicine providers

in a meeting on _____. They explained to me that, because of this condition, the special
(Date)
risks for me are as follows: _____.
(List all concerns. If you need more room, write on the back of this form. <u>Write legibly</u>.)
I understand these concerns and agree to follow all directions and recommendations of my

physicians and the sports medicine providers in this program. I also agree to accept these

additional risks to me as a condition of my participation in this program.

_____   _____
Date   Signature

DO NOT SIGN THIS FORM IF YOU HAVE ANY QUESTIONS OR CONCERNS!

---

  * For Use At Group Meeting.
** For athletes with pre-existing conditions that increase risk of injury/illness. If this section does not apply to you write "not applicable" in the first space.

Taken from *Sport RISK: YOU Be The JUDGE Instructional Guide.* 1995. Phoenix, AZ: The BASIC Foundation.

Another useful technique is videotaping the meeting, including a portion of each of the breakout sessions. This tape should include all the presentations in the general session along with several views of the audience. It needs to have a strong audio feed for presenter comments and questions from parents and athletes. The tape will serve a dual purpose as discussed below.

Other Topics to Address

Keep in mind the two-fold purpose of creating awareness of risk and instilling knowledge about prevention. This requires educating people about the full range of concerns relating to sport injury. Examples of issues to discuss are:

Clarification of your sport medicine structure. Introduce the providers and discuss their qualifications, indicate the nature of their involvement (full-time, part-time, occasional, employed, independent contractor, volunteer, etc.) and how athletes and parents can access their services. Many people harbor an impression of sport medicine based upon the media's portrayal of professional and major college sport programs. It is important to assure that athletes and parents understand the realities of their own situation.

Referrals and self-referrals to family physicians, specialists and other outside providers. Indicate procedures as well as the criteria for and control over the decision about return to activity following a serious injury.

Preparticipation screening. Explain the process employed by the program and, for athletes who go to outside providers, provide written guidelines to be followed in both the selection of the examiner and administration of the exam.

Emergency medical plan. Explain its application in various circumstances. With minor athletes, discuss the challenges of handling emergencies when the parent is not present and cannot be quickly contacted. Reinforce the importance of current and complete information on each athlete's emergency treatment card.

Travel issues. Discuss the risks attendant to travel as well as special concerns when an athlete is injured or becomes ill on a trip. With minors, address the problem of athletes being returned to the organization's facility with no means of transportation to their home and the procedures which will be followed in that situation.

Insurance coverage. Explain what is (or is not) provided by the organization, the cost and benefits of any such coverage, and the ramifications of certain types of personally owned coverage, including limitations on who can provide treatment and where, the effect of capitated coverages on full rehabilitation and the potential problem of delayed treatment while awaiting the approval of managed care plans. A commonly held misbelief by athletes and parents is that sport organizations pay for any medical care necessitated by participation. This notion is one of those which may not be dispelled by simply sending information home to the parents. Failure to make people aware of the realities of the situation could lead to litigation if an athlete is deprived of necessary treatment because of a lack of adequate insurance coverage.

Participation by athletes with legally defined and protected "disabilities" must also be handled appropriately during the risk warning and informed consent process. Laws protecting individuals with disabilities prohibit discriminating in the consent process as well as in allowing participation. To avoid claims of discrimination you must use the same procedures with *all* athletes and not single out the individuals with disabilities for a special approach. This is accomplished by addressing pre-existing conditions "generically" and having a provision in all consent forms which acknowledges the added risk to affected athletes as a result of such a condition (Figure 2, above).

Standardized Materials

Various materials are available to assist in the presentation of risk warning information and documenting informed consent. While any such support material must be evaluated on its merits, using professionally prepared tools affords numerous advantages. One benefit of commercial programs is the uniformity and consistency they bring to the process from sport to sport and year to year. If athletes or parents protest seeing the same video or receiving the same handouts several times, administer a short pre- and post-test each time to see how well they retained the information from the last meeting as compared with their awareness immediately following a "refresher" session.

A broadcast-quality video will also command the attention of meeting participants and add impact to the general risk message. Many school districts, colleges and universities have video production departments capable of producing such videos under the guidance of knowledgeable experts in sport risk management. Use of a video is preferable to program personnel attempting to present the entire message orally or with handouts. Such a video also becomes powerful evidence for the defense in future litigation.

It is a mistake, however, to rely solely on a video. Program personnel must take the time to develop supplemental materials addressing specific issues and applying general risk information to their situation. This is particularly true regarding guidelines pertaining to injury prevention, reporting of symptoms and following medical guidance.

Standardized documents prepared by knowledgeable experts in sport risk management will also be superior to materials developed by someone who does not possess that expertise. This includes consent forms as well as permanent records prepared by program personnel to document the informed consent process (Figure 3).

Alternative Opportunities

When dealing with minors, there will always be athletes and parents who cannot attend the group meeting, necessitating other options. The best alternative is for them to meet with a staff member and go through the same process used in the group setting. Showing them a videotape of the group meeting helps assure that these individuals receive the same message as other athletes and parents. They must also view the warning video, receive any applicable handouts and have an opportunity for their questions and concerns to be addressed. This approach requires a slightly different informed consent form which accurately reflects the process.

The final approach, which is less ideal but may be acceptable when there is no alternative, is sending materials home for the athlete and parent(s) to view together. These include the warning video, the video of the meeting, the handouts provided during the meeting, and the appropriate consent forms. The consent form used in this instance must have different language to provide reasonable assurance that the parents were actually involved, that the information was actually viewed and understood, and

Figure 3. School Record
Risk Warning & Informed Consent Meeting (Group)

Meeting Date _____ Sport(s) _____

Team Level(s) _____

Meeting Planner _____ Moderator _____

Staff members present (List all names and specific assignment. Add a page if necessary.)

_____ _____

_____ _____

Number of athletes present _____ (Roll/Sign-in sheet attached.)

Number of parents/guardians present _____ (Sign-in sheet attached.)

Name of video shown _____

Titles of handouts _____

Video of meeting by _____; Length _____ Minutes; Retained by _____

Presentations by (Name, title and subject; attach additional page if necessary.)

_____

_____

Comments _____

_____

Date _____ Prepared by _____ Signature _____

Taken from *Sport RISK: YOU Be The JUDGE Instructional Guide.* 1995. Phoenix, AZ: The BASIC Foundation.

that they realize they can personally discuss their questions or concerns with a staff member.

Annual Review

Administrators and coaches commonly question the need to repeat this process every year, arguing that athletes and parents object to "having their time wasted" in this manner. These attitudes cannot be allowed to govern organizational policy.

If the process is handled correctly, it will never be perceived as a waste of time. Athletes and parents will appreciate the honesty, concern, awareness of risk, and willingness to involve them in the process of protecting themselves and their children which is evident in a properly conducted meeting.

For minor athletes the risks increase as the level of experience and intensity increases. Athletes and parents who clearly understand the risks at the entry level may be very naive about the situation when they reach a higher level of competition. "Informed consent" means they appreciate how the situation changes as an athlete progresses through sport.

Understanding injury cause and prevention is also a dynamic process. New awareness is continually forthcoming in sport medicine and it is imperative that athletes and parents have the benefit of the latest information. This is also the key to overcoming objections to annual review of the information. Providing them new insights which will help prevent harm or otherwise produce healthier, stronger athletes, further validates the process in their minds.

Finally, to be effectively retained and understood, educational information must be repeated. To suggest that athletes or parents attending a meeting upon entry into the program will retain the information three or four years later is contrary to all accepted principles of education.

Complete Documentation

Legally, the best risk warning methods are of no value unless they can be documented in court. This is achieved through accurately maintained records and the testimony of key participants, including other parents and athletes in the process. In addition to the consent forms, a designated staff member must also prepare a report of the risk warning circumstances, whatever they may have been, and assure that these "records" are properly preserved for use in the event of litigation.

Where no significant injury has occurred during a season, retaining records for two years is probably adequate. If there *has* been an injury, the records must be preserved until you are certain they will never be needed as evidence in litigation. This depends on the age of the athlete, the nature of the injury and the statute of limitations in the particular state.

Evidence for the Defense

Those who follow the outlined procedures but are one of the unfortunate few to experience a serious injury and ensuing litigation will have the strongest defense possible to a claim of failure to warn. Not only can they present the signed consent forms, the video and other warning materials to the jury, but they will have a room full of witnesses who can and, from this author's experience, will testify that they attended the same meeting as the plaintiff and understood and appreciated the risk based upon the information provided. This is also another valuable usage for the videotape of the group meeting.

Once again, however, the attitude of school personnel and their commitment to the process is critical. If administrators or coaches have negative attitudes, attempt to "soften" the message in order to encourage participation, or communicate conflicting messages during the season, the "room full of witnesses" may become their worst nightmare. Similarly, failure to provide complete information, and take reasonable precautions to assure it is understood, will result in the effort being wasted.

Waivers and Releases

Either independently or in conjunction with an informed consent document, many sport programs attempt to eliminate liability for athletic injuries by having athletes and/or parents of minors sign a document which purports to waive the participant's right to sue for injury or release the program from liability for any injury which may occur. This approach raises legal issues too complex to thoroughly address in this context. Simply stated, however, they are of dubious value in most instances.

The problems with these documents result from certain basic legal tenets. First, to be binding, both parties must fully understand the nature of the agreement. This includes awareness of all rights they are waiving *and* of the circumstances which may lead to future injury. The most stringent of these agreements include a specific statement that injury may arise from the negligence of program personnel and that the waiver or release applies even in that circumstance. Without such a provision the document may be held ineffective in a case of alleged negligence, but even with it included, the participant or parent may be ignorant of the meaning of that language and therefore the court may find that they are not bound by its terms. Courts also construe such agreements very strictly and if the actual cause of the injury is not appropriately addressed by the document, the court may rule that it would be effective as to certain injuries but not to those suffered by the plaintiff.

The second problem lies in the fact that minors cannot be bound by their own agreements and parents cannot waive the legal rights of their minor children without court approval. Thus, even if the agreement is found to be enforceable against the parents, after becoming an adult the child can file a lawsuit in which that agreement will have no effect. Some of these agreements attempt to circumvent this problem by including language to the effect that the parents "indemnify" the sport program against any expense or liability relating to athletic injuries suffered by their children, which means that they will reimburse the program for any expenses or judgments resulting from a lawsuit by the child. Even if this provision withstands legal challenge, it is only effective to the extent that the parents have the financial wherewithal to reimburse the program for such loss.

Finally, in many jurisdictions the courts have held that agreements to relieve a person or organization from liability for their own negligence are void as against public policy. Examples are found in *Debell v. Wellbridge Club Management* (NY 2007) and *Connolly v. The Peninsula Group*, (NY 2008), both case arising out of injuries suffered at fitness facilities by facility members while being instructed by facility employees, and *Berlangieri v. Running Elk Corporation*,(NM 2002), in which a guest sued a lodge for injuries suffered while he was riding a horse provided by the lodge and as a part of a group being led by a lodge employee. In the *Berlangieri* case, the court held "that such exculpatory agreements are unenforceable because commercial operators of recreational premises are subject to a non-disclaimable duty to exercise ordinary care to protect patrons from foreseeable risk of physical injury or death" (*Berlangieri*, p. 4.) In cases arising out of injuries to minors while participating on school or youth sport teams, courts are even more likely to find that these types of agreements violate public policy.

There have been other cases involving adult participants in which the courts have upheld pre-injury waivers and releases. For the most part, however, these have been situations where the activity was high risk, such as auto racing and sky diving, or where there was a separate contractual component to the relationship between the participant and the organization, such as membership in a health club or payment of a fee to compete in an event (*Gure v. Tri County Raceway, Inc.* 1974). Even in high risk activities, however, such exculpatory agreements provide no guarantee. *Phelps v. Firebird Raceway* (AZ 2005), was a case brought by a racecar driver against the racetrack for severe injuries he suffered during a race. In ruling that the very explicit "release" and "assumption of risk" document signed by the driver did not, in and of itself, provide an absolute defense for the racetrack, the court referred to a provision in the state constitution which requires that certain issues in negligence cases, including "assumption of risk," be decided by the jury and not by the judge. The court held that it was up to the jury in the case to determine whether or not the document signed by the plaintiff was sufficient to indicate that he had assumed the risk of his injuries, thus relieving the defendant of liability.

The problem with reliance upon such documents is that, as with the cases cited above, one never knows whether it will be effective until a court rules on the issue in a lawsuit filed after the injury occurs. If the participant's injury resulted from risks which are fairly straight-forward and apparent *and* there is no obviously neglectful conduct on the part of the defendant, there is a chance that such a lawsuit will be dismissed on the basis of the pre-injury waiver. If, however, the injury is severe and the plaintiff offers proof of substantial negligence, courts will be less willing to relieve the defendant of responsibility for its conduct. Additionally, even when binding upon the participant, the agreement may be ruled ineffective as to the participant's spouse or children (*Bowen v. Kid-Kare* 1992).

Another dilemma arises from the integration of waiver or release language into an informed consent document. Some courts are of the view that inclusion of terms or conditions which are improper or unenforceable may void the entire agreement. Thus, an informed consent document which would otherwise be effective to eliminate a claim of failure to warn and/or lack of informed consent, may be ruled inadmissible on the basis that it improperly attempted to limit the rights of the injured person (*Kay v. Pennsylvania R.R. Co.* 1952).

The final concern about waivers and releases is the effect they can have on the attitudes and behaviors of program personnel. The use of such documents generally becomes known to administrators, coaches, supervisors and others in positions of responsibility. Too often they adopt the philosophy that preventive measures are not required because the participants have "assumed the risk" and the program cannot be held responsible for any injury that occurs. This may lead to a failure to educate coaches in critical areas of injury prevention and response, develop appropriate medical emergency plans, adopt reasonable transportation policies or implement other critical safety procedures. Not only is this a violation of the program's moral responsibilities to participants, but it is the kind of situation which is likely to cause judges to declare the agreement to be unenforceable as a violation of public policy.

In My Opinion

Risk warning and informed consent may be the most critical aspects of sport risk management, but also the least understood. Myriad excuses are advanced by administrators and coaches for refusal to implement reasonable measures, but none are sufficient to override the legal and moral responsibilities related to these procedures.

Comprehensive risk warning is not only essential to injury prevention, but builds respect for the program in the minds of participants and parents. It establishes a foundation for implementation of other risk management measures and for educating athletes and parents about their responsibilities for preventing injuries. While a significant degree of discipline and commitment are required to effectively carry out risk warning and informed consent procedures, the effort will produce substantial rewards, particularly in litigation arising out of serious sport injuries.

The use of waivers and releases, while occasionally effective in eliminating litigation, provides no guarantees and also carries substantial risk. It must not supplant risk warning and informed consent procedures, and if allowed to diminish attention toward essential measures for reducing risk and preventing injury, may result in *increased* liability exposure.

References

Ball, R.T. (1981) Anecdotal reports to author by legal counsel involved in the case of Thompson v. Seattle School District, et al., King County Superior Court.

Berlangieri v. running Elk Corporation, 48 P.3d 70 (NM 2002).

Bowen v. Kid-Kare, Inc., 585 N.E. 2d 384 (Oh. 1992).

Caine v. Cleveland Parachute Training Center, 9 Ohio App. 3rd 27 (1983).

Cass v. American Home Assurance Company and Granite Risk Corporation, 699 N.W.2d 254 (Wis. 2005), also reported in From The Gym To The Jury, Vol. 18, NO.2

Connelly v. Peninsula Group, 852 NYS2d 104 (AD 2008).

Debell v. Wellbridge Club Management, Inc., 835 NYS2d 179 (AD 2007).

"Despite Drop of 24 percent in 8 Years, Car Crashes Still Top Teen Killer," *The Arizona Republic,* December 6, 1996, A20.

Garrison v. Combined Fitness Centre, Ltd., 559 N.E. 2d 187 (Ill. App. 1st Dist. 1990).

"Guns, Car Crashes the Top Youth Killers," *The Arizona Republic,* March 3, 1996, A4.

Gure v. Tri-County Raceway, Inc., 407 F.Supp. 489 (M.D. Ala. 1974).

Herbert, David. "The Death of Hank Gathers," *The Sport Medicine Standards and Malpractice Reporter* vol. 2, no. 3, June, pp. 41–45.

Hidding v. Williams, 578 So.2d 1192 (La. App. 5th Cir. 1991).

Kay v. Pennsylvania R.R. Co., 156 Ohio St. 503 (1952).

Kleinknecht v. Gettysburg College, 989 F.2d 1360 (3rd Cir. 1993).

Krueger v. San Francisco Forty-Niners, 234 Cal Rptr. 579 (1987).

Mueller, Cantu, and VanCamp. 1996. *Catastrophic Injuries in High School and College Sport.* Champaign-Urbana, IL: Human Kinetics.

Mueller and Cantu. 2011. *National Center for Catastrophic Sport Injury Research Annual Survey of Catastrophic Football Injuries, 1977–2010.*

Mueller and Cantu, 2011, *Catasrophic Sports Injury Study, Twenty-Eighth Annual Report, Fall 1982–Spring 2010.*

"NATA High School Injury Survey." 1989. *Journal of the NATA* vol. 24, no. 4, Winter, pp. 385–388.

NIAAA Publications Committee. 1996. "Sport Litigation: Criteria Developed for Legal Duties of Athletic Coaches, Administrators," *Interscholastic Athletic Administration* vol. 23, no. 1, Fall, pp. 10–13.

Thompson v. Seattle Unified School District, King County Superior Court (1977).

Chapter 5

Product Liability

The usual target of product liability claims is the manufacturer rather than the seller.

Richard T. Ball

The term "product liability," while widely used among sport professionals, is often misunderstood. In fact, it is such a complex legal concept that lawyers and judges often have difficultly correctly applying it to particular situations.

The proper technical term for this doctrine is strict liability in tort. Under given circumstances, it holds the defendant liable for harm regardless of any wrong-doing. The theory applies only to the manufacture or sale of products, as distinguished from liability for negligence related to products, which has a much broader application.

Potential Defendants

Allegations of strict liability in tort can only be brought against one who is engaged in the business of manufacturing and/or selling products. Occasional transactions by individuals or organizations do not expose them to strict liability, but the repeated activity of making or selling products creates such exposure even if that is not their primary business interest. For example, a school that purchases athletic equipment for the use of its students is not a potential defendant in a product liability case, even if it occasionally conducts a sale of surplus equipment as a fund-raising activity. However, if the school regularly *sells* equipment to its students or to outside individuals or organizations, it may be subject to such claims.

This point was clarified in a case filed by a collegiate football player who became quadriplegic during a game. He sued not only the helmet manufacturer but the university's athletic director, athletic trainer and football coach under the theory of strict liability in tort. The court dismissed the strict liability allegations against those individuals on the basis that they were "not part of the original producing and marketing chain. Liability will not be imposed upon a defendant who is not a part of the original producing and marketing chain" (*Hemphill v. Sayers* 1982).

The usual target of product liability claims is the manufacturer rather than the seller. Most states have adopted the rule that the seller is entitled to be indemnified by the manufacturer from any liability so long as the seller passes along the product unchanged. If the manufacturer is still in business, is financially solvent and is subject to the jurisdiction of the courts, the seller is usually a nominal participant in litigation.

Origin of Legal Theory

The concept of strict liability in tort was created by judicial decision. It originated in early common law, being applied in cases in which plaintiffs had been harmed by the consumption of unwholesome foods. It was later expanded to any product intended for application to or ingestion by the human body such as personal care products and medications.

The underlying philosophy was that the manufacturers and sellers of these products had total control over and knowledge of their methods of production and distribution, and that consumers relied upon them to provide products which were safe for consumption. The courts felt that it was unrealistic to require plaintiffs to determine and prove that there had been negligence in the production of the product and held that, if the product was harmful, the manufacturer was liable regardless of whether there was evidence of fault (Restatement of Torts 1965).

As commonly occurs with legal theory, the doctrine eventually took on a life of its own and was expanded far beyond the scope of products for personal consumption. California courts are generally credited with pronouncing the modern version of product liability in a 1962 case brought by a man who was injured when using a power tool purchased as a gift for him by his wife (*Greenman v. Yuba* 1962). Earlier decisions related to such products had been based upon elaborate notions about breach of contract between the buyer and seller, or breach of warranty, and often made a distinction between the legal obligations of the manufacturer to one who *used* the product as opposed to the purchaser.

The California court did away with any pretense about the meaning and purpose of the doctrine, stating that a manufacturer is strictly liable if it places any product on the market that is defective and causes an injury to any user of the product. The court stated that the doctrine was intended "to insure that the costs of injuries resulting from defective products be borne by the manufacturer that put such products on the market rather than by the injured persons who are powerless to protect themselves" (*Greenman v. Yuba* 1962). Legal scholars have justified the theory on the basis that the manufacturer can easily provide this financial protection as a cost of doing business by simply buying insurance to cover such injuries (Restatement of Torts 1965). There is a legal axiom that "hard cases make bad law" and product manufacturers commonly believe that this is a case in point. For example, the philosophy that the solution for manufacturers is to purchase liability insurance fails to take into account the fact that insurers are under no legal obligation to provide such coverage, or to price it at a rate which can be realistically embraced as a cost of doing business. Nonetheless, the concept of strict liability in tort has been adopted in most states and in some instances has been embodied in state legislation. It is still the most common allegation in injury claims against manufacturers and sellers of products.

Basis of Liability

Although strict liability in tort is a very challenging standard, the mere occurrence of an injury while using a product does not create liability. The plaintiff must establish certain elements to recover.

The most critical questions are whether the product is defective (possesses some injury-producing characteristic) and whether it is unreasonably dangerous. Different definitions of the latter term have evolved over the years but the most commonly applied is that the product is *more dangerous than the ordinary user would anticipate.*

A landmark Arizona case applied the doctrine of strict liability to the sport setting in 1976 (*Byrns v. Riddell* 1976). The plaintiff was a high school player who suffered a debilitating brain injury during a football game and sued the manufacturer of his helmet. The case is important in two respects: 1) It established that the questions of whether the product was defective and unreasonably dangerous is to be decided by the jury; and 2) it set forth the criteria to be considered in reaching that decision. These criteria, derived from various legal treatises and court decisions are:

1. The usefulness and desirability of the product;

2. The availability of other and safer products to meet the same need;

3. The likelihood of injury and its probable seriousness;

4. The obviousness of the danger;

5. Common knowledge and normal public expectation of the danger (particularly for established products);

6. The avoidability of injury by care in the use of the product (including the effect of instructions or warnings); and

7. The ability to eliminate the danger without seriously impairing the usefulness of the product or making it unduly expensive.

The court was also careful to point out that these criteria cannot be applied in the abstract, but must be considered in light of the specific facts of the case (*Byrns v. Riddell* 1976). While not universally applied, they are widely accepted as the method for determining whether a product is defective and unreasonably dangerous.

In 2001, the U.S. Court of Appeals, Fifth Circuit, employed a more succinct and somewhat modified version of the *Byrns* criteria in another case against Riddell arising out of a football brain injury. Employing the standard legal precept that federal courts follow the law of the state in which the claim arose, the court adopted language from various Texas cases (and one earlier case in a Texas-based federal district court) to outline the basic issues to be addressed by the court in a product liability case:

1. To evaluate whether a product has a design defect in light of the economic and scientific feasibility of safer alternatives, noting that the degree of feasibility is one factor to be weighed in balancing the utility of a product versus its risks;

2. If there are no safer alternatives, a product is not unreasonably dangerous as a matter of law; and

3. The manufacturer is not required to destroy the utility of a product in order to make it safe (*Rodriguez v. Riddell Sports Inc., et al.* 2001).

More recently, the New York court, in setting forth the criteria in that state for determining whether a product is not reasonably safe, stated that "the proper inquiry is 'whether it is a product which, if the design defect were known at the time of manufacture, a reasonable person would conclude that the utility of the product did not outweigh the risk inherent in marketing a product designed in that manner' (citing *Voss v. Black & Decker Mfg. Co.*NY 1983)." In setting forth seven criteria to be followed in deciding that issue, the court used language somewhat similar to that in the *Bynes* decision, but containing two important modifications, i.e., "the potential for designing and manufacturing the product so that it is safer but remains functional *and reasonably priced*, (and) the manufacturer's ability to *spread any cost* related to improving the safety of the design[emphasis added]" (*Anaya v. Town Sports International*, et al. NY 2007).

Unlike negligence cases which primarily focus on the knowledge and conduct of the defendant, in product liability cases the primary issue is the expectation of the typical user regarding dangers related to use of the product. This means that it is not only a question of whether school administrators responsible for purchasing sport equipment appreciate the dangers involved in using a product such as a protective helmet, but whether the students who will use the helmet share that appreciation.

Another essential component of product liability is proof that the defect *caused* the injury. For example, a plaintiff might claim that a softball batter's helmet was defective because it contained microscopic cracks in the shell which destroyed the ability of the helmet to protect against a blow from a softball. Even if this allegation was true, a plaintiff injured when struck on a part of the face not covered by the helmet would not have a valid claim of strict liability in tort.

Jurisdiction Over Lawsuits and Applicable Law

Another challenge for manufacturers is that persons injured using their products may file suit where they live or where the injury occurred. This means that a manufacturer must be prepared to defend litigation in every state in which its products are used. More importantly, the court where the suit is filed will apply the law of its state, not the home state of the manufacturer. Thus, as demonstrated by the *Byrns, Rodriguez* and *Anaya* cases referred to above, the legal standard imposed on the manufacturer may vary in different lawsuits, even though the products and the injuries may be the same.

Common Allegations

Product liability claims focus on either the design of the product, the manufacture of the product, the labels and instructional materials which accompany the product or a combination of these issues. Design claims are the most complicated and usually involve a great deal of technical evidence.

An interesting example of a claim of "design defect" is the *Anaya* case referred to above, in which the plaintiff was a novice "rock climber" injured while using an indoor rock-climbing wall at a facility owned by the defendant Town Sports International (TSI). He was provided a "harness" manufactured by Petzl America, Inc., another defendant in the case. The plaintiff's injury occurred because a TSI employee attached the safety line he used to a non-weight-bearing gear loop on the harness, rather than to the "anchor point" to which it should have been attached. While the plaintiff was 30 feet off the floor, the gear loop tore away from the harness, causing him to fall. TSI settled with the plaintiff, and Petzl moved for summary judgment on the product liability claims, which the trial court granted. The appellate court reversed that decision and sent the case back for trial. On the issue of design defect, Petzl had admitted that novice climbers like the plaintiff had been known to mistakenly attach safety lines to these gear loops. Rather than eliminating them, or designing them to be weight-bearing, however, the company decided to make these loops *appear* "flimsy" as a way of discouraging people from using them for safety purposes. The appellate court commented that it was up to a jury to determine whether this was an effective approach to making the product "reasonably safe."

Claims of manufacturing defect allege that the particular item used by the plaintiff is defective, rather than attacking the entire product category. Perhaps the plastic used to make the product was substandard, or someone on the manufacturer's assembly line failed to properly attach a critical part. In these cases the plaintiff may prevail by simply comparing the suspect item with other units of the same make, model, vintage and/or with the manufacturer's specifications. However, the plaintiff must also prove that the problem was caused by the manufacturer and did not arise due to some untoward event that occurred after the product left the manufacturer's possession.

Defects related to labeling or instructional materials occur when information outside the awareness of the ordinary consumer is necessary to properly use the product or avoid dangers inherent in its use. For example, most people do not realize that many types of paints and cleaning materials will cause deterioration of the plastics from which athletic helmets are made, reducing their ability to protect against impact. The manufacturer must attach a warning label advising the consumer of this fact and include instructional materials regarding proper procedures for cleaning and painting the product; otherwise, the helmet may become unreasonably dangerous when cleaned or painted with the wrong product.

In the *Anaya* case the plaintiff also alleged failure to warn. Knowing that novice climbers might mistakenly attach safety lines to the gear loops, Petzl had warned against this, *but these warnings were contained in the user manual and in a technical notice*, which the plaintiff never saw. There was a small label on the harness with a skull and cross-bones symbol directing the user to these publications, but nothing on the harness warned against tying a safety line to the gear loop. The trial court had held that the label on the harness and the content of the manual and technical notice satisfied the manufacturer's duty to warn. The appellate court reversed, saying that a jury must be allowed to decide whether these warnings were sufficient to make the product "reasonably safe."

Users may also fail to appreciate the limitations in the ability of a product to protect against harm, even when used as intended by the manufacturer. In 1981 a Texas court ruled that a football helmet which did not contain a label warning the user of the possibility of sustaining a brain injury despite wearing a helmet was defective and unreasonably dangerous (*Rawlings v. Daniels* 1981). The National Operating Committee on Standards in Athletic Equipment (NOCSAE) has incorporated into its standards for football helmets a requirement that each helmet bear a warning label advising the wearer of its limited ability to protect the head and its inability to protect the neck. The standard even specifies the type of language which must be used in the label (NOCSAE Football Helmet Standard 2009.)

Allegations of defective design are more difficult to prove. The plaintiff must demonstrate that because of its design, the product created a risk beyond the expectation of the ordinary consumer. This amounts to an attack on the entire line of products, meaning that every item sold is defective. Consequently, manufacturers must go to great lengths to overcome these claims.

A widely-publicized example of design defect allegations is litigation against football helmet manufacturers. Over the past three decades literally hundreds of claims have been presented, most of them involving allegations of defective design.

Football helmet lawsuits have been divided almost equally between claims of brain injury and claims of neck injury. In brain injury cases, plaintiffs claim their helmet failed to protect them to the degree that ordinary users anticipate. Neck injury cases have included both claims of inadequate protection and claims that the shape of the helmet increased the risk of injury.

Lawyers often refer to design defect cases as a "war of experts." In football helmet lawsuits, plaintiffs commonly hire medical and engineering experts to render opinions about how the injury occurred, the probable forces involved, and ways the injury could have been avoided. These experts generally suggest an alternative design approach which they claim would have reduced the impact forces to levels at which the injury would not have occurred. While these opinions may be based, in part, upon scientific experiments or analysis, they typically are not supported by testing of an alternative product which has proven effective in the field of play.

Manufacturers counter that no helmet can provide absolute protection against brain injury and that ordinary users are aware of this. They assert that modern football helmets do an excellent job of protecting the scalp and skull, but that the anatomy and physiology of the head and the mechanism by which serious brain injury occurs make it impossible to substantially reduce that risk without changing the nature of the game.

They allege, however, that modern designs have reduced the rate of catastrophic head injuries and that the incidence is extremely low given the nature of the game. It has been estimated that there are more than 300,000,000 head impacts in football every year (Powell 1996). Nonetheless, following the adoption of the NOCSAE football helmet standard in 1973, the annual rate of catastrophic head injury dropped by more than 50 percent and has remained at less than one per 100,000 players for more than two decades (Mueller, Canter and Van Camp 1996). More importantly, the rate is essentially the same for *all* designs (Clarke and Powell 1979). Manufacturers claim that, if poor design was the cause of serious head injuries, there would be many more such events each year. Since the presentation of these opposing theories of helmet design involves complex scientific testimony which jurors find difficult to assess, and since jurors tend to sympathize with catastrophically injured plaintiffs, manufacturers must also demonstrate in graphic ways the protective capabilities and qualities of their products. This is often accomplished through videotaped demonstrations of helmet testing under extreme conditions which reveal that, using the most stringent scientific standards currently in place, the helmet in question provides remarkable protection.

In neck injury cases, the initial claims against football helmet manufacturers were that the configuration of the back rim of the helmet shell imposed dangerous forces on the neck when the helmet was struck from the front. When scientific study proved this theory to be unsound, plaintiffs began claiming that the helmet could prevent neck injuries if designed with more effective padding. This theory, too, has been scientifically refuted, leaving plaintiffs with only the claim that manufacturers have failed to effectively warn players of the risk of neck injury due to head first contact. This allegation led to the addition of warning labels to all football helmets, along with the inclusion of risk information in company catalogues and other literature.

Defenses to Product Liability Claims

One way to refute a claim of strict liability in tort is to show that there was a substantial change in the product following the time it left the manufacturer. This may be due to removal of essential components, e.g. interior padding from a protective helmet; modification of the product, e.g. cutting out a portion of the wires in a face guard; or deterioration due to excessive use. In each of these instances, but especially the claim of deterioration, the manufacturer must show that it provided consumers with clear instructions and warnings regarding changes in the product and how they create risks which the user might not otherwise appreciate.

Another defense is misuse of the product. Examples would be putting "youth" helmets, generally intended for pre-high school athletes, on more mature participants or using a baseball catcher's chest protector in a kick-boxing activity. Products are designed and manufactured with a specific purpose in mind, and they may not only fail to provide adequate protection for another activity, but may actually create added risk. Again, the manufacturer must provide users with clear instructional information in order to successfully use this defense. Referring again to the *Anaya* case discussed above, the defendant manufacturer claimed that the actions of the TSI employee (who admitted to being new, inexperienced and not well-trained in her job) in attaching the safety line to the gear loop, constituted a "misuse" of the product which obviated the manufacturer's liability. The appellate court disagreed, noting particularly Petzl's admission that inexperienced people had been known to make that very mistake, and ruled once again that the question of whether the employee's error was foreseeable and should have been considered by the manufacturer in the design of the product, was a decision for the jury.

A number of state legislatures have established certain statutory defenses in product liability cases. One of the biggest problems for manufacturers relates to claims arising from the use of out-dated products, particularly when design standards have changed considerably since the allegedly defective product was made. Typical provisions establish a "state-of-the-art" defense which holds that the defendant is not liable if the product conformed to state-of-the-art standards at the time it was made (ARS). Without such a defense, manufacturers can be held to standards in place at the time of the trial rather than when the product was manufactured.

Another protection for manufacturers implemented by state legislatures has been the establishment of statutes of limitation related specifically to product liability claims. These have come about because of instances in which suits were filed relating to injuries that occurred as much as 15–20 years after the product was sold, and occasionally even longer. In Arizona, the statute of limitation on product liability suits is 12 years after the product was sold, unless the claim relates to negligence of the manufacturer or seller, or to a breach of express warranty provided by the manufacturer (ARS 2011). In Oregon the limit is only 10 years (ORS 2011). In the case of football helmets, which are commonly used well past the 10–12 year limitations period, this has resulted in plaintiffs directing their litigation against the school or team organization that supplied the helmet, and/or the company which reconditioned the helmet, who must defend against claims alleging negligence for allowing and even encouraging the continued use of these "outdated" products, long after allegedly "safer" designs became available. As a result, the National Athletic Equipment Reconditioners' Association (NAERA) has adopted a requirement that it's members refuse to recondition helmets which are more than 10 years old (NAERA 2011).

Liability for Negligence

Strict liability is not the only basis for suing manufacturers. Whether or not that theory is recognized in the state where suit is filed, the plaintiff can also claim that the manufacturer was negligent in the design, manufacture or distribution of a product. These claims require proof of the same four elements of liability which are essential to any negligence lawsuit:

1. That the manufacturer had a duty to the plaintiff;
2. That there was a breach of the duty;
3. That the breach caused the injury; and
4. That the plaintiff suffered damages.

The fundamental distinction between negligence cases and strict liability cases is that in a negligence case it is the awareness of the manufacturer which is important, not the awareness of the plaintiff. If the manufacturer knew or should have known of a risk related to the product but did nothing to reduce that risk, there is strong evidence of negligence. If, however, the manufacturer had no way of knowing of the risk until after the injury occurred, and acted reasonably in other respects, it may be difficult for the plaintiff to establish liability.

Solutions for Manufacturers

While there is no guaranteed protection against litigation, there are certain measures which manufacturers can employ to reduce the likelihood of suit and to increase the likelihood of a favorable outcome if they are sued. In some respects these preventive measures may adversely impact programs which purchase the manufacturers' equipment.

Care must be taken in the wording, design and distribution of company literature, product instructions and labels. In this respect there is often a "tension" between those responsible for marketing and sales, and those charged with designing products or reducing liability risk. Marketing people want to assure that all company literature encourages sales and avoids communicating any message which might discourage purchasers. They often fail to appreciate the close scrutiny given to this documentation in a lawsuit or, in the context of a severe injury, how much emphasis may be placed upon particular words or phrases.

An example is the information provided in product catalogues and literature, which accompany the product, regarding procedures for fitting protective equipment. Administrators, coaches and equipment managers want the fitting process to be quick and simple. Consequently, marketing people want company catalogues and fitting instructions to portray the process in that manner in order to encourage purchase of the product. In actual practice, however, there are always challenges in assuring proper fitting of equipment for *every* athlete. Unless the company provides written instructions in sufficient detail to address all those concerns, the result may be poorly-fitted equipment which leads to liability for unnecessary injuries.

Another example of these conflicting viewpoints is the warning labels on protective helmets. In the late 1970s claims began to emerge that helmets were defective because of the absence of warning labels advising users of the risk of brain injury despite wearing a helmet. For lawyers, the simple solution was to add clear and explicit warning labels, which would immediately eliminate those claims. Marketing executives, however, feared that such labels might discourage purchase of the product, particularly if competing companies did not attach the same warning to their products.

Care in the Wording of Company Advertising

In the mid-1970s, a manufacturer introducing a new football helmet published advertisements which claimed it to be "the type of helmet a neurosurgeon would want his son to wear if his son played football." Other advertising language as well as company press releases and literature proclaimed the superior capability of this helmet to prevent brain injury (Ball 1997). Once the helmet achieved significant market penetration and wide-spread usage, however, brain injuries occurred to some of its users. Since the core issue in a product liability case is whether the product is more dangerous than the ordinary user would anticipate, this type of language increases the difficulty in defending claims filed by brain-injured athletes who assert that they used that helmet because they thought it would provide greater protection.

Research and Quality Control Which Demonstrate Maximum Concern for the Safety of Product Users, and Record Keeping Which Documents That Concern

Sporting goods manufacturers now have the benefit of standards from recognized standard-making organizations such as NOCSAE and the American Society for Testing and Materials (ASTM), which provide guidelines relating to the design, manufacture and testing of many products, e.g. protective helmets, face guards, eye guards, landing mats and even sport bras. They must be able to document compliance with applicable standards, but also prove that they have addressed safety issues not covered by the standards. Although "fault" is not an issue in a strict liability case, jurors tend to be strongly influenced by the fact that the product was carefully designed and meets a widely-accepted standard. Additionally, by showing a strong commitment to research and development and demonstrating the high quality of its products, a manufacturer stands a much better chance of convincing the jury that its product was not defective. Conversely, if the product fails to meet established standards or the manufacturer has not conducted appropriate research, the jury is likely to find in favor of the plaintiff.

Education of the Marketplace Regarding Safe Use of the Product

Football helmet manufacturers have been very aggressive in making administrators and coaches aware of the need for strict compliance with the rules of football prohibiting initial contact with the top of the helmet. Their efforts have included producing videos for distribution to schools, sending speakers to conferences and clinics, distributing posters for display in locker rooms and making replacement warning labels readily available. Because certain sport programs tend to use products beyond their intended life or in a deteriorated condition, helmet manufacturers have also advocated periodic inspection and reconditioning of their products by qualified suppliers, and have recommended an age limit beyond which their products are not to be used. These educational measures not only reduce risk, but create awareness of risk in the minds of consumers. This makes it more difficult for a plaintiff to show that the product was more dangerous than the ordinary consumer would anticipate.

Raising the Price of Products to Cover the Cost of Litigation

In addition to the cost of liability insurance, such policies often impose a substantial self-insured retention or deductible which the manufacturer must pay before the insurance company provides coverage. Additionally, litigation drains manufacturer resources by necessitating in-house research which would not otherwise be undertaken; requiring time (and often travel expenses) of company employees cooperating with defense lawyers, complying with the plaintiff's discovery requests and attending proceedings in the locale where the litigation is conducted; and creating negative publicity which must be overcome by aggressive marketing efforts. Whenever possible, manufacturers pass these costs on to the consumer in the price of their products.

Placing Responsibility on Others for Causing the Injury

In addition to pointing out misuse or modification of the product, the manufacturer may blame the plaintiff's coaches, administrators or sport medicine advisors for failing to follow company guidelines relating to the selection, fit, use, maintenance and replacement of the product, or to properly instruct the plaintiff regarding safe use of the product. While this can be a dangerous tactic, particularly for an out-of-state manufacturer trying to convince a jury to impose liability upon a local sport program, many trial lawyers, insurance companies and manufacturers believe in this strategy.

States have varying legal standards for how the conduct of the plaintiff may be raised as a defense. Some have held that, since the fault of the manufacturer is not an issue in a strict liability case, neither is the plaintiff's negligence an issue. Others allow manufacturers to raise the issue of the plaintiff having caused or contributed to the injury in strict liability cases, as well as in cases alleging negligence by the manufacturer, where the conduct of the defendant is always an appropriate issue. Again, however, the defense runs the risk of incurring the wrath of the jury for "blaming the victim," and the wiser strategy is to be able to show that the product was not defective or that the manufacturer was not negligent rather than relying on the jury to hold the plaintiff responsible.

Litigation Outcomes

Despite all the apprehension about product liability and the sensationalized results in a few cases, manufacturers have been relatively successful in this type of litigation. Several multi-million dollar verdicts have been widely publicized, but the majority of cases that have been decided by a jury have resulted in defense verdicts (Ball). Unfortunately, the media do not consider these outcomes to be as "newsworthy" as a high-dollar verdict, so they receive very little publicity.

The more imposing aspect of product litigation, from the standpoint of the manufacturer, is the cost of defending claims. Successful defense of a catastrophic injury claim against a sporting goods manufacturer can easily cost several hundred thousand dollars for attorneys fees, expert witnesses, special testing and research, travel and other expenses related to the lawsuit (Ball). This is the reason that the vast majority of claims are settled before trial, but even in those instances the combination of pre-settlement defense costs and the payout to the plaintiff may still amount to a substantial sum.

Another dilemma created by the concept of strict liability is the availability and affordability of insurance coverage. In times of financial crisis in the insurance industry it may be impossible to find a carrier that will provide product liability coverage. Even when available, the cost may be so prohibitive that to incorporate it into the cost of doing business would put the price of products out of reach of most consumers. This is particularly true in an industry which has a small market, such as protective athletic helmets.

Impact Upon Sport Programs

While the law of product liability does not directly apply to sport programs and their employees, such lawsuits produce numerous indirect effects. The most obvious result is the increased price of equipment to cover the cost of potential litigation. While all manufacturers attempt to remain competitive in their pricing, the danger in purchasing solely based upon "low bid" is that the product may be substandard because the manufacturer is concerned only with short-term profits and not with long-term financial stability. This type of manufacturer may also be out of business when a lawsuit is filed, leaving the plaintiff to look for others, such as the sport organization, to hold responsible.

Another possibility is the loss of programs or activities. Rising costs of equipment may force a school or organization to abandon equipment-intensive sport for less costly activities. Administrators or governing boards frightened by publicity of substantial plaintiffs' verdicts may insist on discontinuing the activity even though the losing defendants were manufacturers and not sport programs. Similarly, insurance carriers unwilling to distinguish between claims against manufacturers and claims against programs may refuse coverage to the program unless activities involving certain equipment are eliminated. A rash of litigation against trampoline manufacturers (accompanied by substantially fewer against programs) in the late 1960s and early 1970s led to virtual elimination of the trampoline from school campuses, despite the fact that under proper supervision and instruction it is a relatively safe device and an excellent teaching tool (AAHPERD 1978).

Even when the sport program is not a defendant, program personnel are inevitably drawn into litigation. Normally, one or more employees are witnesses to the injury event. Employees are also responsible for selecting and fitting the equipment, instructing the athletes in its use, and warning them of risks. All these may become issues in the litigation, leading to program personnel spending endless hours in interviews by investigators and lawyers, interrogation in depositions and testifying in trial. In addition to the imposition upon their time, program personnel suffer considerable emotional drain from being torn between concern for a tragically injured student and loyalty to a manufacturer that has been a long-standing provider of quality equipment.

The last element of exposure for sport programs is being targeted as a defendant. This may result from the manufacturer being out of business or being a foreign company not subject to the jurisdiction of the court, or a manufacturer that takes legal steps to involve the program in the litigation as a way to avoid or reduce its own liability exposure. The fact that product litigation has called attention to issues like selection, fit, maintenance, replacement and instruction relating to use of equipment, and that many product manufacturers have an excellent record of success in product liability cases, may also cause the plaintiff's lawyer to target the sport program. Many sport injury lawsuits involve claims of strict liability against the manufacturer and of negligence against the sport program in which the plaintiff participated (Ball).

Liability of Programs Related to Equipment

While not subject to true product liability claims, sport programs must be concerned about claims of negligence related to products. These generally fall into the following categories:

1. Modification or misuse of products;

2. Failure to follow manufacturers' guidelines related to selection, fit, maintenance or replacement of products;

3. Inadequate instruction of athletes related to use of products; or

4. Failure to warn athletes and parents of the limited ability of products to reduce the risks of participation.

A product may be *modified* intentionally by cutting the ear flaps off of a batter's helmet or removing sections of protective padding; or inadvertently, such as by using improper paint or cleaning agents. Such actions by program personnel would clearly be the responsibility of the program. If undertaken by athletes or their parents, the program may be held responsible for failing to properly educate them about these concerns, supervise their conduct or inspect their equipment. Misuse may result from the indiscretion of the individual user or from an error on the part of program administrators or coaches. Examples are issuing baseball/softball batter's helmets to hockey or lacrosse players, allowing a batter to use a catcher's helmet, and providing "youth" helmets to high school varsity players.

Failure to follow company guidelines related to the use of products is a common problem in sport programs. To protect themselves against product litigation, manufacturers have undertaken substantial efforts to provide educational and instructional materials to consumers in the form of catalogues and other advertising literature, instruction booklets and charts, and warning labels. Program personnel must familiarize themselves with, and carefully adhere to this information, in order to avoid liability. They must also assure that essential information is passed along to athletes and their parents.

Critical areas where company advisories are often disregarded are the *fitting* of helmets and other protective equipment, regular *inspection* of equipment during the season, *reconditioning* of helmets and *replacement* of products which have exceeded a certain age. The new NAERA requirement alluded to above, which prohibits reconditioning of helmets more than 10 years old, will place an added burden on schools and other team organizations to assure that they are not supplying players with outdated equipment, or face potential liability claims for doing so.

Inadequate instruction and supervision of athletes is the most prevalent claim against sport programs, and this responsibility pertains to their use of equipment just as it does to all other aspects of participation. Athletes must be taught how to inspect their equipment and what actions to take when problems are detected. They must also be taught to avoid abusing their equipment and the types of usage which can create risk.

Claims of inadequate *risk warnings* have become very common and are the most difficult to defend. Many manufacturers have filled their catalogues and instruction booklets with risk warnings in addition to placing warning labels on their products, but it is up to the program to assure that athletes receive and adhere to this information. Very few programs provide players with a copy of the fitting instructions for their helmets even though most companies ship a booklet with every helmet. Programs also often fail to replace damaged warning labels on helmets even though they are readily available from manufacturers, dealers and reconditioners, and the absence of a label means that the helmet does not meet the NOCSAE standard.

Solutions for Programs

1. *Establish and enforce written policies and procedures related to equipment.*

These must be distributed to, and adhered to, by all program personnel. It is imperative to educate those who purchase equipment as well as administrators, coaches, equipment personnel, athletes and parents regarding essential product issues. Too often, people in the purchasing department of the sport organization have no appreciation of differences in the nature and quality of equipment and allow price to control their buying decisions. In addition to properly assigning and fitting equipment, equipment managers, coaches *and* athletes must be educated in how to inspect protective equipment to assure continuation of proper fit and to identify problems which require repair. Equipment personnel must be aware of manufacturers' guidelines regarding repairs and maintenance of their products. They should also be certified by that National Equipment Managers' Association as possessing the minimum knowledge and skill required for their position.

2. *Provide a structure for expediently resolving equipment problems.* If coaches and athletes perceive that reporting equipment problems will interfere with participation, problems are more likely to be ignored. This requires putting a knowledgeable person in charge of equipment, and providing the tools and replacement parts required for immediately completing necessary repairs.

3. *Use care in administering and documenting the risk warning process.* Informed consent has become the standard in sport programs and, without awareness of the risks related to the use of protective equipment and of the limited ability of that equipment to reduce the risks of participation, athletes and parents cannot provide legally-binding informed consent.

4. *Use care in reconditioning and replacement of protective equipment.* Most manufacturers provide guidelines relating to these issues and experienced vendors should be relied upon to assist in identifying items which require reconditioning or should be replaced.

5. *Preserve critical evidence following injuries which may relate to the use of equipment.* This includes not only the particular item of equipment involved, but documents relating to the purchase, usage and maintenance of that equipment; any video or other photographic documentation of the event; written reports or statements of supervisory personnel or eyewitnesses; copies of educational materials or risk warning information provided to athletes and parents; and the athlete's informed consent documents. It is also important to immediately report the injury to the manufacturer and provide any information the manufacturer may request regarding the occurrence. In general, manufacturers have far more experience dealing with these matters than most sport programs, and they can become a valuable ally in fending off potential claims. Conversely, by establishing an adversarial relationship with the manufacturer, the sport program may be inviting unnecessary litigation and place itself at a disadvantage in the event of a lawsuit.

In My Opinion

In spite of many years of widely publicized litigation, manufacturers, reconditioners and sport programs still do not cooperate effectively to reduce their liability risk related to products. These entities must all work together more closely to reduce the likelihood of product liability claims and suits for negligence related to equipment. Certain manufacturers have taken important steps to provide sport programs with educational materials and training related to safer use of products, but this needs to be an on-going process with new and updated materials being periodically provided. Sport programs need to be more attentive to information that is forth-coming from manufacturers and reconditioners and more aggressive in the education of parents and athletes. There is also a need for greater dialogue between manufacturers and consumers regarding injury risk and how improvements in equipment might reduce that risk. Sport programs need to be more aggressive in hiring certified athletic trainers and certified equipment managers, and assigning them responsibility for addressing injury prevention and other equipment concerns. This will improve safety by not only reducing the liability exposure of those programs, but decreasing the negative effects upon them which result from product liability suits against manufacturers.

References

American Alliance for Health, Physical Education, Recreation and Dance. 1978. *The Use of Trampolines and Minitramps in Physical Education*. A policy statement. Washington, D.C.

Anaya v. Town Sports International, Inc., et al., 843 NYS 2d 590 (2007).

Arizona Revised Statutes (ARS) Section 12-551 & 12-683 (1).

Ball, R.T. Anecdotal experience of author.

Byrns v. Riddell, 550 P.2d 1065 (Ariz. 1976).

Clarke, K. and John Powell. 1979. "Football Helmets and Neurotrauma—An Epidemiologic Overview of Three Seasons." *Medicine and Science in Sport* vol. 11, p. 138.

Greenman v. Yuba Power Products, Inc., 377 P.2d 897 (Cal. 1962).

Hemphill v. Sayers, et al., 552 F. Supp. 685 (S.D. Ill. 1982).

Mueller, Frederick, Robert Cantu and Steven VanCamp. 1996. *Catastrophic Injuries in High School and College Sport*, p. 44. Human Kinetics.

NOCSAE Standard Performance Specification For Football Helmets, updated 2009. National Operating Committee on Standards for Athletic Equipment.

Oregon Revised Statutes (ORS) Section 30.905.

Powell, John. 1996. "Epidemiology of Mild Brain Injury in Sport." Paper presented at Conference on Sport Related Concussions: Neurologic and Neuropsychologic Evaluations and Management, sponsored by Allegany General Hospital, The Medical College of Pennsylvania and Hahnemann University.

Rawlings Sporting Goods Co., Inc. v. Daniels, 619 S.W.2d 435 (Tex. 1981).

Restatement of Torts 2d. 1965. Sec. 402A, Comments b & c, vol. 2, pp. 348–350. American Law Institute Publishers.

Rodriguez v. Riddell Sports Inc., et al., 242 F.3d 567 (CCA 5th Circuit 2001).

Chapter 6

Safe Transportation

Know your duties as they relate to transportation responsibilities within the organization.

David LaVetter

Whether you are a coach or sport manager in youth recreational sport, club sport, public or private high school, collegiate athletics, professional sport, or other similar situations, you will most likely be faced with transportation decisions that will significantly affect your organization and its participants. Consider these questions related to transporting participants and staff: Am I required to transport participants to our sports event? Which mode of transportation should we use? Who will do the driving? Is there any driver training that must be completed prior to travel? How safe are the vehicles? How do I respond if a parent wishes to transport their own child? Is there an emergency plan in case of an accident? Should I continue to drive in inclement weather? The responses to these questions will certainly depend on the type of organization, the responsibilities of your job, and the legal duties associated with providing safe transportation. The most common transportation issues currently arising in sport-related settings are modes of transport (size of group), budget, driver training, insurance, maintenance, and state codes for transporting students. Even if the sport administrator is not directly responsible for vehicle maintenance, each vehicle should be properly inspected by the driver prior to departure.

Duty to Provide Safe Transportation

If you are working for club sport, or a recreational setting, it is essential to ask your administrator about the organization's current transportation policies. If they do not have any policies, develop them! Know your duties as they relate to transportation responsibilities within the organization. In school settings, athletics are considered extracurricular activities sponsored by the school, thereby establishing a principal/agent relationship. The corresponding duty to provide safe transportation for team members to off-campus athletic events rests with the institution (van der Smissen, 1990; Pittman, 1994; Appenzeller, 2003). The duty to provide safe transportation begins with securing or checking current travel insurance policies, gaining required authorized travel forms, selecting the appropriate mode of safe transportation for your group, selecting a qualified driver, supervising the entire group from the point of meeting at the vehicle and throughout the entire trip, and finally ensuring all passengers are safely in their vehicles to return to their destinations.

Unfortunately, these duties are often overlooked and present an increased risk to the organization and each passenger's safety. Not having a transport-related accident for decades does not guarantee the next trip will be free from danger. Therefore, establishing transportation policies that align with the recommended travel procedures and practices help minimize risk and potential liability and, more importantly, increase safety. These policies must be consistent. That is, if exceptions and inconsistencies prevail, then prudent practices begin to slacken and the institution increases its risk for lawsuits. For example, in a recent school case, a school district had mandated seat belt use in vans for all passengers at all times. In the deposition, the coaches would turn around and ask all the passengers to fasten their seat belts, yet would begin driving prior to the actual fastening of all seat belts. The coach is not the absolute insurer of a passenger's safety; however, many staff may know the policies but do not regularly enforce them.

Transportation Options

Each of the various modes of transportation described below carries a certain level of risk and measure of institutional liability. Many factors influence the decision concerning which modes of transportation are best suited for each sport and each trip. Each organization has the responsibility to select the best mode which will fulfill their legal obligation to safely transport the passengers, regardless of financial constraints.

Chartered Plane

Some institutions may use aircraft under certain conditions (e.g. long distance traveled, post-season competition, or inclement weather). Approximately one-third of NAIA and NJCAA schools use aircraft when traveling longer distances for their athletic events (LaVetter, 2010). After the fatal crash in 2001, Oklahoma State University issued prudent requirements regarding future use of aircraft. Policy changes after the Wichita State University and Marshall University accidents have also greatly assisted other collegiate athletics programs to develop more careful travel polices today. Teams may use commercial air carriers, charters, and other aircraft; however, all air travel, except on commercial airlines, is subject to review by the institution's aviation consultant. Proper certificates and qualifications are provided by chartered flights, and aircraft owners must furnish proof of insurance in advance. The sport organization's liability may not be avoided if reasonable care was not taken in choosing a competent air carrier (van der Smissen, 1990).

Chartered Bus

In order to transfer most of the transportation risk to an independent contractor, an organization may elect to use chartered buses. For the most part, these practices usually represent a safer practice for your transportation needs, notwithstanding an increased cost compared to vans or organization-owned buses. Again, organizations may still be held liable if they are negligent in the selection of the independent contractor. One must take prudent steps to ensure the screening and selection of an appropriate independent contractor has been made (Pittman, 2004, Appenzeller, 2003).

15-Passenger Van

Another mode of transportation common for youth group organizations, churches, military academies, and schools is the 15-passenger van. Even if the organization owns and operates these vans itself, they carry much risk and liability. Passenger vans handle very differently from smaller passenger vehicles because they are typically longer, higher, and wider. They require additional reliance on the side mirrors for changing lanes, more space, additional braking distances, and have a higher risk of crashes and rollovers if not properly driven and maintained. Fifteen-passenger vans were originally designed as cargo vans. This mode of transportation is still commonly used in high school and college athletics. Today, 80% of small colleges employ 15-passenger vans to help meet their transportation needs (LaVetter, 2005). This practice represents a continued risk management problem facing these schools as well as other organizations.

The National Highway Transportation Safety Administration (NHTSA) has addressed the risks and dangers of rollover and accidents associated with continued use of 15-passenger vans. The NHTSA (2004a) issued an updated report pertaining to fatalities that occurred in 15-passenger van rollover crashes between 1990 and 2002. More than 75 percent (556/725) of all fatalities were in vans involved in single-vehicle accidents. Approximately 53 percent of the 15-passenger vans were involved in fatal, single-vehicle rollover crashes (NHTSA, 2004a). Fifteen-passenger vans are at high risk for rollover under certain conditions (e.g., curved roads, inclement weather, overloading, and speeding). When traveling with 10 or more occupants, with equipment behind the rear wheel axel, or with equipment on top, the vehicle is at risk for rollover (NTSB, 2002; NHTSA, 2004a). Among several other warnings, the NHTSA cautioned that 15-passenger vans are three times more likely to roll over when carrying more than 10 passengers than when carrying fewer than 10 passengers, or lightly loaded (NHTSA, 2004a).

Some administrators may claim it's a question of budget, but many schools are aware of the increased dangers of using these vans and consequently, have changed their policies (i.e., discontinued 15-passenger van usage). For example, after hearing of repeated warnings issued in 2001 and 2003 from the NHTSA, a school district in Ann Arbor, MI now prohibits the use of 15-passenger vans. The district's policy allows smaller roster teams, such as golf, tennis, cross-country, water polo, and gymnastics to take 7-passenger vans driven by coaches, district school buses, or charter coaches. For them, there was only a $20 difference in renting two 7-passenger vans instead of a 15-passenger. Additionally, the decision to take the district's buses costs about $80–$100 more compared to the 15-passenger vans (Schimke, 2004). Some may question the inefficiency of such decisions (taking district buses or chartered buses for small teams), but the focus must be on passenger safety, not money. Administrators should strongly consider the rollover statistics, NHTSA recommendations, and expert arguments. In a recent lawsuit involving a 15-passenger van accident during an athletics away game, it was determined that the drivers had no specialized driver training for vans. Additionally, equipment and heavy ice chests were stored in the back of the van (behind the rear axle). The district's transportation policies were found to be vague, incomplete, and not updated to reflect the latest NHTSA recommendations. The school district was found liable, appealed, and the case was then settled out of court. The organization's transportation policies related to van use should be very clear, implemented in the transportation handbook and in staff meetings, placed on the organization's website, and most importantly, enforced. Some states do not allow the purchase of new vans for student-related travel (see Figure 1). It is strongly recommended to not use 15-passenger vans for team travel.

Figure 1. State Laws for 12- and 15-Passenger Vans
Used for School Transportation

State	To & From School	To & From School-Related Events	Comments
Alabama	No*	No*	*State laws do not apply to private schools.
Alaska	No*	Yes*	*State laws do not apply to private schools.
Arizona	No	Yes	
Arkansas	Yes	Yes	
California	No	No	
Colorado	Yes*	Yes*	*State-wide, self-insurance pool for school districts ceased insuring vans after July 1, 2005.
Connecticut	No	Yes	
Delaware	No	No	
Florida	No*	No*	*Does not apply to private schools or companies that contract directly with parents.
Georgia	No*	Yes*	*State laws do not apply to private schools.
Hawaii	Yes	Yes	
Idaho	No*	Yes	*State statute allows for some exceptions, e.g., students with special needs in remote locations without school buses. *State laws do not apply to private schools.
Illinois	No	Yes	
Indiana	No*	Yes**	*Special education students may be transported in vans. *Vans prohibited after June 2006. State laws do not apply to private schools.
Iowa	No	No	
Kansas	No	No	
Kentucky	No	No	
Louisiana	No*	No*	*State laws do not apply to private schools.
Maine	No	No*	*Private schools are exempt from this state regulation.
Maryland	No	No	*State law not clear on private schools.
Massachusetts	Yes	Yes	
Michigan	No	No	
Minnesota	No	No	
Mississippi	Yes*	Yes*	*State law does not prohibit the use of vans but Department of Education will not approve van purchases.
Missouri	No*	Yes*	*State laws do not apply to private schools.
Montana	No*	No*	*State laws do not apply to private schools.
Nebraska	Yes	Yes	
Nevada	No	Yes	
New Hampshire	No	No	

New Jersey	No	No	
New Mexico	No	No	
New York	No	No	
North Carolina	No*	Yes*	*Private schools not covered by state rules.
North Dakota	Yes*	Yes*	*Prohibiteded after June 1, 2008. Vans no longer allowed to be purchased for these purposes after March 1, 2003. State laws do not apply to private schools.
Ohio	No	No	
Oklahoma	No	No	
Oregon	No	No	
Pennsylvania	No*	No*	*Unless the van was registered as a bus in Pennsylvania prior to March 1, 1993, or titled to a public private or parochial school prior to March 1, 1993, and was registered as a bus to such school prior to September 15, 1993.
Rhode Island	No*	No**	*Child care organizations are exempt and can use vans for transportation to and from school. **Vans purchased prior to January 1, 2000 could be used until January 1, 2008.
South Carolina	No*	No*	*Vans purchases prior to July 1, 2000, could be used until June 30, 2006.
South Dakota	No	No	
Tennessee	No	Yes	
Texas	No*	Yes	*Private schools not covered by state rules.
Utah	No	No	
Vermont	Yes	Yes	
Virginia	No*	No*	*State laws only apply to public schools.
Washington	No*	No*	*State rules only apply to public schools.
West Virginia	No	Yes	
Wisconsin	Yes	Yes	
Wyoming	No*	No*	*State rules only apply to public schools.

National Highway Transportation Safety Administration, November, 2004.

12-Passenger Van or SUV

This option has not been proven to be a safer mode of transporting people. The NHTSA (2004a) affirmed that 12-passenger vans or SUVs were found to have similar rollover statistics to those of the 15-passenger vans. Due to a similar propensity to rollover, it is not recommended to use 12-passenger vehicles for student or youth travel.

Mini-Bus

Mini-buses usually accommodate between 20–30 passengers. They are ideal for athletic team travel and should be strongly considered for purchase by sport organizations. These mini-buses have a wider wheelbase than 15-passenger vans, and therefore are safer. Research reveals that just fewer than 50% of schools employ the safer, wider-base minibuses. Many of the administrators surveyed indicated they occasionally rent minibuses, but acknowledged their department needs to more closely consider making a minibus purchase in the future (LaVetter, 2010).

Organization-Owned Vehicles (Buses)

Organizations have a duty to make sure all buses are in proper condition prior to any travel. Detailed records of vehicle maintenance must be kept to reduce liability. This is a safer option than the aforementioned 15-passenger vans, but in the event of legal action, it is the organization's complete responsibility to ensure transportations policies, approval forms, maintenance records, driver qualifications, emergency plans, passenger emergency information, and insurance are all documented for each trip.

Personal Vehicles

Personal vehicles may appear to be a minor issue for athletic administrators. Many sport organizations continue to have policies that generally allow their staff to use personal vehicles for various athletic-related needs. Only 8% of colleges and universities, by policy, do not allow personal vehicles to be used for athletic-related travel (LaVetter, 2010).

If personal vehicles are used for job-related responsibilities, then adequate insurance should be provided for the vehicle and driver by the institution. The driver's records should be kept on file in the athletic department. The department should have a policy for the number of speeding or alcohol citation limits. Whether the driver intends to transport student-athletes, or simply use the personal vehicle for recruiting or scouting responsibilities, the policy should still be the same as recommended pertaining to insurance coverage and strict driving records. Even when a private vehicle is used, the organization may be held liable (through vicariously liability) for employee negligence committed within their scope of employment. If your organization allows for the use of personal vehicles as a service to the organization, good risk management policies would reveal that all drivers of personal vehicles conform to safety standards imposed by the organization (Appenzeller, 2003). For example, zero reckless driver incidences, or zero alcohol-related violations could be imposed for the safety of future passengers. Additionally, proof of insurance and vehicle maintenance could be required for those using personal vehicles.

Youth Drivers

Organizations are strongly recommended not to use student drivers. Young drivers present a difficult risk management problem given their youth and relative lack of driving experience, especially with large vans. Students should not be generalized as incapable of driving vans; yet, if other employed staff, or hired, qualified drivers are available and have passed a defensive driving course, it is recommended they be required to do the driving. This decision should not only originate from an institutional liability viewpoint, but also a from a safety perspective; drivers should be trained, qualified, and have experience driving the specific vehicles they will be assigned to drive. It takes a great deal of skill to safely navigate 15-passenger vans in all kinds of weather and terrain, especially when fully loaded. In a study of collegiate athletics policies, 46% indicated drivers must be 21 or older to drive vehicles for team travel (LaVetter, 2010).

Student drivers using personal vehicles to transport fellow students on field trips create another serious exposure. This creates a situation in which the student drivers and their vehicles become an institutionally approved or endorsed form of transportation. Should a student's poor driving or unsafe vehicle result in an accident, the institution may be held liable. Lastly, the insurance coverage for an organization's travel may exclude youth or student drivers behind the wheel during organization-sponsored extra-curricular activities.

Hierarchy of Risk

Fried (1999) explained a hierarchy of transportation risk pertaining to student transportation. Essentially, it is a best-to-worst case scenario describing levels of risk and potential liability in transporting participants.

- First, hire an independent contractor. This mode presents the least amount of risk and liability to a school. However, Fried warns administrators that some liability continues to exist despite the institution hiring a private transportation company.

- Second, public transportation is considered the next best method of transporting athletes. The use of city transportation is perhaps outdated and not as common among today's recreational programs, interscholastic athletics, and intercollegiate athletics. Commercial aircraft are considered public transportation since airlines retain most of the liability for negligence, unless the sport organization failed to properly select a competent agency.

- Third, using school vehicles. It is not unusual for an administrator or coach to transport students in schools today. Since the administrator is making all the transportation decisions, the risk has been decreased. However, rigorous safe transportation policies must be in place.

- Fourth, the participants drive themselves to the event. However, as mentioned earlier, most educational institutions have a duty to provide safe transportation for their participants. In most high school and college athletic departments, unless the travel is local, this option is usually not the best alternative. The distances required to travel may be typically too great and costly for participants to travel individually.

- Fifth, parents drive the participants to the event.

- The last and worst option in transporting student-athletes is assigning students to drive. The administrator or institution will be putting himself or herself at greatest risk because the responsibility for safe transportation has been transferred to students.

State Law

While most states require school buses to transport students to extracurricular activities, some still use vans. The National Association of State Directors of Pupil Transportation

Services surveyed (NHTSA, 2004b) its State Director members to determine the current state-by-state laws/regulations on the use of 12- and 15-passenger vans to transport students to and from school or on school-related activity trips (see Figure 1).

Federal law prohibits the sale of new 15-passenger vans for school-related transportation of high school or younger students. Twenty-nine states have laws or regulations that prohibit the use of vans for transporting public school students to and from school and school-related activities. However, 12 states have laws and regulations that prohibit the use of vans for transporting public school students to and from school, but allow the use of vans for school activity trips. Additionally, nine states allow the use of vans for transporting public school students to and from school and school-related activities. In many states, the laws and regulations that apply to public schools may not apply to private and church-sponsored schools.

Driver Training

Licensing and Testing Requirements

Both the driver and the organization can be liable in an accident resulting from driver negligence. Organizations should require all drivers (whether employee or volunteer) complete a driver-training program prior to any travel. In order to also protect the organization from liability, it is strongly recommended that drivers meet other qualifications such as age, experience, special licenses, training, and verification of driver record (Pittman, 2004). Effective policies will address whether a driver has a driving record that is not clean (e.g. reckless driving or DUI citations).

Vehicle Maintenance and Inspections

A well-run maintenance and inspection program can inspire driver confidence and improve morale while reinforcing the institution's commitment to vehicle safety. In addition, written records of maintenance and inspection can be critical documents in accident investigations, claims handling, and potential lawsuits. A maintenance and inspection schedule should be established and adhered to, and all work on every vehicle should be clearly documented, including the date and nature of the work. Vehicles should meet all local, state, federal, and manufacturer's requirements and pass state inspections. Some institutions may limit the use of vehicles that have passed a certain age or mileage. For example, a policy might state those vehicles more than three years old or that have more than 60,000 miles may only be driven locally. This can help prevent mechanical breakdowns on out-of-town trips.

Inspections

A good maintenance program requires frequent, documented inspection of all vehicles and prompt transmittal of the inspection results to the appropriate parties if work is required. All persons driving organization-owned vehicles should be trained in inspection procedures, and every vehicle should be inspected by the driver before it is used. A standardized pre- and post-trip vehicle inspection form should be developed and utilized. A post-trip inspection is frequently overlooked by many institutions but can allow the driver(s) to report any problems experienced during the trip.

Preventive Maintenance

A well-defined and consistently applied preventive maintenance program will result in the safest vehicles as well as the lowest total maintenance cost. The basis for any good preventive maintenance program is the manufacturer's recommended program based on a time or mileage frequency.

Budget Issues

The rising cost of team travel for most sport organizations only adds to overall budget concerns. Interestingly, in the study of small college athletic administrators, only a few (3.1%) felt increased budgets would solve their transportation safety problems (LaVetter, 2010). In this study, budget figures did not have best decision-making factors for transportation policies. Respondents commented that despite the increased cost of taking buses, aircraft, or mini-buses compared to vans, they are willing to make these policy changes, which reflect a strong desire to increase transportation safety.

The number of passengers that were traveling most commonly (27.8%) determined the transportation mode to be used. This finding may be an indication that many sport administrators perceive passenger safety as more important than finances.

Administrators are generally knowledgeable about their organizations' needs. Combining their resourcefulness and abilities with the goal of establishing safe transportation policies and practices, may result in fewer accidents and less litigation. The management style, resourcefulness, and transportation safety education of sport administrators may have greater effects on adherence to transportation policies by departmental staff than other factors, such as budget.

Resources

Transportation Request Form (Sample)

ABC SCHOOL DISTRICT
TRANSPORTATION REQUEST FORM

A) REQUEST INFORMATION Current Date _____

Requestor _____ School/Department _____

Requesting transport for (circle one): Field Trip Athletic/Co-Curricular Special Services

Destination _____ Event Day/Date(s) _____

Departure Time _____ Return Time _____

Number of Students _____ Grade Level(s) _____

Will students be away for the lunch period? Y N

Requestor Signature _____ Principal/Director Signature _____

B) REQUEST CONFIRMATION

Bus Transportation has been scheduled as requested. In the event of a cancellation, notify the Transportation Supervisor at _____ or fax _____. In the event of a last minute cancellation please notify the assigned driver.

Driver Assigned _____ Contact Number _____

Confirmation Date _____

Transportation Supervisor Signature _____

C) SPECIAL SERVICES REQUIRED

Are special accommodations/Behavior Plan required (circle one)? Yes No

If yes, please explain _____
_____

If yes, please describe location and accessibility _____
_____

Transport frequency (circle all applicable) M T W TH F One day only

Please attach the transportation portion of the IEP page to this request form.

D) GENERAL INFORMATION

– All trips should be scheduled *at least one week* (five school days) prior to the event date.

– All Field Trips should be scheduled to occur between the hours of 8:30am–2:00pm. Longer trips are possible, but will require advanced scheduling.

– All Field, Athletic, and Special Services trips require that a staff member(s) be on board who is responsible for student safety and discipline.

– All passenger emergency contact and insurance information is on file in office Yes _____ No _____

E) BUS DRIVER TRIP LOG INFORMATION (to be completed by assigned driver)

Bus number assigned _____ Trip Mileage _____ Fuel used _____

Trip Time: _____ Hours _____ Minutes

Driver Signature: Driver comments on reverse

Consent to Travel Form (Sample)

An example of a consent form that a parent or guardian would sign prior to any organization-sponsored athletic trip:

XYZ ORGANIZATION
Athletic Travel Consent Form (2011)

Name of Student: _____

I, the undersigned, hereby grant permission for my son/daughter named above to be transported via bus, the private vehicle of a parent or coach, or the best means possible as required to get to practice or games.

AUTHORIZATION:

_____   _____   _____
Parent/Guardian's Name   Parent/Guardian's Signature   Date

Away Game Policy

In most situations, student athletes will travel as a team to and from all AWAY games. All student athletes must return to school with the team unless leaving with a parent/guardian or if a parent/guardian gives permission to do otherwise.

If on a particular day a student athlete wishes to leave directly from a game without a parent or guardian and not return to school with the team, she/he is required to either: have a note from her/his parent/guardian stating so, or authorize your student athlete to return from games with specific people recorded below.

I give permission for my child _____ to leave directly from the location of any AWAY games with the following people listed below.

_____

_____

_____   _____

Parent Signature   Date

References

Appenzeller, H. (2003). *Risk management in sport.* Carolina Academic Press.

Athletic Travel Consent Form. Retrieved August 31, 2011 from http://dosportseasy.com/ncces/travel_form.pdf.

Fried, G. B. (1999). Safe at first: a guide to help sports administrators reduce their liability. Durham, NC: Carolina Academic Press.

LaVetter, D. (2005). Safety must drive decisions in van use. *National Collegiate Athletic Association (NCAA) News 42(25),* 4–5.

LaVetter, D. (2010). Transportation practices in community college athletics. *Journal of Community College Research & Practice* 34 (6), 1–13.

National Highway Traffic Safety Administration (2004a). NHTSA repeats rollover warning to users of 15-passenger vans. Found at http://www.nhtsa.dot.gov/15PassVans/

National Highway Transportation Safety Administration (2004b). *NHTSA Action Plan for 15-passenger van safety.* Retrieved February 8, 2005 from http://www.nhtsa.dot.gov/.

National Transportation Safety Board (2002*). Safety report: Evaluation of the rollover propensity of 15-passenger vans.* Washington, DC: NTSB, 2002.

Pittman, A. (1994). Legal and safety issues in school transportation. *Journal of Legal Aspects of Sport,* 4 (1), 18–28.

Schimke, A. (2004). High school drops vans' use. *The Ann Arbor News.* September 6, 2004.

van der Smissen, B. (1990). *Legal liability and risk management for public and private entities.* Cincinnati: Anderson.

Websites

http://www.nasdpts.org/ (National Association of State Director of Pupil Transportation Services)

http://www.nhtsa.dot.gov/15PassVans/ (National Highway Transportation Safety Administration)

http://www.ntsb.gov/safety/safetystudies/sr0203.html (National Transportation Safety Board)

Chapter 7

Youth Sport and the Law

The problem is not the courts, the problem is educating people.

Thomas Appenzeller

What a difference 34 years makes in youth sport. In 1978, James Michner, the noted author, wrote in *Sports in America* that "laws exist to protect children at work and in school, but their play as governed by adults goes unchecked." Today in the United States, youth sport is no longer immune from rules, regulations and litigation. It seems that every day someone associated with youth sport is involved in a lawsuit. Ten years ago there were very few youth sport lawsuits to be found. Today this is no longer true. What used to be problems for interscholastic, intercollegiate and professional sport are now issues for youth sport programs. The number of youth sport programs continues to escalate with an estimated 40 million youth participating in sport in the United States. Never have so many children wanted to participate in such varied sport activities. That is good news. The bad news is that with the record number of children participating in sport, more lawsuits involving youth sport will be filed in court.

Youth Sport and Litigation

Americans sue for practically any and every reason. Former Supreme Court Justice Warren Burger summed up the sue syndrome in the United States when he said, "the nation is plagued with an almost irrational focus—a virtual mania—on litigation as a way to solve all problems." Court cases involving youth sport involve assaults on participants, players, spectators and officials, injuries, sexual abuse, discrimination (gender, race, and disability), contracts, eligibility questions, constitutional issues, employment, and criminal law.

It has been said that information is power and one of the positive results of litigation is the information and guidelines set by the courts that benefit youth sport. Granted that there are frivolous lawsuits, but the benefit is the information that can make youth sport safer. The problem is not the legal system and the courts, the problem is educating people.

Youth sport began with the best of intentions for children; and parents, coaches, officials, and administrators still have good intentions. However, having good intentions is not enough. The challenge is to educate youth sport leaders as to what is current, practical and safe. A few years ago coaches would not allow water breaks during a two- or three-hour practice session because they believed that water would make players sick, weigh on the stomach, slow them down and cause cramps. A very successful football coach did not want his players lifting weights because he thought it ruined them as players, by making athletes muscle bound. These coaches were not bad or mean people, in fact they were very dedicated and caring individuals, but times have changed and there is new information and strategies available regarding risk in youth sport. Unfortunately, much of the new information has come from lawsuits. It is time this information made its way to the public, because an educated public will produce a better product, and that product is our children. We may not like the idea of litigation today, but we have to live with it. Utilizing risk management strategies can be helpful in reducing and preventing injuries and subsequent lawsuits.

Two major issues will be examined in this chapter, liability for injuries and the right to participate. Examples of actual cases and incidents will be given with guidelines for parents, coaches, officials, and administrators. It has been said that the value of law lies not in the happiness it creates, but rather in the misery and suffering it prevents.

For the purposes of this chapter, youth sport is sport for young people up to the age of 18 engaged in sport activities outside interscholastic, intercollegiate or professional levels. With high school athletes being drafted and playing in the National Basketball Association, and young women participating on the professional golf, basketball, and tennis circuit, the care and treatment of young athletes is very important. Many sport organizations are starting children at a younger age with all-star, select, and elite travel teams, more opportunities for year-round participation is available. Youth sport, when compared to interscholastic sport, is relatively inexpensive. Unfortunately, many young athletes are ill-equipped, ill-trained, and ill-prepared by volunteer coaches who devote countless hours and free time to make sport available to children in the local community. The very nature of sport makes injuries a possibility, but when athletes are not trained, equipped, or prepared properly the risk of injury increases. The question becomes, when is an injury an accident that could have been avoided or prevented, and who is liable?

Court Cases Involving Facilities

Alex Castro, a Little League baseball player, was hit by a foul ball while seated on the bench during a game. His parents brought a charge of negligence against the park district, the president of the baseball league, and the team manager. The allegation was of unsafe facilities. The parents felt that the facility was unsafe because there was an opening in front of the dugout. The trial court ruled for the defendants, but the appellate court reversed the decision. The appellate court held that the baseball league and the president had a duty to supervise and safeguard the participants. The appellate court stated:

> The duties and responsibilities of an organization to which the care or control of children is entrusted are sometimes said to be akin to the duties and responsibilities of parents. Such an organization is not an insurer of the safety of children involved. On the other hand, such an organization may not avoid liability for injuries resulting from failure to exercise reasonable care (*Castro v. Chicago Park District* 1988).

The court went on to say:

> The President of the league must be held accountable for the league's activities. A duty voluntarily assumed must be performed with due care or such competence and skill as one possesses. A person cannot escape a duty of ordinary care simply

because he is a volunteer, particularly where the welfare of children is entrusted to him (*Castro v. Chicago Park District* 1988).

This case demonstrates that coaches, whether paid or volunteer, are given the same responsibility for the health, safety, and welfare of the participants as the highest paid college or professional coach. The trained or untrained volunteer who puts children at risk is liable and competence is not based on salary or status.

Areas of Concern

Failure to Warn

Adam Lloyd was a 14-year-old boy practicing with the local swim team at the Jewish Community Center when he was told to begin swimming laps. Adam did a "pike" dive off the starting blocks in three and one-half feet of water and suffered a broken neck. His parents sued the Jewish Community Center, the coaches, and United States Swimming, Inc. (*Lloyd v. Jewish Community Center* 1988). The issue was the failure to warn about the dangers of doing a "pike" dive in shallow water. The case was settled out of court for $4.1 million. This case brings up several issues and questions. First, while coaches need to warn about the inherent risk in an activity, how do coaches warn an athlete without scaring the athlete, and do we want to start off practices or activities with a worst case scenario? How an athlete is warned is still up to the coach or administrator, but it is important that children understand the inherent risk of the activity.

Unsafe Facilities

Many pools now have starting blocks in the deep end, instead of the shallow area of the pool, but others still have the blocks in the shallow end. Just moving the starting platforms to the deep end makes the pool safer, which is a positive step, and should serve to help prevent future unnecessary accidents.

Safety Rules

Another area of concern is whether the coaches had a list of safety rules about what swim team members could or could not do, and whether the rules had been enforced before the time of the accident. Coaches need safety rules posted around facilities and the rules should be emphasized during practice and enforced. An ounce of prevention is still worth a pound of cure.

A 10-year-old goalie in a junior soccer league, playing for the Canterbury Soccer Club, was struck on the head when a 175-pound portable steel goal fell on him. The young boy suffered bruises, lacerations, headaches, and bouts of dizziness. The boy and his mother filed a suit against the club and affiliated state soccer association claiming the defendants failed to properly secure the soccer goal (*From the Gym to The Jury* 1995). A former maintenance man was going to testify that he had informed the club president that the goal was dangerous because it was not anchored to the ground. The parties settled out of court for $340,000. Facilities used by children need to be checked and inspected on a regular basis to ensure their safety. Children do not concern themselves with safe facilities and equipment, they just want to play. Safety is the responsibility of the adult.

Instruction

Joey Fort was a 10-year-old Little League all-star second baseman in Runnemede, New Jersey. For all-star competition, Joey was moved to the outfield and during pre-game practice lost a pop-up in the sun and was hit in the left eye, causing an injury that required several operations to correct. His parents sued the coaches for negligence on their son's behalf for $750,000. The case was settled out of court for $25,000; $20,000 more than the unpaid hospital bills. One issue was the failure to teach proper technique for outfield play in the sun. The parents claimed that their son should have been taught how to use his glove to shade his eyes or been given flip-up sun glasses for protection (*ABA Journal* 1986). Teaching players how to slide correctly in baseball or softball, to tackle in football, or to use a spotter in gymnastics is more important today than ever before. Proper technique can reduce the possibility of injury and while it cannot prevent all injuries, proper techniques in sport can make the activity safer. The coach is a teacher, and the teacher should be concerned with the welfare of the pupil. Ignorance of proper sport techniques is no longer acceptable by the courts (*City of Miami v. Cisneros* 1995).

Landmark Case in Soccer

Julian Nabozny was playing goalkeeper for the Honsa soccer team when he received a pass from a teammate, went down on his left knee, and pulled the ball to his chest (*Nabozny v. Barnhill* 1975). The defendant, David Barnhill, a member of the opposing Winnetka team, kicked the left side of Julian's head, causing severe injuries. The match was played under "Federation of International Football Association" (F.I.F.A.) rules in which the goalkeeper is the only member of a team who is allowed to touch the ball in play, as long as he remains in the penalty area. Any contact with the goalkeeper in possession of the ball in the penalty area is an infraction of the rules. The appellate court ruled that organized athletic competition does not exist in a vacuum, and that the restraints of civilization accompany every athlete onto the playing field. An athlete has a duty to play by the rules, and it is the coach and administrator's responsibility that participants know and understand the rules, and officials and coaches enforce the rules (*Nabozny v. Barnhill* 1975).

Equipment

The previous cases involved facilities, instruction, warnings and rules. Two other leading causes of lawsuits are improper equipment and inadequate supervision. Tony Clark was a 13-year-old youth league football player for the Boca Raton Jets in Florida. While making a tackle in a game, Tony broke his neck and became the youngest player ever paralyzed in a youth football contest. Tony's parents sued the helmet company claiming that the helmet was defective and caused the injury. The helmet manufacturer defended its product, but chose to settle the case out of court for $16 million (*The Trentonian* 1987). Coaches need to make sure that all protective equipment is fitted properly and that the equipment is appropriate for the age and competitive level of the participant to provide equipment that provides protection. Children need safe and proper equipment. Jerseys and uniforms may look nice, but protective equipment must be a priority.

Supervision

Robert Foster, a member of a Special Olympics basketball team, was a 17-year-old youth with an I.Q. of 52 and a mental age of seven years. In order to practice for an upcoming tournament, Robert and 10 other players walked four blocks from their usual outdoor facility to an indoor gymnasium. On the way to the gym, Robert ran out between two parked cars and was struck by a motorist and killed. The trial court concluded that one coach was not adequate supervision under the circumstances, and Robert's mother was awarded $65,000 (*Foster v. Houston General Insurance Company* 1982). Lack of adequate supervision is one of the leading cause of litigation in sport when an injury has occurred. The youth league coach or administrator have to assume the responsibility of *in loco parentis* (in place of parents) for the children. The younger the child, or the more dangerous the activity, the greater the need for close supervision. Adults who are given the care of children have to use sound judgment when carrying out that duty. Injuries and accidents will always happen in sport, such is the nature of sport activities. However, the parent, coach, official, and administrator need to provide safe, adequate supervision and eliminate unnecessary risks.

Violence

One of the fastest growing concerns today in Youth Sports is the increasing level of violence at games and practices. Almost every day television and newspapers report brawls involving parents fighting other parents or parents attacking officials or coaches. Occasionally the violence occurs between children but all too frequently, it is the adults that are the problem. Several of the incidents have resulted in criminal charges being brought against the adults involved in the fracas. The most famous example of parental violence is the story of the two hockey dads who came to blows after a team practice. One father died and the other dad went to prison. Thomas Junta was charged with involuntary manslaughter for his role in the fight that killed 40-year-old Michael Costin. Junta was convicted and sentenced to six to ten years for beating Costin to death. The fight was witnessed by about a dozen children, including Junta's son and Costin's three sons.

Youth Sport in the 21st Century has become the ticket to the Major League, Olympic glory, or at least a four-year college athletic scholarship. The cost associated with Youth Sport and paying to play on a Travel, Select, or All-Star team has risen tremendously over the last decade. Because of the money and time invested, parents have become more vocal and aggressive towards administration, coaches, officials, and other parents. Children are no longer playing to have fun, win or lose, children participating in sport are an investment, and it is an investment that parents expect to pay dividends. The pressure to take the sport to the next level seems to impact the parents more than the children.

The key in violence prevention is two fold: being proactive and adequate supervision. Several Youth Sport organizations, and city and county recreation departments have experimented with silent games, where adults are not allowed to speak or cheer during the contest. Additional strategies have been to require parents and children to sign a good sportsmanship pledge, giving parents red or yellow cards, suspending the coach for an unruly parent, and even anger management classes.

The Youth Sport administration today has to operate in a crises management mode and do everything possible to protect the health and safety of the participants and spectators.

Written policies need to be developed to explain what is and what is not acceptable behavior and the consequences for unacceptable behavior. There needs to be adequate supervision, security if necessary, and rules enforced to curb the rise in violence. Parents have to be reminded from time to time that even though they are paying the bill, sport is still about the child.

Sexual Abuse

Unfortunately, of an even greater concern than violence today in youth Sport is the issue of sexual abuse. Sexual abuse is a concern because of the long-term emotional impact that this crime has on the victim. According to a *Sports Illustrated* article in 1999, the average preferential molester, the kind most common in Youth Sport, victimizes about 120 before being caught. The magazine went on to add that the child molester has found a home in the world of Youth Sports, where as a coach he or she can gain the trust and loyalty of kids and then prey on them. Former National Hockey League and Boston Bruin Sheldon Kennedy declared that he and other young boys were sexually abused by Graham James, a former youth hockey coach in Canada. Olympic Swimmer Diana Nyad has also come forward to publicly talk about the abuse she suffered at the hands of her swimming coach. Nyad has stated that, even though years have passed, she still has to go to weekly therapy sessions to try and deal with the abuse.

The recent Jerry Sandusky scandal at Penn State University has also focused national attention on the problem of sexual abuse of young people. Even though Sandusky was not coaching these young men, Penn State Football has been seen as an uninformed, but innocent co-conspirator.

Administrators have to do everything in their power to prevent sexual assaults from happening. A criminal history and background check is important on the state and national level for anybody who will come in contact with children. In-depth interviews have to be conducted with youth coaches, references need to be contacted, and past supervisors need to be contacted. Every organization should have a written sexual abuse policy and all coaches should sign the policy. Administrators need to hold meetings with coaches and parents to explain the policies. Some issues to discuss are:

overnights

room assignments

photographs

removing clothing

locker room behavior

transportation

physical contact

Parents also play a key role in preventing sexual abuse. The coach/athlete relationship has always been special, but it can be perverted if not supervised. Parents have to be alert to the warning signs of sexual abuse and also talk to their children about inappropriate touching. Parents need to feel free to observe practice and to drop by unannounced.

Youth Sports seem to be a magnet for sexual molesters, so administration and parents need to be vigilant at all times.

Recommendations

- *Always put the safety and welfare of the participant first.* This is the simplest and most common sense guideline and yet it may be the most difficult to follow. In the heat of competition, playing in the big game, championship on the line, parents, coaches, and administrators sometimes get carried away by the desire to win. Short term goals and rewards often replace long-range values and beliefs. Even when the child wants to ignore injuries and participate, always put health and safety first. Youth sport is a game for children, not the NFL Super Bowl, and the excitement of the moment should never replace the reality of the consequences. Do not rush to judgment when it concerns the health and safety of children.

- *Warn participants about the dangers and inherent risks of the activity.* The mother who warns her child about the dangers of touching a hot stove does not always guarantee that the child will never touch a hot stove again and get burned. However, it is important to warn children about certain inherent risks, because in certain situations it may prevent an unnecessary injury. It is not exactly clear how a coach or administrator effectively warns children. It is important that children be told what the risks are for a certain activity.

- *Teach proper technique and correct skills.* In every sport, there is a right way to do something and a wrong way. The correct way is usually the safest and will help eliminate certain unnecessary accidents. Techniques have changed over the years, and most of the changes are an attempt to make sport safer. Teaching a baseball player to run over the catcher, or even jump over the catcher was a common practice at one time, but no longer. The coach needs to be up-to-date when teaching children how to do something. Clinics, college courses, workshops, and camps all are places where coaches can go to learn correct techniques and how to teach the needed skills of the sport. Just as yesterday's meal will not satisfy today's hunger, the old way of doing something may no longer be appropriate. Coaching is teaching and teaching is a lifelong process of learning.

- *Explain and demonstrate safety rules.* Sport rules serve the purpose of making the activity safer and better. Coaches need to be certain that players know what the rules are and why they exist. A football player that knows what "spearing" is and understands what can happen is less likely to spear someone in a game or practice. Posters about why it is important to wear a helmet in baseball or a mouth piece in football can be very useful. Ignorance of the rules by coaches and players is no longer acceptable.

- *Check facilities on a regular basis.* Unsafe facilities are a leading cause of injuries and accidents on every level of sport. The coach and administrator have an obligation to inspect facilities on a regular basis, and if necessary postpone or cancel an activity when a dangerous condition exists. Wet floors, unsafe backstops, and holes in the playing surfaces are a few examples of unsafe playing conditions. Look for potential hazards to prevent unnecessary accidents and document the inspections.

- *Inspect equipment on a regular basis.* Football helmets, catchers' equipment, and gymnastic mats are examples of equipment that need to be checked regularly. Using outdated or worn-out equipment is not a good idea. Good equipment, fitted properly, worn correctly, and well maintained is critical for today's athlete.

- *Post warning signs in facilities explaining dangerous areas and proper behavior.* A picture is worth a thousand words and the administrator or coach should make sure that every athlete gets the picture. Swimming pools, gymnastic equipment, and locker rooms all have the potential to cause injuries. It is very important that the children see examples of proper behavior, and that improper behavior will not be tolerated. Children are most susceptible to injuries and accidents when they are doing things that they should not be doing. Running in a pool area is dangerous behavior and is an example of something that cannot be allowed. Post warning signs and then enforce proper behavior. In areas where English may not be the first language, put signs in both English and the other language used by the children.

- *Always supervise activities.* Young people need supervision, that is one reason parents want their child involved in youth sport. A coach or administrator becomes a surrogate parent and should supervise children accordingly. It is when the coach is not present that children tend to get out of hand, and injuries occur. Always supervise, and the younger the child and more dangerous the activity, the better the supervision provided should be.

- *Develop a plan in case of emergency.* The coach and administrator need to prepare and develop a plan to deal with serious injuries, especially since most youth league teams will not have a team doctor or an athletic trainer at practice or at contests. We have made strides in sport medicine over the past few years, but medical personnel are just beginning to be found on the high school level. On the youth sport level, the coach often serves as the athletic trainer. First aid and CPR training are critical factors in emergencies. Have an emergency medical plan available and have everyone know his/her role.

- *Never assume anything with children, be prepared for the unexpected, and anticipate problems.* One of the rules of leadership is to never assume anything and with children that is a good policy. Children, by their young age, lack experience and what is standard knowledge for an adult might be a lesson not learned yet by a child. The innocence of youth may be caused by an ignorance of the possible dangers of an activity and it is the adult that serves as the protector. Remember that children and adults do not have the same frame of reference. Be prepared for everything and anticipate problems.

- Written policies should be created to explain what is and what is not acceptable behavior on the field and in the stands. Emphasis should be crowd control and security officers may need to be used.

- Criminal background checks should be conducted on all individuals directly involved with children.

- Policies on sexual abuse should be created and coaches should be required to sign the policy.

- The topic of sexual abuse should be addressed by administrators, coaches, and parents.

- Parents should observe practice and always be alert to the warning signs of sexual abuse.

Two Revolutions

The United States has seen two revolutions in sport participation over the last 20 years. First there was Title IX and more recently the Americans with Disabilities Act (ADA). These laws were designed to provide opportunities for classes of people that historically were denied access to sport; women and individuals with disabilities. Initially these laws, and other court decisions, were aimed at interscholastic and intercollegiate sport. However, the trickle down effect is being felt today on the youth sport and community level.

Gender Equity in Youth Sport

There appear to be three trends in sport participation for females. The first is that women want to compete. In the 1960s male athletes on the high school and college level were being dismissed from teams because of long hair, dress codes, and other violations. Several of these athletes pleaded in court for the right to participate. The argument was that athletic competition was important in the physical, moral, and character development of young men. Athletic competition was seen as a critical component of education, a learning lab, part of the curriculum, but outside of the normal school day. People saw sport as being important for young men. Soon mothers and daughters began to ask the question, if it is so important for boys and men, then why would it not be important for girls and young women? If sport is good, then it should be good for both genders. The first trend was the recognition of the value and importance of sport as an extracurricular activity. The second trend was allowing young girls to compete on male teams. In the 1970s the only teams available for sport participation were the boys teams. Allowing females to compete with males was not exactly a popular idea, and girls were not usually welcome. Little League baseball was one of the first sport organizations to be involved in a gender discrimination lawsuit. With young girls asking for the right to play baseball in the early 1970s, Little League coaches and administrators began requiring that players wear athletic supporters and protective cups in order to discourage young girls from participating. There was concern for the physical safety of the female and the ego of the males, if girls were allowed to play. Gender discrimination for safety is permissible, but before the onset of puberty, females have a tendency to be bigger, faster, and better athletes than many males of the same age. Allison Fortin was a 10-year-old girl who wanted to play Little League baseball in Pawtucket, Rhode Island. Little League officials said that they were afraid for Allison's safety so she went to court to be able to play. The Judge ruled in favor of Fortin, saying that the difference between boys and girls at that age could not be accepted as a valid reason to deny participation. Also in the Fortin case, Little League baseball was using public facilities, and the court held that there should not be any gender discrimination. In *Clinton v. Nagy* the court struck down a rule that girls could not participate in football. Again there was no evidence to show that females could not participate safely with males. Many youth sport teams today are coed, particularly with younger children, and it is no longer acceptable to exclude someone arbitrarily because of gender.

In 1978, an Ohio judge, in a widely publicized decision, supported the efforts of two girls to play on the boys' basketball team. The facts of the case are interesting and helped advance the desire of girls to play on boys' teams. Judge Carl Rubin reasoned that the rules that prohibit girls from trying out for mixed gender competition go beyond the state level and are unconstitutional (*Yellow Springs v. OHSAA* 1978). He then said:

> It has always been traditional that boys play football and girls are cheerleaders. Why so? Where is it written that girls may not, if suitably qualified, play football? There may be a multitude of reasons why a girl may elect not to do so. Reasons of stature, or weight, or reasons of temperament, motivation or interest. This is a matter of personal choice. But a prohibition without exception based upon gender is not.

Judge Rubin made a profound statement that was not a popular one in 1978, but prophetic of things that did develop as female participation in sport at every level became a reality. Rubin concluded:

> It may well be that there is a student today in an Ohio high school who lacks only the proper coaching and training to become the greatest quarterback in

professional football history. Of course the odds are astronomical against her, but isn't she entitled to a fair chance to try (*Yellow Springs v. OHSAA* 1978).

The third trend, V. M. I. and The Citadel not withstanding, seems to be a move to more gender segregated teams. Women now want to participate with and against other females at the highest level. Thirty years ago girls just wanted a chance to compete on the boys' team, today they want their own team, and they want the same level of facilities, equipment, and coaches as the boys. If there are going to be separate teams, segregated by gender, then the community organization would do well to adopt policies similar to high school and colleges regarding gender equity. Some suggestions to ensure gender equity are as follows:

1. Male and female teams should have equal access to facilities and equipment. For practices and games, facilities should be scheduled fairly, and there should be equal expenditure for equipment.

2. Efforts should be made to publicize teams equally; sign-ups, registration, and advertisements should be similar for each gender.

3. Expenditures and budgets should be as equal as possible. There has to be a valid reason to spend more money on one team or league than another.

4. Awards, trophies, and banquets should be as equal as possible. There should be no second class treatment given either gender.

5. Every effort should be made to have the same quality of officials at contests. Officials should be paid the same whether it is a boys' or girls' athletic contest.

6. An effort should be made to recruit quality coaches for both genders.

7. If teams are coeducational, there should be an equal opportunity to participate for both genders.

8. If a gifted female athlete wants the challenge of competing against males, and if there are no extreme safety risks, the opportunity should be available (Public Law 92-318 of the Education Act of 1972).

Individuals with Disabilities

Since the mid-1970s, there has been an on-going effort in the United States to give people with disabilities more opportunities. The opportunities have been in education, employment, public access, and sport. One of the first pieces of major legislation was Public Law (93-112), the Rehabilitation Act of 1973, followed in 1975 by the Education for all Handicapped Children Act (Public Law 94-142, now Individuals With Disabilities Education Act (IDEA)). The purpose of these two laws was to bring people with disabilities into the mainstream, especially in public education. President George Bush, in July 1990, signed a third major piece of legislation, the Americans with Disabilities Act (Public Law 101-336 ADA). Called the Civil Rights Act for People with Disabilities, the ADA extended the rights of people with disabilities into the private sector and protected the rights of a wide range of individuals with disabling conditions. Now people with substantial limits, on one or more life activities, must be given access to YMCAs, YWCAs, Boys' Clubs, and Little League sport. Efforts have to be made to ensure universal participation in facilities and programs. The language of the ADA classifies individuals who have an impairment in walking, seeing, hearing, speaking, breathing, learning, or working as having a disability and as such are protected under the law (Dougherty 1994). According to the ADA, these individuals must be given the opportunity to participate unless their participation presents a direct threat to the health and safety of other participants. Sport is such an important part of life, that before an individual can be prohibited from participating, three criteria have to be met. In order to exclude someone based on the threat to health and safety factor, the threat must be real, it must be based on objective and unbiased information, and attempts must be made to reduce or eliminate the risk (Dougherty 1994).

In the past the American Medical Association (AMA) established standards and guidelines for participation, and it was the doctor who made the call on participation. Today, programs and facilities have to be accessible to everyone, and every effort must be made to accommodate all who want to participate. Today, that decision is being made by the parents and the athlete, or the courts if the individual is prohibited from participation (see Chapter 15 for guidelines).

Special Olympics and Challenger Program

Since the late 1960s and early 1970s, sport organizations have been created to offer individuals with disabilities the opportunity to participate in sport and recreational activities with other people with the same or similar disability. Providing segregated sport opportunities is just not enough anymore, especially in light of the current legal climate. People with disabilities want to be able to compete with able-bodied people whenever possible. As with gender equity, Little League baseball has not been on the cutting edge of tolerance and acceptance. In 1987, Little League Baseball, Inc. threatened to lift the charter of the entire 32 team Brockton, Massachusetts, Little League unless three teams of physically and mentally handicapped players were banned from competing. The National Organization stated that children with disabilities were not covered by insurance and should be coached by professionals, not volunteers. In 1990, Little League began its Challenger Division for children with disabilities and now there are over 29,000 children competing in 820 leagues in the United States, Canada, and Puerto Rico. However, for some the Challenger Division is not enough, because they see discrimination and segregation in this type of league. Valerie and Ronald Suhanosky of Milford, Connecticut, do not want to see the Challenger Program eliminated, but they are suing Little League baseball on behalf of their daughter, Lauren. When Lauren's Challenger team wanted to play a regular team, they were told that the league charter and insurance provisions would not allow it. The Suhanosky's want more opportunities for a comparable game for their daughter. The National Little League also adopted a policy that a coach in a wheelchair could coach from the dugout, but not in the coaches' box. Little League had a concern about the dangers a wheelchair presented to the players. An Arizona Little League baseball coach who uses a wheelchair, but with three years of experience, was told he could no longer coach on the field. The coach filed a lawsuit against Little League baseball insisting that he be allowed to coach from the field. The challenge was based on the Americans with Disabilities Act, and the court granted a temporary restraining order stating that the League had not met the requirements of ADA. There had been no individual assessment of the actual risk imposed on the players and there had been no effort made to examine reasonable modifications to reduce any risk. It was determined that with three years' experience, the coach was a positive role model for the players and the U.S. District Court of Arizona issued a preliminary injunction allowing the coach to go back on the field (*Anderson v. Little League Baseball, Inc.* 1992).

Nicholas Devlin was disqualified by the Arizona Youth Soccer Association because he needed crutches to walk. Nicholas played soccer for the Elgin Eagles and also participated in basketball and baseball. After the Youth Soccer Association barred him from practicing and playing in contests, Steve Palevitz, an attorney for the Arizona Center for Disability Law, filed a suit in the U.S. District Court against the Soccer Association. The lawsuit sought reinstatement and unspecified damages claiming that the Soccer Association violated the Americans with Disability Act. One question that the court will have to decide is whether or not using crutches changes the nature of the game, and does using crutches put the other participants at risk? (Appenzeller and Baron 1997).

Recommendations for Individuals with Disabilities

1. Children and coaches with disabilities should be given the opportunity to participate in as many activities as possible. Federal legislation does not allow discrimination against individuals with disabilities and encourages mainstreaming in community sport teams.

2. A blanket policy that excludes groups and classes of people will not be tolerated. Decisions about participation must be made on an individual case by case basis. Policies need to avoid labeling and stereotyping groups of people.

3. Facilities and programs should be accessible to everyone, and an effort made to make sure that people are given an opportunity for success.

4. When necessary, accommodations should be made for the participant during tryouts, practices, and games. If special equipment is needed, it should be provided, as long as the activity is not altered and an unfair advantage is created (see Chapter 27 for ways of accommodation for individuals with disabilities).

5. Make sure that participation has been approved by a physician. The family physician should be responsible for clearing the individual to play.

6. There should be a meeting of the coaches, parents, officials, and children to discuss all potential dangers and hazards of the activity, as well as other players. If the individual with the disability poses a legitimate threat to the health and safety of others, then the individual can be denied the opportunity to play.

7. The threat of injury to the individual with the disability is of concern, but is not a valid reason to exclude one from participation. However, the inherent dangers of the activity should be discussed with the parents and the child before participation is allowed.

8. Discuss alternative options such as Special Olympics and Challenger Baseball. If at all possible, these options need to be made available in every community. A good sporting experience will hopefully create a lifelong participant.

9. Discuss the situation with the parents and children of the team, and explain the consequences and encourage their cooperation. We are not afraid of change, we are afraid of the unknown. Keep parents and team members as informed as possible.

10. Remember, the activity is for children, and the children should be the first priority. The purpose of the ADA is to provide more life experiences for people with dis-

abilities. Acceptance into the mainstream of society is the goal and it is a goal that will ultimately benefit everybody. The young person who has a disability is not disabled, is not handicapped, but rather is a person who has to deal with an unusual condition.

The Christopher Reeve story has emphasized to many Americans the fact that a disability can strike at any time, any place, and any age. Many coaches, administrators, and officials recognize the struggle that goes on in many lives today, and work to reduce the burden, instead of creating new obstacles.

In My Opinion

Times have changed and will continue to change as we enter the next century. Youth sport is no longer fathers coaching, sons playing, and sisters cheering while mothers bake cakes and work the concession stand.

Sport in the United States today is big business. It is a multi-billion dollar a year industry, where the possibility for fame and fortune are unlimited. When Albert Pujols signs a $240 million dollar contract with the Los Angeles Angels, people notice. When an 81-year-old woman sues McDonald's after she spilled coffee in her lap, and wins $2.9 million in damages, people notice. History tells us that sport and law will continue to be important in our society in the 21st century. Now, with a college scholarship, Olympic Gold Medal, multi-million dollar pro contract, or an endorsement contract all on the line, the stakes are very high. Sport has become the goose that lays the golden eggs. The good news is that all of the publicity has created interest and we have more people than ever before involved in youth sport. The bad news is that with more participants, we are experiencing more lawsuits.

There are two keys for developing an excellent youth sport program. First, coaches, parents, administrators, and officials have to be better educated about today's legal climate. We have to do a better job of training the countless volunteers who operate the youth leagues. We want our children to be able to participate, to have a positive experience, and to use that experience to develop a lifetime pattern of sport and physical activity. We cannot accomplish this without education. Second, we have to make the health, safety, and welfare of the children the number one priority. Several years ago, the Ford Motor Company developed a slogan, "Quality is Job 1" and that slogan is even more important for our children than our cars. All of your children deserve a quality program and the emphasis has to be on the child, not the adult or on winning championships. Progress is being made, and progress has to continue as we strive to make Quality Job 1 in youth sport a reality.

References

ABA Journal, The Lawyer's Magazine. 1986. Vol. 72, February.

Anderson v. Little League Baseball, Inc., 794 F. Supp. 342 1992.

Appenzeller, H.T. and R. Baron. 1995. *From The Gym To The Jury* vol. 6, no. 1.

Castro v. Chicago Park District, 533 N.E. 2d. 504 (1988).

City of Miami v. Cisneros, 662 So. 2d 1272 (1995).

Dougherty, Neil J. 1994. *Sport, Physical Activity and the Law.* Champaign, IL: Human Kinetics.

Foster v. Houston General Insurance Company, 407 So. 2d 759 (Texas, 1982).

Lloyd v. Jewish Community Center, Montgomery Circuit Court, No. 0260, Oct. 31(1986).

Nack, William and Don Yaeger 1999 (1999, September 13). Who's coaching your kids? Sports Illustrated, 41–53.

Public Law 92-318 of the Education Act of 1972.

The Trentonian. 1987. February 8.

Yellow Springs Exempted Village School District v. Ohio High School Athletic Assn, 443. F. Supp. 753 (Ohio 1978).

Part III

Risk Management Issues

The very nature of sport makes injuries a possibility, but when athletes are not trained, equipped or prepared properly, the risk of injury increases.

Thomas Appenzeller

Chapter 8

Liability and Risk Management Principles for Property Owners' Associations

---

Developing and implementing a comprehensive risk management plan is the key to avoiding and/or successfully defending the association in the event a lawsuit is filed.

Paul L. Gaskill

Introduction

Not-for-profit Property Owners' Associations (POA) are becoming more prevalent throughout the United States in order to insure that the common interests of the residents of subdivisions are met. As part of the quality of life in a residential subdivision, these associations have determined that recreational opportunities must be provided. Their responsibilities have expanded to include the construction and operations of recreational facilities or resources such as lakes, pools, spas, golf courses and trail systems. As the provision of recreation services has increased, so have the POA risk and liability concerns. The purpose of this chapter is to discuss the history and background of this trend, to review the legal and statutory foundations of these associations, to address the issue of association board member liability and to present a summary of risk management considerations that all property members' associations should follow.

History and Background

For centuries, humans have congregated in common areas to seek shelter, security and the resources necessary for their survival. Housing has always been one of the most important of these quests, and people have actually pooled their physical and financial resources to secure adequate housing since the time of ancient Rome. Many attributes that people sought in a residence were unaffordable to the individual, but could be obtained by the collective.

Throughout American history, villages, towns and cities provided the vast majority of these required services, supported by the tax dollars and volunteer contributions of the citizens. Neighborhoods within these governmental entities often had to meet the specific needs of their residents through the volunteer labors of the inhabitants. Neighborhood services often included self-policing, beautification, maintenance and recreation.

For decades, the development of condominium residences was another housing trend that has addressed the collective need of home owners in America. The term "condominium" actually derives from the Latin word for co-ownership, and is a housing practice that has actually existed since the Middle Ages. The concept is often predicated on the owner's desire to gain access to common facilities (pools, spas, tennis courts, club houses, etc.) while delegating all or some of their home maintenance duties to others, often for an annual fee. Condominium owners may also become involved in the governance of the overall development through participation in property owners' or homeowners' associations (Freeman & Alter, 1992).

As America suburbanized throughout the latter half of the twentieth century, subdivisions were also created that essentially provided for the need of its residents in the same fashion that urban neighborhoods had once done. Legally, a subdivision is a piece of real property that has been divided into two or more units according to a development plan. They generally include common areas or facilities that belong to the owners collectively and are intended for the exclusive use and enjoyment of the property owners. In order to insure that the common interests of the residents of the subdivision are addressed, not-for-profit property owners' associations (or homeowners' associations) have been formed. The members of these property owners' associations are either legal residents or property owners of the subdivision. Originally, property owners' associations were charged with the duties of establishing by-laws and covenants; collecting dues or fees from residents; placing liens on delinquent property owners; foreclosing on property owners; maintaining water systems, roadways and common areas; and often providing snow removal. Today, however, as common areas and facilities have expanded, property owners' associations have assumed a myriad of new tasks and responsibilities.

Many of these responsibilities include the construction and operation of recreation facilities and programs. Examples include, but are not limited to: lakes, pools, spas, golf courses, racquetball courts, tennis courts, trails (hiking, biking, greenways), fishing and camping areas, fitness centers, marinas, club houses and social centers, playgrounds, skate parks, game rooms, multi-purpose fields, recreational vehicle storage areas and concession stands. As facilities were constructed, many POA's have began to establish recreation programs for residents. For example, instructional activities in a variety of programs as well as youth league swimming or soccer teams were organized.

Legal and Statutory Foundations

The legal foundations of property owners' associations for both condominia and subdivisions in the United States date back to the 1950s. From the Federal perspective, associations generally seek Internal Revenue Service not-for-profit (501(c)(3)) status. IRS Publication 4220 presents the general guidelines for organizations that seek tax-exempt status from federal income taxes. This publication describes the eligibility requirements, responsibilities, benefits and application procedures for each applicant. The three key components in determining not-for-profit status include: 1) evidence of *organization* (statement of purpose, articles of incorporation, by-laws); 2) *operational guidelines* consistent with the IRS; and 3) a succinct statement of *exempt purpose.* Preparing for tax exempt status enables the homeowners' or property owners' association to review and refine their articles of incorporation, operational by-laws and procedures.

The Federal Tort Claims Act provides a limited waiver of the federal government's sovereign immunity when its employees are negligent within the scope of their employment. The act also specifies that a tort claim can only be filed against the government in accordance with the law of the place where the act or omission occurred. In allowing suits, the Federal Tort Claims Act enabled the establishment of State Tort Claims Acts which vary from state to state, and define the degree to which liability issues will impact the association. The conclusion is evident: agents of a homeowner's association (board members, volunteers, and employees) may be sued pursuant to the state tort law.

Every state has its own set of state statutes that establish, authorize and define the roles of homeowners'/property owners' associations. These statutes have a variety of titles, many referred to as subdivision or platting acts. In North Carolina, for example, Chapter 47F, the North Carolina Planned Community Act of the N.C. General Statutes, authorizes the establishment of community associations. This act also describes the rights and re-sponsibilities of the association. The state in which the subdivision is located will determine the specific contents of these criteria.

Property owners/homeowners' associations additionally have a legal relationship with the state with respect to the dedication of portions of the subdivision to the exclusive use of recreation or open space. Within the general governmental powers of eminent domain, mandatory dedication statutes of most states allow the state and local government to dictate to the subdivision planners a percentage of land that is dedicated to open space or recreation. The percentage of property dedicated to these purposes varies by municipality. Legal issues involved in the application of these mandatory dedication standards include the actual percentage of land and the specific parcels to be dedicated. Developers have contested the ability of the government to both force the owners to dedicate such lands as well as to choose which specific properties should be used for recreation.

Many legal cases have ensued. In the case of *Dolan v. City of Tigard* (Nebraska) the U.S. Supreme Court examined the principle of "reasonable relationship" and the leverage of the city in granting building permits to developers. The court determined that the city may not use the mandatory dedication principle as a criterion for determining whether the subdivision would be granted or denied a permit to proceed with the development. However, it importantly decided that a "rough proportionality analysis" would be appropriate given the position of most state courts (Kozlowski, 1994). The crux of this decision is based on the assumption that "no precise mathematical calculation is required, but the city must make some sort of individualized determination that the required dedication is reasonable in scope."

In another interesting case, a developer contested the ability of the city to dictate to the developer the specific piece of property that was to be placed in recreational use. In *Messer v. Chapel Hill*, the developer preferred to dedicate a less desirable tract of land for recreation purposes and filed suit. The North Carolina Court of Appeals and the Supreme Court of North Carolina decided that the town was justified in its insistence that the developer comply with its demands, and noted that:

Under the authority granted by Section 160A-372 of the North Carolina General Statutes, every subdivision for residential purposes shall include a portion of land permanently dedicated for the purpose of providing open space, park or recreational areas to serve residents of the immediate neighborhood within the subdivision.

With the increased population that will follow development of the subdivision, comes a need for recreational space. A careful reading of the statute also reveals that these recreational areas can be used by the public, in addition to the subdivision residents. G.S. 160A-372 allows city ordinances to provide for the dedication or reservation of recreation areas. This distinctive phase is important because dedication of private property contemplates public use and falls short of the power of eminent domain.

In proposing a code after review of this and similar cases over the last twenty years, the American law Institute (Kozlowski, 1994) has concluded that a "reasonable connection" analysis should serve to limit legal contests of this nature in the future. It noted that:

> Developers may be required to provide streets and utilities but only of a quality or quantity reasonably necessary for the proposed development. Similarly, a developer may be required to provide land or fees for parks or other open space. The code limits the extent of such demands to that reasonably allocable to the development, measured in terms of the need created by the development.

The implications of the mandatory dedication issue for the property owner's/homeowner's association is significant. If existing subdivisions expand their holdings, members of boards of directors and property owners need to be aware of the state and local government mandates that require their association to comply with existing codes. Potential litigation and expense can hence be kept at a minimum if all of the parties involved are appraised of the powers of the sovereign.

In other inter-relationships with the local government, property owners' associations can work hand in hand with Recreation and Park Departments in planning park spaces and recreation programs. For example, in Lewis and Clark County, Montana, subdivision planning has been addressed in their Parks, Recreation and Open Space Plan. This type of master plan is common throughout the United States. In this instance, the county has outlined the requirements for open space and recreational improvements within subdivisions, and has offered professional planning assistance for these areas. These examples illustrate that the government/private developer relationship need not be adversarial, but rather function as a relationship that benefits all citizens of a geographic area. In other communities, Recreation and Park Departments have entered into agreements with privately owned subdivisions and offered professional recreation programming assistance to property owners' associations engaged in the provision of recreation and leisure services to its residents.

Landowner liability is another important issue with which property owners' associations need to be familiar. Again, most states have enacted landowner liability statutes, also called recreational use statutes, which serve to limit the personal liability that landowners assume when their property is used for recreational purposes. For example, the North Carolina General Statutes, Chapter 38A state:

> Except as specifically recognized by or provided for in this Chapter, an owner of land who either directly or indirectly invites or permits without charge any person to use such land for educational or recreational purposes owes the person the same duty of care that he owes a trespasser, except nothing in this Chapter shall be construed to limit or nullify the doctrine of attractive nuisance and the owner shall inform direct invitees of artificial or unusual hazards of which the owner has actual knowledge. This section does not apply to an owner who invites or permits any person to use land for a purpose for which the land is regularly used

and for which a price or fee is usually charged even if it is not charged in that instance, or to an owner whose purpose in extending an invitation or granting permission is to promote a commercial enterprise.

Recreational use statutes have a significant impact on property owners' associations that operate recreation facilities and programs. Generally, the association owes the invitees the same standard of care that the government would owe to its patrons, and hence the statute would afford no legal protection under the law from land owners who have paid dues or membership fees. However, if no fees are charged, the association would enjoy immunity from any user who is an invitee of the association or of homeowners in the subdivision. As an example, in *Clontz v. St. Marks Evangelical Lutheran Church*, both the church and the landowner were sued for damages when a patron at a church festival was injured. Since neither the church nor the landowner received any financial remuneration nor were willfully or wantonly negligent, the suit was dismissed.

Association Board Member Liability

Officers and board members of property owners' associations in subdivisions or condominia are subject to liability for commission or omission of acts which may lead to the injury of persons on properties under their jurisdiction. In general, courts have applied a business judgment rule (see Appendix A) to uphold their good faith exercise of authority. These rulings have often been based on the volunteer nature of board membership. Alternatively, in *Francis T. v. Village Green Owners' Association*, a condominium owner sued the association and its board following her rape inside her condominium. The plaintiff charged that the association was negligent in failing to install adequate exterior lighting and for refusing to allow her to install additional lighting outside her unit. Noting that a board member may not escape liability by hiding behind the shield of their corporate positions and are liable for their own acts of omission or commission, the court found just cause for the plaintiff and damages were awarded.

Risk Management Considerations

Board members and officers are obviously held to a high standard of care, and can be held liable for decisions and actions since they are agents of the property owners' association. Minimizing the risk of lawsuits is not always easy, but it can be done. Developing and implementing a comprehensive risk management plan is the key to avoiding a lawsuit and/or successfully defending the association in the event a lawsuit is filed. This plan needs to be based on the legal duties of the association, which include the duty to warn of unknown risks, to advise of inherent risks, to inspect the POA properties and facilities, to maintain and repair all facilities and to generally keep all areas safe.

The risk management plan should contain procedures to insure the following actions are taking place. These include, but are not limited to:

1. Review of the articles of incorporation, by-laws and restrictive covenants to assure that the actions and practices of the association are consistent with legal foundations. If they are not, the board needs to take immediate action to modify either the practice or the by-laws.

2. Knowledge of and adherence to all industry standards, particularly those standards that may become more stringent over time through court decisions. State and local housing codes must also be reviewed to assure that the POA is in compliance.

3. Review and modification of all safety and security documents which have an impact on the safety of residents. Consult with a law enforcement agency or private security consultant and document such contact.

4. Secure the services of a qualified attorney familiar with the legal issues involved with property owners' associations.

5. Procure adequate liability insurance for all board members, officers and employees. Routinely review all insurance coverage to see if the policies afford adequate protection. Update all policies as needed.

6. If inadequacies are discovered in any facility or program, promptly execute corrective measures.

7. Perform a background and performance review of all employees to assure that they themselves do not pose a security risk.

8. Make all residents aware of all safety codes, rules and regulations, and make sure all are enforced. Create a vehicle that allows all residents easy access to the board to report all incidents or evolving safety or liability concerns.

9. When possible, make sure new facilities have safety built in, through both design and construction.

10. Conduct a routine safety audit which outlines the frequency of inspections and document all information.

11. Make sure all routine maintenance on all facilities is performed according to a master maintenance schedule. Document the completion of all maintenance tasks.

12. Develop and implement an accident and injury reporting system that is employed regardless of the severity of the injury.

13. Enforce the use of waivers and informed consent agreements. These can be very effective tools in avoiding liability and making participants assume responsibility for risks associated with an activity. By using these documents, the participant enters into a contractual agreement (indirectly in the case of an informed consent agreement) not to hold the service provider liable. Be aware that even the best waivers may not hold up in court.

14. Review all of the position descriptions of all employees to make sure that the employee is acting within the scope of his duties at all times. When discrepancies are discovered, modify the position description immediately.

15. Provide in-service training for all employees, board members and officers, and remember that standards for the credentialing of employees and board members are rising.

16. Use public recreation agencies as consultants to develop a risk management plan that will reduce the risk for property owners' associations.

17. Hire a private property management organization to conduct a risk management assessment for the POA.

18. For the smaller POA, contact a larger POA that has established risk management plans and model after their approaches and philosophies.

Assistance in Risk Management Planning and Legal Decision Making

The Community Associations Institute, a trade association that represents over 250,000 property owners associations, provides training programs, conferences and workshops leading to the CAI Professional designation. One of these professional designations is for the Community Insurance and Risk Management Specialist (CIRMS). It is advised that at least one board member of the property owners' association seek and complete this professional designation. Raising association dues to finance these educational efforts may be necessary. As a portion of its educational mandate, the CAI offers continuous online learning opportunities and offers a national Community Association Law Seminar, annually attended by managers and board members from all over the country.

Additional legal services are readily available to property association employees and board members from the Community Associations Institute. The CAI provides resources, tools and educational opportunities for board members, community managers and association management companies. It provides up-to-date liability insurance advice and information, and has a publications division that provides association managers and board members electronic and print materials such as books, bimonthly newsletters and magazines.

The CAI also has an important government affairs function, and its collective membership has had a significant effect on decisions and legislation effecting property owners' associations. In the past, it has lobbied the Federal Housing Administration on issues that affect the operation and governance of associations, most often condominium associations. The CAI operates a Government and Public Affairs Department which has an Advocacy Center that coordinates the activities of its State Legislative Action Committees. This important arm of the CAI has had numerous successes in positively influencing specific aspects of state and federal legislation.

In My Opinion

This chapter has addressed the legal structure and liability of property owners' associations in the United States. These associations and their agents are exposed to the possibility of lawsuits. Until tort reform can be accomplished by the courts, every agency which provides services to constituents must be diligent in recognizing and managing their risks. This maxim applies to an increasingly frequent and increasingly important system of governance, the property owners' association.

References

http://www.caionline.org.

Clontz v. Saint Marks Evangelical Church, 578 S.E.2D 654, 2003.

Cureman, D., Jackson, ES & Hebard, E.L. (1984). Condominiums and cooperatives. New York: John Wiley and Sons.

Dolan v. City of Tigard. In J. Kozlowski, Parks and Recreation Magazine, 31034.

Francis T v. Village Green Owners' Association, 723 P.2n573 (Cal., 1986).

Freedman, W. & Alter, J.B. (1992). The law of condominia and property owners' associations. New York: Quorum Books.

Internal Revenue Service Publication 4220, Tax Exempt Organizations.

Kozlowski, J. (1994) State mandatory dedication opinions illustrate "rough proportionality" analysis. Parks and Recreation Magazine, 29(9), 31–34.

Kozlowski, J. (2003) Developers challenge fee for parks and recreation. Parks and Recreation Magazine. 38(9), 36–42.

Landowner Liability, Chapter 38A, North Carolina General Statutes, (1995).

Messer v. Chapel Hill, 59 N.C. App. 692; 297 S.E. 2d 632; (1982).

North Carolina Planned Community Act, 47F, North Carolina General Statutes, (1998).

Subdivision Control, Chapter 160A-372, North Carolina General Statutes.

Taylor, S. & Thomas, E. (2003, December 15) Cival Wars. Newsweek Magazine, 42–51.

Appendix A

Section 4.01(a) of the American Law Institute's 1985 project, "Principles of Corporate Governance: Analysis and Recommendations" imposes upon directors and officers a standard of care that an ordinarily prudent person would reasonably be expected to exercise in a like position and under similar circumstances. Specifically, it states:

(a) A director or officer has a duty to his corporation to perform his functions in good faith, in a manner that he reasonably believes to be in the best interest of the corporation, and with the care that an ordinarily prudent person would reasonably be expected to exercise in a like position and under similar circumstances.

   (1) This duty includes the obligation to make, or cause to be made, such inquiry as the director or officer believes to be appropriate under the circumstances.

   (2) In performing any of his functions (including his oversight functions), a director or officer is entitled to rely on materials and persons in accordance with Section 4.02.03.

   (3) Except as otherwise provided by statute or by a standard of the corporation and subject to the board's ultimate responsibility for oversight, in performing its functions (including oversight functions), the board may delegate, formally or informally by course of conduct, any function (including the function of identifying matters requiring the attention of the board) to committees of the board or to directors, officers, employees, experts, or other persons; a director may rely on such committees and persons in fulfilling his duty under this Section with respect to any delegated function if his reliance is in accordance with Section 4.02.03.

(b) A director or officer who makes a business judgment in good faith fulfils his duty under this Section if:

   (1) he is not interested in the subject of his business judgment;

   (2) he is not interested with respect to the subject of his business judgment to the extent he reasonably believes to be appropriate under the circumstances, and;

    (3) he rationally believes that his business judgment is in the best interest of the corporation.

(c) A person challenging the conduct of a director or officer under this Section has the burden of proving a breach of duty of care (and the inapplicability of the provisions as to the fulfillment of duty under subsection [b] or [c]), and the burden of proving that the breach was the legal cause of damage suffered by the individual (Freeman, pp. 104–105).

Chapter 9

Risk Management Strategies for Physical Educators

A sound risk management plan and the practice of proper risk management techniques are the keys to a safe and enjoyable physical education program.

J. Jason Halsey

Although it is rare, lawsuits are occasionally brought against colleges and universities for accidents and injuries that have occurred in physical education courses. For example, a student sued his college after suffering an eye injury following an errant golf shot by his teaching assistant during a physical education class (*DeMauro v. Tusculum College, Inc.,* 1980). Another individual brought a lawsuit against his university because of injuries sustained during a collision in an advanced football class (*Fortier v. Los Rios Community College Dist.,* 1996). These two examples illustrate a trend that has increased over the last two decades. During the past 20 years, physical educators have witnessed a rise in the number of lawsuits in secondary and collegiate physical education programs as schools have slashed budgets, expanded programs, and experimented with new and varied equipment. Although public institutions were traditionally protected by sovereign immunity statutes, today's trend is for states to waive their immunity and allow themselves to be sued under state tort claims acts (Cotten, 1995).

Obviously, risks are inherent in sports and physical activity. Any time a student or athlete is involved in a physical activity the chance of injury exists. No program, whether it is recreational, professional, or educational, can totally safeguard itself from accidents. However, it is imperative that these programs develop and utilize procedures and strategies to control and minimize damage from potential risks (Appenzeller, 1998).

In the context of managing risks, "risk refers to uncertainty or chance of loss, usually accidental loss, one that is sudden, unusual, or unforeseen," (van der Smissen, 1990b, chap. 23, p.3). The need for risk management arose from the development of insurance to cover accidental and unforeseen losses, and its popularity has increased due to the inability of experts in selected fields to precisely predict outcomes in specific situations (Head & Horn, 1997). Therefore, due to the inability to predict or foresee accidents or injuries in sports and physical activities, physical education programs must incorporate risk management strategies to protect themselves from liability and their students from injuries.

Risk management is a multiple step process. On a very broad scale, the process can be outlined in three steps, occasionally labeled the "D.I.M." process (Ammon, 2001). The first step involves Developing a sound and appropriate risk management plan. The next step is to Implement the plan, and the final step includes Managing the plan. A more specific way of defining risk management as a decision making process is the five-step plan developed by Head and Horn (1997). This process is outlined as follows:

> a) Identifying and analyzing exposures to accidental and business losses that might interfere with an organization's basic objectives; b) examining feasible alternative risk management techniques for dealing with those exposures; c) selecting the apparently best risk management techniques; d) implementing the chosen risk management techniques; and e) monitoring the results of the chosen techniques to ensure that the risk management program remains effective (p. 5).

The following paragraph explains this process more thoroughly, and specifically, in terms of physical education.

Risk management is used for a variety of businesses and operations; however, its application to physical education has become a necessity. An example of this is illustrated below in Eickhoff-Shemek's (2001) modification of Head and Horn's five-step approach into four steps, and its adaptation to the standards of practice of a physical education program. Step one entails developing and establishing a risk management committee and a risk management plan to identify all potential loss exposures. The next step is developing risk management strategies that require construction of detailed descriptions of responsibilities of all individuals in charge of teaching and/or supervising activity classes as well as administering the program. These responsibilities should be included in a handbook or manual. Step three is the implementation of the risk management strategies and requires proper training for the instructors. Step four consists of the evaluation and monitoring of the effectiveness of the risk management plan, to which proper supervision and evaluation are essential (Eickhoff-Shemek, 2001). The following sections highlight the most crucial areas in physical education with regards to developing sound risk management procedures.

Supervision

Supervision is recognized as one of the most important areas in the relationship between physical education and risk management and is called into question almost every time a negligence lawsuit is initiated (Dougherty, 1993). "Supervision can be defined as the quality and quantity of control exerted by teachers … over the individuals for whom they are responsible," (Dougherty et al., 1994, p.252). Some of the most important principles of supervision are illustrated in this section and include general and specific supervision, location of supervisor, competence of supervisor, supervisory planning, and various functions of supervision (van der Smissen, 1990b).

Both specific and general supervision are a part of any physical activity program. The term "specific supervision" refers to a supervisor or instructor directly supervising a small group or an individual, while "general supervision" occurs when a supervisor manages control over an activity in a facility or given area (van der Smissen, 1990b). According to Dougherty (1993), "the intensity and specificity of the supervision is inversely proportional to the ability of the student to understand and appreciate the dangers of the activity, to assess his/her performance and skill level, and to adhere to required safety procedures" (p. 24). Specific supervision is required in situations where instruction is given or there are incapable participants (van der Smissen, 1990b). Specific supervision is also required for all high-risk activities. It is extremely important for physical education instructors to understand the duty of supervision owed to the student in various situations.

The responsibility for appropriate supervision in physical education rests with both the instructor and the administration. Some guidelines for appropriate supervision include; the presence of a supervisor being required at all times and during all activities; never leaving a student or a class unsupervised (Dougherty et al., 1994, Tillman, Voltmer, Esslinger, McCue, 1996); the instructor always supervising individuals who are attempting difficult skills or trying a skill for the first time (Tillman, et al., 1996); safety rules and regulations always being posted, explained, and emphasized by the instructor on a regular basis (Dougherty et al., 1994, Tillman et al., 1996); and the instructor eliminating potential dangers when planning his/her lessons (Tillman et al., 1996).

The legal concept of *respondeat superior,* upon which administrators and supervisors can be found liable for the actions of their employees, is important in the area of supervision. Not only is supervision of the students an imperative aspect of controlling risk, the administrator's duty to supervise employees is equally as important. According to van der Smissen (1990a), there are five categories of functions for which an administrator or supervisor is responsible and may be held liable in the event of negligent behavior. They are:

> a) Employing competent personnel and discharging employees shown to be unfit; b) providing proper supervision and having a plan of supervision; c) directing certain services as to manner they should be done; d) establishing rules and regulations for safety and complying with policy and statutory requirements; e) remedying dangerous conditions and defective equipment or giving notice of same when there is knowledge of the condition (chap. 3, p. 108).

Also, the instructors hired must be properly qualified to teach and supervise (Dougherty et al., 1994, Langley & Hawkins, 1999, Tillman et al., 1996, Wong, 1994). The administration must ensure that their instructors and supervisors understand all emergency procedures in case of accidents or injuries (Dougherty et al., 1994, Tillman et al., 1996). There must also be some type of employee evaluation system in which the administrator assesses the instructor's adherence to rules, regulations, and proper risk management procedures (van der Smissen, 1990b). Finally, it is imperative that all supervisory rules and regulations be documented in writing and given to all supervisors and instructors (McGregor & Associates, 2000).

Instruction

Proper instruction and selection of appropriate activities, sometimes associated with supervision, is another key element in the risk management process. Proper instruction in physical education not only helps ensure the safety and well-being of the students but also serves to eliminate negligent conduct (Hronek & Spengler, 1997).

The teacher is responsible for providing proper instruction to the student. There are various risk management techniques that a teacher must utilize while instructing students. One of the most important techniques is teaching skill progression. According to Langley and Hawkins (1999):

> The provider of the activity must be aware of the status of the participants at all times and foresee the potential for risks of improperly selected activities ...

This will involve the use of appropriate lead-up activities and protocols to assure that participants who are behind have the opportunity to advance their skill level (p. 219).

Instructors must also make the students aware of the inherent risks of particular activities (Langley & Hawkins, 1999, McGregor & Associates, 2000, van der Smissen, 1990b). This includes explaining the challenges of an activity in relationship to a student's skill level as well as the safety practices, rules, and regulations associated with a particular activity (Dougherty et al., 1994, van der Smissen, 1990b). An instructor's selection of activities must reflect the characteristics of the participants' ability, skill level, and fitness level (Dougherty et al., 1994, Langley & Hawkins, 1999, McGregor & Associates, 2000, Tillman et al., 1996, van der Smissen, 1990b). Lesson plans should be detailed and documented, and they should include techniques used for the progression of various activities (Langley & Hawkins, 1999, McGregor & Associates, 2000, van der Smissen, 1990b). Also, administrators need to periodically review an instructor's lesson plans (McGregor & Associates, 2000).

Other risk management strategies for instructional practices include the matching of students by age, size, experience, and strength (Langley & Hawkins, 1999, McGregor & Associates, 2000, Tillman et al., 1996), making sure that teaching procedures are consistent with commonly accepted procedures within the profession, and that all curriculum is approved by administrators (Langley & Hawkins, 1999, van der Smissen, 1990b). According to Langley and Hawkins (1999), it is necessary to have alternative methods of instruction when training or participation is interrupted for students who have been ill or injured.

Training

Training is another indispensable part of a risk management program, especially for physical education departments. According to van der Smissen (1990b), "the sound judgment and decision-making capabilities of the personnel becomes a critical element to carrying out properly the reduction of risk program" (chap. 24, p. 21). Administrators may be held liable if they have not hired qualified personnel and ensured that they are properly trained (Wong, 1994). All instructors should attend workshops, conferences, and in-service programs to maintain and update their knowledge and skills concerning the activities they teach (Tillman et al., 1996, van der Smissen, 1990b). It is imperative that all instructors and personnel be trained on any changes in teaching methodologies and any new equipment used (Langley & Hawkins, 1999). Instructors should also be supervised and trained by their administrators in order to illustrate they are effectively performing their duties (McGregor & Associates, 2000). Instructors should take steps to maintain all of their certifications, which imply an awareness of basic knowledge, at the highest possible level (Dougherty et al., 1994, McGregor & Associates, 2000). Proper risk management techniques should be part of the job training (McGregor & Associates, 2000), as should cardiopulmonary resuscitation (CPR) training, first aid training, and emergency procedures training (McGregor & Associates, 2000, Tillman et al., 1996).

Medical Care

One of the most important risk management strategies involves the safety of the participant and includes medical care and first aid. When an injury occurs to a student, the instructor is under a duty of care to render "reasonably prompt and capable" medical assistance to the injured participant (Wong, 1994, p. 422). Public institutions should be aware that recent trends have illustrated that the concept of sovereign immunity has deteriorated in fairness to injured plaintiffs (Wong, 1994). Because of this responsibility, administrators must adopt strict procedures in regard to medical standards. All physical educators should have some type of courses or training that explain the types of injuries most commonly associated with their sports or activities (Tillman et al., 1996). All personnel should be certified in CPR and first aid, and they should be able to render assistance when called upon (Dougherty et al., 1994, McGregor & Associates, 2000, Tillman et al., 1996, van der Smissen, 1990b). Other risk management strategies involving medical care include implementing proper emergency procedures and maintaining proper documentation of all accidents and injuries.

An emergency plan, defined as a "predetermined plan to deal with an emergency in an organized and efficient manner," (McGregor & Associates, 2000, p. 47), is essential for a physical activity program, especially with the rise in the number of sports injuries over the past few decades. A proper plan will take into account the nature and size of a program, the number of participants in the program, and the proximity to emergency and medical care services (van der Smissen, 1990b). Any plan should be well organized and documented in writing (Tillman et al., 1996, van der Smissen, 1990b). When developing and initiating the emergency plan, van der Smissen (1990b) suggests the following:

a) All persons involved in the implementation of the plan should have a part in its development.

b) All personnel should be apprised of the plan, and it should be part of the written manual they receive.

c) There should be an in-service program to enhance the skills of the personnel, both in understanding what the procedures are and in reviewing first aid procedures (Ch. 24, pp. 31–32).

In addition, all emergency plans should include the availability of first-aid kits and access to all relevant emergency phone numbers (Tillman et al., 1996), as well as procedures for locating all emergency services and apparatus, emergency vehicles, and alarms (van der Smissen, 1990b).

Following an injury or accident, it is imperative that the situation is documented and the information regarding the incident be readily available (Tillman et al., 1996). Accident forms should be completed by the instructor and supervisor as soon as possible following the incident (McGregor & Associates, 2000), and they must include important information such as the activity/class in which the accident occurred, date and time of the accident, person in charge at the time of the accident, complete information about the individual who was injured, and any statements from witnesses (van der Smissen, 1990b). Other relevant information concerning the accident should be noted, including the location of the accident, the sequence of the activity, procedures followed in rendering aid, and any preventative measures taken by the injured individual (van der Smissen, 1990b).

Facilities and Equipment

The correct use of equipment and facilities is another sound risk management strategy. Although success has been limited in litigation against institutions involving equipment and facilities, the number and nature of the lawsuits indicate potential liability areas (Wong, 1994). Inspections and maintenance constitute the two major risk management areas when dealing with equipment and facilities.

Inspections of all equipment and facilities should occur on a regular basis (Dougherty et al., 1994, McGregor & Associates, 2000, Tillman et al., 1996). As van der Smissen (1990b) states, "The validity of the inspection depends upon the quality of the inspection system established, including both policies and procedures of implementation" (chap. 24, p.33). A written and detailed schedule of inspections should be kept, as well as recorded documentation on any damaged or faulty equipment or unsafe facilities (Langley & Hawkins, 1999). It is recommended that all grounds be inspected for debris, slippery or uneven surfaces, or other environmental hazards before commencement of an activity (Dougherty et al., 1994). Finally, according to Dougherty et al. (1994) and Tillman et al. (1996), it is a good practice to instruct the students how to do periodic checks on both the equipment and facilities they will be using for an activity.

Maintenance is an important aspect in the correct and safe use of facilities and equipment. All unsafe equipment should be discarded or stored securely until fixed, and unsafe facilities should never be used (Tillman et al., 1996). If needed, Dougherty et al. (1994) suggested modifying an activity until the proper maintenance is performed on broken equipment.

Other risk management techniques in the area of equipment and facilities include securing and locking all equipment and facilities when not in use (Dougherty et al., 1994, Tillman et al., 1996), providing all necessary protective equipment (Tillman et al., 1996), and warning, either verbally or in writing, the students of the status of all equipment and facilities (van der Smissen, 1990b).

The following discussion highlights some risk management practices that need to be included in any comprehensive physical education risk management plan and program.

Accident and Injury Data

When developing a comprehensive risk management plan, it is imperative that those persons responsible for safety in a physical education program understand where the possibilities of risk exist. An annual analysis of accidents and injuries can provide data used to create and update standards within a physical education department. For example, if a program notices an alarming number of eye injuries in racquetball classes, it may choose to develop a policy of requiring all students to wear protective eye guards rather than eliminating the program from the curriculum.

An inclusive analysis of minor injuries with a subsequent enhancement of safety measures should help a program limit the number of serious incidents that occur. In addition, because risk management is the process of balancing the control of hazards with the addition of controlled risks, it is imperative that a physical education department understands the actual danger versus the apparent danger of an activity (Horine, 1999). The first, and most important, step in analyzing accident data is accurately reporting and recording all accidents and injuries on a comprehensive accident report form. This allows a physical education department to compare the number and types of injuries and/or accidents that occur in a particular activity class. Often physical education departments have these forms, but the information gathered is used only to follow up on a specific case and not to examine trends and possible problems in the supervision or instruction of an activity.

Training Workshops and Seminars

An effective and operative risk management plan is dependent on the individuals who implement the risk reduction strategies and procedures. Therefore, the credentials and expertise of the physical activity instructors are vital to any risk management plan. All instructors should be properly licensed and certified; however, formalized certifications are not a guarantee that instructors will perform in a manner consistent with the most current and accepted risk management practices. It is far more important for an instructor to update and enhance their expertise in the crucial areas of risk management and their area of specialization (van der Smissen, 1990b). One of the most effective ways to do this is by participating in formal trainings, in-service workshops, seminars, and conferences specifically designed for risk management in physical education.

Tillman, et al. (1996), stressed that teachers must attend workshops and participate in in-services training programs. McGregor and Associates (2000) suggested that institutions should encourage all relevant staff to upgrade their qualifications on an ongoing basis, while Dougherty, et al. (1994) insisted that instructors must keep instructional skills and certifications at the highest possible level. While most instructors would be unlikely to have a problem with attending additional trainings or workshops on risk management, institutions should make the opportunities more readily available and require their instructors and educators to attend. In a field such as physical education it would be wise for colleges and universities to promote and prioritize safety and risk management training.

Emergency Care Drills

The possibility of injury and even catastrophic injury exists within any physical education program. Therefore, everyone in the department, including the administrators and instructors, should be well rehearsed in emergency care procedures. According to Wong (1994), two main responsibilities exist for a teacher dealing with an injured student. First, the instructor may be required to give medical assistance to the student before medical personnel arrive. Also, the instructor must exert reasonable care in sending an injured student for medical treatment. Instructors may be well trained in knowing what to do, where to go, and who to contact, but an actual emergency is far different than any training or certification program. McGregor and Associates (2000) recommended that all staff have formal training in emergency procedures, and that communicating, training, and rehearsing the emergency response plan are keys to emergency care. All emergency plans are different; therefore, formal training alone will not effectively ready someone for an emergency in their specific program. My research suggested that a majority of physical education departments do not conduct emergency care drills and training. Benefits of conducting these drills include examining the effectiveness of the staff during an emergency response, discovering the length of time it takes for emergency personnel to arrive at the school or injury site, and exposing any shortcomings of the program's emergency response plan.

CPR and First Aid Training

In addition to specific emergency care training, all staff and instructors who interact with physical education students should be formally trained in both CPR and first aid.

According to Wong (1994), instructors have a duty to obtain reasonable and capable medical assistance for injured participants. It is possible for an instructor to be held liable for not properly assisting an injured student. My research suggests that while programs may offer CPR and first aid training, many institutions do not require their instructors to be formally certified. These schools are exposing themselves to potential liability if a student is injured and requires some basic and immediate medical care before emergency personnel can arrive.

Physical educators have a responsibility to reduce their student's exposure to risk and to have protocols in place to deal with accidents and emergencies. No educator can effectively prevent all accidents or injuries; however, both instructors and administrators can choose to take the proper steps and make the correct decisions when these unfortunate incidents occur. A sound risk management plan and the practice of proper risk management techniques are the keys to a safe and enjoyable physical education program.

References

Ammon, R., Jr. (2001). Risk Management Process. In D. J. Cotten, J. T. Wolohan, & T. J. Wilde (Eds.), *Law for Recreation and Sport Managers* (2nd ed., pp. 265–277). Dubuque, IA: Kendall/Hunt.

Appenzeller, H. (1998). Risk Management in Sport. In H. Appenzeller (Ed.), *Risk Management in Sport* (pp. 5–10). Durham, NC: Carolina Academic Press.

Cotten, D. J. (1995). Liability of Educators for the Negligence of Others (Substitutes, Aides, Student Teachers, and New Teachers). *Physical Educator, 52*, 70–77.

DeMauro v. Tusculum College, Inc., 603 S.W. 2d 115 (1980).

Dougherty, N. J., IV. (1993). Legal Responsibility for Safety in Physical Education and Sport. In N. J. Dougherty IV (Ed.), *Principles of Safety in Physical Education and Sport* (pp. 18–25). Reston, VA: American Alliance for Health, Physical Education, Recreation, and Dance.

Dougherty, N. J., IV, Auxter, D., Goldberger, A. S., & Heinzmann, G. S. (1994). *Sport, Physical Activity and the Law.* Champaign, IL: Human Kinetics.

Eickhoff-Shemek, J. (2001). Standards of Practice. In D. J. Cotton, J. T. Wolohan, & T. J. Wilde (Eds.), *Law for Recreation and Sport Managers* (2nd ed., pp. 293–302). Dubuque, IA: Kendall Hunt.

Fortier v. Los Rios Community College Dist., 45 Cal. App. 4th 430 (1996).

Hart, J. E., & Ritson, R. J. (1993). *Liability and Safety in Physical Education and Sport.* Reston, VA: American Alliance for Health, Physical Education, Recreation, and Dance.

Head, G. L., & Horn, S., II. (1997). *Essentials of Risk Management* (3rd ed., Vol. 1). Malvern, PA: Insurance Institute of America.

Horine, L. (1999). Administration of Physical Education and Sport Programs (4th ed.). Boston, MA: WCB/McGraw-Hill.

Hronek, B. R., & Spengler, J. O. (1997). *Legal Liability in Recreation and Sports.* Champaign, IL: Sagamore.

Langley, T. D., & Hawkins, J. D. (1999). *Administration for Exercise Related Professions.* Englewood, CO: Morton.

McGregor, I., and Associates. (2000). *Sport Risk — The Ultimate Risk Management Planning and Resource Manual.* San Rafael, CA: McGregor and Associates.

Tillman, K. G., Voltmer, E. F., Esslinger, A. A., & McCue, B. F. (1996). *The Administration of Physical Education, Sport, and Leisure Programs* (6th ed.). Boston, MA: Allyn and Bacon.

van der Smissen, B. (1990a). *Legal Liability and Risk Management for Public and Private Entities* (Vol. 1). Cincinnati, OH: Anderson.

van der Smissen, B. (1990b). *Legal Liability and Risk Management for Public and Private Entities* (Vol. 2). Cincinnati, OH: Anderson.

Wong, G. M. (1994). *Essentials of Amateur Sports Law* (2nd ed.). Westport, CT: Praeger.

For sample forms, see Chapter 36 by Gary Rushing, "A Risk Management Checklist for Secondary School Athletic Programs."

Chapter 10

Risk Management for Cheerleading

"Cheerleading programs raise a unique set of challenges for coaches and administrators."

Elizabeth Appenzeller

Cheerleading programs raise a unique set of challenges for coaches and administrators in regards to risk management. Although programs differ, from the recreational to the collegiate, there are some basic principles that can be applied to all cheerleading groups.

Cheerleading, for many, is a competitive activity with National Championships while for others it is an activity that takes place on the sidelines, supporting athletic teams. Many of these teams are at different levels of cheerleading participation and are involved with a variety of cheerleading industry organizations. Your team's purpose could be to publicize your school or your city; to evoke pride and spirit for your school, city or team; increase attendance at athletic events; add excitement to events; and encourage sports teams to represent the school or city at competitions and/or community events. However, all teams should recognize that participating in cheerleading provides an opportunity for young men and women to build self confidence, stay healthy and have fun (NCSSE).

Today there are a variety of different types of cheerleading programs. They include (1) Recreational Cheerleading; (2) Interscholastic Cheerleading; (3) Special Needs; (4) All-Star Cheerleading; (5) Collegiate Cheerleading; (7) STUNT teams and Acrobatics and Tumbling; and (8) Professional Cheerleading.

Developing a Risk Management Plan and Strategies

The following strategies should be a part of the school/gym/organization's risk management plan:

1. Organize a Risk Management Safety Committee.

2. Document in writing that a preseason staff meeting was held. Keep a copy of the agenda and list those in attendance. Keep minutes of the meeting.

3. Update all department policies and procedures.

4. Review eligibility rules, pre-participation physical examinations, insurance coverage (including pre-existing physical conditions), HMO and PPO policies, catastrophic insurance and liability coverage for all personnel. Discuss any exclusion with cheerleaders and, when appropriate, notify parents of minors of exclusion and coverage.

5. Discuss warnings and consent and participant agreements. Designate who will meet with the cheerleaders and parents and discuss and implement the participation agreement before it is signed.

6. Require certification in emergency first aid, cardiopulmonary resuscitation (CPR) and use of automatic external defibrillators (AEDs) for coaches and other cheerleading personnel.

7. Discuss the policy and procedure for a medical response plan. Include the coach's role in the plan.

8. Check all first aid kits, cell phones, walkie talkies and on-site telephones to determine that they are operative. Plan to check prior to every practice or competition that they are in working order.

9. Conduct regular inspections of facilities and equipment and document the inspection. Designate who will conduct the inspections.

10. Have a policy for administering accident injury reports and claims.

11. Develop a comprehensive plan for transporting cheerleaders (avoid 15-passenger vans).

12. Check Title IX compliance when appropriate.

13. Check compliance with the Americans with Disabilities Act (ADA).

14. Review proper signage in areas that need signage.

15. Review catastrophic injury protocol.

16. Supervise high-risk activities with competent, certified coaches.

17. Conduct a background check of all cheerleading personnel (including volunteers).

18. Constantly identify risks and evaluate the cheerleading program with a periodic risk assessment.

19. Know the rules of cheerleading and follow them in the program. Utilize national cheerleading guidelines and certification requirements (Appenzeller, Mueller and Appenzeller 128–129).

Implementing Risk Management Strategies

The Risk Management Safety Committee should meet on a periodic basis to prioritize the risk in the program.

Warnings and Consent

It is important for cheerleading administrators and/or coaches to conduct a preseason meeting to discuss the risks that individuals may experience and how the organization will attempt to minimize the inherent risk of cheerleading.

Emergency Action Plan

An emergency action plan (EAP) is a formal, written plan designed to create safety awareness among coaches and athletic trainers. An EAP should prepare coaches and athletic trainers for all foreseeable emergencies that could happen in practice, game and competition settings. This includes everything from sprained ankles to field evacuations. Below is a partial list of what the plan should cover:

1. Bomb Threats
2. Crisis Communication Planning
3. Catastrophic Injury Planning
4. Emergency Evacuations
5. Severe Weather Policies

Developing an EAP should be an ongoing project. You can also improve on your plan, and practicing your EAP will keep it fresh in your coaches' and trainers' minds.

Catastrophic Injury Plan

All athletic departments should have a catastrophic injury plan (CIP). The CIP should include individual team's and their coach's responsibilities. A Catastrophic Injury Plan is a formal, written plan that provides protocol on how to handle an injury such as a spinal cord injury, a campus death, etc.

There are four main phases to handling a catastrophic injury. They are:

1. Handling the injury
2. Working with the injured person's family
3. Addressing the media
4. Working with students and faculty.

Cheerleading coaches must know their roles when handling a catastrophic injury involving one of their team members. Understanding their responsibilities will help minimize confusion about the incident and better prepare them to deal with the injured person's family and properly handle any media.

Personnel Management:
Questions for Cheerleading Personnel

1. Do participants sign a participant agreement before they compete? Who meets with the cheerleaders to discuss the agreement and answer questions before they sign the document?

2. Number of grants for cheerleading? What are the guidelines to get a grant? To keep a grant?

3. Are cheerleaders and mascots required to have a pre-participation physical exam? How often? Is there a standard medical form used?

4. How do the cheerleaders travel? Do they use 15-passenger vans? Who drives the vans or cars on trips? What is the policy for travel?

5. Does the coach or do other staff members always participate in over-night trips to provide supervision?

6. Can we see an accident-injury report used for cheerleaders?

7. What are the risk management strategies used by the cheerleading program? Are they in writing? Who sees that they are followed?

8. Is there a medical response plan? In writing?

9. Is there a catastrophic injury plan in effect?

10. Is an AED available for the cheerleaders at home? On trips? Does everyone know where the AED is located?

11. Do the coaches have certification in training? First Aid? CPR? AED's?

12. Are the coaches certified by a national organization for cheerleading?

13. Is competent supervision furnished at every practice of gymnastic stunts and competitions?

14. Do the cheerleaders use mats? ASTM approved?

15. Are competitive cheerleaders considered athletes and do they count toward Title IX compliance?

16. Are ADA and Title IX guidelines followed?

17. What are the eligibility requirements for cheerleading?

18. Is there a risk management checklist? Who is responsible for inspections of facilities, etc.?

19. Who reports injuries and to whom?

20. Do the cheerleaders get evaluated? Do they evaluate the coaches and program? Is there an exit interview and evaluation?

21. Do the cheerleaders have a cheerleading manual?

22. Can we see a waiver form? Participant Agreement?

23. Are there questions they want to ask us (administrators, coach, participant, athletic trainer, etc.)?

24. Are there any claims against the coach, school, etc.?

25. Are standards of eligibility different from those of other campus groups?

26. Who funds the program?

27. Are tutors provided?

Supervision

Cheerleading and the Law outlines the Importance of Risk Management for Cheerleading administrators and coaches and Risk Management Strategies.

The AACCA states the following in reference to supervisory guidelines:

Providing adequate supervision is a fundamental prerequisite to managing the risk in cheerleading.

A certified coach should be present at all athletic department-sponsored events where spirit squad members are making an appearance.

Legally the courts expect supervision to exist when activities are in progress that can be dangerous to the participant. Although there is no standard regarding the number of supervisors, adequate and competent supervision is required at practices and games. Negligence may be established when cheerleaders are assigned activities that are judged to be beyond their skill and ability. Coaches can be held responsible for injuries if failure to warn of the possible dangers is not discussed (Appenzeller, Mueller and Appenzeller 2008).

Training of Coaches

It all starts with a qualified coach. Coaches should be qualified at every level. There are a variety of coaching certifications available, including the American Association of Cheerleading Coaches and Administrators (AACCA), the National Council for Spirit Safety and Education (NCSSE) and the United States All-Star Federation (USASF). Administrators should also perform background checks on all coaches and support staff that will be working with the cheerleading team.

Safety Certifications

Previous research shows that cheerleading requires a high degree of flexibility, strength, agility and balance. The various lifts, throws, catches, tumbling runs and jumps that comprise most performance routines require a high degree of athletic skill (Cook, Seegmiller, Thomas, & Young 2004). Unlike most sports, cheerleading is year-long and requires often complex gymnastics as well as team stunts. In girls' and women's sports, more than half of catastrophic injuries resulting in paralysis or death happen in cheerleading ("Three Cheers for Safer Cheering," 2006). There are several factors that may contribute to cheerleading injuries, one of which may be the lack of a certified cheerleading coach.

In today's litigious society, many cheerleading organizations have recognized the need for safety. These cheerleading organizations produce educational materials stressing the importance of safety. It is very important for individuals coaching or overseeing a cheerleading program to be properly trained and certified. All-Star Cheerleading teams are governed by the United States All-Star Federation (USASF). The USASF organization has industry standards that require the coaches of All-Star teams to be certified within their organization.

Cheerleading organizations feel that having safety-certified cheerleading coaches and advisors will have an effect on reducing cheerleading injuries. In 2006 the cheerleading community focused on safety and the NCAA changed its catastrophic injury insurance program for cheerleaders by requiring cheerleaders to be directly supervised by a safety-certified coach and or advisor. The NCAA put forth a cheerleading safety initiative to undertake the important issue of cheerleading risk management. The NCAA's goal was to enhance safety for college cheerleaders. The NCAA's Catastrophic Injury Insurance Program includes a requirement for an institution's cheerleading program to be included as a covered event under the policy. The requirement states that cheerleading activities must be supervised by a safety-certified coach or advisor. This change came as a response to data collected on cheerleading injuries. The NCAA believes that a safety-certified coach and or advisor will reduce cheerleading injuries dramatically. The NCAA recognizes collegiate coaches' certifications from both the American Association of Cheerleading Coaches and Administrators (AACCA) and the National Council for Spirit Safety and Education (NCSSE).

Additionally, coaches should be required to be certified in emergency first aid, cardiopulmonary resuscitation (CPR) and in the use of automatic external defibrillators (AEDS).

Instruction

Have **general rules**, **regulations** and **expectations** written down for all team members and parents. This should also include information about the organizational structure of the team, disciplinary procedures, suspension and dismissal procedures. There are systems of rules that if broken result in a disciplinary action such as a warning, suspension or dismissal. Make sure the rules and their results are clear. As in other sports, clubs and activities, hazing exists in cheerleading. It is best to have a written and expressed zero tolerance policy against hazing. Hazing can have some very serious consequences and hazing by cheerleaders should have a disciplinary action for the individuals and/or the team.

The general rules should also include your uniform policy. Cheerleaders may be purchasing some items that they are allowed to keep. For cheerleaders borrowing school or college uniforms you may need to include a return policy for uniforms that includes cleaning or damages. You may also want to set rules about alterations for uniforms and establish a procedure for returning cheerleading items at the end of the year or if quitting or dismissed from the team. Many cheerleading programs limit the wearing of team uniforms and apparel outside of official events.

Social Media Concerns

In today's society, access to media such as the internet, facebook and YouTube is quick and easy. Set a policy for your team members regarding photos, videos, comments, etc. Some teams do not allow videos of competition routines or practices to be placed on facebook or YouTube. Some programs may not allow photos of team members in uniform to be placed on the internet or facebook, while others may welcome photos and videos of their team as a way to promote, recruit or share information. Many colleges have rules against photos on facebook and MySpace for their athletes and they require certain privacy settings be maintained for any of their athletes using such sites. Decide what limitations, if any, you need to place on your team members and/or parents regarding social media and place that information in your general rules.

For teams where scholarship money may be involved, it is essential to also outline how scholarship money is awarded and distributed along with how one's scholarship award may be lost or reduced due to disciplinary action. Many teams award senior team members or captains more scholarship aid while others award equal amounts to all. You can also stipulate that if an individual breaks a team rule they forfeit all scholarship award money. Team members that quit or are dismissed could also automatically forfeit all scholarship award money. Again, regardless of the way you choose to distribute scholarships, make sure the procedure is in writing and is clear to the cheerleaders and their parents.

Time Commitment

The most important part of being a member on a cheerleading team is understanding the time commitment. Be very clear about what your expectations are and the estimated time that being a member of the cheerleading team will require. Often cheerleaders and parents commit to a cheerleading team without really understanding and embracing the amount of time and hard work that will be demanded. One of the differences between cheerleading and some other team sports is the level of choreography and safety of stunting skills required. It is easier to substitute one absent child on the soccer or basketball team for another, but in cheerleading every team member is needed every day to perform the correct choreography and to safely perform stunts. A flyer is not easily subbed for a base or a back spot and vice versa. The entire team suffers when a cheerleading team member is not committed to practices, games or competitions. The ability of the team to move forward with stunting and advanced choreography is often jeopardized by undisciplined and uncommitted team members.

Scheduling

Once you have a group of committed cheerleaders that understands the rules and expectations of the team you can begin practices. Setting practices can be a challenge with every cheerleader and parent's busy schedule. Many gyms and schools also have multiple groups that they need to accommodate. It may be difficult to set the ideal practice schedule based on everyone's schedule and the availability of the facility, but work to set a schedule that everyone can manage and that also gives you the proper practice time you need to develop your team's skills and prepare for games, events and competitions.

Transportation

Cheerleading teams and their members often have to travel to and from practices, games, events and competitions. "Organizations and schools that sponsor cheerleading programs have a duty to provide safe vehicles and qualified drivers when transporting cheerleaders" (Appenzeller, Mueller and Appenzeller 2008). Develop a plan for transporting cheerleaders and avoid 15 passenger vans. The ideal method of transporting any team is with a charter vehicle. The charter company assumes liability and has risk management strategies in place, including a safe vehicle, qualified driver, background checks, references and a contract.

Equipment and Facilities

Your actual practice space should be a safe environment for your cheerleaders, free of distractions and with access to bathrooms and water. Distractions at practice include parents, friends and other teams. Stray basketballs, footballs, soccer balls, softballs, baseballs or frisbees can all pose a serious danger to cheerleaders tumbling and stunting. The coach should inspect the facility before practice and games to ensure a safe environment for the athletes. If it is not safe the coach is responsible for following proper procedure to correct the problem.

Practice space does not always need to be state-of-the-art facilities with a spring floor, but you do need to have a space that provides for the safety of your team. AACCA rules govern the type of skills you can perform on a given surface. If you are practicing in a basketball gym, you must follow AACCA rules as to what tumbling and stunting skills are allowed on that type of surface. Being outside in the grass is also an acceptable practice space but you need to be aware of your surroundings. Having mats available is ideal but you can still have productive practices without mats as long as you have a coach that is doing skill-appropriate and surface-appropriate exercises.

Tumbling mats and other equipment should be stored in a secure location when not being used by cheerleading team members for the following reasons:

1. To reduce the chance of damage to the mats from improper use by gym users and event spectators

2. To reduce the chance of injury from a mat falling on a child or other spectator at an athletic event.

3. To not be considered an out-of-bounds risk during other sports practices and or games

4. To avoid causing interference while extending and retracting the bleachers

5. To avoid causing interference in regards to blocking exits during an emergency

6. To reduce the chance of megaphones, signs, poms and equipment being stolen or vandalized.

Game days can present challenges for coaches and administrators in regards to safety. The same surface rules apply to game day situations (football, basketball, volleyball, etc.) and in addition to the game day distractions there is the added element of crowd control. AACCA notes that cheerleaders should be aware of not only the crowd but also the action on the field or court and restrict stunting and tumbling to times when the action is taking place away from or opposite the section where the cheerleaders are located. Fans can throw items onto the field or court and the game day sidelines are often crowded with fans, game day personnel and camera crews. All of the above actions can pose a real danger to cheerleaders.

AACCA requires additional restrictions on cheerleaders for basketball games. Just as the game management staff and athletic training staff have an emergency action plan for the event and for the teams and personnel involved, cheerleaders must be considered. How will the cheerleaders be protected in various situations? How will they move in and out of the arena or stadium? Coaches and administrators should be familiar with game day venues and the challenges they may pose for cheerleaders. Make it a point to communicate with the game day management and or security team about not only your own team but also any visiting cheerleading teams. Ask that the sideline area where the cheerleaders will be performing be kept clear and that security is available to cheerleaders if there is ever a situation that gets out of hand or one where they need to be escorted safely out of the venue or off the sidelines.

The athletic department should provide a safe zone for the cheerleaders to perform, considering the following:

1. Potential collisions with television crews and equipment

2. Safe exit in the event of severe weather

3. Safe exit in the event of crowds rushing the field

4. Protection of cheerleading equipment involving the situations number 2 and 3.

Medical Care/Pre-Participation Physicals

It is imperative that all cheerleaders, dance team members and mascots not be allowed to participate in practices or games without first receiving medical clearance. A pre-participation physical should be administered by a team physician or personal physician. All team members and incoming students trying out must have proof of insurance and a completed pre-participation form from their doctor before trying out.

Insurance

It is the athletic department's duty to make sure that all cheerleading members and coaches understand the insurance policy. In most departments, Primary health insurance must be provided by the student athlete. Secondary insurance will be provided by the athletic department, with limitations. Catastrophic injury insurance is also provided by the NCAA. Below is the NCAA explanation of benefits:

> The NCAA catastrophic policy covers the cheerleading squad's activities at NCAA varsity team competitions scheduled by the NCAA member institution (cheering at an NCAA varsity football or basketball game, for example). The policy also covers practice sessions and pep rallies that are authorized by, organized by and directly supervised by a safety-certified official coach or advisor of the NCAA member institution in preparation for a varsity team competitions. The coach or advisor must have a current safety certification by a nationally recognized, formal credentialing program for safety certification. The supervisor cannot be a full-time undergraduate student, student coach or member of the team.

> The NCAA catastrophic policy does not cover any activities not directly associated with the activities of an NCAA varsity sport team. Examples of activities that are not covered include camps, clinics, national competitions, conference competitions, fundraisers, alumni events or functions and any events not conducted by the NCAA member institutions.

> Performance s outside the stadium on game-day may be covered but only if this activity is part of the member institution's scheduled cheerleading activities for the game and only if the requirements outlined above for practice sessions and pep rallies are met.

Athletic Trainers

Unfortunately, one of the aspects of any sport or physical activity is the possibility of injury. Athletic Trainers should be assigned and available to cheerleading teams.It is recommended that Athletic Trainers should be available for all cheerleading practices and games and be present at tryouts. Athletic Trainers can assist in lightning and severe weather detection at practices, games and events. The presence of an athletic trainer increases the chance for a quick medical response when injuries occur at practices or tryouts. An Athletic Trainer is usually more qualified to diagnose injuries and begin proper treatment than a coach is. The athletic training staff has a catastrophic injury plan in place. Thus, the trainer is more capable of determining whether outside medical assistance will be needed based on the severity of the injury. Athletic Trainers, along with the team physician, should determine when an injured team member is given clearance to participate in activities again. A qualified Athletic Trainer is able to provide education about weight and nutrition. The athletic training staff can also help enforce team and school rules regarding drugs, drug testing, alcoholic beverages and tobacco and can help provide education in those areas.

Risk Assessment Audit: Suggestions for Administrators and Coaches

Meetings

- Meet Athletic Director (AD) or athletic department representative who oversees cheerleading program

- Meet the cheerleading coach and/or coaches
- Meet the faculty advisor
- Meet the dance coach(es)

Dance Team

- Is the dance team considered separate from the cheerleading program? If the dance team is considered to be equivalent to the cheerleading program then the questions below should also pertain to the dance team. One exception is the NCAA catastrophic injury insurance policy that only deals with cheerleading. However, the issue of insurance still pertains to the dance team.

Coaching Certifications

- Are your coach and assistant coaches AACCA or NCSSE certified?
- Are the coach and assistant coaches CPR, first aid and AED certified?

Supervision of Coaches and Program

- Who directly supervises the cheerleading program?
- Who does the coach report to?
- Who is the liaison between the cheerleading program and the admissions office?
- Who is the liaison between the cheerleading program and the financial aid office (scholarships)?
- How are the program and coach evaluated?
- How often are the program and coach evaluated?

Emergency Care

- Does someone (e.g., athletic trainer or coach) have contact cards for cheerleaders in case of an emergency?
- Does the team have an emergency action plan?
- Does the team have access to the athletic training room?
- Does the team have an assigned Athletic Trainer?
- If the team has an assigned trainer, does that individual attend all practices, games and competitions?

Insurance

If the coach is certified then the NCAA grants an additional catastrophic injury policy for the cheerleading team that protects them only at practices that prepare them for NCAA games and NCAA-sanctioned games.

- How are the cheerleaders insured?
- Are dance team members insured?
- How are your other athletes insured?
- Is there a school insurance policy for student-athletes?

Facilities

All facilities for practice and performances need to be checked for safety and have risks assessed.

- Football field
- Basketball court

Scholarships

- How are scholarships administered?
- Who administers scholarships?
- How and when are scholarships awarded?
- Can scholarship money be taken away (e.g., student falls below team GPA, quits the team, is dismissed, etc.)?

Participation

- Do the cheerleaders sign a participation agreement?
- Do the dance team members sign a participation agreement?
- Is there a team contract that exists that outlines the rules of the team and expectations of individuals?

Competitions

- How are competitions budgeted?
- How does/do the team(s) travel to competition?
- What competitions does/do the team(s) usually compete in?
- Does the competition carry its own insurance policy?
- Does the competition provide medical care?

Travel

- Do the teams travel to away games?
- How is away game travel budgeted?
- What mode of transportation does/do the team(s) use?

All who are involved in cheer programs at every level should utilize risk management strategies to protect cheerleaders and mascots from injuries. In addition, risk management strategies are important to those who administer cheer programs.

References

American Association of Cheerleading Coaches and Administrators (AACCA).

Appenzeller, H., Mueller, F. and E. Appenzeller 2008. *Cheerleading and the Law: Risk Management Strategies.* Durham, NC: Carolina Academic Press.

Cook, T.I., Seegmiller, J.G., Thomas, D.Q. and Young, B.A. 2004. "Physiologic Profiles of the Fitness Status of Collegiate Cheerleaders." *Journal of Strength and Conditioning Research*, 18 (2), 252–254.

The National Council for Spirit Safety and Education (NCSSE)

"Three Cheers for Safer Cheering," 2006. *Magna's Campus Legal Monthly*, 21 (2), 1–6.

Chapter 11

Playground Risk Management and Safety

The most important safety standard for the playground is the proper, appropriate, and adequate supervision of children using the equipment.

Leonard K. Lucenko & Thomas Bowler

Introduction

It is well known that play is an integral part of the development of children. Playgrounds offer them the opportunity to grow socially, mentally, and physically. It is therefore incumbent upon owners and operators of public playground areas, including schools, municipalities, public parks and recreation departments, and other public entities, to make certain that the playground is designed, constructed, and managed to provide a safe and healthy environment for play activities. The importance of providing a safe playground environment is highlighted by the fact that the CPSC has reported that from 2006–2008, an average of 218,851 children received emergency room care for injuries related to playground equipment and areas. Thus, organizations responsible for the design, construction, and operation of public playgrounds must be knowledgeable about the above guidelines and standards. They must be certain that the equipment and surface selected for the public playground area meet these standards. At the heart of this effort should be a comprehensive playground risk management and safety plan. This plan must cover all aspects of playground safety and include the policies, procedures, practices, and rules that need to be established and enforced to reduce the risk of injury to children using the playground equipment.

History of Playground Risk Management and Safety

In 1981 the U.S. Consumer Product Safety Commission (CPSC), at the request of the National Recreation and Park Association, issued the first set of safety guidelines for public playgrounds. Volume I of its Handbook for Public Playground Safety, now the Public Playground Safety Handbook, provided the first voluntary guidelines for owners, operators, and maintenance staffs regarding the safety of the playground equipment and facilities

115

on public playgrounds. Volume II provided technical guidelines for manufacturers of this equipment. The CPSC has since issued a one-volume Handbook in 1991, 1994, 1997, 2008, and the current Handbook, issued in 2010. In addition to providing public playground operators with information on topics such as the age-appropriateness of certain playground equipment, the importance of supervision of the playground area and the training of playground supervisors, and the layout of the playground area and safety specifications for certain equipment, the CPSC also provides suggested maintenance checklists and tools and testing methods for common playground hazards. In addition, the CPSC has published several special studies regarding the number of injuries and deaths related to playground activities.

ASTM International, formerly American Society for Testing and Materials, assumed responsibility for the technical guidelines for playground equipment that were published as Volume II of the (CPSC) 1981 Handbook. In 1993, ASTM adopted Standard F 1487, Standard Consumer Safety Performance Specifications for Playground Equipment for Public Use. This voluntary standard provides the methodologies and standards that manufacturers are required to follow and meet in the design and manufacture of playground equipment. This standard provides requirements for equipment intended for preschool children (ages 2–5) and school age children (ages 5–12). Standard F 1292, Standard Specification for Impact Attenuation of Surface Systems Under and Around Playground Equipment, provides the requirements and methodologies manufacturers must use in measuring the impact attenuation of playground surfacing materials installed beneath playground equipment.

In addition to Standards F 1487 and F 1292, other ASTM Standards that have been developed relative to playground equipment and surfacing include: F 2223 Standard Guide for ASTM Standards on Playground Surfacing; F 1951 Standard Specification for Determination of Accessibility of Surface Systems Under and Around Playground Equipment; F 2075 Standard Specification for Engineered Wood Fiber for Use as a Playground Safety Surface Under and Around Playground Equipment; F 2479 Standard Guide for Specification, Purchase, Installation and Maintenance of Poured-In-Place Playground Surfacing; and F 2373 Standard Consumer Safety Performance Specification for Public Use Play Equipment for Children 6 Months through 23 Months.

Together, the CPSC Handbook and ASTM standards are used by courts as voluntary standards when evaluating the safety of the playground environment. This is reflected in the fact that the following states have either adopted all or incorporated parts of the CPSC Handbook and ASTM Standards into their playground safety statutes and regulations: Arkansas; California; Connecticut; Florida; Illinois; Michigan; New Jersey; New York; North Carolina; Ohio; Oklahoma; Oregon; Rhode Island; Tennessee; Texas; Utah; and Virginia.

The International Play Equipment Manufacturer's Association (IPEMA) provides third-party certification of playground equipment and playground surfacing. IPEMA certification assures that a specific piece of equipment meets the safety requirements of ASTM Standard F 1487 and playground surfacing that meets requirements of ASTM Standards F 1292 and F 2075. In order to become certified, the equipment is tested by an independent laboratory for compliance to the ASTM's standards. IPEMA then issues a certificate of compliance which can be downloaded from its website at www.ipema.com.

National organizations concerned with playground safety include the National Program for Playground Safety (NPPS) and the National Playground Safety Institute (NPSI) of the NRPA. The NPPS and the NPSI both provide professional certification programs for playground safety inspectors. NPPS also provides seminars and training on playground safety.

In addition, NPPS provides playground safety guidance through its S.A.F.E. Model. This model consists of four components—Supervision, Age-Appropriate Design, Fall Surfacing, and Equipment Maintenance. The S.A.F.E. Model also provides recreation and park personnel, school administrations, teachers, teachers' aides, and other playground supervisors, as well as parents, with the tools to create an effective playground risk management and safety program. Through the S.A.F.E. Model, the NPPS advocates the following:

- Properly and appropriately supervising children, especially young children, on playgrounds
- Designing and constructing playgrounds with age-appropriate equipment and areas
- Making certain that the surfacing under and around playgrounds meets industry standards and requirement
- Establishing and implementing an effective playground maintenance program

The Centers for Disease Control (CDC) has published playground injury statistics as well as important safety information on preventing fall injuries. The CDC reports that approximately 8,000 children sustain injuries from falls every day, including falls from playground equipment. This startling fact should alert all playground operators to the importance of playground safety and risk management (CDC, Falls Fact Sheet).

The U.S. PIRG, a federation of state Public Interest Research Groups (PIRGs), along with the Consumer Federation of America, has conducted several surveys of public playgrounds throughout the United States, with particular attention to those areas of the playground where injuries occur most often. These surveys indicate that there is much work to be done to improve the risk management and safety of all public playgrounds, including making certain that the playground surface meets industry standards and that the equipment complies with industry standards as well as addressing entrapment, protrusion, and tripping hazards on the playground.

Another standard for playground safety has been promulgated under the Americans With Disabilities Act (ADA), which was passed into law in 1990. In 2000, the Architectural and Transportation Barriers Compliance Board (Access Board) issued accessibility guidelines to serve as the basis for standards to be adopted by the Department of Justice for new construction and alterations of play areas. In 2010 the final ADA Accessibility Guidelines were signed into law. The guidelines provide scoping requirements for play areas in Section 240 and technical requirements in Section 1008. These guidelines will apply to the construction of all new playgrounds as well as renovation of existing playgrounds.

Playground Injury Statistics

The importance of providing a safe playground environment is highlighted by the fact that the CPSC has reported that from 2006–2008, an average of 218,851 children received emergency room care for injuries related to playground equipment and areas. Of these injuries, 57 percent occurred on public playground equipment. Falls to the surface and equipment failure resulted in 67 percent of these injuries. In addition, the CPSC has also investigated and reported 40 deaths attributed to injuries sustained on playgrounds between 2001 and 2008. This data clearly shows that playground injuries are readily foreseeable and that owners and operators need to take proactive steps to provide children with a safe play experience (O'Brien 2009).

The importance of playground safety is also highlighted by the fact that there has been an explosive increase in the number of lawsuits filed related to injuries sustained on public playgrounds. Playground safety research shows that the most common allegation in these cases is the lack of proper surfacing, the lack of proper inspection and maintenance procedures and, most importantly, the lack of proper supervision of children using the equipment. Research also indicates that the majority of these injuries result from falls from playground equipment, leading to sprains, contusions, lacerations, fractures, and in some tragic cases, even death. The current litigation environment requires that owners and operators of public playground facilities implement policies and procedures to reduce the risk of injuries.

Data Collection

The National Electronic Surveillance System (NEISS) of the CPSC collects playground product-related data from a selected sample of more than 100 hospital emergency rooms located throughout the United States. Thus, only emergency room injuries are recorded and form the national statistics estimates. All statistics have been adjusted to reflect out-of-scope cases that were reported to NEISS. Using this information, analysts provide estimates on a yearly basis as to the number of injuries related to playground equipment, including swings, slides, monkey bars, and horizontal ladders. This information is published in the NEISS's Annual Product Summary Report in the "All Products" category.

Safety Committee

As part of a risk management program, every entity that provides playground equipment should form a safety committee to make sure that the playground is operating safely. These committees play an important function by raising safety awareness in the daily operation of the organization. They identify hazards and dangers that may be present on the playground and analyze various risks that will confront children. They also investigate incidents and accidents, and provide information for the development of policies to address problems for prevention of injuries. Safety committees also become a vehicle for parental, staff, and children's feedback and suggestions for improvement of safety on the playground. The safety committee becomes a team that can have a positive effect on the playground environment for prevention of injuries.

Supervision of the Playground Area

It is a common perception that playing on the playground is considered to be a common and very safe activity. Thus, owners and operators often do not see the need to provide a comprehensive training program for playground supervisors. However, as almost half of all playground injuries are due to lack of supervision and inappropriate behavior, owners and operators must clearly take steps to make certain an appropriate supervisory plan has been developed and implemented and that all supervisory staff are provided with appropriate in-service training regarding important risk management and safety concepts for playgrounds. The most important safety standard for the playground is the proper, appropriate, and adequate supervision of children using the equipment. This is reflected by the fact that 44 percent of all playground injuries are caused by the lack of proper supervision and inappropriate behavior on the part of the child—the most common complaint in litigated cases.

An important component of the playground risk management plan is the development of an appropriate supervisory plan and the establishment of pre-service and in-service training programs for the teachers, teachers' aides, and other staff members given the responsibility to supervise the playground area. An appropriate supervisory plan provides the framework for the proper location and positioning of the playground supervisors. Depending on the equipment located on the premises, it is important for supervisors to be positioned at the most dangerous areas of the playground. This includes, for example, positioning a supervisor at horizontal bars, overhead rings and other overhead equipment from which children may fall. A supervisor should also be actively aware of the swing area and the slides. Supervisors also should also be roaming around the playground, overseeing the activities and intervening when necessary to prevent injuries due to the potentially inappropriate behavior of a child. What should not take place on the playground is two or more supervisors standing together in one location and conversing. This is not the time or place to socialize with colleagues or friends.

To facilitate the successful implementation of the supervisory plan, the owner/operator of the playground must make certain that the supervisory staff is provided with adequate and appropriate pre-service and in-service training. The lack of appropriate training provided to those responsible for supervising the children during recess or play periods is often a contributing factor to the circumstances surrounding the injury. It is critical that playground operators design, develop, implement, enforce, and re-evaluate an appropriate in-service training program.

The CPSC's Handbook states the following, on pages 7–8, regarding the basic safety principles that supervisor should know and understand:

Supervisors should understand the basics of playground safety such as:

- Checking for broken equipment and making sure children do not play on it.
- Checking for and removing any unsafe alterations, especially ropes tied to equipment, before letting children play.
- Checking for properly maintained protective surfacing.
- Making sure children are wearing footwear.
- Watching and stopping dangerous horseplay, such as children throwing protective surfacing materials, jumping from heights, and attempting flips or other dangerous actions while on the equipment.
- Watching for and stopping children from wandering away from the appropriate play area.

The CPSC also provides the following in its Public Playground Safety Checklist, available on the CPSC website, to assist playground supervisors to properly discharge their responsibility for providing for the safety of children:

1. Make sure surfaces around playground equipment have at least 12 inches of wood chips, mulch, sand, or pea gravel, or that mats are made of safety-tested rubber or rubber-like materials.

2. Check that protective surfacing extends at least 6 feet in all directions from play equipment. For swings, be sure surfacing extends, in back and front, twice the height of the suspending bar.

3. Make sure play structures more than 30 inches high are spaced at least 9 feet apart.

4. Check for dangerous hardware, like open "S" hooks or protruding bolt ends.

5. Make sure spaces that could trap children, such as openings in guardrails or between ladder rungs, measure less than 3.5 inches or more than 9 inches.

6. Check for sharp points or edges in equipment.

7. Look out for tripping hazards, like exposed concrete footings, tree stumps, and rocks.

8. Make sure elevated surfaces, like platforms and ramps, have guardrails to prevent falls.

9. Check playgrounds regularly to see that equipment and surfacing are in good condition.

10. Carefully supervise children on playgrounds to make sure they're safe.

Supervisors should also be aware of the age-appropriateness of the equipment located on the playground and take affirmative steps to prevent situations such as preschool children using overhead equipment that is intended for school age children. Supervisors should be instructed on the recommended safety rules and requirements for each piece of equipment and then make certain that the children comply with the rules. This means being alert to behavior where children may be misusing equipment and placing themselves, and others, at risk for serious injury.

Supervisors need to understand and appreciate that children have a propensity to engage in sudden and inappropriate behaviors and thus supervisors need to be constantly attentive to the children's activities while they are playing on the playground. This means intervening and stopping hitting, pushing, shoving, and other inappropriate behaviors before they deteriorate into more serious situations that can lead to injuries. The importance of recognizing these dangerous situations and taking immediate action is compounded by the fact that young children are often unaware of the risk involved in the misuse of equipment and do not understand the danger they place themselves in by engaging in this behavior. Thus, it is important for the supervisor to be vigilant in making sure the children use the equipment in a safe and proper manner.

Selection and Installation of Protective Surfacing

Along with supervision, the installation of protective surfacing materials for playgrounds is critical for the safety of users. With this in mind, several types of protective surface materials may be used. Traditionally, within indoor environments, rubber tile surfacing and/or poured in place material is used. For example, this type of material is used at fast food restaurants and family activity centers. Generally, within outdoor domains and depending on the region of the country, the following types of materials are available to the public: shredded/recycled rubber, sand [various granular types, i.e., coarse v. fine], pea gravel, wood mulch, wood chips, rubber tiles and poured in place materials.

There are certain surfaces that are *NOT* acceptable and *NOT* recommended within the playground industry. These surfaces are grass, macadam (i.e., blacktop), concrete, and bare ground. All of these types of surfaces do not meet the playground industry's standard of care. The critical issue for surfacing is the ability for the substance to absorb shock upon a landing. The material must be able to disperse and attenuate the fall. Certainly, grass, blacktop (i.e., macadam), concrete, and bare ground would not be able to absorb shock from a fall and disperse it. Children can suffer debilitating injuries by falling onto surfaces that do not meet the playground industry's standard of care. It is recognized the human skull is the most vulnerable body part at risk during a fall. The playground industry standard is based upon the benchmark of 200 *gs* of force or less. When 200 *gs* are exceeded during a fall, a serious head injury may occur. Unfortunately, there are no benchmarks for long bone injuries within the playground industry. Therefore, one cannot predict if a long bone fracture will occur at an unknown amount of *gs* of force.

When designing and installing playgrounds, the CPSC recommendations regarding the depth of loose fill material should be reviewed and consulted. It is important to understand that the original loose fill material should be at an uncompressed depth of 12 inches. With constant use the loose fill surface will become packed down or compressed. According to the CPSC, loose fill material compresses up to 25 percent (Handbook, page 10). Thus, the CPSC, as well as the NPPS, recommend that 12 inches of loose fill material be initially installed to assure that the surfacing selected meets these requirements. As provided in the Minimum Compressed Loose-Fill Surfacing Depths Table of the 2010 CPSC Handbook, the minimum compressed depth of loose fill material is nine (9) inches.

As the table shows that the fall height will vary depending on the loose material used. At this time, shredded/recycled rubber at six (6) inches and wood chips at nine (9) inches will attenuate a fall up to ten (10) feet. This means that in all likelihood a serious, life-threatening injury to the head will not occur. Basically, sand, pea gravel, and wood mulch (non-CCA) at nine (9) inches will attenuate falls up to four (4), five (5), and seven (7) feet respectively.

Each type of surface has its advantages and disadvantages.

The composition of shredded/recycled rubber actually provides a great amount of attenuation (i.e., absorption) with only six (6) inches of depth. There are three main drawbacks with installing this type of product: it retains heat; it will not support wheelchair use; and it is easily vandalized.

The advantage of using sand is that it is readily available throughout the United States. However, one disadvantage is the fact that it will only attenuate to five (5) feet. Therefore, most swings, slides, and climbers should not be utilizing sand as their protective surfacing agent.

Pea gravel is a stone of approximately the size of a garden pea. This protective surfacing needs tilling to keep the material loose and retain its attenuation qualities. Bear in mind, any protective surfacing material is only as good as the air it traps between the individual particles.

Wood mulch does have a higher attenuation value for absorbing falls from heights, however its drawback is that it needs constant maintenance. If the wood mulch is not commercially prepared, the chances of large twigs, poison sumac, poison ivy, and thorny bushes being present could create a problem. In a risk management sense, one needs to carefully know the make-up of the wood mulch. As an aside, certain nut trees can also cause allergic reactions in some children.

Wood chips are uniform in size. This is a commercial product without the hazards of various large twigs, poison bushes, and types of nut trees being mixed into the fray. Engineered

Minimum Compressed Loose-Fill Surfacing Depths Table

Inches	of	(Loose-Fill Material)	Protects to	Fall Height (feet)
6*		Shredded/recycled rubber*		10
9		Sand		4
9		Pea Gravel		5
9		Wood mulch (non-) CCA		7
9		Wood chips		10

* Shredded/recycled rubber loose-fill surfacing does not compress in the same manner as other loose-fill materials. However, care should be taken to maintain a constant depth as displacement may still occur.

wood chips, if installed correctly, should have a stone drainage layer with a geotextile fabric (i.e., felt fabric) placed over this stone layer material. The loose-engineered wood mulch is then placed on top of this fabric to approximately twelve (12) inches in depth.

Commercial rubber tiles are another option for satisfying the protective surfacing issue. Thermal burns are quite real, since this product will become hot. Children should *not* take their shoes off to access the playground equipment. Warning signage should be placed at a prominent place on the playground to warn of such hazards.

Lastly, poured in place surfacing is very expensive, however it does not have the typical spaces that rubber tiles do. It also requires low maintenance. Therefore, from a risk management standpoint, it is a viable option. However, the cost may be too prohibitive for many agencies.

The Detroit Testing Laboratories, a third party endorser for IPEMA, has instrumentation to test surfacing. This is usually done via laboratory conditions with the proposed tested protective surfacing material contained in a wooden box. Instrumentation of a head form attached to a cable is dropped from various heights. (It should be noted that prior to sophisticated instrumentation, human cadavers were dropped to determine what consequences would occur. It goes without saying that the playground industry is much more sophisticated now.) Today's instrumentation will show the peak G-force which impacts the protective surfacing material at that height. Any G-force figure under 200 *gs* of force would imply a life-threatening serious head injury *would not* occur. The human benchmark within the playground industry is the "head" as the designated most vulnerable body part. Therefore, it is imperative that protective surfacing materials are within the range of 200 *gs* of force or less.

As shown in the table, loose filled materials should be kept at a minimum of nine (9) inches of compressed material. Some playground companies are placing a demarcation line on their vertical posts to show caregivers the appropriate maintenance depth. If your old vertical uprights are not marked, you can paint a dot or line on the post as to where the protective surfacing material should be for complying with the playground industry's standard of care. This can work against an agency within litigation, if the markings are clearly visible and an incident does occur which could implicate lack of protective surfacing maintenance.

Under the Accessibility Guidelines of the ADA, there must be an accessible route to the playground for children with disabilities. Once a child can access this route and get to the playground, it must be usable. There should be ground level components and elevated play components based on a formula. This will ensure a variety of components for the disabled (Accessibility Play Areas, 2007). Inside the playground area, the playground equipment should be compliant with the appropriate sections of ASTM F-1487, which pertains to play elements for the disabled. The impact attenuation material must comply with ASTM F 1951, which addresses accessibility for wheelchairs.

Selection and Installation of Equipment

The playground industry has become more refined with regard to the age-appropriateness of equipment. As noted earlier, the industry now recognizes that there are three age groups for children. The toddler category covers children from six (6) months through twenty-three (23) months of age. The preschool designation covers children from the age of two (2) through five (5) years of age. The elementary school category covers children from age five (5) through twelve (12) years of age. Within each distinct category, there are certain pieces that fit the child developmentally. For example, in the toddler category, the climbing apparatus should not be higher than thirty-two (32) inches. Spiral slides must be less than 360 degrees. Swings should have the wrap-around bucket type of seat. Within the preschool category, horizontal ladders must be equal or less than sixty (60) inches for ages four (4) and five (5). Swings can be of the belt variety or the full bucket variety for the two (2) through four (4) year olds. In the elementary category, track rides, swings of the belt type, rotating tire swings, and fulcrum seesaws are types of equipment that developmentally fit the elementary range.

It should be pointed out within each category that there are exceptions as to who can safely use the equipment. For example, within the preschool category, some five-year-olds may exhibit more of the motor characteristics of an elementary child. The converse can be true as well, (i.e., some five-year-olds may developmentally perform like a toddler who is three (3) years old). Supervision needs to come into play when steering children towards age-appropriate equipment. The playground equipment manufacturers and the playground industry must recognize the fact that chronological age is not always the best indicator of child development.

The layout of the playground is critical to the safety of children and supervision by adults. There should be distinct play areas for children for the preschool category versus youngsters within the elementary range. Sometimes landscaping barriers will assist in letting the public realize this distinction. Signage, as previously mentioned, will direct the caregiver by showing them the age distinction. One word of warning should be noted here. Children in the preschool category, as well as their parents, will sometimes play on the elementary-aged equipment for additional challenges. Parents will ignore the signage presented to them. Therefore, from a risk management point of view, the playground signs need to be visible and at the entrance to the playground. If there is more than one entrance, it is incumbent upon the agency to provide additional signs at various points of entry.

Clear sightlines of equipment and children are extremely important in supervision. Linear placement of playground equipment all in a row for several hundred feet will obscure the supervisor from seeing a child who will be hidden by intervening equipment. Solid tunnels, solid panels and enclosed tubular slides will limit the supervisor from having adequate vision at all times. From a risk management perspective, illicit drug activity and sexual activity in the evening hours by adolescents can take place within hidden modules located on playgrounds.

The risk manager needs to take precautionary steps to involve the local police in patrolling playgrounds at night, if this is a continual problem. In selection of playground equipment, the risk manager needs to discuss the selection of tunnels etc. with see-through panels to limit the agency's risk. In composite, or linked structures (commonly referred to as playscapes), when architects use wood throughout the design, this is especially troublesome. The solid-wood tunnels, houses, turrets, and crawl-through spaces present a supervision dilemma for the caregiver. From a risk management standpoint, the agency involved in a community-built project needs to discuss this issue with the playground architect.

Adequate use zones for equipment are crucial from a risk management standpoint. Many injuries on the playground occur due to faulty placement of equipment. The owner/operator needs to know the specifications for the various pieces of equipment. Basically, swings, rotating equipment, rocking equipment, slides and stationary equipment have distinct use zones. Swings take up the most space on a playground and should be positioned at the outskirts of the entire design. By placing the use zone at the appropriate distance, from a risk management point of view, the owner/operator will be lessening potential litigation against their agency.

Rotating equipment, such as merry-go-rounds, need at least six (6) feet of use zones for safety. Children will be running along the outside of the circumference, as well as dismounting. Therefore, plenty of space is desirable from a risk management point of view.

Stationary equipment requires six (6) feet on all sides of the equipment for safety. If a child falls, there should be no other pieces of equipment a child can fall upon. In composite structures, professional judgment comes into play when deciding if six (6) feet is absolutely necessary.

There are several pieces of equipment the owner/operator of a playground environment should be aware of from a risk management point of view. The following pieces should not be present on the playground: trampolines, swinging gates, giant strides, climbing ropes (not secured at both ends), heavy metal swings (animal figure swings), multiple occupancy swings, (basically addressing bench swings, etc., not multiple occupancy tire swings) rope swings, swinging dual rings, and trapeze bars. All of the above-mentioned items have the potential for serious injury and/or death. Because of the bulk of many of the above-mentioned items, the threat of injury is imminent.

Signage

Signage will assist the caregiver in directing them towards the most age appropriate design. Playgrounds should be "signed" for appropriate risk management. These signs should be very visible to the public entering into a playground. For example a sign indicating "This Playground Is Intended for Ages 2–5" will assist the caregiver in selecting an appropriate designed play area. It will also show the intent on the part of the owner/operator to limit the activity to a particular age group. Signage will not totally insulate the agency from getting sued, however, it will help by showing the agency's knowledge of the industry and their intent.

Steps to Solve Common Playground Hazards

The owner/operator responsible for playground safety within the community should act immediately to solve any playground hazard. The following items will show the owner/operator in charge of risk management some typical playground hazards which can lead to serious injury. Some of these items which can lead to potential injury and/or death are: protective surfacing material not being maintained, "S" hooks not crimped sufficiently, insufficient use zones, protrusions, entrapments, entanglements, and crush and shear points. The owner/operator will need to retrofit/eliminate playground equipment that is out of compliance with the CPSC Handbook and ASTM standards. Additionally, the owner/operator will need to focus on the accessibility with the Access Board for compliance with the ADA. With appropriate paper work, owner/operator should be able to document and remove logically equipment which is hazardous.

For most municipalities, it *will not* be feasible to tear out all equipment immediately. Therefore, a priority system is desirable from a risk management point of view. The equipment removal system based on a Priority 1–5 classification would be advantageous to any playground equipment manager. It is a simple way of removing the most dangerous equipment first and proceeding to the least dangerous. By phasing out certain pieces, all components do not have to be removed immediately. Priority 1 is based on the concept of removing any piece of equipment which would cause death or dismemberment. Certainly, the risk manager will want to eliminate any and all pieces that could cause a potential death or dismemberment. For example, some old free-standing slides still have spaces between 3.5 inches to 9.0 inches on their step ladders, which potentially could entrap a child's head and cause asphyxiation.

Priority 2 is based on any piece that could cause temporary disability. For example, a rung missing on a horizontal ladder may cause a child to lose his/her grip by over reaching for the next rung, and thus falling and fracturing an arm. Although not life threatening, the injured child will be in a cast for six (6) weeks.

Priority 3 may be a minor infraction of the playground standards. For example, a bolt may extend beyond the fastening nut more than two (2) threads under a slide bedway inaccessible to children. While a child may get scratched, if they reach under the bedway, the injury is minor in nature. While the standards will impose a two (2) thread limit protrusion, this is not just cause to eliminate this module immediately at the detriment to the children.

Priority 4 is a minor non-compliant issue, in which the chance for injury is very limited. For example, a slide exit may be one inch higher than is acceptable, however the chance for injury is very minor.

Priority 5 is a playground operating under the standard of care and no action is needed other than ongoing maintenance (Kutska, 2009).

Compliance with the ADA Accessibility Guidelines needs to be reviewed to ensure your playground fits the abilities of special needs youngsters. Is there an adequate approach and access to your playground? Are there ramps to ensure that children in wheelchairs have the ability to play with their peers? Are there adequate ground interactive modules, as well as above ground modules for the disabled? Are transfer stations located at convenient places to enable children to access the equipment from a wheelchair?

The owner/operator should make sure the groundcover complies with the CPSC Handbook and ASTM standards. When dealing with a vendor, documentation should be sought that will give you a paper trail, indicating their installed product meets the requirements of ASTM F 1292. A complaint in many lawsuits is the lack of appropriate protective surfacing. Therefore, the owner/operator should make certain to replenish loose filled material periodically throughout the year. Budgeting will need to be predicated on how much the playground is used. Heavy usage will require monitoring the protective surfacing closely to make certain the stress areas under slides, swings, and merry-go-rounds do not fall below safety levels. Maintenance personnel will need to be trained in knowing when to rake back loose fill material. They will also need to know when and how to order additional materials. The maintenance staff also should be trained from a risk management point of view. This training should be reviewed each year by a qualified person, who is well versed in the safety of the equipment and the protective surfacing.

When a playground is newly installed, it should have an audit performed by a Certified Playground Safety Inspector, who is credentialed by the NRPA or NPPS, to make sure it complies with the CPSC Handbook and ASTM standards. The written audit should be retained by the agency for any future questions that may come up regarding the playground's compliance within the field. However, if any of the standards change, it would be wise to perform another audit to see if use zones, distances on equipment, and signage need updating. Some equipment may have to be moved to conform with new existing standards. Some equipment may have to be cordoned off from children, if it is out of compliance. The risk manager should get involved in sealing off a non-compliant playground. Yellow caution tape is *NOT* acceptable for this purpose. The owner/operator should cordon off the area with fencing to ensure the area is inaccessible. No gate should be provided to the public. Signage on the chain link fencing should indicate the playground is closed. The sign may suggest an alternate playground site for the public within close proximity.

Some of the equipment may have to be relocated to comply with the CPSC Handbook or ASTM standards. For example, swings may not have the proper use zones, since they were installed many years ago. Most playground equipment is anchored in cement, which cures into concrete. To remove this equipment, it is imperative to dig around all footings and remove the concrete base at each vertical. Using heavy-duty machinery and pulling it out of the ground without taking off the concrete anchors will likely bend and destroy any galvanized pipes and prevent further salvage. By using a jackhammer device, the concrete can be removed and the pipes can be salvaged. Care must be taken in relocating playground equipment to make certain that connecting hardware has not been compromised. Any type of connecting elbows, chain, and fittings must be secured from the playground distributor or playground manufacturer. The local hardware store may use metals of different tensile strength, which will not meet the playground manufacturer's specifications.

Any noticeable rust on pipes, chain, connecting elbows, and connecting fittings should be analyzed for defects from a risk management perspective. At shoreline communities, near salt sea air, playground equipment made out of metal is particularly vulnerable to corrosion. The playground manager should be skeptical about relocating any and all playground equipment in these locales, if salt air presents an issue.

Summary

This chapter discussed the importance of developing, establishing, and implementing an appropriate risk management plan for public playgrounds. It is important for owners/operators to design a plan incorporating these risk management principles. By doing so, they will provide a safe playground environment for the children using the equipment. They will also be able to provide a strong defense in the event an injury does occur and a lawsuit is filed.

References

2010 ADA Standards for Accessible Design [2010] Department of Justice.

American Society for Testing & Materials International. [2007]. *Standard consumer safety performance specification for playground equipment for public use.* F 1487-07a. West Conshohocken, PA.: American Society for Testing & Materials International.

American Society for Testing & Materials International. [2009]. *Standard specification for determination of accessibility of surface systems under and around playground equipment.* F 1951-09b West Conshohocken, P.: American Society for Testing & Materials International.

American Society for Testing & Materials International. [2010]. *Standard specification for impact attenuation of surfacing materials within the use zone of playground equipment.* F 1292-09. West Conshohocken, PA: American Society for Testing & Materials International.

Centers for Disease Control. *Falls Fact Sheet.* Atlanta, GA: Centers for Disease Control.

Guidance on the 2010 ADA Standards for Accessible Design, [2010] Washington D.C.: Department of Justice.

Kutska, K. S. [2009]. *Playground Safety Is No Accident.* [4th ed.]. International Playground Safety Institute, LLC.

O'Brien, Craig W., [2009] *Injuries and Investigated Deaths Associated with Playground Equipment, 2001–2008,* Washington, D.C.: U.S. Consumer Product Safety Commission.

Playing It Safe: A Fifth Nationwide Safety Survey of Public Playgrounds [2000] U.S. Public Interest Research Group and the Consumer Federation of America.

Playing It Safe: The Sixth Nationwide Safety Survey Of Public Playgrounds [2002] U.S. Public Interest Research Group Education Fund and the Consumer Federation of America.

Public Playground Safety Checklist, Washington, DC: U.S. Consumer Product Safety Commission, CPSC Document. No. 327.

Ramsey, L. F. & Preston, J. D. [1990]. *Impact Attenuation Performance of Playground Surfacing Materials.* Washington, D.C.: U.S. Consumer Product Safety Commission, Mechanical Engineering Division, Directorate for Engineering Sciences.

Thompson, Donna, Susan D. Hudson, Heather M. Olsen, [2007] *S.A.F.E. Play Area,* Human Kinetics Publishers, Champaign, Ill.

Tinsworth, D. and McDonald, J. *Special Study: Injuries and Deaths Associated with Children's Playground Equipment.* [2001]Washington, D.C.: U.S. Consumer Product Safety Commission.

U.S. Consumer Product Safety Commission. [1997]. *Handbook for Public Playground Safety.*Washington, D.C.: Office of Information and Public Affairs.

U.S. Consumer Product Safety Commission. [2010]. *Public Playground Safety Handbook.* Bethesda, MD.: U.S. Consumer Product Safety Commission.

www.ipema.com.

www.cdc.gov/HomeandRecreationalSafety/Playground-Injuries.

Chapter 12

Risk Management in Motorsports

Managing the risks associated with motorsports is a very complex and layered topic.

Travis L. Teague

Introduction

Motorsports are about speed, and speed is inherently dangerous. Since the earliest days of motorsports, dangers have been a significant aspect of the competition and appeal of the sport. Managing the risks associated with motorsports is a very complex and layered topic. Unlike other forms of sport, motorsports involve, in most instances, several heavy machines travelling at very high rates of speed. Whether the venue is a NASCAR race drawing well over 100,000 spectators, or a weekly karting track with a handful of participants, the risks are very real, as is the potential for litigation and asset loss due to an incident occurring.

While motorsport management is a new field of study within academia, this chapter will attempt to identify some of the more common types of risk situations that exist in motorsports and the potential management strategies that may be utilized to reduce the risk(s) involved. Specifically, the chapter will focus on a brief history of four marker events associated with motorsport risk management; the categories of motorsport stakeholders; the categories of motorsport facilities; the types of hazards associated with the various facility categories and the consequences of injuries to the motorsport stakeholders; and finally a brief discussion about some of the advancements that have been implemented to reduce risks and subsequent injuries within the sport.

Historical Perspectives

When examining risk management history within motorsports, it becomes necessary to focus on several "marker events" that have led to significant changes in the policies and procedures governing the sport. Let's look at four such events, two of which occurred within the United States, and two of which took place in Europe. As is often the case with regard to safety changes within a sport, the changes are usually a result of an accident and catastrophic injury or injuries that result. Unfortunately, three of the four marker events we will examine involved the loss of life. The 1955 24 Hours of LeMans endurance race was a marker event of tragic proportions. Although statistics vary based on which account is reviewed, approximately 100 lives were lost during this race, the vast majority of those being spectators.

During the early stages of the race, as competitors were jockeying for position entering the pits, two of the cars collided, with one careening into an embankment. As the car hit the embankment, debris from the vehicle flew into the crowded grandstands with disastrous results. Within seconds, dozens were dead or dying in the grandstands, while the involved vehicle burst into flames, leaving the driver dead as well. From this tragedy, some countries banned racing outright, while others closely scrutinized the rules and procedures for races within their borders. The involved manufacturers also suffered great scrutiny and some even pulled out of racing altogether, in part because of the negative publicity associated with such catastrophic results. Just two years later, in the famous Mille Miglia road race event, another accident occurred where nine spectators, along with a driver and mechanic, were killed. This incident occurred as a race car crashed and veered off the road course, striking several spectators who were standing alongside the venue. The results of this accident marked the end of the event and further global scrutiny on the sport and its rules, especially those related to safety. The United States has seen its share of deadly events as well. Two marker events of note include an incident at Talladega Super Speedway involving popular driver Bobby Allison, and the other, the accident that claimed the life of American icon, Dale Earnhardt Sr., at Daytona International Speedway. Both of these incidents occurred within America's most popular form of racing, the National Association of Stock Car Auto Racing (NASCAR). The incident involving Bobby Allison occurred when a tire blew out and the car spun sideways. The spin and ensuing lift that was created on the car sent the car climbing like a wing on a plane at takeoff into the catch fence. The incident occurred when speeds on the track were reaching all-time highs, well over 200 miles per hour. Although the fence did its job and kept the vehicle from going into the spectator seating area, the height that the car obtained and the outright destruction of the car and catch fence lead to a monumental competition change within NASCAR's, at that time, Winston Cup Series racing. The change was technical in nature with regard to the rules of the sport. On the super speedways, which are Talladega and Daytona, the competitors were now required to use "restrictor plates" on their engines. The effect of these plates basically reduced the amount of horsepower the cars could generate, thereby reducing speeds. The likely hope was that the cars, at reduced speeds, would be less likely to become airborne, reducing the chance of one getting over the fence and into the grandstand seating. Through today, this has proven to be an effective strategy. However, it is important to note that several other safety strategies and innovations have been implemented that have also reduced the likelihood of this type of incident occurring. We will focus on some of these strategies later in the chapter.

In February of 2001, on the last lap of the Daytona 500, racing legend Dale Earnhardt Sr. was killed as his car struck the outside retaining wall in turn four of Daytona International Speedway. His death shocked not only the motorsport world, but the general public as well. In the aftermath of Earnhardt's death, a number of significant safety changes were initiated within motorsports; from personal protective equipment now required by the sanctioning bodies, to the race cars, to the tracks where they raced, many rules and safety modifications occurred. From the introduction of the "Car of Tomorrow" (COT) in NASCAR; to the requirement of the HANS device, which focuses on head restraint during an impact; to the wide implementation of the Steel and Foam Energy Reduction system or "SAFER" Barriers around the outside of the tracks, the focus on safety in NASCAR, and motorsports in general, was heightened after Earnhardt's death. Again, we will look at some of these changes in more detail later in the chapter.

Categories of Motorsport Stakeholders

At first glance, it may appear that the only danger in motorsports is related to those who are driving or piloting the competing vehicles. However, upon closer scrutiny, it becomes evident that there are many more individuals and non-human assets that are also exposed to risk. This includes members of the media, track workers, and officials, as well as the thousands of spectators that attend many national touring events on a weekly basis across the globe. As one might expect, the nature of the exposure to risk within motorsports is complex.

With regard to risk management, those involved within the motorsport industry can be sub-divided into two primary categories: Motorsport Participants and Motorsport Spectators. Let's begin with the latter, which is somewhat less complex. In most instances, spectators are defined as those being invited to attend a motorsport event and view the race from the grandstands, infield, or a hospitality suite. In the vast majority of instances, these persons would be considered invitees to the venue, with track operators owing them a standard of care to protect from unreasonable risk involved with the event. However, when discussing spectators, the gray area seems to be when the spectator is allowed to move from a more traditionally defined spectator seating, such as the grandstands, to an area primarily designed for competitors, such as pit road or the garage. This is not uncommon in most forms of motorsport for the "credentialed" spectator to gain access to one of these more dangerous competition areas. While the spectator is usually required to complete some type of release or waiver to enter these competition areas, the related risk is no doubt increased and must be closely scrutinized.

Participants within motorsport events are somewhat more complex to define. Obviously, the drivers or pilots of the vehicles are considered to be participants in the competition. They face the greatest risk from the dangers associated with crashes into other cars, the retaining walls/fences, and in some cases, fixed structures such as trees or rocks in rally car or off-road truck racing. After the driver, the next highest risk categories for participants are those individuals who are considered to be "over-the-wall" personnel. These are primarily the pit crew members who service the vehicles during pit stops, which many times take place during "green flag" scenarios where full speed competition is occurring on the track. Other personnel who are exposed to "green flag" situations on the track include the sanctioning body officials in most instances. Whether the officials are standing on pit road observing pit stops or serving as a flagman behind a wall somewhere on a road course, the risks they are exposed to in these situations should be examined and treated to some degree to reduce the exposure as much as possible.

Others in the participant category include safety workers for the track such as fire, medical, or safety crew personnel. These individuals normally enter the race environment during a "caution" period where the speeds on the track slow considerably, but the dangers present are still many and have proven to be fatal in multiple situations. Another group that is in the participant category is the various members of the media. At most races there is one form or another of media coverage; from a sports writer at a local paper to the dozens, if not hundreds, of media personnel that cover most national touring motorsport events. These media members include participation from print, radio, television, and other forms of electronic broadcast. Finally, it is also important to make sure that you have considered a final segment of the participation category called ancillary participants. This ancillary participant category includes vendors, such as those selling merchandise or food; security or ticket workers; and finally any volunteers that are being utilized to execute your event. In most instances these are groups that assist with parking and traffic control, ushering, selling souvenir merchandise, and food services. All of these participants are critical to having a successful event, and it is the duty of facility operators to protect them from the risks associated with the sport of motor racing.

Categories of Motorsport Facilities

Several different aspects of motorsport facilities have been identified for inclusion in discussions regarding risk management (Teague and Kiser, 2009). Similar to the stakeholder classifications from the previous section, race facilities were similarly sub-divided into two primary categories of Participant and Spectator Areas. Defining the spectator areas of a motorsport facility can be quite complex. It is necessary to look at all the areas of the facility where a spectator is expected or invited to visit during the course of an event. The category of motorsport spectator facilities can be sub-divided into two areas: at-track and ancillary areas. The at-track sub-category includes the traditional grandstand seating and luxury seating, such as suites and "club level" seating. Also included within the at-track sub-category for spectators are the competition areas where special credentialing/ticketing allows entry to the garage, pits, or some special pre-race activities, such as driver introductions. This type of access usually requires spectators to sign some form of release or waiver to gain entrance. Usually some age limitation excluding minors also exists for access to these areas. There are some forms of motorsport, such as NHRA drag racing, that allow all ticketed spectators in the "garage area." Regardless of the policies on access to these competition areas, it is critical that the facility operators consider the security risks, as well as the risks that may cause injury to the spectators allowed in these areas. Finally, another at-track area is the concourse where concessions and merchandise are sold, as well as where other facilities such as restrooms exist.

The ancillary sub-category of motorsport spectator facilities includes a variety of areas that are important for those responsible for risk management to examine. One of the most important traditions to thousands of motorsport fans is the opportunity to camp at the track or in close proximity on other, usually private, property. Campgrounds are areas that are unique to motorsports. Basically, all the services needed for a small city are required to safely operate the campgrounds at several national motorsport events. Therefore, if camping is a part of the revenue stream for the track, it is the track operator's responsibility to examine the facilities and related policies with regard to keeping spectators safe. Everything from well-placed signage regarding the dangers of high voltage power lines when setting up flagpoles and antennas from recreational vehicles, to the dangers of carbon monoxide poisoning from improperly ventilated heater,s are concerns for the track operator. Planning for access and egress for campers during inclement weather, providing sufficient numbers of security personnel to control intoxicated spectators and prevent asset loss via vandalism or theft, and managing the use of four-wheelers or other forms of personal transportation of campground guests are all front burner items for those responsible for managing campgrounds. Other ancillary areas for spectators are the numerous hospitality areas that are located on most speedway properties. Issues arising from foodborne illness, providing for appropriate security for guest check-in, as well as insuring that hospitality tents or other structures are constructed in such a manner as to withstand inclement weather, especially high winds, are all concerns related to risk management. Finally, security plans should be in place when bringing "personalities" into the hospitality areas, such as drivers, team owners, and various celebrities from other sports or forms of entertainment. A final ancillary motorsport spectator facility is known as the midway. This is usually the area where a wide variety of merchandise is sold from various vendors. In addition to the driver and team merchandise, a major aspect of the midway areas are the mega-activation displays that the numerous corporate sponsors of the sport utilize to market their companies. Some of the companies also utilize the midway to distribute product samples or give spectators the opportunity to try their products. This is especially true of companies promoting technology-related devices such as phones or computers, as well as various hand and power tool companies. Each of these merchandise and sponsor areas has their own unique risks. From the dangers of experimenting with a power drill, to having a policy for cleaning up a spilled beverage that creates a slip hazard at a sponsor display, the facility manager should know and treat the risks in the most prudent manner possible. While it is true that some of these risks, especially those associated with the midway area, may be transferred through the use of an independent contractor, it is still likely that the track operator will be named in any ensuing litigation resulting from a spectator injury. A wise and prudent operator will insure that appropriate language is within any independent contract to relieve the track of as much risk as possible.

The category of motorsport participant facilities also has several sub-categories that need to be examined with regard to real and perceived risks. It is important to again note that participants include several different professions in addition to the drivers. Media, emergency workers, security personnel, etc. must also be considered when examining the risks involved. The first sub-category is the competition area(s) associated with racing. There are three areas that facility operators must consider in this sub-category. They include the risks that occur on the actual race track itself. The other two areas are the pits, or pit road, and finally, the garage area where the cars are prepared throughout the weekend.

There are also several ancillary areas for participants. These areas may not exist at all tracks, but they certainly need to be considered if they are present. The ancillary sub-categories include areas in which the cars or external fuel tanks are filled and where hazardous wastes are disposed or recycled. In addition, there are specific areas where car inspections occur that should be examined with regard to risks to inspectors/officials inspecting the vehicles. Other ancillary areas where participant risks occur include timing and scoring areas, such as the flag stand, and areas where spotters (individuals who keep in radio contact with drivers to alert them of accidents or other situations on the track) are placed to view the race. From the flag stand, where the flagman controls on-track activity, to places around the racing circuit where individuals are stationed to monitor timing and scoring equipment, it is critical to insure that these ancillary areas have been studied to reduce undue risks associated with participants fulfilling their jobs.

Some additional ancillary areas where participants work at the race include the media center and medical centers/areas that are located at the facility, as well as numerous security posts that both uniformed and non-uniformed security personnel are responsible for controlling.

Types of Motorsport Risks and Related Injuries

The different types of risks within motorsports are as numerous as the types of racing that exist. When discussing risks in motorsports, it is important to look at the "who" piece of the equation. That is, who is facing the risks? Again, we will separate the types of risk based on the established categories of participants (see previous section for identification of different participant categories) and spectators.

Let's examine the spectator risks first. With regard to spectators, the risks that are involved are similar to most other sporting venues, with the primary issues such as spectator falls, medical emergencies, fan-to-fan violence, food illnesses, etc., all needing to be considered and addressed by the facility management. However, there are some critical differences between motorsports and other sporting venues with regard to spectator dangers. For example, as pointed out earlier in the chapter, the risks associated with debris from crashes, including entire vehicles, vehicle parts, or hazardous fluids, including flammable ones, escaping through or going over the safety catch fences are of the utmost concern. These dangers are ever-present and must be front-of-mind for track operators and those in management. It is important to consider the non-competition risks as well with regard to spectator safety. Several motorsport venues also involve spectator risks on-property from issues related to camping and tailgating. Dangers from carbon monoxide exposure when improper heaters or grills are used in tents or other enclosed areas, propane explosions from grills or other devices, and dangers from overhead power lines coming in contact with flag poles that fans display are all relevant risks that motorsport venue operators will face. Finally, with regard to spectators, some risks may be associated with simply being on the property. For example, many incidents have occurred from spectators being struck by golf carts that are quite common at many national touring race series events.

Participant risks obviously include the numerous ways in which the drivers could be injured during a crash on the track, but perhaps not so obvious is the potential harm that can occur as a result of close interaction with fans. For the fan, one of the major thrills of motorsports is to be able to get close to the action. Motorsport has long been known for providing opportunities for fans to have close interaction with the drivers, and in many instances, the vehicles. As the popularity of the sport of racing has grown, the opportunities for fans to have this close access has been greatly reduced, especially as drivers have more sponsor and media obligations they are being required to fulfill. With this dilemma in mind, some tracks have spent millions of dollars in an effort to enhance the spectator experience. Areas generally described as "Fan Zones" have begun to spring up, especially within the infield areas of some tracks. These fan-friendly areas enable fans to view the teams working on the cars, take pictures, and even get autographs from their favorite driver or crew chief, and all of this is being done in close proximity, such as through overhead walkways or through glass windows. The primary reason for these modifications has been to simply enhance the experience of the customer, i.e., the fan. However, with this increased accessibility also comes the additional risks associated with close interaction with the drivers, team members, vehicles, and other team equipment. The types of risks in these situations range from potential assault or injury of one of the participants, to the loss of physical assets in the form of theft or vandalism. It is important to note that the spectators in these fan-friendly areas are in addition to the hundreds of "V.I.P." fans who are credentialed to be in the garage or pit areas, especially prior to the race. Most of these V.I.P. fans are either participating on a garage tour via one of the corporate sponsors, are a friend or family member of one of the team members, or have received the credential via some other route, most likely through the sanctioning body or track. While it is true that this type of access pleases the fans and corporate sponsors in the sport, there should be specific plans and protocols set in effect to counter the risks that this type of interaction between fans and competitors may bring.

In addition to the risks associated with a crash, other risks that those in the participant category may be exposed to include pit or garage fires; an accident in the pits, such as a jack inadvertently dropping the car on a crew member; various eye injuries that may occur through working on the car; or even a burn or injury that could occur as a result of contact with a hazardous material leaking from the vehicle. While these types of dangerous scenarios and potential injuries may seem common for the driver or team member to encounter, the difficulties for the track operator are multiplied when you expose those other individuals in the participant category to such situations. For example, a crew member should have a fire retardant suit on while fueling the car, but the media person with a microphone standing three feet away may very well not have this same level of protection or professional training to react in the event of a pit fire. Therefore, it is critical for the track operator to plan appropriate risk reduction strategies with regard to issues like "who should have access to certain areas?" or "what level of training should our emergency response personnel be expected or required to obtain?"

With regard to others in the participant categories at the venue, it is also important that the track operator consider possible risk scenarios when planning traffic-related staffing for both vehicular and pedestrian traffic. For example, it is not uncommon for traffic jams to occur at motorsport venues. What strategies and training have been discussed and employed with regard to traffic access and egress? Have the volunteer or paid ticket gate workers been prepared to deal with the multiple tickets and credentials that will be used during the weekend? Do they have training in dealing with individuals who are frustrated because they are being told that the cooler they have can't be brought into the venue? Have all workers, specific to their responsibilities, been trained or prepared to some degree for the risks that they may encounter on race day? With all these questions and issues, some method of training, however developed and implemented, may very well improve the experience for the customer while at the same time reducing the likelihood of a situation escalating.

What measures have been taken to insure that the television crew members are appropriately tethered when recording footage high above the track? Have specific areas been discussed and communicated to the media with regard to where photographers or videographers may take footage during the event? These are a few of the questions that should be addressed in risk management planning meetings that could reduce the impact of an asset loss.

Finally, some forms of risk apply across both participant and spectator categories. These risks include those associated with severe weather-related emergencies such as tornados or thunderstorms. In addition, track operators must also be concerned with the risks associated with terrorist activity. This applies to all venues, but especially those that are televised or involve thousands of spectators.

Addressing the Risks

In recent years there have been several attempts by industry leaders to mitigate many of the risks that have been mentioned in this chapter. From a spectator standpoint, various policies have been put in place to screen fans when entering facilities. While these actions are predominately focused on major national touring motorsport events with large crowds, the concepts should be examined at the local and regional levels of the sport as well. Methods and policies to search backpacks, coolers, and other enclosures, and in some cases prohibiting these items, has become a standard procedure in several venues. Spectators have also benefited from improved and higher catch fences that surround the tracks, but again, these changes have been mostly reserved for those facilities with larger crowds and greater budget potential. The unknown in spectator protection with regard to catch fences in particular, seems to lie in the lack of recognized construction standards for tracks, especially those that don't have significant financial resources. While there are many reasons for the lack of standards, such as that different vehicles may race at different speeds dependent on the track, it seems that a greater examination of an industry-recognized standard is needed to insure spectator safety, especially at the hundreds of smaller tracks across the country where organizational budgets do not allow for the hiring of engineers to examine specific needs.

With regard to participants, especially drivers, many safety innovations have occurred in the last decade. As mentioned in the beginning of the chapter, the design and implementation of the Steel and Foam Energy Reduction (SAFER) Barrier has been highly lauded as reducing serious injuries and potential fatalities in the sport. The SAFER barrier basically serves as a means of spreading the energy of a crash over time. Before the installation of the barrier, a car would hit the retaining wall at the track, usually constructed of concrete, and there was no "give" from the wall; a lot of the energy from the sudden stop was then transferred into the driver, thereby greatly increasing the chance of serious injury. Now, with the barrier in place, with a combination of steel and foam, the wall does "give" upon impact. While it may not seem like much, the dissipation of the energy has proven to be lifesaving.

There have also been several modifications to the cars. NASCAR created what was termed a few years ago as the "Car of Tomorrow" or COT. The COT had several safety innovations, including moving the driver's seat more towards the center of the car, adding shock-absorbing foam in the door panels, and creating a safer fuel cell for the vehicles. It should be noted that other sanctioning bodies have also studied data from crashes to improve safety for their drivers.

It seems that other than the drivers, the best way to reduce accidents and resulting injuries in the participant categories is to develop, communicate, and enforce policies and procedures aimed at specific facility areas around the venue. For example, are there steps facility operators can borrow from other professional leagues with regard to protecting members of the media? Can greater scrutiny be given to how emergency medical or track service workers are trained to be safe while performing their duties? Again, these issues are especially applicable to those tracks without the resources perhaps available to larger venues.

Conclusion

With regard to motorsports management, safety is the primary concern. It is the responsibility of the motorsport manager to ensure that all facilities are safe, clean, and prepared for both spectators and participants. Since all forms of motorsports involve machinery going fast, the potential for injury is ever-present, both for participants and spectators. It is the job of the facility manager to make sure that all steps have been taken to provide the safest environment possible. The responsibilities involve everything from managing the parking lots and campgrounds associated with the event to the grandstand, concourse, garage, and pit areas. Successful operations within this realm depend on proper planning and pre-event preparation, as well as the organization of a qualified and trained staff of both paid and volunteer workers (Teague, 2008).

The manager must stay current on the latest safety advances for facilities such as catch fences around the track, while instituting and enforcing policies related to crowd management and spectator behavior before, during, and after the event. Failure to implement and enforce proper policies and procedures in any of these areas can result in litigation against the facility and/or organization.

It is impossible to predict all the incidents that could occur at race venues. However, it is possible to examine your facility, look at the risk-related incidents that have occurred in the past within motorsports, and then determine what the best risk management plan is for your particular track or venue. Finally, it is critical that the organization can document their efforts in identifying the potential risks at the venue and the steps taken to treat or reduce those potential risks. With prudent examination of identified risks, adequate personnel training, and policy implementation, today's motorsport facility operator can provide the safest environment possible.

References

Teague, T. & Kiser, J. (November, 2009). *Facility-Related Motorsport Injuries.* North Carolina Alliance for Athletics, Health, Physical Education, Recreation, and Dance. Winston-Salem, NC.

Teague, T. (2008). *Motorsport Management.* Successful Sport Management (Book Chapter). G. Lewis & Appenzeller, H (Eds.), Charlottesville, VA: The Michie Company.

Chapter 13

Liability and Property Insurance for Sport Organizations

"Determine the different types of insurance policies that are required to prevent the potential causes of loss."

John M. Sadler

All Sport Organizations Must Carry Adequate Insurance

All sports organizations, from the single team to the national governing/sanctioning body, need to be covered and protected by a number of different liability and property insurance policies which comprise what is commonly known as a property & casualty insurance program. The need to protect the assets and the continued ability to operate and provide services goes to the core mission of all sports organizations whether private or public, amateur or professional.

And it's not just the sports organizations as legal entities that are at risk. It's of equal importance to protect the respective directors, officers, employees, and volunteers who operate these sports organizations as their personal assets are often "on the chopping block" during litigation. In order to continue to provide their talent and labor, these individuals must feel comfortable that they are personally protected from liability.

Even a single youth team has multiple and significant exposures to losses and the resulting need for different types of insurance policies. The different types of insurance policies needed usually increase with the number of participants and teams, the number of employees and volunteers, the assets accumulated, and the complexity of the operations.

In addition, statutory requirements may mandate the carrying of certain policies such as Auto Liability and Workers' Compensation. Furthermore, contractual agreements with lending institutions and third parties such as facility owners may require the carrying of other policies such as General Liability, Property, Equipment, and Auto Physical Damage.

Concerns of Management of Larger Sports Organizations

The directors and officers of sports organizations are entrusted with making important decisions about the selection of insurance brokers, insurance carriers, policies to be carried, the quality of coverages within each policy, and risk management services that are needed. In larger sports organizations such as associations and governing/sanctioning bodies, these decisions are not just made on behalf of the sports organization as an entity and its respective directors, officers, employees, and volunteers, but also on behalf of the members of the organization, whether they are individuals, teams, or clubs.

Most insurance decision makers of larger sports organizations have the following major concerns as regards their property & casualty insurance program:

1. **Managerial Negligence**—They don't want to be embarrassed if a large lawsuit or property loss is not covered by the insurance program due to their lack of due diligence. The resulting financial hardship or bankruptcy will result in finger pointing. Failure to carry adequate insurance can result in litigation against directors and officers for managerial negligence.

2. **Personal Liability**—They don't want to incur personal liability in the event of litigation. Whenever the sports organization as an entity is sued, directors and officers are often shot gunned into the lawsuit as individual defendants. Therefore, it's important that the various liability policies adequately cover the individual directors and officers.

3. **Membership Benefits**—They want to offer their members an excellent insurance program offering more competitive prices and broader coverages as compared to what the members could individually purchase. A strong member insurance program can aid in the recruitment and retention of members.

4. **Overpaying**—They want to make sure that they are not overpaying for their insurance policies and want to test the waters every several years by approaching different carriers just to be safe. Or, in the alternative, they want their current insurance carriers to reduce rates when warranted by overall industry pricing trends and loss experience.

5. **Offset Expenses of the Sports Organization**—Many larger sports organizations want to be reimbursed for their expenses in promoting the insurance program to their members. It is permissible in many states for a sports organization to receive a marketing fee or similar fee in exchange for the performance of non-insurance services. However, the sports organization must not cross the line and engage in services that require an insurance license such as approving applications or explaining coverages.

Important Steps in the Risk Management Decision Making Process

Many sports organizations and their insurance agents make the mistake of primarily concentrating on the insurance bidding process in an effort to find the least expensive insurance carriers. Unfortunately, this single-minded pursuit ignores the traditional risk management process (or it is only paid "lip service") and actually raises the cost of risk over the long term. Insurance agents and carriers are the primary providers of risk management services for sports organizations, as most can't afford a full time risk manager on their staff. The long term cost of risk (and insurance) can be reduced to the greatest extent only when qualified insurance agents implement the following risk management process:

1. **Exposure Identification** — Exposures to loss include losses to property, net income, liability, and personnel. They should be identified by the use and review of historical loss data of the sports organization, loss data of similar organizations, surveys/questionnaires, financial statements, inspections, interviews with management, and interviews with outside experts.

2. **Analyze Threat Levels** — Once identified, the sports organization's exposures to loss should be analyzed in terms of frequency of loss and severity of loss. The threat level should be measured by those that interfere most directly with the sports organization in terms of income, growth, continuity of services or operations, and humanitarian goals.

3. **Priority of Treatment** — Those losses that pose the highest threats should receive priority of treatment. Sports organizations should spend the most time and money addressing the potential causes of loss that could have the biggest negative impact.

4. **Apply Risk Control Techniques** — Risk control techniques key in on preventing or reducing actual losses. Examples include avoidance (ex: 15 passenger vans, overnight sleepovers), loss prevention (ex: criminal background checks), loss reduction (ex: mandate safety equipment), segregation of loss exposures (ex: set up separate entity to hold scholarship funds), and contractual transfer for loss control (ex: subcontract out risky activities such as transportation of participants, serving of liquor, or fireworks).

5. **Apply Risk Financing Techniques** — Risk financing techniques key in on figuring out the best and least expensive way to pay for losses that can't be controlled. Examples include retention of losses (ex: paying smaller and/or predictable losses out of funded reserves or under insurance deductibles) and transfer through the purchase of insurance or the use of contractual transfer for risk financing (ex: waiver/release, hold harmless/indemnification provisions).

6. **Emerging Risks** — Study and prepare for emerging risk issues such as advanced concussion diagnosis and treatment, updated CPR techniques, and AED's.

7. **Monitor Results** — Set acceptable performance standards; compare actual results to standards; and correct substandard performance.

Important Steps in the Insurance Process

For those risks that are to be insured under the risk management decision-making process, the following considerations should be taken into account:

1. **Determine Types of Policies Needed** — Determine the different types of insurance policies that are required to address the potential causes of loss such as General Liability, Accident, Workers' Compensation, Business Auto, Directors & Officers Liability, Cyber Liability, Property, Crime, etc.

2. **Customize Coverages and Avoid Unacceptable Exclusions** — Checklists should be used to carefully analyze each policy with an eye towards eliminating unacceptable policy exclusions and negotiating special coverage enhancements. General property & casualty checklists from reputable industry sources should be combined with customized checklists that are specific to the sports industry.

3. **Carry Adequate Policy Limits** — Carry policy limits that are high enough to cover a worst-case scenario. The decision over how high a General Liability, Business Auto Liability, or Umbrella/Excess Liability limit to carry is as much art as science. Factors to be considered include value of assets at risk, exposure units creating the risk (ex: the greater the number of participants, the greater the chance of a catastrophic injury and resulting claim), recent court cases, limits carried by peer organizations of similar size, affordability, and the particular severity risks that are faced by a sports organization (ex: transportation of participants, sex abuse/molestation).

4. **Choose Carriers with Adequate Financial Strength** — Only do business with insurance carriers that have at least an A-rating by A.M. Best Company for financial strength. However, keep in mind that an A-rating is by no means a guarantee of long-term financial strength as carrier financials can deteriorate rapidly. It's important to pay attention to any adverse media reports about your carrier and to consult other financial rating organizations such as Standard & Poor's and Moody's when in doubt.

5. **Loss Analysis and Rate Justification** — Perform quarterly, semi annual, or annual audits of property & casualty insurance loss data to assess the effectiveness of the risk control and risk financing program. The audit should include a review of carrier generated loss runs paying special attention to frequency problems and individual large losses with open reserves. Problem claims should be analyzed with an eye towards the implementation of risk control techniques for prevention and reduction.

On an annual basis, carrier premium and loss runs should be summarized in a chart to show premiums, incurred losses (includes paid losses, reserves set in anticipation of future payments, and claim expenses) and loss ratios for the current year and four prior policy years. Loss ratios are computed by dividing incurred losses by premiums. As a general rule, a loss ratio of around 60% is considered to be the break-even point for most policy types. In other words, insurance carriers lose money when loss ratios exceed the break-even point. As a rule of thumb, loss ratios in excess of 60% may indicate the need for a rate increase or non-renewal and loss ratios that are well under 60% may indicate that the sports organization deserves a rate reduction. By the use of simple algebra, a rate change factor can be computed that would allow for a target loss ratio (ex: 60%) to be achieved.

However, these rate justification rules of thumb are over simplistic for at least two reasons. One reason is because most individual sports organizations are not statistically large enough to be rated on their own premium and loss experience. As a result, most are class rated based on the aggregate results of similar sports organizations. When class rating is used, the rates tend to stay within a range with small deviations (debits or credits) being allowed for above average or below average loss experience. Another reason is because losses that are shown on carrier loss runs tend to be immature and understated since they have not been adjusted for medical inflation trending or loss development. Rate justification analysis requires more accurate loss information than what is shown on carrier loss runs.

Additional trending and loss development analysis to determine an ultimate loss ratio for each policy type is required to show how the insurance carrier underwriters view the real profitability of the policy. The ultimate loss ratios will have a bearing on the carrier's decision to non-renew a policy or to apply rate changes. The first adjustment is to convert past loss amounts into current dollars. Appropriate trending factors should be applied to losses from past years to account for price inflation for medical care and other claim expenses. As a rule of thumb, an annual medical inflation trending factor of 5% is commonly used. The second adjustment is to predict how loss amounts will mature over time. Appropriate loss development factors should be applied to losses from past years to account for unknown and unreported claims that may be reported in the future and for the likely under reserving of known claims. The application of loss trending and development factors often have the impact of greatly increasing the loss dollars over and above those that appear on the carrier loss runs. Therefore, an account that appears to have an acceptable loss ratio may in fact be a money loser for the insurance carrier after the losses have been adjusted. While the application of loss trending and loss development factors for rate justification are often accurate on a macro basis for an insurance carrier's entire book of business, they are often not accurate for an individual account.

Insurance carrier underwriters often make self-serving assumptions when applying trending and loss development factors and when analyzing claims with open reserves. These assumptions can result in requests for unwarranted rate increases. Savvy insurance agents must understand rate justification analysis techniques and their strengths and weaknesses in order to negotiate with underwriters. Armed with this knowledge, insurance agents can effectively argue against rate increases or for rate decreases where warranted. Unfortunately, most insurance agents don't have an understanding of these techniques and are at the mercy of the carrier underwriters when representing their clients.

Choosing the Most Qualified Insurance Agent and Carriers/MGA's*

The Problem with the Traditional Bidding Process

Many sports administrators make the common mistake of allowing multiple insurance agents to bid on their sports insurance program. After all, the more opinions and quotes, the better, right? Also, doesn't the introduction of competition between insurance agents create the best result in terms of the lowest price? In my opinion, these commonly held beliefs could be counterproductive in the sports insurance marketplace.

The sports insurance marketplace has a limited number of insurance carriers that are capable of providing quality General Liability coverage. As a result, it does not make sense to cut loose multiple insurance agents who are in mad rush to be the first agent to approach the same handful of carriers. The insurance agents will bombard each underwriter with multiple applications that may contain contradictory information that will raise red flags

---

* MGA is an abbreviation for Managing General Agency. An MGA is an insurance organization that provides some of the services that are normally provided by insurance carriers in exchange for a fee. Examples of common MGA services include underwriting, policy issuance, loss control, claims administration, and marketing. The MGA as a middleman does not increase the cost of doing business since they provide services that the insurance carrier would be required to otherwise provide. Therefore, the existence of MGA's reduces the expenses of the insurance carriers.

about the truthfulness of any single application. In addition, the insurance carrier underwriters may believe that too many insurance agents chasing an account is an indication that the account is a "price shopper" and is not interested in a long-term relationship. The likely result is that the application will be moved to the bottom of the stack and will not receive priority treatment by the underwriters.

Furthermore, the various insurance agents who are quoting may become frustrated when they find that other agents have "blocked" their markets with prior application submissions and they will request "broker of record" letters to alter this outcome. Typically, an insurance carrier will only work with the agent who was the first to submit an application. However, if a subsequent agent can convince the sports organization to sign a "broker of record letter," such agent will take over the rights to represent the insurance carrier. The insurance carrier that receives a "broker of record letter" must inform the first submitting agent and give such agent a certain period of time, such as five days, to receive a countermanding "broker of record letter" to offset the effect of the first "broker of record letter." The end result is that many stressful and time consuming communications will go back and forth between both insurance agents and the sports organization administrator who is overseeing the bid process.

In my opinion, the better way to handle the process is to choose the most qualified insurance agent based on a predetermined set of criteria and then to allow that agent to approach the limited marketplace to obtain proposals from various insurance carriers. Such a process will result in the best of both worlds as the sports organization will benefit from working with the most qualified insurance agent and will still gain access to all the insurance carriers and will do so in a setting that is less likely to cause underwriter mistrust. This process should produce the best combination of insurance and risk management advice and service for the lowest possible cost.

The sports risk creates some unique exposures to loss that must be anticipated and then addressed with the negotiation of specialized coverage modifications. It takes many years of experience in the sports niche for any insurance agent to become familiar with the unique exposures to loss and the special coverage modifications that are required to address these exposures. This experience is acquired after reviewing dozens of actual claims and lawsuits in specific areas and noting the insurance carrier responses to these claims under a number of different coverage forms. A sports organization definitely does not want to hire an insurance agent without this specialized experience.

Selection Criteria

Insurance Agency Qualifications

- Special department dedicated to sport insurance risks
- Number and names of similar sports organizations insured
- Premium volume of similar sports organizations insured
- Carriers or MGA's represented for each policy type
- Premium volume and special relationships with each carrier/MGA to be approached
- Resumes of key servicing staff including experience in sports insurance niche
- Specific staff that will be assigned to service account
- Claims management services

- Loss analysis, forecasting, and rate justification services
- In house authority to issue certificates of insurance
- Injury tracking services and automation
- Training on employee injury reduction, premises safety, auto safety, special events safety, etc.
- Special risk management services for sports organizations
- Agency license for both Property & Casualty and Life, Accident, & Health for all states of sports organization's operations
- Website services including online enrollment; self-issuance of certificates of insurance; educational blogs; risk management reports, forms, articles, programs, etc.

Insurance Agent Qualifications

- Resume of insurance agent
- Number of years of experience in insurance industry
- Number of years dealing with sports accounts
- Title or position within insurance agency
- Ownership in insurance agency
- Special training and designations such as CPCU, CIC, etc.
- Producer license for both Property & Casualty and Life, Accident, & Health for all states of sports organization's operations
- Carriers/MGA's to be approached for each policy type
- Names and contact information of similar sports organization clients for reference check
- Membership in professional trade organizations in insurance industry
- Board of director positions or committee assignments on behalf of sports organizations
- Publications on insurance and risk management on behalf of sports organizations
- Number of proposed client meetings throughout year to review insurance and risk management programs
- Renewal strategy philosophy
- Disclosure of commissions and fees earned
- Meetings/trade shows/speaking engagements on behalf of sports organization

Carrier/MGA Qualifications

- AM Best rating for financial strength
- Number of years in sports insurance niche
- Number of similar sports insurance clients
- Premium volume of similar sports insurance clients
- Names of similar sports insurance clients

- Philosophy on acceptable loss ratios
- Claims services offered
- Risk management services offered
- Licensed in all states where sports organization operates
- Other services provided

Types of Policies Needed

To follow is a listing and general explanation of the various types of insurance policies that should be considered by sports organizations. Of course, smaller sports organizations with more limited operations will not need all of these types of insurance policies. Special attention is given to common policy exclusions and coverage enhancements that can have the biggest impact (negative or positive) on sports organizations due to their unique operations.

General Liability

General Liability is perhaps the most important insurance policy for sports organizations due to the prevalence of spectator injury and participant injury claims. Likewise, it is the most difficult policy to place due to the limited number of insurance carriers in the marketplace that offer quality coverage forms. There is a perception in the insurance industry that sports organizations generate a higher than normal risk of severity claims and are difficult to underwrite. However, in recent years, several new carriers have entered the marketplace, resulting in more options than in past years.

General Liability policies cover certain lawsuits alleging "bodily injury" (ex: spectator injury or participant injury) or "property damage" caused by an "occurrence" which are not subject to the standard policy exclusions or non-standard exclusions that may be added by policy endorsements. In addition, the policy responds to certain lawsuits alleging "personal injury" (ex: slander, libel, invasion of privacy, false imprisonment, etc.) and "advertising injury" (ex: disparagement of a third party in advertising material). The policy provides an attorney for legal defense and will pay up to the policy limits in the event of settlement or adverse jury verdict.

Occurrence vs. Claims Made

A sports organization should always purchase an "occurrence" policy form instead of a "claims made" policy form whenever possible. The superior "occurrence" policy form pays covered claims as long as the policy is in force when the injury occurs. It does not matter if the policy is subsequently cancelled and if a claim is later filed after the policy expiration date. On the other hand, the inferior "claim made" policy form pays covered claims only if 1) the policy is in force when the injury occurs and 2) the same policy, a renewal policy with a properly set "retroactive date," or an expired policy with an "extended reporting period" is in effect when the claim is filed. A "claims made" policy is risky for a sports organization because a sports participant who is a minor can wait until the age of majority (usually 18 in most states) plus an additional two years for the statute of limitations to run before filing a lawsuit. In some cases, this could be a period of 15 years.

"Claims made" policy forms provide too many opportunities for problems to arise if a new carrier is selected upon renewal (and if the insurance agent does not know how to coordinate the "retroactive date") or if the policy is non renewed or cancelled due to non payment of premium.

Definition of Bodily Injury

The standard ISO definition of "bodily injury" is "… bodily injury, sickness or disease sustained by a person, including death resulting from any of these at any time."

Some carriers offer an important General Liability endorsement to broaden the definition of "bodily injury" to include mental anguish, mental injury, shock, fright, humiliation, or emotional distress or death resulting from bodily injury, sickness, or disease.

Common Policy Limits

A General Liability policy should include the following basic limits of coverage at a minimum:

Each Occurrence: $1,000,000

General Aggregate: $2,000,000

Products/Completed Operations Aggregate: $1,000,000

Personal/Advertising Injury: $1,000,000

Damage To Premises Rented To You: $300,000 (also known as Fire Damage Legal Liability on older policy forms)

Premises Medical Expense Payments: $5,000 (does not apply to injury to athletic participants)

The following additional limits may appear on some policies:

Participants Legal Liability: $1,000,000

Sex Abuse/Molestation Each Claim: $1,000,000

Sex Abuse/Molestation Aggregate: $1,000,000

Non-Owned And Hired Auto Liability: $1,000,000

Employee Benefits Liability: $1,000,000

Each Occurrence and General Aggregate Limit

The Each Occurrence limit caps the payout of losses arising from any one occurrence or accident. A single occurrence could involve injuries to a single claimant or to multiple claimants (ex: lightning strike, bleacher collapse). The General Aggregate limit caps the payout of losses that arise throughout the policy year from multiple occurrences. It is the insurance industry standard that the General Aggregate limit should be twice the Each Occurrence limit.

To follow is an example to illustrate how these limits work:

Assume that the Each Occurrence limit is $1,000,000, the General Aggregate limit is $2,000,000, and three claims occur sequentially in the policy year with total liabilities owed of $1,200,000, $600,000, and $800,000 respectively. As regards the $1,200,000 claim, the carrier would only pay $1,000,000 of this claim due to the $1,000,000 Each Occurrence limit and the sports organization (and possibly its administrators and staff) would be "out of pocket" for the balance of $200,000. As regards the $600,000 claim, it would be paid in full as it is under the Each Occurrence limit and has not tripped the General Aggregate limit. As regards the $800,000 claim, the carrier would only be responsible for paying $400,000 of this claim since any amounts in excess of $400,000 would trip the General Aggregate limit of $2,000,000 for all claims during the policy period.

Sports organizations with large number of participants or teams would be better served by not having a General Aggregate on their policy (designated by a showing of "NONE" on the policy) or by having a special endorsement that reinstates the General Aggregate per team, league, or event.

It is also common to see a single master General Liability policy covering an entire sports association or sanctioning body and its member teams/leagues under a single General Aggregate limit. This is dangerous since those filing claims later in the policy year may find that they have no General Aggregate limits left to pay their claims.

Products/Completed Operations Limit

The General Aggregate limit applies to covered "bodily injury" or "property damage" losses that occur on owned or rented premises. On the other hand, the Products/Completed Operations limit applies to covered "bodily injury" and "property damage" losses that occur away from premises owned or rented and that arise out of "your product" or "your work."

Products that are typically sold by sports organizations include concession foods/drinks, t-shirts, equipment, and fundraising products. On occasion, such products are defective and result in injuries to purchasers and other members of the public. Examples include food poisoning (off premises) and injuries from the sale of sports equipment such as helmets, kayaks, etc.

Work (ex: construction operations) performed by staff or by hired contractors may include the building of sheds, bleachers, fences, and other structures. Such work may initially be on premises owned or rented by the sports organization but the sports organization may later sell the premises or discontinue the lease. Completed construction operations may later result in injuries such as from bleacher collapse, electrocution from faulty wiring, and fire from faulty wiring.

In the sports context, since the majority of claims arise from spectator or participant injury on owned or rented premises, the General Aggregate usually plays a larger role than the Products/Completed Operations Aggregate.

Personal/Advertising Injury Limit

The Personal/Advertising Injury limit applies to certain lawsuits alleging slander, libel, or disparagement of a person's or organization's goods, products, or services; invasion of privacy; false arrest or imprisonment; malicious prosecution; wrongful eviction; the use of another's advertising idea in your advertisement, or infringing upon another's copyright, trade dress, or slogan in your advertisement.

The definition of "advertisement" is "a notice that is broadcast or published to the general public or specific market segments *about your goods, products, or services for the purpose of attracting customers or supporters.* For the purposes of this definition: a. notices that are published include material placed on the internet or similar means of electronic communication; and b. regarding web-sites, only that part of a website that is about your goods, products, or services for the purposes of attracting customers or supporters is considered an advertisement."

Notable *exclusions* include Personal/Advertising Injury arising out of knowing violation of rights of another; oral or written publishing of material with knowledge of its falsity; criminal acts; assumption of liability normally belonging to another under a contract (ex: indemnification/hold harmless); breach of contract; failure of goods or services to conform with statement of quality or performance in your "advertisement;" insureds in media and internet business (ex: advertising, broadcasting, publishing, telecasting, designing websites, internet search/content/service provider; however, the linking to others or advertising for yourself or others on the internet is not by itself considered to be in the business of advertising, broadcasting, publishing, or telecasting); electronic chat rooms or bulletin boards, unauthorized use of another's name or product (ex: email address, domain name, meta tag, or similar misleading tactics); and distribution of material in violation of statutes (ex: TCPA, CAN-SPAM, or similar).

To follow are common situations that arise in the sports context that may be covered by Personal/Advertising Injury (if not otherwise excluded):

- A slanderous statement is made about a coach, umpire, or parent arising out of the heat of competition.

- The results of a criminal background check are not kept confidential resulting in a claim for slander and invasion of privacy.

- Promotional materials for the sports organization, such as photos or videos, use the image of a member without such member's permission, resulting in a claim for invasion of privacy.

- Publication of normal member related newsletters, magazines, or website content results in a claim for libel or invasion of privacy.

- Publication of normal member related newsletters, magazines, or website content for the purpose of promoting member services (falls under definition of "advertisement") results in a claim for trademark or copyright infringement.

The following activities are not likely to be covered under Personal/Advertising Injury due to the above mentioned exclusions:

- Providing blogs, chat rooms, electronic bulletin boards, where users can post potentially libelous comments.

- Advertising, broadcasting, publishing, telecasting, and designing websites on behalf of others that goes beyond normal membership services.

- Entering into contracts with technology vendors for member services (ex: website templates, telecasting, video, private social media, etc.) where the sports organization assumes the liability of the vendor under an indemnification/hold harmless provision.

- Publishing material that is not part of the "advertisement" of the sports organization that infringes upon the copyright or trademark of others.

- Engaging in Search Engine Optimization (SEO) techniques based on the use of competitor names or similar names in meta tags or domain names.

Need for Cyber Liability and/or Media Liability Insurance

Due to the Personal/Advertising Injury exclusions listed above, sports organizations with operations that may fall under these excluded areas should seriously consider purchasing Cyber Liability and/or Media Liability insurance.

In addition, some of the broader Directors & Officers Liability policies may include coverage for "personal injury" and "publishers liability.'" One particular policy form offered by the Chubb Group Of Insurance Companies defines publisher liability as the infringement of copyright or trademark, unauthorized use of title, plagiarism or misappropriation of ideas. This is important protection because such Directors & Officers policies provide the coverage grant of "personal injury" and "publishers liability" without most of the exclusions that are found under the General Liability policy form. Of course, the addition of these enhancements under a Directors & Officers policy are not as broad as the coverages that can be obtained under a good Media Liability or Cyber Liability policy form.

Damage to Premises Rented to You Limit (Formerly Fire Damage Legal Liability)

The Damage To Premises Rented To You limit (usually $100,000 or $300,000 depending on the carrier) applies to situations where the sports organization rents or leases premises (buildings or other structures) from a landlord and where the negligence of the sports organization results in "property damage" to the rented premises. Such rentals could take the form of a long-term lease for the purposes of office space or storage, short-term rental of a motel room to conduct a seminar or meeting, short-term rental of a gym for practice, or short-term rental of an arena for an athletic competition.

Whether of not coverage applies for property damage liability to the rented premises depends on a number of factors including whether the loss is caused by fire (ex: electrical outlet overloaded by too many pieces of equipment plugged into daisy chain) or other than fire (ex: water damage from sprinkler discharge, skylight broken by batted baseball, floor scratched and marred), whether loss is to rented contents in addition to the building (ex: tables, chairs, audio-visual equipment), and whether the rental is for a period of seven or fewer consecutive days.

Rentals of Eight or More Consecutive Days:

- Limit applies only to property damage liability to the part of the premises that are rented
- Limit does not apply to property damage liability to contents that are rented along with the premises
- Limit only applies to property damage liability *caused by fire*
- Limit does not apply to property damage liability *caused by other than fire*. If coverage for this exposure is needed, there are two possible solutions: 1) add coverage under Commercial Property Policy with Legal Liability Coverage Form

Endorsement (CP 00 40 04 02) or 2) amend the lease so that tenant is not responsible for damage to premises

Rentals of Seven or Fewer Consecutive Days:

- Limit applies to property damage liability *caused by fire* to the part of the premises that are rented but not to contents that are rented
- Limit applies to property damage liability *caused by other than fire* for both part of the premises that are rented plus contents that are rented

In cases where the replacement cost value of the rented premises exceeds the limit of coverage, a higher limit should be requested from the carrier (may be difficult to negotiate and/or expensive). As an alternative, the lease should be amended with a joint waiver of subrogation provision so that both the landlord and tenant would release each other from liability for damage to the other's property and depend solely on their own Property insurance to cover any damage to their respective property.

It's important to note that the Damage To Premises Rented To You Limit and corresponding coverage only applies to that part of the premises that is the subject matter of the rental. It does not apply to other premises inside the same building that are not being rented or to neighboring buildings. Any damages to such other premises or contents due to the negligence of the tenant would be addressed under the Each Occurrence limit.

Premises Medical Expense Payments Limit

The Premises Medical Expense Payments limit applies to situations where a spectator or other third party is injured due to a "slip and fall" or similar premises related accident on premises owned by or rented to the sports organization or on other premises on which operations are being conducted. This coverage will pay ambulance, hospital, and doctor's bills on behalf of the injured party regardless of fault on the part of the sports organization in an attempt to appease the injured party to dissuade them from hiring an attorney. The limit of coverage is typically $5,000. If the medical bills exceed $5,000 and/or if a lawsuit is filed, the Each Occurrence limit would then be applicable.

It's important to note that Premises Medical Expense Payments coverage does not apply to injury to any sports participants since this coverage excludes injuries arising from athletic activities. Therefore, it only applies to injuries to spectators and other third parties who may be injured. Athletic participants such as players, coaches, managers, etc. must look towards a separate Accident insurance policy for similar coverage.

Some insurance carriers that specialize in the sports niche believe that liberal use of the Premises Medical Expense Payments limit allows them to get involved with small claims earlier in the process to prevent them from turning into larger claims due to attorney involvement. Other carriers have a different philosophy and prefer to take a hard line approach of denying any responsibility from the beginning. Such carriers exclude Premises Medical Expense Payments coverage from the policy.

Participants Legal Liability Limit

Due to the prevalence of the dangerous "Athletic Or Sports Participants Exclusion" (excludes lawsuits arising out of injuries to athletic participants) which can be hidden deep in the policy exclusions with no requirement to disclose on a certificate of insurance, some insurance carriers that specialize in insuring sports risks choose to distinguish themselves from the competition by adding an affirmative grant of coverage called "Participants Legal Liability" (covers lawsuits arising out of injuries to sports participants). Such grant of coverage allows the carrier to show the existence of such coverage on a certificate of insurance that provides evidence of the non-existence of the "Athletic Or Sports Participants Exclusion.'"

Participants are generally defined under a "Participants Legal Liability Endorsement" as those persons who are granted access to restricted areas of the sports facility that are generally "off limits" to the general public. Examples of such participants include athletes, coaches, managers, umpires, etc.

However, a General Liability policy that is silent on the issue automatically includes coverage for "Participants Legal Liability" even without affirmatively showing a limit as long as the policy does not include an "Athletic Or Sports Participants Exclusion." The endorsement that grants coverage for "Participants Legal Liability" may actually include some exclusions that restrict coverage (ex: Participant vs. Participant, Player vs. Player, Warranty Of Waiver/release) that may not be found on a policy without a separate endorsement for "Participants Legal Liability." Therefore, the existence of a "Participants Legal Liability" limit and corresponding endorsement may not necessarily be advantageous if these other exclusions are found within the endorsement.

An advantage to having a separate limit for "Participants Legal Liability" includes injury scenarios. such as lightning strikes, where multiple spectators and participants may be injured at the same time. Such situations are considered to be a single occurrence and as such the "Each Occurrence" limit may be exhausted. However, the existence of the "Participants Legal Liability" limit allows coverage for injury to participants to be segregated under a separate limit that frees up the "Each Occurrence" limit to be allocated to spectators.

Sex Abuse/Molestation Limit

When there is an incident of sex abuse/molestation within a sports organization, it's not just the alleged abuser who is likely to be sued. The entire board of directors and the officers are likely to be sued for failure to screen (applications, criminal background checks, etc.) and failure to implement a specific risk management program to protect the children against child predators.

A General Liability policy may cover allegations of sex abuse/molestation if it is silent on the issue as long as there is no specific Abuse/Molestation exclusion. Coverage under such situations is not guaranteed and will depend on state case law and the exact nature of the allegations. However, most carriers that insure sports organization are likely to insert an exclusion for Sex Abuse/Molestation.

Some carriers offer a buy-back with a specific limit for sex abuse/molestation via a special endorsement in order to clarify that coverage exists. Such an affirmative coverage grant removes all coverage doubts that may exist under the silent approach. When a specific limit is offered, it is usually in the form of a per claim limit and a separate aggregate limit.

Carriers that offer this coverage use specific language to place a cap on their overall exposure due to fears generated by some courts that have ruled that each abuse/molestation incident is a new occurrence and that successive policies can be stacked on top of each other to multiply the total aggregate limits available to pay a claim. In addition, it's common knowledge that abusers/molesters tend to have multiple victims. Furthermore, specific wording may be added to exclude coverage for the perpetrator himself or herself and for other directors or officers who remained silent and did not take action despite knowledge of an incident.

It is also common to see a single master General Liability policy with a Sex Abuse/Molestation limit covering an entire sports association or sanctioning body and its member teams/leagues under a single Sex Abuse/Molestation Aggregate limit. This is dangerous since those filing claims later in the policy year may find that they have no General Aggregate limits left to pay their claims. As a result, such sports organizations should attempt to negotiate reinstatement of the Sex Abuse/Molestation aggregate on a per league or per team basis.

Coverage for Sex Abuse/Molestation can be difficult to negotiate with the carriers unless the sports organization applying for coverage can prove that it has implemented certain loss controls such as mandatory criminal background checks on all adults with access to youth, mandatory staff and parent education, policies and procedures to make an incident less likely to occur (ex: prohibition of overnight sleepovers, buddy system where a single adult is never alone with a single child, etc.), and mandatory reporting of occurrences to board and police.

Non-Owned and Hired Auto Liability Limit

Non-Owned And Hired Auto Liability insurance can be written as either part of a Business Auto policy or as an endorsement to a General Liability policy. Typically, it is written as an endorsement to a General Liability policy only when the sports organization does not have any owned vehicles titled in its name.

See the section on Business Auto insurance for a detailed description of Non-Owned And Hired Auto Liability.

Problem General Liability Exclusions

All General Liability policies grant broad coverage for "bodily injury" and "property damage" caused by an "occurrence" under the insuring agreement that is found in the beginning of the policy. In addition, all General Liability policies use exclusions to remove coverage for certain situations that are deemed to not be insurable for various reasons (ex: too risky, moral hazard, against public policy) or that should be insured under a different type of policy (ex: Workers' Compensation, Auto, Property). The exclusions include both standard exclusions that are found in the exclusion section of the General Liability policy as well as exclusions that are found in endorsements (i.e. policy amendments) that are attached as pages near the end of the policy.

To follow is a list of some of the most common "problem" exclusions for sports organizations that are found on General Liability policies. Every attempt should be made to negotiate the removal or modification of these exclusions to a more acceptable version. If negotiation does not yield acceptable results, serious consideration should be given to finding a new insurance carrier. However, this list is not all-inclusive as there are a number of other "problem" exclusions that are found less frequently.

Athletic or Sports Participants Exclusion — This exclusion takes away coverage for bodily injury to any person while practicing for or participating in any sports or athletic contest or exhibition that is sponsored by the insured.

Insurance carriers that don't specialize in insuring sports organizations commonly use this exclusion to control what they perceive to be as an unacceptably high risk. Its existence often slips by insurance agents and risk managers who don't carefully review the policy form or who aren't aware that quality sports insurance coverages can be obtained through multiple sources.

The use of this exclusion for most sports organizations is totally unacceptable since athletic participant injuries and resulting lawsuits are a common occurrence. Furthermore, they represent a "severity risk" since damages from catastrophic sports injuries can be high. The existence of this exclusion reduces a sports organization's General Liability policy to what is commonly known as a "spectator liability policy."

Knowledgeable underwriters lower the risk of paying General Liability claims for athletic participant injury lawsuits by mandating the existence of Accident Insurance (amateur sports), Workers' Compensation Insurance (professional sports), and waiver/release forms. For more information on why waiver/release forms are "worth the paper they are written on," go to www.sadlersports.com/riskmanagement.

Participant vs. Participant Exclusion—This exclusion takes away coverage for instances where one participant sues another participant. Since participants are broadly defined (see definition above under Participants Legal Liability section), this could include situations such as player vs. player, coach vs. coach, or player vs. coach. It's important to note that most versions of this exclusion don't penalize other parties that could be dragged into the lawsuit such as the sport organization as an entity, directors, officers, or other staff members.

Not providing coverage for player vs. coach situations is a totally ridiculous result that must be avoided due to its common occurrence. One negotiation strategy is to narrow the context of the Participant vs. Participant exclusion by changing it to a Player vs Player (or Athlete vs. Athlete) exclusion.

Some argument can be made for the existence of a Player vs. Player Exclusion (or Athlete vs. Athlete Exclusion) to provide a disincentive in adult sports situations where one adult athlete recklessly endangers the safety of another adult athlete.

However, it is becoming increasingly common for carriers to remove the Player vs. Player exclusion in youth sports. On the other hand, it could be argued that the Player vs. Player exclusion is not a problem in youth sports since youth players aren't normally targets in lawsuits due to lack of assets to satisfy judgments.

Volunteer vs. Volunteer Exclusion

The 2001 and later editions of the standard Insurance Services Office (ISO) General Liability policy form added what is commonly referred to as the Volunteer vs. Volunteer exclusion (see policy section "Who Is An Insured") which can have a detrimental and unexpected impact in the sports context. Lawsuits that may fall under the scope of this exclusion include coach vs. coach, umpire vs. coach, manager vs. coach, etc. It's not uncommon for one coach to accidentally (but negligently) injure another coach during skills demonstrations or drills. For example, one of our youth baseball clients recently filed a claim for a lawsuit arising from batting practice where the head coach hit a ball that struck an assistant coach who was not paying attention. It's possible to negotiate the removal or modification of this exclusion with many carriers.

Assault & Battery Exclusion

The standard ISO General Liability policy form has an exclusion for "bodily injury" or "property damage" expected or intended from the standpoint of the insured. However, this exclusion does not apply to "bodily injury" resulting from the use of reasonable force to protect persons or property.

When the Assault & Battery Exclusion is added to the policy, the exception is removed for the use of reasonable force to protect persons or property. This can result in some unexpected denials of coverage in the sports context. For example, a coach or umpire could be denied coverage for engaging in self-defense against an aggressor who is injured and files a lawsuit. Also, lawsuits have been filed against coaches who accidentally injured a participant while trying to break up a fight.

In addition, most versions of the Assault & Battery Exclusion specify that coverage does not apply to the insured (sports organization) for incidents committed by its employees, volunteers, or any other person; for failure to suppress or prevent an incident; or for negligent hiring, supervision, or training.

It's common for the sports organization and its officers and board of directors to be named as defendants along with the staff member who allegedly committed the assault & battery. The most common theory of recovery is for negligent hiring when the accused staff member is found to have a criminal background that should have been an indication of a propensity for violence. This is another reason (other than the concern over sexual offender crimes) why staff members should be screened with background checks for suitability.

Warranty of Waiver/Release

Some General Liability policies may have a warranty provision that voids coverage in the event of a participant injury lawsuit if the sports organization can't produce a signed and dated waiver/release agreement on behalf of the injured participant filing the lawsuit. Waiver/release agreements are to be strongly encouraged; however, many sports organizations don't have strong administrative and record keeping procedures and it's possible for a single document to slip between the cracks despite the best intentions of the administrators.

A less severe version of this warranty provision requires the sports organization merely to have a procedure in place for the collection of signed and dated waiver/release agreements on behalf of all participants. Such wording may not result in coverage denial in the event that a single waiver/release can't be produced so long as there is evidence that a procedure was in place and there was a good faith attempt to administer such procedure. However, the wording of such warranty provisions must be carefully reviewed to gain a clear understanding of the requirements for coverage.

Punitive Damages Exclusion

Most summons & complaints (lawsuit papers) in the sports context for bodily injury incidents request punitive damages and refer to the lack of care by the negligent party as being grossly negligent, willful, wanton, and reckless. Proof of such extreme misconduct is necessary to support a claim for punitive damages. Punitive damages are damages over and above the regular compensatory damages such as medical expenses, lost income, pain and suffering, etc. Punitive damages are meant to punish and make an example of the grossly negligent party. Even though punitive damages are often difficult to prove, it does not makes sense for a General Liability policy to exclude punitive damages and subject the covered parties to needless worry.

Some states have case law or statutes that may not allow insurance carriers to insure punitive damages since it may be considered to be against public policy.

Sex Abuse/Molestation Exclusion

The Sex Abuse/Molestation Exclusion endorsement is commonly used by underwriters for youth sports risks due to the difficulty in implementing adequate loss controls, the severity risk, and the risk of multiple claimants and incidents. This endorsement is usually attached near the end of the policy.

Other forms of child abuse are often included within the scope of this exclusion including physical abuse and emotional abuse. These often take the form of excessive exercise as punishment and verbal insults.

Sports organizations should always attempt to negotiate a buyback of this coverage and should stand ready to adopt and implement required loss controls. For more information on the abuse/molestation risk including specific risk management programs and training videos, go to www.sadlersports.com/riskmanagement.

Contractual Liability Limitation

Sports organizations frequently enter into contracts that include indemnification and hold harmless provisions where they assume the tort liability that would ordinarily belong to the other party to the contract. Such assumption of contractual liability can be covered under General Liability policies (depending on the exact wording of the provisions). However, General Liability policies that include the Contractual Liability Limitation Endorsement can take away this needed protection.

An example of the application of this exclusion would occur when a sports organization sends a travel team to play in a tournament and as part of the registration process, the sports organization signs an agreement with the tournament host that includes an unfavorable hold harmless/indemnification provision in favor of the tournament host. Such a provision may require the sports organization to assume all liability for injury to its players, even if arising out of the sole negligence of the tournament host. In the event that a player drowns during a tournament host sponsored and supervised swimming party, the sports organization may be legally responsible due to the contractual assumption of such liability. In such a circumstance, the Contractual Liability Limitation Endorsement could result in a claim denial that could have a devastating impact on the sports organization and its administrators and staff.

Collapse of Temporary Structure

Some General Liability policies may have a Collapse Of Temporary Structure Exclusion that can have the impact of removing coverage in the event of certain bleacher collapses. Bleacher collapses often involve multiple claimants with serious injuries. Whether or not a particular bleacher is temporary or permanent can be subject to debate. The insurance carrier may argue that any bleacher that is not permanently anchored or affixed is temporary.

Ownership/Maintenance/Management of Athletic Fields or Facilities Exclusion

This exclusion is often used by insurance carriers to limit their responsibility to pay for claims that arise out of incidents that occur during sanctioned and supervised operations or activities such as practices, games, tournaments, banquets, meetings, field work days, etc.

Such an exclusion would preclude coverage that arises out of the mere ownership, maintenance, or management of the athletic field or facility. Many serious injuries occur on property at times other than during sanctioned and supervised events. Athletic fields, if not properly secured, often draw members of the public who may participate in pick up games or who may play on playground equipment such as swings and slides. Property owners, lessors, and managers are often found to be liable when a premises related condition is the cause of the injury.

Field/facility owners and lessors (that are responsible for what happens 24/7 under the provisions of a lease agreement) need to verify that their General Liability policy covers the 24/7 ownership or management risk exposure.

Note: The coverage form referenced is ISO CG 00 01 12 07

Accident

Accident insurance pays covered medical expenses on behalf of injured participants who are injured during covered activities. Coverage is normally designed to be "excess" or "secondary" so that it only pays after existing family health insurance has already responded to a claim. Excess Accident coverage is more affordable than Primary Accident coverage since it does not duplicate benefits.

First Line of Defense

There are two primary reasons for the use of Accident insurance in the sports context: 1) satisfies a moral obligation of the sports organization to make sure that injured participants get quality medical treatment and 2) is required by the General Liability carrier as a pre-condition for covering a participant injury lawsuit claim.

From the General Liability insurance carrier's point of view, the Accident policy is the first line of defense against lawsuits resulting from participant injury. If there is no Accident insurance in force and if there is a significant injury to an uninsured (no family health insurance) or inadequately insured (high deductible, coinsurance, or unfavorable exclusions under family health insurance) participant, such participant is likely to incur significant medical bills. After receiving dunning letters and phone calls from unpaid medical services providers, such participant (or parent) will likely visit an attorney who will recommend a negligence based lawsuit against the sports organization and its administrators and staff. On the other hand, If the Accident policy guarantees that the injured participant (or parent) will not incur significant out of pocket medical expenses, it takes away much of the incentive for them to file a lawsuit against the sports organization as a "deep pocket."

Some Recommended Minimum Coverage Standards

Medical Limit—The medical limit should be at least $25,000 per person per accident. A policy with a medical limit of $5,000 or $10,000 won't be enough to cover even a moderate injury. For example, ACL injuries, which are common in sports, can easily exceed $20,000 after surgery and rehabilitation. Furthermore, most General Liability carriers require an Accident policy with a medical limit of at least $25,000 as a pre-condition of covering a participant injury lawsuit claim. Higher limits such as $100,000 or $250,000 should be strongly considered due to the additional protection offered at rate that can be surprisingly affordable.

No Internal Payout Limitations — Many Accident policies have internal payout limitations, which are also known as sublimits or allocations. Examples include limits on certain categories of medical expenses such as surgeon's fees ($1100), daily hospital room and board ($100), doctor's visits ($20), physiotherapy ($10), etc. Some plans include so many internal payout limitations that it would be impossible for the policy to ever get close to paying even 50% of the overall medical limit. Such plan designs that result in significant unpaid medical bills increase the chances of litigation against the sports organization in an effort to find a "deep pocket." The better Accident plans don't have these internal payout limitations (with the common exception of dental benefits).

Excess vs. Primary — Excess Accident insurance requires other collectible insurance, such as family health insurance, to respond first. There are three scenarios that can arise with high quality Excess Accident coverage: 1) if the existing family health insurance pays 100% of the bills, the Excess Accident policy will not respond to the claim, 2) if the existing family health insurance only pays 80% of the bills (due to it's own deductible or coinsurance), the Excess Accident policy should pay the remaining 20% less any deductible, 3) if there is no existing insurance, the Excess Accident policy becomes primary and pays for 100% of the bills, less any deductible.

Primary Accident insurance can be purchased that will pay without regard to other collectible insurance. However, in order to make it affordable, most carriers will "water down" the benefits by inserting an oppressive schedule of internal payout limitations (see section above). If such internal payout limitations are present, they can result in extreme dissatisfaction if the payout does not come close to covering the medical bills.

Therefore, in most cases, high quality Excess Accident insurance is superior to Primary Accident insurance since high quality Excess Accident insurance will guarantee that the injured participant (or parent) does not incur significant out of pocket medical expenses. The fact that the payout is excess to any existing family health insurance does not diminish the important role that is played by Excess Accident insurance.

Mandatory vs. Optional Participation — Participation in an Accident plan should always be mandatory instead of optional. Mandatory plans require coverage for all participants and a premium to be paid on behalf of all participants by the sports organization. On the other hand, optional plans allow individual participants to choose whether or not they want to pay to be covered. Optional participation plans are unacceptable for two reasons: 1) not every participant who needs coverage will purchase it and as a result some will be uninsured, and 2) the General Liability policy will likely have a warranty provision that requires Accident insurance to be carried on an injured participant as a pre-condition of coverage for a resulting lawsuit.

Deductibles — Deductibles commonly range from $0 to $500. Deductibles can result in significant premium savings. For example, increasing a deductible from $0 to $100 may result in a premium savings of 20%. From the point of view of the injured participant (and parent), deductibles in excess of $500 may result in financial hardship. However, sports organizations that only carry Accident insurance to satisfy the requirements of the General Liability carrier (and don't perceive it as a member benefit) may want to investigate higher deductibles such as $1,000 or $2,500.

Payout Period—The payout period is the time period for which incurred medical bills will be paid from the date of the injury. The payout period should always be at least one year. However, in cases where the medical limit is $100,000 or more, the payout period should be extended to two or three years. The insurance carrier will require a small additional premium for this enhancement. Any injury that approaches $100,000 in medical bills will likely result in the performance of medical services after one year.

Covered Activities—The Accident policy should cover all sports organization approved and adult supervised activities including tryouts, practices, games, tournaments, non-sport outings, and travel to and from. In youth sports, many of the more serious claims arise from non-sport outings such as awards banquets, backyard cookouts, swimming parities, and celebration trips to restaurants, etc. As a result, coverage should extend to these activities unless they are not approved by the sports organization's policies and procedures. As concerns coverage for travel to and from, some Accident policies cover only supervised group travel to and from whereas others cover individual travel to and from that is provided by a licensed driver.

Covered Persons—All players and staff (paid and volunteer) should be covered. Staff normally includes but is not limited to coaches, assistant coaches, managers, umpires, referees, scorekeepers, concession workers, field maintenance workers, and administrators such as directors and officers. The definition of covered persons under the Accident policy should always be at least as broad as the General Liability carrier's requirement to cover certain persons under an Accident policy.

Business Auto

A Business Auto policy (i.e., Commercial Auto) should be written to cover all owned, non-owned, and hired autos of the sports organization. An owned auto is one that is titled in the name of the sports organization. A non-owned auto is one that is owned by an employee or staff member but is used to run errands or make trips on behalf of the sports organization. A hired auto is one that is rented from a car rental company or that is borrowed.

Owned Autos

The various state financial responsibility laws set minimum insurance requirements for owned vehicles. Most require the owner of the vehicle to provide proof of Auto Liability in an amount of $30,000 per person, $60,000 per accident, and $25,000 property damage. Some states require higher limits. In addition, many require Uninsured Motorists and Personal Injury Protection/Medical Payments (no fault) coverage. The minimum insurance limits set by state financial responsibility laws are too low to cover the damages resulting from an auto accident resulting in moderate to serious bodily injury or property damage. For this reason, it is strongly recommended that sport organizations carry limits that are significantly higher than the minimum state requirements.

To follow are the typical coverages and limits that should be carried on owned autos:

- **Auto Liability:** $1,000,000 Combined Single Limits—Auto Liability pays for bodily injury and property damage claims from injured third parties (ex: passengers in insured vehicle, passengers in other vehicles, pedestrians, and damage to other vehicles) resulting from the negligence of the owner/driver of the insured vehicle.

Since auto accidents tend to result in serious injuries to multiple passengers, it does not make sense to carry a limit lower than $1,000,000. If available, combined single limits are preferred to split limits since combined single limits offers more flexibility in the allocation of available limits between bodily injury and property damage and multiple injured persons.

- **Uninsured Motorists:** $1,000,000 — Uninsured Motorists reimburses the insured in the event the insured incurs bodily injury and/or property damage due to the fault of an uninsured motorist. The Uninsured Motorist limit will reimburse the insured for the amount that the insured is legally entitled to recover had the negligent party carried insurance. It is recommended that the Uninsured Motorist limit should match the Auto Liability limit.

- **Underinsured Motorists:** $1,000,000 — Underinsured Motorists reimburses the insured in the event that the insured incurs bodily injury and/or property damage due to the fault of an underinsured motorist. The Underinsured Motorist limit will reimburse the insured for the amount that the insured is legally entitled to recover had the negligent party carried insurance. It is recommended that the Underinsured Motorist limit should match the Auto Liability limit.

- **Personal Injury Protection/Medical Payments (no fault):** $2,500 — Personal Injury Protection or Medical Payments is a type of no fault coverage to compensate injured insureds for medical expenses, lost wages, etc. without regard to fault. Many states mandate a minimum limit but higher limit may be purchased of an additional premium charge.

- **Collision:** Actual Cash Value Of Auto — Pays for damage to covered auto due to collision with another object or the auto's overturn.

- **Comprehensive:** Actual Cash Value Of Auto — Pays for damage to the covered auto due to any cause other than collision.

Note: Many states have versions of no fault coverage, a discussion of which is beyond the scope of this article. In addition, a discussion of other, less important coverages such as Towing And Labor and Rental Reimbursement has been omitted.

Non-Owned and Hired Autos

A sports organization can be vicariously liable for auto accidents resulting from non-owned vehicles (those not titled in the name of the sports organization) that are owned by employees or volunteer staff but used to run errands on behalf of the sports organization. Such errands could include a trip to the post office or a sporting goods supply store. Non-Owned Auto Liability coverage protects the sports organization but not the individual driver who would need to look towards his or her own Personal Auto Policy for protection.

A sports organization and its driver can be liable for auto accidents resulting from the use of rented (ex: rented from Hertz, Avis, etc.) or borrowed (ex: borrowed from church) vehicles. Hired Auto Liability coverage protects both the sports organization and its authorized driver while using such vehicles on official business of the sports organization.

Many insurance carriers in the sports niche are reluctant to provide Non-Owned And Hired Auto Liability due to the severity risk of a serious auto accident involving multiple injuries and high medical bills. Furthermore, the risk is difficult to underwrite due the failure of most sports organizations to run motor vehicle record checks on its drivers and to provide driver training.

It is customary for insurance carriers to attempt to control the severity risk under Non-Owned And Hired Auto Liability by excluding from coverage the use of 15 passenger vans and by limiting coverage for the transportation of participants. Both of these areas represent a significant severity risk due to the possibility of serious injuries to multiple passengers.

It's important to note that Hired Auto Liability does not extend physical damage coverage (i.e., comprehensive or collision) to the vehicle itself and as a result separate coverage arrangements must be made either through the purchase of Hired Car Physical Damage from the insurance carrier or through the Collision Damage Waiver from the rental car company. This matter is also complicated by the possible availability of similar coverage when using certain credit cards for payment of the rented vehicle. The decision on the best way to insure the physical damage exposure for rented vehicles is a complicated matter and beyond the scope of this article. An insurance agent should be consulted prior to renting a vehicle.

Note: Coverage form referenced is ISO CA 00 01 03 06

Workers' Compensation

Workers' Compensation policies consist of two coverage parts: Part One—Workers' Compensation and Part Two—Employers Liability.

Part One: Statutory Workers' Compensation

Pays the statutory benefits to injured workers as prescribed by the controlling state's Workers' Compensation Act. State Workers' Compensation laws were developed to provide efficient compensation to injured workers and to protect employers against tort based lawsuits. As a result, Workers' Compensation is a no fault system that pays without regard to any negligence or wrongdoing on the part of the employer.

Workers' Compensation Benefits

Workers' Compensation insurance pays the following benefits to employees or employees of uninsured subcontractors who suffer occupational injuries or diseases while "on the job" and "in the course of employment." Benefits vary per state.

- 100% of past and future medical bills.
- Rehabilitation expenses.
- Weekly lost wages based on a formula (usually 66.6% of average weekly wages for the prior year) for a pre determined number of weeks subject to a waiting period and a minimum and maximum payroll amount.
- Lump sum awards for disabilities.
- Lump sum awards for disfigurements.
- Death benefits to dependents.

Part Two: Employers Liability

Employers Liability responds to legal liability arising from occupational injuries and diseases to employees where recovery is allowed by law. Employers Liability claims are somewhat rare due to strong "exclusive remedy" doctrines in many states where an injured worker's exclusive remedy is to file for Workers' Compensation benefits under Part One. However, injured workers and third parties can sometimes file lawsuits to trigger coverage under Employers Liability. Examples of such lawsuits include loss of companionship or consortium by spouse, loss of household services by family member, dual capacity lawsuits (employer sued as manufacturer of defective product that caused injury), third party or action over, and consequential bodily injury (family member injury suffered as consequence of employee's injury).

Basic Employers Liability Limits

$100,000 Bodily Injury By Accident Limit

$500,000 Bodily Injury By Disease — Policy Limit

$100,000 Bodily Injury By Disease — Employee Limit

Higher limits may be purchased for a very small additional charge.

State Law Requirements to Carry Workers' Compensation

Whether a particular sports organization is required to carry Workers' Compensation can be a complex issue and the answer may vary from state to state. However, the consequence of failure to carry a policy when required by law to do so can be severe.

For larger sports organizations with many employees, it's a "no brainer" that Workers' Compensation must be carried. On the other hand, the issue is less clear for many smaller sports organizations such as teams and leagues. Several states have enacted laws that exempt sports leagues from carrying Workers' Compensation. However, in the vast majority of states, the requirement for smaller sports organizations remains somewhat of a "gray area."

Many smaller sports organizations are volunteer run, but they sometimes pay individual workers or businesses for services such as umpiring, janitorial, concessions, field maintenance, etc. Whenever these organizations host a large tournament, many more workers than normal are hired. Of course, most sports organizations consider these workers to be independent contractors and not employees for various reasons such as to reduce payroll tax liability.

These smaller sports organizations tend to purchase Accident and General Liability insurance but forgo the purchase of Workers' Compensation. The Accident policy often covers all players, coaches, managers, umpires, scorekeepers, and other staff and pays a medical expense benefit ranging from $25,000 to $250,000, depending on the limit selected. Accident coverage is normally excess or secondary to other collectible family health insurance. From the point of view of the Accident insurance carriers, the Accident policy is meant to cover volunteers and other paid workers who don't come under the Workers' Compensation Act.

The existence of Accident insurance does not excuse a sports organization that is otherwise required to carry Workers' Compensation. Also, Accident insurance benefits usually fall well short of the extensive benefits offered by a Workers' Compensation policy. For example, most Accident policies don't pay benefits for lost wages resulting from work related injuries. In addition, Workers' Compensation policies don't have a limit for medical expenses whereas Accident policies always have a medical limit.

Analysis of Requirement to Carry Workers' Compensation Under South Carolina Law

It is instructive to study the requirement for businesses (sports organizations) to carry Workers' Compensation in a particular state such as South Carolina, since other states may follow a similar thought process. The conclusions drawn below are based on selected statutes from the SC Workers' Compensation Act and an interview with the Director Of Compliance Division of the South Carolina Workers' Compensation Commission. Of course, other states may have different requirements and a competent insurance agent and attorney should be consulted to provide guidance in this area.

Liability for Injuries to Workers Who Are Not Paid in SC — Workers who are not paid are considered to be "gratuitous workers" and as a result their injuries are generally not compensable under the Workers' Compensation Act in SC. Workers whose compensation is considered to be expense reimbursement (ex: umpires who are paid to offset travel expense and cost of uniform) are likely to be considered "gratuitous workers."

Liability for Injuries to Employees Who Are Paid in SC — Businesses are exempt from carrying Workers' Compensation if they regularly employ fewer than four employees within the state or had a total annual payroll during the previous year of less than $3,000, regardless of the number of persons employed during that period.

Just because a sports organization considers a paid worker to be an independent contractor instead of an employee does not mean that a Workers' Compensation Commissioner will agree with such a classification. This is true even if there is a contract that states the worker is an independent contractor. Such a contract is just one factor to be considered. In these cases, after consultation with their attorney, the injured worker almost always claims to be an employee instead of an independent contractor. The Commissioner will apply a test based on case law and will look at about 20 different factors. The Commissioners tend to be very sympathetic to injured workers and will go to great lengths to find that they are employees and that their injuries are compensable.

Liability for Injuries to Workmen of a Subcontractor in SC — The terms independent contractor and subcontractor are interchangeable for Workers' Compensation purposes. Businesses that hire subcontractors to perform or execute work that is part of the "trade, business, or occupation" of the business are liable for injuries to workmen of such subcontractors just as if they were employees of the business. However, injuries to a subcontractor worker who is a sole proprietor, partner, or LLC owner of the business are not compensable under the Act. However, as already stated, these workers will usually claim that they are employees instead of subcontractors (independent contractors).

If the subcontractor carries its own Workers' Compensation policy, such policy will pay benefits to the injured workmen. For this reason, it is critical to require subcontractors to provide a certificate of insurance evidencing Workers' Compensation before they are hired.

Liability and Penalties for Failure to Carry Workers' Compensation When It Is Required

If an employee or workman of a subcontractor suffers an injury that is compensable under the Act and if they seek Workers' Compensation benefits from a sports organization that was required to carry Workers' Compensation but failed to do so, the consequences can be severe. In most states, penalties can be assessed against the sports organization to make up for past Workers' Compensation premiums that should have been paid. In addition, the injured worker can file for Workers' Compensation benefits against the state's Uninsured Employers Fund. After paying the prescribed Workers' Compensation benefits to injured worker, the Fund will then place a lien against the sports organization in an amount that is equal to the benefits paid. This can result in insolvency for the sports organization since the total benefits can be extremely large depending on the seriousness of the injury.

Operations in Multiple States

Workers' Compensation policies should be customized to account for multi-state operations since each state has its own Workers' Compensation Act with its own unique requirements and benefits. Failure to properly set up the policy can result in uncovered claims. Unfortunately, it is often difficult to find a single insurance carrier that is licensed in all states of operation and this can result in a hodgepodge of separate insurance policies and the corresponding administrative hassle of separate billings and policy audits.

It is important to properly list all states with both known and unknown exposure under sections 3A and 3C of the policy. Otherwise, coverage in a particular state will not be triggered. This can be a problem since injured employees and their attorneys "forum shop" to bring their claim for Workers' Compensation in the state that will have the highest level of benefits. The various state Workers' Compensation acts may allow choice of state between state of hire, state of residence, state of primary employment, state of pay, state of injury, or state in agreement between employer and employee. For example, assume that the claimant has a choice between filing for benefits in the states of SC and VA and that the VA benefits are $20,000 greater and that VA was not properly added as a covered state. In this scenario, it is possible that the Workers' Compensation carrier would pay benefits up to the SC level but the insured sports organization would be responsible to pay the remaining $20,000 out of pocket.

Section 3A (Known State Exposure): Section 3A of the policy triggers coverage for each state where the insured "knows" that an employee or uninsured sub will be working as of the effective date of the policy. The definition of "known work" is subject to varying interpretations. Some insurance experts advise that 3A should be limited to states where an employee is domiciled or where there is an existing contract for work as of the effective date. These experts don't see the need to list states through which salesmen will be traveling or in which executives will be attending trade shows. However, other experts and some state Departments of Insurance would advise listing all states within which employees have even minimal contact under Section 3A.

Section 3C (Unknown State Exposure): Section 3C of the policy triggers coverage for states in which the insured is not aware of potential exposure as of the effective date of the policy. This section should included all states except those listed in Section 3A and the monopolistic states. It is important to note that Section 3C will not provide benefits for any state which should have been listed as a Section 3A state. The insurance carrier should be notified immediately if work begins in a 3C state after the effective date of the policy.

Monopolistic States: Sports organizations with worker exposure in the monopolistic states of ND, OH, WA, and WY must purchase Workers' Compensation coverage directly from the respective state fund. Coverage for these states can't be purchased through the private insurance marketplace. Since Employers Liability coverage is not available through the monopolistic state funds, a coverage known as "Stop Gap Employers Liability" should be endorsed onto either a private marketplace Workers' Compensation policy or the General Liability policy.

Federal Compensation Laws

Some sports organizations may have operations that fall under various federal compensation benefit laws that are not covered by the standard Workers' Compensation policy form. If such exposure exists, it must be endorsed onto the existing Workers' Compensation policy or a stand-alone policy must be purchased. Failure to address these federal exposures can create large uninsured liabilities as the benefits owed under these federal laws tend to be much higher than those under state Workers' Compensation.

Examples of federal benefit laws creating liability include US Longshoremen And Harbor Act (USL&H) (operations over navigable waters), Jones Act (seamen on vessels), and Foreign Defense Base Act. USL&H and Jones Act may apply to certain water-based sports organizations.

Sports Risks Are Perceived as High-Risk by Insurance Carriers

Insurance carriers that write Workers' Compensation insurance may perceive sports organizations as high-risk business and often are not willing to voluntarily write this coverage. As a result, many end up being placed in state assigned risk pools that result in higher rates and less flexibility to add needed states of coverage. Of particular concern to insurance carriers are sports organizations with employee exposure in the areas of professional athletes, coaches, and umpires. On the other hand, organizations with employee exposure limited to the areas of clerical, officer travel, and event management are not considered to be high risk.

Note: Coverage form referenced is National Council on Compensation Insurance (NCCI) WC 00 00 00 A.

Umbrella/Excess Liability

Sports organizations purchase Umbrella/Excess Liability insurance to protect against catastrophic lawsuits that exceed the liability limits of underlying policies such as General Liability, Business Auto, and Employers Liability. Umbrella/Excess policies can provide additional peace of mind and should be considered as part of a comprehensive insurance program. At a minimum, sports organizations should at least get a quote for an Umbrella/Excess Liability policy just to find out the cost.

In past years, Umbrella Liability policies provided broader coverages than Excess Liability policies. However, most modern Umbrella Liability forms are "watered down" to provide only slightly broader coverages than Excess Liability forms. The important thing to remember is that there is usually only a slight difference between the terms "Umbrella Liability" and "Excess Liability" as regards the true protection provided.

Here is an example of how an Umbrella/Excess Liability policy increases the limits of an underlying policy. Assume that a sports organization carries an Umbrella/Excess

Liability policy with a limit of $1,000,000. Also assume that the same sports organization carries a General Liability policy with an Each Occurrence Limit of $1,000,000 and a Business Auto policy with an Auto Liability limit of $1,000,000. In this example, the total limits of coverage to respond to a claim would be $2,000,000 for General Liability type claims and $2,000,000 for Auto Liability type claims.

True Umbrella Liability Policy Fulfills Three Major Purposes

1. **Increases Limits of Coverage** — The first purpose (as illustrated in the example above) is to provide additional limits of coverage over and above the underlying General Liability, Auto Liability, and Employers Liability (Part 2 of Workers' Compensation Policy) policies. Before this "excess" coverage is provided, the insured must maintain the underlying policies at a certain limit of liability to coordinate with the Umbrella policy requirements. The most common underlying limit requirements are as follows:

    *   General Liability — $1,000,000 Each Occurrence; $2,000,000 General Aggregate; $2,000,000 Products/Completed Operations Aggregate; $1,000,000 Personal/Advertising Injury

    *   Business Auto Liability — $1,000,000 per claim

    *   Employers Liability — $500,000 Each Accident; $500,000 Disease — Policy Limit; $500,000 Disease — Each Employee

    Coverage can be customized to increase the limits of all or just one of the above underlying policies. For example, some sports organizations may choose to only purchase an Umbrella/Excess Liability policy to increase the limits of their General Liability policy.

2. **Provides Drop Down Coverage Feature** — The second purpose is to provide "drop down" coverage in the event that an underlying policy's aggregate limits are exhausted. In such a circumstance, an Umbrella policy will "drop down" and pay for covered liability on a primary basis. For example, assume that an underlying General Liability policy has an Each Occurrence limit of $1,000,000 and a General Aggregate limit of $1,000,000. During the policy year, the General Liability policy pays a $1,000,000 claim and then has another claim of $500,000. The Umbrella policy will pay the $500,000 claim under the drop down feature.

3. **Provides Broader Coverage Feature** — The third purpose is to provide broader coverage for certain liability risks that are not covered by the underlying policies. This most often occurs when the Umbrella policy has fewer or narrower exclusions than the underlying policy. For example, a General Liability policy may exclude liability arising from non-owned watercraft 26 feet or more in length whereas an Umbrella policy may exclude liability for non-owned watercraft 51 feet or more in length. Therefore, an Umbrella Liability policy may pick up a claim arising out of a non-owned watercraft between 26 and 51 feet in length. The broader coverage feature is usually subject to a self-insured retention (similar to a deductible). Self-insured retentions are typically $10,000 and must be paid out of pocket before the broader coverage feature will respond.

    Other areas of broadened coverage may include broader coverage territory; broader definition of personal injury; fellow employee exclusion deleted; non owned aircraft chartered with a crew; and coverage for certain types of property in the care, custody, or control of the insured.

A true Umbrella Liability policy provides coverages under 1., 2., and 3. above, whereas an Excess Liability policy only provides coverages under 1. and 2.

Both Umbrella and Excess Liability Policies May Provide Narrower Coverage Than Underlying Policies

In the context of sports organizations, it's common for Umbrella and Excess policies to have exclusions that are not found on the underlying General Liability policy. The most common examples of such exclusions include Non Owned And Hired Auto Liability (if endorsed onto General Liability) and Sex Abuse And Molestation. However, the Umbrella or Excess Liability carrier may provide a buy-back for these common exclusions.

Limits and Pricing

Umbrella/Excess Liability policies may be purchased in increments of $1,000,000. Each $1,000,000 increment is subject to a minimum premium ranging from $500 to $2,500 depending on the carrier. The actual premium may be higher than the minimum premium depending on the loss exposures. The most common premium basis for exposures to loss includes number of participants, number of teams, payroll of employees, revenues, number of vehicles, etc. Umbrella/Excess Liability quotes are often expressed as a percentage of the underlying premiums. For example, some policies are priced at a rate of approximately 20% of underlying premiums for the first layer of $1,000,000. Further discounts may be applied to each additional layer of $1,000,000 due to the decreasing probability of a claim breaching the additional limits.

How High a Limit Is Needed?

There is no definitive way to answer this question. Factors to be considered include value of assets at risk, exposure units creating the risk (ex: the greater the number of participants, the greater the chance of a catastrophic injury and resulting claim), recent court cases, limits carried by peer organizations of similar size, affordability, and the particular severity risks that are faced by a sports organization (ex: transportation of participants, sex abuse/molestation).

Liquor Legal Liability

Sports organizations that serve or furnish beer, wine, or liquor may be held liable for injuries to patrons or other third parties under the following legal theories of recovery:

1) The patron was under the legal drinking age

2) The patron was obviously intoxicated

3) Statutes, regulations, or ordinances (ex: "dram shop" acts or alcoholic beverage control laws) or case law that imposes "strict liability" for the sale of alcoholic

beverages even if it can't be proved that the serving of the alcoholic beverage was the "proximate cause" of the injury.

Common examples of alcohol related incidents resulting in potential liability for sports organizations include auto accidents with injuries to the intoxicated driver, passengers, or other third parties; fights resulting in injuries to participants; and vandalism damages to property. The frequency of these incidents tends to be low but the severity potential is very high.

Host Liquor Liability Coverage under General Liability

The standard General Liability policy form has an exclusion for insureds " ... in the business of manufacturing, distributing, selling, serving, or furnishing alcoholic beverages." The key is to correctly interpret the meaning of "in the business of." Some courts have ruled that *not-for-profit* organizations are not "in the business of" even if they regularly sell alcoholic beverages and as a result have what is known as "host liquor liability" coverage under their existing General Liability policy. However, there is at least one high profile decision that reached the opposite conclusion based on a number of additional factors. Also, insurance carrier claims adjusters are hesitant to provide "host liquor liability" coverage for the sale of alcohol because they believe that it is contrary to the intent of the drafters of the policy form. As a result, some experts advise that not-for-profits that sell alcohol (cash bar or as part of an admission ticket) or that are required to take out a liquor license or permit should not rely on the "host liquor liability" coverage under their General Liability policy.

Furthermore, some General Liability policies include endorsements (ex: CG 21 50) that amend the terms of the standard policy form which has the effect of definitively taking away the "host liquor liability" coverage for organizations that make a charge (ex: cash bar or part of the admission price) or if the event requires a liquor license or permit.

Sports organizations should closely examine their policy form with their insurance agent and review case law in their state before relying on "host liquor liability" coverage.

Liquor Legal Liability Coverage

Some sports organizations can't rely on the "host liquor liability" coverage under their General Liability policies because they may be considered to be "in the business of manufacturing, distributing, selling, serving, or furnishing" or their policy has an endorsement that restricts coverage. Such sports organizations should purchase Liquor Legal Liability insurance. This coverage may be purchased as either a stand-alone policy or as an endorsement to the General Liability policy.

Sports organizations may sell alcoholic beverages to patrons on a direct basis with their own staff or may contract out the sales of alcoholic beverages to a vendor. *Primary Liquor Legal Liability* insurance is needed in the event that the staff of the sports organization makes the alcohol sales. On the other hand, *Contingent Liquor Legal Liability* insurance is needed if a vendor that holds the liquor license makes the alcohol sales.

Estimated Premium Costs

A leading source for Liquor Legal Liability insurance for sports organizations, K&K Insurance Group, Inc., provides the following guidelines for premium indications:

Minimum Premium: Range from $300 to $1,000 depending on the type of risk, the state where risk is located, and risk management controls.

Rate Per $1,000 Of Beer, Wine, and Liquor Sales For Primary Liquor Legal Liability: varies from $5 to $25 depending on past loss experience, state where sports organization is located (states with strong Dram Shop acts are more expensive) and the type of alcohol served (ex: more expensive to serve liquor).

Rate For Contingent Liquor Legal Liability: The rates are the same as for Primary except that the sales are based on the percentage that is received by the sports organization. For example, if the contract provides that the sports organization is to receive 25% of the alcohol sales made by the vendor, the rate would only be applied to such 25%.

Additional Considerations if a Vendor Sells Alcohol for Sports Organization

1) A written contract should be in place to protect the legitimate interests of the sports organization.

2) Such contract should include strong indemnification/hold harmless language in favor of the sports organization and its directors, officers, employees, and volunteers against any and all claims, damages, and expenses (including reasonable attorney's fees) arising out of the sale of alcoholic beverages.

3) In addition to providing evidence of the normal insurance policies that are required of vendors such as Workers' Compensation, General Liability, Business Auto, etc., the vendor must provide evidence of currently valid Liquor Legal Liability coverage with an insurance carrier that is rated at least A- by A.M. Best and such policy must have a limit of at least $1,000,000 Each Claim (even though it is recommended that a limit of $5,000,000 or more be carried). In addition, the sports organization should be named as an "Additional Insured."

Why Contingent Liquor Legal Liability Is Needed If a Vendor Sells Alcohol

Even if the vendor provides an indemnification/hold harmless provision in favor of the sports organization and carries its own Liquor Legal Liability policy, things can still go wrong. For example, the vendor's insurance policy may cancel due to non-payment of premium or its aggregate limit may be exhausted by a prior claim during the policy year.

Sports organizations that contract out the sales of alcohol are usually "shot gunned" into liquor liability lawsuits under the following theories of recovery:

- The sports organization was negligent in its hiring and retention of the alcohol vendor that was known to cut corners and turn a blind eye to safety rules in serving patrons.

- The security provided by the sports organization should have noticed that a patron was intoxicated and should have ejected him before he purchased additional drinks.

- The ticket taker provided by the sports organization should have noticed that a patron was intoxicated and denied admission.

For additional risk management controls to protect against liquor lawsuits, visit www.sadler-sports.com/riskmanagement and see article entitled "Liquor Liability For Sportsplexes."

Management Liability

Management Liability insurance is the modern term for the various types of coverages that protect an insured organization against certain liabilities resulting from managerial negligence by its officers, board of directors, and other staff. Management Liability policies take a modular approach where the insured can pick and choose from an array of coverages including Directors & Officers Liability, Employment Practices Liability, and Fiduciary Liability.

Most commercial insurance policies such as General Liability, Workers' Compensation, Business Auto, Property, etc. use policy language that is standardized to a great degree. Standardized policy language that has been tested by the courts allows for predictability in determining whether coverage is likely to exist in a particular claim scenario. As a result, insurance agents can more easily advise their clients on coverage issues relating to these policies. On the other hand, Management Liability policies do not use standardized policy language as one policy form may vary greatly from another in terms of organizational structure, coverage grants, definitions, exclusions, and conditions. As a result, Management Liability policies are more difficult to interpret and compare and the coverage outcomes can be more difficult to predict.

Under some of the older policy forms that are still in use, Directors & Officers Liability policies may automatically include coverage for Employment Practices Liability. However, under the many of the more modern policy forms, Directors & Officers Liability and Employment Practices Liability are different coverage parts under the same policy and a separate premium must be paid for each to trigger coverage.

Directors & Officers Liability (D&O)

Directors & Officers Liability insurance protects the insured entity and its directors, officers, employees, and volunteers against certain types of lawsuits such as financial mismanagement; discrimination based on race, sex, age, or handicap; violation of rights of others under state, federal, and constitutional law; and failure to follow rules or bylaws when making an administrative decision.

It's important to note that these types of lawsuits are not covered under a General Liability policy which only responds to lawsuits alleging "bodily injury" (ex: spectator and participant injury), "property damage,"" "personal injury" (ex: slander, libel, invasion of privacy), and "advertising injury" (ex: disparagement of competitor in advertising materials). Likewise, a Directors & Officers Liability policy specifically excludes from coverage the types of lawsuits that are covered by a General Liability policy.

One of the most common misconceptions is that a Directors & Officers Liability policy covers directors and officers against all types of lawsuits, including those alleging "bodily injury" (ex: spectator or participant injury). This is why it is critical for directors and officers to be protected by a General Liability policy as well.

Claims Made Coverage Form Challenges

Directors & Officers Liability is written on a "claims made" form instead of an "occurrence" form. Under the "claims made" form, coverage problems can arise in the event that the policy is cancelled, non-renewed, or transferred to a new carrier. The insurance agent must provide guidance on how to handle these situations including advice on "retro dates," "pending or prior dates," and "extended reporting periods."

Not-for-Profit vs. For-Profit

Directors & Officers Liability policies for "not-for-profit" sports organizations are relatively inexpensive and typically include broad coverage terms. Minimum premiums may start out at $300 for smaller leagues and $1500 for larger associations or sanctioning bodies. Of course, pricing will increase with higher revenues, weak financial statements, high-risk nature of operations, if members are to be included under a group program, or if there is a past history of losses. On the other hand, the premiums for "for-profit" sports organizations tend to be more expensive, with less favorable coverage terms.

Some Favorable D&O Coverage Provisions:

- The insurance carrier must "Pay On Behalf Of" instead of "Indemnify."
- Broad definition of "Wrongful Act" as "any" error, misstatement, misleading statement, act, omission, neglect, breach of duty, etc. instead of "negligent" error, misstatement. . . .
- Defense is included outside of the limits of coverage
- Broad definition of insured persons to include the entity and its directors, officers, trustees, managers, employees, volunteers, committee persons, etc.
- Addition of coverage for "personal injury wrongful act" and "publishers wrongful act."
- Loss prevention and consultation services.

Some Common D&O Policy Exclusions:

- Deliberately fraudulent act or willful violation of statute or regulation
- The gaining of any in fact profit or advantage to which the insured person was not legally entitled
- Any wrongful acts that occurred prior to any "retro date" or "pending or prior date"
- Prior claims subject to any notice given in any application for coverage
- Violation of certain securities laws such as Securities Act of 1933
- Bodily injury or property damage (should be covered under General Liability)
- Release of pollutants
- ERISA violations (should be covered under Fiduciary Liability)
- Employment related wrongful acts (should be covered under Employment Practices Liability)
- Punitive or treble damages exclusions
- Insured vs. Insured exclusions are common to provide a disincentive for internal lawsuits between insured persons. Some insurance carriers will eliminate or modify this exclusion.
- Breach of contract (should try to negotiate removal of exclusion or defense only)
- Liability assumed under contract

- Claims arising from serving on board of any outside entities
- Non-monetary damages such as injunctive relief

Some Problem D&O Exclusions for Sports Organizations to Avoid:

- Breach of Contract—If this exclusion is on the policy, attempt to remove it or amend it so that it does not apply to legal defense for breach of contract. Some lawsuits filed against sports organizations for failure to follow their own rules or bylaws are framed as breach of contract with members.

- Antitrust or Restraint of Trade—This type of litigation occurs in the sports context when a sports organization implements rules that inhibit participation in other sports organizations.

- Certification, Accreditation, and Peer Review—Many sports organization have training programs where coaches, umpires, or instructors are certified or accredited. Even if this exclusion is not on the policy, a strong argument could be made for a Professional Liability policy to cover this exposure.

- Non-Monetary Relief or Injunctive Relief Claims—If this exclusion is on the policy, an attempt should be made to amend it so that coverage applies for legal defense. Many lawsuits arise in the sports context when a player is disqualified from participation in a tournament and such player files an action with a judge for injunctive relief to have the tournament postponed until a determination can be made.

Employment Practices Liability (EPLI)

Employment Practices Liability insurance covers liability arising out of the employer—employee relationship. The primary types of liabilities that are covered include wrongful discipline or termination, discrimination, and sexual harassment. The better coverage forms typically cover a number of other workplace liabilities that are created by state and federal statutes and case law.

To follow is a sample of the types of employment offenses that are covered by one of the broader forms on the marketplace through Chubb:

- Breach of Employment Contract—oral, written, or implied contract including obligations arising out of employee handbooks, employee manuals, etc.

- Employee Discrimination—violation of employment discrimination laws including wrongful termination, demotion, denial of tenure, refusal to hire, refusal to promote, etc. based on person's race, religion, creed, national origin, disability, sex, HIV status, sexual orientation or any other status protected by local, state, or federal laws or common law.

- Employment Harassment—sexual harassment, unwelcomed sexual advances, or requests for sexual favors that is a condition of employment or basis for employment decisions creates an intimidating and hostile work environment. In addition, non-sexual workplace harassment that creates an intimidating and hostile work environment.

- Retaliation—retaliation against an employee for exercising rights under law, refusing to violate law, or disclosing or threatening to disclose violation of law.

- Workplace Tort—employment related defamation; invasion of privacy; negligent evaluation, wrongful discipline, retention, supervision, hiring, misrepresentation, infliction of emotional distress/mental anguish/humiliation, failure to consistently enforce corporate policies and procedures.

- Wrongful Employment Decision—wrongful demotion, denial of tenure, or failure to promote.

- Wrongful Termination—wrongful termination, dismissal, discharge, or constructive termination.

Third Party Discrimination/Third Party Liability

Many of the modern policy forms break out an optional coverage for third party discrimination or third party liability. A "third party" is often defined as someone other than an employee, such as a customer, vendor, service provider, or other business invitee of the insured. In order to trigger coverage for "third party" claims alleging discrimination (ex: race, religion, creed, sex, disability, national origin, sexual orientation, or other protected statuses) or sexual harassment, this coverage option must be triggered.

Common EPLI Policy Exclusions for Liability or Benefits Arising Out of

- Employment Retirement Income Security Act (ERISA)
- Consolidated Omnibus Budget Reconciliation Act (COBRA)
- Occupational Safety & Health Laws (OSHA)
- Fair Labor Standards Act
- National Labor Relations Act
- Benefits under Workers' Compensation, Unemployment Insurance, Disability Insurance or similar local, state, federal, or common law benefit laws
- Racketeer Influenced And Corrupt Organizations Act (RICO)
- Sherman Anti-Trust Act or similar laws
- Punitive or treble damages
- Intentional or criminal acts
- Assumption of contractual liability (ex: indemnification/hold harmless provisions in PEO or employee leasing contracts)
- Costs to modify building under Americans With Disabilities Act
- Employee benefit stock options
- Any employee practices wrongful acts that occurred prior to any "retro date" or "pending or prior date"
- Prior employment practices claims subject to any notice given in any application for coverage

Important EPLI Underwriting Considerations

Some important underwriting considerations for acceptability of a risk or for pricing discounts include recent terminations, turnover rate, layoffs, mergers/acquisitions, salary ranges, incident and loss history, and risk management practices that have been implemented, including the existence of an employee handbook.

Fiduciary Liability

The Employee Retirement Income Security Act of 1974 (ERISA) governs employers with certain employee benefit plans, such as traditional pension plans, cash balance plans, 401(K) plans, profit-sharing plans, and employee welfare benefit plans.

ERISA was enacted to protect employees who participate in employer-sponsored employee benefit plans. It imposes a fiduciary duty on those who exercise discretionary authority over administration and management of plan assets and investment advice. ERISA fiduciaries include directors and officers who have personal liability in the event they don't act in the best interests of the plan participants.

Fiduciary Liability Insurance protects the business as an entity and its directors, officers, employees, and trustees against certain fiduciary wrongful acts in the handling of employee benefit plans.

Fiduciary Liability Insurance coverage is normally inexpensive and a prudent investment in light of the personal liability faced by directors and officers. Many make the mistake of believing that they have no liability for the investment performance self-directed 401(K) plans; however, liability can still exist for negligent hiring or failing to monitor the performance of investment advisors.

Professional Liability
(i.e., Errors & Omissions)

The use of the terms Professional Liability insurance and Errors & Omissions Liability insurance are historically distinguishable but are now almost interchangeable in the insurance industry. For the purposes of discussion of their impact on sports organizations, they are considered to be one in the same.

Whereas a General Liability policy covers certain lawsuits alleging bodily injury and property damage, a Professional Liability policy covers certain lawsuits alleging pure economic damages with no accompanying bodily injury or property damage.

Sports organizations with the following exposures may benefit from a Professional Liability policy:

- Player alleges that improper instruction by coach has resulted in loss of college athletic scholarship or professional sports career.

- Player alleges that mistake made in recruiting service profile has resulted in loss of college athletic scholarship or professional sports career. Sports organizations that publish player statistics or strengths and weaknesses may have this exposure.

- Member team/league alleges that negligent management or financial advice provided by sanctioning sports organization has resulted in economic loss to team/league. This exposure is common when the relationship between the sanctioning body and team/league is that of franchisor — franchisee in a for-profit model.

- Applicant or member has certification or accreditation denied or revoked and as a result alleges economic damages.

Some General Liability carriers may be willing to add a Professional Liability endorsement for minor Professional Liability exposures for no charge or a small charge. Otherwise, a stand-alone Professional Liability (Errors & Omissions) must be purchased. The premium for such a policy will be based on revenues and minimum premiums start in the $1,500 to $2,500 range.

Media Liability

Sports organizations that advertise, broadcast, publish, and telecast may have media liability exposure for alleged offenses such as slander, libel, invasion of privacy, and violation of intellectual property rights such as copyright, trademark, and trade name infringement, etc. Some of these exposures may be covered by the Personal/Advertising injury coverage under a General Liability policy as was explained in a prior section. However, due to numerous exclusions, a General Liability policy will not be sufficient for sports organizations with more than incidental media liability exposures.

A Cyber Liability policy may be sufficient for sports organizations with online media exposures. However, those with more traditional exposures (ex: magazines, books, videos, etc.) may need to purchase a Media Liability policy.

Cyber Liability

Due to the increasing advance of technology, sports organizations face cyber liability exposure from the following common operations:

- Collection of member confidential data such as social security numbers, bank account numbers, credit card numbers, drivers license numbers, etc. on websites, computers, and laptops
- Use of email to transmit communications
- Collection of information on minors under age 13
- Website chat rooms and blogs
- Website e-commerce stores that accept payment via credit card or ACH
- Publishing website media and content
- Social media such as facebook to promote organization
- Exclusive social media websites for members
- Delivery of services over websites
- Collecting criminal background checks on staff
- Medical records from injury databases

The following types of increasingly common occurrences are not covered by General Liability or Directors & Officers Liability policies:

- Hacker accesses computer system and obtains clients' "personally identifiable information" such as names in combination with corresponding driver's license numbers, account numbers, credit card numbers, social security numbers, etc.; employment files; and employees' or clients' medical information.

- The resulting potential liabilities from data breach (whether caused by the negligence of the sports organization or its IT service providers); from violation of state and federal privacy laws (requiring expensive notification, credit card monitoring, and fines); class action lawsuits; HIPAA violations for release of medical records; and violation of other consumer protection laws such as Fair Credit Reporting Act and California Consumer Credit Reporting Agencies Act.

- An email is sent with an attachment that contains a virus resulting in damage to the recipient's data.

- Laptop is stolen or lost and confidential information falls into hands of unauthorized users.

- Disgruntled employee intentionally releases confidential information.

- Disgruntled employee intentionally destroys computer records.

- Electronic media liability if website or email content results in libel, invasion of privacy, or violation of intellectual property rights (ex: copyright or trademark infringement).

- Administrative or operational error by employee or outsourced provider damages your computer system or records.

- Cyber extortion attacks on your computer system.

- Loss of income or payment of extra expenses while your computer system or website is shut down due to a covered peril.

To follow is a listing of typical Cyber Liability coverage sections:

Third Party Coverages (liability for damages to third parties)

- Security and Privacy Liability—Failure of computer security and wrongful release or failure to protect confidential or personally identifiable information.

- Transmission Liability—Transmission of virus, Trojan, malware, etc. through email or from website.

- Media Liability—Invasion of privacy or intellectual privacy violations arising from electronic media.

- Privacy Breach Notification and Credit Monitoring—Pays advertising expenses, mailing costs, and credit monitoring costs arising from breach.

First Party Coverages (damages to insured):

- Loss of Information—Pays to restore lost data, information, programming, etc. resulting from covered loss.

- Business Interruption and Extra Expense—Pays for lost income and extra expenses due to failure of computer systems from covered loss.

- Cyber Extortion—Pays extortion costs to prevent release or misuse of confidential information.

- Cyber Terrorism—Pays for income lost due to denial of service attacks.

- Crisis Management—Pays for public relations costs to rehabilitate reputation after a covered incident.

Minimum premiums for Cyber Liability policies start out in the $2,500 range and increase with revenues. Underwriting factors that can impact acceptability of a risk or pricing debits/credits include the industry of the applicant, types of confidential data that is maintained, operations, computer security controls, media review practices, and financial strength.

For up to date information on the devious techniques that hackers are using to access confidential information and on risk management steps to protect against this exposure, visit www.insurancefortechs.com/blog and select the category for "Cyber Liability."

International

Sports organizations have foreign exposures when their participants and teams travel outside of the US for training or competitions or when their managing personnel travel on organization related business. In addition, some sports organizations may have workers who are permanently located outside of the US.

US Insurance Policies Have the Following Limitations as Regards Foreign Exposures:

General Liability: The "coverage territory" is limited to the US (including territories and possessions), Puerto Rico, and Canada for lawsuits brought in such covered territories. Coverage may also apply to injuries occurring in all other parts of the world *if resulting lawsuits are brought in the "coverage territory"* and result from 1) the sales of products in the "coverage territory" or 2) for the activities of a person whose home is in the "coverage territory," but is away for a short time on organization business.

Sports organizations with foreign exposures should request their General Liability carrier to broaden the coverage territory by special endorsement.

Accident: Some policy forms have a worldwide coverage territory whereas others may limit coverage to medical services performed in the US.

Business Auto: The coverage territory is limited to the US (including territories and possessions), Puerto Rico, Canada. Worldwide coverage applies only to the extent that a) the vehicle is a private passenger type and is leased, hired, rented, or borrowed without a driver for 30 days or less; and b) *the lawsuit is brought in the US (including territories and possessions), Puerto Rico, or Canada.*

Workers' Compensation: Workers who are temporarily outside of the US (rule of thumb 30 consecutive days or less) may have statutory Workers' Compensation benefits for their state of hire depending on their state's Workers' Compensation laws. However, the regular Workers' Compensation policy form does not cover the following exposures: employees who are outside the US for more than 30 consecutive days (rule of thumb depending on state's Workers' Compensation laws), emergency medical evacuation to closest qualified medical facility, repatriation of body in the event of death, and endemic diseases (such as those caused by tropical parasites).

Foreign Package Policy

A Foreign Package Policy may be purchased from several carriers for as little as $2,500. A Foreign Package policy typically provides the following coverages:

- Voluntary Compensation—Provides voluntary Workers' Compensation benefits for work related injuries and illnesses for foreign based employees who are US Nationals (based on state of hire), Third Country Nationals (based on country of origin), or Local Nationals (based on country of origin).

- Employers Liability—Satisfies local Employers Liability laws for work related injuries and illnesses of foreign based employees.

- Medical Evacuation/Repatriation—Emergency medical evacuation is a primary concern when visiting third world countries without advanced medical care. Serious medical conditions such as a heart attack warrant advanced medical treatment. Emergency medical evacuation benefits include the cost to hire a charter airplane staffed with a doctor and nurse for transportation to the closest qualified medical facility.

- Endemic Diseases—Visits to tropical counties can result in endemic diseases such as those caused by local bacteria and parasites. These endemic diseases are not normally covered by US based Workers' Compensation insurance.

- Executive Assistance Services—Includes emergency and travel assistance services via toll free international calling or web for medical and legal contacts, personal services, and political evacuation or repatriation.

- Kidnap and Extortion—Pays up to policy limits for kidnap or extortion demands.

- International Medical and Accidental Death & Dismemberment—Fills in coverage gaps of domestic health insurance policies and provides accidental death and dismemberment benefits.

- Foreign General Liability—Provides General Liability protection for claims arising from incidents in foreign countries where lawsuits are filed in such foreign countries. However, it may be difficult to obtain this coverage without an Athletic Participants Exclusion.

- Contingent Auto Liability—Extends the limits of auto liability and physical damage coverage arising from foreign auto rentals. Typically, foreign rental car companies only offer basic auto liability and physical damage limits to comply with local laws. Additional limits are needed through Contingent Auto Liability due to the potential for auto accidents with a high severity potential.

- Foreign Property and Equipment—Provides Property Insurance coverage for real and personal property that is permanently located in a foreign country or is temporarily out of the US.

Property and Equipment

Sports organizations commonly own the following types of property that should be covered under a properly customized and endorsed Commercial Property insurance policy:

- Buildings, sheds, fences, bleachers, scoreboards, and other structures
- Personal Property such as furniture, fixtures, office equipment, supplies, and inventory
- Tenant's improvements and betterments
- Computer hardware, software, and data
- Sports equipment
- Field maintenance equipment

Commonly covered perils include fire, windstorm, hail, theft, vandalism, auto collision, etc.

Whenever possible, the Special Perils Of Loss coverage form should be used and all property should be insured for its full replacement cost value. Computer hardware and software should be insured under a special Electronic Data Processing (EDP) coverage form that insures against certain common perils that are excluded under the regular Commercial Policy coverage form. In addition, equipment that leaves scheduled premises should be insured under an Inland Marine coverage form so that coverage will follow the equipment to other locations.

A sports organization should carefully review its Property insurance needs with a property & casualty insurance professional who specializes in business insurance. Such insurance agent should use a detailed checklist to make sure that all special coverage needs and exclusion buy backs have been addressed.

Sports organizations commonly enter agreements where they lease buildings and personal property. These lease agreements should be carefully reviewed for insurance requirements as the tenant or lessee is commonly required to carry certain types of insurance to protect the interests of the landlord or lessor. An experienced property & casualty insurance agent should review all such agreements to advise the sports organization on contractual requirements as pertains to Property Insurance (in addition to Liability insurance requirements and indemnification/hold harmless provisions).

Business Income and Extra Expense

Property Insurance covers direct damage to property from covered perils and pays for its repair or replacement. On the other hand, Business Income insurance pays for indirect damage to a sports organization's financial statement as a result of a covered direct damage loss to property.

For example, if a sports organization's headquarters were to burn down, it's possible that a disruption of operations would occur and the sports organization would incur financial loss (ex: lost profits and ongoing expenses) during the period of restoration of its building, contents, and important business records.

Or, in the alternative, if the sports organization were to immediately relocate to a temporary location and immediately resume operations, it would still incur extra expenses such as lease payments, rush delivery of phones and computers, information technology consulting fees for set up, etc.

Business Income and Extra Expense insurance was designed to reimburse insureds for these types of losses and has been statistically proven to significantly lower the resulting chances of business failure and bankruptcy. Due to the complexities of determining the proper limit of coverage to purchase and the various coverage options, it is imperative to consult with a property & casualty insurance agent who specializes in business insurance for the proper plan design.

Crime

Sports organizations can have significant assets at risk from the traditional perils of employee or volunteer embezzlement and the modern perils of funds transfer fraud and computer fraud. Most sports organizations are not properly insured for these exposures and don't have adequate risk management controls in place.

The Commercial Crime policy form (ISO CR 00 20 05 06 and CR 00 21 05 06) offers the following coverage parts that may be individually purchased:

Employee Dishonesty—Provides coverage for employee theft of money, securities, or other property such as equipment. The definition of employee includes regular employees; temporary workers (except for theft outside of premises); leased workers; trustees of employee benefit plans; interns (except for theft outside of premises); managers, directors, or trustees while performing within scope of usual duties as an employee or acting as a member of a committee elected or appointed by board resolution to perform specific acts (as distinguished from general directorial acts).

If applicable, it is critical that sports organizations request special endorsements to extend coverage to theft from volunteers (other than fund solicitors), non-compensated officers, chairperson and members of specified committees, specified directors and trustees on committees, partners, LLC members, computer software contractors, agents, brokers, or independent contractors.

It is also important to purchase Employee Dishonesty coverage on a blanket basis that protects against theft from all employees or others in a designated class as opposed to specified employees or others who must be individually named on the policy. Sports organizations have frequent turnover of personnel and as a result it is likely that an organization will fail to update the list of specified employees or others.

Forgery & Alternation—Provides coverage for forgery or alteration of a check, draft, or promissory note that is drawn against the insured's accounts.

Money & Securities—Provides coverage for theft, disappearance, or destruction of money & securities from either inside the premises/banking premises or outside the premises. Coverage may also be extended to robbery or safe burglary of other property.

Computer Fraud—Provides coverage for financial loss due to a hacker gaining access to the computer of a business and effecting a fraudulent transaction. An example of computer fraud occurs when company A sells services to company B. An employee of company B hacks into the computer of company A and changes the bank routing and bank account numbers to his own. The next time a payment is made for services, the funds are fraudulently transferred to the employee instead of company A. (Example provided by Travelers Insurance Company.) According to a 2008 survey by Computer Security Institute, the average financial loss due to computer fraud was $289,000.

Electronic Funds Transfer Fraud—Provides coverage for financial loss due to a hacker gaining access to the computer of a financial institution, accessing an online account, and circumventing normal online authentication controls to affect a fraudulent wire transfer. An example of Electronic Funds Transfer Fraud occurs when a hacker gains bank account and password information by planting a Trojan horse virus in an email attachment sent to the bookkeeper of a company. The bookkeeper opens the attachment and a keyword logger is launched that secretly obtains the account and password information. The hacker accesses the online banking system and completes a fraudulent electronic wire transfer. According to a 2008 survey by Computer Security Institute, the average financial loss due to funds transfer fraud was $500,000.

Money Orders and Counterfeit Money—Provides coverage due to loss by good faith acceptance of money orders that are not honored or counterfeit money.

Traditional Crime Risk Management Controls

Many smaller sports organizations are not run as serious businesses and as a result don't have strong risk management controls to protect against employee and volunteer dishonesty. The key to preventing insider dishonesty is to have a separation of duties so that no single person has total control over any one process or audit procedure. To follow are recommended controls:

- Require a countersignature on all checks or on checks over a certain amount.
- Someone who is not authorized to deposit or withdraw must handle bank account reconciliation.
- If credit cards or debit cards are used, make sure that someone who is not authorized to use the cards reviews the monthly statements.
- Keep detailed inventory records of all equipment and require a log to be maintained when equipment is assigned or checked out.
- Create an audit committee to review all financial records, account statements, and to take an inventory of all equipment.
- Collect checks instead of cash during fundraisers.

Electronic Crime Risk Management Controls

Phishing scams, Trojan horses, key loggers, and similar techniques allow hackers to gain access to online banking transactions and to circumvent standard online authentication controls. Internal controls such as antivirus, firewalls, and employee training are critical, but won't protect against 100% of attacks. Therefore, Computer Fraud and Electronic Funds Transfer Fraud coverages are strongly recommended.

Conclusion

This article provides a basic education and framework to assist sports administrators in better understanding their property & casualty insurance needs and in managing the performance of their insurance and risk management experts. The concepts, insurance policies, exclusions, special coverage enhancements, and risk management controls and programs discussed in this article provide a basic overview but are by no means a complete account of all considerations. Sports organizations should seek the counsel of the very best sports insurance and risk management experts with the qualifications that are outlined in this article.

Disclaimer

This article has been prepared for the purpose of explaining general insurance coverage and risk management concepts for sports organizations. It should in no way be considered to provide specific insurance or legal advice for any particular sports organization. As regards actual coverages provided by any insurance policy, only the actual policy itself should be relied upon as it provides all coverages, exclusions, conditions, and limitations.

Descriptions of coverage for General Liability, Business Auto, Property, and Crime policies refer to policy forms issued by Insurance Services Office (ISO). Descriptions of coverages for Workers' Compensation refer to the policy form issued by the National Council On Compensation Insurance (NCCI). All sports organizations should consult with competent insurance agents, risk managers, and attorneys to devise a specific insurance and risk management plan that is customized to fit their particular needs.

References

Cyber Liability: Cyber Security Liability, Philadelphia Insurance Companies, http://www.phly.com/products/CyberSecurity.aspx; Chartis Net Advantage, Chartis, Inc., http://www.chartisinsurance.com/us-network-security-and-privacy-insurance_295_182553.html.

Employment Practices Liability: The Chubb Group Of Insurance Companies, http://www.chubb.com.

International Insurance: The ACE Group, http://www.acegroup.com/us-en/businesses/international-casualty.aspx.

Liquor Liability: K&K Insurance Group, http://www.kandkinsurance.com.

Umbrella/Excess Liability: Excess Liability/Commercial Umbrella Coverages, David Viola, CIC Commercial Casualty Institute, The National Alliance For Insurance Education And Research.

Part IV

Medical Issues

Sport medicine specialists, such as a physician or athletic trainer, may be held liable for malpractice when a general practitioner rendering the identical treatment will not be liable.

Schubert, Smith & Trentadue
Sport Law

Chapter 14

Administering a Sport Medicine Program

The quality of any program is directly related to the personnel who are responsible for its success.

Jerald D. Hawkins

In the fast-paced, technical world of sport medicine, administrative responsibilities are often neglected in favor of more urgent (and often more interesting) issues. It is all too common for critical administrative duties to be poorly performed or, in some cases, disregarded altogether. Consequently, the failure to execute these administrative responsibilities in a competent and timely manner has become a commonly-cited cause of action in sport litigation. This chapter focuses on four important aspects of effective administration: personnel administration, facility management, record-keeping, and emergency preparedness. If neglected, these key administrative responsibilities may provide fertile ground for litigation. However, when properly performed, they can help the sport medicine administrator reduce his/her negligence litigation.

Personnel Administration

The quality of any program is directly related to the personnel who are responsible for its success. One of the most effective methods of providing sport medicine services in a timely, competent, and professional manner is through the systematic development of a "sport medicine services team" made up of a variety of sport medicine professionals. The precise size and make-up of the team must be determined by the specific needs of each program, and the personnel resources available within the program and in the surrounding community. Therefore, there is no single "sport medicine services team" model which will work for every program. There are, however, some basic concepts which will apply to most, if not all sport medicine services programs.

Every sport medicine services team should have an administrative coordinator, a head athletic trainer, a program or team physician, and a small core group of other medical specialists. This group may be referred to as the Primary Team because they are the ones who will be primarily responsible for establishing program policies and making major decisions based on those policies.

Administrative Coordinator

The larger the sport medicine services program, the greater the need for an administrative coordinator. This person should have expertise in both sport medicine and program administration, and will be responsible for long-range administration and overall supervision of the program. Also, as the title implies, he/she will facilitate the coordination of the program's daily activities with other ancillary programs such as an institution's academic sport medicine program, student internship program, and community service programs. Furthermore, the administrative coordinator may also (with the assistance of the head athletic trainer) assume responsibility for such administrative tasks as budget preparation.

The intent here is not to usurp the authority of the head athletic trainer, but, rather, to relieve him/her of some administrative responsibilities which may be beyond the scope of his/her expertise, thus allowing him/her to devote more time to the daily operation of the sport medicine services program. The need for a specific administrative coordinator is most acute in those programs in which the head athletic trainer possesses little or no administrative expertise or experience. In some programs, the position of administrative coordinator may be assumed by the head athletic trainer (if he/she has administrative expertise), or the director of athletics (if he/she has sport medicine expertise). However, it is recommended that the duties of administrative coordinator be performed by a professional other than the head athletic trainer and director of athletics.

Head Athletic Trainer

The head athletic trainer is obviously the central figure in every sport medicine services program. He/she should be nationally certified (preferably NATA), and state certified/licensed where such certification/licensure is available. It is also recommended that the head trainer have substantial experience as an assistant athletic trainer prior to assuming the position of head trainer. The head trainer is responsible for the day-to-day functional operation of the sport medicine services program, including all injury management services, supervision and coordination of assistant athletic trainers, fiscal management, and record-keeping.

Program Physician

Every sport medicine services program should identify one physician with the designation of program physician (often referred to as the team physician).

This physician should be selected on the basis of his/her medical expertise, medical specialty (family practice physician, orthopedic surgeon, etc.), geographic proximity to the program, and, possibly most important, his/her interest in sport medicine. The program physician is often recruited from the ranks of institutional board members or alumni.

The specific responsibilities of a program physician will depend upon the specific needs and desires of the organization and program with which he/she works. However, a program physician should have the following responsibilities:

- Compile and maintain a medical history of each athlete in the program.
- Conduct preparticipation physical examinations.

- Attend all games or matches, and as many practices as feasible.

- Supervise and provide instruction to sport medicine services personnel.

- Be available to see injured athletes during regular office hours, and provide treatment or referral as deemed appropriate.

- Be "on call" for the emergency care of injured athletes at times other than during office hours.

- Make decisions relative to when and under what conditions injured athletes should return to participation.

- Work closely with the other members of the sport medicine team in establishing policy and coordinating services.

Unlike the administrative coordinator and head athletic trainer, the program physician is rarely an institutional employee. Therefore, it is important that his/her relationship with the program be carefully spelled out in a written contract. This document should specify the precise role and responsibilities of the program physician, along with the form and amount of compensation (if any) he/she will receive for his/her services. It is recommended that the contract be renewable on an annual basis.

Other Medical Specialists

In addition to the program physician, the Primary Team should also utilize the services of a small group of other medical specialists. This group may include a team dentist, team ophthalmologist, team podiatrist, etc. These specialists are identified as the primary care-givers for the program in their individual specialty areas, and may also function in this role under a written, annually-renewable contract (even though no compensation other than normal and customary fees may be involved). The size and precise make-up of this group is directly dependent upon the specific needs of each individual program.

Not all sport medicine services personnel are members of the Primary Team. This is not to imply that their roles and responsibilities are of less importance than those of the Primary Team members, but simply that they are not directly involved in policy-making decisions. This group may be referred to as the Extended Team, and will include assistant athletic trainers, graduate assistant athletic trainers, student athletic trainers, and a host of other sport medicine and/or exercise science professionals, possibly including an exercise physiologist, nutritionist, sport psychologist, gynecologist, etc. The assistant, graduate assistant, and student athletic trainers are primarily responsible for daily injury care services under the direction of the head athletic trainer, while the other professional specialists on the Extended Team provide specialized services as deemed appropriate and desirable by the head athletic trainer in consultation with the other members of the Primary Team.

The "team" method of personnel development is designed to maximize the coordination and effectiveness of the wide spectrum of services provided by the sport medicine services program. Although initial attempts to develop a comprehensive, functional team may be difficult and time-consuming, the ultimate results will be worth the effort.

Facility Management

A sport medicine services facility (athletic training room) is a highly specialized medical facility, and should be maintained with the injury care needs and safety of athletes in mind.

Facility Maintenance

An athletic training room is a medical facility, not unlike a physician's office or hospital emergency room. For this reason, regular maintenance must be a high priority to ensure that sanitation and safety standards are maintained at all times.

1. Floors in the service areas should be swept or vacuumed at the end of each work day. Athletes should not be allowed to wear cleated, outdoor shoes into the athletic training room. Even if this rule is observed, normal daily traffic flow will leave dirt on the floor, creating an unsanitary environment.

2. If not carpeted, floors in the service areas should be mopped at least twice weekly. While daily sweeping and/or vacuuming will control loose dust and dirt, regular mopping is necessary to keep the floors clean and sanitary.

3. The hydrotherapy area floor should be disinfected at least twice weekly. Moisture (especially when combined with warmth) offers a favorable environment for fungal and bacterial growth. Therefore, care must be taken to regularly disinfect wet areas.

4. Waste baskets and other trash containers should be emptied and disposed of throughout the work day as needed, and at the end of each work day. Waste materials are not only unsightly, they are often unsanitary.

5. Blood and other bodily fluids should be cleaned up and disposed of immediately according to universal precautions procedures. With the recent concern about blood-borne pathogens (e.g., HIV, HBV, etc.), universal precautions should be strictly followed.

6. Treatment tables, taping tables, and other frequent contact surfaces should be cleaned and disinfected at the end of each work day. Contact surfaces such as treatment and taping tables may serve as a medium for infectious pathogen transmission. Therefore, daily cleaning and disinfection of all such surfaces is mandatory for maintaining desirable sanitation standards and preventing the spread of disease.

7. Sinks and whirlpools should be cleaned and disinfected at the end of each work day. Sinks and whirlpool baths pose a potential threat of infectious disease transmission because of their frequent use by a wide variety of athletes and sport medicine services personnel. Failure to clean and disinfect them on a daily basis may promote fungal, bacterial, and/or viral growth, and enhance the probability of infectious transmission.

8. Other modalities, rehabilitation equipment, etc. should be cleaned and inspected weekly. Modalities, rehabilitation exercise equipment, and other frequently used equipment items must be kept clean and in good, safe working order. Weekly cleaning not only enhances the overall appearance of the facility, but protects the equipment from needless wear and tear. Also, such equipment should be inspected on a weekly basis to assure that it is safe for athlete use, or, if found to be unsafe, can be withdrawn from use until necessary repairs can be made.

9. Wet and/or soiled towels, elastic wraps, etc. should be disposed of (taken to the laundry room or collection site) throughout the work day as needed, and at the end of each work day. Once towels, elastic wraps, or other personal fabric items have been used, they should not be reused until they have been properly washed and dried. Wet and/or dirty towels are unpleasant and unsanitary, and should be freshly laundered between uses. Furthermore, wet towels should never be left in the training room overnight, and each work day should begin with an adequate supply of fresh, clean, dry towels.

10. All open containers (e.g., skin lubricant, ultrasound gel, alcohol, etc.) should be wiped clean and tightly capped, and all treatment items (e.g., tape scissors, modality electrodes, etc.) returned to their proper place at the end of each work day. Ointments, creams, gels, and liquids which are left open may lose their potency and/or become contaminated. Therefore, all jars, bottles, tubes, and other containers should be wiped clean and sealed at the end of each work day (preferably after each use) to retain the original effectiveness and minimize the possible contamination of their contents.

Facility maintenance is not a pleasant or enjoyable task. However, as stated earlier, the athletic training room is a medical facility, and should be maintained according to the same standards. Every member of the sport medicine services staff should take an active role in facility maintenance, with specific duties assigned and scheduled on an equitable basis.

Record Keeping

One of the most important, yet often neglected, administrative functions in any sport medicine services program is record keeping. The development and implementation of a comprehensive record keeping system 1) serves to enhance the effectiveness of organizational communication while, at the same time, 2) helping to minimize the ever-present threat of litigation resulting from the failure to adequately document the nature and extent of care provided to an injured athlete or other program participant.

As previously noted, the first purpose of establishing a comprehensive record keeping system is to maximize communication within the sport medicine services program so as to deliver optimal services to the athlete/patient. Organizational communication may be classified as "formal," the exchange of important information or ideas which require written documentation, and "informal," the exchange of less important information which usually takes place verbally and requires no written documentation. Most of the communication within a sport medicine services program is sufficiently important to be considered "formal" in nature. However, such communication is often treated some-what informally, resulting in needless miscommunication. In the event of a negligence claim against the program or one of its members, such miscommunication may become the basis for litigation. It is quite obvious that omissions in sport medicine record keeping are not likely to be viewed in a court of law as reasonable and prudent behavior. On the other hand, while record keeping in and of itself cannot shield one from litigation, carefully written documentation of services rendered can be a powerful weapon for refuting claims of negligent behavior. This is assuming, of course, that such documentation reflects a pattern of reasonable, prudent, and competent care.

The development and implementation of an effective record keeping system is a highly personalized process in that the finished product must accurately reflect the specific needs and functions of the program for which it has been designed. Likewise, the number and types of specific record keeping forms utilized will vary significantly from one organization to another. Although the specific nature of the record keeping system will depend upon the needs and functions of the program, there are a few basic recommendations which should be considered when attempting to maximize record keeping effectiveness.

1. When in doubt, put it in writing! Every member of the sport medicine services team should be instructed and expected to document every communication, recommendation, and procedure concerning his/her function as an agent of that program. Making written documentation a regular part of day-to-day staff duties will go a long way toward establishing record keeping as an integral and vital part of the sport medicine services delivery process, and will minimize the likelihood that inappropriate and/or inadequate care will be rendered as a result of poor communication. Furthermore, such practice will maximize the documentation needed to establish the precise nature of services provided in response to a lawsuit based on a claim of negligent behavior on the part of the program and/or employees thereof.

2. Cross-file records to provide duplicate documentation. One of the most important concepts in the record keeping process is that of maintaining records of important information in more than one location. For example, the basic information concerning an acute sport injury (i.e., name, date, type of injury, immediate care rendered, etc.) should be maintained in several locations including the athlete's personal medical file, a central file of all injury reports, and in a computer data file if the record keeping system is computerized. The purpose of this procedure is twofold. First, practicing cross-file duplication minimizes the danger of losing important data in the event that one of the file sources is misplaced, destroyed, or, in the case of computerized data, erased. Second, maintaining multiple file sources is one way of establishing an image of prudent and conscientious behavior on the part of the organization and its staff.

3. Utilize multicopy forms where appropriate. The use of carbonless, multicopy forms is one effective way of implementing the cross-file plan recommended in the preceding paragraph. When multiple copies of an important form are available, the task of creating multiple file sources is an easy one. Simply file one copy of the form in the athlete's file, another in the central file, and others in other appropriate locations. In this way, information recorded on one form may serve multiple purposes with a minimal amount of effort. A second important benefit of using multicopy forms is that of improved communication. When multiple copies of a form are available, one or more of these copies may be routed to appropriate members of the organization outside the sport medicine services program (e.g., administrators, coaches, etc.), providing them with written information about a specific injury situation. This eliminates many of the problems inherent with verbal communication.

4. Utilize interactive forms whenever possible. An interactive form is one which requests and/or requires two-way communication before the form is considered complete and ready for action and/or filing. Interactive forms are especially beneficial for establishing clear communication and precise documentation of information among various members of the sport medicine services team, and/or between members of the sport medicine services team and others (e.g., physician specialists, coaches, etc.) who are not members of the sport medicine services team. When an injured athlete is referred to a physician for evaluation and

treatment, a written reply from the attending physician is always preferable to a verbal reply since the physician's opinion may be the basis for such important decisions as when and if the athlete may return to activity, and/or how the injury should be cared for during the important time of recuperation and rehabilitation. Using a form which requires such written interaction enhances both the quantity and quality of communication among the sport medicine services program, the medical community, coaches, and administrators.

One of the most common forms found in any sport medicine services program is some type of injury report form. The injury report form is an excellent example of the type of form which may be best suited for the carbonless, multicopy, and interactive design. A carbonless four-copy injury report form maximizes communication between the sport medicine services program, the attending physician(s), and other appropriate agencies such as medical insurance providers.

5. Design and utilize forms which reflect the unique needs and functions of the program in which they will be used. It is not generally recommended that standard or stock forms be utilized. Although the use of such forms is more convenient than investing the time and effort required to design custom forms, stock forms often request information which is not needed while omitting other desired information.

Finally, the information presented in this section pertains exclusively to conventional, written records. In recent years, a variety of computer-based record keeping systems have been developed and marketed for use in sport medicine services programs. Computerized record keeping offers the distinct advantages of time and space economy. However, three factors should be considered before adopting a computer-based record keeping system. First, just as with stock forms, canned or stock computer programs rarely match the specific needs and functions of the programs which adopt them. Second, if a computerized system is to be established, it is recommended that a computer program be custom designed to meet the specific needs and functions of the sport medicine services program. Third, even if a computerized record keeping system is utilized, a hard copy (printed copy) of all important records should be maintained.

Chapter 15

Blood Borne Pathogens

Hepatitis B is the ninth leading cause of death worldwide.

T. Ross Bailey

Blood borne pathogens are disease-causing microorganisms that can potentially be transmitted through blood contact. The blood borne pathogens of concern include (but are not limited to) the Hepatitis B (HBV) and the human immunodeficiency virus (HIV). The frequency of infection from these microorganisms has increased during the last decade among all portions of the general population.

Facts about Hepatitis B

According to the Center for Disease Control, fourteen people die each day from Hepatitis B-related illnesses, such as cirrhosis and liver cancer (Center for Disease Control 1990). Three hundred thousand persons are infected yearly. New cases have increased approximately 50% in the last ten years. While many of those infected have no symptoms or mild flu-like illnesses, one third (1/3) will have severe hepatitis which will result in death for 1% of that group (*NCAA Sport Medicine Handbook* 1996–97). Currently in the United States there are over one million chronic carriers. Hepatitis B illnesses account for more than 10,000 hospital admissions yearly.

Types of Hepatitis

Hepatitis A: Fecal-oral route of transmission; enteric virus (able to live in the digestive system).

Hepatitis B: Transmitted through blood/body fluids; blood transfusions as well as through sexual contact.

Hepatitis C: Transmitted through blood/body fluids; transfusions. Known as non A or non B.

Hepatitis D: Transmitted through blood/body fluids; transfusions. Requires active Hepatitis B, either acute or chronic.

What Is Hepatitis B?

By basic definition, hepatitis is an inflammation of the liver. The liver cells are damaged and gradually replaced by scar tissue. It is usually accompanied by the following clinical symptoms:

Fever, jaundice, enlarged liver, fatigue, malaise, vomiting, anorexia, dark colored urine.

Incubation period is 15 to 50 days with the norm being 28 to 30 days (*Taber's Cyclopedic Medical Dictionary, 18th edition, Feb. 1997*). The disease is caused by a virus and some people can become carriers of the disease. In the 8% of the total population exposed, 25% will develop chronic active Hepatitis (Hadler and Margolis 1996). Teenagers and adults are the most susceptible to contracting the disease. Health care workers and others that handle soiled dressings, clothes, etc. are at the greatest risk.

The Hepatitis B virus has been detected up to seven days after the carrier's blood or body fluids have dried on a counter top or other surfaces (Seasholster 1992). The virus is inactivated quickly after being exposed to chemical cleaning agents such as *Omega (AirChem)* or household bleach (1:10 mixture). It takes approximately ten minutes of contact by isopropyl alcohol 70 percent to deactivate the virus.

A vaccine is available to health care workers, police, firefighters, emergency personnel, morticians, and others at risk to immunize against the virus. The American Pediatric Medical Association and the American College Health Association have recommended that newborn infants, children, and collegiate age young adults be immunized against the virus. If workers are exposed routinely to body fluids and/or blood, they are required to be immunized against the virus, sign a statement as to their wish not to be immunized, or show that they have the antibody present in their blood stream. OSHA recommends that the employer provide for the vaccination at no cost to the employee (OSHA Directive 1991). The records of the immunizations must be kept on file for 30 years. The vaccine is given in a three-day regimen. The second injection follows the first by one month, the third follows six months later.

The Center for Disease Control (CDC) reports that 12,000 cases occur among public safety and health care workers yearly and almost 300 die yearly after accidental exposure to the virus or its long-term effects. The risk for health care providers contracting the disease is 10 times that of the average employed person (CDC 1990). The American Liver Foundation reports that a carrier's risk of developing primary liver cancer is *300 times greater* than the risk of non-disease carriers (American Liver Foundation 1996).

How BIG Is the Problem?

Hepatitis B is the ninth leading cause of death worldwide. Approximately two million people die each year, primarily from Hepatitis B related cirrhosis and liver cancer. This disease affects an estimated five percent of the entire world population. More than 200 million people are chronic carriers of the Hepatitis B virus. The Hepatitis B virus is often linked to HIV, the virus that causes AIDS, but the Hepatitis B virus is far more widespread throughout the world and *300 times* more contagious. However, the routine mandatory testing of student athletes for either HBV or HIV for participation purposes is not recommended. Individuals who desire voluntary testing should be assisted in getting such services.

HIV-AIDS Issues

Stages of HIV Disease

Primary infected: Infected, but no antibodies are present for six weeks to three months. The detection tests are generally negative at this stage.

Chronic Asymptomatic: The test is positive, however, no symptoms are present.

Chronic Symptomatic: Repeated episodes of illness.

Advanced AIDS: Develop opportunistic infections. The T4 Cell count is below 200.

Facts about AIDS

- It is estimated that 5,000 people worldwide are infected daily (World Health Organization 1996).

- Seventy-five percent of all global HIV cases to date are estimated to have been spread through vaginal intercourse. This figure is approximately 6% in the USA.

- It is estimated that there are 1.5 million cases of HIV infection and this figure is growing daily.

- One in every 250 Americans is infected with the virus.

- One person dies every 10 minutes from the virus in the USA. (Total cases, as of March 13, 1992; 206,392 in the USA).

- It was estimated that by the end of 1993, AIDS would be the second leading cause of death in people aged 20–25 (Wiley 1992).

- More females will become infected in the future than will males.

- The incidence of infection among African Americans and Hispanics will continue to rise (Wiley 1992).

- The incidence of homosexual transmission will decrease, while the cases contracted from heterosexual contact will increase.

- Fewer cases from hemophiliacs and transfusion recipients will be reported.

- Specific guidelines and testing for athletes involved in contact and collision sport will be established.

NCAA Guidelines and Participation with HBV or HIV

HBV

The specific epidemiologic and biologic characteristics of HBV form the basis for the following recommendation:

> If a student athlete develops acute HBV illness, it is prudent to consider removal of the individual from combative, collision types of sport until loss of the infectivity is known. The best marker for infectivity is the HBV antigen which may persist up to 20 weeks in the acute stage. Student-athletes in such sport who develop chronic HBV infections should probably be removed from competition (*NCAA Sport Medicine Handbook* 1996–97).

HIV

In general, the decision to allow an HIV positive student-athlete to participate in athletics should be made on the basis of the individual's health status. If the student is asymptomatic and is without evidence of immunologic deficiencies, then the presence of the HIV infection does not mandate removal from play (Arnold 1995). The Team Physician must play an important role in helping the student-athlete make these decisions. The disease must be recognized as a chronic illness that may create a series of complex issues surrounding the advisability of continued exercise and athletic competition. There is no evidence that exercise and training of moderate intensity is harmful to the health of HIV infected individuals. No research data is available for looking at the effects of intense training and competition for the elite athlete with HIV.

There have been no validated reports of transmission of HIV in the athletics setting (*Journal of the American Medical Association* 1992).

The administrative issues are of great importance. The identification of individuals with a blood borne pathogen must remain confidential. Only those persons in whom the infected student chooses to confide have a right or need to know about this aspect of the student's medical history (*Journal of the American College of Health* 1991).

Universal Precautions

This system should be used for all patients, not just those infected with the Hepatitis B or HIV virus.

Barrier Protection

- *Gloves must be worn whenever:*
    - direct contact with blood or body fluids is expected to occur;
    - the health care provider is examining abraded, lacerated, burned, blistered or other non-intact skin conditions during *any invasive* procedures;
    - the health care worker has cuts, lesions, dermatitis, or chapped hands;
    - the health care worker is dealing directly with contaminated instruments.
- *No gloves* should ever be used or reused on more than one patient at a time.
- *Masks, protective eye wear, and gowns* should be used anytime there is a risk of splattering of contaminated fluids into the eyes, ears, nose, or mouth of the health care worker. The health care worker should always wash their hands as soon as possible if they become contaminated with body fluids. The use of gloves does not preclude any hand washing.
- All *disposable surgical instruments, needles, scalpels* and other sharp instruments should be disposed of in a proper *Sharps Container* (a closable, puncture proof, sealable properly labeled container to hold used needles and other sharp instruments that may be contaminated with blood or body fluids). Any soiled dressings, gauze pads, wound dressings, Band-Aids, bloody clothing, towels, etc. should be disposed of using a *Bio-Hazard Red Bag* (bio-hazard bags/cans require special disposal precautions and are not to be thrown away with normal household or business related trash). The physical plant facility should make arrangements with a company specializing in Bio-Hazard Bag disposal. Containers should be provided for any visiting teams or outside groups that may be using athletic facilities.

- Never handle dental appliances, mouth guards, or other saliva-contaminated items without gloves.

- Do not share eating or drinking utensils.

- Never share shaving utensils. Hair clippers should be sanitized between patients.

- All wounds on athletes should be properly covered.

In My Opinion

The health care provider in the athletic setting must be aware of the presence of the various hepatitis strains and their potential presence in society and thus in the athletic setting. Practicing good common sense and established preventative measures can protect not only the health care provider, but the other student athletes or patients as well. Immunization of all persons who have the potential for exposure is recommended. These would include the professional medical staff, the student athletic trainers and managers, as well as the laundry room personnel and janitorial staff. OSHA standards encourage employees to pay for the cost of immunizations for the above personnel.

On a football sideline, one person should be designated as the "blood person." This person stays gloved up during the course of the contest and has a waist pack that contains all of the necessary supplies for dealing with a bloody exposure. He/she should be able to treat the wound of the athlete as well as treating the uniform. Prior planning will not only increase the efficacy of the athletic training staff on the sideline, but help to protect the others who might be accidentally exposed.

Sharps containers are rarely if ever needed on a sideline, but biohazard containers are used everyday. They should be present at every practice and game setting. A plan should be established on how "soiled and bloody" towels are dealt with by the staff. Whenever possible, the use of scissors instead of needles to open blisters or boils should be encouraged in the athletic training room. This will lower the potential for accidental needle sticks to the staff athletic trainer, therapist, team physician, or student-athletic trainer. The use of bio-hazard containers, sharps containers, and continuing educational seminars to keep the various personnel up-to-date on new findings and information is a must if we are going to help eradicate this disease. This is not a problem that another school or facility down the road will have, this is a problem now and must be addressed by administrators, medical staffs, and other support personnel.

References

"AIDS Education on the collegiate campus." 1991. *Journal of the American College of Health* vol. 40, no. 2, pp. 51–100.

American Liver Foundation Publication. 1996. *Hepatitus B, Patient Information.*

Arnold, B.L. 1995 "A review of selected blood borne pathogen statements and federal regulations." *Journal of Athletic Training* vol. 30, no. 2, pp. 171–176.

Center for Disease Control. 1990. "Protection against Viral hepatitus." Recommendations of the Immunization Practices Advisory Committee (ACIP), MMWR 39 (RR-2), 1.

Hadler, S.C. and H.S. Margolis. 1996. Hepatitis B immunization: vaccine types, efficacy, and indications for immunization. In Remington and Swartz, *Current Topics in Infectious Diseases* vol. 12. Boston: Blackwell Scientific Publications.

Journal of the American Medical Association. 1992. Vol. 267, no. 10, pp. 1311–1314.

NCAA Sport Medicine Handbook 1996–97, pp. 24–28.

OSHA Directive, December 6, 1991.

Seasholster, Dr. Lynn. 1992. Presentation, Southwest Athletic Trainers Association, TX.

Taber's Medical Dictionary. 18th Edition, pp. 884, 885, 886.

Wiley, David C, Ph.D. 1992. Southwest Athletic Trainers Association presentation.

World Health Organization. Expanded Program on Immunization (EPI). http://www.who.org/programmes/gpv/gEnglish/epi/epihbv.htm.

Chapter 16

A Catastrophic Injury Plan

The most effective way to deal with an emergency catastrophic accident is to plan in advance.

Michael Clopton

The Importance of Planning

The most effective way to deal with an emergency or catastrophic accident is to plan in advance. Proper planning and training will reduce confusion and eliminate unnecessary errors when an emergency occurs. Although statistics tell us that some activities are more likely to result in catastrophic accidents, no institution, sport or individual is exempt from an emergency. Planning is critical for everyone. In the event of a catastrophic accident, whether it occurs in the training room, during practice, during an event or while traveling, the proper procedures should be followed.

If the accident occurs on campus, immediate contact with emergency personnel is critical. The senior most trainer or most qualified coach should attend to the injured person immediately and send the second person in charge for help. It is a good idea to have a mobile phone at all events where telephones are not readily available.

The individual who makes the call should contact 911 first. There is not enough time to notify other people. Be prepared to give the 911 operator an exact location of the accident and the best way to get directly to the injured person. This person should have keys to all of the gates in the area. Trying to find a maintenance person to unlock gates uses precious time (often these accidents occur after normal working hours). Another individual should be positioned in an area where he/she can be recognized by the emergency vehicle. This person should wave their arms or do whatever is necessary to be seen and then lead the emergency personnel directly to the accident site.

Protect the Site of Accident

Once the athlete has been transported, the site should be left as it was when the accident occurred. Photos and videos should be taken of the area. All relevant items should be tagged, secured and held in the legal counsel's office. If any item was removed from the scene, it should be recovered and the reason for removal noted. For example, if a spinal cord injury occurs during football practice, the helmet and shoulder pads should be retrieved from the emergency room and returned to the university. All television angles of the accident (if applicable) should be delivered to the university legal counsel immediately. All individuals who witnessed the accident should be contacted and provide a statement which is notarized and filed in the accident report. Keep all consent forms and agreement to participate forms with the accident report.

If the accident occurs during travel, videos, pictures, maintenance records of the vehicle, weather reports and police reports must be delivered to the legal counsel immediately. Once the injured person has been transported and the accident site secured, the following procedures should be followed:

Notification of Parents

The athletic director or coach, if the athletic director is not present, should call the athlete's parents to inform them of the situation and arrange transportation to the hospital. Since accidents can occur while away from campus, the trainers should have accurate home and work phone numbers of the athlete's parents in their briefcase at all times. If the athlete's parents do not live together, phone numbers should be accurate for each of them. The proper time to gather this information is the first day the athlete arrives on campus and to update it when a change occurs.

It is critical that parents are notified by athletic department staff first. Word travels rapidly in today's media communications and parents should not be made aware of their son or daughter's injury by watching television news or a call from local media members.

The National Collegiate Athletic Association (NCAA) and many other governing organizations allow the institution to pay parents' expenses to travel to the attending hospital. Athletic department staff members should be aware of the phone numbers to call to arrange all travel needs for the family.

Under no circumstance should athletic department employees assume any responsibility or cast any blame for the injury. That information can come later and does not benefit anyone. The call should simply be placed to notify the family of the injury and arrange travel plans.

Notification of Administration

If the athletic director is not present, he/she must be notified after the parents are notified.

The athletic director should notify the president of the university and chief legal counsel of the accident. Just as the parents deserve immediate notification, the administration must be aware of situations that have such a huge impact on the institution. Anyone who has experienced a catastrophic accident knows that it is devastating to the university community.

Notification of Insurance Carrier

If the injured athlete has insurance, the carrier should be notified. Again, the athletic trainer should have already compiled this information and have it at all times.

NCAA member institutions must contact the NCAA Catastrophic Insurance Program at (800) 233-6222. The insurance company will work with the family, institution and medical personnel to ensure that every aspect of the treatment is handled properly.

The NCAA Insurance Company must be notified whether the family has insurance or not.

If the institution is not a member of the NCAA, the appropriate insurance company must be notified immediately. It is important to have a 24-hour emergency phone number to contact the appropriate company.

Whether the injured athlete's family has insurance or not, the institution's catastrophic insurance carrier should be notified. Most companies will assign a case manager to ensure that every aspect of the treatment is handled properly.

Designate a Spokesperson

In a catastrophic accident, there is intense media attention at the local and national level. The university should designate one spokesperson. It is advisable for the spokesperson to be a member of the university president's staff. The role of this individual is to:

1.   Inform the media of the accident. The first press conference should include a brief explanation of how the accident occurred and up-to-date medical information. At no time should the spokesperson assume or assign responsibility for the injury. Concern for the injured person and family should be of primary interest to the spokesperson.

     Daily briefings should occur until the media's interest is reduced. By nature, many members of the media are curious and become suspicious when they feel that information is withheld. Briefings should include written releases and faxes to all interested media outlets.

2.   After the initial press conference, the spokesperson should avoid specifics concerning medical information. Only with parental consent should medical information be provided to the media. The attending physician should be the only person to provide specifics about the injury or prognosis and not until the parents or guardians approve.

3.   The spokesperson should not conduct one-on-one or private interviews with individual members of the media. No one is entitled to a scoop.

It is critical for the spokesperson to be the only person to address the media concerning the specifics of the accident. Administrators, coaches, trainers and athletes should comment only about their concern for the injured athlete and the family.

Statements like: "I knew that move was dangerous. I can't believe he/she tried it;" "I never felt safe in the university van;" or similar statements can prove damaging in court.

Communications with Student Athletes/Coaches

Teammates and coaches of the injured athlete should meet as a group and discuss the accident and anything else related to the injured person. People deal with tragedies differently. The individual's need must be met. Counseling may be necessary and must be provided for those who request it. If the accident resulted in a fatality, long term counseling may be necessary.

Team members should be notified that all official comments must be made by the spokesperson. Athletes and coaches should be encouraged to address the media about their concern for the athlete and their family members. Analyzing the cause of the situation or specifics should be discouraged.

Relations with Immediate Family Members

Before the injured person was a member of the institution, he/she was part of a family. The families should receive up-to-date information as soon as it is available. They should be treated with great respect and concern.

Institutional personnel should be at the hospital on a daily basis.

These procedures were implemented at the University of Oklahoma in 1993. It is important to note that each institution should develop their own program. There are numerous details that can be adjusted to suit the particular needs of an institution.

Fortunately, the University of Oklahoma has not had an occasion to use these procedures, but are confident they would be successful if needed.

In My Opinion

Procedures for dealing with catastrophic accidents must be developed and included in the institution's handbook and followed if the occasion arises. These risk management procedures are often seen as unnecessary since the chance of a catastrophic accident is so small. Administrators are so busy with daily operations that there is not enough time to prepare for things that, statistically, have little chance of happening. This position is understandable but irresponsible. We have a duty to the athletes to ensure that they have every opportunity to be successful and safe.

Preparation is the key to being successful in many situations and always the case in risk management areas. For example, what would happen if an athlete had a severe spinal cord injury in an athletic contest and the trainer did not have the parents' home phone number. There is a good chance that the family would be notified by a media outlet. Parents deserve better and our duty to the athlete extends to the parents. Take time to prepare.

A worthwhile exercise would be to contact institutions who have faced catastrophic accidents in the past 10 years and see how they handled their tragic accidents. The ones who were prepared and extended support to the families will be the ones who experienced less confusion and financial loss.

Chapter 17

The Preparticipation Physical Examination

The decision to declare an athlete medically ineligible for sport participation is extremely complex.

Martin E. Block

Can Athletes Be Excluded from Sport If They Fail Their Physical Examination?

Tim Parse is the leading scorer for the Colby-Sawyer (New Hampshire) soccer team. He is the leading scorer despite being born with Klippel-Feil syndrome, a fusion of the cervical vertebrae in his neck. He suffers back pain, has only partial hearing in his left ear, is legally blind in his left eye, and has asthma (Tkach and Timanus 1996), yet he was allowed to play soccer. On the other hand, Alani Pahulu, a college football player at the University of Kansas, was declared medically ineligible by the team physician to play football when it was discovered that he had a congenitally narrow cervical canal. The team physician felt that Alani's condition significantly increased his risk for severe injury in a collision sport like football. Interestingly, three other specialists said that Alani could participate in football with no more risk of injury than any other player (*Pahulu* 1995). Still, Alani was not allowed to play football at Kansas. Why should Tim be allowed to play with a cervical problem but not Alani?

A preparticipation medical evaluation should be required upon a student-athlete's entrance into the institution's intercollegiate athletics program (see NCAA Bylaw 17.1.5). This initial evaluation should include a comprehensive health history, immunization history as defined by current Centers for Disease Control and Prevention (CDC) guidelines, and a relevant physical exam, with strong emphasis on the cardiovascular, neurologic, and musculoskeletal evaluation. After the initial medical evaluation, an updated history should be performed annually. Further preparticipation physical examinations are not believed to be necessary unless warranted by the updated history or the student-athlete's medical condition. The American Heart Association has modified its 1996 recommendation for a cardiovascular screening every two years for collegiate athletes. The revision recommends cardiovascular screening as a part of the physical exam required upon a student-athlete's entrance into the intercollegiate athletics program. In subsequent years, an interim history and blood pressure measurement should be made. Important changes in medical status or abnormalities may require more formal cardiovascular evaluation (NCAA 2009).

Results also showed that approximately 13% of student-athletes examined required follow-up but did not preclude athletic participation (cleared with follow up or CFU). Approximately 2% of student-athletes examined had abnormalities that precluded athletic participation until further evaluation and treatment were administered (not cleared or NC). Musculoskeletal abnormalities accounted for over 40% of those student-athletes receiving NC and over 25% of those receiving CFU. Most of the NC and CFU student-athletes had a previous musculoskeletal injury which was considered a major risk factor for re-injury. The authors noted the difficulty in determining the threshold for risk or for CFU for student-athlete with abnormalities such as inflexibility, asymmetric strength, and abnormal mechanics.

Physical examinations as a prerequisite for participating in interscholastic sport programs are as common a fall ritual as assigning lockers and back-to-school nights. While the quality of the examination is sometimes questionable (particularly in high schools where in some cases all that is required is a urine sample and a quick listen of the athlete's heart), one probably cannot find a middle school, high school, or college program in the United States that does not require some type of physical examination (Kibler 1990).

Yet, what if a prospective student-athlete fails a physical examination? In most school districts and intercollegiate programs, failing the physical examination simply means the student-athlete is declared medically ineligible and cannot participate in interscholastic sport. Case closed, end of story—or is it? What if the athlete claims that the medical problem is a disability? Is it legal to exclude a student-athlete with disabilities from participating in sport solely on the basis of a failed physical examination, or would it be considered discriminatory?

Many athletes have had very successful interscholastic, intercollegiate, and even professional sport careers despite having significant health problems or disabilities. For example, Terry Cummings plays professional basketball with a heart condition that is controlled by medication (Eskenazi 1990). At the 1984 Olympics in Los Angeles, 67 of the 597 members of the U.S. Olympic team were diagnosed with exercise-induced asthma. Of the 174 medals earned by U.S. athletes in those games, 41 were won by athletes with asthma, including four by swimmer Nancy Hogshead (Bingham 1990). Gail Devers won a gold medal in the 100 meter dash in the 1992 Summer Olympics even though she has Graves disease (Lee 1992).

Certainly there are tragic stories of young, seemingly healthy athletes who have died while participating in sport (Pai 1996). Who could forget video footage of Hank Gathers suffering a fatal heart attack while playing collegiate basketball (Bonkowski 1996; Smith 1991)? Olympic volleyball player Flo Hyman, basketball star Pete Maravich, and professional football player Chuck Hughes all died from sudden cardiac death while playing sport (Fay and Torg 1990). Certainly there are medical conditions that increase an athlete's risk of injury or even death, but isn't it the athlete's decision (along with his parents and personal physician) whether or not to take that risk?

The purpose of this chapter is to review the issue of physical examinations and medical ineligibility as it relates to participation in sport. First, there will be a review of guidelines established by the National Collegiate Athletic Association (NCAA) and state high school leagues regarding physical examinations. This will be followed by a review of recommendations established by physician organizations regarding when to exclude an athlete due to medical conditions. Finally, there will be a review of Section 504 of the Rehabilitation Act as it relates to physical examinations and participation in scholastic sport.

Athletic Association Guidelines: College and University

The National Collegiate Athletic Association (NCAA), the major governing body for intercollegiate athletics in the United States, recently published its annual Sport Medicine Handbook, which contains the organization's recommendations on sport medicine issues (Benson 1996). NCAA members do not have to follow these recommendations, nor are members subject to disciplinary action for non-compliance. Rather, each NCAA member institution establishes minimum health/fitness qualifications for athletes in a particular sport.

The handbook does recommend a preparticipation medical examination to "determine whether the student-athlete is prepared to engage in a particular sport" (Benson 1996). The handbook suggests that the exam include a comprehensive health history, immunization history, and physical examination including an orthopedic evaluation (Benson 1996). Furthermore, the handbook clearly recognizes the right of athletes with disabilities to participation in intercollegiate sport if the athlete qualifies for the team without lowering the team standards and if the athlete does not impose risk on others. The handbook recommends joint approval from the physician most familiar with an athlete's disability, the team physician, an appropriate school official, and parental consent (if the athlete is a minor) before permitting an impaired athlete to participate in athletics. The handbook suggests that impaired athletes should be medically disqualified from participating only if the impairment presents "unusual risk of further impairment or disability to the individual and/or to other participants."

High School

The National Federation of State High School Associations (NFHS)'s acting recommendations for the NVHS Sports Medicine Advisory Committee, has stated that pre-participation physical evaluations for high school student-athletes are a necessary and desirable precondition to interscholastic athletic practice and competition.

The majority of state high school athletic associations require some type of preparticipation physical examination (Feinstein, Soileau, and Daniel 1988). The quality of this examination and subsequent approval for participation depends on the sport medicine knowledge of the examining physician (Feinstein, Soileau, and Daniel 1988). However, very few state athletic associations provide specific guidelines for conducting a preparticipation examination or for excluding an athlete from participation for medical reasons (American Academy of Family Physicians 1992; Feinstein, Soileau and Daniel 1988). What most state associations do require is the medical clearance by at least one physician before allowing an athlete to participate in a school-sponsored athletic program. For example, a New York statute permits an athlete with a disability to participate in school-sponsored athletic programs if the athlete obtains affidavits from two licensed physicians certifying that he/she is capable of participating safely in the particular sport (Mitten 1992; see Table 1 for list of state requirements).

In summary, the NCAA and the vast majority of high school athletic associations require a preparticipation physical examination, and the NCAA and most high school athletic associations provide general guidelines for these examinations. However, neither the NCAA nor the vast majority of state athletic associations have established rules or recommendations regarding the exclusion of athletes with disabilities from participation in competitive sport (Mitten and Maron 1994). Apparently, most athletic teams rely on the team physician's recommendations regarding medical clearance of prospective athletes.

Table 1. State Requirements for Preseason Exams

State	Required Frequency of Exam	Official State Form	Medical History	Exam Guidelines	Recommendations for Exclusion from Sports
Alabama	Yearly	Yes	No	Yes	No
Alaska	Yearly	Yes	Yes	Yes	No
California	Not specified	No	—	—	—
Colorado	Yearly	Yes	No	No	No
Connecticut	Yearly	Yes	Yes	Yes	No
D.C.	Yearly	Yes	Yes	Yes	Yes
Florida	Yearly	Yes	Yes	Yes	No
Georgia	Yearly	Yes	Yes	Yes	Yes
Hawaii	Yearly	Yes	Yes	Yes	No
Idaho	Yearly	Yes	Yes	Yes	No
Illinois	Yearly	Yes	No	Yes	No
Indiana	Yearly	Yes	Yes	Yes	Yes
Iowa	Yearly	Yes	Yes	Yes	No
Kansas	Yearly	Yes	No	Yes	No
Kentucky	Yearly	Yes	No	No	No
Maine	Not specified	No	—	—	—
Maryland	Yearly	Yes	Yes	Yes	No
Massachusetts	Yearly	Yes	Yes	Yes	No
Michigan	Yearly	Yes	No	Yes	No
Minnesota	Every 3 years	Yes	Yes	No	No
Mississippi	Yearly	No	—	—	—
Missouri	Yearly	Yes	No	Yes	No
Montana	Yearly	No	—	—	—
Nebraska	Yearly	Yes	No	Yes	No
Nevada	Every 3 years	Yes	Yes	No	No
New Hampshire	Once	No	—	—	—
New Jersey	Yearly	No	—	—	—
New Mexico	Yearly	No	—	—	—
New York	Yearly	Yes	Yes	Yes	Yes
North Carolina	Yearly	Yes	Yes	Yes	No
North Dakota	Yearly	Yes	Yes	Yes	No
Ohio	Yearly	Yes	Yes	No	No
Oklahoma	Not specified	Yes	Yes	Yes	No
Oregon	Not specified	No	—	—	—
Pennsylvania	Yearly	Yes	No	No	No
Rhode Island	Not specified	No	—	—	—
South Carolina	Yearly	Yes	Yes	Yes	No
South Dakota	Yearly	Yes	Yes	Yes	No
Tennessee	Yearly	Yes	No	No	No
Texas	Every 3 years	Yes	Yes	Yes	No
Utah	Yearly	Yes	Yes	Yes	No
Virginia	Yearly	Yes	Yes	Yes	No
Washington	Yearly	Yes	Yes	Yes	No
West Virginia	Yearly	Yes	Yes	Yes	No
Wisconsin	Yearly	Yes	No	No	No
Wyoming	Not specified	Yes	Yes	Yes	No

Note: Arizona, Arkansas, Delaware, Louisiana, and Vermont did not provide any information. A dash (—) indicates that information was not provided.
From: Feinstein, R.A., E.J. Soileau, and W.A. Daniel. 1988. "A national survey of preparticipation physical examination requirements." *The Physician and Sportsmedicine* vol. 16, no. 5, pp. 51–58.

Table 2a. Classification of Sports According to Contact

Contact	Limited-Contact	Noncontact
Basketball	Adventure racing	Badminton
Boxing	Baseball	Body building
Cheerleading	Bicycling	Bowling
Diving	Canoeing or kayaking	Canoeing or kayaking
Extreme sports	(white water)	(flat water)
Field hockey	Fencing	Crew or rowing
Football, tackle	Field events	Curling
Gymnastics	High jump	Dance
Ice hockey	Pole vault	Field events
Lacrosse	Floor hockey	Discus
Martial arts	Football, flag or touch	Javelin
Rodeo	Handball	Shot-put
Rugby	Horseback riding	Golf
Skiing, downhill	Martial arts	Orienteering
Ski jumping	Racquetball	Power lifting
Snowboarding	Skating	Race walking
Soccer	(Ice)	Riflery
Team handball	(Inline)	Rope jumping
Ultimate Frisbee	(Roller)	Running
Water polo	Skiing	Sailing
Wrestling	Cross-country	Scuba diving
Skateboarding	Water	Swimming
Softball	Table tennis	
Squash	Tennis	
Volleyball	Track	
Weight lifting		
Windsurfing or surfing		

Adventure racing has been added since the previous statement was published and is defined as a combination of 2 or more disciplines, including orienteering and navigation, cross-country running, mountain biking, paddling, and climbing and rope skills. The American Academy of Pediatrics opposes participation in boxing for children, adolescents, and young adults.

The American Academy of Pediatrics recommends limiting bodybuilding and power lifting until the adolescent achieves sexual maturity rating 5 (Tanner stage V).

Extreme sports have been added since the previous statement was published.

The American Academy of Pediatrics recommends limiting the amount of body checking allowed for hockey players 15 years and younger, to reduce injuries.

Martial arts can be sub-classified as judo, jujitsu, karate, kung fu, and tae kwon do; some forms are contact sports and others are limited-contact sports.

Orienteering is a race (contest) in which competitors use a map and a compass to find their way through unfamiliar territory.

From: Rice, S.G. (2008). Medical conditions affecting sport participation. *Pediatrics, 121*, 841–848.

Medical Associations

American Academy of Pediatrics

The American Academy of Pediatrics Committee on Sports Medicine revised their recommendations for participation in competitive sports (Bernhardt & Roberts, 2010; Rice, 2008) These guidelines provided two types of information: (1) classification of sport into contact and non-contact sport, and (2) recommendations for participation according to medical disability within each sport classification (see Tables 2a and 2b). The Committee noted that these recommendations "do not indicate an exclusive course of treatment or procedures to be followed" and that "variations taking into account individual circumstances may be appropriate" (AAP 1988). The Committee suggested that the physician's clinical analysis be used when making a final decision regarding a particular athlete. Furthermore, the Committee suggested that the physician, the athlete, and the athlete's parents jointly discuss the medical condition and make an informed decision whether or not participation in a particular sport is "worth the risk" (AAP 1988; Mitten 1992).

American Academy of Family Physicians

In 2010, the American Academy of Family Physicians, along with the American Academy of Pediatrics, the American College of Sports Medicine, the American Medical Society for Sports Medicine, the American Orthopaedic Society for Sports Medicine, and the American Osteopathic Academy of Sports Medicine have created an updated Preparticipation Physical Evaluation (PPE), for use by physicians and other healthcare professionals in evaluating the physical condition of student-athletes (Bernhardt & Roberts, 2010). The new PPE is designed to be the conclusive guide for pediatric, family, and team physicians when examining athletes before training or competition. PPE provided detailed information covering issues that could place athletes at risk during practice or competition, such as heart and lung problems, head injuries, heat exhaustion, hydration, overuse, overscheduling, and cultural issues. In addition, screening and education can possibly detect and prevent complications related to conditions such as diabetes and sickle cell disease.

Table 2b. Medical Conditions and Sports Participation

CONDITION	ALLOW PARTICIPATION?

Atlantoaxial instability (instability of joint between cervical vertebrae 1 and 2)—**Qualified Yes**
Explanation: Athlete (particularly if he or she has Down syndrome or juvenile rheumatoid arthritis with cervical involvement) needs evaluation to assess the risk of spinal cord injury during sports participation, especially when using a trampoline.
Bleeding disorder—**Qualified Yes**
Explanation: Athlete needs evaluation.
Cardiovascular disease
Carditis (inflammation of the heart)—**No**
Explanation: Carditis may result in sudden death with exertion.
Hypertension (high blood pressure)—**Qualified Yes**
Explanation: Those with hypertension_5 mmHg above the 99th percentile for age, gender, and height should avoid heavy weightlifting and power lifting, bodybuilding, and high-static component sports (Fig 1). Those with sustained hypertension (_95th percentile for age, gender, and height) need evaluation. The National High Blood Pressure Education Program Working Group report defined prehypertension and stage 1 and stage 2 hypertension in children and adolescents younger than 18 years of age.
Congenital heart disease (structural heart defects present at birth)—**Qualified Yes**
Explanation: Consultation with a cardiologist is recommended. Those who have mild forms may participate fully in most cases; those who have moderate or severe forms or who have undergone surgery need evaluation. The 36th Bethesda Conference defined mild, moderate, and severe disease for common cardiac lesions.
Dysrhythmia (irregular heart rhythm)—**Qualified Yes**
Long-QT syndrome
Malignant ventricular arrhythmias
Symptomatic Wolff-Parkinson-White syndrome
Advanced heart block
Family history of sudden death or previous sudden cardiac event

Implantation of a cardioverter-defibrillator

Explanation: Consultation with a cardiologist is advised. Those with symptoms (chest pain, syncope, near-syncope, dizziness, shortness of breath, or other symptoms of possible dysrhythmia) or evidence of mitral regurgitation on physical examination need evaluation. All others may participate fully.

Heart murmur—**Qualified Yes**

Explanation: If the murmur is innocent (does not indicate heart disease), full participation is permitted. Otherwise, athlete needs evaluation (see structural heart disease, especially hypertrophic cardiomyopathy and mitral valve prolapse).

Structural/acquired heart disease

Hypertrophic cardiomyopathy **Qualified No**

Coronary artery anomalies **Qualified No**

Arrhythmogenic right ventricular cardiomyopathy **Qualified No**

Acute rheumatic fever with carditis **Qualified No**

Ehlers-Danlos syndrome, vascular form **Qualified No**

Marfan syndrome **Qualified Yes**

Mitral valve prolapse **Qualified Yes**

Anthracycline use **Qualified Yes**

Explanation: Consultation with a cardiologist is recommended. The 36th Bethesda Conference provided detailed recommendations.

Most of these conditions carry a significant risk of sudden cardiac death associated with intense physical exercise. Hypertrophic cardiomyopathy requires thorough and repeated evaluations, because disease may change manifestations during later adolescence

Marfan syndrome with an aortic aneurysm also can cause sudden death during intense physical exercise. An athlete who has ever received chemotherapy with anthracyclines may be at increased risk of cardiac problems because of the cardiotoxic effects of the medications, and resistance training in this population should be approached with caution; strength training that avoids isometric contractions may be permitted. Athlete needs evaluation.

Vasculitis/vascular disease—**Qualified Yes**

Kawasaki disease (coronary artery vasculitis)

Pulmonary hypertension

Explanation: Consultation with a cardiologist is recommended. Athlete needs individual evaluation to assess risk on the basis of disease activity, pathologic changes, and medical regimen.

Cerebral palsy—**Qualified Yes**

Explanation: Athlete needs evaluation to assess functional capacity to perform sports-specific activity.

Diabetes mellitus—**Yes**

Explanation: All sports can be played with proper attention and appropriate adjustments to diet (particularly carbohydrate intake), blood glucose concentrations, hydration, and insulin therapy. Blood glucose concentrations should be monitored before exercise, every 30 min. during continuous exercise, 15 min. after completion of exercise, and at bedtime.

Diarrhea, infectious—**Qualified No**

Explanation: Unless symptoms are mild and athlete is fully hydrated, no participation is permitted, because diarrhea may increase risk of dehydration and heat illness (see fever).

Eating disorders—**Qualified Yes**

Explanation: Athlete with an eating disorder needs medical and psychiatric assessment before participation.

Eyes—**Qualified Yes**

Functionally 1-eyed athlete

Loss of an eye

Detached retina or family history of retinal detachment at young age

High myopia

Connective tissue disorder, such as Marfan or Stickler syndrome

Previous intraocular eye surgery or serious eye injury

Explanation: A functionally 1-eyed athlete is defined as having best-corrected visual acuity worse than 20/40 in the poorer-seeing eye. Such an athlete would suffer significant disability if the better eye were seriously injured, as would an athlete with loss of an eye. Specifically, boxing and full-contact martial arts are not recommended for functionally 1-eyed athletes, because eye protection is impractical and/or not permitted. Some athletes who previously underwent intraocular eye surgery or had a serious eye injury may have increased risk of injury because of weakened eye tissue. Availability of eye guards approved by the American Society for Testing and Materials and other protective equipment may allow participation in most sports, but this must be judged on an individual basis.

Conjunctivitis, infectious—**Qualified No**
Explanation: Athlete with active infectious conjunctivitis should be excluded from swimming.

Fever—**No**
Explanation: Elevated core temperature may be indicative of a pathologic medical condition (infection or disease) that is often manifest by increased resting metabolism and heart rate. Accordingly, during athlete's usual exercise regimen, the presence of fever can result in greater heat storage, decreased heat tolerance, increased risk of heat illness, increased cardiopulmonary effort, reduced maximal exercise capacity, and increased risk of hypotension because of altered vascular tone and dehydration. On rare occasions, fever may accompany myocarditis or other conditions that may make usual exercise dangerous.

Gastrointestinal—**Qualified Yes**
Malabsorption syndromes (celiac disease or cystic fibrosis)
Explanation: Athlete needs individual assessment for general malnutrition or specific deficits resulting in coagulation or other defects; with appropriate treatment, these deficits can be treated adequately to permit normal activities.

Short-bowel syndrome or other disorders requiring specialized nutritional support, including parenteral or enteral nutrition
Explanation: Athlete needs individual assessment for collision, contact, or limited-contact sports. Presence of central or peripheral, indwelling, venous catheter may require special considerations for activities and emergency preparedness for unexpected trauma to the device(s).

Heat illness, history of—**Qualified Yes**
Explanation: Because of the likelihood of recurrence, athlete needs individual assessment to determine the presence of predisposing conditions and behaviors and to develop a prevention strategy that includes sufficient acclimatization (to the environment and to exercise intensity and duration), conditioning, hydration, and salt intake, as well as other effective measures to improve heat tolerance and to reduce heat injury risk (such as protective equipment and uniform configurations).

Hepatitis, infectious (primarily hepatitis C)—**Yes**
Explanation: All athletes should receive hepatitis B vaccination before participation. Because of the apparent minimal risk to others, all sports may be played as athlete's state of health allows. For all athletes, skin lesions should be covered properly, and athletic personnel should use universal precautions when handling blood or body fluids with visible blood.

HIV infection—**Yes**
Explanation: Because of the apparent minimal risk to others, all sports may be played as athlete's state of health allows (especially if viral load is undetectable or very low). For all athletes, skin lesions should be covered properly, and athletic personnel should use universal precautions when handling blood or body fluids with visible blood. However, certain sports (such as wrestling and boxing) may create a situation that favors viral transmission (likely bleeding plus skin breaks). If viral load is detectable, then athletes should be advised to avoid such high contact sports.

Kidney, absence of one—**Qualified Yes**
Explanation: Athlete needs individual assessment for contact, collision, and limited-contact sports. Protective equipment may reduce risk of injury to the remaining kidney sufficiently to allow participation in most sports, providing such equipment remains in place during activity

Liver, enlarged—**Qualified Yes**
Explanation: If the liver is acutely enlarged, then participation should be avoided because of risk of rupture. If the liver is chronically enlarged, then individual assessment is needed before collision, contact, or limited-contact sports are played. Patients with chronic liver disease may have changes in liver function that affect stamina, mental status, coagulation, or nutritional status.

Malignant neoplasm—**Qualified Yes**

Explanation: Athlete needs individual assessment.

Musculoskeletal disorders—**Qualified Yes**

Explanation: Athlete needs individual assessment.

Neurologic disorders

History of serious head or spine trauma or abnormality, including craniotomy, epidural bleeding, subdural hematoma, intracerebral hemorrhage, second-impact syndrome, vascular malformation, and neck fracture—**Qualified Yes**

Explanation: Athlete needs individual assessment for collision, contact, or limited-contact sports.

History of simple concussion (mild traumatic brain injury), multiple simple concussions, and/or complex concussion—**Qualified Yes**

Explanation: Athlete needs individual assessment. Research supports a conservative approach to concussion management, including no athletic participation while symptomatic or when deficits in judgment or cognition are detected, followed by graduated return to full activity.

Myopathies **Qualified Yes**

Explanation: Athlete needs individual assessment.

Recurrent headaches—**Yes**

Explanation: Athlete needs individual assessment.

Recurrent plexopathy (burner or stinger) and cervical cord neuropraxia with persistent defects **Qualified Yes**

Explanation: Athlete needs individual assessment for collision, contact, or limited-contact sports; regaining normal strength is important benchmark for return to play.

Seizure disorder, well controlled—**Yes**

Explanation: Risk of seizure during participation is minimal.

Seizure disorder, poorly controlled—**Qualified Yes**

Explanation: Athlete needs individual assessment for collision, contact, or limited-contact sports. The following noncontact sports should be avoided: archery, riflery, swimming, weightlifting, power lifting, strength training, and sports involving heights. In these sports, occurrence of a seizure during activity may pose a risk to self or others.

Obesity—**Yes**

Explanation: Because of the increased risk of heat illness and cardiovascular strain, obese athletes particularly needs careful acclimatization (to the environment and to exercise intensity and duration), sufficient hydration, and potential activity and recovery modifications during competition and training.

Organ transplant recipient (and those taking immunosuppressive medications)—**Qualified Yes**

Explanation: Athlete needs individual assessment for contact, collision, and limited-contact sports. In addition to potential risk of infections, some medications (eg, prednisone) may increase tendency for bruising.

Ovary, absence of one—**Yes**

Explanation: Risk of severe injury to remaining ovary is minimal.

Pregnancy/postpartum—**Qualified Yes**

Explanation: Athlete needs individual assessment. As pregnancy progresses, modifications to usual exercise routines will become necessary. Activities with high risk of falling or abdominal trauma should be avoided. Scuba diving and activities posing risk of altitude sickness should also be avoided during pregnancy. After the birth, physiological and morphologic changes of pregnancy take 4 to 6 weeks to return to baseline.

Respiratory conditions

Pulmonary compromise, including cystic fibrosis—**Qualified Yes**

Explanation: Athlete needs individual assessment but, generally, all sports may be played if oxygenation remains satisfactory during graded exercise test. Athletes with cystic fibrosis need acclimatization and good hydration to reduce risk of heat illness.

Asthma—**Yes**

Explanation: With proper medication and education, only athletes with severe asthma need to modify their participation. For those using inhalers, recommend having a written action plan and using a peak flowmeter daily. Athletes with asthma may encounter risks when scuba diving.

Acute upper respiratory infection—**Qualified Yes**

Explanation: Upper respiratory obstruction may affect pulmonary function. Athlete needs individual assessment for all except mild disease (see fever).

Rheumatologic diseases—**Qualified Yes**

Juvenile rheumatoid arthritis

Explanation: Athletes with systemic or polyarticular juvenile rheumatoid arthritis and history of cervical spine involvement need radiographs of vertebrae C1 and C2 to assess risk of spinal cord injury. Athletes with systemic or HLA-B27-associated arthritis require cardiovascular assessment for possible cardiac complications during exercise. For those with micrognathia (open bite and exposed teeth), mouth guards are helpful. If uveitis is present, risk of eye damage from trauma is increased; ophthalmologic assessment is recommended. If visually impaired, guidelines for functionally 1-eyed athletes should be followed.

Juvenile dermatomyositis,

idiopathic myositis,

Systemic lupus erythematosis,

Raynaud phenomenon

Explanation: Athlete with juvenile dermatomyositis or systemic lupus erythematosis with cardiac involvement requires cardiology assessment before participation. Athletes receiving systemic corticosteroid therapy are at higher risk of osteoporotic fractures and avascular necrosis, which should be assessed before clearance; those receiving immunosuppressive medications are at higher risk of serious infection. Sports activities should be avoided when myositis is active. Rhabdomyolysis during intensive exercise may cause renal injury in athletes with idiopathic myositis and other myopathies. Because of photosensitivity with juvenile dermatomyositis and systemic lupus erythematosis, sun protection is necessary during outdoor activities. With Raynaud phenomenon, exposure to the cold presents risk to hands and feet.

Sickle cell disease—**Qualified Yes**

Explanation: Athlete needs individual assessment. In general, if illness status permits, all sports may be played; however, any sport or activity that entails overexertion, overheating, dehydration, or chilling should be avoided. Participation at high altitude, especially when not acclimatized, also poses risk of sickle cell crisis.

Sickle cell trait—**Yes**

Explanation: Athletes with sickle cell trait generally do not have increased risk of sudden death or other medical problems during athletic participation under normal environmental conditions. However, when high exertional activity is performed under extreme conditions of heat and humidity or increased altitude, such catastrophic complications have occurred rarely. Athletes with sickle cell trait, like all athletes, should be progressively acclimatized to the environment and to the intensity and duration of activities and should be sufficiently hydrated to reduce the risk of exertional heat illness and/or rhabdomyolysis. According to National Institutes of Health management guidelines, sickle cell trait is not a contraindication to participation in competitive athletics, and there is no requirement for screening before participation. More research is needed to assess fully potential risks and benefits of screening athletes for sickle cell trait.

Skin infections, including herpes simplex, molluscum contagiosum, verrucae (warts), staphylococcal and streptococcal infections (furuncles boils, carbuncles, impetigo, methicillin-resistant *Staphylococcus aureus* cellulitis and/or abscesses), scabies, and tinea—**Qualified Yes**

Explanation: During contagious periods, participation in gymnastics or cheerleading with mats, martial arts, wrestling, or other collision, contact, or limited-contact sports is not allowed.

Spleen, enlarged—**Qualified Yes**

Explanation: If the spleen is acutely enlarged, then participation should be avoided because of risk of rupture. If the spleen is chronically enlarged, then individual assessment is needed before collision, contact, or limited-contact sports are played.

Testicle, undescended or absence of one—**Yes**

Explanation: Certain sports may require a protective cup

This table is designed for use by medical and nonmedical personnel. "Needs evaluation" means that a physician with appropriate knowledge and experience should assess the safety of a given sport for an athlete with the listed medical condition. Unless otherwise noted, this need for special consideration is because of variability in the severity of the disease, the risk of injury for the specific sports listed in Table 1, or both.

From: Rice, S.G. (2008). Medical conditions affecting sport participation. *Pediatrics, 121,* 841–848.

Figure 1. Classification of Sports According to Cardiovascular Demands (Based on Combined Static and Dynamic Components)

INCREASING DYNAMIC COMPONENT ⟶

	A. Low (< 40% Max O$_2$)	B. Moderate (40-70% Max O$_2$)	C. High (> 70% Max O$_2$)
III. High (>50% MVC)	**IIIA** **(Moderate)** Bobsledding/luge[a,b] Field events (throwing) Gymnastics[a,b] Martial arts[a] Sailing Sport climbing Water skiing[a,b] Weight lifting[a,b] Windsurfing[a,b]	**IIIB** **(High Moderate)** Body building[a,b] Downhill skiing[a,b] Skateboarding[a,b] Snowboarding[a,b] Wrestling[a]	**IIIC** **(High)** Boxing[a,c] Canoeing/kayaking Cycling[a,b] Decathlon Rowing Speed-skating[a,b] Triathlon[a,b]
II. Moderate (20-50% MVC)	**IIA** **(Low Moderate)** Archery Auto racing[a,b] Diving[a,b] Equestrian[a,b] Motorcycling[a,b]	**IIB** **(Moderate)** American football[a] Field events (jumping) Figure skating[a] Rodeoing[a,b] Rugby[a] Running (sprint) Surfing[a,b] Synchronized swimming[b]	**IIC** **(High Moderate)** Basketball[a] Ice hockey[a] Cross-country skiing (skating technique) Lacrosse[a] Running (middle distance) Swimming Team handball
I. Low (< 20% MVC)	**IA** **(Low)** Billiards Bowling Cricket[d] Curling Golf Riflery	**IB** **(Low Moderate)** Baseball/softball[a] Fencing Table tennis Volleyball	**IC** **(Moderate)** Badminton Cross-country skiing (classic technique) Field hockey[a] Orienteering Race walking Racquetball/squash Running (long distance) Soccer[a] Tennis

INCREASING STATIC COMPONENT ⟶ (vertical axis)

Figure 1. Classification of sports according to cardiovascular demands (based on combined static and dynamic components). This classification is based on peak static and dynamic components achieved during competition. It should be noted, however, that the higher values may be reached during training. The increasing dynamic component is defined in terms of the estimated percentage of maximal oxygen uptake (Max O$_2$) achieved and results in increasing cardiac output. The increasing static component is related to the estimated percentage of maximal voluntary contraction (MVC) reached and results in increasing blood pressure load. Activities with the lowest total cardiovascular demands (cardiac output and blood pressure) are shown in box IA, and those with the highest demands are shown in box IIIC. Boxes IIA and IB depict activities with low/moderate total cardiovascular demands, boxes IIIA, IIB, and IC depict activities with moderate total cardiovascular demands, and boxes IIIB and IIC depict high/moderate total cardiovascular demands. These categories progress diagonally across the graph from lower left to upper right.[a] Danger of bodily collision.[b] Increased risk if syncope occurs.[c] Participation is not recommended by the American Academy of Pediatrics.[d] The American Academy of Pediatrics classifies cricket in the IB box (low static component and moderate dynamic component). (Reproduced with permission from Mitchell JH, Haskell W, Snell P, Van Camp SP. 36th Bethesda Conference. Task force 8: classification of sports. *J Am Coll Cardiol*. 2005; 45(8): 1364–1367.)

From: Rice, S.G. (2008). Medical conditions affecting sport participation. *Pediatrics, 121*, 841–848.

Table 3. The 12-Element AHA Recommendations for Preparticipation Cardiovascular Screening of Competitive Athletes

Medical history*

Personal history

1. Exertional chest pain/discomfort
2. Unexplained syncope/near-syncope[†]
3. Excessive exertional and unexplained dyspnea/fatigue, associated with exercise
4. Prior recognition of a heart murmur
5. Elevated systemic blood pressure

Family history

6. Premature death (sudden and unexpected, or otherwise) before age 50 years due to heart disease, in > 1 relative
7. Disability from heart disease in a close relative < 50 years of age
8. Specific knowledge of certain cardiac conditions in family members: hypertrophic or dilated cardiomyopathy, long-QT syndrome or other ion channelopathies, Marfan syndrome, or clinically important arrhythmias

Physical examination

9. Heart murmur[‡]
10. Femoral pulses to exclude aortic coarctation
11. Physical stigmata of Marfan syndrome
12. Brachial artery blood pressure (sitting position)[§]

* Parental verification is recommended for high school and middle school athletes.

† Judged not to be neurocardiogenic (vasovagal); of particular concern when related to exertion.

‡ Auscultation should be performed in both supine and standing positions (or with Valsalva maneuver), specifically to identify murmurs of dynamic left ventricular outflow tract obstruction.

§ Preferably taken in both arms with Valsalva maneuver, specifically to identify murmurs of dynamic left ventricular outflow tract obstruction.

From: Maron, B.J., Thompson, P.D., Ackerman, M.J., Balady, G., Berger, S., Cohen, D., Dimeff, R., Douglas, P.S., Glover, D.W., Hutter, A.M., Kraus, M.D., Maron, M.S., Mitten, M.J., Roberts, W.O., & Puffer, J.C. (2007). "Recommendations and considerations related to preparticipation screening for cardiovascular abnormalities in competitive athletes" 2007 Update: A scientific statement from the American Heart Association Council on Nutrition, Physical Activity, and Metabolism. *Circulation, 115*, 1643–1655.

American College of Cardiology

AHA Screening Guidelines

The concern for sudden death in student athletes due to undetected cardiomyopathy had lead many pediatric cardiologists to call for additional screening of student-athletes for cardiovascular diseases including screening by electrocardiograms (Chandra, Papadakis, Sharma 2010; Giese et al., 2007; Maron, 2009; Mozes et al., 2010; Myerburg & Vetter, 2007; Papadakis, Whyte, & Sharma 2008; Papadakis & Sharma, 2009; Siddiqui & Patel, 2010). In 2007 the American Heart Association Council on Nutrition, Physical Activity, and Metabolism, endorsed by the American College of Cardiology, created recommendations for screening for cardiovascular disease of high school and college student-athletes (see Table 3). The 2007 AHA recommendations consist of 12 items (8 for personal and family history and 4 for physical examination). At the discretion of the examiner, a positive response or finding in any 1 or more of the 12 items may be judged sufficient to trigger a referral for a more detailed cardiovascular evaluation by a cardiologist.

In 1984, the American College of Cardiology held a conference in Bethesda, Maryland, in which experts in cardiac medicine established guidelines for developing recommendations regarding the medical eligibility of athletes with cardiac problems in competitive sport (Maron, Epstein, and Mitchell 1985). Ten years later, organizers of the original conference felt the need to update and revise the recommendations because (a) of advances in the diagnosis, treatment, and understanding of cardiovascular diseases, (b) of sudden interest in sudden cardiac death after highly-publicized deaths of well-known collegiate and professional athletes, and (c) previous recommendations were read by cardiologists but not by physicians who typically conduct medical examinations of competitive athletes (Mitchell, Maron, and Raven 1994). This later issue was somewhat resolved by simultaneous publishing the recommendations in the *Journal of the American College of Cardiology* and *Medicine and Science in Sport and Exercise* (Maron and Mitchell 1994).

As with the AAP recommendations, the Bethesda Conference classified sport into levels based on peak dynamic and static components during competition: (1) dynamic exercise (low, moderate, or high) which involves changes in muscle length and joint movement resulting in small intramuscular force, and (2) static exercise (low, moderate, or high) which involves development of a relatively large intramuscular force with little or no change in muscle length or joint movement (Mitchell, Haskell, and Raven 1994; see Table 3). They then provided recommendations for participation within these classifications for congenital heart conditions (Graham, Bricker, James, and Strong 1994), acquired valvular heart disease (Cheitlin, Douglas, and Parmley 1994), hypertrophic cardiomyopathy and other myopericardial diseases (Maron, Isner, and McKenna 1994), systemic hypertension (Kaplan, Deveraux, and Miller 1994), coronary artery disease (Thompson, Klocke, Levine and Van Camp 1994), and arrythmias (Zipes and Garson 1994). It is beyond the scope of this paper to review all their recommendations. However, there were two general points that came out of the conference that are important to note here. First, it was concluded that many decisions regarding whether or not an athlete with a heart condition should be allowed to play a particular sport often are not clear cut and require the "art of medicine." Second, it was suggested by several conference speakers that physicians make recommendations, not final decisions (e.g., Hutter 1994; Maron et al. 1994). As noted by Hutter (1994) "the physician makes recommendations to the athlete and to the team, and should not be put in a position of being solely responsible for whether or not an athlete is permitted to participate."

In summary, several physicians' groups have established guidelines and recommendations for determining what conditions warrant restrictions in sport participation. However, all of these groups noted that their guidelines tended to be conservative and not applicable to all situations. They suggested that the physician most knowledgeable about each athlete's unique condition and circumstances make final recommendations to the coach and athlete regarding medical eligibility.

Legal Right to Participate in Sport

Do athletes with medical disabilities have a legal right to participate in competitive, interscholastic, or intercollegiate sport? Most cases dealing with the right of athletes with disabilities to participate in sport fall under two federal laws: Section 504 of the Rehabilitation Act (Act) and the Americans with Disabilities Act (ADA). Both acts protect "otherwise qualified individuals" from discrimination solely on the basis of a disability. While Section 504 covers program and activities that receive federal funding or assistance,

ADA includes private programs, facilities, and activities that are open to the general public (Block 1995). Since most of the court cases to date have been filed on the grounds of violation of Section 504, this law will be examined in more detail.

Section 504 of the Rehabilitation Act

Section 504 of the Rehabilitation Act of 1973 (PL 93-112) was the first federal civil rights law protecting the rights of individuals with disabilities. Section 504 mandates that "no qualified handicapped person shall, on the basis of a handicap, be excluded from the participation in, be denied the benefits of, or otherwise be subjected to discrimination under any program or activity which receives or benefits from Federal financial assistance" (Federal Register 1990). In essence, the Act was designed to prevent the common practice of discriminating against individuals with disabilities who had the necessary skills for particular jobs or to participate in particular activities (e.g., sport) just because they had a disability.

In terms of sport participation, the Act bars excluding athletes with disabilities from participating in interscholastic or intercollegiate sport if the athlete possesses the skills and abilities required of the sport. For example, an athlete with the skills necessary to try-out and make a high school basketball team cannot be excluded from that team solely because he/she has mental retardation, one eye, or one arm. On the other hand, an athlete with disabilities can be excluded from participation in sport if the school shows "substantial justification" such as (a) physical inability to perform (lacks speed, stamina, strength, co-ordination, and/or understanding of the game), (b) increased risk of injury to other participants (e.g., athlete who needs to use a wheelchair to play basketball), (c) the need to fundamentally alter the activity to accommodate the athlete (athlete with a severe visual impairment needs a beach ball to be successful in volleyball), or (d) undisputed medical testimony against playing (i.e., athlete cannot find at least one competent physician to clear him to play a sport) (Mitten 1992).

It is important to note that the Act (as is the case with ADA) limits schools from excluding athletes from participation solely because of concern for the student's own health and safety (Block 1995; Mitten 1992). If an athlete with a disability (or in the case of a minor, the athlete and his/her parents) chooses to participate in a particular sport even though participation may increase his/her risk of injury or harm, then that athlete has the right to choose to participate. As noted by Mitten (1992), the legal right to participate in a sport even though it may cause a person harm is similar to the legal right to accept or refuse medical treatment even though some physicians disagree with the decision.

Courts have tended to reject claims by schools that paternalistic concerns for an athlete with a disability justifies exclusion from participation in sport. For example, in *Wright v. Columbia University* (1981) the court argued that "such motives, while laudably evidencing Columbia's concern for its students' well-being, derogate from the rights secured to plaintiff under Section 504, which prohibits 'paternalistic authorities' from deciding certain activities are 'too risky' for a handicapped person." Similarly, in *Poole v. South Plainfield Board of Education* (1980) the court found that "The Board of Education decided that it was part of its function to protect its students against rational judgments reached by themselves and their parents.... Here the Board has acted in a manner contrary to the express wishes of parents, who, together with their son, have reached a rational decision concerning the risk involved in wrestling." In contrast, the *Pahulu* court upheld University of Kansas' physicians' decision to exclude Alani Pahulu from playing football even though three specialists gave him medical clearance. This ruling seems contrary to the Act's provision of barring schools from excluding athletes to protect them from harm when there is conflicting medical testimony. As noted by Mitten (1992): "A university may violate the Act's reasonable accommodation requirement if it refuses to permit a handicapped athlete to participate in a sport in accordance with team physician's credible recommendation but contrary to another competent physician's credible recommendations."

The Act does not provide an athlete with a disability an absolute right to participate in sport. Rather, it is reasonable for a school to base participation on medical clearance by a competent physician. As noted above, a school can claim a "substantial justification" to bar an athlete from participation in sport if no physician provides medical clearance (Mitten 1992). For example, Stephen Larkin, a high school football player with hypertrophic cardiomyopathy (HCM) could not find a physician who would clear him to play high school football. Thus, the court found that Moeller High School did not violate the Act when they declared Stephen to be medically ineligible (*Larkin v. Archdiocese of Cincinnati* 1991). On the other hand, when there are conflicting medical recommendations, then the Act suggests that the athlete, along with his family, make the participation decision (Mitten 1992). For example, the University of Arizona allowed Mark Tingstad, a football player with spinal stenosis (abnormally narrow spinal canal) to decide if he should play football when there was conflicting medical evidence. Mark chose to play football, however, he quit after suffering temporary paralysis while making a tackle during a game (Demak 1989).

Definition of Handicapped and Otherwise Qualified

Two key terms that are defined in more detail are "handicap" and "qualified." Both terms are important for athletes who claim rights under Section 504. "Handicapped persons" means any person who (1) has a physical or mental impairment which substantially limits one or more major life activities, (2) has a record of such an impairment, or (3) is regarded as having such an impairment. "Physical impairment" means any physiological disorder or condition, cosmetic disfigurement, or anatomical loss affecting one or more of the following body systems: neurological; musculoskeletal; special sense organs; respiratory; including speech organs, cardiovascular; reproductive; digestive; genito-urinary; hemic and lymphatic; skin; and endocrine. "Mental impairment" means mental or psychological disorder, such as mental retardation, organic brain syndrome, emotional or mental illness, and specific learning disabilities. "Major life activities" means functions such as caring for one's self, performing manual tasks, walking, seeing, hearing, speaking, breathing, learning, and working. "Has a record of such an impairment" means has a history of, or has been classified as having, a mental or physical impairment that substantially limits one or more major life activities. "Is regarded as having an impairment" means (a) has a physical or mental impairment that does not substantially limit major life activities, but is treated by a recipient as constituting such a limitation; (b) has a physical or mental impairment that substantially limits major life activities only as a result of the attitudes of others toward such impairment; or (c) has none of the impairments listed above, but is treated by a recipient as having such an impairment (Federal Register 1990).

"Qualified handicapped person" was defined as follows: (1) With respect to employment, a handicapped person who, with reasonable accommodations, can perform the essential functions of the job in question ... (4) With respect to other services, a handicapped person who meets the essential eligibility requirements for the receipt of such services" (Federal Register 1990).

Courts have made it clear that in order to make a case of discrimination under Section 504, the student-athlete must demonstrate that he/she (1) is an individual with a handicap, (2) is otherwise qualified to participate, (3) has been excluded solely by reason of the handicap, or (4) has been excluded from a program or activity receiving federal funds (Mitten 1992).

Does a Medical Disability Constitute a Handicap?

The vast majority of student-athletes who fail medical examinations would qualify as "handicapped" under the law. As Mitten (1992) noted, courts have considered an array of medical conditions as "handicaps" under the Act, including heart conditions, congenital back abnormalities, permanent osteoarthritis, knee and back injuries, and loss of a paired organ. However, the mere presence of a handicap alone does not qualify an individual. The handicap must "substantially limit one or more of the person's major life activities" (Federal Register 1990). For the most part, courts have found that participation in inter-scholastic and intercollegiate sport constitutes a major life activity for many athletes in that participation can be an integral part of a students' education and learning experience (*Knapp* 1996; Mitten 1992). For example, the *Knapp* court (1996) found that basketball held a unique educational value for Nicholas Knapp, and that simply having him take a different role on the team (e.g., manager) or participate in a different sport or extracurricular activity would not provide the same learning experiences. However, an interesting inter-pretation by the *Pahulu* court (1995) found that Alani Pahulu was not disabled within the meaning of the Act. The court argued that, while intercollegiate football may be a major life activity (i.e., learning), not allowing Alani to participate in football would not substantially limit his ability to learn since he still would be on scholarship and have continued access to academic services and extracurricular activities on campus. The court further noted that Alani also would have the opportunity to participate in the football program in other roles (*Pahulu* 1995).

Otherwise Qualified

Once it is established that the student-athlete in fact is "handicapped" under the Act, the next question is whether or not the student-athlete is "otherwise qualified." The standard for determining "otherwise qualified" was established by the Supreme Court in *Southeastern Community College v. Davis* (1979). The court held that a college nursing program did not have to admit an applicant with a hearing problem to a surgical training program, because the applicant could not satisfy the school's "legitimate" qualifications necessary for patient safety even with reasonable accommodations (Mitten 1992). A "handicapped person" must meet the minimal qualifications to participate in a particular program, and a school or program does not have to lower or substantially modify its standards to accommodate that person. In other words, a "handicapped person" is "otherwise qualified" if that person is able to meet all of a program's requirements (with reasonable accommodations) in spite of his/her disability (Mitten 1992; *Southeastern Community College* 1979; Stein 1978).

The concept of "otherwise qualified" can be somewhat confusing. Criteria or qualifications cannot be made that would exclude a class of people based solely on their disability (Block 1995). For example, making "the ability to run" or "having normal eye sight in both eyes" a qualification for participation in high school tennis discriminates people who use wheelchairs or who have visual problems. A better qualifier is one that is simply based on abilities such as being able to hit 90% of the balls back over the net including balls that are played towards the sidelines. Reiterating this key point, the Office of Civil Rights of the Department of Health, Education, and Welfare provided an interpretation of one of the typical medical disqualifies of the 1970s—having only one paired organ: "Students who have lost an organ, limb or appendage but who are otherwise qualified may not be excluded by recipients from contact sport. However, such students may be required to obtain parental consent and approval for participation from the doctor most familiar with their condition. A school cannot assume that such a child is too great a risk for physical injury or illness if permitted to participate in contact sport" (Office of Civil Rights 1978).

Recent courts have upheld the rights of athletes with one paired organ to participate in interscholastic and intercollegiate sport. For example, in *Poole v. South Plainfield Board of Education* (1980), the courts found South Plainfield violated the Act by denying an athlete with one kidney a chance to wrestle. The school argued that the athlete was not "otherwise qualified" because he failed the team physician's physical exam. However, the court noted that the athlete met the sport training requirements and was cleared to participate by another physician. Similarly, in *Grube v. Bethlemeh Area School District* (1982), the court found that the school district violated the Act by denying an athlete with one kidney from playing football based on a team physician's recommendation. The court argued that the school district did not find "substantial justification" for excluding this athlete since the athlete's personal physician had cleared him to play. And in *Wright v. Columbia University* (1981), the court held that the school was in violation of the Act by not allowing an athlete with sight in one eye to play football based on a team physician's examination. The court noted that the athlete's personal opthamologist concluded that there was no substantial risk of serious eye injury related to participation in football.

In all of the above cases, it was determined by at least one physician that the risk of injury to the athlete was not "substantial." This notion of substantial risk seems to be a grey area for physicians and the courts. While schools have a rational basis for declaring an athlete medically ineligible based on a team physician's recommendations, the Act requires more than just a rational basis for discriminating against an athlete with a legitimate disability. The school must show "substantial justification" (*Grube v. Bethlehem Area School District* 1982; Mitten 1992; *Wright v. Columbia University* 1981). For example, the *Pahulu* court found that the medical findings of "substantial risk of serious injury" by the Kansas University physicians were reasonable and rational even though three specialists cleared Alani Pahulu to play football. This was a rather peculiar finding given that the Act clearly implies that a school cannot exclude an athlete if the athlete has received clearance to play by at least one competent physician. In contrast, the U.S. District Court for the Northern District of Illinois ruled that the risk of injury to Nicholas Knapp given his heart condition was not substantial based on testimony of four cardiologists despite Northwestern University's team physician not giving Nicholas medical clearance (*Knapp* 1996). The *Knapp* ruling seemed to be more consistent with previous rulings (e.g., Grube 1982; Poole 1980; Wright 1981) and more consistent with the Act. However, this ruling was overturned by the appeals court noting that "medical determinations of this sort are best left up to team doctors and universities, as long as they are made with reason and rationality (*Knapp* 1996).

An interesting question is whether or not a medical examination in and of itself can be used as a qualifying standard. In *Pahulu* (1995), the courts found that a medical examination constituted a "technical standard" which was required for admission and subsequent participation into a program. Similarly, *Knapp* (1996) found that an individual is not qualified if there is a "genuine substantial risk" that he/she could be injured or could injure others. One of the benchmark cases regarding the use of a physical examination is *Larkin v. Archdiocese of Cincinnati* (1991). As noted earlier, Stephen Larkin wanted to play football at Moeller High School in Cincinnati, but a physical examination detected hypertrophic cardiomyopathy (HCM), one of the leading causes of sudden death in young athletes. Informed of his condition and the inherent risks of playing a strenuous sport with HCM, Stephen still wanted to play interscholastic football at Moeller. He claimed Moeller's refusal to allow him to play football violated the Act. He argued that he was a "handicapped person" who was "otherwise qualified" to play football under the Act. He further argued that Moeller's refusal to allow him to play football was based solely on his disability and thus violated the discrimination mandate of the Act. His lawyer pointed out that there was no evidence that Stephen was at increased risk of sudden death from strenuous activity, noting that Stephen ran and lifted weights regularly without any ill effects. He also noted that Stephen's family was fully aware of his condition and was willing to waive any tort claims against the school if Stephen were allowed to play football.

In deciding the case, the judge found Stephen was an "individual with a handicap" under the Act. However, the court found that Moeller did not violate the Act, because Stephen was not otherwise qualified since he could not pass the physical examination. The court noted that none of the physicians who examined Stephen recommended that he be allowed to play. Furthermore, the court argued that Stephen's inability to pass the Ohio High School Athletics Association's by-law requiring a "physician certification" before participating in interscholastic sport was a "substantial justification" for the school's decision (*Larkin* 1991; Mitten 1992). Thus, obtaining a physician's approval via a physical examination prior to participation in interscholastic sport can be viewed as a reasonable "qualifier" to sport participation without violating Act. Furthermore, a school can claim "substantial justification" for excluding athletes who have not obtained a competent physician's medical approval to play a particular sport (Mitten 1992). The NCAA recently adopted new guidelines for participation of athletics with disabilities in NCAA sanctioned sports.

NCAA Guideline 3a "Participation by the Impaired Student-Athlete" defined "impaired student athlete" as follows:

1. Those confined to a wheelchair;
2. Those who are deaf, blind, or missing a limb;
3. Those who have only one of a set of paired organs;
4. Those with severe chronic illness;
5. Those with severe reduction in normal physiologic function;
6. Those who may have a physical, behavioral, emotional, or psychological disorder or abnormality that substantially limits a major life activity.

The NCAA recognized the right of individuals with impairments to an equal opportunity to participate in high-quality sport or recreational programs. These individuals should be eligible for intercollegiate program if they qualify for a team without any lowering of standards for achievement, attendance, or completion of required tasks, and if their participation does not put others or themselves at significant risk of substantial harm.

Medical exclusion of a student with an impairment for an athletics program should occur only when the impairment presents a significant risk of substantial harm to the health or safety of the individual and/or other participants that cannot be eliminated or reduced by reasonable accommodations.

Recent judicial decisions have upheld a university's legal right to exclude a student-athlete with an impairment from competition if the team physician has a reasonable medical basis for determining that athletic competition creates a significant risk of harm to the student-athlete or others.

Participant Considerations

Before allowing any student-athlete with an impairment to participate in an athletic program, it is recommended that an institution require joint approval from the physician most familiar with the student-athlete's impairment, the team physician, an appropriate official of the institution, and the parents. In all cases, the decision to participate should include:

1. Available published information on the risks of participation;
2. The current health status of the student-athlete;
3. The sport and position played;
4. Availability of acceptable protective equipment or measures; and
5. The ability of the student-athlete (and, in the case of a minor, the parents) to understand the risks.

Organ Absence or Non-Function

In the specific instance in which the absence or non-function of one of a set of paired organs constitutes the specific impairment, the following specific issues need to be addressed with the student-athlete and his/her parents. The discussion, and subsequent process by which the decision for or against participation is made, should take into account the following factors:

1. The quality and function of the remaining organ;
2. The probability of an injury to the remaining organ; and
3. The availability of current protective equipment and the likely effectiveness of such equipment to prevent injury to the remaining organ.

Medical Release

When the decision is made to allow the student-athlete with an impairment to compete, it is recommended that a properly executed document of understanding and a waivermedical release concerning the ramifications of sports participation relative to the impairment should be executed.... Such statements are not a guarantee against legal action should an unfortunate circumstance occur, but serve to document the student-athlete's understanding of his or her medical condition and potential risks of participation and the institution's and medical staff's intentions and efforts on behalf of that student-athlete.

Since laws and local conditions vary, however, the NFHS Board of Directors determined that the creation of a standardized national pre-participation physical evaluation procedure would not be practical.

* American Academy of Pediatrics: Committee on Sports Medicine and Fitness *Medical Conditions Affecting Sport Participation.*

In My Opinion

The decision to declare an athlete medically ineligible for sport participation is extremely complex and is compounded by expectations and feelings of the player, his/her parents, teammates, and the coach (Kibler 1990; Mitten 1992). Still, anyone with any interest in sport would agree that some athletes have disabilities that preclude participation in certain sport, and certainly no one wants to see young athletes get hurt or even die because of sport participation. In an effort to prevent athletes with severe medical disabilities from further harm, high school and college athletic programs require athletes to pass a preparticipation physical examination given by a competent physician.

However, neither state high school athletic associations nor the NCAA provide clear guidelines on what type of medical problems warrant a team physician to declare an athlete medically ineligible. Several medical associations provide published recommendations that are available to team physicians regarding sport participation. Other individual physicians have provided further opinions regarding whether or not athletes with one eye or kidney should participate in contact sport (Dorsen 1986; Vinger 1987). Yet, these medical associations and independent physicians make it clear that their recommendations are only guidelines. As noted by Maron and Mitchell (1994) regarding cardiovascular problems, "There are few definitive data demonstrating that either strenuous exertion predisposes an athlete with a cardiovascular abnormality to a death that otherwise would not have occurred, or that withdrawal from competitive athletics will necessarily prolong life ... they (the recommendations) are presented here in the context of guidelines and therefore should not be regarded as inflexible or absolutely restrictive" (p. 224).

To complicate matters, Section 504 of the Rehabilitation Act and the Americans with Disabilities Act, civil rights laws protecting the rights of individuals with disabilities, prevent discrimination of athletes with disabilities solely due to their disability. If an athlete has the skills necessary to participate in an interscholastic or intercollegiate sport, then that athlete has the right to participate even if participating might jeopardize his/her health and well being. However, participation in high school and collegiate sport is not unconditional. If a school has "substantial justification" to exclude an athlete with a disability, then the school is not in violation of the Act. Courts have held that schools can claim substantial justification to exclude athletes with disabilities if the athlete does not receive medical clearance by at least one competent physician familiar with the athlete's condition. And some courts (e.g., *Knapp* 1996; *Pahulu* 1995) have gone as far as to rule that medical eligibility be left to universities regardless of conflicting testimony by outside physicians.

It appears then that schools have the right to ask an athlete to take a preparticipation physical examination given by a competent physician as qualification for participation in school-sponsored sport programs. If the athlete fails this examination, then the athlete has the right to get a second opinion from another competent physician. When no physician gives an athlete medical clearance to participate in a given sport, then clearly the school has substantial justification under the Act to exclude the athlete. However, if there is conflicting medical testimony, such that at least one competent physician provides medical clearance, then the Act would seem to empower the athlete and his/her parents to make the participation decision. Unfortunately, recent rulings such as *Knapp* and *Pahulu* continue to make this a grey area in medical eligibility.

References

Bernhardt, D.T., & Roberts, W.O.(2010). *Preparticipation Physical Evaluation* (4th ed.). Elk Grove Village: American Academy of Pediatrics.

Chandra, N., Papadakis, M., Sharma, S. (2010). Preparticipation Screening of Young Competitive Athletes for Cardiovascular Disorders. *The Physician and Sports Medicine, 38*(1), 54–63.

Giese, E., O'Connor, F.G., Brennan, F.H., Depenbrock, P.J., Oriscello, R.G. (2007). The athletic preparticipation evaluation: Cardiovascular assessment. *American Family Medicine, 75*, 1008–1014.

Maron, B.J. (2009). Distinguishing hypertrophic cardiomyopathy from athlete's heart physiological remodeling: clinical significance, diagnostic strategies and implications for preparticipation screening. *British Journal of Sports Medicine, 43*, 649–656.

Maron, B.J., Thompson, P.D., Ackerman, M.J., Balady, G., Berger, S., Cohen, D., Dimeff, R., Douglas, P.S., Glover, D.W., Hutter, A.M., Kraus, M.D., Maron, M.S., Mitten, M.J., Roberts, W.O., & Puffer, J.C. (2007). Recommendations and considerations related to preparticipation screening for cardiovascular abnormalities in competitive athletes" 2007 Update: A scientific statement from the American Heart Association Council on Nutrition, Physical Activity, and Metabolism. *Circulation, 115*, 1643–1655.

Mozes, A., Homoud, M., Link, M., Weinstock, J., Garlitski, A., & Estes, N.A.M. (2010). Screening for sudden death in the athlete, *Cardiovascular Pathology, 19*, 340–342.

Myerburg, R.J., & Vetter, V.L. (2007). Electrocardiogram should be included in preparticipation screening of athletes. *Circulation, 116*, 2616–2626.

NCAA. (2009). Guideline 1b: Medical Evaluations, Immunizations and Records. *Sports Medicine Handbook (19th Ed.)*. Indianapolis, IN: Author.

Papadakis, M. Whyte, G., & Sharma, S. (2008). Preparticipation screening for cardiovascular abnormalities in you competitive athletes. *British Medical Journal, 337*, 806–811.

Papadakis, M., & Sharma, S. (2009). Electrocardiographic screening in athletes: The time is now for universal screening. *British Journal of Sports Medicine, 43*, 663–668.

Rice, S.G. (2008). Medical conditions affecting sport participation. *Pediatrics, 121*, 841–848.

Siddiqui, S., & Patel, D. R. (2010). Cardiovascular screening of adolescent athletes. *Pediatric Clinics North America, 57*, 635–647.

Chapter 18

The Problem of Sudden Death in Competitive Athletes

A quality history, physical and thorough screening examination are still the best means to identify athletes at risk for sudden cardiac death.

Richard A. Weintraub

Introduction

Sudden death among young competitive athletes is a rare, but devastating event that touches the lives of all concerned. Families, coaches, administrators, the lay and medical communities are horrified by the completely unexpected sudden death of athletes who were previously thought to be in excellent health (Maron, Thompson et al. 1996; Hackel and Reimer 1993). Few occurrences in our society are as agonizing, have such a profound impact, and engender such a high level of concern and public scrutiny (Ali 1991; Christensen 1989). It is a vexing and elusive problem that has far-reaching and extensive social, ethical and medical-legal implications.

Probably the first reported incident of sudden death in an athlete was in 490 BC. Pheidippides, a young Greek messenger, ran 26.2 miles from Marathon to Athens, delivered a message of the Greek victory over the Persians, and then collapsed and died (McMicken 2011; Wikipedia 2011). In modern history, the media publicity engendered by the untimely demise of several high profile athletes such as Hank Gathers (College basketball), Flo Hyman (Olympic volleyball), Reggie Lewis (NBA basketball), Lenny Bias (College basketball), Sergei Grinkov (Olympic figure skater) and Pete Maravich (NBA basketball), and others has further heightened our awareness and strengthened the need to approach the practical and ethical issues of this problem (Maron 1993). In our society, trained athletes are generally perceived as the healthiest segment of our population and tend to epitomize the benefits of physical conditioning. The realization that many such athletes may harbor occult and potentially lethal malformations and still perform at exceptionally high levels for long periods of time has further highlighted this problem (Maron, Shirani et al. 1996). A compelling desire and need to prevent further occurrences has thus become of paramount importance in athletic programs.

Table 1. Cardiac Causes of Sudden Death

I. Coronary artery disease
    A. Coronary atherosclerosis
    B. Congenital coronary anomalies
    C. Thromboemboli to coronary arteries
    D. Arteritis
    E. Coronary spasm
II. Non-coronary cardiovascular disease
    A. Valvular heart disease
        1. Valvular Stenosis (i.e., Aortic Stenosis)
        2. Myxomatous degeneration of the mitral valve (MVP)
        3. Rheumatic heart disease
    B. Infectious (bacterial, viral, auto-immune)
        1. Myocarditis
        2. Bacterial endocarditis
        3. Pericarditis
        4. Parasitic
    C. Primary myocardial disease
        1. Hypertrophic Cardiomyopathy (HCM)
        2. Dilated Cardiomyopathy
        3. Idiopathic
    D. Cardiac conduction system disease
        1. Ion Channelopathies (i.e., Long QT syndromes, Brugada syndrome)
        2. Wolf Parkinson White (WPW)
        3. Arrythmogenic Right Ventricular Dysplasia (ARVD)
    E. Connective Tissue Disease (i.e., Marfan's Syndrome)
    F. Blunt chest trauma (i.e., Commotio Cordis, Cardiac contusion)
    G. Drugs and Alcohol

Preventive measures such as comprehensive and often expensive screening programs have not yet proved to be cost-effective, nor are they consistently able to identify all athletes at risk (Maron, Shirani et al. 1996; Rich 1994). The development of consensus recommendations and guidelines for the most prudent, practical and cost-effective screening procedures, along with strategies to implement them represents an immense challenge to all concerned. Fortunately, through the efforts of many dedicated researchers and practicing physicians, the many causes of cardiac death in athletes has been well-defined. Controversy remains about the best and most practical inclusion criteria in theses evaluations. What is still lacking are more uniform standards for conducting sports screening programs, certifying health professionals who perform these evaluations and implementing these programs.

Scope of the Problem

Sudden death among athletes is an infrequent event and as such, the design of a preventive program must take this into account. Even the most common cause of sudden death in trained athletes in the United States, Hypertrophic Cardiomyopathy (HCM), occurs relatively infrequently in the general population (Van Camp et al. 1995; Maron, Gardin et al. 1995). Since cardiovascular causes of sudden death are by far the most common, this chapter will focus primarily on these (see Table 1).

The scope of the problem is huge owing to the large number of competitive athletes in the United States. There are estimated to be approximately five million high school

Figure 1. Effect of Race on Cardiovascular Sudden Death in Competitive Athletes

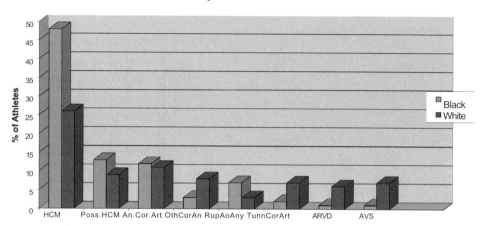

Figure 1: Effect of race on 139 autopsy confirmed cases of sudden death in competitive athletes, shown for those diseases with 5 or more deaths. 5 Asian, Hispanic, or Native American athletes were not included in this analysis. Possible hypertrophic cardiomyopathy (HCM), denotes those hearts with some morphological features consistent with, but not diagnostic of HCM. An.Cor.Art indicates anomolous origin of coronary artery; OthCorAn, other coronary anomalies; RupAoAny, ruptured aortic anyeursm; TunnCorArt, tunneled coronary artery; ARVD, arrhythmogenic right ventricular dysplasia; AVS, aortic valve stenosis. Adapted from Maron, Shirani et al. (1996) with permission of the author.

athletes in the United States in addition to one half million collegiate and over 5,000 professional athletes (Maron, Thompson et al. 1996).

The incidence of sudden cardiac death (SCD) in National Collegiate Athletic Association (NCAA) student athletes during a recent 5 year study (2004–2008) revealed an incidence of SCD to be 1 per 43,770 athletes per year. Cardiovascular sudden death was the leading cause of death (56%) and represented 75% of sudden deaths during exertion. Despite best efforts these data were likely biased by the current poor methods of data collection which clearly underestimate the risk of SCD (Harmon 2011).

The overall prevalence of participating athletes affected appears to be in the range to 1:200,000 per year (Maron 1998), among high school athletes and is disproportionately higher in males and black athletes (see Figure 1) (Maron, Shirani et al. 1996; Van Camp, Vloor et al. 1995; Williams 1991). Past published accounts of deaths suggested an average of only 11 autopsy-confirmed cardiovascular deaths per year from 1985 to 1995, which because of the inconsistencies in reporting and selection bias almost certainly underestimated the frequency of these events (Maron, Shirani et al. 1996). Importantly, the more recent estimates based on the results of a 27 year US National registry, instituted by the Minneapolis Heart Institute Foundation, found the overall sudden death rate to be substantially greater than prior estimates. This registry was largely autopsy based but included multiple sources, including medical and lay news reporting. This registry included those who died suddenly or were successfully resuscitated and survived between 1980 and 2006. It included organized major and minor sports at all competitive levels (Maron, Doerer, 2009). There were a total of 1,866 athletes who died suddenly (or survived cardiac arrest) in 38 diverse sports. Interim analysis showed that the reports of sudden deaths had increased by 6% per year,

Figure 2. Number of Cardiovascular (CV), Trauma-Related, and Other Sudden Death Events in 1,866 Young Competitive Athletes, Tabulated by Year

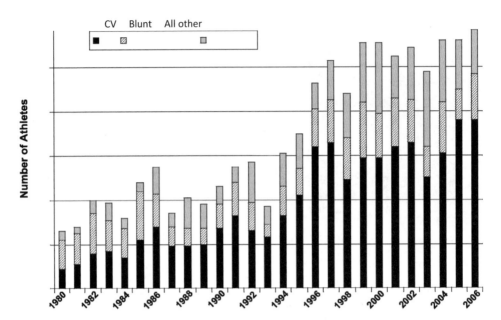

Adapted from Maron Barry J.: Doerer Joseph J. et al.; Circulation 2009; 119: p. 1087.

with an average of 66 deaths per year over the last 6 years of the study (see Figure 2). The availability of a National Registry, enhanced public awareness, and media attention probably contributed to the increase in reported cases rather than to an actual increase in the occurrence of sudden death. This showed a higher frequency of sudden deaths in athletes than previously reported and was about 0.61 deaths per 100,000 person years. The cardiac diseases relevant to these discussions probably account for an estimated combined prevalence of 0.3% in the general athlete population (Maron, Doerer 2009).

Causes of Cardiac Sudden Death in Competitive Athletes

The competitive athlete can be defined as one who participates in an "organized team or individual sport requiring systematic training and regular competition against others while placing a high premium on athletic excellence and achievement" (Maron and Mitchell 1994). Sudden death on the athletic field is usually due to underlying cardiovascular disease and most often is precipitated by intense physical activity. It usually occurs during or just after this activity, although the immediate risk for sudden death is highest during activity (Burke, Farb et al. 1991; Maron, Epstein and Roberts 1986; Maron 1993).

Most commonly, the pathophysiologic mechanism of sudden death is cardiac arrhythmia (disorders of conduction of electrical impulses in the heart). This can result in ventricular fibrillation, a condition in which the ventricular chambers of the heart contract in such a chaotic manner that the heart stops pumping and cardiac arrest ensues

Table 2. Non-Cardiac Causes of Sudden Death

I.   Neurologic
   A.   Cerebral hemorrhage
   B.   Epilepsy
   C.   Meningitis
   D.   Traumatic
II. Ruptured aortic aneurysm
III. Blunt chest or head trauma
IV. Allergic
   A.   Asthma
   B.   Angioneurotic edema
   C.   Acute hypersensitivity
V.   Environmental
   A.   Heat stroke
   B.   Drugs
      1.   Recreational
         a.   Alcohol
         b.   Cocaine
         c.   Volatile inhaled agents (toluene, butane, chlorinated hydrocarbons, chlorofluorocarbons, i.e., Freon)
      2.   Therapeutic
         a.   Antiarrythmic agents
         b.   Anti-cancer agents (anti-metabolites)
         c.   Tranquilizers
         d.   Anti-depressants, psychotropic drugs
         e.   Performance enhancing drugs
   C.   Unknown (no autopsy or normal autopsy)

(Maron, Shirani et al. 1996; Maron and Garson 1994). This may be a primary arrhythmia resulting from the specific underlying cardiac condition or it may be a result of other factors, such as blunt trauma, associated illness, or drugs — either therapeutic, recreational, or elicit. Sudden intracranial or intrathoracic bleeding from ruptured brain aneurysms, or major blood vessels (aorta) can occur spontaneously or as a result of blunt trauma. These sudden events are often catastrophic and can result in sudden death of the individual (see Table 2).

Specific Conditions Known to Cause Cardiac Sudden Death

The 27-year Minneapolis National Registry found that 56% of deaths were due to cardiovascular disease (Maron, 2009). Twenty-two percent were due to blunt trauma causing structural damage to the heart, 4% were due to commotion cordis (blunt chest trauma initiating a cardiac arrhythmia) and 2% were due to heat stroke.

It has been known for two decades and reconfirmed in multiple studies that in athletes younger than 35 years of age (in North America), Hypertrophic Cardiomyopathy (HCM) is the most common cardiac condition associated with sudden death (Maron 1993; Van Camp, Vloor et al. 1995; Maron, Roberts et al. 1980; Maron, Doerer 2009). A spectrum of over 20 structural cardiovascular abnormalities implicated in causing SCD has been further defined (Maron, Shirani et al. 1996).

Arrhythmogenic Right Ventricular Dysplasia (ARVD) (a common cause in other countries, such as reported from Italy) (Corrado, Thiene et al. 1990; Thiene, NAVA et al. 1988), idiopathic left ventricular hypertrophy, coronary anomalies, premature atherosclerosis, and Marfan's syndrome comprise the majority of the remaining causes of sudden death in athletes (Maron, Shirani et al. 1996; Cheitlin, DeCastro and McAllister 1974; Roberts 1987; Maron 1996; Wight and Salem 1995; Fudderman and Lemberg 1995; Thompson 1993; Kenny and Shapiro 1992; Burke, Farb and Virmani 1992; Vaska 1992; Firor and Faulkner 1998; Epstein and Maron 1986). In the athlete older than 35 years, coronary atherosclerosis is the leading cause of sudden death followed by those conditions responsible for sudden death in younger athletes (Thompson, Stearns et al. 1979; Thompson, Funk et al. 1982; Waller and Roberts 1980; Virmani, Robinowitz and McAllister 1982). Aortic dissection, ruptured aorta, myocarditis (cardiac muscle inflammation often leading to cardiac arrhythmias), myxomatous mitral valve degeneration (MVP), and anomalous origin of the coronary arteries are next in frequency. These are followed in frequency by non-cardiac causes such as cerebral aneurysms, sickle cell trait, non-penetrating blunt chest trauma, bronchial asthma, therapeutic use of medications, and, all too frequently in our society, recreational use and abuse of drugs (Kark, Posey et al. 1987; Maron, Poliac et al. 1995; Virmani, Robinowitz et al. 1988; Isner, Estes et al. 1986; Pretre and Chilcott 1997). Not surprisingly, the distribution of cardiovascular causes of sudden death was nearly identical when comparing data from 1996 (Maron, Thompson 1996) to the longer period of the Minneapolis Registry (Maron 2007) (see Figure 3).

The occurrence of these events is most commonly found in basketball and football participants, followed by track, soccer, and others (see Figure 4). Sudden death in women on the athletic field is much less common (estimated to be about 12% of all sudden death cases) and may possibly be explained by lower participation rates, different demands of training or cardiac adaptions (Pelliccia, Maron et al. 1996; Maron, Doerer 2009). Also, the important cause of cardiac sudden death, Hypertrophic Cardiomyopathy, is less common in women (Wigle, Sasson et al. 1985; Maron, Bonow et al. 1987; Louie and Edwards 1994; Klues, Schiffers et al. 1995; Maron, Wolfson et al. 1983).

Screening Programs

Screening is an initial step in identifying conditions known to place athletes at high risk (Jensen-Urstad 1995). In view of the low prevalence of disease in the general population at large and low occurrence of sudden death, screening programs to provide medical clearance for participation in competitive sport must be designed to identify many pre-existing and suspicious abnormalities. Preparticipation screening involves the systematic practice of medically evaluating large, general athletic populations before participation in sports for the purpose of identifying or raising the suspicion of abnormalities that could provoke life threatening diseases or sudden death (Maron 1996, Corrado 2005). The overall low yield of clinically significant cardiac abnormalities from screening has generated debate as to the usefulness of the Preparticipation Physical Evaluation (PPE). It is estimated that 200,000 athletes would have to be screened to detect 1,000 athletes who might be at risk for sudden death and one athlete who would actually die (Lyznicki 2000). Currently there is no cost effective battery of tests to identify all of the potentially life threatening conditions. The efficacy of various national and international screening programs is not readily resolved in the context of evidence-based investigative medicine, but rather supported by expert concensus. Issues relating to the methodology and

Figure 3. Distribution of Cardiovascular Causes of Sudden Death in 1,435 Young Competitive Athletes

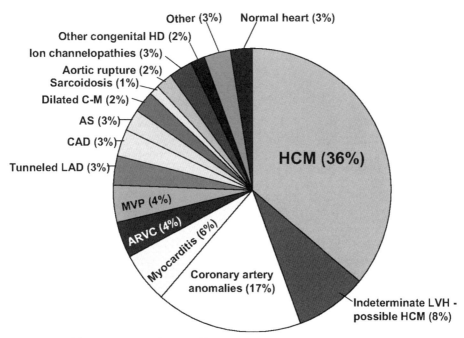

Maron B J et al. Circulation 2007;115:1643-1655

From the Minneapolis Heart Institute Foundation Registry, 1980 to 2005. HCM indicates Hypertrophic Cardiomyopathy; ARVC arrhythmogenic right ventricular cardiomyopathy; AS, aortic stenosis; CAD, coronary artery disease; C-M, cardiomyopathy; HD, heart disease; LAD, left anterior descending; LVH, left ventricular hypertrophy; and MVP, mitral valve prolapse. Adapted from Maron et al. (2007).

justification for preparticipation screening, including the use of the 12 lead electrocardiogram (ECG), have become a complex area of debate (Maron, 2007 update). Various screening approaches, including history and physical exam alone or in combination with screening 2-D echocardiography and electrocardiography have not been shown to be cost effective (Lyzinicki et al. 2000). Nevertheless, based on ethical, legal and medical grounds some form of cardiovascular preparticipation screening is both justifiable and compelling. PEPs are recommended and fully endorsed by a multitude of medical and sports societies. Recommendations for PEPs have been published by the American Heart Association (Maron et al. 2005). The overwhelming consensus is that the implementation of a screening program that includes a quality history and thorough cardiac screening physical examination is currently the best means to identify athletes at risk for sudden death. Also, proper screening can hopefully assist in structuring an effective means to pursue further evaluation and testing of the individual athletes identified to be at increased risk. The ultimate hope is that this early detection will not only prevent an episode of sudden death but will trigger further evaluation and likely specialty referral that will permit therapeutic interventions that may alter the clinical course and natural history of the disease.

Expert scientific documents addressing the issues involved and detailing the recommended requirements for screening and PPE were published in 1996 (Maron,

Figure 4. Sports Engaged in at the Time of Sudden Death in 134 Young Competitive Athletes

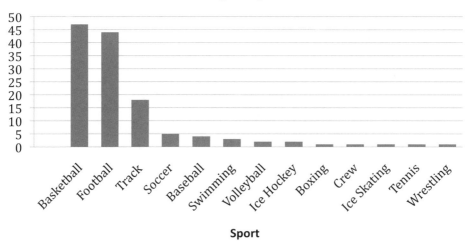

Those competing in track events were either distance runners or sprinters. Adapted from Maron, Shirani et al. (1996) with permission of the author.

Thompson 1996) in the AHA preparticipation screening scientific statement and updated a decade later in the 2007 updated AHA scientific statement (Maron, Thompson 2007).

History and Physical Examination

Since many conditions are familial or inherited, historical information about pre-existing non-cardiac and cardiac conditions, such as congenital cardiac abnormalities and cerebrovascular conditions, along with the knowledge of any family history of sudden death is crucial. This information can provide clues or raise the necessary suspicion to better proceed in individual evaluation and testing of the athlete in question. Any history of symptoms such as palpitations (heart fluttering), syncope (passing out), seizures, or chest pain are important and necessary considerations in recognizing and preventing effort related tragedies (Whittington and Banner 1994).

In the older athlete, and on even rarer occasions the young athlete, a history of premature coronary disease may be present. In the younger athletes, a family history of this or congenital heart disease is useful. Since most young athletes are reluctant to be excluded from sport, historical information should be obtained or forms filled out with the help of parents. When pertinent findings are present, intensive investigation of identifiable or worrisome symptoms can then be performed on an individual basis.

The detailed recommendations for the necessary personal and family history were initially proposed in the 1996 26th Bethesda Conference scientific Statement. These recommendations were retained and unaltered in the updated 36th Bethesda Conference (Maron 2005). They consist of 12 items (8 for personal and family history and 4 for physical examination) (see Table 3) (Maron 2007).

Table 3. The 12-Element AHA Recommendations for Preparticipation Cardiovascular Screening of Competitive Athletes

Medical history*

Personal history

1. Exertional chest pain/discomfort
2. Unexplained syncope/near-syncope†
3. Excessive exertional and unexplained dyspnea/fatigue, associated with exercise
4. Prior recognition of a heart murmur
5. Elevated systemic blood pressure

Family history

6. Premature death (sudden and unexpected, or otherwise) before age 50 years due to heart disease, in ≥ 1 relative
7. Disability from heart disease in a close relative < 50 years of age
8. Specific knowledge of certain cardiac conditions in family members: hypertrophic or dilated cardiomyopathy, Long QT syndrome or other ion channelopathies, Marfan syndrome, or clinically important arrhythmias

Physical examination

9. Heart murmur‡
10. Femoral pulses to exclude aortic coarctation
11. Physical stigmata of Marfan syndrome
12. Brachial artery blood pressure (sitting position)§

* Parental verification is recommended for high school and middle school athletes.

† Judged not to be neurocardiogenic (vasovagal); of particular concern when related to exertion.

‡ Auscultation should be performed in both supine and standing positions (or with Valsalva maneuver), specifically to identify murmurs of dynamic left ventricular outflow tract obstruction.

§ Preferably taken in both arms.

Adapted from Maron, Thompson, Ackerman et al., Recommendations and Considerations Related to Preparticipation Screening for Cardiovascular Abnormalities in Competitive Athletes: 2007 Update, Circulation 2007, 115: p1646.

The physical examination can then be used to pick up additional signs of these disorders and help quantify these findings. Some examples of this are significant cardiac murmurs, irregularities of heart rhythm and severe hypertension (Rich 1994). For instance, a history and physical examination can detect Aortic Stenosis and a portion of people with HCM and Marfan's syndrome. If the physical examination is suggestive of Marfan's syndrome and a chest x-ray is done, a large portion of athletes with this disorder (cystic medial necrosis) will be found. When an EKG is added to this series, most of the Hypertrophic Cardiomyopathy patients at risk for sudden death can be diagnosed. In addition, if a 2-D echocardiogram is added, most patients with significant valvular stenosis (obstruction to blood flow leaving the heart due to a narrowed heart valve), HCM, and cystic medial necrosis can be identified (Lazar 1996). If an exercise stress test is then performed, approximately 20% of coronary artery disease and congenital artery anomalies may be identified.

Ancillary Testing

Additional non-invasive and invasive studies include Holter monitor recording, tilt table testing, Cardiac computerized tomography (Cardiac CT/CCT), cardiac magnetic resonance imaging (CMR), standard treadmill exercise test and radionuclide cardiac scanning. More sophisticated electrophysiologic studies and cardiac catheterization can be added to identify further, high risk athletes. However, because some asymptomatic patients present with sudden cardiac death as their initial manifestation of disease, it is virtually impossible to identify comprehensively all patients at risk.

By knowing what questions to ask, performing a thorough cardiac screening examination and being aware of potential diagnostic clues, the knowledgeable health professional can feel comfortable in identifying most patients at risk for sudden cardiac death (Rich 1994). Importantly, if an athlete has any symptoms that arouse suspicion of cardiovascular disease, he must be meticulously investigated, as an underlying life-threatening illness may be present (Jensen-Urstad 1995). The further edition of ancillary tests may then be necessary to more thoroughly define the presence and extent of disease (Wigle, Sasson et al. 1985; Maron, Bonow et al. 1987; Klues, Schiffers et al. 1995; Maron, Wolfson et al. 1983; LaCorte, Boxer et al. 1989; Maron, Bodison et al. 1987).

When a definitive diagnosis is made, the excellent resource of the Consensus Panel Guidelines of the 26th Bethesda Conference and the updated 36th Bethesda Conference can be used to make recommendations for continued participation or disqualification from competitive sport (Isner and McKenna 1994), (Maron, Zipes 2005). These recommendations focus primarily on population base screening of high school and collegiate athletes and apply to competitors of all ages in both sexes. These recommendations are based on the probability that intense athletic training and competitive participation is likely to increase the risk for SCD (or disease progression) in athletes with clinically significant underlying structural heart disease. Specific diseases and cardiovascular conditions are outlined in this document. In each, the goal is to try to determine eligibility for participation in competitive athletics for each disease, the magnitude of the risk for sudden death with continued participation in competitive sports and address the criteria to determine whether disqualification is appropriate. The consensus recommendations for each disease state takes into account the nature and severity of the condition as well as the nature and general physical demands of specific sports and training. Also, early detection of significant conditions through screening may in many cases allow for appropriate treatments and interventions that may cure or control the disease, and thereby prolong life. Furthermore, it may sometimes permit the athlete to compete.

Genetic Testing

Currently, genetic testing to identify many hereditable cardiac conditions is not only readily available, but can now be performed at a relatively reasonable cost. Genomics is recognized as a monumentally important advance in medical diagnostics, and has become increasingly more relevant. The identification of many genetic diseases such as HCM, ARVD, Ion Channelopathies such as Long QT and Brugada syndromes and others are currently available. However, applications for medical screening have significant limitations. For example, at least 12 different genetic mutations have thus far been linked to the many forms of the Long QT Syndome. Hypertrophic Cardiomyopathy, the most common genetic heart disease, has over 1,000 mutations in 13 or more genes described. It has a very heterogeneous spectrum and phenotypic expressions, thereby limiting its usefulness for screening purposes. To date, the identification of specific mutations has, unfortunately, little value in predicting prognosis in HCM patients because of the marked variability in phenotypic expression and heterogeneity of expression in this condition. The primary role of such genetic testing is for the diagnosis of relatives in families with documented

HCM, or in probands for whom definitive diagnosis is ambiguous by standard clinical evaluation and testing, i.e., in distinguishing HCM from the normal physiologic variant of the "athlete's heart" (Maron, Semsarian 2010).

Further testing and longitudinal studies with long term follow up will be necessary to help answer the challenging questions about carriers of certain gene mutations and development of disease. In the interim, athletes deemed to be at high risk for SCD may be eligible for primary preventive therapy of SCD with an Implantable Cardioverter Defibrillator (ICD).

At present genetic testing may be useful but reserved for the further evaluation of borderline cases and in athletes of families where there is a strong history or propensity for premature sudden cardiac death. I do believe that in the not too distant future that combinations of genetic testing will be able to better identify phenotypic expressions of disease that are at risk for cardiac sudden death, as suggested recently in Long QT syndromes (Itoh 2010).

AED's and ICD's

Since the mechanism of sudden cardiac death is usually ventricular fibrillation, prompt strategies to defibrillate victims of SCD have emerged and been refined, particularly with the advent and development of the Automatic External Defibrillator (AED). AEDs have been shown to be effective for the immediate resuscitation of athletes with ventricular arrhythmias and cardiac sudden death. They are potentially life-saving, relatively inexpensive and easy to use. They work automatically when applied properly in detecting and confirming life-threatening cardiac rhythms and automatically delivering defibrillation therapy shocks. They are currently available, even to minimally trained or untrained lay responders mostly through public support, in many public places, such as airports, stadiums, coliseums and hospitals. Furthermore, AEDs are recommended pieces of equipment at all training and stadium facilities (Caffey 2002; Maron, Zipes 2005; Myerberg, 2005). It is currently considered reasonable, and recommended by the 36th Bethesda Task Force, to have these devices available for use at training facilities, sports arenas and stadiums. They may, however, not always be successful in the prevention of sudden death, which again emphasizes the importance of preparticiapation screening for the prospective identification of at-risk athletes and the prophylactic prevention of cardiac sudden death by selective disqualification (Maron 2007). Most important is the fact that availability of an AED at a sporting event should not be construed, nor does it provide, absolute protection against a fatal outcome from cardiac arrest. Moreover, it should not supersede restrictions against participation in competitive athletics.

Since the initial advent and reports of the ICD by Dr. Mirowski in 1980 (Mirowski, Mower, 1980), the Implantable Cardioverter Defibrillator (ICD), one of the most significant medical advancements in this medical era, has evolved as a highly effective device. Moreover, ICDs are the most effective medical treatment of life-threatening arrhythmias. Genetic diseases, which are responsible for a great proportion of sudden deaths in young athletes, have over the last decade been targeted for ICD therapy for both primary and secondary prevention. These genetic diseases, such as Hypertrophic Cardiomyopathy (the most common cause of CSD in young athletes in the USA) and other inherited diseases such as Ion Channelopathies (Long or Short QT syndromes, Brugada syndrome, catecholinergic polymorphic ventricular tachycardia) and Arrythmogenic Right Ventricular Cardiomyopathy/Dysplasia (ARVC/D) (the most common cause in some European countries) can have their arrhythmias successfully terminated with the ICD. This, however, remains a secondary prevention of cardiac sudden death syndromes, and does not impart primary treatment or cure of the underlying disease. Hence, ICD placement, although usually successful, does not allow the participation of athletes in most strenuous athletic endeavors. Specific guidelines addressing participation of athletes with implanted ICD's are well outlined in the 36th Bethesda Conference Scientific Statements (Maron, Zipes 2005).

Limitations and Problems of Screening Programs

Confusion does abound, since some published reports of cardiovascular screening programs of large athletic populations, unfortunately, have to date detected only relatively few lethal abnormalities in athletes despite incorporating noninvasive testing (i.e., 2-D echocardiogram and 12-lead electrocardiograms) (LaCorte, Boxer et al. 1989; Weidenbener, Krauss et al. 1995; Feinstein, Colvin and Oh 1993; Risser, Hoffman et al. 1985; Murray, Cantwell et al. 1995; Louis, Maron et al. 1989). Preparticipation screening alone (without non-invasive testing) lacks sufficient sensitivity to guarantee detection of all cardiovascular abnormalities connected with sudden death in young athletes. Current screening problems in the US may be encumbered by significant numbers of false negative results. Also, many cardiac abnormalities must be distinguished from normal variants (false positive results) often seen in the "athlete's heart," which is a normal physiologic adaption and variant to exercise and conditioning. There is also a significant area of overlap and a "gray area" when using the ECG, between normal and diseased conditions when comparing an athlete's heart to abnormalities such as HCM, hypertension, myocarditis and ARVD (Maron, Douglas, JACC 2005).

Prior studies have investigated the clinical, demographic, and pathological profiles of young competitive athletes who died suddenly and unfortunately emphasizes the low percentage of athletes (3%) that had suspicious cardiovascular abnormalities on the pre-participation examination (Maron, Shirani et al. 1996). Furthermore, an even lower percentage were correctly identified (0.9%) by routine pre-screening programs. It has been repeatedly pointed out in the literature that pre-participation screening appears to be of only limited value in identification of underlying cardiovascular abnormalities (Rich 1994; Thompson, Stearns et al. 1979; Feinstein, Colvin and Oh 1993; Risser, Hoffman et al. 1985; Louis, Maron et al. 1989). Nevertheless, the prevailing consensus, particularly within our society, is that there is a responsibility on the part of administrators and physicians to institute prudent efforts to identify life-threatening diseases in athletes and hopefully minimize the cardiovascular risks associated with these highly competitive sports. There is likewise an implicit ethical (and possibly legal) obligation on the part of educational institutions to implement the most efficient cost-effective strategy to insure that their athletes are not subject to unacceptable medical risks (Maron, Brown et al. 1994).

There are usually limited resources available to high school and smaller collegiate programs, although some screening programs that incorporate noninvasive tests at a greatly reduced cost have been described (Weidenbener, Krauss et al. 1995; Feinstein, Colvin and Oh 1993; Louis, Maron et al. 1989). Also recognized is that there may not be a high motivation amongst professional and even collegiate teams or athletes to implement proper cardiovascular screening, because of the possible exclusion of these athletes from competition (Maron, Brown et al. 1994). Appropriate strategies are further hampered at any level of competitive athletics by real life cost considerations along with the awareness that it may not be possible to achieve an ideal zero risk in competitive sport (Maron 1993; rich 1994; Maron, Brown et al. 1994).

For example, from a financial standpoint alone, the theoretical cost of a mass US screening program for competitive athletes could approach $2 billion per year. The amount to detect each athlete with the suspected cardiac disease would be $330,000 and the cost of preventing each theoretical death would be $3.4 million (Maron, et al. 2007). This may not be considered excessive by many for preventing a sudden death in a young individual, but the possibility of a continuous national program, considering these financial constraints, would certainly be arguable and hotly debated.

Specific Limitations of Screening and Diagnostic Evaluation

Other reasons for this contradiction about screening includes the recognition that specific cardiovascular adaptations occur in response to regular physical exercise, and the extent of these changes must be well understood in evaluating participants. The type and duration of exercise as well as the gender and race of the athlete are important considerations. The cardiac adaption to intense physical training are morphologically different from those conditions associated with cardiac sudden death. The cardiovascular adaption to regular physical exercise lead to normal morphological and structural changes in the myocardium (heart muscle) that may influence the cardiac examination, the ECG and other noninvasive tests such as the stress test and 2-D echocardiogram (Wight and Salem 1995). Precise knowledge and recognition of these changes can allow a knowledgeable clinician to distinguish normal physiologic changes from cardiac abnormalities. For instance, the ECG may be abnormal in up to 75% to 95% of people with HCM. It may be able to identify many patients with hereditary channelopathies, such as Brugada, Long QT syndromes, ARVD and myocarditis (Maron, McKenna 2003). False positive tests may occur, especially in borderline instances, and it can be particularly difficult to differentiate these abnormalities from normal cardiac adaption to exercise. An ECG can also frequently identify the important, but less frequent, Wolff-Parkinson-White syndrome (WPW), as well as other electrical abnormalities of the cardiac conduction system (Moss, Schwartz et al. 1991; Vincent, Timothy et al. 1992).

The distinction between normal physiologic changes from those cardiac abnormalities detected among athletes is, however, often difficult (Maron, Wolfson et al. 1983;Maron, Douglas, 2005). Although the addition of noninvasive diagnostic tests to the screening process in young athletes has the potential to enhance detection of certain cardiovascular defects, the problem of over diagnosis and false positive tests is an additional recognized limitation (Houston, Puffer and Rodney 1985; Maron 1986; Pelliccia, Maron et al. 1991; Maron, Pelliccia and Spirito 1995; Pellicia and Maron 1995). On the other hand, false negative tests may occur, particularly since some conditions may not become overtly manifest until adolescence or later.

A recent study from Harvard compared the standard PEP alone with the inclusion of an ECG. The inclusion of an ECG improved the overall sensitivity of screening from 45.5% to 90.9%. However, including the ECG reduced the specificity of screening from 94.4% to 82.7%, with a false positive rate of 16.9%. Although no definitive conclusions regarding the effect of ECG inclusion on sudden death rates could be made, there was improved sensitivity at the expense of an increased rate of false positive results. This further highlights the statistical problems encountered and the perceived value of adding tests to screening programs (Baggish 2010).

Other considerations include the social and ethical dilemmas created when available testing does not resolve this distinction, often resulting in heavy emotional, financial and medical burdens to the athletes and their families. Of equal concerns is the anxiety and uncertainty engendered by the requirement for additional testing and possible athletic competition exclusion.

A striking example of this often occurs in athletes with Marfan's syndrome. Tall athletes are often considered a premium for many competitive sports (i.e., basketball and volleyball) and since most patients with Marfan's syndrome are not only tall, but also have long and very flexible extremities, they often excel at many sports. Vigorous exercise unfortunately poses significant risks for most of these athletes. Unhappily, a diagnosis of Marfan's syndrome carries with it a certain amount of bad news, including a decreased life expectancy. These people can harbor cardiovascular manifestations (including mitral valve degeneration and aortic root disease) which left undiagnosed can have catastrophic consequences and result in sudden death of the athlete. This is particularly true for those engaging in strenuous physical activities. This syndrome has an autosomal dominant mode of inheritance in 85% of those affected but with variable clinical expression. The fact that Marfan's has distinct skeletal, ocular, and body habitus hallmarks allows trained personnel to suspect or make this important diagnosis on physical exam. In addition, a history, especially of sudden death in family members and aortic or mitral valve abnormalities, particularly if associated with tall stature, can aid in the suspicion of this diagnosis (Lazar 1996). The 2D echocardiogram test is essential in this group since 85% of Marfan's patients have mitral valve prolapse and most have aortic root dilitation (Pyeritz and Wappel 1983). It can help to not only make the diagnosis, but to stratify the degree of cardiovascular involvement. In addition, a normal test can help to rule out this frequently devastating diagnosis and differentiate those with Marfan's syndrome from normal athletes. Patients with documented Marfan's syndrome are at risk of aortic dissection, rupture, or lethal arrhythmias and should not engage in contact sport marked isometric or rigorous activities. Newly revised recommendations for Marfan's patients without aortic root dilatation, aortic valvular insufficiency, or mitral regurgitation allow them to participate in low and moderate static and low dynamic sport (such as golf, bowling, billiards, and archery) (Graham, Bricker, James et al. 1994; Maron, Ackerman 2005). Fortunately, with a precise diagnosis, current medical and surgical treatment can avert disasters and significantly prolong life in these individuals.

Ion Channelopathies such as the Long Q-T syndromes are an inherited electrical abnormality that usually involves young people. It is both an autosomal dominant and recessive, inherited disease that is often misdiagnosed as epilepsy or simple fainting. The ECG is currently the best way to diagnose Long Q-T syndrome. Genetic testing is today, readily available for over 12 genetic mutations associated with the multiple forms of this disease. Another important inheritable channelopathy disease is the Brugada syndrome. Unfortunately, with these diseases simple diagnosis is not always possible and inheritance is not always clear. Recent data indicates that a certain proportion of genetically affected relatives with this syndrome of prolonged QT interval may have few or no abnormalities on the ECG, making historical clues and identification most problematic (Van Camp, Vloor et al. 1995). ICD therapy is available for symptomatic individuals, but medical therapy with Beta blockers still holds a major role as first line prophylactic therapy.

The Wolff-Parkinson-White syndrome (WPW) is a congenital abnormality of the conduction system. In patients with WPW, accessory electrical pathways or connections between the pumping chambers of the heart exist that may lead to symptomatic and/or life threatening arrhythmias. In many young people the clinical manifestations of palpitations may be minimal and easily be ignored. This disorder can easily be suspected or diagnosed from the ECG (Wiederman, Becker et al. 1987).

In most other disorders, however, the ECG alone has a relatively low specificity as the only ancillary screening procedure in athletic populations. This is largely due to the high frequency of electrocardiographic abnormalities that may be associated with normal physical adaptations of the heart to athletic training. Hence, routine use of ECG's and even exercise testing may be limited by low specificity.

Definitive identification of congenital coronary anomalies is much more problematic. These usually require more sophisticated imaging procedures such as CCT, CCTA (coroary computerized tomographic angiography), CMR or cardiac cathereterization for an accurate diagnosis to be established.

Routine screening of individuals with exercise testing (usually used in older athletes for coronary artery disease identification) has the marked limitation of low specificity and pretest probability in this population of otherwise young, healthy, low-risk athletes.

Also, there is concern that the widespread application of non-invasive testing in athletic populations could inevitably result in large numbers of false-positive results, creating unnecessary anxiety among substantial numbers of athletes and their families, as well as unjustified exclusion from competitive athletics. Although non-invasive testing can improve upon the diagnostic power of the preparticipation history and physical, it is considered by many to not be practical or prudent to recommend the routine use ECG, 2D echocardiography or treadmill exercise testing for the detection of cardiovascular disease in large populations of young athletes (Williams, 1998)

More sophisticated screening with genetic DNA testing (such as for HCM, Long Q-T syndrome and other Ion Channelopaties), as stated, is currently becoming more widely available, but is not yet practical due to the marked heterogeneity of this and several other disorders (Greisterfer-Lowrance, Kass et al. 1990; Thierfelder, Watkins et al. 1994; Watkins, Conner et al. 1995). Therefore the routine use of some or all of these screening modalities (i.e., 2D-echocardiogram, genetic testing) cannot currently be recommended because of the previously discussed low prevalence of disease and relatively high cost in screening large numbers of athletes and should be reserved for those identified as high risk or those with diagnostic problems.

The scope, extensive resources, and limitations of screening were well pointed out in a recent study by Dr. Fuller et al. from Reno, Nevada (Fuller, Spring, Arger et al. 1995). In this large prospective study, one of the larger cohorts of high school athletes was screened for possible causes of sudden cardiac death during pre-participation exams. As is usually the case, the interest for this study stemmed from the societal impact of the sudden death of a young basketball player. In this study, the question raised was whether the addition of an ECG to the standard history and physical at initial pre-participation screening was helpful or not. Five thousand six hundred fifteen high school athletes (3,378 boys and 2,237 girls) at 34 different high schools were evaluated prospectively for 3 years and followed for up to 4 years. An ECG was added to the pre-participation exam, which included the normal history and physical examinations. Abnormalities of the ECG prompted the performance of a cardiac ultrasound (2-D echocardiogram). One hundred fifteen (2%) of athletes had an abnormal history. One hundred ninety-six (3.5%) had an abnormal cardiac exam and 193 (3.5%) had an abnormal ECG. One hundred twenty-six (2%) had combined abnormalities. All 630 (11%) with abnormal screening underwent a 2-D echocardiogram. In this population, only one sudden cardiac death occurred in which the athlete was fortunately successfully resuscitated from ventricular fibrillation. This patient had a normal ECG, history, and physical examination and turned out to have a congenital coronary anomaly (anomalous right coronary artery) as the cause of sudden death. Also, despite the expected occurrence of HCM in one in every 500 people of the general population, no cases of this were uncovered. Other conditions that were specifically sought were Marfan's syndrome (which can be suspected from the physical examination), anomalous coronary arteries, myocarditis, and primary electrical conduction abnormalities of the heart such as WPW. Soft grade 1–2 cardiac murmurs (usually benign or functional) did not appear to require further evaluation since all of these patients had normal echocardiograms. It was further recognized that louder cardiac murmurs associated with palpable thrills (grade 4 or above), diastolic murmurs, carotid bruits, or Marfan habitus were "red flagged" for further investigation. Severe hypertension was found at a low incidence of only one per 1,000. Forty-three high school athletes (7% of the ultrasounds performed) were found to have minor abnormalities and no further serious undetected abnormality was noted on the 2-D echocardiogram. Five thousand one hundred forty (91.5%) were approved for competitive sport. Four hundred thirty-five (7.8%) were approved after follow up with their local MD (primarily for hypertension). The ECG alone led to disqualification of the athlete in sixteen or one in every 350 of those screened. Once again, no cases of HCM were detected, and even with the addition of a treadmill exercise test, no cases of anomalous coronary artery or premature coronary artery disease were found (16 athletes required a treadmill, all of which were normal). Only a small number (2–3%) required more specific testing for abnormal electrocardiographic findings such as left ventricular hypertrophy (LVH), significant T-wave abnormalities, Q-waves, Wolff-Parkinson-White syndrome (WPW), bundle branch block, or serious rhythm disturbances. In this study, patients with the syndrome of WPW were picked up and referred for appropriate treatments, which with modern medical technology using catheterization and radio-frequency catheter ablation techniques, can now lead to complete cures.

In the most recent published study of adding ancillary testing to the PEP, a single University incorporated an ECG and 2D echocardiogram with the medical history and physical exam and used the 36 th Bethesda recommendations for exclusion. In 964 consecutive athletes 35% were abnormal and 10% of these were classified as distinctly abnormal. 2-D echocardiogram and ECG findings initially resulted in exclusion of 9 athletes from competition. Seven of these athletes with WPW syndrome were ultimately cleared for participation (4 received treatment and 3 did not require treatment). This process identified 9 athletes with significant cardiovascular conditions and only 2 were excluded from competition. This study not only supports the use of ancillary testing but also offers a framework for further preparticipation programs (Magalski 2011).

This study emphasizes the scope and extensive resources necessary in a well-run screening program. It also emphasized that even the more common causes of cardiac sudden death are often found to be exceedingly rare in any one particular study. It further suggests that the addition of an ECG to the history and physical exam increases the ability to detect potentially serious abnormalities that necessitate further testing before approval for competitive sport. Importantly, the marked low incidence of only one occurrence of sudden death may well represent a biased population because of pre-selection of patients not seen fit to participate to begin with. Another arguable interpretation is that it may actually represent excellent screening to allow exclusion of those few athletes at risk.

The failure to reduce the incidence of SCD by adding an ECG to the screening protocol (as well as adding an exercise ECG) was again supported by a study in Israel comparing two time periods before and after 1997, when a mandatory national Sport Law (screening law) was enacted for competitive athletes. The rate of sudden death in athletes for these periods of time was essentially identical, at 2.6 events per 1000,000 athlete years. It was further suggested that false positive ECGs may occur in over 10% of athletes being screened and that a huge number would have to undergo expensive additional testing (Steinvil, Tamar, 2011). This study has been criticized on methodological grounds because the data (number of SCDs) was derived from limited sources and not from a prospective registry. This may have underestimated the total number of sudden deaths. Also, the population at risk was estimated based on prior years (Pellicia, Corrado 2011). This study does have merit, since, as aptly pointed out by the authors, the mean incidence of sudden death was within the same range of the events reported in Italy, the US and Denmark. Also it did compare the post-screening with the pre-screening period, which were of similar duration (Viskin 2011).

Further limitations of athletic screening also relate to the implementation of recommended or existing programs. A report on cardiovascular screening of US collegiate athletes pointed out that preparticipation screening was a requirement at 97% of the 1,110 schools surveyed between 1995 and 1997. The report was based on the 79% (879) of schools that actually responded to the survey. Screening was performed on campus by 81% of those schools responding to the survey. Only 26% of the history and physical exam screening forms (performed by team physicians or nurse practitioners) contained at least 9 of the recommended 12-point AHA screening guidelines and 24% contained 4 or fewer parameters and were considered to be inadequate. Important components, such as a family history of premature sudden death and others, were omitted in over 40% of screening forms. The screening practices used in these NCAA member colleges and universities were clearly felt to limit the potential to detect cardiovascular abnormalities that could lead to sudden death (Pfister 2000).

Medical-Legal Implications

Medical-legal considerations are a legitimate concern to educational institutions and sport organizations. Currently, there is no clear legal precedent regarding the duty or requirement to perform or conduct pre-participation screening of athletes to predict possible medically significant, predisposing abnormalities. There is currently an absence of binding requirements by law or athletic governing bodies, and most institutions and teams rely on their own physicians or other medical personnel to determine appropriate medical screening procedures. Dr. Maron, a leading researcher and expert in medical aspects of sudden cardiac deaths, has ably pointed out that there are no generally accepted and binding criteria for the removal of athletes with cardiovascular disease from competition. "For athletes with cardiovascular disease, the precise risk incurred by participation in competitive sport is uncertain" (Maron 1993). Johnson has also pointed out that the causes of sudden death in exercise, age 35 and younger, are generally not preventable because they are typically structural and difficult to detect. He states that "the best a physician can do is to be alert to important information in the family and patient history and to the occasional sign or symptom that may warrant further evaluation" (Johnson 1992).

The physician who has medically cleared an athlete to participate in competitive sport may not necessarily be legally liable for an injury or death caused by an undiscovered condition. Malpractice liability for failure to discover a latent asymptomatic cardiac condition would require proof that a physician deviated from customary or acceptable medical practice in his or her specialty in performing the pre-participation screening of athletes and that the use of established diagnostic criteria and methods would have disclosed the medical abnormalities.

Currently, the law permits the medical profession to establish the appropriate nature and scope of pre-participation screening of athletes based on its collective medical judgment. Despite the emotional extremes of present legal malpractice debates, the legal standards defined for physician liability are fairly clear. "Physicians are not legally or ethically liable to save patients from all harm nor are they directed to take all steps that would reduce harm" (Mitten 1993).

The legal precedent is that "a physician is under a duty to use that degree of care and skill which is expected of a reasonably competent practitioner of the same class (or specialty) to which he belongs, acting in the same or similar circumstances" (Weistart 1985; *Shilkret* 1975).

The central ethical issue in medical litigation should be to improve the standard of care applied. Establishment of formal standards may limit the extraneous effects of legal contests that are often based primarily on the expertise of the lawyers involved. In this same light, it is the medical profession's responsibility to periodically upgrade and update the medical recommendations as more data and scientific information become available.

In 1994, the 26th Bethesda Conference updated the previous 16th Bethesda Conference (1984) by formulating their recommendations for participation in competitive athletics. At that time the courts had not yet considered whether an athlete with a cardiovascular abnormality could be involuntarily excluded from a competitive sport.

These guidelines for pre-participation cardiovascular screening of athletes were hoped to constitute some evidence of the proper medical standard of care. These guidelines were felt to help establish the legal standard of care if generally accepted, customarily followed by physicians (Mitten 1993) or relied upon by the courts in determining the nature and scope of legal responsibility born by sponsors of competitive athletes in determining medical fitness (Maron, Thompson et al. 1996; *Shilkret* 1975).

Subsequently, in 1996 there was a lawsuit filed on behalf of an athlete claiming the legal right to play an intercollegiate sport despite the team's physician recommendation for disqualification. The other physician disagreed with this decision. This lawsuit (Knapp vs. Northwestern) has served to begin a medico-legal framework for medical decisions regarding disqualifications upheld by universities. The athlete in question had suffered a previous cardiac arrest during basketball participation in high school, and had an ICD placed for the purposes of primary prevention of SCD. There was disagreement among the medical expert testimony and the trial court ruled that he could compete. However, the appellate court ruled in favor of the university and upheld the school's decision to medically disqualify him (1997 Court; Maron 1998MEJM;Maron Ackerman 2005). This decision basically upheld the appropriateness of a physician's reliance on current consensus medical guidelines (26th Bethesda Conference,1994) in making a participation recommendation for an athlete with a cardiovascular abnormality to medically disqualify him. The appellate court stated that Knapp's exclusion was legally justified by the University and did not violate the federal Rehabilitation Act of 1973. This case essentially, formed a legal precedent by recognizing the appropriateness of physician's reliance on consensus guidelines in making medical decisions about athlete disqualification from competitive sports (Maron 2005 — 36th Bethesda Conference).

The law and legal precedent do, however, require that these recommendations be applied on an individual basis rather than used to exclude all athletes who have a particular cardiovascular abnormality.

On the other hand, in considering potential malpractice liability for medically clearing an athlete, the law still requires a physician to have and use current knowledge, skill and care in making these recommendations for participation. The legal standard remains "good medical practice," which includes reasonable, customary and accepted medical care under the circumstances. It is anticipated that the 36th Bethesda Conference recommendations (2005) will now be legally accepted and recognized by physicians and the legal community. Also that compliance with these guidelines should represent evidence that a physician has satisfied the legal requirements and may be the basis of defense against any malpractice allegations.

Practical Aspects of Screening Programs

Currently there are no universally accepted or mandated standards or requirements for the screening of high school and college athletes. Also there is no approved certification for those healthcare professionals who perform the screening examinations. In high schools, there are individual state associations that design and implement performance standards and the National Federation of State High Schools has not played a regulatory role. A 1997 study found high school screening processes to be significantly lacking. Forty percent of the individual states had either no formal screening requirement or a history & physical questionnaire that was found to be incomplete or inadequate (Glover 1998). Fortunately, a follow up analysis eight years later, in 2005, showed a striking improvement in state questionnaire forms and eighty-one percent of states are now judged to have adequate questionnaires (Glover, 2006).

In contrast, colleges and universities usually conduct preparticipation screening within a preexisting infrastructure (i.e. dedicated team physicians and health centers). Member institutions of the NCAA have been independently responsible for their own preparticipation process and design of their own screening history and physical examination. The NCAA has long recommended evaluation of student athletes before participation. More recently, a major advance by the NCAA Committee on Competitive Sports and Medical Aspects of Sports has mandated a preparticipation evaluation for all collegiate athletes in Divisions I, II and III before their first practice or competition. The NCAA also recommends that this be performed by a qualified physician according to guidelines outlined in the Preparticipation Physical Evaluation monograph (PPE 2005 Minneapolis; Maron, Ackerman 2005). It adopted most but not all of the AHA preparticipation history and physical exam items. This was a combined effort of the American Academies of Family Physicians and Pediatrics, the American College of Sports Medicine, and several other medical societies. Though there are screening protocols that incorporate noninvasive testing at reduced costs, these efforts have been unique and have involved donation of equipment and professional time for all but technician related costs (Weidenbener, Krauss et al. 1995; Feinstein, Colvin and Oh 1993). These have been based on public service projects largely through volunteer efforts and cannot be expected to be consistently reproduced or applied. In the real world there are many priorities for the use of available resources on the large scale necessary to provide effective screening of high school and college athletes.

Trained health workers, in lieu of physicians, can perform screening as long as they have the requisite skills and background to obtain a detailed cardiovascular history, perform a physical examination and recognize the presence of obvious cardiovascular and other abnormalities that should be further evaluated. It may be preferable that such an individual be a licensed physician, but this is not always feasible and often a trained registered nurse or physician's assistant can function in these settings. Importantly, parents should be responsible for helping to complete history forms, at least for high school athletes.

In Italy, there has been government mandated preparticipation athletic screening in all athletes engaged in competitive sports since 1982. The state-subsidized national program includes athletes between the ages of 12 to 35 years of age engaging in organized team or individual sports. There must be annual medical clearance, which includes an ECG, carried out by certified sports physicians with special training in identifying cardiovascular abnormalities. Clearance is based on the preparticipation history, physical and ECG. In 2004–2005 the IOC and ESC also advocating adding the ECG to their screening programs (Corrado, 2005; IOC, 2004; Bille, 2005).

This different strategy has resulted in the fall of Italian cardiac deaths of athletes by over 90%, predominantly due to the mortality reduction in the subgroup of cardiomyopathies in their Northern region. In Italy these evaluations are done by specially trained and certified examiners. Despite this, there still remains debate as to whether this process results in lower athlete sudden death rates when compared to the US preparticipation strategy that does not include an ECG. One recent analysis found no difference in mortality between these two systems (Maron, Haas 2009). The European approach, at present, advocates combining non-invasive testing with the standard history and physical exam (Corrado, 2006).

National screening in the US does not currently exist & most experts concede that a de-novo comprehensive national screening program is highly unlikely to occur. In particular, given the size of the U.S. (with five times the population of Italy), large number of athletes to be screened (approximately 10 million) exclusive of youth sports and masters athletes, as well as the geographic variations and numerous rural areas, a legally-mandated process of screening or athletic disqualification is problematic and highly unlikely at present in the US (Maron 2007). The necessary federal subsidization, cost and manpower required would be enormous and are currently considered impractical. Also, strong opposition would likely be incurred based on cost-effectiveness alone. The Italian experience, although admirable, cannot be translated into the current US medical system and environment.

The issues and problems of false positive test results, especially ECG results in athletes (reportedly 10–25%) (Maron 1987:Corrado, 1998), would further expand the cost and complexity of more ancillary testing that would be generated by these results. It is important to re-emphasize the fact that False positive results can generate marked athlete, family and school anxiety and uncertainty and possibly unnecessary disqualification.

In My Opinion

Clearly, all abnormalities in competitive athletes cannot be reliably detected. The efficacy of existing and proposed screening strategies has been debated and not easily resolved by evidence-based medicine. Despite this seeming contradiction there remains overwhelming support for the principles of cardiovascular screening initiatives in both the medical and lay communities (Maron,2007; Maron,Doers,2009). The early detection of significant cardiac disease by preparticiapation screening will in some cases allow for further tiered cardiac specialty evaluation and timely therapeutic interventions, such as

ICD implantation, that can treat and terminate life-threatening arrhythmias, alter the clinical course and natural history of the disease and prolong life.

Failure of screening with PPE may be due to the asymptomatic nature of many of these disorders, the paucity, or lack, of abnormal or suspicious clinical findings or related to the poor sensitivity of currently available testing. Some abnormalities may even defy sophisticated available evaluations. It is precisely for these reasons that a therapeutic program and emergency contingency plans are of the utmost importance. Those athletes who develop sudden death and require immediate resuscitation should have this capability readily available on the scene. This can be done by having trained personnel present who can administer immediate resuscitative measures. This can be accomplished by trainers, coaches, nurses, physicians, or emergency medical technicians with appropriate resuscitative equipment at athletic events or practices. In this regard, AEDs for primary and secondary prevention should be readily available. This can, of course, be lifesaving. This highlights the fact that a well-outlined emergency plan needs to be strongly encouraged and established. Appropriate training includes basic first aid and cardiopulmonary resuscitation training. This is felt by many to be mandatory for anyone working extensively with athletes. The emergency procedures should include on-site treatment and a mechanism to immediately contact emergency personnel with proper transport to a qualified emergency treatment facility.

It must be clearly understood by all that the purpose of this process is not to undermine athletic programs or simply to disqualify athletes. Rather it is to avoid a potential catastrophe. Once again, the misconception must be dispelled that affected athletes that achieve excellence are not affected despite being asymptomatic. There are definite and extensive logistic, time, and cost considerations and constraints in structuring and implementing these programs. Understandably, this may be far in excess of the actual public health problem. Fortunately in our society, people with obvious predisposing factors or conditions, such as congenital heart problems, are usually steered away from competitive athletics at an early age. Because of this pre-selection bias and lack of mandatory reporting, the effect of screening is not altogether known, nor is the entire pool of athletes at risk known.

There is a convincing desire and need to prevent any further occurrences of this important and challenging problem of SCD. A quality history and thorough screening physical examination are still the best means to start to identify athletes at risk for sudden death. It is worth restating that a meticulous personal and family history is the cornerstone of a successfully applied athletic screening program. Additional initial screening tests (i.e., ECG, 2-D echocardiogram) do add value, particularly in unsuspected abnormalities, but will undoubtedly depend on the resources (monetary and personnel) available to each program. Ancillary testing, both screening and more definitive testing and specialty referral, should not be delayed or avoided in individual suspicious cases.

There is an inherent need for responsible organizations and institutions, such as the NCAA, to recognize and accept their responsibilities in these matters. Furthermore, in making decisions about withdrawing athletes from competition, confusion still abounds and the lines of communication and responsibility frequently become muddled (Maron 1993). The loyalties of the team physician may become divided between responsibility to the athlete and desire for success of the team.

Fortunately there is continued ongoing research to help answer many of the debated and unanswered questions about both screening and limitation or disqualification from athletic participation. A current pilot study is underway in the NFL in which all incoming athletes get a 2D echocardiogram. A two year study is in progress in the NBA which includes a stress echocardiogram on all participants every year. These results will hopefully help further our understanding and help guide us in further recommendations.

Currently, the ultimate responsibility for making individual athletic participation recommendations is from the physician, but the ultimate responsibility of removing an athlete from competition is not clear. There is often an ethical and legal controversy based on the personal freedom of the athlete and on the physician's inclination to remove the athlete from competition judged to involve unacceptable risks. Misplaced priorities, particularly among college and professional sports, including potential financial gains for talented young men and women, has resulted in catastrophes in our society. The problems associated with screening programs are often not the programs themselves, but the extent of the process and the recognition of contributing or suspicious factors that may need further evaluation. The implementation and organization of these programs may need to be revised, more structured, more standardized and definitely followed through.

Despite the stated practical and theoretical limitations of screening programs, the AHA and many other medical associations do support the necessity of medical screening of athletes as an important public health issue that is compelling on ethical, medical and legal grounds. Presently, the AHA's relatively conservative recommendations do not believe it to be prudent or practical to recommend the routine addition of the ECG or 2D echocardiogram despite the known fact that it may enhance the diagnostic accuracy of the standard history and physical. It also recognizes that there are significant current medical manpower limitations (lack of a physician group currently to do and interpret these exams), that would not support mass screening at present.

Although lacking the power to detect all cardiovascular abnormalities, a quality, focused history and physical exam by an experienced physician or health professional should continue to be utilized and expanded to areas where this is not the current practice. Furthermore, diligence and proper training in performing these exams and ECG interpretations by certified examiners trained to recognize these abnormalities (as in the Italian model) is required. This remains our most prudent and practical approach to screening and the best defense against the inexplicable horror of a sudden death in an athlete. I do personally feel that the addition of an ECG to the focused PPE is a reasonable, easy to perform and low cost measure that may improve the accuracy of the screening process, although, admittedly this is still yet to be proven. Whether the Italian and European advocated inclusion of an ECG in the screening process is valuable is still arguable and will have to await further results from ongoing research to be answered. Despite these variations in screening the death rates among athletes in the USA, Italy & Europe remain very similar. These differences in approach to the same problem underscores the complexity and controversial questions that have both cultural and societal overtones (Maron, Doerer, 2009).

In view of the differences and variation in the current practices of preparticipation examinations, I would recommend that a systematic national standard be developed. This should include a thorough and complete targeted personal and family history to include all the currently AHA recommended questions. A qualified and preferably certified medical examiner who is knowledgeable in the above aspects should perform the evaluation. The history should include the 12 key points outlined by the AHA. Physical exams that are designed to identify these conditions should be performed prior to participation. This type of screening is obtainable, is a reasonable objective in our society and should be mandatory for all competitive athletes. If there is evidence or suspicion of a potentially lethal cardiovascular condition that is known or might be likely to cause sudden death then appropriate ancillary testing and specialty consultation can be obtained, and then, if necessary, available criteria for eligibility can be addressed. Eligibility and disqualifications issues and decisions should currently be made in accordance with the 36th Bethesda conference recommendations. The clear message is in using medical personnel that are educated, certified and vigilant in the specifics of looking at athletes.

In order to make necessary and accurate decisions about further recommendations and guidelines, it is essential that accurate data be available to our dedicated researchers in this field. Because of pre-selection bias and lack of mandatory reporting, the effect of screening is not altogether known, nor is the entire pool of athletes at risk known. The current lack of a systematic and mandatory reporting registry makes accurate data collection and the true magnitude of the problem even more difficult to obtain. A nationally-mandated reporting systems needs to be established to accurately assess the true prevalence of sudden death in competitive athletes. Only then will we be able to more accurately assess the impact and adequacy of different types of screening programs.

The problem is ubiquitous; in just the last few weeks there have been five deaths reported in the press. Fortunately, through the concern and reporting of the media, both locally and nationally, the level of public awareness about the issues of sudden death in athletes has remained of prominent importance (e.g.,*USA Today* Aug.16, 2011; *Parade Magazine* Aug.7, 2011). Young athletes continue to die suddenly and we need to continue to strive for a solution that is both feasible and cost effective.

Glossary of Medical Terms

Ablation—An invasive electropysiologic method actually disrupting or cutting a specific abnormal electrical conduction pathway in the heart wall. Strong local energy is delivered at a precise location, usually with radio-frequency current (see also Invasive, Electropysiology).

Automatic External Defibrillator (AED)—An automatic external device that recognizes ventricular fibrillation through the use of skin surface pads and then automatically delivers an external shock to defibrillate the heart and restore a normal rhythm.

Aneurysm—A weakening of a portion of the blood vessel wall resulting in a "balloon-like" outpouching. This may be prone to rupture, tearing, or leaking of blood into surrounding tissue or structures.

Aorta—The major blood vessel carrying oxygenated blood away from the heart. Arteries supplying all the body organs arise from this blood vessel or its branches.

Aortic Dissection—A tearing of the aortic wall which may extend for variable lengths, causing obstruction to blood flow and/or leaking of blood into surrounding structures.

Aortic Stenosis—A narrowing and obstruction of the aortic valve which controls the flow of blood from the main pumping chamber of the heart (left ventricle) to the whole body. It may be congenital or acquired later in life.

Arrhythmia—Abnormalities of electrical stimulation or impulse conduction in the heart. These abnormalities can lead to rapid heart rates (tachycardia), slow heart rates (bradycardia), or chaotic heart rhythms (i.e., ventricular fibrillation).

Arrhythmogenic Right Ventricular Dysplasia (ARVD)—A congenital abnormality in the development of the right-sided pumping chamber of the heart (right ventricle) that pumps blood to the lungs to become oxygenated. Often associated with ventricular arrythmias such as ventricular tachycardia and fibrillation.

Asymptomatic—When the patient does not experience or perceive any symptoms despite the presence of an abnormality.

Atherosclerosis—Deposition of fatty plaques in the walls of arteries. This can lead to obstruction of blood flow (i.e., heart attack—myocardial infarction).

Autosomal—Refers to a genetic mode of inheritance that is not "sex-linked" (i.e., autosomal dominant or recessive).

Bundle Branch Block—An electrical pattern caused by a specific blocked conduction pathway in the heart. It may be congenital or acquired, and may be a normal variant or an abnormal finding.

Cardiac Murmurs—Heart sounds that are associated with blood flow across the heart valves and picked up by listening with the stethoscope. Murmurs may be due to obstruction or leakage of the valves. There are many normal variants (functional murmurs) as well as pathologic murmurs associated with a wide spectrum of cardiac diseases.

Cardiac Catheterization—An invasive technique used to visualize and study the heart chambers, coronary arteries, and associated blood vessels. Radio-opaque contrast material (dye) and an X-ray are used to outline chambers or blood vessels (see also Invasive).

Cardiomyopathy—A primary disease of the cardiac muscle tissue (i.e., Hypertrophic Cardiomyopathy, congestive cardiomyopathy).

Carotid Bruit—An abnormal sound or murmur occurring over the carotid artery. This is often a clue to significant obstruction of blood flow and usually caused by atherosclerosis, but can be heard with dilitation or abnormal tortuosity.

Cerebrovascular—Blood vessels of the brain and associated structures.

Commotio Cordis—Sudden death due to ventricular fibrillation, caused when a projectile (e.g., baseball, lacrosse ball, hockey puck) strikes the chest wall with forceful, sudden, blunt non-penetrating chest trauma in an individual with no underlying cardiac disease.

Congenital—Occurring at birth and usually persisting throughout life.

Coronary Anomalies—Variations and abnormalities of development, origin, or position of the coronary arteries. These arteries arise from the aorta, just above the aortic valve, and supply the heart itself with nutrients and oxygenated blood.

Cystic Medial Necrosis—Abnormalities of the muscular and supporting tissue layers of blood vessels. The primary pathologic abnormality seen in Marfan's and some other related syndromes.

Diastolic Murmur—A cardiac murmur occurring during the filling of a heart chamber with blood.

2-D Echocardiogram—A non-invasive (external) technique of visualizing cardiac chambers and structures using reflective ultrasound waves.

ECG—A 12 lead external surface recording that displays the electrical activity of the heart.

Electrophysiologic Studies (E-P study)—A specialized invasive study of the cardiac conduction system within the heart. Usually done by cardiac catheterization techniques. It is used to diagnose and evaluate cardiac arrhythmias.

Exercise Stress Test—An exercise test using a treadmill or bicycle ergometer with associated continuous ECG monitoring. This is used to detect narrowing of the coronary arteries and/or arrhythmias precipitated by the stress of exercising. Often used in the diagnosis and evaluation of coronary artery disease. Also called a Treadmill exercise test.

Familial—A condition with a marked tendency to occur frequently in related family members but without a direct or consistent pattern. It can also skip generations. Usually implies a genetic or hereditary mode of transmission that may not, as yet, be proven.

Functional—Usually used to denote a normal cardiac murmur in distinction to abnormal murmurs that indicate valvular obstruction or incompetence (insufficiency or regurgitation).

Genomics—A discipline in genetics concerning the study of the genomes of organisms.

Holter Monitor Recording—Continuous external ECG recording of the heart rate and rhythm using a tape recorder or digital recording system.

Hypertrophic Cardiomyopathy (HCM)—A hereditary disease of cardiac muscle cells (fibers) characterized by abnormal thickening and disarray of muscle fibers. This can lead to abnormal heart chamber and wall thickening. This can be associated with obstruction to outflow of blood from the main pumping chamber of the heart (left ventricle). It can be a cause of cardiac arrhythmias, syncope (passing out), and heart failure. Symptoms are most often exertional and include dizziness, syncope, palpitations, chest pain, and exertional shortness of breath.

Idiopathic—Of unknown cause (or etiology).

Implantable Cardioverter-Defibrillator (ICD)—An implanted device that monitors the electrical heart rhythm and can be programmed externally to deliver an internal cardiac shock or electrical pacing to terminate life-threatening arrhythmias such as ventricular tachycardia and ventricular fibrillation.

Intracranial—Within the brain.

Intrathoracic—Occurring within the chest cavity including the compartment containing the aorta and great vessels.

Invasive—Testing that requires direct entrance into the arteries, veins (blood vessels), or heart chambers. Usually done by per cutaneous technique (i.e., through the skin by a needle puncture).

Ion Channelopathies—Hereditary disorders of ion channels that control and regulate electrical conduction in the heart.

Left Ventricular Hypertrophy—Abnormal thickening of the main pumping chamber of the left side of the heart (left ventricle), which pumps oxygenated blood to the whole body.

Long Q-T Syndrome—A genetic electrical abnormality of cardiac muscle depolarization characterized by a long Q-T interval on the electrocardiogram (ECG). It may be associated with rapid and chaotic forms of ventricular tachycardia.

Marfan's Syndrome—A hereditary disease of the supporting tissue of the cardiovascular system including the great vessels (aorta) and valves (i.e., mitral valve prolapse). This disease affects the muscular and supporting tissue components of these structures. It can lead to valvular incompetence (mitral valve prolapse) or weakening of the arterial walls (cystic medial necrosis) with subsequent aneurysm formation, tearing (dissection), or rupture of the blood vessel. Usually associated with a distinct body habitus.

Mitral Valve Prolapse—Abnormality of the mitral valve which controls flow between the left-sided cardiac pumping chambers. This may be associated with valvular leaking (incompetence or regurgitation) and is often associated with cardiac arrhythmias. It tends to be familial.

Morphological—Structural.

Myocarditis—Inflammation of cardiac muscle cells that may lead to weakening of the heart muscle with associated heart failure and/or cardiac arrhythmias.

Myocardium—Heart muscle tissue.

Non-invasive—External diagnostic test that does not require actual entrance into the circulation (i.e., 2-D Echocardiography, Electrocardiogram (ECG)).

Palpitations—This sensing of heart activity by the patient. Usually described as fluttering, racing, irregularities, or pounding of the heart.

Radionuclide Scanning—Nuclear heart scanning done after injection of radio-nuclear isotopes with a short half-life, that accumulates in viable ("alive" or "stunned") heart muscle or in cardiac chambers. Most often done with exercise testing (and ECG monitoring) or pharmacologic (use of drugs) agents to simulate the stress of exercise. It is used to define "dead" (nonfunctioning) or oxygen starved (ischemic) areas of the heart as an aid to the diagnosis of coronary artery disease. A much more sensitive and specific technique than treadmill testing alone.

Sickle Cell Trait—A partial genetic abnormality of red blood cell hemoglobin synthesis. Hemoglobin is the component of the red blood cells that carry oxygen. This may lead to poor oxygenation, particularly during physical stress, and can be associated thrombosis (formation of blood clots) of arteries and/or abnormal bleeding.

Sudden Death—Sudden collapse of an individual without known direct antecedent symptoms or cause. Most commonly due to ventricular fibrillation (see fibrillation). This may result in the death of an individual unless prompt resuscitation is accomplished. The exact time of death resulting from this event is usually defined by the author in any particular study.

Syncope—Passing out.

Tachycardia—Refers to abnormal and inappropriate rapid heart rates and rhythms.

Therapeutic—Used to treat specific medical condition.

Tilt Table Test—A non-invasive test used to vary the patient's body position and uncover abnormal episodes of low blood pressure (hypotension) and/or slow heart rate (bradycardia) causing syncope (passing out). Used as a diagnostic tool in patients to distinguish between an exaggerated normal response to changes in body position from a disease entity.

TTE—Transthorasic echocardiography, A non-invasive (external) technique of visualizing cardiac chambers and structures using reflective ultrasound waves (same as 2D Echocardiography).

Ventricular Fibrillation—Rapid and chaotic stimulation of the heart resulting in ineffectual blood flow, cardiac asystole (cardiac standstill), and sudden death.

Ventricular Tachycardia—Rapid electrical stimulation and contraction of the heart usually associated with diminished blood flow to the brain and passing out. This may degenerate into ventricular fibrillation and cause sudden death. It is associated with many cardiac abnormalities and is felt to be the pathophysiologic mechanism in most cases of sudden death.

Wolff-Parkinson-White Syndrome (WPW)—A variety of congenital abnormalities of the cardiac conduction system characterized by one or multiple accessory electrical pathways or connections between the upper (atrium) and lower (ventricle) pumping chambers of the heart. This may result in several forms of rapid heart rates caused by bypassing the normal conduction pathways and may degenerate into serious ventricular arrhythmias such as (ventricular fibrillation).

References

Ali, T. 1991. "Sudden Death In Athletes in Trinidad and Tobago." West Indian Med J vol. 40, December, pp. 192–194.

Baggish A.L., Hutter Jr., Wang F., Yared K., Weiner R.B., Kupperman E., Picard M.H., Wood M.J., "Cardiovascular screening in college athletes with and without electrcardiography: A cross-sectional study." Ann Intern Med. 2010 Mar 2; 152(5): 269–75.

Bille K., Schamasch P., Brenner J.I., Kappenberger L., Meijboom F.J., Meijboom E.J., Sudden deaths in athletes: the basics of the "Lausanne Recommendations" of the International Olympic Committee. Circulation. 2005; 112 (suppl II): II-830. Abstract.

Burke, A.P., A. Farb, and R. Virmani. 1992. "Causes of Sudden Death in Athletes." Cardiol Clin vol. 10, no. 2, May, pp. 303–317.

Burke, A.P., A. Farb, et al. 1991. "Sport related and non-sport-related sudden cardiac deaths in young adults." Am Heart J vol. 121, pp. 568–575.

Caffey S.L., Willoughby P.J., Becker L.B., "Public Use of automatic external defibrillators", N Engl J Med 2002; 347: 142–7.

Cheitlin, M.D., C.M. DeCastro, and H.A. McAllister, Jr. 1974. "Sudden death as a complication of anomalous left coronary origin from the anterior sinus of Valsalva: A not so minor congenial abnormality." Circulations vol. 50, pp. 780–787.

Christensen, R.E. 1989. "Sudden Unexpected Death In Young Athletes: A Review." Alaskan Med J vol. 31, July–December, pp. 144–147.

Corrado D., Basso C., Shiavon M., Thiene G., "Screening for hypertrophic cardiomyopathy in young athletes". N Engl J Med. 1998; 339: 364–369.

Corrado D., Basso C., Pavei A., Michieli P., Schiavon M., Thiene G., "Trends in sudden cardiovascular death in young competitive athletes after implementation of a preparticipation screening program". JAMA. 2006; 296: 1593–1601.

Corrado D., Pelliccia A., Bjørnstad H.H., Vanhees L., Biffi A., Borjesson M., Panhuyzen-Goedkoop N., Deligiannis A., Solborg E., Dugmore D., Mellwig K.P., Assanelli D., Delise P., van-Buuren F., Anastasakis A., Heidbuchel H., Hoffman E., Fagard R., Priori S.G., Basso C., Arbustini E., Blomstrom-Lundqvist C., McKenna W.J., Thiene G., "Cardiovascular pre-participation screening of young competitive athletes for prevention of sudden death: proposal for a common European protocol: consensus statement of the Study Group of Sport Cardiology of the Working Group of Cardiac Rehabilitation and Exercise Physiology and the Working Group of Myocardial and Pericardial Diseases of the European Society of Cardiology". Eur Heart J. 2005; 26: 516–524.

Corrado, D., G. Thiene, et al. 1990. "Sudden death in young competitive athletes: Clinicopathologic consultations in 22 cases." Am J Med vol. 89, pp. 588–596.

Epstein, S.E. and B.J. Maron. 1986. "Sudden Death In The Competitive Athlete: Prospectives on Pre-participation Screening Studies." Jam Coll Cardiol vol. 7, no. 1, January, pp. 220–230.

Feinstein, R.A., E. Colvin, and M.K. Oh. 1993. "Echocardiographic screening as part of a pre-participation examination." Clinical J of Sport Med vol. 3, pp. 149–152.

Firor, W.B. and R.A. Faulkner. 1998. "Sudden Death During Exercise: How Real A Hazard?" Can J Cardiol vol. 4, no. 6, September, pp. 251–254.

Fudderman, L.G. and L. Lemberg. 1995. "Sudden death in athletes." Am J Crit Care no. 3, May, pp. 239–243.

Fuller, C.M., D.A. Spring, Arger, et al. 1995. Prospective Screening of 5,615 High School Athletes for Sudden Cardiac Death. Abstract. American College of Cardiology, Annual Scientific Sessions, JACC, February.

Glover D.W., Glover D.W., Maron B.J., "Evolution over 8 years of the US preparticipation screening process for unsuspected cardiovascular disease in US high school athletes." Circulation. 2006; 114 (suppl II): II-502.

Glover D.W., Maron B.J., "Profile of preparticipation cardiovascular screening for high school athletes." JAMA. 1998; 279: 1817–1819.

Graham, T.P., Jr., J. Bricker, F.W. James, et al. 1994. "American College of Cardiology and American College of Sport Medicine: Cardiovascular abnormalities in the athlete: recommendations regarding eligibility for competition: Task Force 1: Congenital heart disease." J Am Coll Cardiol vol. 24, pp. 876–883.

Greisterfer-Lowrance, A.A., S. Kass, et al. 1990. "A molecular basis for familial hypertrophic cardiomyopathy: A B-cardiac myosin heavy chained gene missense mutation cells." Cell vol. 62, no. 5, September 7, pp. 999–1006.

Hackel, D.B., and K.A. Reimer. 1993. Sudden death cardiac and other causes. Durham, NC: Carolina Academic Press.

Harmon K.G., Asif I.M., Klossner D., Drezner J.A., "Incidence of sudden cardiac death in national collegiate association athletes", Circulation, 2011 Apr 19; 123(15): 1594–600.

Houston, T.P., J.C. Puffer, and W.N. Rodney. 1985. "The athletic heart syndrome." N Engl J Med vol. 313, pp. 224–232.

IOC Medical Commission, International Olympic Committee. Sudden Cardiovascular Death in Sport: Lausanne Recommendations: Preparticipation Cardiovascular Screening. December 10, 2004. Available at: http://multimedia.olympic.org/pdf/en_report_886.pdf.

Isner, J.M., N.A. Estes, III, et al. 1986. "Acute cardiac events temporally related to Cocaine abuse." N Engl J Med vol. 315, pp. 1438–1443.

Itoh H., Shimizu W., Hayashi K., Yamagata et al., "Long QT syndrome with compound mutations is associated with a more severe phenotype: A Japanese multicenter study", Heart Rhythm 2010; 7: 1411–1418.

Jensen-Urstad, M. 1995. "Sudden death in physical activity in athletes and non-athletes." Scand J Med Sci Sport vol. 5, pp. 279–84.

Johnson, R.J. 1992. "Sudden Death During Exercise. A Cruel Turn of Events." Post Grad Med vol. 92, no. 2, August, pp. 195–198, 201–202, 205–206.

Kark, J.A., D.M. Posey, et al. 1987. "Sickle-Cell trait as a risk factor for sudden death in physical training." N Engl J Med vol. 317, pp. 781–787.

Kenny, A. and L.M. Shapiro. 1992. "Sudden Cardiac Death in Athletes." Br Med Bull vol. 48, no. 3, July, pp. 534–545.

Klues, H.G., A. Schiffers, et al. 1995. "Phenotypic spectrum and patterns of left ventricular hypertrophy and hypertrophic cardiomyopathy: Morphologic observations and significant as assessed by 2-dimensional echocardiography in 600 patients." J Am Coll Cardiol vol. 26, pp. 1699–1708.

LaCorte, M.A., R.A. Boxer, et al. 1989. "EKG screening program for school athletes." Clin Cardiol vol. 12, pp. 42–44.

Lazar, J.M. 1996. "Marfan's Syndrome: Cardiovascular manifestations and exercise implications. Your Patient and Fitness in Cardiology vol. 10, no. 6, November/December, pp. 6–15.

Louie, E.K. and L.C. Edwards, III. 1994. "Hypertrophic cardiomyopathy." Prog Cardiovasc Dis vol. 36, pp. 275–308.

Louis, J.F., B.J. Maron, et al. 1989. "Pre-participation echocardiographic screening for cardiovascular disease in a large, predominantly black population of collegiate athletes." Am J Cardiol vol. 64, pp. 1029–1033.

Lyznicki J.M., Nielson N.H., Schneider J.F., "AMA policy on cardiovascular screening of student Athletes", Am Family Physician, 2000 Aug 15; 62(4); 765–74.

Magalski A., McCoy M., Magee L.M., Goeke J., Main M.L., Bunten L., Reid K.J., Ramza B.M., Am J Med, 2011 Jun; 124(6): 511–8.

Maron, B.J. 1996. "Triggers of Sudden Cardiac Death In the Athlete." Cardiol Clin, vol. 14, no. 2, May, pp. 195–210.

Maron, B.J. 1993. "Sudden death in young athletes: Lessons from the Hank Gathers affair." N Engl J Med vol. 329, pp. 55–57.

Maron, B.J. 1986. "Structural features of the athlete's heart as defined the echocardiography." J Am Coll Cardiol vol. 7, pp. 190–203.

Maron, B.J., "Diversity of views from Europe on national prepartication screening for competitive athletes", Heart Rhythm, vol. 7, Issue 10, October 2010, pp. 1372–1373.

Maron B.J., "National electrocardiography screening for competitive athletes: Feasible in the United States?", Am J Cardiol. 2009 Jul 15; 104(2): 276–80. Epub 2009 May 18.

Maron B.J., "National electrocardiography screening for competitive athletes; Feasible in the United States?", Ann Intern Med 2010, July 20; 153(2); 131–133.

Maron, B.J., S.A. Bodison, et al. 1987. "Results of screening a large group of intercollegiate competitive athletes for cardiovascular disease." J Am Coll Cardiol vol. 10, pp. 1214–1221.

Maron, B.J., R.O. Bonow, et al. 1987. "Hypertrophic cardiomyopathy: Interrelations of clinical manifestations, pathophysiology and therapy, 1." N Engl J Med vol. 316, pp. 780–789.

Maron, B.J., R.W. Brown, et al. 1994. "Am Journal ethical, legal and practical considerations effecting medical decision making in competitive athletes." J Am Coll Cardiol vol. 24, pp. 854–860.

Maron Barry J., Joseph J. Doerer, Tammy S. Haas, David M. Tierney, MD; Frederick O. Mueller, PhD, Sudden a March 3, 2009.

Maron B.J., Haas T.S., Doerer J.J., Thompson P.D., Hodges J.S.. "Comparison of U.S. and Italian experiences with sudden cardiac death in young competitive athletes and implications for preparticipation screening strategies". Am J Cardiol. 2009, Jul 15; 104(2): 276–280.

Maron Barry J., MD, FACC, Chair, Pamela S. Douglas, MD, FACC, Thomas P. Graham, MD, FACC, Rick A. Nishimura, MD, FACC and Paul D. Thompson, MD, FACC, "Task Force 1: Preparticipation screening and diagnosis of cardiovascular disease in athletes", J Am Coll Cardiol, 2005; 45:1322–1326, doi:10.1016/j.jacc.2005.02.007.

Maron, B.J., S.E. Epstein, and W.C. Roberts. 1986. "Causes of sudden death in competitive athletes." J Am Coll Cardiol vol. 7, pp. 204–214.

Maron, B.J., J.M. Gardin, et al. 1995. "Prevalence of hypertrophic cardiomyopathy in a general population of young adults: Echocardiographic analysis of 4,111 subjects in the Cardia study—coronary artery risk development in (young) adults." Circulation vol. 92, pp. 785–789.

Maron, B.J. and A. Garson. 1994. "Arrhythmias and sudden cardiac death in elite athletes." Cardiol Rev vol. 2, pp. 26–32.

Maron B.J., Gohman T.E., Aeppli D., "Prevalence of sudden cardiac death during competitive sports activities in Minnesota high school athletes." J Am Coll Cardiol. 1998; 32: 1881–1884.

Maron B.J., Haas T.S., Doerer J.J., Thompson P.D., Hodges J.S., "Comparison of U.S. and Italian experiences with sudden cardiac deaths in young competitive athletes and implications for preparticipation screening strategies", Am J Cardiol. 2009, Jul 15; 104(2); 276–280.

Maron, B.J., J.M. Isner, and W.J. McKenna. 1994. "26th Bethesda Conference: Recommendations for determining eligibility for competition in athletes with cardiovascular abnormalities. Task Force 3: Hypertrophic cardiomyopathy, myocarditis, and other mild pericardial diseases and mitral valve prolapse." J Am Coll Cardiol vol. 24, pp. 880–885.

Maron B.J., McKenna W.J., Danielson G.K., et al. American College of Cardiology/European Society of Cardiology clinical expert consensus document on hypertrophic cardiomyopathy: "A report of the American College of Cardiology Foundation Task Force on Clinical Expert Consensus Documents and the European Society of Cardiology Committee for Practice Guidelines." J Am Coll Cardiol 2003; 42: 1687–713.

Maron, B.J. and J.H. Mitchell. 1994. "Revised eligibility recommendations for competitive athletes with cardiovascular abnormalities." J Am Coll Cardiol vol. 24, pp. 848–850.

Maron B.J., Mitten M.J., Quandt E.F., Zipes D.P., "Competitive athletes with cardiovascular disease—the case of Nicholas Knapp". N Engl J Med 1998; 339: 1632–5.

Maron, B.J., A. Pelliccia, and P. Spirito. 1995. "Cardiac disease in young trained athletes: Insights into message with distinguishing athlete's heart from structural heart disease, with particular emphasis on hypertrophic cardiomyopathy." Circulation vol. 91, pp. 1596–1601.

Maron, B.J. and L. Poliac, et al. 1995. "Blunt impact to the chest leading to sudden death from cardiac arrest during sport activities." N Engl J Med vol. 333, pp. 337–342.

Maron, B.J., W.C. Roberts, et al. 1980. "Sudden death in young athletes." Circulation vol. 62, pp. 218–229.

Maron, B.J., Semsarian C., "Emergence of gene mutation carriers and the expanding disease spectrum of hypertrophic cardiomyopathy" editorial, Eur Heart J, 2010.

Maron, B.J., J. Shirani, et al. 1996. "Sudden death in young competitive athletes: Clinical demographic and pathological profiles." JAMA vol. 276, no. 3, July, pp. 199–204.

Maron B.J., P.D. Thompson, et al. 1996. "Cardiovascular pre-participation screening of competitive athletes: A statement for health professionals from the sudden death committee (Clinical cardiology) and congenital cardiac defects committee (Cardiovascular disease in the young), American Heart Association: AHA medical/scientific statement." Circulation vol. 94, pp. 850–856.

Maron J., Thompson J., Ackerman M., Balady G., Berger S., Cohen D., Dimeff R., Douglas P., Glover D., Hutter A., Krauss M., Maron M., Mitten M., Roberts W., Puffer J. "Reccomendations and Considerations Related to Prepartication Screening for Cardiovascular Abnormalities in Competitive Athletes: 2007 Update." Circulation 2007, 115: 1643–1655.

Maron, B.J., Thompson P.D., Puffer J.C., McGrew C.A., Strong W.B., et al. "Cardiovascular prepartication screening of competitive athletes; a statement for Health Professionals from the Sudden Death Committee (Clinical Cardiology) and Congenital Cardiac Defects Committee (Cardiovascular Disease in the Young), American Heart Association". Circulation 1996; 94; 850–856.

Maron Barry J., Williams, Richard A. editor, The Athlete and Heart Disease, "Diagnosis, Evaluation & Management", Chapter 16: "Cardiovascular Prepartication Screening of Competitive Athletes", Maron; pp. 273–284.

Maron, B.J., J.K. Wolfson, et al. 1983. "Relation of electrocardiographic abnormalities and patterns of left ventricular hypertrophy identified by 2-dimensional echocardiography in patients with hypertrophic cardiomyopathy", Am J Cardiol vol. 51, pp. 189–194.

Maron B.J., Zipes Doerer et al. 36th Bethesda Conference: eligibility recommendations for competitive athletes with cardiovascular abnormalities. J Am Coll Cardiol. 2005; 45: 1312–1375.

McMicken   D.,   "Sudden   Death   in   Athletes,"   available   at: http://www.hughston.com/hha/a_16_4_4.htm,2011.

Mirowski M., Reid P.R., Mower M.M., Watkins L., Gott V.L., Schauble J.F., et al. "Termination of malignant ventricular arrythmias with an implantable automatic defibrillator in human beings". N Engl J Med. 1980; 303: 322–4, Am J Cardiol vol. 51, pp. 189–194.

Mitten, M.J. 1993. "Team physicians and competitive athletes: Allocating legal responsibility for athletic injuries." University of Pittsburgh Law Review vol. 55, pp. 129–169.

Moss, E.J., P.L. Schwartz, et al. 1991. "The long QT syndrome: Perspective longitudinal study of 328 families." Circulation. vol. 84, pp. 1136–1144.

Murray, P.N., J.D. Cantwell, et al. 1995. "The role of limited echocardiography in screening athletes." Am J Cardiol vol. 76, pp. 849–850.

Myerburg R.J., Estes NAM III, Fontaine J.M., Link M.S., Zipes D.P., Task Force 10: automated external defibrillators. J Am Coll Cardiol. 2005; 45: 1369–1371.

Pelliccia A., Corrado D., "The Israel Screening Failure-Analyzing the Data to Understand the Results", Letters to the Editor, JACC vol. 58, no. 9, 2011: 989–90.

Pelliccia, A., B.J. Maron, et al. 1991. "The upper limit of physiologic cardiac hypertrophy in highly trained elite athletes." N Engl J Med vol. 324, pp. 295–301.

Pelliccia, A., B.J. Maron, et al. 1996. "Athletes horror in women: Echocardiographic characterization of highly trained elite female athletes." JAMA vol. 276, pp. 211–215.

Pelliccia, A. and B.J. Maron. 1995. "Pre-participation cardiovascular evaluation of the competitive athlete: Perspectives from the 30 year Italian experience." Am J Cardiol vol. 75, pp. 827–829.

Pelliccia, Faggard et al., "Reccomendations for competitive sports participation in athletes with cardiovascular disease: a consensus document from the European Society of Cardiology", Eur Heart J. 2005; 26; 1422–1445.

Pfister G.C., Puffer J.C., Maron B.J., "Preparticipation cardiovascular screening for US collegiate student-athletes", JAMA 2000, Mar 22–29, 283(12): 1597–9.

Preparticipation Physical Evaluation. 3rd ed. Minneapolis, Minn: McGraw-Hill/The Physician and Sports-Medicine; 2005.

Pretre, R. and M. Chilcott. 1997. "Blunt trauma to the heart and great vessels." N Engl J Med vol. 336, pp. 626–632.

Pyeritz, R.E. and M.A. Wappel. 1983. "Mitral Valve dysfunction in the Marfan's syndrome; clinical and ecchocardiographic study of prevalence and natural history." Am J Med vol. 74, no. 5, pp. 797–807.

Rich, B.S. 1994. "Sudden death screenings — review article" Med Clin North Am vol. 2, pp. 267–88.

Risser, W.L., H.M. Hoffman, et al. 1985. "A cost-benefit analysis of pre-participation sport examination of adolescent athletes." J Sch Health vol. 55, pp. 270–273.

Roberts, W.C. 1987. Congenital coronary artery anomalies unassociated with major anomalies of the heart or great vessels in: Adult congenital heart disease, p. 583. Philadelphia, PA: S.A. Davis Company.

Shilkret v. Annapolis Emergency Hospital Association, 276 Md. 187, 200, 349 A.2d 245, 253 (1975). See also J. Waltz and F. Inhau, 1971, Medical Jurisprudence vol. 42.

Steinvil, Chundadze, Zeltser, Rogowski, Halkin, Perluk, Viskin, "Mandatory Electrocarf-diographic Screening of Athletes to Reduce Their Risk For Sudden Death Proven Fact, or Wishful Thinking?", JACC, 2011; 57(11): 1291

Thiene, G., NAVA, et al. "Right Ventricular Cardiomyopathy and Sudden Death in Young People." N Engl J Med vol. 318, pp. 129–133.

Thierfelder, L., H. Watkins, et al. 1994. "A-tropomyosin and cardiac troponin mutations cause familial hypertrophic cardiomyopathy: A disease of the sarcomere period cell." Cell vol. 77, no. 5, June 3, pp. 701–712.

Thompson, P.D. 1993. "Athletes, Athletics, and Sudden Cardiac Deaths." Med Sci Sport Exerc vol. 25, no. 9, September, pp. 981–984.

Thompson, P.D., M.P. Stearns, et al. 1979. "Death during jogging or running: A study of 18 cases." JAMA vol. 242, pp. 1265–1267.

Thompson, P.C., E.J. Funk, et al. 1982. "Incidences of deaths during jogging in Rhode Island from 1975–1980." JAMA vol. 247, pp. 2535–2538.

Van Camp, S.P, C.M. Vloor, et al. 1995. "Nontraumatic sport deaths in high school and college athletes." Med Sci Sport Exerc vol. 25, pp. 641–647.

Vaska, P.L. 1992. "Sudden Cardiac Death in Young Athletes. A review for nurses." AACN Clin Issues Crit Care Nurs vol. 3, no. 1, February, pp. 243–254.

Vincent, G.M., K.A. Timothy, et al. 1992. "The spectrum of symptoms and QT intervals and carriers of the genes for the long-QT syndrome." N Engl J Med vol. 327, pp. 846–852.

Virmani, R., M. Robinowitz, et al. 1988. "Cardiovascular effects of Cocaine: An autopsy study of 40 patients." Am Heart J. vol. 115, pp. 1068–1076.

Virmani, R., M. Robinowitz, and H.A. McAllister, Jr. 1982. "Nontraumatic deaths in joggers: A series of 30 patients at autopsy." Am J Med. vol. 72, pp. 874–882.

Viskin S., Halkin A., Steinvil A., Zeltser D., "Reply", Letters to the Editor, JACC vol. 58, no. 9 2011; 991–92.

Waller, B.S. and W.C. Roberts. 1980. "Sudden death while running in conditioned runners age 40 years or over." Am J Cardiol vol. 45, pp. 1292–1300.

Watkins, H., D. Conner, et al. 1995. "Mutations in the cardiac myosin binding protein-C gene on chromosome 11 caused familial hypertrophic cardiomyopathy" Nat Genet vol. 11, December, pp. 434–437.

Weidenbener, E.J., M.D. Krauss, et al. 1995. "Incorporation of screening echocardiography in the pre-participation exams." Clin J Sport Med vol. 5, pp. 86–89.

Weistart, John C. 1985. "Legal consequences of standard setting for competitive athletes with cardiovascular abnormalities." J Am Coll Cardiol vol. 6, pp. 1101–1197.

Whittington, R.M. and Jeea Banner. 1994. "Sport-related Sudden Natural Deaths in the City of Birmingham." JR Soc Med vol. 87, no. 1, January, pp. 18–21.

Wiederman, C.J., S.E. Becker, et al. 1987. "Sudden death in a young competitive athlete with Wolff-Parkinson-White Syndrome." Eur Heart J vol. 8, no. 6, pp. 651–655.

Wight, J.N., Jr. and D. Salem. 1995. "Sudden Cardiac Death In the "Athletes Heart." Archives Internal Medicine vol. 155, no. 14, July 24, pp. 1473–1480.

Wigle, E.D., Z. Sasson, et al. 1985. "Hypertrophic cardiomyopathy: The importance of the site and extensive hypertrophy—a review." Prog Cardiovasc Dis vol. 28, pp. 1–83.

Wikipedia "Pheidippides", available at http://en.wikipedia.org/wiki/Pheidippides.

Williams, R.A. 1991. "Sudden cardiac death in blacks, including black athletes." Cardiovasc Clin vol. 21, no. 3, pp. 297–320.

Chapter 19

Emergency Medical Preparedness

It is imperative that all sport medicine personnel be prepared to render effective emergency care when a medical emergency occurs.

Jerald D. Hawkins

Medical emergencies in sport medicine are relatively rare. However, they do occur and when they do, they often pose life-threatening danger to the victim. Therefore, it is imperative that all sport medicine services programs and personnel be prepared to render effective emergency care when a medical emergency occurs. Emergency preparedness involves 1) development, maintenance, and implementation of an emergency response plan (including efficient interfacing with local emergency medical care services); 2) timely and accurate assessment of emergency injuries; and 3) performance of specific emergency care procedures. This chapter focuses on the delivery of comprehensive emergency sport medicine care.

Three critical issues must be addressed when designing a comprehensive emergency preparedness plan: qualifications of personnel, availability of emergency equipment, and the specific plan itself.

Personnel

It is safe to assume that the quality of emergency care available in a sport medicine services program can be no better than the qualifications of the personnel responsible for providing such care. Since the primary concern of emergency care is to prevent death by maintaining cardiovascular and central nervous system functioning, all sport medicine services personnel should be prepared to perform cardiopulmonary resuscitation. The American College of Sports Medicine has recommended that all personnel involved in exercise-related programs be trained and certified in basic cardiopulmonary resuscitation (CPR) and preferably Advanced Cardiac Life Support (ACLS). Likewise, the National Athletic Trainers' Association requires that all certified athletic trainers must possess certification in first aid and CPR. Given the potentially grave consequences of inadequate emergency care, and the relative ease of obtaining such training from local American Heart Association and American Red Cross chapters, these recommendations would appear quite reasonable.

Equipment

Since many life-threatening emergencies in sport medicine settings involve the possibility of cardiac and/or respiratory arrest, it would be wise to have emergency equipment available, some of which will allow trained personnel to administer Advanced Cardiac Life Support. While only personnel with appropriate training should utilize advanced life support equipment, in the absence of qualified personnel, it is still valuable to have such equipment available for the attending physician or other qualified personnel who may be on site or summoned to the scene. The following advanced life support equipment should be available at practice and game venues:

- crash cart or kit with appropriate drugs
- oxygen
- suctioning apparatus
- defibrillator

Although advanced life support is rarely required, when such action is necessary to save the life of a participant or spectator, the availability of this equipment may be the difference between life and death.

In addition to advanced life support equipment, other emergency care equipment should be readily available at practice and game sites:

- blood pressure cuff
- stethoscope
- bolt cutters for rapid removal of football face masks
- spine board
- scoop-type stretcher
- air or vacuum splints
- bleach for bleach/water blood clean-up

Finally, every athletic trainer should carry the following emergency care items on his/her person at practice and game venues:

- scissors
- tongue forceps
- oral screw
- plastic airway
- pen light flashlight
- sterile gauze pads
- latex gloves

Emergency Plan

Even with qualified personnel and emergency equipment available, competent emergency care requires that appropriate functions be carried out in the most efficient manner. Many sport medicine-related programs (e.g., cardiac rehabilitation programs) have discovered that the most efficient way to ensure quality emergency care is through the development, maintenance, and frequent rehearsal of a formal emergency care plan. This plan should include: 1) the establishment of the basic responsibilities of all program personnel in the event of an emergency; 2) the posting of telephone numbers of emergency assistance services throughout the facility and in all field kits; 3) the development of a system for daily assignment of specific emergency responsibilities to on-duty personnel; and 4) the frequent review and rehearsal of emergency procedures.

General Personnel Responsibilities

The American College of Sports Medicine (ACSM 1988) suggests that exercise and fitness program personnel should know the basic emergency response plan without having to read it in an emergency situation. These general responsibilities include:

a. knowing how to activate the emergency plan,

b. knowing the location of all necessary communication equipment,

c. knowing how to describe the location of the incident, how to get there, and the location of exits,

d. knowing the location of all emergency equipment,

e. knowing the responsibilities for people assisting with the incident,

f. being able to provide first responder assistance,

g. knowing how to prepare a crash cart and defibrillator for those trained to use it (if applicable), and

h. preparing an accurate account of the incident and what was done.

Every member of the staff in a sport medicine services program should be thoroughly familiar with and well-versed in carrying out these basic responsibilities.

Critical Telephone Numbers

Important emergency telephone numbers, such as those for ambulance services, emergency medical services (EMS), physicians, and local emergency medical facilities, should be posted throughout the facility, especially immediately adjacent to all telephones. In those areas where the 911 emergency response system is available, this recommendation may be modified accordingly.

Specific Emergency Responsibilities

In addition to the general emergency responsibilities identified above, specific staff responsibilities should be assigned on a daily basis. These responsibilities may be clearly spelled out on small "emergency assignment cards," which may be attached to each staff member's clothing at the beginning of the work day or shift, and referred to in an emergency situation. Some examples of specific emergency assignments for staff members assigned to the training room are as follows:

Emergency Assignment #1 (Head Athletic Trainer)

　　1. Take charge of emergency situation in absence of physician.

2. Assess patient and initiate emergency care.

3. In absence of Head Athletic Trainer, the senior staff member present should assume Emergency Assignment #1 responsibilities.

Emergency Assignment #2 (Assistant Athletic Trainer or Student Athletic Trainer)

1. *Assist with direct emergency care.*

2. Record information regarding vital signs and/or other pertinent data.

Emergency Assignment #3 (Assistant Athletic Trainer or Student Athletic Trainer)

1. *Activate emergency response system by using the nearest telephone to contact Emergency Medical Services or other appropriate medical assistance (e.g., 911)— Emergency phone numbers _____*

2. Describe clearly and precisely the nature of the emergency and location where medical assistance is needed.

3. Meet and assist emergency assistance personnel to emergency site.

Emergency Assignment #4 (Assistant Athletic Trainer or Student Athletic Trainer)

1. *Terminate other athletic training room activities (e.g., treatments in progress).*

2. Assist with direct emergency care.

3. Other assignments as directed. Specific assignments may be rotated on a daily or weekly basis.

When an athletic trainer is on the field or court he/she must assume Emergency Assignment #1 responsibilities. If a second athletic trainer is on site, he/she should assume Emergency Assignment #2 responsibilities. An Emergency Assignment #3 card (containing specific emergency telephone instructions) should be carried in every athletic training field kit, and, in the event of an emergency, used by a coach or other responsible individual to summon emergency medical assistance. At practice or game sites where several athletic trainers are present (e.g., football), an emergency response plan similar to that employed in the athletic training room should be considered. It is highly recommended that sport medicine personnel at remote game or practice venues have portable two-way radios for immediate access to the athletic training room in case of emergency.

Emergency Plan Review and Rehearsal

As stated earlier, every staff member should be thoroughly familiar with and well-versed in carrying out the emergency response plan. The most effective way of developing these competencies is through frequent review of the procedures, and actual drills during which the emergency plan is implemented as designed. These drills should be conducted at least quarterly; preferably monthly, if feasible. Written records should be kept documenting the date, time, and specific nature of each drill. Also, the effectiveness of each drill should be carefully evaluated, and the emergency plan modified as needed.

References

American College of Sports Medicine: Resource Manual for Guidelines for Exercise Testing and Prescription. 1988. Philadelphia: Lea & Febiger. Reprinted with permission.

Chapter 20

A.T.,C. and EMTs — Confrontation or Cooperation?

From a liability point of view, it does not make sense to have a confrontation when time is essential.

Michael J. Welch

One assumption that all athletes face is that eventually they might become injured. In most cases, these injuries are not life threatening. Unfortunately, however, there are several cases each year where the athlete is severely injured. It is at this point that the injured athlete must be removed from "the fields of friendly strife" and transported to a medical facility for emergency treatment. In addition, the injured athlete deserves the highest quality of care during the entire episode. However, each year there are reports that this may not occur. One area that often appears to be a problem is the transfer of the injured athlete to the medical facility. What would normally seem to be a rather simple process falls apart and the problem usually centers around a conflict between the on-site athletic trainer and the Emergency Medical Service (EMS), called for the transportation of the athlete. Thus, the purpose of this chapter is to discuss this process and recommend mechanisms to ensure that this transfer is as safe and quick as possible. What will not be discussed is whose treatment is best for the injured athlete.

EMT and A.T.,C. Certification

Certified athletic trainers (A.T.,C.) are well-trained to handle emergencies that result from athletic injuries. A certified athletic trainer must pass a rigorous exam developed by the National Athletic Trainers Association (NATA). However, before one is eligible to sit for the exam, he/she must meet basic criteria. He/she must have graduated from college that has an approved curriculum by the Commission on Accreditation of Allied Health Education Programs (CAAHEP). As part of the curriculum students "work" numerous hours alongside mentors who are currently certified. Obviously, the majority of these courses are focused on the care and prevention of athletic injuries. During this time valuable experience is gained by working "shoulder to shoulder" with a certified trainer. There can be no substitute for this experience. Lastly, one must also possess a valid CPR card in order to sit for the exam.

An equally well-trained group that responds to emergencies is the Emergency Medical Technician (EMT). However, it is difficult to discuss the procedures of gaining certification as each state has its own set of criteria. This is, therefore, a basic difference between the A.T.,C. and the EMT. The A.T.,C. is certified by a national organization and all have to pass the same basic competencies, whereas the EMT passes the basic competencies as established by each state. In general, it appears that most states require about 125–150 hours of classroom instruction and approximately 25 hours of practical work either in an emergency room or with an emergency medical service before one is eligible to take the state examination.

Since both the A.T.,C. and the EMT are committed to giving the highest quality of care to the injured athlete, why do problems sometimes arise in the transportation of the injured athlete off of the field and to the medical facility? I believe that there are two reasons. The first is a lack of communication between the two parties. The second is the misunderstanding of each other's role in ensuring that the athlete receives the highest quality of care.

In almost every case, the athletic trainer will be the first person to arrive at the scene to treat the injured person. As stated in the preceding paragraph, the A.T.,C. is well qualified to handle the medical emergency that may develop. In doing so, the A.T.,C. will evaluate the situation and determine if transportation to a medical facility is necessary. If the athlete needs to be transported, the EMS is called for this purpose. In order for this process to occur properly and without delay, an open line of communication should have been established well before the summons to the field. By doing such, the role that the A.T.,C. and EMT play in this transfer will be better understood.

For general discussion purposes, let's discuss a hypothetical situation that occurs on a regular basis. During football practice, a player appears to have suffered a head/neck injury. The player is in the prone position and does not get up. The A.T.,C. is summoned to the site and he/she begins to make an initial assessment. Obviously, the first objective is to determine the level of consciousness. Once this has been established, other vital signs can be obtained such as breathing rate, pulse rate, and blood pressure. These should all be recorded and used as a baseline for a reference. Monitoring of these vital signs needs to continue to determine if the condition of the injured athlete begins to deteriorate and more drastic measures have to be taken. For this discussion, the individual is conscious and, therefore, has a pulse and is breathing. However, because of paralysis it is deemed necessary that the athlete be transported to a medical facility and the call goes out to the EMS.

Upon arrival, the EMT should take a few seconds to gather some very important information concerning the injured athlete. The A.T.,C. will have gathered information about the mechanism of injury as well as initial symptoms and a record of the vital signs. This is all very useful and the EMT should take the time to gather this information. At this point the EMT is ready to assume his/her role in transporting the athlete. The A.T.,C. must realize that the EMT will begin to perform his/her own initial assessment of the injured athlete. This should not be looked upon as doubting the work of the A.T.,C., but as necessary medical protocol. It is necessary for two reasons. One is the fact that EMS operate under a strict protocol as established by either his/her medical director or a medical board. Any deviation from this process is a serious violation of the protocol by which they operate. In most states the protocol requires that the EMT performs an initial evaluation of the injured party upon his/her arrival.

At this point, the cooperation usually is smooth. In most cases that I have heard where discrepancies arise, it is usually over the question of equipment removal, i.e., the removal of the helmet or shoulder pads. In the view of most A.T.,C.'s; helmet removal should rarely occur until one reaches the medical facility. Even with the presence of face masks, CPR can be given if necessary without the removal of the helmet. Face masks can be easily cut off in order to render CPR and not risk further or possible injury to the head and neck of the unconscious athlete.

Preseason Meeting

Athletic trainers must realize that in most states once the EMT physically touches the injured athlete, the EMT now assumes all responsibility and the injured person is his/her patient. The athletic trainer must be able to make this transfer. This may be difficult for some because of the emotional attachment to the injured athlete. There is almost a sense of ownership. The athletic trainer views this athlete as his or hers. The athletic trainer feels personally responsible for the care of "his/her" athletes. Now one is seriously injured and the athletic trainer is not totally sure about the person who is about to assume all responsibility. This is the reason that if these two parties had communicated before the season began, many problems could and would be avoided. I advocate that before every season begins the A.T.,C. and the EMS need to meet to discuss several critical issues concerning the transportation of the injured athlete.

The first issue that should be discussed is the concept of equipment removal. The A.T.,C. will be able to express his/her opinions with regard to this issue as well as discuss the guidelines of helmet removal as published by the National Athletic Trainers Association (1995), as listed below:

Athletic Helmet Removal Guidelines

The National Athletic Trainers' Association has adopted the following guidelines with regard to the on-site removal of the athletic helmet.

Removing helmets from athletes with potential cervical spine injuries may worsen existing injuries or cause new ones. Removal of athletic helmets should, therefore, be avoided unless individual circumstances dictate otherwise.

Before removing the helmet from an injured athlete, appropriate alternatives such as the following should be considered:

Most injuries can be visualized with the helmet in place.

Neurological tests can be performed with the helmet in place. The eyes may be examined for reactivity, the nose and ears checked for fluid and the level of consciousness determined.

The athlete can be immobilized on a spine board with the helmet in place.

The helmet and shoulder pads elevate the supine athlete. Removal of helmet and shoulder pads, if required, should be coordinated to avoid cervical hyperextension.

Removal of the face mask allows full airway access to be achieved. Plastic clips securing the face mask can be cut using special tools, permitting rapid removal (NATA 1995).

In all cases, individual circumstances must dictate appropriate actions.

In turn, the A.T.,C. will be able to review the protocol that the particular medical service is operating under. If there are some major concerns on either side, they can be settled now, not on the field. In addition, if a discrepancy cannot be solved, it would be an excellent idea to allow the medical director of the EMS and the team physician for the school to discuss this issue. Usually these two individuals have different specialities and may have different viewpoints. Usually the team physician is an orthopedic physician whereas the medical director is in the field of emergency medicine or internal medicine. These two individuals can discuss and set the protocol and reduce liability for the athletic trainer and the responding medical technician.

I would also recommend that the athletic trainer take a helmet and shoulder pads to this meeting. I feel that many of the EMTs have never seen how football helmets or shoulder pads fit. Or if they have, it has been many years ago and styles have changed. In fact, one physician told me that he saw no big problem with EMTs removing the helmet because he is sure they have had training in removing motorcycle helmets. There is a tremendous difference between these two helmets and, in addition, motorcyclists are not wearing shoulder pads. Removing the helmet from a football player, but leaving the shoulder pads on, may result in a severe extension of the neck and exacerbate the injury.

Issues other than equipment removal can and should be discussed at this meeting. What are the credentials of the EMTs who arrive? Will any of the responding team be certified in Advanced Life Saving (ALS) or will they possess their Basic Life Saving certificates (BLS)? In discussing this issue with one athletic trainer, this was a specific concern. This university was located partially in the city limits and partially in the county, outside of the city. This particular athletic trainer had more confidence in the EMS from the county because of their level of training and certifications. He felt that these individuals were much more capable of dealing with life-threatening emergencies. There is no doubt in my mind that he is much more comfortable in turning over one of his athletes to this particular EMS.

Advances in Equipment

Advances in first aid equipment are constantly being made and both the athletic trainer and the EMT need to keep abreast of these advances. A new mattress has been designed to make transportation of someone with an injured back or neck safer and more comfortable. Instead of placing the injured athlete on a backboard, the mattress conforms to all body parts and spaces. Because the spine board is hard, pillows or towels must be used to support various body parts. The air mattress fills in these areas and appears to be easier to handle. Exchanging information on such advances can only ensure that the injured athlete will receive the highest quality of care.

The most important outcome of these meetings, however, will be the mutual respect that will develop between these two professions. The A.T.,C. will understand the guidelines that the EMTs operate under and will also become more familiar will their training and expertise. The EMT will also find that the athletic trainer is an excellent resource. The athletic trainer has been trained to specifically deal will athletic injuries and has the expertise to do so. The special equipment that many athletes wear may present a problem to the EMT, since they do not have to deal with it as an everyday occurrence. Therefore, they need to be aware of this equipment and follow the guidance of the A.T.,C.

The injured athlete deserves the highest quality of medical attention when injured. The A.T.,C. and the EMT will provide this only when they work as teammates. In order to be teammates, it is imperative that the two meet before the actual emergency and there are no doubts or questions about the care to be rendered. Unfortunately, this may be a problem because of the number of individuals who might work for an emergency medical service. However it is possible to meet with the operations officer or the medical director to ensure that these issues can be discussed and then disseminated to the remainder of the members of the EMS.

By having these meetings, the role that each plays will become much clearer. Both the A.T.,C. and the EMT play important roles in the treatment of the injured athlete to ensure quality care. However, because their roles are different it is only through open and continuous dialogue that one can ensure the safe transfer of the injured athlete from the A.T.,C. to the EMT.

In My Opinion

Several athletic trainers I interviewed said that not one had ever had any problem with the transfer of an injured athlete to an EMS team. These athletic trainers were from different states, but all had a common thread. They all stated that they had several meetings with the EMS that serves their school and that they work very well together. It is obvious that these two teams have communicated with each other before an emergency when tensions might be high and time is paramount. It is also clear that they each have a mutual respect for each other's profession.

From a liability point of view, it does not make sense to have a confrontation when time is essential. The first order of business is to make sure that the injured athlete is transported to a medical facility. Therefore, planning for the future will eliminate any unnecessary conflicts.

One A.T.,C., when asked when he thought the EMTs should assume control responded: "Why should I risk a lawsuit for something that could go wrong when the EMTs are there! They are trained to handle the emergency and I let them."

Chapter 21

Who Should Provide Medical Care: Athletic Trainer or First Responder?

While watching a high school football game you notice a player go down and not move on the field. You notice an individual run on the field to attend to the injured athlete and may think to yourself, "Good, the athlete is going to get medical care since the doctor or certified athletic trainer (AT) is on their way out." Scary enough, there is a good chance the individual is neither a physician nor an AT. It is estimated that less than 42% of public high schools across the United States employ an AT (Stevens & Van Der Horst, 2008) and very few are privileged to have a physician readily available. Therefore, there is a very good chance the individual attending to the athlete is not an AT and potentially lacks the ability to provide appropriate care. The question then becomes, what credentials or qualifications does this individual have and why are they even in a position to attend to the athlete, considering it may be a life-threatening head injury such as a concussion?

Craig Eilbacher

High School Athletic Participation and Injury

During the 2010–2011 high school athletic seasons, there were more than 7.6 million interscholastic athletes (including men and women) across the United States (National Federation of State High School Associations, 2011). Football alone contributes approximately 1.1 million (14%) of those athletes. With a steady increase in overall athletic participation in high school athletics each year, the risk of injury is also predicted to increase (Nelson, et al., 2007; Rauh, Marshall, Powell, Mueller, & Queale, 2001). Football, a high-risk sport, compiled nearly 517,726 injuries during the 2005–2006 season (Rechel, Yard, & Comstock, 2008; Shankar, Fields, Collins, Dick, & Comstock, 2007). Injuries range from minor cuts, bruises, and sprains to the more serious broken bones or catastrophic injuries, such as brain injuries (e.g., concussions). Research indicates sprains and strains to be the most common injury in football. Concussions and fatalities are a close second (Nelson et al., 2007; Ramirez, Schaffer, Haikang, Kashani, & Kraus, 2006;

Rechel et al., 2008; Shankar et al., 2007). Boden et al. (2007) indicates catastrophic head injuries or fatalities are greater in high school athletics than college. Therefore, one may believe that is where providing the most appropriate medical personnel should be of the utmost importance.

The most notable medical problems plaguing high school athletes, especially early in the football season, are environmental illnesses such as heat cramps, exhaustion, and stroke. According to Coris, Walz, Konin, & Pescasio (2007), exertional heat stroke is the leading cause of death in high school athletes. Ironically, it is also the most preventable if the appropriate personnel are in place to ensure proper prevention, recognition, and treatment. It seems that every year, especially in the hot month of August; a high school death in football hits the news. In 2011, from July to September, there were six high school deaths in football. Increased temperature was believed to be a contributing, if not the main factor in all six deaths (Siegel, 2011). While further research into the causes of death and the care provided, coaches were the primary care provider in all six incidents. It is easy to question whether coaches push the limit when it comes to training. Therefore, the question remains, isn't it a conflict of interest when coaches are dually responsible for looking out for the health of their athlete and deciding when to remove a player from a game due to injury; especially if it is their star? If so, then who should be providing the care?

Athletic Trainer vs. First Responder

For decades, high school football has seen a number of deaths every year. Professional and collegiate athletes benefit from the services of an athletic trainer, while high schools, many times, are left with a coach or volunteer certified in first aid and CPR. Athletic trainers have been providing athletic health care for student athletes for many years, dating back to the turn of the nineteenth century. Many considered athletic trainers to be a "jack of all trades" with responsibilities as equipment managers, laundry men, and first aid providers (Scheider, 1986). According to the National Athletic Trainers' Association (NATA), an AT is a nationally certified allied health care professional who specializes in the prevention, diagnosis, and intervention of emergency, acute, and chronic medical conditions involving impairment, functional limitations, and disabilities (www. NATA.org). Preparation to become an athletic trainer in the early years relied heavily on learning through experience, or what is known to many older athletic trainers as the "internship" or "apprenticeship." As of 2011, athletic trainers' preparation is a combination of formal classroom and extensive clinical instruction coupled with countless hours of hands on clinical experiences. The American Red Cross (ARC) clearly defines a first responder as a person trained only in emergency care (e.g., rescue breathing, CPR) who may be required to provide care in the community at a place of employment (The American Red Cross, 2005). The following table represents the academic requirements of athletic trainers and first responders.

As identified in Table 1, the academic preparation of a FR pales in comparison to the athletic trainer. To become an AT an individual must graduate from either an entry-level undergraduate or master's degree program accredited by the Commission on Accreditation of Athletic Training Education (CAATEE). In addition to extensive coursework and clinical experiences, an AT must pass the National Athletic Trainers' Association Board of Certification (BOC) examination. In contrast, any individual can become a first responder by completing a course with no longer than 4.5 to 6 hours of instruction, skill demonstration, and successful completion of the course exam by the ARC or American Heart Association (AHA). Course content by the ARC includes: before providing care

Table 1. Athletic Trainer and First Responder Education

Educational Preparation	AT Educational Preparation	First Responder Educational Preparation
CPR/AED/First Aid Certification		
ARC Professional Rescuer Training	✓	
ARC First Aid-Responding to Emergencies or ARC First Aid/CPR/AED for the Workplace		✓
Injury Management Workshop (20 hours)		✓
Professional Content	*Completed in a college or university program*	
Risk Management and Injury Prevention	✓	
Pathology of Injuries and Illnesses	✓	
Orthopedic Clinical Examination and Diagnosis	✓	
Medical Conditions and Disabilities	✓	
Acute Care of Injuries & Illness	✓	
Therapeutic Modalities	✓	
Conditioning, Rehabilitative Exercise, and Pharmacology	✓	
Psychosocial Intervention and Referral	✓	
Nutritional Aspects of Injuries & Illnesses	✓	
Health Care Administration	✓	

Created by Craig Eilbacher March 12, 2009/doctoral dissertation.

and checking an ill or injured person (49 minutes), cardiac emergencies (35 minutes), automated external defibrillator (27 minutes), breathing emergencies (34 minutes), sudden illness (30 minutes), environmental emergencies (22 minutes), soft tissue injuries (38 minutes), and injuries to muscles, bones and joints (27 minutes).

Two additional, yet very distinct, differences between the AT and first responder is the required "license to practice" act (in 48 states) and the amount of continuing education credits required. First, an AT in North Carolina must work directly under the supervision of a licensed physician (Athletic Trainer Licensing Act, known as Senate Bill 660: Article 34). The athletic trainers' licensure act reduces the first responder's chances and ability of claiming to provide athletic training services. As of 2011, first responders are not required to obtain a license or be supervised by any medical professional or pass a certification exam. Therefore, first responders are in positions to provide medical care (possibly beyond their scope of training) without physician supervision. The AT is required to obtain75 hours of continuing education credits every three years, which can be obtained by attending professional conferences, publishing research in the field, and giving professional presentations at athletic training conferences and symposiums. In contrast, the first responder is not required continuing education credits, only recertification every two years for CPR/AED and three years for first aid (American Red Cross standards). While the overwhelming difference in training is obvious; in the state of North Carolina, the Board of Education Injury Management Policy indicates schools can employ either an AT or have a first responder at football games and practices. Based on the information presented, ask yourself, "Who would I want on the sideline treating my son or daughter in the event of a medical emergency?"

Medical Coverage in High Schools across the United States

In 2011, approximately 42% of high schools employed an AT; therefore, in the majority of high schools, athletic health care was left to a coach or a volunteer first responder. Additionally, there is no current mandate that requires public or private high schools to employ an athletic trainer. Hence, state officials have acknowledged the inadequacy of care and relatively slow progress in implementing even minimal acceptable coverage (Aukerman et al., 2006; Bell et al., 1984; Culpepper, 1986; Koabel, 1995; Lackland et al., 1985; Lindaman, 1992; Mathews & Esterson, 1983; Porter, Noble, Bachman, & Hoover, 1980; Redfern, 1980; Sherman, 1985; Vangsness et al., 1994; Wrenn & Ambrose, 1980). The National Athletic Trainers' Association position statement on care at the high school level (National Athletic Trainers' Association, n.d.-a) states:

> The best way to protect the public is to allow only Board Certified athletic trainers and state licensed athletic trainers to practice. Athletic trainers have the education and skills to properly assess and treat athletic injuries. In coordination with the team physician, they are qualified to make decisions regarding return to play. Other allied health professionals are not qualified to perform these tasks. Most situations that athletic trainers encounter should not be left to a coach or layperson that does not have the proper training.

While states have been slow with any type of health care reform regarding the standard of care being provided at high schools, many have made valuable strides in addressing the issue, more importantly with concussion protocols. Even though Alaska, California, and Hawaii were the only three states that did not regulate the athletic training profession as of 2011 (NATA News, 2011); in a span of two years, 2009–2011, 30 states passed a concussion bill, with nine of them indicating the ATC as a qualified allied health professional able to make a return to play decision.

In California, on January 27, 2010, an organization called Advocates for Injured Athletes (AIA) spoke with state legislators to push for the employment of athletic trainers in the schools. The AIA was developed by Beth and Tommy Mallon following the shattering of Tommy's cervical vertebrae during a lacrosse game in which the athletic trainer appropriately managed and treated what could have been a catastrophic injury. At that time the California National Federation began requiring that all coaches have CPR/First Aid certifications completed and on file. Additionally, bill 1647 was presented to legislators. It would require automated external defibrillators (AED) and a state regulation on the athletic training profession.

Similar events took place in Kentucky, when the death of a high school football player in 2008 prompted the state's high school athletic association to require coaches to complete a sport safety course (Spears, 2009). Coaches could complete an online course that highlights important information such as concussions and heat illnesses. Additionally, the high school athletic association and Department of Education embarked on a state wide study on sport safety (Spears, 2009). The state's quick response was crucial, considering the head football coach was being indicted for the athlete's death. He was later acquitted.

New York does not recommend that schools have an AT but does require all coaches to maintain CPR/First Aid/AED certification and complete the NYS coaching certification program. Coaches are required to seek certification by either the American Red Cross, American Heart Association, American Safety & Health Institute, or the National Safety

Council. Additional avenues include a State Education Department in-service course or a college first aid course.

The lack of an AT employment mandate in high schools across the United States continues to put coaches and parent volunteers in a position to provide athletic health care with minimal training. While many states have implemented a coaching course or seminar, it is virtually impossible to attain medical preparation as an athletic trainer and then guarantee proper care would prevail in the event of an emergency. Regardless the percent of schools in each state that have an AT, the potential for improper care will continue be an issue.

The Growing Issue in North Carolina

In North Carolina it is clear to see the battle between the athletic trainer and first responder. In North Carolina, the State Board of Education (NCSBE) Injury Management Policy (16 NCAC 06E.0203) mandates that all high schools have either a licensed AT or a first responder providing medical coverage for football games and practice. In addition, were a school to seek to have a volunteer or paid first responder, they would be required to attend the twenty hour Injury Management Workshop (IMW) held in conjunction with the North Carolina High School Coaches Convention.

The IMW was designed to provide first responders the opportunity to increase their medical knowledge beyond their basic first aid and cardiopulmonary resuscitation course by either the ARC or AHA. Additionally, a continual review of heat-related illnesses, concussion information, and skills necessary for physical exam and assessment of athletic injuries are typically common themes. The workshops are organized by level of knowledge and years of experience. For example, a Level I participant's primary focus is first aid and basic injury management. Upon completion of Level I and one year of field experience at a high school, an individual would enter Level II the following year, which is considered to contain more advanced content and skills. Ironically, the workshops are coordinated and taught by NC licensed athletic trainers, the ones who are pushing state legislators to mandate that all high schools employ an athletic trainer. It seems athletic trainers are teaching first responders to do their job with only a 20 hour workshop.

It is imperative that individuals keep in mind the unequivocal differences in professional training between an AT and first responder. As of 2008, North Carolina had roughly 49% of high schools with an AT, therefore, leaving greater than 50% of medical care for high school athletes to first responder with minimal, if any, medical training. According to the law, a stranger off the street can take the ARC course and 20 hour IMW, then stand on the sideline of a football game and make medical decisions even in a life-threatening situation.

A Closer Look at First Responders in NC

In the wake of three North Carolina high school football player deaths during the 2008 season, the medical care provided to high school athletes came under fire. Many people had begun to scrutinize the level of care being provided, in particular by first responders. At the time only two studies had been conducted and concluded that medical care was inconsistent or lacking (Aukerman, et al., 2006; Eilbacher & Tritschler, 2004).

Previous studies across the United States had thoroughly examined whether coaches, acting as first responders, possessed knowledge regarding first aid and athletic injury (Barron, 2004; Kujawa & Coker, 2000; Ransone & Dunn-Bennett, 1999). Findings indicated coaches lacked sufficient knowledge, considering they were in a position as the primary medical provider. In fact, coaches typically rely more on their personal experiences as an athlete regarding the care and prevention of injuries, rather than a background of medical knowledge (Flint & Weiss, 1992). A study conducted by Eilbacher (2010) was designed to shed light on the issues surrounding first responders providing athletic health care for high school student athletes.

The study examined (N = 93) first responders' perceived knowledge and the likelihood of skills and behaviors with a survey administered at the Injury Management Workshop, held in conjunction with the NC coaches clinic, in 2009. Because first responders attended different levels of workshops it was hypothesized that individuals with four or more years of experience would perceive more knowledge than those with three or fewer years of experience. Additionally, the same should have been consistent with their likelihood to perform specific health care skills and behaviors. Perceived knowledge and the likelihood of skills and behaviors were examined in five content areas: (a) upper extremity; (b) lower extremity; (c) head, neck, cervical spine and low back; (d) general medical/internal; (e) environmental conditions. Results indicated that regardless of years of experience, first responders perceived themselves to have enough knowledge in all content areas except head, neck, cervical spine, and low back content. Additionally, first responders were likely to perform athletic health care skills and behaviors in all content areas if given the opportunity. However, first responders with four or more years of experience were more likely to perform skills and behaviors associated with environmental conditions than those with less years of experience. A moderate to high positive correlation was found for perceived knowledge and likelihood of skills and behaviors content areas. Meaning, first responders were likely to perform athletic health care skills and behaviors only if they perceived to be knowledgeable in the five content areas.

Two additional issues identified from the study included the lack of compliance by public schools regarding the state's injury management policy that all first responders had to attend the workshop annually; and that participants who actually attended completed the entire 20 hour workshop. First, according to the North Carolina High School Athletic Association, there were 379 North Carolina high schools in 2009. Approximately 156 schools had an AT, leaving 223 schools to seek the services of a first responder. With 17 ATs at the IMW, a total of 114 schools were not represented. As of 2011, North Carolina school systems lack administrative management of the policy. Additionally, there are no penalties for schools that do not comply. Lastly, participants enter and leave the workshop at their own leisure. According to the coordinators of the workshop there are many individuals that only attend one or two days of a three day workshop. It is these individuals that are standing on the sideline making medical decisions for our student athletes.

Eilbacher's (2010) study should raise major concerns, considering first responders did not perceive themselves to have enough knowledge in head, neck, cervical spine, and low back content area. More importantly, it's first responders in North Carolina high schools that are responsible for identification and analysis of potential catastrophic injuries, such as spinal injuries and concussions; considering concussions rank second to sprains and strains as the most common injury in football (Nelson et al., 2007; Ramirez, Schaffer, Haikang, Kashani, & Kraus, 2006; Rechel et al., 2008; Shankar et al., 2007). Concussions have received national attention in the past two years in the NFL, the NHL, college football, and more importantly, high school football. It is well known that athletes participating in high school football are at greater risk of catastrophic head injuries or fatalities than those in college (Boden, Tacchetti, Cantu, Knowles, & Mueller, 2007). Treating an athlete with a concussion can be complex and should be the primary responsibility of trained professionals with the ability to recognize the signs and symptoms, and determine the appropriate time an athlete may return to play (Boden et al., 2007; Mueller, 2001). Spinal injuries pose a similar threat of a catastrophic injury to concussions if not treated properly. When speaking about the severity of spinal injuries, Cendoma & Rehberg (2007) stated:

> In a single instant, the athlete is transformed from a competitive athlete into a critically injured person … and see the fear in a injured athletes eyes. It is at this moment that the sports health care professional realizes that prior preparation, practice, and mental rehearsal can mean the difference between a person living or dying, between the person walking away from a serious injury or living life with a devastating disability.

Therefore, it is inconceivable to think a first responder is qualified to address and manage a concussion or spinal injury with very limited training. Furthermore, it is even more inconceivable for these types of injury to be left to the coaching staff to manage when their main focus is winning a ball game.

Where We Go from Here

Participation in high school sports will continue to rise; therefore, athletes, parents, and coaches should expect injuries to be commonplace. It is difficult to prevent many injuries, however, proper personnel is critical to ensure athletes are receiving the best care possible. I applaud states that are seeking to further educate their coaches and parents on how to better address injuries. However, we spend an uncontrollable amount of time worrying about getting the best football coach for high schools but seem to sacrifice who is providing medical care on the sidelines. Athletes are constantly at risk of injury, so why should they also be at risk of receiving care from unqualified individuals?

In My Opinion

In my opinion, proper coverage in high school sports is going to continue to be a problem. Many school districts across the United States are facing financial constraints. This is evident in that many public middle schools and high schools are either dropping sports programs or making them "pay to play" because of the financial burden. In North Carolina, schools choose to have or not have a sports program. Since athletics is viewed as "extra-curricular," many school systems are not willing to help fund an AT unless they have a teaching degree. Therefore, if schools cannot find an AT with a teaching license to both teach and provide athletic training services (another issue in the athletic training profession) they must rely on the first responder or obtain an AT through a clinical outreach program with a hospital or physical therapy clinic. If schools cannot employ an AT it is important that proper steps be taken to ensure at the minimum basic care is available for athletes. Below is a list of recommendations for public and private high schools:

1. *Emergency Action Plan (EAP):* Each school should design and implement an emergency action plan according to the NATA recommendations. Proper development of an EAP is critical when trying to reduce the risk of liability in the event of an emergency. Therefore, I highly recommend consultation by an athletic trainer to assist in composing such a document. Injury management protocols should include heat illness, concussion, sudden cardiac arrest (SCA), and sickle cell. For example, the plan should clearly indicate where the automated external defibrillators (AED) are located for easy access by medical personnel in the event of a SCA. The plan should be covered with the coaching staff at the beginning of the year and assessed regularly after every emergency situation. Constant updating of the EAP will assure the protocols are effective. A shortened version of North Carolina's EAP template submitted by the North Carolina High School Athletics Association, is provided in Table 2. A more detailed document can be found at www.nchsaa.org, under the health and safety section of the website.

2. *First Aid/CPR/AED Training:* Require every coach (head and assistants) to take a basic first aid class and, if possible, a sport safety class. Additionally, it is imperative that the school's athletic director keeps records ensuring training is done and continued annually.

3. **Community Outreach:** Develop a partnership with a local orthopedic/PT clinic that is interested in working your athletic program to begin the development of a sports medicine team if you do not employ one. Obtaining the services of an AT may be possible through an outreach program with a local clinic.

4. *Push for AT:* Make it a priority to provide the best care possible; that is, employ an AT at your high school. Work with school system personnel to demonstrate the value of employing an AT. Additionally, get involved with state legislators and your state athletic training association to support a push for a state wide mandate to employ an AT.

Below is a list of additional resources that will assist athletic programs in further developing a safe environment for high school athletes.

- Drezner et al. (2007). Inter-Association Task Force Recommendations on Emergency Preparedness and Management of Sudden Cardiac Arrest in High School and College Athletic Programs: A Consensus Statement. *Journal of Athletic Training.* 42(1):143–158.

- Swartz et al. (2009). National Athletic Trainers' Association Position Statement: Acute Management of the Cervical Spine-Injured Athlete. *Journal of Athletic Training.* 44(3):306–331.

- For heat related illness information visit the Kory Stringer Institute at *ksi.uconn.edu.*

- The National Federation of State High School Associations at www.nfhs.org. Click on the "Sports Medicine" link and then "NFHS SMAC Position Statements and Guidelines".

Conclusion

The care being provided to high school athletes should be a top priority for all athletic programs. Athletic Directors and school administrators should be cognizant that

Table 2. General Guidelines for Developing Emergency Action Plans

1. Establish Roles—adapt to specific team/sport/venue, may be best to have more than one person assigned to each role in case of absence/turnover
   - Immediate care of the athlete
   - Activation of Emergency Medical System
   - Emergency equipment retrieval
   - Direction of EMS to scene
2. Communication
   - Primary method
     - May be fixed (landline) or mobile (cellular phone, radio)
   - Back-up method
   - Test prior to event
   - Activation of EMS
     - Identify contact numbers (911, ambulance, police, fire, hospital, poison control, suicide hotline)
     - Prepare script (caller name/location/phone number, nature of emergency, number of victims and their condition, what treatment initiated, specific directions to scene)
   - Student emergency information
     - Critical medical information (conditions, medications, allergies)
     - Emergency contact information (parent/guardian)
     - Accessible (keep with athletic trainer for example)
3. Emergency Equipment
   - e.g. Automated External Defibrillators, bag-valve mask, spine board, splints
   - Personnel trained in advance on proper use
   - Must be accessible
   - Proper condition and maintenance
4. Emergency Transportation
   - Ambulance on site for high risk events (understand there is a difference between basic life support and advanced life support vehicles/personnel)
   - When ambulance not on site
     - Entrance to venue clearly marked and accessible
     - Identify parking/loading point and confirm area is clear
   - Coordinate ahead of time with local emergency medical services
5. Additional considerations
   - Must be venue specific (football field, gymnasium, etc)
   - Put plan in writing
   - Involve all appropriate personnel (administrators, coaches, sports medicine, EMS)
   - Post the plan in visible areas of each venue and distribute
   - Review plan at least annually
   - Rehearse plan at least annually
   - Document

Additional Considerations for Specific Conditions When Developing an EAP
1. Sudden Cardiac Arrest
2. Heat Illness
3. Head and Neck Injury
4. Asthma
5. Anaphylaxis
6. Lightning

catastrophic injuries are always a possibility when athletes step on a field for practices or games. Therefore, programs should be well prepared to handle any medical emergency to assure the most appropriate and efficient care is provided. As a society we are consumed with having the best coach; but need to be even more concerned about who is providing medical care and the kind of care being provided. We cannot prevent every injury but we can have the best professional to care for it: an athletic trainer.

References

Aukerman, D. F., Aukerman, M., McManama, M., & Browning, D. (2006). Medical coverage of high school athletics in North Carolina. *Southern Medical Journal, 99*(2), 132–136.

Barron, M. J. (2004). *The assessment of first aid and injury prevention knowledge and the decision making of youth basketball, soccer, and football coaches.* |dissertation|. Michigan State University.

Bell, G. W., Cardinal, R. A., & Dooley, J. N. (1984). Athletic trainer manpower survey of selected Illinois high schools. *Athletic Training, 19*(1), 23–24.

Boden, B., Tacchetti, R., Cantu, R., Knowles, S. B., & Mueller, F. O. (2007). Catastrophic head injuries in high school and college football players. *The American College of Sports Medicine, 35*(7), 1075–1081.

Cendoma, M. & Rehberg, R.S. (2007). Management of spinal injuries. In R. S. Rehberg. *Sports Emergency Care: A Team Approach.* Thorofare, NJ: SLACK Incorporated.

Coris, E., Walz, S., Konin, J., & Pescasio, M. (2007). Return to activity considerations in a football player predisposed to exertional heat illness: A case study. *Journal of Sport Rehabilitation, 16*, 260–270.

Culpepper, M. J. (1986). The availability and delivery of health care to high school athletes in Alabama. *The Physician and Sports Medicine, 14*(1), 130–137.

Eilbacher, C. (2010). *North Carolina high school football first responders' perceived knowledge and their likelihood to perform athletic health care behavior.* |dissertation|. Greensboro, NC: University of North Carolina at Greensboro.

Eilbacher, C., & Tritschler, K. (2004). Survey of North Carolina public high school administrators: Opinions and attitudes toward athletic training services. *The North Carolina Journal for Alliance for Athletics, Health, Physical Education, Recreation, and Dance, 40*(2).

Flint, F. A., & Weiss, W. R. (1992). Returning injured athletes to competition: A role and ethical dilemma. *Canadian Journal of Sport Sciences, 17*(1), 34–40.

Koabel, B. P. (1995). *Assessment of the need for certified athletic trainers in New York state high schools.* Eugene, OR: Microform Publications, Int'l Institute for Sport and Human Performance, University of Oregon.

Kujawa, R., & Coker, C. A. (2000). An examination of the influence of coaching certification and the presence of an athletic trainer on the extent of sport safety knowledge of coaches. *Applied Research in Coaching,* 14–23.

Lackland, D. T., Testor, J. M., Akers, P. C., Hirata, I., Knight, R. M., & Mason, J. L. (1985). The utilization of athletic trainer/team physician services and high school football injuries. *Athletic Training, 20*(1), 20–23.

Lindaman, L. M. (1992). Athletic trainer availability in interscholastic athletics in Michigan. *Journal of Athletic Training, 27*(1), 9–16.

Mathews, E., & Esterson, P. (1983). Sports medicine in Northern Virginia high schools. *Athletic Training, summer,* 181–183.

National Athletic Trainers' Association. (n.d.-b). What is an athletic trainer? Retrieved September 22, 2011, from http://www.nata.org/about_AT/whatisat.htm.

NATA. (2007). Appropriate Medical Care For Secondary School-Age Athletes: Consensus Statement. Retrieved August 2007, from http://www.nata.org/statements/support/secondary_school_medcarecommunication.pdf.

NATA News. (2011). State legislation: Progress Report. *NATA News*(September), 24.

National Federation of High School Association. (2008). 2007–2008 High School Athletics Participation Survey. Retrieved 10/10/08, from http://www.nfhs.org/core/content manager/uploads/200708%20Participation%20Survey.pdf.

Nelson, A. J., Collins, C. L., Yard, E. E., Fields, S. K., & Comstock, D. (2007). Ankle injuries among United States high school sports athletes, 2005–2006. *Journal of Athletic Training, 42*(3), 381–387.

Porter, M., Noble, B., Bachman, D. C., & Hoover, R. L. (1980). Sportsmedicine care in Chicago-area high schools. *The Physician and Sports Medicine, 8*(2).

Ramirez, M., Schaffer, K., Haikang, S., Kashani, S., & Kraus, J. (2006). Injuries to high school football athletes in California. *American Journal of Sports Medicine, 34*, 1147–1158.

Rauh, M., Marshall, S. W., Powell, J. W., Mueller, F. O., & Queale, W. (2001). Sports injury epidemiology among high school athletes: Past, present and future perspectives. *The American College of Sports Medicine, 33*(5), S1. Ransone, J., & Dunn-Bennett, L. R. (1999). Assessment of first-aid knowledge and decision making of high school athletic coaches. *Journal of Athletic Training, 34*(3), 267–271.

Rechel, J. A., Yard, E. E., & Comstock, D. (2008). An epidemiologic comparison of high school sports injuries sustained in practice and competition. *Journal of Athletic Training, 43*(2).

Redfern, R. W. (1980). Emergency medical skills in high school coaches. *The Physician and Sports Medicine, 8*(11), 115–116.

Scheiderer, L., (1986). *Program director and department chairperson preferences for undergraduate professional preparation of athletic trainers.* |dissertation|. Athens, OH: Ohio University.

Seigel, J. (2011, September 3). High school football player dies; sixth athlete death this summer. ABC News. Retrieved September 21, 2011 from http://www.abcnews.go.com.

Shankar, P. R., Fields, S. K., Collins, C. L., Dick, R. W., & Comstock, D. (2007). Epidemiology of high school and collegiate football injuries in the United States, 2005–2006. *American Journal of Sports Medicine, 35*(5), 1295–1303.

Sherman, B. (1985). A new approach to athletic training in southern Wisconsin high schools. *The Physician and Sports Medicine, 13*(1), 57–64.

Spears, V. (2009). High school sports law is signed: Stronger safety measures required at practices, events. Retrieved February 23, 2010, from http://www.kentucky.com/2009/03/25/737304/high-school-sports-law-is-signed.html.

The American Red Cross. (2005). *First Aid-Responding to Emergencies.* Stay Well.

Vangsness, T. C., Hunt, T., Uram, M., & Kerlan, R. (1994). Survey of health care coverage of high school football in southern California. *American Journal of Sports Medicine, 22*(5), 719–722.

Wrenn, J. P., & Ambrose, D. (1980). An investigation of health care practices of high school athletes in Maryland. *Journal of Athletic Training*, 85–92.

Chapter 22

Six Minutes to Live or Die: Automatic External Defibrillators

---

Lives are saved or lost within six minutes.

Kenny Morgan

In the United States each year, sudden cardiac arrest occurring outside of a hospital kills 250,000 people, which is approximately 685 people per day (Davis, 2003). Studies have shown that two out of three deaths occur before the victim even reaches the hospital, usually at home, work, or in a public place such as a golf course (American Heart Association, 2001). In fact, according to the American Heart Association (2001), the top five places where people suffer cardiac arrests are airports, jails, stadiums, golf courses, and shopping malls. The most determinant factor in whether an individual suffering from cardiac arrest lives or dies is elapsed time until treatment. For years expert opinion stated that help must arrive within ten minutes, but new findings from the Mayo Clinic show that lives actually are saved or lost within six minutes (Davis, 2003). The installation of automatic external defibrillators (AED) in public areas is quickly becoming an invaluable tool to rescuers and victims alike in reducing response times and increasing lifetimes.

AEDs

An AED is a battery-driven device that administers an electric shock through the chest wall of a person who has suffered a cardiac arrest (Connaughton & Spengler, 2001). The devices are called "automatic" because there is little operator involvement required. The operator has only three things to do: turn on the machine, attach the pads to the patient's chest, and follow visible and audible instructions the machine provides (Sarkis, 2000). AEDs are approximately the size of a laptop computer and weigh between four and seven pounds. At present, AEDs are available at an approximate cost of $3,000 to $5,000 (Peterson, 2000). The purpose of an AED is to assist first-responders, such as police, EMT's, firefighters, security guards, flight attendants, lifeguards, and others in sudden cardiac arrest episodes (Connaughton & Spengler, 2001). The American Heart Association recommends that AEDs be placed where a reasonable probability exists of one sudden cardiac arrest occurring every five years (Schnirring, 2001).

AEDs and Sport Medicine

AEDs are increasingly being placed in a wide variety of sports, recreation, and fitness settings (Mitchell, 1999). According to Van Camp et al. (1995), an average of sixteen sudden cardiac deaths occur annually among U.S. high school and college athletes, although additional deaths may go unreported. Just as important, there are many other people at sports events, including officials, coaches, and fans, who are at risk for cardiac arrest. The fatal heart attack suffered by Major League Baseball umpire John McSherry, before a national television audience on opening day 1996, is just one example.

The entry of AEDs into the sporting arena has become attractive as the results of numerous studies documenting increased survival rates have been known. Most professional football and basketball teams have AEDs on the sidelines, according to AED manufacturers, and the devices are becoming more common in professional baseball dugouts (Cantwell, 1998). In addition, some high schools are beginning to implement AED programs.

AEDs are beginning to make their way onto the golf course as well. According to Smith (1999), sudden cardiac arrest is the number one cause of death on the golf course. Due to size, poor accessibility, and often remote location, a golf course is usually one of the worst places to be when your heart stops (Smith, 1999). Smith (1999) explains that golf courses have to solve a three part problem of establishing an AED program in large part because an AED does not do much good when it is sitting in the shop cabinet while the victim is on the thirteenth fairway a mile and a half away. The first step involves acquiring an AED and training the proper number of people on how to use it. Secondly, some form of communication has to be established between the golfers on the course and the golf shop. Finally, there has to be some form of transportation that can quickly reach the victim and, if necessary, transport that person to an ambulance.

AED programs are not only being implemented for participator use, but programs are also being established for where they are proportionately needed most, in the stadiums and arenas themselves, for spectator use. For example, Scott Johnson of the Greensboro Coliseum reported that the Coliseum partnered with the Moses Cone Health System Foundation in the spring of 2001 and purchased four AEDs for the Coliseum Complex. These four AEDs are strategically placed throughout the facility and office areas for quick and easy access. According to Johnson, the Coliseum has approximately 32 staff that has been certified for use, with plans to certify an additional 18 to 28 in the next year. The staff that is targeted for training includes those that are around mass groups of people at the venue's larger events. The Coliseum's four new AEDs are only a supplement to the contingent of paramedics that normally accompany the major events.

Regulatory and Legal Implications of AED Use

The acquisition of an AED is regulated by the U.S. Food and Drug Administration (FDA), but use is controlled by individual state codes. The FDA requires a workplace to have medical approval in order to buy or lease an AED (Starr, 1999). In addition, physicians have to submit a written request to the FDA in order to obtain an AED. Once authorization is received, the state has jurisdiction over use and management of the equipment (Starr, 1999).

According to Starr (1999), the state considers two categories of AED users. Medical users are health care and allied health care responders in medical centers and EMS systems who would use an AED as part of their well-defined emergency medical procedures. State medical practice acts, as well as health and EMS codes, regulate the use of AEDs by these people.

Secondly, public access users are nonmedical, lay, and workplace first-aid responders who are not associated with a medical center or EMS agency. These groups are those who would use an AED as part of basic life support procedures until arrival of EMS or advanced responders (Starr, 1999). Public Access Defibrillation Legislation (PADL) addresses the education of nonmedical users and their use of defibrillators. PADL is being spearheaded by the American Heart Association and public interest groups (Starr, 1999).

Despite the relatively low cost of a machine, AED program implementation has progressed at a significantly slow rate across the country. Greaney (2000) notes that given our litigious-driven environment, AEDs have not yet earned widespread acceptance because of potential civil liabilities posed to AED operators, owners, trainers, and prescribing physicians. This situation is beginning to change, however, now that 49 states and the District of Columbia have passed legislation that gives critical protection from lawsuits to all or some AED operators, such as lay persons (Good Samaritans), rescuers, athletic trainers, medical directors, and AED trainers (Greaney, 2000). In addition, in November of 2000 President Clinton signed into law the Cardiac Arrest Survival Act that extends immunity for Good Samaritans in those states that do not offer protection from liability. Moreover, it is beneficial to know that AED manufacturers offer indemnification programs for their devices. These programs generally indemnify users against liability as long as the users are certified by a nationally recognized program (American Heart Association or Red Cross) and have properly maintained the defibrillator (Vander Neut, 1999). The manufacturer HP Heartstream went so far as to indemnify those purchasing, renting, or leasing its AEDs against claims emerging from their use, providing the devices were properly used and maintained (Zolkos, 1998).

While the historic Cardiac Arrest Survival Act is a step in the right direction, many proponents of AED implementation feel that it is still not quite enough. Peterson (2000) notes that not only is it important to indemnify users, but also prudent to indemnify acquirers, trainers, and maintenance personnel as well. Good Samaritan laws do not go far enough for some business leaders to achieve the level of comfort that would allow them to endorse and participate in public access defibrillation (PAD) (Peterson, 2000). Therefore, it is important that potential buyers, operators, trainers, and users of AEDs refer to individual state codes to determine the limited liability of AED use in their state.

Public Access Defibrillation Programs

As more PAD programs have been implemented over the past years, studies have been conducted to determine the programs' efficiencies and deficiencies. Results from the National Institutes of Health PAD trial show that twice as many lives were saved in public places that had AEDs, however, researchers say there are several areas where improvement is needed, especially in designing strong response plans (Davis, 2003, p. 8D). Many experts are quick to give the credit of a life saved by an AED to the quality of the PAD program and not to the machine itself. According to Tom Aufderheide of the Medical College of Wisconsin, programs require significant initial input, and they are very high maintenance (Davis, 2003, p. 8D). In many ways, an AED is only as effective as the human being who is operating the machine. Poor decision making and human missteps that waste valuable time can render the devices useless.

Potential users of AEDs must be able to understand when to use the device, how to use it, and where it is located. Davis (2003) tells the story of a person who collapsed at a gym where the staff was trained in AED use. On the day in question the person who normally worked the front desk was absent and his replacement did not even know what an AED was when asked to retrieve the device. The victim died as a result of not being treated in time. Sport managers who elect to implement PAD programs must be aware of problem areas in an effort to save lives. The human error mentioned above was the neglect for training for all staff members, regular and part time. Other problem areas in PAD programs in include attrition. A study conducted by *USA Today* to determine how well PAD programs located across the U.S. and Canada work revealed that half the volunteers trained to use an AED left their jobs within a year (Davis, 2000). Similarly, retention rates for trained volunteers decline over time. According to the National Institutes of Health, CPR skills fell to 87% proficiency when volunteers were tested a year after their initial training. The attrition and declining retention rates are problems that require large amounts of time for administrators to solve or offset.

An easier problem to solve in PAD programs is the security and placement of the AEDs. Davis (2003) notes in the *USA Today* study that in 55% of the programs studied the AEDs were hidden and sometimes locked away from the public while only 31% were accessible to the public. From these PAD efficacy studies, administrators must understand the importance of implementing and maintaining quality PAD programs.

Legal Trends

The most significant obstacle to large-scale AED distribution in the business world is fear of exposure to negligence liability lawsuits (Lazar, 1997). It is reasonable for businesses to take this issue into consideration when analyzing the risks and benefits of AEDs. According to attorney Richard A. Lazar (1997), four essential elements must be proven in order for a plaintiff to successfully sue an AED purchaser or user. These include duty, breach of duty, causation of injury, and legally recognized damages. The failure to prove any one of these elements is fatal to a plaintiff's case. The most important element in the context of an AED case is that of duty (Lazar, 1997).

According to Lazar (1997), duty in negligence law is defined as "an obligation, to which the law will give recognition and effect, to conform to a particular standard of conduct toward another." If no legal duty exists, no liability suit can be filed. In the context of duty, businesses contemplating the purchase of AEDs must consider whether a legal obligation to render medical aid to patrons exists and, if so, the scope of the obligation (Lazar, 1997). This particular issue is one that many risk managers have had to analyze very closely in an effort to avoid liability. While bystanders generally have no legal obligation to provide affirmative medical aid to ill or injured persons, the existence of certain relationships between a victim and one in position to render aid may create a duty to provide assistance (Lazar, 1997). Business sectors including common carriers, innkeepers, and commercial establishments open to the public may be compelled by law to render a minimum level of first aid care and to timely summon outside emergency medical assistance (Lazar, 1997). Lazar (1997) says that the scope of this duty is generally defined by appellate case law, trial courts, and juries.

Of all the court cases that have been mentioned the most important issue that arises out of all of these is the standard of care issue. Owners of AEDs and potential acquirers of the devices are all wanting to know what is the standard of care, or duty owed, to sudden cardiac arrest victims in today's society? That question still remains relatively unanswered, but if these cases are any indication, and AEDs keep becoming more and more prevalent, the standard of care will be increasing. As is evident in some of the aforementioned cases and as many experts have suggested, once AEDs become more widely adopted at facilities, the question of liability will focus not on the deployment of AEDs, but on their absence at a facility. If laws are changed and AEDs are made more widely available, health and fitness facility owners believe that the standard of emergency response care in their facilities will undoubtedly move toward requiring the use of AEDs (Herbert, 1998). Dr. Don Vining, a radiologist in Naples, Florida who has been instrumental in establishing an AED-based safety initiative at Olde Florida Golf Club says, "In five years, when there are twenty golf clubs in your community and eighteen of them have this equipment on site, and you don't, I think you're going to be liable for not having it." (Smith, 1999).

It is also important to remember that, according the American Heart Association, no known judgments have been rendered against the operator of an AED for negligent or improper use of an AED. Liability claims associated with negligent operation of an AED are mitigated by the difficulty in establishing that the operator proximately caused harm to the victim. The operator is attempting to resuscitate an individual who, without the AED, will likely remain dead. This point, coupled with the fact that an AED will not allow defibrillation to a victim that does not need it, all but indemnifies an operator in most cases.

Legal risks associated with adoption and implementation of business-based AED programs, while not zero, appear quite negligible (Lazar, 1997). Many risk managers believe greater risks can arise from failure to acquire and adopt AED programs. According to Lazar (1997), four main factors constitute why business-based AED programs are generally a low-risk endeavor. 1) No lawsuits, verdicts, or appellate cases are identified involving the use of an AED to help a victim of sudden cardiac arrest. 2) Sudden cardiac arrest victims are, in effect, already dead. Use of an AED can only help, it cannot hurt. 3) Many if not most businesses carry liability insurance coverage protecting the business in the event of an AED lawsuit. 4) Most states have laws limiting the types and scope of negligence lawsuits permissible against lay individuals rendering emergency medical care.

Statutory Immunity Provisions

Forty-nine states and the District of Columbia now provide statutory immunity or limitations on liability for those involved in some manner with an AED, however, these provisions vary greatly as to the person or entity listed (Connaughton & Spengler, 2001). At the time of this writing the only state that did not have specific AED immunity provisions in its state law is Iowa. Jurisdictions with legislation relevant to AEDs provide limitations on liability for the user of the AED, the person or entity providing the AED and related training, the person responsible for the site placement of the AED, the one responsible for the site where the AED is located, the one providing supervision, and the purchaser of the AED (Connaughton & Spengler, 2001). The person who uses an AED in an emergency is often protected from liability where his or her conduct does not amount to gross negligence or willful misconduct (Connaughton & Spengler, 2001). Potential AED users in the sport setting include coaches, stadium and arena security personnel, lifeguards, golf pros, ski patrol, and athletic trainers.

AED State Code Statutory Immunity Provision Table

States requiring that the AED user be properly trained (28)
AK, AZ, CA, CT, HI, IL, IN, KS, LA, MA, MD, ME, MO, MT, NE, NJ, NM, NV, NY, OK, OR, PA, RI, UT, VA, VT, WV, WY

States requiring that the user acts without compensation (25)
AL, AR, CA, CO, DC, FL, HI, IL, KS, KY, MA, MN, MO, MS*, ND, NH, NV, NY, OK, OR, RI, SC, UT, VA, WV, WY

States providing immunity to those that provide training in CPR and AED use (17)
AL, AR, AZ, CA, DC, DE, KY, LA, MS, NC, NJ, NM, NV, OR, RI, TN, WY

States providing immunity to those that provide AED training only (7)
FL, IL, MI, MT, ND, SD, WI

States providing immunity to person or entity where an AED is located (23)
AL, AR, AZ, CA, CO, DC, DE, IL, IN, KY, LA, MI, MT, NC, ND, NJ, NM, NV, NY, OR, TN, WI, WY

States providing broad immunity (4)
ID, NH, OH, WA

States providing immunity to person providing supervisory services in AED use (11)
AR, LA, MD, MI, MT, ND, NJ, NM, OR, SD, WI

States providing immunity to the purchaser of an AED (16)
AZ, IL, IN, LA, NH, NJ, NM, NY, OH, OK, OR, PA, SC, TX, VT, WY

* Provides immunity to user who acts with or without compensation.

It is evident that because of liability concerns many sport managers are reluctant to implement AED programs, but according to Connaughton and Spengler (2001), knowledge of immunity provisions in state laws might encourage the use of AEDs in sport settings. Information relevant to the person or entity protected by statute is necessary to reduce the fear of litigation and encourage the use of AEDs in sport and recreation (Connaughton & Spengler, 2001). If recent trends are any indication, having an AED might provide less exposure to liability than not having one on site.

This statutory immunity provision table is intended to be used as a general reference only. It is important to remember that state law is always in flux and any diligent person would need to check current legislation applicable to their state. Within the last decade many states have passed new AED bills, so one need also pay attention to when these laws take effect. If you feel that your state immunity laws are not sufficient and you are still concerned about litigation, there are AED manufacturers that provide indemnification programs for their properly maintained equipment, where the users are certified by the Red Cross or the American Heart Association (Nohr, 2011).

References

Ala. Code § 6-5-332 (2001).

Alaska Stat. § 09.65.090 (2001).

American Heart Association. (1998). American Heart Association report on the second public access defibrillation conference. *Circulation, 13*, 1309–1304.

American Heart Association News Release-health clubs not fit for cardiac emergencies. (2001). *Exercise Standards and Malpractice Reporter, 15(1)*, 8–9.

Ariz. Rev. Stat. § 36-2263 (2000).

Ark. Code Ann. § 17-95-605 (2001).

Automatic external defibrillators for public access defibrillation: recommendations for specifying and reporting arrhythmia analysis algorithm performance, incorporating new waveforms, and enhancing safety. (1997) *Circulation, 95*, 1677–1682.

Cal. Civ. Code § 1714.21 (2001).

Cantwell, J.D. (1998). Automatic external defibrillators in the sports arena: the right place, the right time. *Physician and Sportsmedicine, 26(12)*, 33–34; 76.

Col. Rev. Stat. § 13-21-108.1 (2001).

Conn. Gen. Stat. § 52-557b (2001).

Connaughton, D.P., & Spengler, J.O. (2001). Automated external defibrillator in sport and recreation settings: an analysis of immunity provisions in state legislation. *Journal of Legal Aspects of Sport, 11(51)*, 51–67.

Davis, R. (2003, July 28). Many lives are lost across USA because emergency services fail. *USA Today*, pp. 1A, 6A.

Davis, R. (2003, November 12). Study: defibrillator plans can fail in a heartbeat. *USA Today*, p. 8D.

Del. Code Ann. tit. 16, § 3005C (2000).

D.C. Code Ann. § 6-3803 (2001).

Fla. Stat. Ann. § 768.13 (2000).

Ga. Code § 31-11-53.1 (2000).

Ga. Code § 51-1-29.3 (2000).

Greaney, P.P. (2000). AEDs: not as common as the office water cooler — but a lot more helpful in saving lives. *Osh.Net Newsletter Article*. Retrieved November 15, 2001 from the World Wide Web.

Gundry, J.W., Comess, K.A., DeRook, F.A., Jorgensen, D., & Bardy, G.H. (1999). Comparison of naïve sixth-grade children with trained professionals in the use of an automated external defibrillator. *Circulation, 100*, 1703–1707.

Haw. Rev. Code § 663-1.5 (2000).

Herbert, D.L. (2001). Another AED lawsuit may go to trial. *Fitness Management, 17(6)*, 52.

Herbert, D.L. (2001). Failure to have AED suit results in defense verdict. *Exercise Standards and Malpractice Reporter, 15(3)*, 42–43.

Herbert, D.L. (2000). Alleged failure to have AED litigation in Florida results in another defense verdict — but the plaintiff receives $2.25 million. *Sports, Parks, and Recreation Law Reporter, 14(2)*, 23–24.

Herbert, D.L. (2000). Failure to defibrillate litigation results in another defense verdict. *Exercise Standards and Malpractice Reporter, 14(1)*, 11–13.

Herbert, D.L. (2000). More on AEDs. *Exercise Standards and Malpractice Reporter, 14(3)*, 42–43.

Herbert, D.L. (1999). Large verdict returned against Busch Gardens in emergency response case (failure to use AED). *Sports Medicine Standards and Malpractice Reporter, 11(5)*, 29.

Herbert, D.L. (1998). Are defibrillators part of the emergency response standard of care owed to patrons by health and fitness facilities? *Exercise Standards and Malpractice Reporter, 12(4),* 49;52.

Idaho Code § 5-337 (2000).

745 Ill. Comp. Stat. § 49/12 (2001).

Ind. Code § 16-31-6-2 (2001).

Ind. Code § 34-30-12-1 (2001).

Kan. Stat. Ann. § 65-6124 (2000).

Kan. Stat. Ann. § 65-6149a (2000).

Ky. Rev. Stat. § 311.668 (2001).

Kyle, J.M., Leaman, J., & Elkins, G.A. Planning for scholastic cardiac emergencies: the Ripley Project. *Scientific Newsfront — The West Virginia Medical Journal.* Retrieved November 15, 2001 from the World Wide Web.

La. Rev. Stat. § 40:1236.14 (2001).

Lazar, R.A. (1997). Defibrillators enter the business marketplace. *Occupational Health and Safety.* Retrieved November 15, 2001 from the World Wide Web.

Mass. Ann. Laws ch.112 § 12V (2001).

Md. Code Ann., Educ. § 13-517 (2000).

Me. ALS 364 (2001).

Mich. Comp. Laws § 691.1504 (2001).

Minn. Stat. § 604A.01 (2000).

Miss. Code Ann. § 73-25-37 (2001).

Mitchell, E. (1999). More stadiums add lifesaver to lineup. *Sport Business Journal, 1(38),* 11–17.

Mo. Rev. Stat. § 190.092 (2000).

Mont. Code Ann. § 50-6-505 (2001).

Neb. Rev. Stat. Ann. § 71-51,102 (2001).

Nev. Rev. Stat. Ann. § 41.500 (2001).

N.H. Rev. Stat. Ann. § 153-A:31 (2000).

N.J. Stat. Ann. § 2A:62A-26 (2001).

N.M. Stat. Ann. § 24-10C-7 (2000).

N.Y. Pub. Health Law § 3000-b (2001).

N.C. Gen. Stat. § 90-21.15 (2000).

N.D. Cent. Code § 32-03.1-02.3 (2001).

Nohr, K.M. (2011, April 7). Getting to the heart of AED law. *Sport Risk.* Retrieved November 14, 2011, from www.sportrisk.com/2011/04/07getting-to-the-heart-of-aed-law/.

Ohio Rev. Code Ann. § 2305-235 (Anderson 2001).

Okla. Stat. Ann. tit. 76, § 5A (2000).

Or. Rev. Stat. § 30.801 (1999).

Penn. Con. Stat. tit. 42, § 8331.2 (2001).

Peterson, K.F. (2000). Legal implications of lay use of automatic external defibrillators in non-hospital settings. *Journal of Contemporary Health Law and Policy, 17,* 275–320.

R.I. Gen. Laws § 9-1-34 (2001).

Sarkis, K. (2000). AEDs: starting a company program. *Occupational Hazards, 62(4),* 61.

Schnirring, L. (2001). AEDs gain foothold in sports medicine. *Physician and Sportsmedicine, 29(4),* 11; 15–16; 19.

Smith, S. (1999). Saving lives on the golf course: join the battle against golf's deadliest enemy-sudden cardiac arrest. *Golf Digest, 50(1),* 84–88; 90.

S.C. Code Ann. § 728 (1999)

S.C. Code Ann. § 44-76-40 (2000).

S.D. Codified Laws § 20-9-4.1 (2001).

Starr, L.M. (1999). Is an AED in your company's future? *HR Magazine, 44(6),* 114–118.

Tenn. Code Ann. § 63-6-218 (2001).

Tenn. Code Ann. § 68-140-706 (2001).

Tenn. Code Ann. § 68-140-707 (2001).

Terry, G.C., Kyle, J.M., Ellis, J.M., Cantwell, J.D., Courson, R., & Medlin, R. (2001). Sudden cardiac arrest in athletic medicine. *Journal of Athletic Training, 32(2),* 205–209.

Tex. Civ. Prac. & Rem. Code Ann. § 74.001 (2000).

Utah Code Ann. § 26-8a-601 (2001).

42 U.S.C. § 238p (2001).

Valenzuela, T.D., Roe, D.J., Nichol, G., Clark, L.L., Spaite, D.W., & Hardman, R.G. (2000). Outcomes of rapid defibrillation by security officers after cardiac arrest in casinos. *The New England Journal of Medicine, 343(17),* 1206–1209.

Van Camp, S.P., Bloor, C.M., & Mueller, F.O. (1995). Nontraumatic sports death in high school and college athletes. *Medicine and Science in Sports and Exercise, 27(5),* 641–647.

Vander Neut, T. (1999). Putting defibrillators into the hands of employees. *Risk and Insurance,* 7–8.

Va. Code Ann. § 8.01-225 (2001).

Vt. Stat. Ann. tit. 18, § 907 (2001).

Wash. Rev. Code § 70.54.310 (2001).

W. Va. Code § 16-40-3 (2001).

W. Va. Code § 16-40-4 (2001).

Wis. Stat. Ann. § 895.48 (2000).

Wyo. Stat. Ann. § 35-26-103 (2001).

Zolkos, R. (1998). Defibrillators save lives but may create liability. *Business Insurance, 32(32),* 3–4.

Part V

Event and Facility Management Issues

The facility manager has a tiger by the tail. He's got to be part booking agent, part salesman, part fire inspector, and part lawyer to make it through the insurance crisis.

Richard Keystone

Chapter 23

ADA and Sport Facilities

Nowhere can the ADA's effect be seen more prominently than in facilities.

Gil B. Fried

In a watershed event for millions of Americans, President Bush signed the Americans with Disabilities Act (ADA) into law on January 26, 1990. The new law promised millions of Americans the opportunity to receive equality in ways never before experienced by some or long forgotten by others. The ADA has been dubbed the Emancipation Proclamation and the Bill of Rights for individuals with disabilities (Schneid 1992). The number of people that would be covered by the ADA was estimated at 45 million people in the United States (Schneid 1992). By the 2000 census the number of disabled people in the United States had grown to almost 50 million.

The Civil Rights Act of 1964 is considered a sweeping legislative enactment entitling women and minorities the equality they need to be gainfully employed. The ADA is even more sweeping because while it is unusual for someone to change sex, nationality, race or religion; it is not uncommon for a healthy individual to be suddenly stricken by heart disease, diabetes, arthritis, or a variety of other maladies. These unwanted maladies become the basis for potential discrimination or exclusion. The ADA was adopted with several key sections that impact the sport industry. One section focused on places of public accommodations and another section applies to the workplace. One of the primary purposes of the ADA is to ensure that facilities and organizations that provide public accommodations are accessible to all people. The ADA also requires employers to make "reasonable accommodations," for current and future employees who have a disability.

Nowhere can the ADA's effect be seen more prominently than in sport and recreation facilities. Sport and recreational facilities are especially prominent in ADA coverage due to the publicity generated by such facilities and the number of individuals who attend events or engage in activities at such facilities. Sport facilities have become the target for organizations such as the Paralyzed Veterans of America who have engaged in a concerted effort on behalf of their 17,000 members to challenge new sport facilities which do not meet ADA requirements. The group filed claims against several arenas claiming that while spaces are available at each site for wheelchairs, most seats do not offer a clear view of the action when surrounding fans stand up. Regulations under the ADA require all wheelchair seats to be designed so that the wheelchair using patron is not isolated, has the choice of various seats and each ticket price level, and in places where fans are expected to stand, facilities must provide a line of sight "comparable" to the view from seats provided to other spectators. Companion seating also needs to be available for those with disabled guests.

The United States Architectural and Transportation Barriers Compliance Board introduced ADA recommendations for sport facilities. Recommendations were developed for sport facilities, places of amusement, play settings, golf, recreational and other boating and fishing facilities, and outdoor development areas. The sport facility recommendations are set forth in over 200 pages describing the layout of baseball dugouts, entrance turnstiles, and other sport facility components. The Americans with Disabilities Act Accessibility Guidelines (ADAAG) were revised several times to reflect technological and legal interpretations of the ADA. Other regulations can be found in the International Code Council's (ICC's) International Building Code (IBC), which has been adopted by every state in the United States, and regulations such as the Uniform Federal Accessibility Standard (UFAS), which applies to those who receive federal funding.

Other laws work with the ADA to create a complete compendium of laws covering all sport facilities. The 1968 Architectural Barriers Act and the Rehabilitation Act of 1973 provide an extensive regulatory framework for sport facilities. Due to numerous legal challenges and new interpretations the Justice Department, in 2010, issued new ADA Standards for Accessible Design that applied to Title II (to protect qualified individuals with disabilities from discrimination on the basis of disability in the services, programs, or activities of all state and local governments) and III (to provide equal access to services at public accommodations) of the ADA. State and local laws can also affect facility design, construction, and renovations. Building codes determine specific issues such as how many steps can be built without needing a handrail, the number of inches required per person, per seat, in bleacher seating (usually 17–20 inches allocated for each seat), and the number and size of exits based on the number of individuals expected to use each exit.

These laws are all coming into play in a variety of sport facilities, ranging from stadia and arenas to schools and bowling alleys. The scope and applicability of ADA facility requirements are best understood when analyzed in light of the express purpose of the ADA.

Purpose Behind ADA

The underlying principle of the ADA focuses on the equal opportunity for individuals with disabilities to participate in and benefit from programs and facilities in the most integrated setting possible. The goal of the ADA is mainstreaming by allowing individuals with disabilities the opportunity to mainstream into American society. To help bring about mainstreaming, facilities and programs must integrate the individuals with disabilities to the maximum extent possible, provide separate programs when required to ensure equal opportunity, and must not exclude individuals with disabilities from regular programs (unless there is a significant injury risk). The extent of the obligations to integrate people in the best manner possible can be seen in the following excerpt from the U.S. Department of Justice's (DOJ) Highlight of Title III's requirements:

Public accommodations must

- Provide goods and services in an integrated setting, unless separate or different measures are necessary to ensure equal opportunity.

- Eliminate unnecessary eligibility standards or rules that deny individuals with disabilities an equal opportunity to enjoy the goods and services of a place of public accommodation.

- Make reasonable modifications in policies, practices, and procedures that deny equal access to individuals with disabilities, unless a fundamental alteration would result in the nature of the goods and services provided.

- Furnish auxiliary aids when necessary to ensure effective communication, unless an undue burden or fundamental alteration would result.

- Remove architectural and structural communication barriers in existing facilities where readily achievable.

- Provide readily achievable alternative measures when removal of barriers is not readily achievable.

- Provide equivalent transportation services and purchase accessible vehicles in certain circumstances.

- Maintain accessible features of facilities and equipment.

- Design and construct new facilities and, when undertaking alterations, alter existing facilities in accordance with the Americans with Disabilities Act Accessibility Guidelines issued by the Architectural and Transportation Barriers Compliance Board and incorporated in the final Department of Justice title III regulation (http://www.ada.gov/t3hilght.htm, 2011).

ADA Requirements for Sport Facilities

Title III of the ADA covers places of public accommodations and commercial facilities. For a facility to be considered a place of public accommodation, the facility's operation has to affect interstate commerce. This means that a facility needs to be open to the general public and that people can visit the facility from various states. Public facilities which meet this test include, but are not limited to, any establishment serving food and drinks, entertainment facilities (movie theaters, concert halls, etc.), public gathering places (auditoriums, convention centers, stadiums, arenas, etc.), public transportation centers, places of recreation (parks, zoos, bowling alleys, etc.), places of education (private schools), and places of exercise or recreation (gymnasium, golf courses, etc.). The only exceptions from Title III coverage are private clubs and religious organizations. There are an estimated five million facilities that meet the ADA coverage requirement.

Under the ADA, a place of public accommodation is required to remove all architectural barriers to access if such removal is "readily achievable." When an architectural barrier cannot be removed, the facility must provide alternative services. However, any new construction or facility alteration must comply with all ADA accessibility standards. New construction is required to be readily accessible and usable unless it is structurally impracticable.

Commercial facilities are facilities not intended for residential use and whose operation affects interstate commerce. Examples of commercial facilities include factories, warehouses, and office buildings. Existing commercial facilities are not required to remove architectural barriers even if the removal is readily achievable. Commercial facilities also do not need to provide alternative services as do places of public accommodation. Only newly constructed commercial facilities and alterations to existing commercial facilities need to meet ADA requirements.

The primary focus in analyzing sport facilities revolves around the public accommodation requirements. Public accommodations may not discriminate against individuals with disabilities. Disabled individuals cannot be denied full and equal enjoyment of the "goods, services, facilities, privileges, advantages, or accommodations" offered by a covered facility. The ADA applies to covered facilities no matter whether they are owned by the private, non-profit, or government sectors.

Full and equal enjoyment covers more than just facilities. It also covers programs held within the facilities. The landmark case setting forth ADA requirements for sport programs under Title III is *Anderson v. Little League Baseball, Inc.* Little League Baseball adopted a policy in 1991 that prohibited wheelchair-using coaches due to the potential collisions that could occur between a player and coach. Anderson, a wheelchair user who also was an on-field coach, contended that the policy change was instituted to prevent him from coaching during a 1991 season-end tournament. The local Little League office refused to enforce the rule and Anderson's team was eliminated early in the tournament. The issue arose again in 1992 when Anderson coached an all-star team.

The court questioned whether Anderson posed a risk to other participants. The court also examined whether Little League's claimed "direct threat" (to others) was based on generalizations or stereotypes about the effects of a particular disability. The court held that each coach had to be individually assessed. There was no evidence that Little League Baseball, Inc. undertook any type of inquiry to ascertain the nature, duration, and severity of risk, the probability that injury could actually occur or whether reasonable modifications of policies, practices, or procedures could reduce the risk. Thus, any rule developed by an organization (that utilizes places of public accommodation) must provide the opportunity to evaluate each program participant on his/her own merits. Any policy that results in an absolute ban on any handicapped individual(s) will always be struck down if there is at least one person who does not pose a "direct threat" or can prove that he/she does not epitomize a generalization or stereotype.

The unfair and indiscriminate application of stereotypes has resulted in several successful suits against sport facilities. A California ski resort violated the ADA with its policy that prohibited persons in wheelchairs from riding cable cars to the resort's recreational facilities. The court concluded that the resort's policy responds not to an actual risk, but to "speculation, stereotypes, and generalizations." The resort was forced to modify its policies. A Philadelphia gym facing significant legal fees agreed to pay $35,000, adopt a non-discrimination policy, and provide mandatory staff AIDS/HIV education to settle an ADA (Title III) lawsuit. The suit was brought by an AIDS victim who claimed the gym owner publicly humiliated him, threw him out, and told him never to return to the gym because he had AIDS.

Another example involved the Executive Director of the Paralyzed Veterans of America's Michigan chapter, who helped bring a claim under the ADA against Michigan Stadium at the University of Michigan. The Stadium can hold 107,501 fans. Disabled seating selection was limited to 45 wheelchair-accessible spots spread along row 72 in the south end zone, and another 45 in the north end zone. Based on the need for facilities to have wheelchair-accessible seats comprising one (1) percent of a venue's overall seating capacity, the University of Michigan was roughly 985 wheelchair slots shy of compliance. The university had undertaken various renovations of the Stadium, but their initial response was that the facility was built years before the ADA was passed and as such they were grandfathered from having to change their wheelchair seating options. The argument was that any of the modification projects did not constitute significant modifications to the facility to change the ADA grandfathering provision. The parties entered into a consent decree where the University did not admit fault but agreed to specific requirements including the two provisions highlighted below:

4. By the start of the 2008 football season, the University shall provide permanent locations for wheelchair seats and companion seats in the Stadium as follows:

a. approximately 96 wheelchair and 96 companion seats in a continuous permanent row along the east sideline of the Stadium from the south edge of portal 39 through the north edge of portal 7 at row 54, consisting of 12 permanent platforms ("the East Sideline Row 54 Wheelchair Seating")…

b. the University shall continue to provide a total of approximately 81 permanent wheelchair seats and 81 companion seats (i) in the north end zone, from portal 31 through portal 37 at Row 72 ("North End Zone Row 72 Wheelchair Seating") in a continuous permanent row, and (ii) in the south end zone, from portal 9 through portal 15 at Row 72 ("South End Zone Row 72 Wheelchair Seating") in a continuous permanent row….

5. By the start of the 2010 football season, the University shall provide additional permanent locations for wheelchair seats and companion seats in the Stadium as follows:

a. approximately 56 wheelchair seats and 56 companion seats in a continuous permanent row along the east sideline of the Stadium from the south edge of portal 41 through the north edge of portal 5 on row 72, consisting of 8 permanent platforms ("East Sideline Row 72 Wheelchair Seating")…;

b. approximately 24 wheelchair seats and 24 companion seats in a continuous permanent row in the northwest corner of the Stadium from the southwest edge of portal 31 through the north edge of portal 28 on row 72, consisting of 3 permanent platforms ("the Northwest Corner Row 72 Student Wheelchair Seating"), see …; and

c. a minimum of an additional permanent 72 wheelchair seats and 72 companion seats located on the west sideline on the new west concourse, added as part of the University's 2010 Expansion Plan, approximately between column lines 2W and 16W and between 19W and 33W ("the West Concourse Sideline Wheelchair Seating"), …

By the start of the 2010 football season, pursuant to paragraphs 4 and 5, the University was required to provide a minimum of 329 permanent wheelchair seats and a minimum of 329 permanent companion seats vertically and horizontally dispersed throughout the Stadium as described in the Consent Decree (Michigan Paralyzed Veterans of America v. University of Michigan, No. 07-11702 http://www.ada.gov/umichstadium.htm).

What Disabilities Are Covered by ADA?

The ADA employment provision clarifies what constitutes a disability under the ADA. Individuals covered by the ADA include those with *significant physical or mental impairments,* a *record of an impairment,* and those *regarded as having an impairment.* A last category of disabled persons are those who are not disabled themselves, but have a relationship with a disabled person. Such a person could be the son/daughter, husband/wife, or some other relationship where the able-bodied person needs to accompany or assist the disabled person. A person with a record of disability is protected even though they might not currently experience any impairment. Thus, a cancer patient in remission is still covered by the ADA. Furthermore, those regarded as having impairments are protected even if they never had any impairment. Therefore, a person who is extremely short and could be called a dwarf would be covered as a disabled person even if they did not think of themselves as being disabled. The focus is on what others think, because so many people act on their assumptions and that can impact how they treat others. Even though the ADA has been around for almost 20 years, there are still lawsuits focused on what qualifies as a disability.

Not all physical or mental impairments constitute a disability. The impairment has to be *significant*. To help determine significance, the following factors are examined: the length of time the condition has existed, the number and types of life activities affected, the extent to which the disability limits opportunities, and whether the condition is medically diagnosable.

Common examples of protected disabilities include: paralysis, diabetes, arthritis, cancer, epilepsy, asthma, vision impairments, hearing impairments, speech impairments, learning disabilities, muscular dystrophy, heart disease, and manic depressive disorder. Conditions commonly regarded as impairments include dwarfism, albinism, cosmetic deformities, controlled diabetes, and visible burn injuries. The ADA specifically excludes homosexuals, bisexuals, transvestites, transsexuals, pyromaniacs, kleptomaniacs, and compulsive gamblers. Other conditions that are not covered by the ADA include: colds, broken bones, appendicitis, hair color, hair type, or left-handedness. It should be noted that after a recent Supreme Court decision, someone who has a disability such as vision impairment is covered by the ADA, unless they can remedy their medical condition with cures such as medicine or glasses. If someone can resolve their medical condition with such cures then they are no longer considered disabled pursuant to the ADA.

In 2009, the Equal Employment Opportunity Commission (EEOC) developed new guidelines for analyzing a disability and those guidelines provide the following changes:

- The definition of disability—an impairment that poses a substantial limitation in a major life activity—must be construed in favor of broad coverage of individuals to the maximum extent permitted by the terms of the ADA, and should not require extensive analysis;

- Major life activities include "major bodily functions;"

- That mitigating measures, such as medications and devices that people use to reduce or eliminate the effects of an impairment, are not to be considered when determining whether someone has a disability; and

- Impairments that are episodic or in remission, such as epilepsy, cancer, and many kinds of psychiatric impairments, are disabilities if they would "substantially limit" major life activities when active.

The new DOJ regulations adopted in 2010 have the following changes:

1) New definition of "service animal"

2) Changes in requirements for accessible ticketing and seating

3) New definitions of "mobility device"

4) Revised ADAAG standards

These changes help show that the definition of disability is not static and has evolved due to loopholes, litigation, and new diagnosis. The above enumerated rules and definitions present a complicated list of potentially disabled individuals. Unfortunately, most of the disabilities covered under the ADA are not readily visible. Thus, the notion that you can see when a disabled person uses your facility is a fallacy. Therefore, you have to prepare your facility for any and all potential users. The hallmark for proper preparation entails providing reasonable accommodation.

What Constitutes a Reasonable Accommodation?

Reasonable accommodation refers to correcting both architectural- and program-related barriers. An architectural barrier represents a building's physical element that impedes access for disabled individuals. Examples of architectural barriers include: steps and curbs rather than ramps; unpaved parking areas; conventional doors rather than automatic doors; office layouts that do not allow a wheelchair to move through an office; deep pile carpeting which is difficult for wheelchairs to traverse; or mirrors, paper towel dispensers, and sinks that are positioned too high on a bathroom wall. The DOJ or a plaintiff will examine a facility to determine if the facility is really open for all people. If access is limited, the next question is whether the barrier can easily be modified or corrected. Most modifications can be done in a reasonable time frame and at a reasonable cost. The law does not require a facility to be completely rebuilt to accommodate the disabled. Whatever modifications might be required only need to be reasonable and a facility does not need to be completely rebuilt.

All covered facilities must reasonably modify their policies, practices, and procedures to avoid discrimination. Modifications do not need to be undertaken if they would fundamentally alter the nature of the goods, services, facilities, privileges, advantages, or accommodations. A perfect example of this rule was seen at the inaugural Disney World Marathon. One disabled participant, a motorized wheelchair user, sued claiming the race organizers were not reasonably accommodating his needs. The race organizers replied that by having the disabled individual compete, the race would be fundamentally altered. The court agreed with the race organizers. The judge concluded that the race organizers were providing reasonable accommodation to disabled individuals through the running of a wheelchair-user division in the race. However, the disabled prospective participant who filed the claim was no ordinary wheelchair user. He used a motorized wheelchair. The court reasoned that the use of a motorized wheelchair would significantly alter the nature of the event. By allowing a motorized wheelchair, the court would have opened the door for a disabled person to claim the next year that they wished to participate while driving in a customized van. The court was unwilling to let the law go so far as to alter the very nature of the event. Thus, the ADA can require minor changes to an event to accommodate the disabled, but the event does not need to be completely modified.

While events do not need to be significantly changed, new events are being added to comply with the ADA. One of the greatest areas of growth involves intercollegiate athletics. For example, the University of Illinois fields an intercollegiate wheelchair basketball team. Such teams are not the norm, but are gaining in popularity as colleges and universities are being dragged into offering additional competitive sports for the disabled, similar to how some programs were forced by Title IX to add additional women's sports. To help handle the potential increase in demand for disabled sports, the National Collegiate Athletic Association (NCAA) has convened a group called the Student-Athlete Disability Advisory Group to provide advice on how to accommodate disabled students (Disability compliance for higher education, 2004). Furthermore, the NCAA has had to alter their rules to cover student eligibility for student-athletes who have learning disabilities that could have impacted their classroom performance.

There is no need to provide individual prescription devices that must be customized for individual use such as glasses, wheelchairs, or hearing aides. Neither is there a requirement to provide individualized assistance such as eating, dressing and toileting assistance. Thus, while it is fairly easy to determine what accommodations do not need to be provided, it is much more difficult to determine the appropriate level for achieving reasonable accommodation.

What constitutes effective accommodation for the hearing impaired took an interesting turn in 2011, when the 4th U.S. Circuit Court of Appeals upheld a lower court's decision concerning music lyrics at FedEx Field. Starting in 2003, hearing impaired fans had asked for greater access to information. After a suit was filed, FedEx's management started streaming captioning on two LED ribbon boards at the 50 yard line. The streamed information included game information, public address announcements and non-musical halftime entertainment. What was not covered were musical lyrics and that is what the case *Feldman v. Pro Football Inc.* was focused on. The court concluded that music is an important part of the game experience and can arouse enthusiasm and passion. Thus, the facility would need to provide captioning of lyrics, even if they might be nonsensical. The problem with such a ruling is that a facility could comply with the ADA by captioning the lyrics, but such compliance might in fact cause a violation of copyright laws. Thus, ADA compliance can in fact lead to additional legal concerns and should not be viewed in a vacuum.

Do I Have to Prepare for All Potential Disabilities?

Facilities need to try and accommodate disabled users/participants/employees. The major exception to this rule is if the person (and their disability) represents a risk of serious injury to themselves and others. Thus, a person who has Turrets Syndrome can be denied a job opportunity if their inadvertent swearing could possibly cause violence based on the people they would be working with. The law is clear that no employer needs to hire a disabled applicant for a given job. The law requires disabled applicants to be considered similar to all other qualified applicants. It does not mean that an employer has to hire a disabled applicant over a more or better qualified applicant. Disabled applicants need to be given the opportunity to compete and obtain a job if they are the most qualified and best applicant.

Most facility operators, when faced with possible access barriers, struggle with a prioritization process. Which repairs should be completed first? What repairs or changes can be implemented over time? In order to provide guidance, the DOJ has established priority suggestions for removing barriers. The primary concern and priority is the removal of any and all barriers that would prevent individuals with disabilities from entering the facility. The next priority is to provide access to areas where goods and services are made available to the general public. The third priority is to provide access to restrooms. The fourth priority entails removing all barriers to using the facility. Such repairs can include adding floor level indicators in elevators, lowering telephones and lowering paper towel dispensers in bathrooms. These repairs relate only to areas that are not exclusively used by employees as work areas. Thus, an older executive office that has not been modified since before the 1990s would not need to be modified. In contrast, a public restroom or hallway would probably need to e modified to accommodate disabled patrons.

Reasonable accommodation for ensuring equal communication can include a multitude of auxiliary communication aids, such as qualified interpreters, transcription services, audio recordings, speech synthesizers, telecommunication devices for the deaf (TDD's), telephone handset amplifiers, video text displays, written material (including large print), note takers, assistive listening devices, closed caption decoders, or brailed materials. Besides purchasing needed equipment, any and all equipment must be kept in accessible locations and in working condition. Most auxiliary aids are relatively inexpensive, such as amplifiers for telephones. However, purchasing and maintaining a significant amount of auxiliary equipment can become costly for smaller businesses.

No facility administrator knows for sure how many patrons with special needs might show for any given event. Thus, a facility needs to be prepared for almost any contingency. Whether a visually or mobility impaired patron, a facility needs to be ready. The Astrodome, when used for football and baseball, had approximately 60,000 seats and was required to have assistive listening devices for 2% of the seats, which totaled 1,200 devises. The highest number of devices requested for any game was under 20 devices. Similarly, the original ADA regulations required 1% of seating throughout a stadium to be handicapped assessable, with companion seating opportunities.

The new ADAAG guidelines apply to facilities with more than 300 seats and requires each wheelchair accessible location to have a companion seat. However, facilities with at least 5,000 seats need 36 wheelchair seats and one for each every additional 200 seats (Emmons, 2004). Similarly, for venues with over 2,000 seats the new guidelines require 55 assisted listening devices and then one for every 100 additional seats. The seats cannot be just in one section, but need to be distributed throughout the facility, and then made available at each pricing level from luxury seats to bleacher seats. Similar to the numbers required for disabled seating, detailed formulas also exist for assistive listening devices. Under the 2010 DOJ guidelines, for facilities with seating capacities between 1,001 to 2,000 people there need to be at least 35 devices plus 1 for every 50 seats over 1,000 seats. For facilities with over 2,001 patrons there need to be at least 55 devices plus 1 for every 100 seats over 2,000 seats.

How Much Will It Cost?

Public accommodations are only required to remove barriers when such removal is "readily achievable" (ADA Section 302(b)(2)(A)(iv)). "Readily achievable" means that the repairs or modifications can be made without significant difficulty or expense (301(9)).

Several factors influence the costs associated with barrier removal. These factors include the nature and cost of needed remedial action, the financial strength of the facility or organization required to provide the accommodation, and the relationship of the facility in the overall financial picture of the parent company. Companies with significant capital will be held responsible for undertaking more repairs than a financially-strapped business.

Cost is only one factor to be considered when attempting to make a facility barrier free. An alteration is defined as any physical change that affects facility usability. Such changes can include remodeling, renovations, rearranging walls, and other activities that affect a facility's use. Any alterations begun after 1992 must be useable by disabled individuals to the maximum extent feasible. An example of an unfeasible alteration can be demonstrated through analyzing a renovation project for a facility entrance. While performing renovations, the facility manager is told that the only way to increase the doorway size to accommodate a wheelchair would affect the building's structure. Thus, it would be technically unfeasible to widen the entrance. Only that portion of the accommodation plan can be avoided. All other ADA alteration requirements would have to be followed.

Traditionally, landlords are responsible for facility repairs and modifications. Thus, landlords are typically responsible for financing required renovations or repairs. Lease agreements can provide the tenant with a right to modify a facility. If a lease agreement specifically allows a tenant to renovate a facility, it will be the tenant's responsibility to pay for ADA required modifications. If a lease is silent concerning responsibility for required repairs, the DOJ could force both the landlord and tenant to pay.

While some accommodations might seem impossible for a company to afford, tax benefits can make such improvements attainable. Internal Revenue Service (IRS) Code, Section 190, specifies that up to $15,000 of allowable expenditures for ADA required compliance can be deducted rather than capitalized. All expenditures over $15,000 constitute capital expenditures. Furthermore, under IRS Code, Section 44, eligible small businesses with sales less than $1 million and less than 30 employees can receive a credit equal to 50 percent of the accommodation's cost for expenses that do not exceed $10,250 in any tax year, for a maximum credit of $5,000. This credit applies to expenditures that are both reasonable and necessary. These tax benefits are best discussed through an example.

Sam Jones is the owner of Health-T Fitness Facility. Jones employs 15 people and has sales of $400,000 per year. After hiring an ADA compliance consulting company, Jones discovered that he needed to modify the facility's front entrance so a wheelchair could enter through the front door. The company also concluded that a ramp had to be built to provide access between the aerobic area and a soon to be built tennis playing area. In year one, Jones spent $18,000 to modify the front entrance. Jones took a $15,000 tax deduction and capitalized the remaining $3,000 expense. In year two, Jones spent $12,000 on the required ramp. Sam can only use $10,250 for the tax credit, but this number is reduced in half by the IRS regulations. The $5,125 credit is reduced because the maximum allowed tax credit for such repairs is $5,000. Thus Jones was eligible for a $5,000 tax credit on his next tax return.

What Will Happen If I Just Do Nothing?

The ADA is enforced through several means. Private citizens can file their own ADA claim in federal court. Private claims are only entitled to injunctive relief and attorney fees. Thus, if a bowling alley does not provide any reasonable accommodation, a patron can sue to force the alley to build a ramp so a wheelchair user could reach the lanes, but not for monetary damages.

A private citizen can also file a claim with the attorney general. After receiving a complaint, the DOJ can then sue the facility owner and seek injunctive relief. The attorney general can also recover monetary damages and civil penalties.

Practical and Inexpensive ADA Solutions for Sport Facilities

The purpose of this chapter is not to scare sport administrators. However, it should be specifically noted that the DOJ has clearly indicated that the days of ADA education are long over and the DOJ is now in a phase of ADA enforcement.

There are numerous ADA solutions that can be implemented at little or no cost. While facility renovation costs and repairs are hard to reduce, it is much easier to implement program-wide attitude changes which can significantly reduce the chance of incurring an ADA complaint and provide evidence that ADA compliance is being developed and fostered throughout the organizational staff.

For extensive repairs or renovations, facility operators can hire an ADA consulting firm to determine what repairs need to be made. Another option involves performing a complete facility review and program review to discover first-hand what potential problems exist. The first step necessary when undertaking your own ADA review is to designate one individual within your organization as the ADA expert. This "expert" will have to review literature in the field, become familiar with ADA regulations and specifications, and listen to the needs of employees and customers.

The second step involves the undertaking of a comprehensive facility audit. All facility components should be analyzed and evaluated for accessibility. A written evaluation should be prepared to track needed repairs, facility evaluation dates, repair dates, repair costs, priorities, and similar concerns. Such documentation is critical when facing an ADA investigation.

A convenient approach to conducting a facility audit entails working from outside to inside a facility; following the same travel path a disabled person might use. The following represent specific concerns that should be examined. This is not an exhaustive list, but rather a framework for further analysis.

Parking Area

Does your facility have ample parking spaces for individuals with special parking needs?

Are international symbols for the disabled used to identify parking spaces?

Is there adequate spacing between a disabled individual's potential parking space and other spaces so a wheelchair could easily be moved around a car/van's side?

Are there directional signs indicating the facilities entrance?

Sidewalks/Ramps

Are sidewalks at least 68 inches wide, to allow two wheelchairs to simultaneously move past one another on the sidewalk?

Are ramps clearly set apart with colored paint and the international handicapped symbol?

Can the ramp or curb be reached easily by someone parking in the handicapped parking space?

Is the slope at the right angle as to not hinder someone using a wheelchair?

Entrance Ways

Are entrance doors/paths unlocked and accessible?

Is there a minimum of 60 x 60 inches of level space in front of the entrance door to allow maneuvering?

Are doors easy to open? Push or pull doors need to be opened with less than 8.5 pounds of pressure. Sliding doors and interior doors require less than 5 pounds pressure. Fire doors require at least 15 pounds pressure.

Are doormats at the most one-half inch high and in the proper place as not to obstruct access?

Can doors be grasped with one hand without the need for a tight grip or wrist turning?

Are automatic doors set to open only when someone is less than two feet away from the doors? (This could cause an individual in a wheelchair to be hit by the doors.)

Are there accessible doors next to revolving doors?

Is there any metal or wood plating on the very bottom 7-inches of a glass door?

Is the door threshold flush with the floor or entrance surface?

Are interior floors covered with a non-slip surface?

Is high-plush carpeting used in transit areas?

Stairs

Are treads no less than 11 inches and covered with non-slip material?

Are there stair risers and do they run a uniform height?

Are the stair's nosing sharp/pointed and do they extend past the lip by over 1 inch?

Do the handrails extend at least 12 inches past the top and bottom stair?

Is the handrail's height between 34 and 38 inches above the stair treads?

Is the handrail grab bar less than 1 inch in diameter and easy to grip?

Are there tactile designations at the top and bottom of the stair run?

Elevators

Is an elevator required for accessibility to all facility levels?

Is an audible and visual signal provided to identify the elevator's travel direction?

Are elevator call buttons located at most 42 inches above the ground without any obstructions, such as ash trays?

Are Braille or raised/indented floor level designation buttons within the elevator?

Do the elevator doors open at least 32 inches and provide ample wheelchair accessibility within the elevator?

Does the elevator stop flush at each floor level?

Is the elevator equipped with an automatic bumper or other safety closing mechanisms?

Does the elevator have handrails mounted 34 to 36 inches above the elevator's floor?

Is the control panel located no more than 48 inches above the elevator's floor?

If an elevator's automatic doors are not functioning correctly is a maintenance plan in place to make immediate repairs?

Public Restrooms

Is an accessible restroom available for each sex?

Are restrooms and appropriate stalls clearly marked with international symbols?

Are restrooms identified with Braille or raised/incised lettering on the door or by the door frame?

Are mirrors and paper dispenser mounted within 40 inches of the floor?

Is the toilet appropriately placed at the right height and distance from any hot plumbing fixtures?

Is there an area of at least 30 x 48 inches provided in front of the toilet for a wheelchair to move around?

How are faucets activated (levers, handles, or motion detectors)?

Does the handicapped stall have a door that swings out and provides at least 32 inches of clearance?

Are handrails appropriately placed in stall?

Are toilet paper and seat covers within easy reach of a person on the toilet?

Are flush controls mounted lower than 40 inches from the floor and easy to grasp?

Is there unobstructed access to the bathroom?

Telephones

Are the telephone dials and coin slots no more than 48 inches above the floor?

Is the receiver cord at least 30 inches in length?

Are phone directories usable at a wheelchair level?

Is the handset equipped with an amplification mechanism?

Are usage and payment instructions available in Braille?

Water Fountains

Is the fountain at least 27 inches high and 17–19 inches deep?

Are there easy to control buttons, levers, or motion detectors?

Is some signage available showing how to operate the fountain?

Are drinking cups available for fountains that are too high?

The third step involves evaluating policies, procedures, and facility practices. All policies, procedures, or practices that may affect individuals with disabilities need to be addressed. These practices can be modified with little cost or effort. For example, a receptionist could be asked to answer all phones in a loud voice while clearly enunciating the company's name. Waiters could be instructed to ask each party being served how they can accommodate any special needs that any patron might have. The key to any such effort is co-opting all employees into the process with the view that they should not be afraid to ask how they can help or what they can do. For example, a sporting goods store's normal practice might be to require a driver's license when accepting a personal check. If someone does not have a license, the sales clerk should not automatically reject the check. The sales clerk should ask for other pieces of identification, or ask why the customer cannot produce a driver's license. Many individuals with disabilities do not have driver's licenses.

The fourth step involves acquiring and maintaining in readily usable fashion, any necessary auxiliary aids such as interpreters, taped text, Braille text, and assistive listening devises to name a few. There is no requirement that the most expensive method of accommodation needs to be pursued. Any method of accommodation or auxiliary aid needs to be effective for its intended purpose.

The fifth step involves following-up to make sure your plans are acted upon. In one case handled by the author, an individual with a disability defecated on herself in a restaurant even though the restaurant had accessible restrooms. The individual sued the restaurant for violating the ADA. While the restroom met the ADA requirements, a food shipment had been received earlier in the day and the only place the employees thought about putting the boxes was in the hallway to the restrooms. While there was a wide enough path for a person to enter, there was no room for a wheelchair to fit through. Constant vigilance is required to insure that changing circumstances do not render a facility inaccessible.

Lastly, facility owners should always check with their accountant to determine if they could receive a tax break.

Employment Concerns

Facility-related issues are important, but the ADA also covers employing those who are impaired under the ADA. All those individuals covered by the ADA as being disabled preserve the ADA protection during the entire employment process. Thus, someone that is obese cannot automatically be disqualified from applying for a fitness-related position, even if they appear not to be fit. If being fit is not a bona fide occupational requirement (BFOQ), which means someone that is not fit can still perform the job, then it would be an ADA violation not to at least consider that obese applicant with all other qualified applicants. As an example, a health food store could advertise for a sales clerk position. The essential elements of the job entail selling, stocking shelf, ordering merchandise, and dealing with customers. A health food store cannot just hire trim, fit, and able-bodied people. If a disabled person applies for the job and can perform all the elements of the job then they should be interviewed and seriously considered for the job. As stated earlier, this does not mean the disabled applicant needs to be hired if there is an equally qualified applicant who happens to have a better personality.

The ADA requires an employer of more than 20 employees to not discriminate against covered individuals in the hiring, firing, promoting, and handling of all employees. Thus, a non-covered employee could work for years, then become disabled (for example by getting sick with cancer or living with a cancer patient) and then the employer would need to provide reasonable accommodation such as a modified work schedule so the employee can receive therapy. Facility employment concerns can range from creating opportunities for disabled applicants to apply and attend interviews to working with unions to make sure janitors do not have learning disabilities (covered by the ADA) that limit their ability to read chemical labels, which could allow hazardous chemicals to be mishandled.

The ADA employment provisions are very complex and cannot be taken lightly. They cover everything from what questions can be asked during an interview to whether someone can be given a drug test and/or fired for being an alcoholic. A competent attorney should be counseled to avoid any unfortunate miscues.

In My Opinion

The DOJ is past the stage of ADA education and is now aggressively pursuing ADA violators. Sport facility administrators have to develop a mind-set, and co-opt other employees into accepting the mind-set, of providing all potential facility and program users with reasonable assistance. The key to ADA compliance was recently highlighted in a youth baseball case in California. The national governing body for the baseball league backed the youth league in not allowing an athlete to play in part, to prevent the player from "embarrassing himself." The choice of whether or not a person might be embarrassed is solely up to that person, not others. Sport administrators and program coordinators cannot exclude anyone just because someone might be embarrassed. Participants should be provided the opportunity to determine if they, in fact, will be embarrassed. This is the mandate of reasonable accommodation.

References

Anderson v. Little League Baseball, Inc., 794 F. Supp. 342 (DC. Ariz 1992).

Disability Compliance for Higher Education (2004, July 6). Are student-athletes with disabilities the next big compliance worry. LRP Publications, Vol. 9, No. 12.

Emmons, N. (2004, September). Know the code. Venues Today, 25–28.

Feldman v. Pro Football, Inc. http://pacer.ca4.uscourts.gov/opinion.pdf/091021.U.pdf.

Schneid, Thomas D. 1992. *The Americans With Disabilities Act, A Practical Guide for Managers.* New York: Van Nostrand Reinhold.

U.S. Department of Justice, (2010). 2010 ADA Standards for Accessibility and Design. Retrieved http://www.ada.gov/2010ADAstandards_index.htm.

Chapter 24

Event Management: A Practical Approach

With experience and planning you should be able to minimize greatly the risk involved with staging an event.

David R. Maraghy

Introduction

Since the early 1980s, when I began my involvement with the Greater Greensboro Open, one of the oldest stops on the PGA TOUR, I have reveled in the process of marketing, promoting, and operating all manner of events—from golf tournaments to polo matches to rock concerts and even a softball world series. It is most satisfying to sit back after such efforts and reflect on all the many pieces which came together to make the event successful.

A sure sign of the individual who thrives on the frenetic pace and chaos which usually is at the center of any event is the pure enjoyment received moving from one problem to the next and finding solutions, knowing that while all hell is breaking loose, the spectators, participants, and guests at the function think all is well. Now that deception is really fun!

If you have ever been involved in any event you can identify with the above feelings. While you may be normal, and therefore not thrive on the feeling of being in a kind of "war," you also realize that controlled commotion is inherent to every activity which brings together large numbers of people in one place.

With experience and planning you should be able to minimize greatly the risks involved with staging an event. Much of the planning process involves identifying risk areas, and then formulating the right questions related to such risks. Another key to success is to reduce the potential for surprises and the attendant risks which follow.

In writing this chapter the term "risk" is sometimes used broadly to cover not only physical injury and potential litigation, but also financial loss. In fact, risk can even mean failure in terms of not fulfilling the expectations of the spectators and/or participants—maybe even the simple fact they did not have fun. Therefore, the event was not successful, money was probably lost, and the event will not be supported in the future.

The purpose of this chapter is to share my experience and provide some practical advice on avoiding risks. The actual solutions for each challenge you face will vary depending upon the particular event and nature of the risks. Therefore, this chapter emphasizes developing the ability to ask the proper questions as opposed to providing any general panacea.

The patient lying exposed on the surgical table never wants to hear the attending physician utter the word "oops." Hopefully, this chapter will aid you in avoiding use of that same dreaded word in caring for your "patient"—the event.

Planning and Organization

There is an old adage: "Plan your work, and work your plan." The crucial element in striving to reduce risks associated with operating an event is careful planning.

In the proper planning of an event, there is no substitute for experience. Therefore, when facing your first few projects do not be shy about seeking assistance, knowledge, and advice from experienced sources. If live mentors are not available, or experienced individuals are too competitive to lend assistance, then do your research. A trip to the library will reveal articles on planning almost anything: a golf outing, conference, marathon, or car rally.

As you gain experience in this area, you will find that your expertise transcends any one specific field. While the particulars of marketing the event will change based upon the demographics of the target audience, the logistics will be very similar. I find this rule to run true in my dealings with successful event managers for all different sport and activities.

Accordingly, the Organizational Chart provided below was developed through the years primarily in designing and implementing golf events. Nevertheless, it has also been used quite successfully to plan and operate many other events by gearing the questions raised towards that particular sport or activity.

Your concept of planning needs to move beyond thinking in terms of simply following any outline or chart. Instead, sit alone with a pencil and large sheet of paper, computer, (or whatever creative tools you find comfortable), and run through all aspects of the event from the very first stages to the desired conclusion.

For me, this process results in an outline containing many sections and sub-sections. Also, key to this process of analysis is a narrative or editorial comments on those sections where necessary. This exercise also results in an added back-up checklist to the Organizational Chart used to structure and plan the event.

The narrative and comments are such a crucial ingredient in my recipe for success because they reveal the "what ifs...." Again, careful planning like this helps to eliminate risks. More often, events fail, people are injured, or money is lost because the promoter did not anticipate well the risks inherent to the activity or event.

Organizational Chart

Through experience, trial and error, you will develop the form of chart which works the best for you as a planning and operational tool. In the meantime, this section will offer some general considerations for you. The suggestions will be geared towards the issue of avoiding, or at least reducing, risks of injury/liability or financial failure.

In planning any event my organizational structure takes the form of a schematic skeleton. This chart usually results in ten major sections with an average of ten sub-sections or sub-headings of more specific areas of responsibility.

Those sub-sections will vary with the kind of activity, but the ten primary headings seem to cross over very effectively. Therefore, those ten sections are enumerated below, with only those sub-headings pertinent to risk issues being discussed. You will note that some key considerations, such as crowd control, security, and transportation, actually extend beyond just one section and will be addressed in several places.

Sales — Ticket Sales

Plan for the procedures related to sales of tickets at the event site. How will you monitor sales, and enforce spectators' purchasing? Provide necessary security for locations with cash.

In terms of crowd control and possible risk of injury, formulate a well-conceived plan for sales, avoiding long lines and frustrated spectators. Walk through the actual process of selling the ticket, picking up the ticket, adequate staffing, cash versus credit card services, and ingress and egress through narrow entrance areas. Uniformed officers in the area provide a calming effect on customers waiting in line, thereby deterring pushing and possible jostling or injury of others.

Do you need to allow for bilingual or multi-lingual ticket sellers to speed the process and render it more effective? Similarly, will your ticket sellers need to convert money? If so, find bright people and provide them the necessary conversion tables, charts, calculators, etc.

Clear, simple, easy to read, large signs can also quicken the sale process. Prices of tickets, available seating, and the cost of goods or concessions can all be grasped and the appropriate money made ready while customers wait in line. Again, consider whether the signs need to be in several languages, and prices in more than one currency.

Do you need to allow for "Will Call," where spectators can pick up tickets left for them or purchased in advance? Where will such an area be best located to avoid confusion, and the clogging of lines for ticket sales?

Similarly, do you anticipate a large number of individuals with special status for discounted prices, or perhaps free admission: military, students, seniors? If so, the process will be smoother if you provide special lines to accommodate them.

Sponsor Services

Most sub-headings here address the area of promotions and hospitality functions for large dollar sponsors as opposed to any real risk issues. When considering financial risks, however, you better take care of these folks!

Actually, in caring for your sponsors you will face many vital areas of event management, but they are all addressed elsewhere herein. Such issues will be transportation (valet parking), planning and maintaining a safe hospitality area (seating, special tents, etc.), security and credentials, and crowd control.

Contestant Services —
Special Consideration of Accommodations,
Security, and Transportation

What special arrangements need to be made for your contestants, performers, artists, players, or drivers? Consider not only issues of comfort, but also safety.

If you are dealing with a bona fide superstar do you need to find very secure, private accommodations? Will you reserve an entire floor of the hotel? How much of an issue is security at each stage of the event? Do you need to assign security guards to the individual 24 hours a day?

Is transportation an issue? Do you need to provide for reception at the airport? How many cars, vans, or limousines are necessary? Think through every transportation need — air and ground — from start to finish of the event.

How will the contestants get to/from the event? Is a special traffic lane necessary? What about getting to/from a stage, field, track, or course?

What security will be required during the actual performance, race, match, concert, or tournament?

With the disturbing increase of terrorism and other senseless acts, such as the victimization of Monica Seles, one of tennis' brightest stars, where is the event business headed in terms of liability? How much planning and security will be sufficient, both in terms of protecting the contestant, and protecting you from financial ruin through legal actions by an injured performer? You will have to balance carefully your risk of exposure to liability for injury to a contestant versus the potential prohibitive costs of obtaining necessary security, and special expensive accommodations and modes of transportation.

Hospitality — Liquor Liability

Most sub-headings here concern entertaining of guests, sponsors, and special V.I.P.'s. Nevertheless, for all social functions you must again consider all the relevant questions posed in other sections herein: access, ingress/egress, security, traffic flow, crowd control, and other thoughts relating to large numbers of people.

One additional key area of concern is the ever-growing body of law on liability for an event or function serving alcohol. I offer this caveat with a few examples of how others have attempted to prevent problems. Be aware of your very high exposure to potential liability when serving alcohol to someone who is then injured and/or injures others as a result of those actions taken while under the influence, especially driving.

When hosting an event, seek legal consultation on the prevailing law in your jurisdiction. Sound advice on this subject will be worth every penny. Discover if case law or statute offers guidelines to be followed in such circumstances which may help insulate you from liability.

Some examples of preventive measures being employed at events are suggested below. *Nevertheless, nothing contained herein is to be taken as a guarantee that such measures will relieve you of liability in such situations.*

Many stadiums now cease selling alcohol prior to the end of the game. This strategy provides two benefits: it shortens the amount of time spectators can drink, thereby hopefully reducing the number of intoxicated persons; and, also lengthens the time between the last drink and when the spectator climbs behind the wheel of a car. You certainly can consider such a time control device in your event.

Common at many functions is the stringent check of age identification for the purchase of alcohol. Attendant to that process is a manner of identifying legal-aged individuals throughout the duration of the event—hospital-type wrist bands, etc. Again, uniformed officers with power of arrest in the jurisdiction can be quite a deterrent, as well as very useful in case a scene becomes disorderly.

Many events now offer services such as free soda or other non-alcoholic beverage for designated drivers.

Another strategy is to provide access to designated driver services—whether hired by the function or paid for by the user. Some of these services will actually follow you home in your car so it will be there in the morning when you wake up.

Ready access to traditional cab service can also be effective.

Whatever route you choose, know that you are very vulnerable on this point.

Operations — Crowd Management

This area naturally is the heart of any event. Sub-headings, therefore, are many and varied depending upon the type of event. In my organizational chart, however, one sub-heading cries out for consideration in terms of concerns for risks: crowd control. Some of the relevant questions have been posed above and should be reviewed by you as they relate to this issue. A new, very pertinent consideration in avoiding liability, however, is where you place your spectators.

Incredibly, there is a body of law that hints a golf tournament might be liable to a spectator hit by a golf ball straying into the gallery area as marked by gallery ropes. Some courts have indicated that by placing gallery ropes behind which spectators must remain to observe golf action, the tournament has somehow implied that those areas are safe. Actually, I always thought the gallery ropes were intended to protect the players from the crazed fans!

More seriously, whatever happened to the legal theory of "assumption of risk"? That theory holds that whoever attends a golf tournament or baseball game or car race, should be presumed to know that balls go out of play and cars run off the track. Therefore, the event should not be capable of being held liable, providing it exercises reasonable efforts to allow for the safety of the spectator.

Beware. This area of the law may not be working in your favor as much as it once did. Once again, therefore, consult legal counsel for the applicable rule in your geographic area, legal jurisdiction, and your particular event. Standards may well differ for a highly dangerous sport like auto racing as opposed to the professional badminton exhibition of India vs. Korea.

What level of precautionary measures are sufficient? Should the netting behind home plate extend all the way down both the first and third foul lines to prevent injury from one of those wicked foul line drives? How high should the protective glass be in a hockey rink? Is it reasonable to lower that glass on the sides of the rink, but extend it to the ceiling behind both goals where errant shots fly? What areas for the viewers at an auto race are safe from flying debris, tires, and flames when a tragedy occurs?

Assess your event carefully, try to envision the worst thing that could happen no matter how remote or unlikely it may seem, and plan accordingly.

Site Management — Construction, Electrical, Maintenance, and Signage

This section involves several areas of potential risk: construction, electrical, maintenance, and signage. Legal analysis on the duties imposed on you by the first three items would constitute a voluminous treatise on the law of business invitee. Lacking such space, suffice it here to raise real warning flags for you in organizing your event.

You are inviting onto your business premises — be it an arena, stadium, golf course, or race track — potential litigants in large numbers. Are you building or providing bleachers for them to sit? Do not assume the competence of anyone erecting such structures, or the soundness of any provided. Take reasonable, necessary steps to ensure the safety of fans using those seating areas.

Once everything is in place, you will bear the responsibility of maintaining the facilities and grounds in a safe manner. Your actual standard of care under the law may vary in different jurisdictions, but be aware of common hazards: water on the floor, holes on the golf course, loose steps, dead tree limbs.

Are you providing power? If so, has the electrical work been performed competently? Are there exposed power lines? Is the proper current provided where necessary? Are the heaters in the corporate hospitality tents a fire hazard?

Signage is the final sub-section to be considered for purposes of risk. Place warning signs in areas where errant golf balls, baseballs, flying cue balls, if applicable — may somehow come into contact with spectators. Jurisdictions vary on the efficacy of such signage in insulating the event from liability. Nevertheless, risk consultants strongly recommend such signage as a useful piece of evidence when presenting your side of the case.

Provide information plainly, clearly, and often on what to do in case of emergency, lightning, or other dangerous inclement weather. What is the procedure and where should the spectator go if a warning siren screams of approaching lightning?

Exit signs should be clearly marked.

If effective in your area, signs disclaiming any responsibility or liability whatsoever for anything should be displayed.

If you know of the existence of a dangerous condition you cannot rectify, then rope it off and surround it with bold warning signs. If necessary, consider assigning security personnel to the area to prevent entry.

Concessions — Licenses, Taxes

Most of the risks here are financial.

Know the various licenses you may need, and applicable taxes for sales of any kind. Regarding food and beverage, what are the county, state, and ABC licenses or permits needed? What, if any, is the governing tax associated for such sales for which you will be accountable?

If merchandise is the issue (souvenirs, the ubiquitous event T-shirt), again what licenses and taxes apply? Is there a legal way to avoid such taxes: non-profit status, 501(c)(3) status under the Internal Revenue Code, charitable, church, other?

If you are selling items on a consignment basis, know how stringent the accountability will be on you to return either the product or the equivalent in cash.

The bottom line here is to ensure you are not assessed a fine, penalty, tax, or other invoice you were not expecting.

Be aware of freshness of food/beverage products where that is an issue. Are there any special requirements for the preparation of certain foods? You could also be liable to consumers at your event who become ill through bad food.

Finance

If you undertake the sale of tickets on behalf of someone else, be clear regarding your accountability at the end. Too often I have seen situations where someone felt he was acting more as a favor to the promoter in helping to distribute tickets, but at the end of the event a dispute arose regarding an unreal expectation of strict accountability for such sales.

What measures need to be taken to reduce your financial risk? Some events use scrip tickets instead of cash for the purchase of food and beverage. It is easier to control the sale of scrip. You need fewer people to handle the money. You also have an easier accounting system because a quick tally of tickets compared to cash reveals any discrepancies.

Do you have adequate security for people and areas handling large amounts of cash? Are the proper systems in place for dealing with credit card sales? How will you safely transport cash and make deposits? Who will do so?

Establish a sound system of controls for tickets, merchandise, and concessions products. What is your system for monitoring all spectators to ensure display of proper tickets or credentials, and of enforcing sales to those individuals lacking such items?

Insurance is a vital issue falling under this section. Because of its importance, however, it is separately discussed below.

Support Services — Health and Safety, Communications, Traffic Control, Transportation, and Parking

With the litigious nature of society, the topic of Health and Safety deserves special attention from you in your planning. You must guard against any failure to provide reasonably adequate medical care for your spectators and contestants. Certainly at every event site you are not expected to provide a fully-equipped medical unit equivalent to a transportable Mt. Sinai Hospital. You will, however, be expected to provide for some measure of medical care that is reasonable under the circumstances. Anticipate.

What you provide will be dictated by the distance from the nearest medical facility, the size of the crowd, the nature of the event, the demographics of the crowd, and the inherent danger in the event or of the site. Example: an outdoor event in the summer in the South can expect sunburn and dehydration. Take steps to protect against such conditions—water stations, shade areas—and to provide treatment when they do occur. Example: a surfing contest will add to the first example the need for expertise and personnel to provide rescue services in large seas and surf. The medical problems to anticipate will differ greatly—by worlds, in fact—if you are hosting a croquet championship in Newport, Rhode Island, as opposed to being involved in a NASCAR event in South Hill, South Carolina.

While the examples are endless, you should allow for at least an acceptable level of on-site care: EMT's, volunteer doctors/nurses, transportation for such personnel, adequate supplies, and satisfactory treatment area. The key here is to anticipate, do your research, and respond to the data appropriately.

The next sub-section is an essential tool not only in preventing risk situations, but simply for ensuring smooth operation: communications. Have a sufficient number of radios, walkie-talkies, cellular phones, whatever it takes to keep key personnel in contact with each other. You or your designate should be capable of communicating with and monitoring conversations of all necessary department heads. By monitoring you can anticipate problems and defuse the situation. You also want the proper personnel to be able to react quickly to emergencies of any kind and magnitude: medical, parking, traffic, security, inventory control, even running out of ice in the title sponsor's hospitality tent.

In your advanced planning be cognizant of potential traffic control and parking problems. Snarled traffic can mean lost revenue in tickets and concession sales. Moreover, are you allowing a hazardous situation which might result in injury? Has your lack of attention to detail in this area created a dangerous intersection somewhere? Because of your failure to plan for an orderly departure from crowded parking lots, are your spectators engaged in a spontaneous demolition derby?

Do you have adequate security to control traffic and provide safe parking areas? Is your signage directing traffic sufficiently clear and well-placed?

The final pertinent issue hereunder is transportation. In nearly every event of any kind transportation issues tend to be the most bothersome.

Shuttling large numbers of fans brings about images of long lines at shuttle stops, uncomfortable buses, and generally a miserably inconvenient experience.

Transporting a small number of V.I.P.'s—sponsors or celebrities—can also be a nightmare. Nothing will lose a key sponsor faster than when its CEO stands cooling his heels on some sidewalk waiting for his/her ride. My experience is that such little things cost you sponsorship dollars more often than major catastrophes. Therefore, spend plenty of time in planning for these details.

A couple of hints should be most helpful to your planning in this area. Drive the routes to be taken to confirm actual time and distance. Be sure all drivers know the directions well, and even practice driving the routes! Do not laugh. While it is incomprehensible to me, I have seen significant events where the hired drivers show up for work and have no idea of the location of elemental destinations: the airport, the host hotel, even the site of the event. This was a source of criticism during the 1996 Olympics in Atlanta.

Educate your drivers on rush hours to be reckoned with during the event. Discover reliable short-cuts and alternate routes.

Convey all this information in writing to the drivers. Provide simple maps. Provide accurate, detailed, written schedules to everyone. Place a cellular phone in each vehicle.

Realize, too, your tremendous potential liability in hiring drivers and providing transportation. Be a smart consumer. Is it ultimately cheaper and wiser to hire a transportation or destination company with large umbrella insurance coverage, than to try to manage transportation yourself? Under the circumstances, can this step insulate you from disastrous risks?

If you insist on hiring drivers, be aware of a range of issues: obtaining adequate insurance, and screening drivers by running motor vehicle records for DUI's or similar severe violations. Otherwise, you could be held grossly negligent in a legal action. Do your research on this issue in your venue, jurisdiction, and with your insurance advisor and legal consultant.

Advertising, Promotions, Media Relations

Unless you assault an esteemed member of the paparazzi for snapping a photo of you in a compromising position, your likelihood of risk for injury under this section is slight. Nevertheless, several angles are worth considering.

First, you may open yourself up to ridicule and some risk of financial liability if you are not careful with your advertising. While you may be desperate to promote your event and increase sales, do not declare that Michael Jordan will be coming when actually Vernon Jordan is. As a rule, under-promise and over-deliver, and you will be a hero with your sponsors and spectators. By performing well under that guideline you are assured of a long and successful event career.

Be careful around the press. I enjoy working with the media, and have been fortunate to enjoy a good relationship for any event or individual client I was promoting. Remember, nonetheless, the media always has more power, ink and videotape than you ever will, so do not go to war with them. Off-hand remarks, or "off the record" comments made to members of the press you do not really know can end up as headlines. Derogatory comments by you which are broadcast or published can result in your calling yourself by a new name: the Defendant.

Also, use the press to help you. The media may not always cooperate, but often they will aid you in disseminating information. Do not limit their assistance to trying to sell tickets. Use the press to help control traffic by providing a map, and designating alternate routes to your event. Provide necessary information about parking, shuttles, and transportation.

Insurance

To paraphrase an old real estate formula for success: "There are three factors which will reduce your exposure from risks associated with organizing and operating an event: 1) Insurance; 2) Insurance; 3) Insurance." While it is preferable to head off problems by all methods and considerations, such as those contained herein, I am an advocate of insurance. This is not the area in which to cut corners financially. Thus, the issue is important enough to justify dedicating this brief section to offer a few general comments and principles.

Find a good insurance company specializing in the area of your event. Assess its track record in terms of providing service, and any pertinent history of paying off on losses when necessary. A good insurance representative with experience in this field is a useful tool in your planning efforts to reduce your exposure. Find one who has handled similar event business.

Determine a sufficient amount of insurance coverage for your event. Do you need an umbrella coverage for liability of $1,000,000 or $5,000,000?

Moreover, establish a minimum requirement of insurance for any subcontractor who will work on your event. Require such proof of insurance *before* they are allowed on site. Be certain you and your company are named insured on the policy. Identify the other individuals and entities who also should be named insured.

A good insurance group will serve as a clearinghouse for all certificates of insurance which need to be collected from the various subcontractors for your event: caterers, transportation company, golf course, arena, stadium, parking service, contractor, electrical, sanitation company, etc.

Discussed above was the risk associated with hiring drivers. For a fee the insurance company can run the motor vehicle records of your potential drivers to determine past serious violations.

Together with your legal counsel, your insurance representative can advise you on the dangerous area of liquor liability. The representative will want the certificates of insurance covering that risk from the caterer, the site, and any entity serving alcohol at your function.

Over the years the experienced representative I use has been very helpful in creating a trusty checklist of risk factors in a particular event. Find your insurance advisor who can perform the same valuable service for you.

Be cognizant of the specialty insurance coverages which are available. Although somewhat expensive, you should at least consider the viability of event cancellation insurance whenever you conduct an outdoor event. Determine exactly the conditions under which you can recover. Also, define what items you will recover: expenses only, lost profits?

Even narrower kinds of coverage are available. In golf, American Hole In One will insure prizes to reward a hole in one at your golf event. The standards will be very strict as to the yardage required on the hole to be covered under the policy, the number of players participating, the permitted number of shots, the sequence of shots, officials necessary to observe and verify, and whether or not professionals are eligible (this will increase the premium). Naturally, the premium amount will fluctuate depending upon the value of the prize.

We have been very successful creating excitement and promoting a major event with ancillary contests such as a Hole In One for significant cash amounts or a Mercedes, etc. It also is a good way to bring in sponsors who can gain exposure by taking title to the contest. Do not forget to build into the sponsorship package the cost of the premium.

I suspect you can find insurance—for a price—to cover most any promotion you want to stage. Consider creative incentives when examining ways to market your event by adding excitement. Is it financially feasible to offer a bonus for winning three races at your steeplechase race? In your series of Monster Truck Races the tension will be unbelievable by providing a $1,000,000 bonus for winning two races in a row.

A client of yours may want to enhance the value of its title position in several events by offering a similar kind of bonus. Example: a company is the title sponsor of two or three tournaments on the golf or tennis tour. It wants to ensure the highest caliber of the field of participants. As your client, that company may call on you to devise some bonus program to encourage the stars to play all the titled events with a big reward for winning two or more. You will want to be able to respond to that inquiry by seeking the consultation of your trusted agent in the field of specialty insurance.

Waivers

As mentioned above, there is a vast body of law on the issue of waivers. The advice here is simply to obtain the opinions of your legal counsel and insurance representative on the most effective form of waiver for your jurisdiction and event. Incorporate that waiver into your entry process. Be sure every participant has signed such a waiver with the entry blank.

Also, know the law in your area regarding validity of such a waiver. What are the age requirements? Is every participant 18 years of age or older? Is parental consent necessary? If so, is such parental consent evident on the waiver?

Many events include a waiver of liability somewhere on the ticket purchased to gain entrance to the event. Again, how binding such a waiver is will depend on the law of the jurisdiction and circumstances. Nevertheless, it certainly cannot hurt to place that waiver on the ticket. Such language could be one more piece of useful evidence for your side in case the worst happens and you are dragged into our legal system.

Contingency Plans

A solid contingency plan can reduce risk of physical injury, perhaps even save lives, and also affect the other aspects of the term "risk" as contemplated herein—considerations of finances and fun. Once your planning and organization has revealed a potential problem, then you must be creative and flexible to design the appropriate and effective contingency plan.

Anticipation

One of the best examples of the many benefits of a solid contingency plan involves the greatest fear of any outdoor event: dangerous inclement weather. For purposes of this example we examine the most difficult outdoor activity to control, the golf tournament.

Golf tournaments are uniquely difficult because unlike an auto race, tennis match, concert, or ball game, you have many spectators spread out over a vast geographic area watching the athletic activity unfold over that same area. Neither your contestants nor the spectators are concentrated in any one place. Accordingly, all the usual problems associated with those outdoor activities are magnified greatly.

In recent years golf tournaments, especially at the professional level and the knowledgeable level of the United States Golf Association, have become more sophisticated in protecting players and spectators. It was not long ago, however, that various professional players were injured when struck by lightning, and a spectator was killed by lightning at a major golf tournament.

Naturally, the first defense against such disasters is advanced warning. Modern radar and related weather technology now supply very accurate and timely progress reports on approaching bad weather. Be sure to do your research and make the arrangements to take advantage of that technology. Use all such tools available to you.

Do not panic, you do not have to purchase expensive electronic wizardry to render your event headquarters a NASA station. Such services are available for a reasonable fee on a per event basis which will provide you up to the minute reports on approaching weather during the event.

Now, suppose you have determined there is a problem of advancing dangerous weather conditions, what next? In golf, a horn or siren signals play shall stop because of lightning. Nevertheless, both players and spectators remain at risk out on the course. So, you now engage the evacuation plan you devised when you were planning the tournament.

First, the signal is given in ample time for the spectators to seek shelter. Limited space in the clubhouse has resulted in tournaments providing alternative safety areas out on the golf course, i.e., facilities equipped with lightning rods.

Both for considerations of safety and comfort, the players and caddies quite often are treated differently. At the Virginia State Open we have large utility vehicles parked out on the golf course. When play is stopped for lightning the volunteers serving as gallery marshals or scorers near those vehicles are designated to drive the players and caddies back to the clubhouse in those vehicles. Remember, this plan works only if the car keys are accessible to those designated drivers. Do not laugh! It happens. Nothing is quite so frustrating and scary as observing very irate players abusing a poor volunteer while standing in the pouring rain outside a locked evacuation vehicle, outlined against a backdrop of a black sky streaked by lightning flashes.

Unforeseeable

Inherent to the term "unforeseeable" is the inability to guard against such circumstances with any contingency plan because you could not possibly know it was going to occur — hence the concept of the term. Nevertheless, when the unforeseeable does occur you may still be held accountable, no matter how unfair. Accordingly, you better work on your seer imitation.

In that regard you can prepare for the "highly unlikely," and better do so. As an example, I am very proud of a contingency plan developed for a wonderful golf experience titled "Fantasy Golf Camp."

The Fantasy Golf concept is to allow amateurs to spend five nights/four days with PGA TOUR stars in a very close environment. Not only does the amateur receive daily instruction from the TOUR players and then play 18 holes of golf, but at night everyone gathers for drinks, dinner, and camaraderie. The experience far surpasses a one day pro am where the amateur may barely hear a word from the pro for 18 holes.

The socializing with the pros after golf and the intimate access to the TOUR players really make the Fantasy Golf Camp special. Add to that experience the venue of Las Vegas, and everyone involved really had the unique opportunity to become friends.

As you can imagine, such an event requires significant financial underwriting for the hotels, meals, and most of all the fees for the TOUR players. Imagine the investment it takes to assemble the Fantasy Golf "staff" of true luminaries who attended, such as Tom Kite, John Daly, Curtis Strange, Davis Love III, Lanny Wadkins, and Payne Stewart. Therefore, it was crucial to ensure the participants had the fun expected, or else financial failure could result to the organizer.

I go to such great lengths to describe the experience because this particular Camp took place in early November in Las Vegas. Everyone, especially the Las Vegas contacts, assured me that the weather would be acceptable. We might need sweaters and windbreakers, I was told, but it never rains that time of year. Fair enough, I thought. It did not occur to me, however, to inquire about the likelihood of … SNOW!

Yes, the very first day of the Camp, with expectations soaring, and grown men and women acting like children in the presence of the TOUR stars, it snowed. It was so cold I wanted to weep. But wait …

The day would be saved because of a contingency plan. I mentioned earlier I was so proud of this plan, and it is because we ignored all the assurances of pleasant, if not balmy, weather. In fact, the day turned out to be the best possible kick-off for the Camp.

Many months prior to the Camp, arrangements were made with a local golf shop to have indoor golf practice equipment ready, and on standby. A large ballroom was reserved at the host hotel for a practice facility. Within one hour of the first camper facing cold weather we were set up inside, with Tom Kite offering full swing instruction to campers hitting off a moveable practice tee into a net. Noted teaching instructor Scott Davenport, of the famous *Golf Digest* Schools, was providing swing analysis with the aid of the latest technology. Other PGA TOUR stars were working one-on-one with campers on putting mats.

The biggest hit of the day was TOUR player Peter Persons organizing a chipping contest into nets. Peter was also collecting the bets while he cajoled the campers into competing, wagering, and verbally abusing each other. They were having a ball! Cocktails and food were plentiful, and the entire atmosphere reeked of camaraderie.

We finally had to drag people out of there in time for dinner. No one wanted to stop having fun. From that first makeshift day, many friendships were made, and a fantastic tone was set for the rest of the Camp.

In My Opinion

Assess the potential problems applicable to your event, and formulate contingency plans accordingly. Be creative and flexible. Do not let yourself be bound by thinking in terms only of the usual or normal. While precedent and experience are very helpful, also take the time to envision those things "unforeseeable" to other, less successful event managers. Accumulate all the information you can from all sources on ways to organize and operate an event. Speak with experienced individuals. Assemble all the written materials available. Use that research to create your own Organizational Chart, which you trust.

Make a solid attorney and insurance representative a standard part of your event team. Seek advice before the problem occurs. Preventive legal advice is much cheaper than bringing in the attorneys to defend you later in litigation.

Chapter 25

Security Issues at Sports Events

The most accepted approach that guides an organization's effort in preparing against terrorism is risk management (Decker 2001).

John Miller

Before the terrorist attacks on September 11, 2001, sport event managers most often dealt with inebriated fans, medical emergencies, or thefts. While these issues still occur, the terrorist attacks of September 11, 2001, the recent rioting by fans after the Stanley Cup Finals, and bomb threats at baseball stadiums illustrate an era of increasingly diverse and significant violence at sports events. Images of these destructive actions have set into motion a chain reaction that is significantly impacting the sports world. Because they are so strongly associated with the American economy and culture, sports have been considered significant targets of violent attacks (Appelbaum, Adeland, & Harris, 2005; Atkinson & Young, 2002). During a panel discussion, Paul Zoubek, Counsel for the New Jersey Domestic Preparedness Task Force, stated that: "Sports are a very symbolic target of terrorism because they are so associated with the globalization of the American economy and the American culture" (Fallon, 2003, p. 367). As a result, sport venue managers began reassessing their safety procedures, security assessments, and operational plans to identify new ways to provide a safe environment for fans and participants (Fallon, 2003). It is important to note that although the concept of terrorism conjures up certain images, such as the 2001 World Trade Centers, for this chapter "terrorism" will be used as a way to depict any extremely violent occurrences at sports events. Thus, the words "terrorism" and "violence" will be used interchangeably throughout this chapter. Additionally, individuals described as terrorists, in this chapter, are those who unlawfully "use of violence against persons or property to intimidate or coerce a … civilian population, or any segment thereof, in furtherance of … political or social objectives" (FBI, 2006, p. 3).

The Effects of Terrorism on Security

Organized Terrorism

According to Crenshaw (2000): "Terrorism is meant to hurt, not to destroy" (p. 406). Terrorism is allied to collective civil violence in the form of organized or spontaneous activities (Borum, 2007). As such, terrorism may be delineated into two main categories: organized terrorism and spontaneous terrorism. Organized terrorist activities often have a discrete set of objectives when selecting potential targets they believe will further their cause, such as media exposure, economic harm, and significant number of potential casualties (Suder, 2004). Such organized terrorism requires a significant amount of planning, organization, and rehearsal, and includes the incidents at the World Trade Center as well as the Oklahoma City bombing (Cohen, 2001). For example, if a venue manager received a bomb threat indicating when and where an attack would occur, it would be recognized as organized terrorism.

Sports venues should be particularly concerned with organized violence for two primary reasons. First, authorities have begun considering athletic venues among the new types of potential targets. The Federal Bureau of Investigation (FBI) recognized this possibility when it provided sport facility managers a warning after it learned that individuals with possible terrorist connections had downloaded data pertaining to several National Football League venues (Grace, 2002). In fact, then FBI Director Robert Mueller acknowledged that agents had been directed to look at any potential locations that a terrorist might strike, one of which could be a sports venue (Grace, 2002). Additionally, the Department of Homeland Security (DHS) identified a dozen possible strikes it viewed as most devastating, including a truck bombing of a sports arena (Lipton, 2005).

Second, sport venues are attractive targets because, " ... with tens of thousands of people in attendance, an attack on a stadium could cause massive casualties with maximum media exposure" (Wade, 2000, p. 18). As such, these venues are problematical to make safe and secure since large numbers of spectators are constantly entering and leaving the premises. Secondly, sports venues may be categorized as "soft targets," prone to a violent attack. Soft targets are targets that are not well-protected, so terrorists can gain access to them relatively easily (Clonan, 2002).

Spontaneous Terrorism

In addition to organized threats, the amplification of anti-social behavior of spectators has added the potential for an increased exposure of harm to others attending sporting events (Miller & Gillentine, 2006). For such anti-social behavior, also referred to as spontaneous terrorism or violence, the main objective may be to physically act out displeasure of a judgment that went against the home team, an intense dislike of an opposing team, extreme disappointment in the team not winning a championship, or extreme pleasure of the team winning a championship, without any in-depth planning. Spontaneous terrorism is usually sporadic and requires mass participation (Crenshaw, 2000). Such terrorism is often an impetuous representation of discontent that does not possess political goals or organized plans (Merari, 1993). For example, fans throwing beer bottles at the end of a professional football game when an overturned call occurred in the final minutes, or fans burning items due to a team loss in a championship may be regarded as a spontaneous terror attack (Goss, Jubenville, & MacBeth, 2003; Withers, 2002). Moreover, such recent incidents as fans attacking other fans at sports events in San Francisco and Los Angeles may be considered spontaneous terrorist incidents (Associated Press, 2011) and add to the challenges of providing a reasonably safe environment at sports contests. Such added exposure to harm shifts the paradigm for sport event organizers by asking the question: how can identifiable risks be managed at sporting events in today's society?

Risk and Security Management

According to Decker (2001), the most accepted approach that can guide an organization's effort in preparing against terrorism is risk management. Decker stated that a risk management plan is a systematic and analytical process to consider the possibility that a danger will jeopardize an asset (e.g., a structure, individual, or function) and to identify ways that may decrease the risk and diminish the price of an attack. Because external risks such as an organized terrorist incident or spontaneous anti-social behaviors of spectators often lie outside a facility or event manager's influence, managers may be restricted in the direct actions they can take to handle a potentially harmful incident. Nonetheless, a sport manager can still prepare for potential organized or spontaneous violent incidents by developing, implementing, and enforcing plans to deal with them effectively once a problematic risk event occurs. While risk management will not work miracles, it can assist in the preparation to reduce the number of potential untoward surprises.

An integral component of an effective risk management plan is the inclusion of security policies and procedures. Security issues must be considered when developing a risk management plan since a sport venue manager must be able to identify risks that could conceivably cause losses and jeopardize the safety of the staff, patrons, and property (Miller & Veltri, 2001). Whereas risk management plans help to ensure the protection of sport organizations by supplying a structure for managers in finance, security, and human resources, security policies describe the intent of the company in a given area and security procedures satisfy the objectives of the security policy by making the intent of the policies concrete (Cawood, 2002). A risk management plan provides a framework while security management plans and procedures provide a "road map" for the implementation and conduction of the risk management plan.

Foreseeability Issues in Security Management

Within the current climate of "permanent emergency" in the post 9/11 context of the "war on terror," security issues have become important in the successful staging of sport events. Good security management involves operating proactively in order to initiate appropriate action and avoid organizational mini and major crises. In order to possess good security management, the sport event manager should have the ability to foresee the potential for injury. According to *Isaacs* v. *Huntington Memorial Hospital* (1985), " … authorities who know of threats of violence that they believe are well-founded may not refrain from taking reasonable preventive measures simply because violence has yet to occur" (pp. 125–126). For instance, the Rand Corporation developed a model to support the security preparation for the London 2012 Olympics (Rand, 2007). The basis of the model, which included catastrophic and worst-case scenarios, was to "foresee, in a structured and systematic way, a range of different potential security environments that could potentially exist in 2012" (p. 50). The model employed three aspects: adversary hostile intent, adversary operational capability, and potential domestic ? international effects on the security system in the United Kingdom. A total of 27 potential future security environments (FSE) were identified. Within each FSE, specific hypothetical scenarios were developed to gauge operational capabilities. Unfortunately, the model "does not give any specific weight to a particular future scenario, rather, it treats all futures as equally valid' (Rand, 2007, p. 50).

Likelihood and Impact of an Incident

While the Rand model appears to signal an evident willingness to contemplate the potential "unthinkable" likelihood, it may miss the second component that sport venue managers should consider: impact. For example, sport event managers may view the likelihood that a stadium or arena may be the focus of a terrorist incident to be near zero. The perception of likelihood and impact may relate to the theory of the threshold of effective zerohood (Rescher, 1983) which states that once the probability of an incident occurring becomes small enough, the potential of the incident occurring may be viewed as outside the range of appropriate concern. In other words, if it hasn't ever occurred or hasn't happened in a long time the probability of it occurring may be negligible. This prospect is relatively low in risk, even though they realize that if a stadium is actually hit catastrophic consequences would occur. Thus, it is important to clarify whether the principal concern is likelihood or impact. If the probability of an incident occurring is considered to be close to zero, the perception may very well be to set aside the need for security assessment and management. If the analysis of the impact was the primary concern, the scope of the risk would increase. In other words, if the organization can foresee the realization of a threat as well as the negative impact that an attack could create, the level of the security management would be elevated. As such, when a plausible danger is multiplied by the potentially harmful impact, the level of risk increases (i.e., credible threat x potential negative impact = level of risk increases). Even if the prospect of either type of violence (organized or spontaneous) be considered relatively low, it would be tragic if t4 an improbable catastrophic event could have been prevented or mitigated through inexpensive or costless measures, especially if these measures were not taken because the venue manager was unaware of them (Baker & Merriman, 2003). It is the understanding of the likelihood and impact that generates the overall reflection of the security assessments which will be discussed in the following section.

Security Assessments

A key component to any security management plan is the establishment of a security assessment. The security assessment process calls for comprehensive deliberation of likely risks, not necessarily all risks. Risk is the result of the convergence of three variables: threat, vulnerability, and consequence (Chertoff, 2007). Both threat and vulnerability are influenced by the probabilities of events that are highly uncertain (Chertoff, 2007). As such, sport venue management should consider employing security assessments that can assist in revealing possible threats, vulnerabilities, criticalities, and consequences of an incident. Each of these components will be briefly discussed in the following sections.

Threat Assessment

The first step in assessing security risks is to conduct a threat assessment. A threat assessment may be used as a decision support tool to assist in creating and prioritizing security-program requirements, planning, and resource allocations (Decker, 2001). When an organization embarks on a risk assessment effort, the team conducting the assessment is searching for potential sources of concern (Frame, 2003). It deals with such issues as how operations might be negatively affected or what weaknesses can be identified. A variety of factors may be used to assess the threat. Among these: Is the threat credible? Is the threat corroborated? Is the threat specific and/or imminent? How grave is the threat? (International Association of Assembly Managers, 2002). Such questions characterize the threat conditions of a terrorist incident and provide the appropriate protective measures needed to reduce vulnerabilities.

Vulnerability Assessment

Vulnerability refers to the level to which a target is likely to be attacked and the ability that a target can present to fend off an attack (Decker, 2001). A vulnerability assessment is an evaluation of those areas that are susceptible to a strike through a malevolent attack by an individual(s) who desire to create physical or psychological harm to an organization's infrastructure, including its employees or patrons. Thus, a vulnerability assessment assists in the identification of weaknesses that may be exploited and suggests options to eliminate or address those weaknesses (Decker, 2001). For example, a vulnerability assessment might reveal weaknesses in an organization's security systems, training security personnel, avenues of ingress and egress, or the distance from parking lots to important buildings as being so close that a car bomb detonation would damage or destroy the buildings and the people working in them (Decker, 2001). Additional areas of concern in identifying event vulnerabilities include facility access, food vendor access, areas for concealed threats, security protocol, and access to team locker rooms, as well as lighting and entrance inspections. Once potential vulnerabilities are identified, it is wise for the sport venue manager to prioritize the important aspects of the organization. To do so, a criticality assessment should be conducted.

Criticality Assessment

A criticality assessment is a practice that recognizes and calculates important assets, infrastructure, and critical functions based on a variety of factors. These factors include the importance of its mission or function of the event, location of the venue in regards to important governmental and financial centers, the number of people that may be at risk, or the significance of a structure or system. Assessing the criticality of a target can help in determining target attractiveness as well as determining which potential areas will receive attention first (Decker, 2001). Thus, criticality assessments are important because they help identify which assets, structures, or functions are relatively more important to protect from an attack. Once a potential target has been identified, the next step for a risk event manager would be to identify and minimize the liabilities of that target through a vulnerability assessment.

Assessments should be performed on a regular basis. Information from these assessments provides effective gauges as to how successful security practices are achieved and maintained within the assessed areas. The outcomes of these assessments should be presented to relevant decision-makers for use as a way to develop additional guidance. An examination of these assessments will allow the relevant decision-makers an appropriate balance of resources to strengthen security.

Consequences of a Terrorist Incident

After the three components of a security assessment are completed, the sport venue manager should understand the consequences of an organized terrorist incident. Due to the media coverage on sports now being commonplace, a targeted venue would be only one of several entities to feel the effect. News of a terrorist incident, whether spontaneous or organized, at an athletic event would quickly become national news and could have the potential to cause widespread fear in many sports fans, thus affecting economies elsewhere. Lee, Gordon, Moore, and Richardson (2008) conducted a case study to ascertain possible economic losses as the result of an organized terrorist event on a sports stadium. They created a hypothetical situation in which a National Football League stadium, seating 75,000 people, was the subject of a bioterrorism attack. Several computer based simulations determined the economic impact of the attacks. The major areas of economic impact were casualties, illnesses, contamination, and business interruption. Casualties were assumed to be 7,000 among stadium attendees and an additional 3,600 from people within the community. A value of a statistical life computation was used to measure economic impact of lost lives. The researchers estimated that 20,000 attendees and an additional 11,000 people from the community would suffer severe illnesses that would require a hospitalization of seven days as well as follow-up medical appointments, with the quarantine of the stadium and surrounding area for a month. It was estimated that 50% of the buildings would be uninhabitable for six months and the entire decontamination process would last approximately a year. Lastly, the business effects were thoroughly examined, as the incident would probably result in higher risk aversion by the public resulting in less demand for various goods. The study indicated that if a stadium were to be attacked, attendance would drop at least 8% simply due to the cancelling of games for the month of quarantine. Depending on the extremity of reaction by the public, attendance levels are estimated to drop anywhere from 15% to 40%. Business would also be affected in the form of lost jobs in the immediate area. Using the attacks of September 11 as a model, researchers estimated that 3,793 jobs would be lost for the first year. Ultimately, economic impacts could be estimated to range anywhere from $62 billion to $73 billion. While the results of an attack on a college arena would not carry quite the economic impact, it would still undoubtedly have a sizeable effect on the economy.

As these and other potential consequences emerge, the sport venue manager must then consider how the implementation and enforcement of the security plan must be achieved. To do so, several concerns must be addressed. These concerns will be discussed in the next section.

Enforcing Security Plans

Security Implementation Issues

The effective implementation of security policies and procedures requires security personnel trained to understand the balance between the risks to the agency and costs to preserve or protect a particular asset (Cawood, 2002). As the likelihood of spontaneous terrorism incidents increases and the specter of an organized incident looms in the background, the capacity for sport venue managers to fully deal with—or even identify—them becomes a critical challenge. The difficult job is to sustain the facade of complete security or the perception of being able to "feign control over the uncontrollable"(Beck, 2002, p. 41). Security officials must avoid depicting a situation that would be perceived by citizens as being "too great" of a security display. For example, some patrons object to pat-downs, claiming that pat-downs are a violation of their constitutional rights because they are warrantless and unreasonable government searches and seizures (*Johnston v.*

Tampa Bay Sports Authority, 2005; *Sheehan v. San Francisco 49ers*, 2009; *Stark v. Seattle Seahawks*, 2007).

Spectator Pat-Downs

The *Sheehan* (2009) court pointed out that stadium owners "... necessarily retain primary responsibility for determining what security measures are appropriate to ensure the safety of their patrons" (p. 480). One of the security management measures instituted by sports organizations was pat-downs of patrons entering the stadium. Pat-downs have been employed as a means to ensure that improvised explosive devices ("IEDs") which might be carried on a person entering a stadium may be detected (*Johnston v. Tampa Sports Authority*, 2006). The original intent of pat-downs was established by international security and military personnel because suicide vests could be hidden underneath an individual's garments, thereby avoiding detection (Mowbray, 2005). Because pat-downs may detect hidden IED's, some have perceived that they are more apt to dissuade a possible terrorist attack (Wirtz, 2006). However, as presented in the *Johnston, Sheehan, and Stark* cases, pat-downs are arguably intrusive, especially when not communicated well to the patrons.

As a simplistic example, a wider lens approach might suggest that the better use of resources is on less intrusive prevention measures. As such, there are other security search options that sport event managers may employ with less controversy than pat-downs, such as visual checks and metal detectors, as well as container checks or bag searches. Visual checks have been used in which individuals extend their arms away from their bodies with palms up. In doing so, the security personnel may be able to see if any explosive devices are on the body without compromising a patron's personal space (Share, 2008). However, a significant concern is that possible false security may exist due to personnel being inattentive or "rushed" to get the patrons through the turnstiles (Fallon, 2003).

Metal detectors and closed circuit televisions (CCTV) have also been utilized as search mechanisms. The installation of metal detectors, commonly referred to as target hardening, has been thought to increase the security of soft targets such as sports stadiums and arenas (Paraskevas, 2008). Yet, the effective use of metal detectors has been questioned since the September 11th terror hijackers used plastic knives (Fallon, 2003; Picarello, 2005). Closed circuit television (CCTV) cameras are now a common sight on public highways and in shopping malls and arcades. As the number of systems has increased so has their technological sophistication. However, speculation still exists about CCTV's regarding their effectiveness in providing security. A common goal of most CCTV systems has been the prevention of crime and disorder through deterrence. It is also assumed that CCTV will aid detection through its surveillance capability and the opportunity it may afford to deploy security personnel or police officers appropriately. Claims are also made that CCTV provides public reassurance and therefore reduces fear of crime, which may, in turn, increase the use of public spaces (Bennett & Gelsthorpe, 1996). CCTV is also used as a site management tool, for example, to observe traffic patterns or for security control at football matches. Yet, potential concerns exist when using a CCTV for security since there may be few or no personnel available to be deployed who can deter a crime. There is also the possibility that CCTV could lead the public to feel a reduced responsibility for policing because they assume that this is the responsibility of the cameras (Groombridge & Murji, 1994). However, surveillance technology, such as using CCTV's, raises the issue of privacy since it is designed to enable a surveillant to observe that which the subject does not intend to be observed (Lyon, 2003).

Other Security Options

Recent technological advancements have introduced a vast array of security solutions which can help to ensure the safety of patrons and participants at sporting events. Such new innovations offer the flexibility to be attuned to the specific security issues and needs of each sport organization. For example, event passes or identification cards to sports contests can provide an easily visible form of identification which can be recognized in a simple manner and verified immediately. However, technological advancements may be tailored to the level of security required for the event. Among these advancements are the identification of unique serial numbers, barcodes, fine line/guilloche print, magnetic strip, microtext print, UV print, hologram and contact/contactless chip. These improvements allow data to be stored on the pass, allowing automated movement around the event, without the need for human verification. However, the lack of personal interaction during the verification phase may become a concern. Additionally, if these items possess personal information about the individual, privacy issues may also apply. Personal information includes data assigned to an individual, such as a social security number, address, or telephone number. Such assigned personal information may be used to identify the activities and habits of the person, which then can be used without the individual's knowledge (Alpert, 1995).

Container checks and bag searches are also options that a sport event manager may consider instead of other searches. Although less controversial than pat-downs, concerns about bag searches include the lack of attention by security personnel to materials in the bag or bag size (Fallon, 2003). To provide an increased level of security, it is recommended that more than one method of verification be implemented. To make certain that a lack of attention by personnel is avoided, appropriate security training must be implemented.

Personnel Security Training

The analysis of the range of potential incidents is vital for defining capabilities in terms of both the implementation and enforcement of security plans. Previous researchers have reported that security personnel at sporting events seldom possess sufficient anti-terrorist training (Baker, Connaughton, Zhang, & Spengler, 2007; Goss, et al., 2003; Miller, Veltri & Gillentine, 2008). Yet, the most important aspect in securing a facility is the training of personnel. Miller and Veltri (2001) stated that people and procedures are the two primary security components that need to be addressed in a facility. People who need to be considered in a security plan include administration personnel, staff and maintenance personnel, student workers, and volunteers. Another segment of risk control needs to address employee and third-party safety, property protection, emergency participants, and visitors. In fact, many organizations are focusing more and more on the preparedness through appropriate employee training as the principal method for reducing both the frequency and severity of losses over the long term (Cawood, 2002).

Effective security plans are dynamic in nature. Should the training of a security plan become stagnant, in other words if it doesn't change or is not provided in a timely manner, over time its effectiveness will become compromised. A security training program should delineate responsibility for security training, explain the importance of security, detail security personnel responsibilities, discuss present security controls being taken to protect personnel and assets, and serve as a forum to discuss security questions (American Petroleum Institute, 2005).

Figure 1. Elements of Capability

Planning	Collection and analysis of intelligence and information, and development of policies, plans, procedures, mutual aid agreements, strategies, and other publications that comply with relevant laws, regulations, and guidance necessary to perform assigned missions and tasks. Access to robust information-sharing networks that include relevant intelligence, threat analysis, and real-time incident reporting.
Organization and Leadership	Individual teams, an overall organizational structure, and leadership at each level in the structure that comply with relevant laws, regulations, and guidance necessary to perform assigned missions and tasks.
Personnel	Paid and volunteer staff who meet relevant qualification and certification standards necessary to perform assigned missions and tasks.
Equipment and Systems	Major items of equipment, supplies, facilities, and systems that comply with relevant standards necessary to perform assigned missions and tasks.
Training	Content and methods of delivery that comply with relevant training standards necessary to perform assigned missions and tasks are provided on a regular basis (once every 2–4 months). Processes in place to identify and address dependencies and interdependencies to allow for more timely and effective implementation of short-term protective actions and more rapid response and recovery.
Exercise, Evaluations, and Corrective Actions	Exercises, self-assessments, peer-assessments, outside reviews, compliance monitoring, and actual major events that provide opportunities to demonstrate, evaluate, and improve the combined capability and interoperability of the other elements to perform assigned missions and tasks to standards necessary to achieve successful outcomes. Structures and processes that are flexible and adaptable, both to incorporate operational lessons learned and effective practices, and also to adapt quickly to a changing threat or incident environment.

Source: Chertoff, 2007.

According to the National Preparedness Guidelines (2007), the cycle of security preparation is dependent on six elements of capability: 1) planning, 2) organizing and leadership, 3) personnel, 4) equipment and systems, 5) training, and 6) exercise, evaluations, and corrective actions. Further description of these six capabilities may be viewed in Figure 1.

Security as a Value-Added Element

Broadly, it can be said that risk tends to degrade an organization's (or an activity's) value if left unattended (Rescher, 1983). Proper security management of sport venues can save money and ensure greater safety for spectators and participants. Patton (1997) indicated that effective facility security and control will positively impact safety, reduce theft and vandalism, and help control maintenance. Security issues in recreation facilities must be addressed in the early stages of building design or reconstruction. Stolovitch (1995) suggested that security design should not be considered as an add-on as this can result in increased cost and vulnerability to potential security-related lawsuits. Thus, the case can be made that effective security management contributes to organization value

(Williams, Smith, & Young, 1998). However, there is some controversy as to how "value" is measured because it can mean very different things in different settings. For the sports event manager, the value of the event would seem to be derived from an interconnected range of "experience elements," such as ambience, competitiveness of the event, concessions quality, security, and a range of other issues such as convenience or weather. If it becomes too egregious, security stops being reassuring and can paradoxically accentuate the prospect of extreme unmanageable danger. In the extreme, security measures could become so burdensome that they offset reduced ticket prices, attractive concessions, and the general excitement of attending a professional football game. In other words, security measures could degrade the value of the experience. Thus, security management decisions almost invariably involve a generalized risk-reward trade-off (Adams, 2001). It is impossible to drive risks to "zero" without degrading value (and even then, proximity to "zero" comes only at great expense), so the decision process must follow an optimizing rule, balancing the costs and benefits against overall security management objectives (Rescher, 1983).

Conclusion

It is clear that when the specific intents of organized or spontaneous violence have been analyzed, athletic venues provide virtually every component needed as a target selection (National Intelligence Estimate, 2007). Since the level of risk that sporting event organizers face from spontaneous and organized terrorism appears to be continuously increasing, security management of those risks must also be elevated. Security management has been recognized as the:

> "... overall plan consisting of: identifying potential security threats to ... facilities; assessing the risks associated with those threats in terms of incident likelihood and consequences; mitigating the risk by reducing the likelihood, the consequences, or both; and evaluating the risk reduction results achieved" (American Petroleum Industry, 2005, p. 43).

Due to the evolution of security management practices, it is recommended that sport venue managers concentrate on the security goals established after September 11, 2001. First, facility managers must simply accept the fact that any stadium or event exists as a potential target for organized and/or spontaneous acts of terror (Hurst, Zoubek, & Pratsinakis, 2002). Second, these managers must possess the education to be able to handle incidents should they occur (International Association of Assembly Managers, 2002). Third, though it may never be fully possible, venues should work to establish a level of foreseeability in which they address a potential threat without overemphasizing security issues (Piccarello, 2005). Regardless of the different types of security conducted, the provision of a strong security presence must be balanced to be a value-added component of the activity. A sport venue manager would be wise to consider the three-prong balancing test as set forth by the *Jensen v. Pontiac* (1982) court. The court in *Jensen* recognized that a reasonable search included a three-prong test of: 1) the public necessity, 2) the efficacy of the search, and 3) the degree and nature of the intrusion involved. The public necessity inquiry considers the nature of the threat involved along with the likelihood that the threat will materialize (*Collier v. Miller*, 1976). According to the *Jensen* Court, the second prong of the balancing test considers the likelihood that the search procedure will be effective in averting the potential harm (p. 624). Citing *United States v. Skipwith* (1973), the *Jensen* court stated that the final factor that must be balanced was "the degree and nature of intrusion into the privacy of the person and effects of the citizen which the search entails" (p. 19). Thus, the sport event manager should consider the likelihood of a threat and its impact, whether the search will avoid injury, and whether the search could violate the patron's right to privacy. By implementing the security venue issues presented in this chapter, sport venue managers may be able to gain a unique advantage in the development of some of the most secure events in the world today.

References

Adams, J. 2001. *Risk*. London: Routledge.

Alpert, S. A. (1995). Privacy and intelligent highways: Finding the right of way. *Santa Clara Computer & High Technology Law Journal, 11*, 97–118.

American Petroleum Institute. (2005). Security guidelines for the petroleum industry. Retrieved from http://new.api.org/policy/otherissues/upload/Security.pdf.

Appelbaum, S. H., Adeland, E., & Harris, J. (2005). Management of sports facilities: Stress and terrorism since 9/11. *Management Research News, 28*(7), 69–83.

Associated Press. (2011). Los Angeles Dodgers fans attack San Francisco Giants fan. Retrieved from http://www.azcentral.com/sports/diamondbacks/articles/2011/04/01/20110401los-angeles-dodgers-fans-attacks-san-francisco-giants-fan.html#ixzz1WSR6FmQH.

Atkinson, M. & Young, K. (2002). Terror games: Media treatment of security issues at the 2002 Winter Olympic Games. *International Journal of Olympic Studies, 11*, 53–78.

Baker, T.A., Connaughton, D. P., Zhang, J. J. & Spengler, J.O. (2007). Perceived risk of terrorism and related risk management practices of NCAA 1A football stadium managers. *Journal of Legal Aspects of Sport, 13*(2), 145–179.

Baker, K.P. & Merriam, D. W. (2003). Homeland security and premises liability. *The American Law Institute*, 1267–1285.

Beck, U. (2002). The terrorist threat: World Risk Society revisited. *Theory, Culture, and Society, 19*(4), 39–55.

Bennett, T. & L. Gelsthorpe (1996). Public attitudes towards CCTV in public places. *Studies on Crime and Crime Prevention, 5*(l), 72–90.

Borum, R. (2007). Psychology of terrorism. Retrieved from http://oai.dtic.mil/oai/oai?verb=getRecord&metadataPrefix=html&identifier=ADA494527.

Burns, C., Mearns, K., & McGeorge, P. (2006). Explicit and implicit trust within safety culture. *Risk Analysis, 26*(5), 1139–1150.

Cawood, J.S. (2002). Security. In R.W. Lack (Ed.) *Safety, health, and asset protection: Management essentials* (pp. 553–566). New York: Lewis Publishers.

Chertoff, M. (2007). National preparedness guidelines—September 2007. *Department of Homeland Security*. Retrieved from http://www.dhs.gov/xlibrary/assets/National_Preparedness_Guidelines.pdf.

Clonan, T. (2002, October 26). Any time any place, *Irish Times*, W1.

Cohen, A. (2001). Secure in defeat. *Athletic Business, 25*(11), 9–10.

Collier v. Miller, 414 F. Supp. 1357 (S.D. Tex. 1976).

Crenshaw, M. (2000). Psychology of terrorism: An agenda for the 21st century. *Political Psychology*, 21(2), 405–420.

Decker, R. J. (October, 2001). *Homeland security: A risk management approach can guide preparedness efforts.* Retrieved from http://www.gao.gov/cgi-bin/getrpt?GAO-03-102.

Fallon, R. H. (2003). Legal issues in sports security. *Fordham Intellectual Property, Media, and Entertainment Law Journal, 13,* 349–401.

Federal Bureau of Investigation. (2006). *Terrorism in the United States.* Retrieved from www.fbi.gov/publications/terror/terroris.pdf.

Frame, J. D. (2003). *Managing risk in organizations.* San Francisco: Jossey-Bass.

Goss, B. D., Jubenville, C. B., & MacBeth, J. L. (2003). *Primary principles of post-9/11 stadium security in the United States: Transatlantic implications from British practices.* Retrieved from www.iaam.org/CVMS/Post%20911%20Stadium%20Security.doc.

Grace, F. (2002, July 4). *FBI alert on stadiums.* Retrieved from http://www.cbsnews.com/stories/2002/07/03/attack/main514252.shtml.

Groombridge, N. & K. Murji. (1994). Obscured by cameras? *Criminal Justice Matters, 17,* 9.

Hurst, R., Zoubek, P., & Pratsinakis, C. (2002). American sports as a target of terrorism. *Sport and the Law Journal, 10*(1), 134–139.

International Association of Assembly Managers. (2002). *IAAM safety and security task force best practices protocols terrorism response planning for venue managers.* Retrieved from http://www.iaam.org/cvms/TerrorismFacts.pdf.

Isaacs v. Huntington Memorial Hospital, 38 Cal. 3d 112, 211 Cal. Rptr. 356, 695 P.2d 653, 1985 Cal. LEXIS 253 (1985).

Jensen v. Pontiac, 317 N.W.2d 619 (Mich. App.1982).

Johnston v. Tampa Sports Authority, (November 2, 2005). No. 05-09151, Order Granting Plaintiff's Emergency Motion for Preliminary Injunction, at 3–4 (Hillsborough County, Fla. Nov. 2, 2005).

Johnston v. Tampa Sports Authority, 442 F. Supp. 2d 1257 (M.D. Fla. 2006).

Lee, B., Gordon, P., Moore, J., & Richardson, H. (2008). Simulating the economic impacts of a hypothetical bio-terrorist attack: A sports stadium case. *Journal of Homeland Security and Emergency Management, 5(1),* 1–20.

Lipton, E. (2005, March 16). U.S. report lists possibilities for terrorist attacks and likely toll. *New York Times,* A1.

Lyon, D. (2003). Surveillance after September 11. London: Blackwell Publishing.

Merari, A. (1978). A classification of terrorist groups. *Studies in Conflict & Terrorism, 1*(3–4), 331–346.

Miller, L. (2006). The terrorist mind: A psychological and political analysis. *International Journal of Offender Therapy and Comparative Criminology, 50,* 121–138.

Miller, J. & Gillentine, A. (2006). An analysis of risk management policies for tailgating activities at selected NCAA division I football games. *Journal of Legal Aspects of Sport, 16,* 197–215.

Miller, J. & Veltri, F. (2001). Campus recreation centers: An examination of security issues. *Journal of Legal Aspects of Sport, 11*(2), 169–180.

Miller, J., Veltri, F. & Gillentine, A. (2008). Spectator perception of security at the Super Bowl after 9/11: Implications for facility managers. *Sport Management and Related Topics Journal, 4*(2), 16–25.

Mowbray, J. (2005). *Florida judge shockingly halts security searches at NFL games.* Retrieved from http://townhall.com/columnists/JoelMowbray/2005/10/31/florida_judge_shockingly_halts_security_searches_at_nfl_games?page=2.

National Intelligence Estimate. (2007). *The terrorist threat to the US homeland.* Retrieved from www.dni.gov/press_releases/ 20070717_release.pdf.

Patton, J. D. (August, 1997). Mission: Control. *Athletic Business, 21*(8), 63–68.

Paraskevas, A. (2008). Towards safer special events: A structured approach to counter the terrorism threat. In J. Knight (Ed.), *International perspectives of festivals and events: Paradigms of analysis* (pp. 279–295). London: Elsevier Publishing.

Piccarello, C. M. (2005). Terrorism, tourism, and torts: Liability in the event of a terrorist attack on a sports or entertainment venue. *Villanova Sports and Entertainment Law Journal, 12*, 365–392.

RAND Europe. (2007). Setting the agenda for an evidence-based Olympics. Cambridge: The Rand Corporation Europe.

Rescher, N. (1983). *Risk: A philosophical introduction to the theory of risk evaluation and management.* Washington, D.C.: University Press of America.

Share, M. (2008). Pat-down searches and protest cages: How security at the 2016 Olympic Games could affect First and Fourth Amendment liberties in the city of Chicago. *DePaul Journal of Sports Law and Contemporary Problems, 5*, 73–85.

Sheehan v. San Francisco 49ers, 45 Cal. 4th 992, 89 Cal. Rptr. 3d 594, 201 P.3d 472, (2009).

Slovic, P. & Peters, E. (2006). Risk perception and affect. *Psychological Science, 15*(6), 322–325.

Stark v. Seattle Seahawks, 2007 U.S. Dist. LEXIS 45510 (W.D. Wash. June 22, 2007).

Stolovitch, D. A. (1995). Drawing security into building design. *Security Management, 39*(12), 69–72.

Suder, G. (2004). *Terrorism and the international business environment.* Cheltenham, UK: Edward Elgar.

United States v. Skipwith, 482 F.2d 1272, 1276 (5th Cir. 1973).

Wade, J. (December, 2002). Safeguarding the Meadowlands. *Risk Management*, p. 18.

Walker, I., & Augoustinos, M. (2006). *Social cognition—An integrated introduction.* London: Sage Publications.

Williams, C. A., Smith, M. L., & Young, P. C. (1998). *Risk management and insurance* (8th ed.). New York: McGraw-Hill Book Company.

Wirtz, J. J. (2006). Responding to surprise. *Annual Review of Political Science, 9*, 51.

Withers, T. (2002). *Browns ban plastic bottles of beer.* Retrieved from http://bengals.enquirer.com/2002/08/09/ben_browns_ban_sales_of.html.

Part VI

Risk Management Concerns

Risk management is an attempt to educate sport personnel about their re-sponsibilities under the law and upgrade safety for sport participants and spectators.

Thomas Appenzeller

Chapter 26

Drug Testing and the NCAA

Recent court decisions have established a new class of people, athletes, who because of physical talent and ability are not afforded the same constitutional protection that their non-athletic classmates possess.

Tom Appenzeller & Bob Casmus

Introduction

During the 1905 college football season, 18 players were killed and over 100 more were severely injured. Columbia and Northwestern dropped the sport while Stanford University and California switched to rugby. The future of college football looked bleak. President Theodore Roosevelt, an avid football fan, pressured college administrators to take action. Representatives from over 60 institutions, heeding the President's advice, met in New York City and formed the Intercollegiate Athletic Association of the United States. In 1910, the name of the organization was changed to the National Collegiate Athletic Association (NCAA). The purpose of the NCAA, according to its constitution, was, "the regulation and supervision of college athletics throughout the United States in order that the athletic activities in the colleges and universities of the United States may be maintained on an ethical plane in keeping with the dignity and high purpose of education." Member institutions adopted the "Principles of Amateur Sport" (Swanson and Spears 1995) that stated that:

Each institution which is a member of this association agrees to enact and enforce such measures as may be necessary to prevent violations of the principles of amateur sport such as:

a. Proselyting

    1. The offering of inducements to players to enter colleges or universities because of their athletic abilities and of supporting or maintaining players while students on account of their athletic abilities, either by athletic organizations, individual alumni, or otherwise directly or indirectly.

    2. The singling out of prominent athletic students of preparatory schools and endeavoring to influence them to enter a particular college or university.

b. The playing of those ineligible as amateurs.

c. The playing of those who are not bona fide students in good and regular standing.

d. The improper and unsportmanlike conduct of any sort whatsoever either on the part of the contestants, the coaches, their assistants, or the student body (Proceedings of Third Annual Convention 1909).

The NCAA assumed an educational and supportive role for the betterment of intercollegiate sport and encouraged the formation of regional conferences to enforce eligibility and other standards (Swanson and Spears 1995).

Created at the request of President Teddy Roosevelt to save football, the NCAA today controls virtually all areas of college sport. Included in its bylaws are rules and regulations concerning amateurism, recruiting of student-athletes, eligibility requirements, playing and practice seasons, financial aid, number of coaches per sport, postseason competition, and now drug testing. In the pursuit of fair and equitable competition, the NCAA decided at its 1986 annual convention to test college athletes for drugs (Schaller 1991). The National Collegiate Athletic Association formed its Drug Education committee in 1973 and the committee initially administered programs in drug use, prevention, and drug education. From 1973 to 1986, the Drug Education Committee produced a variety of educational materials to help institutions and conferences develop effective drug education programs. However, the 1986 legislation authorized the NCAA to test student-athletes for performance enhancing or harmful drugs (Schaller 1991). In 1999, the NCAA decided to outsource administration of the drug testing program to the National Center for Drug Free Sport. Drug testing can now occur year-round and at any phase of an NCAA championship. All NCAA Division I institutions will be tested at least once per academic year and are subject to year-round testing. Likewise, NCAA Division II programs are subject to year-round testing and can be tested during any phase of an NCAA championship. NCAA Division III institutions that sponsor a Division 1 level sport are accountable under the NCAA Division 1 criteria (NCAA website). The drug testing would be conducted at all postseason championships and at football bowl games (Leeson 1989). With the tragic drug related deaths of Len Bias and Don Rogers, there was a public outcry over the perceived rising popularity of drug use among college athletes. In the United States there was growing support for the drug testing of athletes and colleges, universities, and the NCAA felt pressure to implement a drug testing program for all member institutions. In 1986–1987, the NCAA drug testing program cost $950,000 for approximately 3,000 tests and, in addition, $430,000 was budgeted for drug education programs. For 1987–1988, the NCAA budgeted $1,965,000 for drug testing and education and by 1990–1991 the budget had grown to $3.2 million. Half of the $3.2 million was used by the NCAA for actual testing at championship events and bowl games and the other $1.6 million was used in year-round testing. The 2010–2011 NCAA drug testing budget is now 4.5 million dollars. The NCAA provides a list of banned substances to its members, with more than 70 drugs in eight categories included. The drugs on the NCAA list are considered to be either performance enhancing and or potentially harmful to the health and safety of the student-athlete. The eight categories are:

1. Psychomotor and central nervous system stimulants

2. Anabolic agents

3. Alcohol & Beta Blockers (rifle only)

4. Diuretics and Masking Agents

5. Street Drugs

6. Peptide hormones and analogues

7. Anti-estrogens

8. Beta-2 Agonist (2010–2011 NCAA Handbook)

Note: Any substance chemically related to these classes is also banned.

The institution and the student-athlete shall be held accountable for all drugs within the banned drug class regardless of whether they have been specifically identified.

Drugs and Procedures Subject to Restrictions:

a. Blood Doping. The practice of blood doping (the intravenous injection of whole blood, packed red blood cells or blood substitutes) is prohibited, an evidence confirming use will be cause for action consistent with that taken for a positive drug test. 31.2.2.4.1 (page 16 2011–2012 Drug Testing Program—revised 8/15/89 and 5/4/92)

b. Local Anesthetics (under some conditions).

c. Beta-2 Agonists permitted only by prescription and inhalation.

d. Caffeine if concentrations in urine exceed 15 micrograms/ml.

(2011–2012 NCAA Banned Drugs from the NCAA website)

There are two general exceptions to the NCAA banned drug list. These exceptions involve the use of local anesthetics and asthma- or exercise-induced bronchospasm medications. Medical exceptions may be granted for a prescribed medication that is outlined under the NCAA Drug Testing Exceptions Procedure (NCAA website). For the purpose of sport and the NCAA, there are two general categories of prohibited substances: illegal drugs and performance enhancers. Illegal drugs include marijuana and cocaine, drugs that are sometimes classified as recreational (Dougherty et al. 1994). In 2002, ephedra was included in the NCAA year-round testing program. The NCAA will not grant a medical exception for the use of medical marijuana (NCAA website). Steroids is the best example of a performance enhancing drug. The use of an anabolic agent or peptide hormone must be approved by the NCAA before the student-athlete is allowed to participate in competition while taking these medications. The institution must submit required NCAA medical documentation from the prescribing physician supporting the diagnosis and treatment (NCAA website). Testing of student-athletes is done for one of three purposes:

1. to help preserve the health and well being of the athlete.

2. to ensure equitable competition.

3. to detect violations of applicable laws and league rules.

The drug testing policy of the NCAA is so that no one participant might have an artificially induced advantage, so that no one participant might be pressured to use chemical substances in order to remain competitive, and to safeguard the health and safety of participants. Prior to the beginning of the sport season, the student-athlete signs a consent form allowing the NCAA to conduct a drug test. By voluntarily agreeing to be tested, the athlete allows the NCAA to test the student for the banned substances listed in the NCAA manual. The student is not required to sign the consent form, but failure to sign the form means the athlete is immediately ineligible for NCAA competition. In 2005, a student-athlete who is in breach of the NCAA drug testing program protocol (e.g. no-show, tampering with a sample) shall be considered to have tested positive for the use of any drug other than a "street drug"(18.4.1.5.1.1 2011 NCAA Drug Testing Manual) In 1999, the NCAA decided to outsource administration of the drug testing program to the National Center for Drug Free Sport. During postseason championship events and certified football bowl games the NCAA will randomly select student-athletes for drug testing.

When the student-athlete is selected, a "urine validator" is sent to observe the athlete within the collection station (Leeson 1989). After the athlete has provided an adequate sample, the NCAA follows very precise written guidelines to ensure a good test and to maintain confidentiality. The NCAA uses the Gas Chromatography Mass Spectrometry (G.S./M.S.) method of testing, which is considered the most accurate and the most expensive (Leeson 1989). An athlete may appeal a positive test and the NCAA goes to great effort to maintain the integrity of the sample and the confidentiality of the person being tested. In the first year (1986–1987) of the Drug Testing program, 34 of the 3,511 athletes tested were declared ineligible, and of the 34, 31 were engaged in football, one in track, and two were basketball players. Twenty-five of the football players tested for steroids and the two basketball players tested for cocaine (*Hill v. NCAA* 1994). From 9/1/09 to 12/31/09, there were 37 positive test during the year-round testing program and 45 positive test results occurring during NCAA Championships and Bowl games. Of these positive tests, 1 appeal was granted, 8 appeals were denied, 2 athletes had a 50% reduction of their punishment and 11 had medical exceptions. From 1/1/2010 to 8/31/2010, there were 68 positive tests during the year-round testing program and 82 positive tests occurring during NCAA Championships and Bowl games. Of these positive tests no appeals were granted, 21 appeals were denied, 2 athletes had a 50% reduction of their punishment and 41 had medical exceptions granted (NCAA Drug Testing Program Results Summary from the Center for Drug Free Sport). The majority of the positive test for the 2009–2010 academic year were due to anabolic agents and stimulants.

The NCAA Survey of Institutions in 2009 shows that 65% of all institutions responding to the survey have in operation a drug/alcohol education program for student-athletes, a one percent increase from 2007. There were 491 institutions that responded to this survey (NCAA 2009 Member Institution's Drug/Education Testing Survey: Executive Summary). This same survey also shows results that 54% of the responding institutions have a drug testing program for student-athletes, a four percent increase from 2007. 92–96% of the respondents reported doing drug testing of all sport groups; 69–72% of institutions reported using reasonable suspicion as a deciding factor in whom to test, and 13–16% of institutions used entire team and championship testing as determinants. Respondents reported that the majority of samples are tested for marijuana (95%), cocaine and amphetamines (94%), narcotics (83%), ecstasy (74%), ephedrine (67%) and diuretics (56%). Less than one-half are tested for alcohol (22%) and anabolic agents (22%). Twenty-five percent of institutions reported removing the student-athletes from the team after a 2nd positive drug test; 79% do so after the 3rd positive test. Currently the NCAA testing program screens for marijuana (THC) only at NCAA Championships. Seventy-nine percent of respondents believe that marijuana (THC) testing should be added to the NCAA year-round program.

January 2012 NCAA Study of Substance Use Habits of College Student-Athletes — NCAA Research Staff

Findings from the 2006 Study: Use Among College Students

Among the entire group of student-athletes, the use of amphetamines has continually increased since 1997. The main reason stated for using amphetamines is for the treatment of attention deficit disorder. Anabolic steroid use has decreased slightly from 2001. Almost 60% of student-athletes continue to believe that their use of alcoholic beverages has no effect on athletic performance or on their general health. The number of respondents who believe that the NCAA and their institutions should drug test student-athletes increased from 2001, with nearly two-thirds believing that the NCAA should drug test student-athletes. The number of respondents believing that drug testing by the NCAA and the institutions has deterred college athletes from using drugs has increased. Now twenty-six years later, the NCAA is still committed to drug testing of college student-athletes. That is not to say that every athlete has gone gladly to test as there have been several legal challenges to the right of the NCAA to drug test.

Fourteenth Amendment

Drug testing in college sport by the National Collegiate Athletic Association raises a number of legal issues, including concerns about an athlete's constitutional rights to due process, equal protection, and privacy, as well as protection against illegal search and seizure and self-incrimination. The first legal principle used against the NCAA has been that of state action. Only federal and state actors in public institutions are bound by the requirements of the Constitution and due process (Wong 1994). Private institutions that are free of governmental control do not have due process requirements (Dougherty et al. 1994). A plaintiff must be able to prove state action by a university, association, or other amateur governing body when attempting to invoke constitutional law protection in a drug testing challenge. The university, association, or other amateur governing body must be shown to be part of the federal government, a state government, or an arm or agency of a state government. Private entities are not subject to constitutional challenges (Wong 1994). One of the issues recently has been the change of status of the NCAA as a state actor. The NCAA used to be considered a state actor by the courts. In 1972, in *Curtis v. NCAA,* plaintiffs were being barred permanently from intercollegiate competition by the NCAA (Martin 1986). The plaintiffs, whose academic achievements in college surpassed the minimum 1.600 grade point average, were being barred because they had participated contrary to the rules during their freshman year. The preliminary injunction issued in favor of the plaintiffs in *Curtis* by Judge Arthur C. Wallenberg mentioned only that half of the NCAA's membership consisted of a public institutions, cited no authority, and went officially unreported (Martin 1986). Using the *Curtis* decision, a legal journal in 1972, in attempting to analyze possible judicial relief in connection with disputes between student-athletes and the NCAA, stated:

> Any attempt to invoke the protections available under the fourteenth amendment for a college athlete penalized by the NCAA must be qualified with the caveat that such an invocation resides on the borderline of established constitutional doctrine (Martin 1986).

Beginning with *Buckton v. NCAA,* the court held that the NCAA's intimate involvement with state actors was sufficient to change its otherwise private functions to the category of state action (Dougherty et al. 1994). The concern in *Buckton* was the domination of American college hockey by Canadian student-athletes. United States District Judge Joseph L. Tauro found in *Buckton* that the NCAA had two sets of rules regarding eligibility to participate in hockey, one set for the Americans and another set for foreign students (Martin 1986). Judge Tauro found that regulations setting forth facially disparate conditions for the participation of a foreign student in a sport, as opposed to an American student, has to fall when judicially challenged (Martin 1986). State-supported educational institutions and their members and officers play a substantial, although admittedly not pervasive role in the NCAA's program (Dougherty et al. 1994). State participation in or support of nominally private activity is a well-recognized basis for finding state action (*Parish v. NCAA* 1975). The fifth circuit noted that the Association, as coordinator and overseer of college athletics, was performing a traditional governmental function and that meaningful regulation of this aspect of education is beyond the effective reach of any one state (Martin 1986). The fifth circuit concluded that were the NCAA to disappear tomorrow, government would soon step in to fill the void. The court declared in *Parish v. NCAA* that it would be strange doctrine indeed to hold that the states could avoid the restrictions placed upon them by the Constitution by banding together to form or support a private organization to which they have relinquished some portion of their governmental power (Martin 1986). This reasoning allowed the courts to impose the same type of due process restrictions on private organizations such as the NCAA as they would impose on its individual member institutions (Dougherty et al. 1994). The courts' reason for holding the NCAA to the requirement of state actor were:

1. Public universities make up over half the membership.

2. State funds paid membership dues.

3. Events are held in university facilities.

4. One institution, one vote rule making.

5. Individual members were state actors.

6. Those individual members were intimately involved in the activities of the NCAA.

7. The NCAA exercised regulatory control over those members much in the same way a government might (Dougherty et al. 1994).

However, beginning in 1984, the NCAA went from being a state actor to no longer being a state actor. The courts began to reject this line of reasoning in the *Blum v. Yaretsky* (1982) decision, which indicated a change in the level of involvement necessary for a private entity to be considered as functioning as a state actor. The respondents in *Blum v. Yaretsky* represented a class of Medicaid patients in New York challenging decisions by the nursing home in which they resided to discharge or transfer patients with neither notice nor opportunity for a hearing. The court held in the *Blum* decision that mutual involvement with State actors alone would not suffice to support a finding of state action (Dougherty et al. 1994). The decision would rest instead on the degree of control that the private agency exerted over the actions of its public members. The first Appellate court not to find state action in the operation of the NCAA was *Arlosoroff v. NCAA* (1984), in which it said:

> It is not enough that an institution is highly regulated or subsidized by the state. If the state in its regulatory or subsidizing function does not order or cause the action complained of, and the function is not one traditionally reserved to the state, there is no state action.

The federal courts in *McHale v. Cornell University, Graham v. NCAA, Karamanos v. Baker,* and *McCormack v. NCAA* all ruled that the NCAA did not constitute state action and therefore defendants were not restricted by the due process and equal protection requirements of the Constitution. The most famous case to declare that the NCAA was no longer a state actor was *Tarkanian v. NCAA*. The University of Nevada at Las Vegas (UNLV), a state university, had been investigated by the NCAA and the committee found 38 violations, including 10 against men's basketball Coach Jerry Tarkanian. Following the investigation, the NCAA ordered UNLV to suspend Tarkanian as coach or face additional penalties. UNLV did so, and Tarkanian sued, claiming that the NCAA had violated his constitutional right to due process. The Supreme Court held that:

> The NCAA's participation in the events that led to Tarkanian's suspension did not constitute state action prohibited by the Fourteenth Amendment and was not performed under color of state law within the meaning of 1983. The source of the rules adopted by the NCAA is not Nevada, but the collective membership, the vast majority of which are located in other states. Moreover, UNLV's decision to adopt the NCAA's rules did not transform them into state rules and the NCAA into a state actor, since UNLV retained plenary power to withdraw from the NCAA and to establish its own standards (*Tarkanian v. NCAA* 1988).

The NCAA, then, is a private organization and its rules and regulations are not governed by the United States Constitution and particularly the Fourteenth Amendment. However, individual members that are publicly funded are state actors and therefore may be held individually to the constitutional requirements of due process when employing drug testing procedures (Dougherty et al. 1994). Private institutions that receive no state funds would not face the same constitutional constraints as public universities when deciding to implement additional drug testing procedures above that of the NCAA. Since the athlete has to sign a consent form to be tested, the consent form helps to satisfy the due process requirements. When the athlete consents to be tested, the athlete has waived his or her right to due process, even though failure to sign a consent form means automatic and complete ineligibility. The courts view the act of signing a drug testing release form as voluntary because the person who refuses to sign does not get tested and is not disciplined by being dropped from school or reported to police. The athlete is also not able to show deprivation of a significant liberty or property interest, because legal precedent in this area has most often found that a student-athlete does not have a liberty or property interest in athletics (Wong 1994). Since the NCAA is not a state actor and since athletes voluntarily sign consent forms to be tested, drug testing does not violate the Fourteenth Amendment to the Constitution.

Fourth Amendment

The National Collegiate Athletic Association has the ability to randomly drug test student-athletes in postseason competition. The procedures for drug testing do not violate due process requirements, but does the test violate the athlete's right to privacy? There have been a number of Fourth Amendment challenges to the method of drug testing that the NCAA employs to monitor student-athletes. A drug test through urinalysis is considered a search in the legal sense (Dougherty et al. 1994). The Fourth Amendment of the United States Constitution provides:

> The right of the people to be secure in their persons, houses, papers, and effects against unreasonable searches and seizures, shall not be violated, and no warrants shall issue but upon probable cause, supported by oath or affirmation and particularly describing the place to be searched, and the persons or things to be seized (Norton et al. 1991).

Since the testing of an athlete's blood or urine constitutes a search, the search must be deemed reasonable in order to take place. So far the majority of the cases involving drug testing and the Fourth Amendment have been upheld in favor of the NCAA (Wong 1994).

David Bally challenged Northeastern University's drug testing program for members of its intercollegiate athletic teams (*Bally v. Northeastern University* 1989). Bally alleged that Northeastern's policy requiring student-athletes to consent to drug testing, as a condition of participation in sport, violated his civil rights and his right to privacy under Massachusetts law. A member of the indoor and outdoor track team and cross-country team, Bally refused to sign Northeastern's drug testing form as well as the NCAA's drug testing consent form for the 1987–1988 academic year. Northeastern declared Bally ineligible to participate in track and cross-country even though he had met Northeastern's other conditions for eligibility. Northeastern's program requires that a student-athlete consent to drug testing, through urinalysis, during postseason competition as well as during the regular season. The program requires that student-athletes be tested once annually for certain drugs, viz., amphetamines, barbiturates, benzodiozepine, cannabinoid, cocaine, methaqualone, opiates, and phencyclidine. The program also mandates random testing throughout the academic year and requires testing of athletes before any NCAA postseason competition. Northeastern cites as its reasons for instituting its drug testing program a desire:

a. to promote the health and safety of student-athletes.

b. to promote fair intra team and intercollegiate competitions.

c. to ensure that Northeastern student-athletes, as role models to other students and/or representatives of Northeastern to the public, are not perceived as drug users (*Bally v. Northeastern University* 1989).

Bally did not allege or show state action, rather he asserted his rights under the Massachusetts Constitution and he failed. The Supreme Judicial Court of Massachusetts held that the drug testing program did not violate states' civil rights or privacy statutes. Bally had to prove:

1. his exercise or enjoyment of rights secured by the Constitution or laws of either the United States or of the Commonwealth

2. had been interfered with, or attempted to be interfered with and

3. that the interference or attempted interference was by threats, intimidation, or coercion (*Bally v. Northeastern University* 1989).

Bally was not successful at the Appellate level.

In *O'Halloran v. University of Washington,* a student-athlete at a state university brought action challenging enforcement of the NCAA drug testing program. Elizabeth O'Halloran contended that the NCAA's drug testing program is constitutionally flawed because it interferes significantly with student's privacy rights: the right to live one's life in private, free from governmental interference, the right to be let alone. The plaintiff contended that this interference occurs because urination is monitored and because private facts about student-athlete's activities in addition to the use of drugs may be revealed; for example, pregnancy, or use of pills for birth control, or treatment of depression, epilepsy, or diabetes. O'Holloran also argued that over all, the drug testing program results in an unreasonable search and seizure because the need for search does not outweigh the invasion of privacy rights. The NCAA argued that consent to drug screening as a condition of eligibility for participation in intercollegiate athletics is not prohibited by the United States or State of Washington Constitutions and that NCAA's conduct is not state action (*O'Halloran v. University of Washington* 1988). The NCAA also argued that:

1. the privacy interest alleged does not rise to the magnitude of highly personal family matters addressed in Supreme Court privacy cases.

2.   the privilege of participation in intercollegiate athletics is not a constitutionally protected property or liberty interest.

3.   there is no unreasonable search and seizure since the search is compelled neither by government nor by giving up of a privilege secured by state or federal constitution (*O'Halloran* 1988).

The United States District Court concluded that while a urine test may be a search, it is reasonable, there being a diminished expectation of privacy in the context of a university athletic program and there being a compelling interest by the university and the NCAA that outweighs the relatively small compromise of privacy under the circumstances. The Court concluded in *O'Halloran* that both the basis for and the scope of the NCAA's drug testing program is reasonable. The court relying on the decision in *Railway Labor Executives' Assn. v. Burnley* held that there are certain well-defined exceptions to the warrant requirement for a search, such as searches incident to lawful arrest, the automobile exception, hot pursuit, plain view, border searches, administrative searches of closely regulated industries, searches of school-children's possessions at school, and consent. In the *Railway Labor Executives' Assn. v. Burnley,* the court balanced what it concluded were the railroad employees' reasonable expectations of privacy with the governmental interest in the safe and efficient operation of the railroads for the benefit of railroad employees and the public affected by that operation. The court added that for athletes, the suspicion is not directed at a particular individual but at an activity that has experienced a drug abuse problem. It is laudable that the NCAA and its members are attempting to educate, ferret out, and deter drug use among athletes, and they would be remiss if they were not doing it. It is important that the NCAA make the effort to turn up evidence of inappropriate drug use. The plaintiff's greatest complaint in an invasion of privacy concern is that the testing programs require monitoring of urination. However, in providing a urine sample, the student-athlete is not threatened with the consequences of loss of liberty that would face someone in a criminal investigation. The only consequence is denial of eligibility, which is not a protected right. Low grades, failure to use protective equipment, or medical reasons may also cause loss of eligibility. The primary purpose of the monitor is to preserve the integrity of the sample and this does not constitute an unreasonable invasion of privacy (*O'Halloran v. University of Washington* 1988). Against this background, the larger interest of the health of the student-athlete, as well as the public's and competing athletes' perception of the fairness of intercollegiate athletics, greatly outweighs the relatively small compromise of an individual's privacy interest which is diminished in the context of collegiate athletics.

A notable case in the area of drug testing is *Hill v. NCAA*. In *Hill,* two Stanford University students challenged the NCAA's drug testing program as violating the privacy initiative of the State Constitution of California. Article 1, Section 1 of the California Constitution provides:

All people are by nature free and independent and have inalienable rights. Among these are enjoying and defending life and liberty, acquiring, possessing, and protecting property, and pursuing and obtaining safety, happiness, and privacy.

The phrase, "and privacy" was added to California Constitution, Article 1, Section 1 by an initiative adopted by the voters on November 7, 1972. Stanford intervened in the suit on behalf of the students and adopted the plaintiff's position. Finding the NCAA's drug testing program to be an invasion of plaintiffs' right to privacy, the Superior Court permanently enjoined its enforcement against plaintiffs and other Stanford athletes. The

Court of Appeal upheld the injunction, but the Supreme Court of California reversed and remanded (*Hill v. NCAA* 1994). The Supreme Court held that:

1. The Privacy Initiative of the State Constitution embodies right of action against nongovernmental entities.

2. The Privacy Initiative of the Constitution applies to intercollegiate athletic organizations.

3. Not every assertion of privacy interest under the Privacy Initiative of the State Constitution need be overcome by compelling interest.

4. The Intercollegiate athletic association's drug testing policy involving monitoring of urination, testing of urine samples, and inquiry concerning medications did not violate Constitutional right to privacy (*Hill v. NCAA* 1994).

The Supreme Court of California added that the intercollegiate athletic association's drug testing policy involving monitoring of urination, testing of urine samples, and inquiry concerning medication did not violate constitutional right to privacy; interest in freedom from observation during urination and privacy of medical treatment and information were reduced by students' voluntary participation in intercollegiate athletics and outweighed by the association's interest in safe guarding integrity of competition and protecting the health and safety of student-athletes. As a result of its unique set of demands, athletic participation carries with it social norms that effectively diminish an athlete's reasonable expectation of personal privacy in his or her bodily conditions, both externally and internally. Students and universities have no right to participate in intercollegiate athletic competition. In the decision, the Supreme Court of California held that intercollegiate sport is, at least in part, a business founded upon offering for public entertainment athletic contests conducted under a rule of fair and vigorous competition. Scandals involving drug use, like those involving improper financial incentives or other forms of corruption, impair the NCAA's reputation in the eyes of the sport-viewing public. A well-announced and vigorously pursued drug testing program serves to:

1. provide a significant deterrent to would-be violators, thereby reducing the probability of damaging public disclosure of athletic drug use.

2. assure student-athletes, their schools, and the public that fair competition remains the overriding principle in athletic events (*Hill v. NCAA* 1994).

The Fourth Amendment to the Constitution does not proscribe all searches and seizures, but only those that are unreasonable. As a sponsor of athletic competition, the NCAA was well within its legal rights in adopting a drug testing program designed to eliminate the actual or potential influence of drugs in competitive sport.

The one case where a student-athlete successfully challenged drug testing is the *University of Colorado v. Derdeyn*. The Supreme Court of Colorado held, in 1993, that in the absence of voluntary consent, the university's random suspicionless urinalysis drug testing of student-athletes was an unconstitutional search. The court held that the Fourth Amendment to the United States Constitution protects individuals from unreasonable searches conducted by government, even when government acts as administrator of athletic program at a state school or university (*University of Colorado v. Derdeyn* 1993). University students are not entitled to less protection than other people.

The University of Colorado drug program was implemented in 1984, several years before the NCAA began postseason drug testing procedures. Colorado was one of the first universities to begin drug testing of student-athletes and the policies and procedures were changed several times. The Trial Court found no evidence that an actual drug abuse problem among student-athletes existed, or any evidence that an athlete had been injured in any way because of the use of drugs. The Trial Court concluded that University of Colorado's random urinalysis drug testing of athletes without individualized suspicion violates the Fourth Amendment guarantee against unreasonable search and seizure.

Interscholastic Sport

The *Colorado* case was decided November 1, 1993, but the decision seems to be obsolete in view of the Supreme Court ruling in *Vernonia School District 47J v. Acton.* Even though the *Acton* case involves interscholastic, not intercollegiate, athletics, the Fourth Amendment issue is still the same. The Supreme Court in *Acton* affirmed the random urinalysis requirement for participation in athletics. The Supreme Court, citing precedent in *Schaill by Kross v. Tippecanoe County School Corp., Skinner v. Railway Labor Executives' Assn.,* and *Treasury Employees v. Von Raab* held that students wanting to participate in sport were denied the protection of the Fourth Amendment against search and seizure (*Vernonia School District 47J v. Acton* 1995). In a 5–4 decision, the Supreme Court concluded that since student-athletes have to suit up in communal dressing rooms and shower and change in groups, the athlete is not allowed to be bashful. Further, by choosing to go out for the team, the student-athlete voluntarily submits to a higher degree of regulation than other students. The student-athlete has to have a preseason medical examination with urine sample, must have adequate health insurance coverage, maintain a minimum grade point average, and comply with rules of conduct, dress, and curfew hours that may be established by a coach or athletic director. People who choose to participate in a closely-regulated industry have reason to expect intrusions upon normal rights and privileges, including privacy. The drug testing policy in Vernonia School District applies to all students participating in interscholastic athletics. Students wishing to play sport must sign a form consenting to the testing and must obtain the written consent of their parents. Athletes are tested at the beginning of the season for their sport. In addition, once each week of the season the names of the athletes are placed in a "pool" from which a student, with the supervision of two adults, blindly draws the names of 10% of the athletes for random testing, and those selected are notified and tested the same day, if possible. The Supreme Court acknowledged that a drug problem largely fueled by the role model effect of athletes' drug use, and of particular danger to athletes, is effectively addressed by making sure athletes do not use drugs. "Taking into account all the factors, we, the majority have considered the decreased expectation of privacy, the relative unobtrusiveness of the search, and the severity of the need met by the search and conclude that Vernonia's Drug Testing policy is reasonable and hence constitutional" (*Vernonia School District 47J v. Acton* 1995).

In 2008, the Supreme Court of Washington State disagreed with the United States Supreme Court on the issue of drug testing high school athletes. The parents of Aaron and Abraham York sued the Wahkiakum School District, alleging that the District's random and suspicionless drug testing of student-athletes violated the State of Washington Constitution. The School District asked that the Court adopt a "special needs" exception to the warrant requirement to allow drug testing of student-athletes. The State Supreme Court held that the urinalysis test was a significant intrusion on a student's fundamental right of privacy. The Wahkiakum School District modeled its policy after the one used in Vernonia, but the Washington Supreme Court stated that just passing muster under the Federal Constitution does not ensure survival under the State Constitution. The

Supreme Court explained that in the State of Washington, there was a long history of striking down exploratory searches not based on at least reasonable suspicion. The Washington Supreme Court reversed the Superior Court ruling supporting the School District.

In 2011, the Goshen County School District Number 1 in Wyoming also had its drug testing policy for student-athletes challenged in court. The Wyoming Supreme Court ruled that the School District had a compelling interest in providing for the safety and welfare of its students, and that schools could impose rules that might be inappropriate for adults. The Wyoming Supreme Court found that the School District did not violate the United States Constitution Fourth, Fifth, or Fourteenth Amendments. Drug testing is a bigger issue today from a legal standpoint than when it began back in 1986.

Since the Supreme Court has justified the random, suspicionless, drug testing of a 12-year-old James Acton in the small logging town of Vernonia, Oregon, then it would seem to hold that all athletes may be subject to random urinalysis. The NCAA can mandate drug testing at postseason competition because it is not considered to be a state actor, but is a private, voluntary organization. The athlete, by signing the voluntary consent form, waives his right to due process, even though failure to sign the consent form would mean immediate ineligibility. Private colleges and universities, because they are not state actors, are also able to mandate random drug testing for their athletes. Public institutions, who are state actors, but no more and no less than Vernonia School District, have the go ahead from the Supreme Court to require mandatory year-round drug testing. From analysis of State and Federal cases involving drug testing of college athletes, the evidence indicates that college and university have the legal green light to continue to administer random drug tests

In Our Opinion

The United States Supreme Court in *Tinker v. Des Moines School District* (1969), mandated that students do not shed their constitutional rights at the school house gate. The *Tinker* case was a landmark decision that used the United States Constitution to protect the rights of students. However, recent State and Federal Court decisions on the subject of random drug testing of student-athletes seem to be qualifying the *Tinker* decision. The recent decisions have established a new class of people, the athlete, who because of physical talent and ability are not afforded the same constitutional protections that their non-athletic classmates process. The Supreme Court in *Vernonia School District 47J v. Acton* has successfully taken the word "student" out of the phrase "student-athlete" and has created a suspect classification. Even Justice Ginsburg, in her separate concurrence, made it clear that she would not have accepted the constitutionality of a testing program that would have included the entire student body (Kirkby 1996). Drug testing is all right for athletes, they take showers together, but not for the average student. What we have is guilt by association; if a person is an athlete, we need to test them for drugs. Such a suspicion-by-association method significantly erodes Fourth Amendment interests which have historically been protected by adherence to the traditional notions of probable cause and reasonable suspicion. However, suspicion directed at one individual cannot justify a search of other individuals simply because they are similarly situated and, likewise, information about a class of people does not create reasonable suspicion of the guilt of each member of that class. In her *Vernonia* dissent, Justice O'Connor emphasized:

Whether a blanket search is better … than a regime based on individualized suspicion is not a debate in which we should engage. In my view, it is not open to judges or governmental officials to decide on policy grounds which is better and which is worst. For most of our constitutional history, mass suspicionless searches have been generally considered per use unreasonable within the meaning of the Fourth Amendment. And we have allowed exceptions in recent years only where it has been clear that a suspicion-based regime would be ineffectual (*Vernonia School District 47J v. Acton* 1995).

We do not believe that we need to make athletes a suspect class in the United States; athletes should be treated with the same rights and privileges as any other member of the student body.

Risk Management Strategies

Ten Components of a Good Drug Testing Program

1. A Policy Statement

   Athletes and parents need to know the purpose for the drug testing program.

2. Notification of Testing

   Will the testing be year-round or just in-season, and where and when will the testing actually take place?

3. An Educational Component

   Education and abstinence should be a major part of any drug testing program. Athletes should be informed about the dangers of drug use.

4. Identification of Banned Substances

   There should be a list of drugs that can not be used by the athletes.

5. A Random Testing Component

   How many athletes will be tested per team, what percentage, and how will athletes be selected for testing?

6. Accuracy of Test

   The institution should use a drug testing firm with a good reputation.

7. Sanctions

   What happens to the athlete that tests positive? Punishments and penalties should be clear and in writing before tests are administered.

8. Due Process Considerations

   What is the appeals process for the athlete that tests positive?

9. Confidentiality

   Every effort should be made to protect the athlete from public disclosure, ridicule, and embarrassment. The right or need to know should be limited.

10. Validity

    Test administrators should make sure that the athlete does not cheat on the test. The substance tested should belong to the athlete.

Court Cases

I. State Action

    A. NCAA a State Actor (1973–1984)

        1. Precedent for State Actor:

            Buckton v. NCAA, 366 F. Supp. 1152 (D. Mass. 1973).

            Associated Students, Inc. v. NCAA, 493 F. 2d 1251 (9th Cir. 1974).

            Parish v. NCAA, 506 F. 2d. 1028 (5th Cir. 1975).

            Jones v. NCAA, 392 F. Supp. 285 (D. Mass. 1975).

            Howard University v. NCAA, 367 F. Supp. 926 (D.D.C. 1973), Aff'd., 510 F. 2d. 213 (D.C.Cir. 1975).

            Regents of University of Minnesota v. NCAA, 560 F. 2d. 352 (8th Cir. 1977).

            Colorado Seminary v. NCAA, 417 F. Supp. 885 (D. Colo. 1976), Aff'd., 570 F. 2d. 320 (10th Cir. 1977).

        2. State action narrowed after 1982:

            Blum v. Yaretsky, 102 S. Ct. 2777 (1982).

            Rendell-Baker v. Kohn, 102 S. Ct. 2764 (1982).

            Lugar v. Edmondson Oil Co., 102 S. Ct. 2744 (1982).

    B. NCAA no longer a state actor.

        1. Precedent for no state actor:

            Arlosofoff v. NCAA, 746 F. 2d. 1019 (4th Cir. 1984).

            McHale v. Cornell University, 620 F. Supp. 67 (N.D.N.Y. 1985).

            Graham v. NCAA, 804 F. 2d. 953 (6th Cir. 1986).

            Karamanos v. Baker, 816 F. 2d. 258 (6th Cir. 1987).

            McCormack v. NCAA, 845 F. 2d. 1338 (5th Cir. 1988).

            Tarkanian v. NCAA, 109 S. Ct. 454 (1988).

II. Fourth Amendment

    A. Balancing Test

        1. Precedent drug testing upheld:

            Schaill by Kross v. Tippecanoe County School Corp., 8\64 F. 2d. 1309 (7th Cir. 1988).

            Bally v. Northeastern University, 532 N.E. 2d. 49 (Mass. 1989).

            O'Halloran v. University of Washington, 679. F. Supp. (W.D. Wash. 1988), Rev'd On Other Grounds, 856 F. 2d. 1375 (9th Cir. 1988).

            Hill v. NCAA, 865 P. 2d. 633 (Cal. 1994).

            Vernonia School District 47J v. Acton, 115 S. Ct. 2386 (1995).

        2. Precedent drug testing rejected:

            Odenheim v. Carlstadt-East Rutherford R. School, 510 A. 2d. 709 (N.J. Super. Ch. 1985).

Brooks v. East Chambers Consol. Ind. School Dist., 730 F. Supp. 759 (S.D. Texas 1989), Aff'd Without Opinion, 930 F. 2d. 915 (5th Cir. 1991).

University of Colorado v. Derdeyn, 863 P. 2d. 929 (Colo. 1993).

References

Dougherty, N., D. Auxter, A.S. Goldberger and G. Heinzmann. 1994. *Sport, Physical Activity and the Law*. Champaign, IL: Human Kinetics.

Leeson, T.A. 1989. "The Drug Testing of College Athletics." *Journal of College and University Law* vol. 16, no. 2.

Martin, G.A. 1986. "The NCAA and Its Student Athletes: Is There Still State Action." *New England Law Review* vol. 21, no. 1.

NCAA Drug Testing Program 2011–2012 (NCAA Website).

NCAA 2009 Survey: member Institutions Drug Education and Drug Testing Programs (NCAA Website).

"NCAA Study of Substance Use habits of College Students-Athletes" The NCAA Research Staff. January 2006.

Norton, M.B., D.M. Katzman, P.D. Escott, H.P. Chudacoff, T.G. Patterson, and W.M. Tuttle, Jr. 1991. *A People and A Nation*. Boston, MA: Houghton Mifflin.

Proceedings of the Third Annual Convention of the Intercollegiate Athletic Association of the United States. 1909.

Schaller, W.L. 1991. "Drug Testing and the Evolution of Federal and State Regulation of Intercollegiate Athletics: A Chill Wind Blows." *Journal of College and University Law* vol. 18, no. 3.

Swanson, R. and B. Spears. 1995. *History of Sport and Physical Education in the United States*. 4th Edition. Madison, WI: Benchmark.

Wong, G. 1994. *Essentials of Amateur Sport Law*. 2nd Edition. Westport, CT: Praeger.

Chapter 27

Fitness Center Safety

Management must take a proactive approach when establishing their fitness center.

David L. Harlowe

Introduction

Whether you are starting a new facility or updating an existing facility, this chapter is designed to help fitness center owners, managers, and all support staff understand the risks inherent in this industry. Management must take a proactive approach when establishing their fitness center. Your facility could be a simple, small-town gym or a sophisticated training center for athletes. Regardless of the size or scope of the facility there are certain risks that must be recognized and addressed. While there are no set rules for the fitness industry, the American College of Sports Medicine (ACSM) has developed standards and guidelines for safety in fitness centers. Various ACSM's guidelines will be addressed throughout this chapter.

Facility Layout

There are a growing variety of fitness centers out there today. There are sports-related facilities, circuit-training facilities, cycling studios, etc. Regardless of the format, care must be taken in safely laying out your facility. There are five main things that must be addressed. They are:

- Fitness Center Flooring
- Equipment Positioning
- Facility Lighting
- Facility Environment
- Facility Signs

Fitness Floor Types

When setting up a fitness facility you must take into consideration what each particular area will be used for. There are at least four areas to any fitness facility, each with its own special needs. The first priority is always the safety of the people using the area. Choosing the right floor will help prolong equipment life and reduce the chance of injuries due to equipment failure. Below are the four main areas and the recommendations for the type of floor that should be used.

Free Weight Area

The floor in the free weight area will take the most abuse because dumbbells and weight plates will be in constant use. In theory, these pieces of equipment should be placed back on their respective racks when not in use, but in reality they will be dropped on the floor too many times to count. To help reduce damage to this equipment and the floor in the area, rubber padding should be used. It is recommended that a permanent rubber floor be used throughout the area. The rubber floor should be at least 1/2" to 3/4" in thickness and meet OSHA and ADA minimum standards for traction. When installing permanent flooring it is very important that the edge of the floor be level in the transition from one area to another. At the very minimum the edge of the floor should be leveled as to reduce the chance of someone tripping when entering the area. Consideration should be made in adding extra padding in the dumbbell area since people have a tendency to drop the dumbbells on the floor after use rather than return them to the dumbbell rack.

Selectorized Equipment Area

When choosing the floor type for the selectorized machine area you have more options. This type of equipment is heavy and stationary. The choices for the floor in this area could be rubber, wood, or carpet. If rubber flooring is used then make sure it is epoxy-bonded to the sub-floor to form a non-porous, seamless surface. It is important that the floor is secure so gaps and bulges will not form from machine movement over time. An uneven floor presents a major trip hazard. If wood floors are used then rubber pads should be placed under the equipment frame legs to provide shock absorption and protection to the floor, as well as keep equipment from shifting from continuous use. Carpeted floors are the most common floors found in this area. Carpeted floors should be checked periodically to make sure equipment has not shifted from use and formed raised seams that could make someone to trip.

Cardiovascular Area

Typically you will find the floor in most cardio areas to be carpeted. This is fine as long as the carpet is cleaned regularly to prevent bacteria and fungus build-up resulting from sweat and dirt accumulation. The use of wood floors in the cardio area can be aesthetically pleasing, but can become a problem if the floor becomes wet from sweat or spilled water. Equipment such as treadmills have a tendency to move from their original position when people use the elevation option on wood floors. If you have a wood floor in the cardio area then it is recommended that you place rubber pads under the equipment.

Many fitness centers today are using elevated decks for the cardio area to create a more functional atmosphere for audio/visual purposes. This can pose a danger if the flooring on the platform is a solid color or texture throughout the entire area. There must be a

DIN Floor Standards

Floor Test	DIN Standard	Explanation
Shock Absorption	53% Minimum	Insufficient shock absorption causes activity-related injuries to ankle and knee joints. Correct shock absorption reduces fatigue and significantly lowers the risk of injury.
Resilience	2.3 mm minimum	Inadequate energy return in a floor causes sore ankles and a surface too "hard" for safe, strenuous activity. Excessive energy return creates a trampoline effect and potential for injury.
Surface Friction	0.5 Minimum 0.7 Maximum	Rotating and pivoting motions create strain on joints without the proper friction coefficients to minimize stress. On a friction scale of .1 (ice) to .9 (fly paper), .5–.7 is the DIN Standard.
Impact Isolation	15% Maximum	Without proper impact isolation, participants' movements can interfere with each other, creating the possibility of injury.
Rolling Load	337.6 lbs	Proper foot stability is essential to reducing foot roll-over and other injuries to participants.

clear distinction between walkways and the platform. Steps leading up to the platform must contrast in color from the rest of deck. This will help prevent people from losing their bearings and stumbling or falling.

Group Exercise Area

The floor in the group exercise room is going to see a variety of classes ranging from aerobics to martial arts. It is important that the floor be durable yet forgiving to the people using the room. By forgiving what is meant is that the floor must have proper shock absorption to help cut down on leg injuries to class participants. Most floor manufacturers use the DIN Floor Standards. DIN is short for Deutsches Institut für Normung. The DIN Standards were developed in Germany and are recognized worldwide as the best method for evaluating sports floors. The standards were developed to ensure that aerobic athletes received the greatest degree of safety and performance from a flooring surface when participating in aerobic exercise.

Equipment Positioning

The next important step to setting up a safe facility is to strategically set up your equipment. Overcrowding an area is one of the biggest risks that management can create. ACSM Guideline ACSM 10.G14 is a good rule to follow when setting up equipment in your fitness center. It states:

> The design and layout of a facility should provide at least 20 to 40 square feet for each piece of equipment. The exact amount of space to be occupied is determined by the size of each particular piece of equipment and the recommendations of the manufacturer.

Free Weight Area

The free weight area can be a complex area to safely layout because of the various sizes of benches, machines and accessories available. There will be a lot of traffic moving through this area at various times of the day so it is important that the area is organized in a way that allows users plenty of room. The free weight area should be divided into sections and particular attention should be paid to the storage of the weight plates. There should be a section designated for Olympic style flat benches and incline benches. This area should have its own set of plates and plate trees for proper storage. Weight plate trees should be evenly placed throughout the free weight area to cut down on traffic and to ensure proper storage of the plates. Make sure weight horns are clearly labeled with the poundage the tree is designed to hold. This will cut down on 45 lb plates ending up on 25 lb weight horns which could cause the weight tree to tip over.

There should be a designated dumbbell area within the free weight area. Olympic style benches are not designed for dumbbell use and improper use could lead to an injury. Adjustable benches should be placed in the area to provide a variety of settings so dumbbell users will not attempt to use Olympic benches designed specifically for barbell use. These benches should be positioned with at least three feet of space between them to reduce the chance of a dumbbell striking another person while being used.

Selectorized Equipment Area

The equipment in this area will most likely be placed in a particular order to create a circuit. Regardless of equipment order, positioning should be well thought out. There should be at least two to three feet of unobstructed space between each piece of equipment in this area. The unobstructed area should include an allowance for any moving arms that could extend into traffic areas. A good way to test the range of the equipment is to have someone get on the equipment and move through its entire range of motion while someone else walks by. Simple checks like this can greatly reduce the chance of injuries.

Cardiovascular Area

The cardiovascular section of the gym should be well thought out because there are many risks associated with the area and the equipment used in it. Electrical cord placement is one of the most common risks found in the cardio section. Cardiovascular equipment that requires electricity to function must be strategically aligned close to available outlets. New facilities have the advantage of installing outlets where they are needed. Existing facilities are sometimes victims of pre-existing outlet placement. In any case, equipment must be positioned so cords won't create an unnecessary trip hazard.

Another issue of concern in the cardio area is the placement of treadmills. The distance between treadmills is mainly a comfort issue in that most people do not want any type of interference from someone too close beside them. There should be at least one foot of space between treadmill units. A major concern with treadmills is the amount of space behind each unit. People have been and will continue to be ejected from running treadmills. The only place they have to fall is backward. This creates a major safety concern. While ACSM does not address this risk, several major treadmill manufacturers have recommended that there be at least *three feet of unobstructed space* behind each unit. There should not be any walls, windows, poles, or other pieces of equipment within three feet of the back of the treadmill, ever.

Facility Lighting

Having a low level of light in a facility is a risk because floor edges, cables, etc. can be concealed and become trip hazards.

ACSM guideline 10.G24 simply states:

> The fitness floor should have an appropriate level of light. The level of illumination should be at least 50 foot-candles at the floor surface.

If an area has dark colored carpet or black rubber flooring then the minimum of 50 foot-candles should be exceeded to the point that all traffic areas are clearly visible.

Facility Environment

A facility's environment is important for a number of reasons. First, a warm facility with poor air circulation could create condensation. Condensation can cause rubber floors to become slippery and equipment to rust and ultimately malfunction. Second, elevated temperatures in a club can add to physical demands already placed on a person from normal exercise. This could cause a person to become overheated and possibly pass out, or worse. ACSM Guideline 10.G23 recommends the following:

- Temperature: 68 to 72 degrees Fahrenheit
- Humidity: 60 percent or less
- Air Circulation: 8 to 12 exchanges per hour

Facility Signage

Once the layout of the fitness center is addressed, signs need to be strategically added throughout the entire facility. Signs can play a variety of roles in a fitness center. There are warning signs, policy and procedure signs, directional signs, etc. We will concentrate on warning signs. Warnings signs act as an additional staff member whose sole purpose is to constantly remind members and guests about facility rules and regulations. These rules and regulations are designed to create safety awareness and cut down on incidents. The following guidelines should be followed when using signs to warn members/guests about risks.

- Signs should be professionally printed. Computer printouts and handwritten signs should be avoided. Professional signs will separate themselves from printouts concerning class schedules and other club announcements.

- Signs should be posted no higher than 4'–6' off the ground to ensure that they will be easily viewed.

- Large print and borders should be used when creating a warning sign to make sure it stands out and grabs a person's attention.

- Sign sizes will vary depending on their location and the message they must relay. It is highly recommended that policy and procedure signs be at least 18" x 24" in size to ensure maximum visibility. Individual policy signs can vary in size and makeup. Decals can be used on mirrors to attract attention to rules.

Signs are important, but you don't want to clutter the facility with too many so that you lose the ability to make your point. Below are descriptions of two key signs that should be used in fitness centers and the areas where they should be placed.

Facility Rules

This sign should state a facility's policies in regards to using equipment. There should be at least one of these signs posted at the entrance to the facility, one in the selectorized equipment area, and one in the free weight area.

Spotter Sign

This sign should recommend the use of a spotter when using free weights. Remember, you should only *recommend* a spotter. If you require one then you are ultimately responsible for providing one at all times. The sign should be conspicuously posted throughout the free weight area.

There are numerous other signs that can be placed in a fitness facility. Signs can be placed in the locker rooms stating facility policies about theft, in the free weight area telling members to replace their weights when done, and so on. The ultimate goal of the signs is to help provide a safe, productive environment for people using the facility.

Overall Facility Safety

Now that we have addressed strategies in safely setting up a fitness facility we can address specific safety issues.

Supervision Guidelines

Qualified supervision is very important in cutting down on incidents in a fitness center. Staff members should be trained to periodically walk through all areas to see if anyone needs assistance. This assistance could involve spotting someone at the bench press or giving simple advice on using the correct technique. Supervision duties in a fitness facility consist of:

- Providing new member orientations on equipment use.
- Setting up basic workouts for new members.
- Modifying workouts for existing members.
- Assisting members in adjusting equipment and/or acting as a spotter.
- Patrolling locker rooms and sauna areas.
- Daily maintenance of equipment (i.e. cleaning, lubrication, etc.)
- Cleaning up barbells and dumbbells left by members.

Management should require all personnel who will deal with members on an instructional basis to go through an orientation program that will familiarize them with all equipment and areas of the facility. Equipment orientation should cover everything from seat adjustments to proper equipment operation. It is highly recommended that all instructors be certified in exercise instruction before creating programs for members or instructing them in exercise techniques.

Supervision does not merely consist of watching members exercise. It also involves watching for trouble areas on equipment. Staff members need to watch for torn upholstery, worn cables, broken plastic housing, etc. Maintenance Logs and Schedules should be utilized when carrying out these duties.

Free Weight Area

There should be several rules that are always observed in the free weight area. People performing barbell exercises should be required to use bar collars at all times. The use of bar collars will help reduce incidents in which weight plates slide off the ends of the bars, potentially landing on another person or injuring the user. Spotters should be recommended for all exercise involving heavy loads. This can range from heavy bench press moves to heavy squats. Staff members should make sure that people don't lean weight plates against walls or equipment. This can cause a trip hazard in which someone could hurt their leg or foot. The dumbbell area comes with its own set of risks that can be reduced. The racks on which the dumbbells are stored should be appropriate for the style of dumbbell used. This will ensure that people's fingers and hands won't get pinched or smashed because of improper design. Staff members should periodically check the dumbbells to make sure there is no damage or loose parts. Members should be told not to drop the dumbbells after use to avoid damaging to them. This rule would make a good sign to be posted in the area.

Selectorized Equipment Area

Probably the biggest risk found in this area is misuse of equipment. Proper orientation and instruction will help reduce that risk. However, there are still risks involved with selectorized equipment. The key components that present risks with selectorized equipment are padding, cables, and selector pins. It is important that the padding and upholstery covering it be checked periodically to ensure that there are no tears or missing pieces of pad that could expose a person's leg or arm to bare metal.

Staff members must make sure that weight stack selector pins are the correct size. If a selector pin is too short for the weight stack it is being used in, it could slip out during movement and lead to an injury. One danger in this area that often goes overlooked involves equipment with steel cables. One specific example is the lat pull-down machine. If the cable breaks on this machine then the user will be struck in the head or neck area. Many of today's equipment manufacturers have replaced the steel cable with a Kevlar belt. Routine maintenance is the key to identifying cut or frayed cables.

Cardiovascular Area Safety

The cardiovascular section is one of the most highly used areas in a fitness facility. Treadmill usage alone has increased by 720 percent over the past ten years. The treadmill is a high-risk piece of equipment because if a person falls, they are going to first hit a running belt and then be thrown backward. For these reasons, treadmill safety is very important. Earlier we discussed the importance of unobstructed space behind a treadmill. The next step in promoting treadmill safety is providing proper instruction on how to safely start and stop the treadmill. Instructions are usually found on the console of the treadmill on how to properly operate the unit. Additional operating instructions should be covered during new member orientation.

All treadmills are equipped with an emergency stop button. Newer treadmills are equipped with an emergency stop cord in addition to the stop button. The emergency stop cord is becoming a hot topic in litigation involving ejection from treadmills. Most people do not want to use the emergency stop cord for a variety of reasons. However, management must highly recommend the use of the stop cord while exercising. Some treadmill manufacturers have placed warnings on the console of the treadmill instructing the user to put on the safety cord before exercising. Some treadmills come with stop cords and no warnings. In this case, management should post signs around the area strongly recommending the use of the stop cord. Again, staff members should only *recommend* the use of the stop cord. If people are required to use the cord then management is essentially responsible for having a staff member constantly monitor the area to make sure the cords are being used.

Group Exercise Area Safety

Risks in the group exercise area mainly come from user participation. In other words, most injuries range from sprained ankles to overexertion. It is still important for class instructors to inspect equipment daily. This includes steps, rubber-bands, punching bags, etc. If defective equipment is discovered then it should be removed from use immediately and repaired or replaced. Signs should be placed in the area to help participants monitor their heart rates and rate of perceived exertion (RPE). Class instructors should be trained to spot participants who may be overexerting themselves.

Emergency Planning & Equipment

One of the key elements to having a successful fitness facility is the existence of an Incident Response Plan (IRP). An IRP is a formal plan designed to dictate duties to staff members when handling an emergency. By incident, what is meant is any situation where a person is injured or their life is in danger. This could be as simple as a sprained ankle or as complex as a fire evacuation. The plan should address it all.

Incident response plans should be developed one step at a time. You must remember that you are planning for the unpredictable. It sounds like a contradiction in words, but there is no way you can know what type of accident will happen or when it is going to happen. You must be prepared for anything. You should keep your IRP basic because the simpler it is, the more likely it will be properly carried out. Remember, your IRP should be designed to save lives and/or reduce injuries. Developing an IRP should be an ongoing project. You can always make it better. Practicing your IRP will help you make it strong and also keep it fresh in your mind and your staff members' minds.

Before you start developing your Incident Response Plan you should conduct a risk assessment to determine the most likely risks you might see. You may be at a greater risk of a fire than an earthquake, so be practical and determine what is more likely to happen in your facility setting and geographical location.

The following minimum requirements must be met in order to successfully implement an Incident Response Plan:

- A CPR and first aid certified staff member should always be on duty.

- A working and readily accessible communications system must be in place and available for use in contacting outside emergency assistance.

- Emergency phone numbers must be posted in conspicuous areas located beside all telephones.

- Detailed directions to the facility from the closest emergency service station must be located at all phones. The complete address of the facility must be included with directions.

- 1st and 2nd responders MUST be CPR/first aid certified if whole staff is not. 3rd responder is designated as outside emergency help summoned. Emergency Response Plan must be rehearsed. Rehearsals must be documented.

First Aid Kit

Most of the time, when an injury occurs, outside help is not needed. Sometimes all that is needed is an ice pack or Band-Aid. With this in mind, there must be at least one, adequately stocked First Aid Kit on the premises. In the event an accident occurs and calls for first aid, management must determine if the injured party can administer their own First Aid procedures or if they need assistance from a staff member. If help is needed from a staff member then precautions should be taken. If blood is present then any staff member helping the injured person must wear rubber gloves to avoid possible contact with blood-borne pathogens (AIDS, Hepatitis B, etc.). If medical attention, such as CPR, is needed, then the attending staff member might want to use a mouth guard. Things like this should be addressed in the Emergency Response Plan so a quick decision can be made.

- It is recommended that the following items be available in the First Aid Kit:

Rubber Gloves

Antiseptic Spray

Cotton Swabs

Band-Aids (various sizes)

Gauze Pads

Cold Packs

First Aid Cream

Blankets

Scissors

Current edition of a First Aid Manual

Automated External Defibrillator (AED)

A major issue for discussion today is whether or not fitness facilities should have an Automated External Defibrillator on the premises. An AED is a device used to administer an electric shock through the chest wall to the heart. Built-in computers assess the patient's heart rhythm, judge whether defibrillation is needed, and then administer the shock. Audible and/or visual prompts guide the user through the process. At the time of this printing, New Jersey, Michigan, Illinois, and Rhode Island are the only states close to implementing laws that would require fitness centers to install AEDs.

AEDs are important because they strengthen the chances of survival. They can restore a normal heart rhythm in victims of sudden cardiac arrest. New, portable AEDs enable more people to respond to a medical emergency that requires defibrillation. When a person suffers a sudden cardiac arrest, their chance of survival decreases by 7% to 10% for each minute that passes without defibrillation. An AED is safe to use by anyone who's been trained to operate it. Studies have shown the devices to be 90% sensitive (able 90% of the time to detect a rhythm that should be defibrillated) and 99% specific (able 99% of the time to recommend not shocking when defibrillation is not indicated). Because of the wide variety of situations in which it will typically be used, the AED is designed with multiple safeguards and warnings before any energy is released. The AED is programmed to deliver a shock only when it has detected VF. However, potential dangers are associated with AED use. That's why training—including safety and maintenance—is important.

Member Issues

Orientation/Supervision

It is very important that all novice lifters be required to go through an orientation program to help them learn the basics of using exercise equipment. Simple things like seat adjustment, weight selection, accessory bar selection, etc., can be critical in providing a person with a foundation for safe exercise.

Personnel Qualifications

One of the most prevalent risks found in facilities today is the lack of qualified personnel. Qualified personnel are certified in safety techniques and procedures and, if applicable, sport-specific instruction. Management should create a job description for each position in the facility. This description should dictate what certifications should be obtained to perform the job and state time limits for obtaining these certifications.

CPR Certification

It is recommended that at least 50% of all staff members be certified in CPR. If this percentage has not yet been obtained then it is very important that at least one CPR-certified staff member be on duty at all times. In the event that an unforeseen situation arises and calls for immediate medical attention, proper procedures can be quickly and correctly administered by a qualified staff member. CPR certification prepares staff members for dealing with heart attacks, strokes, diabetic emergencies, epileptic seizures, and complications arising from asthma.

First Aid Certification

It is recommended that at least 50% of all staff members be certified in first aid, or at least one first aid certified staff member be on duty at all times. In the event that an unforeseen situation occurs and calls for immediate medical assistance, proper procedures can be quickly and correctly administered. There is a high probability that first aid techniques will be needed to correct the situation. First aid certification prepares staff members for bone, joint, and muscle injuries (very common in health clubs), heat-related injuries, bleeding, and moving and rescuing victims.

Exercise Certification

It is recommended that all trainers and instructors be certified in exercise instruction through a nationally accredited organization. An accredited organization is one that requires an initial exam be passed (no take home exams) and then certification can only be maintained through yearly re-testing and/or continuing education credits (CEC). Exercise certification provides insight into the different needs for different people. Certification keeps trainers and instructors in touch with the ever-changing fitness industry. Certification teaches trainers the latest in techniques, nutrition, etc.

If not already in existence, facility management should begin keeping personnel records that indicate what certifications are held by each staff member and indicate the renewal date for each certification.

Facility Documentation

Record-keeping is very important in day-to-day operations because it helps ensure that policies and procedures are strictly adhered to by management. Records should be kept for all activities offered at the facility and any maintenance performed on equipment. In the event that a lawsuit arises from an injury/accident, record keeping could be used as proof in a court of law showing that management acted responsibly in carrying out day-to-day operations. Documentation includes:

Liability Waivers

Liability Waivers, if properly written, could release a facility from harm in the event an accident or injury has occurred and the facility has been accused of negligence in a lawsuit. Waivers must be created with the input of an attorney. More and more courts are upholding the validity of waivers today, but waivers must be written in favor of the facility and its staff. All new members and guests must be required to sign a waiver of liability prior to being allowed to use the facility. Waivers should be kept on file for at least two years after a member has left the facility.

Health History Form

Health history forms, or PAR-Q forms, are designed to discover any pre-existing health problems or conditions experienced by a new member, prior to their use of the facility. Health history forms should require a new member to disclose all known injuries and health-related conditions that exist. This includes any family health history conditions. If there is a suspect condition that exists then a doctor's release note should be obtained before they are cleared to exercise in the facility.

Incident Reports

Incident reports are a means for documenting circumstances leading up to an accident or injury and the procedures taken by staff members to correct the situation. Pre-formatted, blank reports must be kept on file at the facility at all times. All managers must know how to properly fill out an injury report. The manager on duty must complete the incident report. If there are any witnesses to the accident, have them complete the witness report. A copy of the incident report should be sent immediately to the facility's insurance carrier.

It is imperative that all staff members understand the importance of reporting any incident, no matter how small the incident might seem. Even if the injured person says they are "okay," the incident must be reported anyway.

Maintenance Schedules

Maintenance schedules are designed to assign and dictate duties to staff members involving basic cleaning and lubricating procedures on exercise equipment. Maintenance schedules should clearly state what pieces of equipment should be cleaned and lubricated and the frequency that this should happen.

Equipment Maintenance Logs

Maintenance logs are a means of documenting major repairs performed on exercise equipment. Maintenance Logs can help provide proof that management has followed the correct procedures in repairing equipment. The document should indicate who performed the work, what repairs were made, what type of parts were used (factory or generic), and what date the work was completed.

Equipment Maintenance

As advanced as today's exercise equipment has become, there is still a chance that a piece of equipment in the facility currently has some type of defective part. Whether the part was defective at the time of shipping or has become defective through heavy use is a fact that must be determined by facility management. This is why maintenance logs and maintenance schedules are so important. If management can prove that it inspected and serviced the equipment consistently and according to manufacturer's standards, then there is a much better chance of being exonerated in the event an incident happens.

To get maximum results from exercise equipment, daily and weekly maintenance routines must be followed. The frequency of maintenance needed on exercise equipment is determined by many factors that include the following: 1) temperature, 2) humidity, 3) use, 4) ventilation, and 5) shielding and friction. There are two types of maintenance that must be performed on equipment. They are *external* and *internal* maintenance. One is just as important as the other, so to make sure that neither type is overlooked maintenance schedules should be used. Cleaning duties should be assigned to individual staff members through the maintenance schedules so that staff members will always know their respon-sibilities. The schedules should be posted or located in a binder so that staff members can view them before beginning their daily maintenance duties.

Most equipment manufacturers today have some type of product liability insurance. You should ask your sales rep if his/her company offers it. When a machine does break down you should immediately take it out of service. Move it off the floor if possible, or at the very least, put a sign on it stating "Out of Service, Do Not Use." A good way to check equipment for defects is to use it yourself. Make sure you pay close attention to the heavily used equipment as these machines will break down the quickest.

Locker Rooms

Locker rooms have two high-risk areas that are often overlooked. They are as follows:

Non-Slip Flooring

Non-slip flooring should be placed in all traffic areas where water could get on the floor. Generally, this is the shower area. Most people step out of the shower to dry off, thus causing water to drip on the floor. Vinyl matting (waffle tile) is highly recommended for these areas because it keeps a person out of direct contact with the tile floor and allows the floor to dry faster when water hits it. Vinyl matting also cuts down on the buildup of bacteria.

Ground-Fault Circuit Interrupters

Ground-Fault Circuit Interrupters (GFCI) are circuit breakers located right on an electrical socket. GFCI's are designed to help prevent electric shock if a person were drying their hair and accidentally stepped in a puddle of water. If your facility is less than five years old, GFCI's are probably already installed. If you don't then it is highly recommended that you have GFCI's installed in all areas where there is a potential water/electricity mix. Ground-Fault Circuit Interrupters are inexpensive and easy to install and their use could prevent a tragic accident.

References

ACSM's Health/Fitness Facility Standards and Guidelines.

American Heart Association, www.americanheart.org, 2003.

On-Site Fitness, March/April 1999.

Chapter 28

Title IX Fundamentals

A complete understanding of the requirements of the law is the key to risk management when dealing with gender equity issues in sports.

Barbara Osborne

Title IX of the Education Amendments of 1972 was passed by Congress on June 23, 1972. Section 901(a) provides:

> *No person in the United States shall, on the basis of sex, be excluded from participation in, be denied the benefits of, or be subjected to discrimination under any education program or activity receiving Federal financial assistance.*

This simple sentence represents landmark Civil Rights legislation mandating equal opportunity for girls in educational endeavors. Although Title IX was enacted to address gender inequities in math, science, and other educational disciplines, it is most popularly known for creating opportunities for girls in athletics. In 1972, only one in twenty-seven high school girls participated in varsity athletics—now almost one in two participates. At the intercollegiate level, participation has expanded from under 30,000 female varsity athletes to over 150,000. As participation levels for female athletes have increased tremendously, it is important to note that the number of males participating in school and university sports has also increased (although not as dramatically) during this time period.

Title IX has been in effect for over forty years, and it is estimated that eighty percent of schools do not comply with the law. Although tremendous gains have been made for girls to participate in school-sponsored sports, discrimination still exists and equity has not yet been attained. In this chapter, the fundamental requirements of Title IX will be reviewed to provide a solid foundation for compliance with the law and to eliminate the persistent misconceptions related to this legislation.

Fundamentals of Title IX

Title IX covers three areas of activity within educational institutions: employment, treatment of students, and admissions. In order for Title IX to apply, the following three things must be present:

1. A claim of discrimination on the basis of sex
2. An educational program or activity
3. The educational institution receives Federal financial assistance.

1975 Regulations

As almost every educational institution in the country receives some sort of Federal financial assistance; the legislation is far-reaching. However, it was not known that Title IX would regulate athletics participation until the Department of Health, Education, and Welfare (the predecessor to the current Department of Education) promulgated Regulations for compliance with Title IX in 1975. Specific requirements for interscholastic, intercollegiate, intramural and club athletics programs are covered by the regulations concerned with the treatment of students. These regulations required:

1. Athletically related financial assistance be allocated in proportion to the numbers of male and female students participating in intercollegiate athletics,

2. All other benefits, opportunities, and treatment afforded participants of each sex are equivalent, and

3. The interests and abilities of students are effectively accommodated to the extent necessary to provide equal athletic opportunity for members of both sexes.

It is important to note that **all** three of these requirements are to be fulfilled in order to achieve compliance with the law. The first two requirements are fairly simple to understand. The first requirement, proportionate financial aid, is simple mathematics. For example — if 60% of the athletes at an educational institution are male and 40% of the athletes are female, then 60% of the athletically related financial assistance (scholarships) must be awarded to the males and 40% to the females.

The Regulations included a list of program factors that should be taken into account to determine compliance with the second requirement — that benefits, opportunities and treatment afforded to participants of each sex are equivalent. Popularly known as the "laundry list," these factors include:

1. Whether the selection of sports and levels of competition effectively accommodate the interest and abilities of members of both sexes

2. Provision of equipment and supplies

3. Scheduling of games and practice time

4. Travel and per diem allowance

5. Opportunity to receive coaching and academic tutoring

6. Assignment and compensation of coaches and tutors

7. Provision of locker rooms, practice and competitive facilities

8. Provision of medical training services

9. Provision of housing and dining facilities and services

10. Publicity

This list should not be considered comprehensive or exhaustive. The Regulations permit the Director of the Office for Civil Rights to consider other factors, such as recruitment of student athletes and provision of other support services, in determining equal opportunity.

The third requirement — that the interests and abilities of students are effectively accommodated — is the most vague and consequently least understood of the Title IX Regulations. By July 1978, the Office of Civil Rights (OCR) had received nearly 100 complaints alleging discrimination in athletics against more than 50 institutions of higher education. In attempting to investigate these complaints, and to answer questions from colleges and universities, it was determined that further guidance on what constitutes compliance with the law was necessary.

1979 Policy Interpretation

In 1979, the Department of Health, Education, and Welfare issued a Policy Interpretation specifically targeted at intercollegiate athletics departments. The Policy Interpretation was intended to clarify the meaning of "equal opportunity" in intercollegiate athletics, as well as to provide guidance to assist institutions in determining whether any disparities which may exist between men's and women's programs are justifiable and nondiscriminatory. The Policy Interpretation is divided into the same three components as the 1975 Regulations: compliance in financial assistance, compliance in other program areas, and compliance in meeting the interests and abilities of male and female students. Guidance in the first two areas is fairly straightforward, however, the Three-Prong Test introduced in the 1979 Policy Interpretation to explain whether colleges and universities meet the third requirement of effective accommodation has spawned significant controversy.

Under the Three-Prong Test (also known as the Effective Accommodation Test), a college or university must satisfy one of the following three standards in order to prove compliance:

1. Substantial proportionality measured by comparing the percentage of undergraduates enrolled to the percentage of student-athletes by sex,

2. History and continuing practice of program expansion which is responsive to the developing interest and abilities of the underrepresented sex, or

3. Demonstrate that the present program has fully and effectively accommodated the interests and abilities of the members of the underrepresented sex.

Although the 1979 Policy Interpretation was targeted at intercollegiate athletics, the general principles also apply to club, intramural and interscholastic athletics programs that are covered by the regulations.

2003 Clarification Letter

The US Department of Education issued a Clarification Letter on July 11, 2003, reinforcing that the Three-Prong Test was still the only way to prove that a school is effectively accommodating participation opportunities for Title IX compliance. The Clarification Letter is significant in that it is the first time that the practice of cutting men's teams to achieve proportionality rather than adding women's teams to satisfy the first prong was expressly cited as a disfavored practice. The Clarification Letter further promised that Title IX enforcement would be consistent across all Department of Education regional offices, and that educational efforts regarding Title IX would be increased.

Title IX Enforcement

Title IX was meant to be self-enforcing, meaning that each institution is responsible for complying with the law. There are two additional ways to stimulate enforcement of Title IX—an administrative option or through private litigation.

Administrative enforcement. The administrative process of Title IX enforcement is set forth in 88.71 of the Title IX regulation. According to the regulation, enforcement may be initiated by periodic compliance reviews of colleges and universities selected by the Department of Education, or as a result of a valid, written and timely complaint alleging discrimination on the basis of sex at an institution receiving Federal funding. The Department has 90 days to conduct an investigation and inform the institution (and the complainant, if applicable) of its findings. If the investigation indicates that an institution is in compliance, the Department states this, and the case is closed.

For those institutions found not in compliance, the Department outlines the violations found and has an additional 90 days to resolve violations by obtaining a voluntary compliance agreement from the institution. Although the legislation required secondary schools to be in compliance by July 21, 1976, and for colleges and universities to be in compliance by July 21, 1978, the Office of Civil Rights has chosen to negotiate compliance rather than withdraw federal funding. The goal of negotiation is agreement on steps the institution will take to achieve compliance. To be acceptable, a plan must describe the manner in which institutional resources will be used to correct the violation, and specify timetables for reaching interim goals and full compliance. When agreement is reached, the Department notifies the institution that its plan is acceptable. The Department then is obligated to review periodically the implementation of the plan.

In theory, if an institution is found in noncompliance and voluntary compliance attempts are unsuccessful, the formal process leading to termination of Federal assistance will begin. Although these procedures, which include the opportunity for a hearing before an administrative law judge, are specified at 45 CFR 80.8–80.11 and 45 CFR Part 81, no institution has ever been denied Federal funding because of noncompliance with Title IX.

Private litigation. An individual that believes he or she is being discriminated against on the basis of sex may choose to file a lawsuit against the institution. In 1979, the Supreme Court held in *Canon v. University of Chicago,* 441 U.S. 677, that although the legislation did not expressly empower an individual to bring a Title IX lawsuit, there was an implied private right to do so.

Legal Developments and Challenges to Title IX

The 1975 Regulations and the 1979 Policy Interpretation provide the foundation for Title IX compliance. However, over the years, legislative and legal challenges have also shaped the law. This section will chronologically review the most significant challenges to Title IX.

Through the mid-1970s, more than a dozen attempts were made by legislators to invalidate or modify Title IX. In 1974, Senator John Tower proposed an amendment to exclude revenue-generating college sports from the scope of Title IX coverage. The Tower Amendment was strongly supported by the leadership of the NCAA. Congress resoundingly rejected the proposal, deferring to the expertise and judgment of the Department of Health, Education, and Welfare, which was concurrently drafting the 1975 Regulations for compliance with Title IX. Unhappy with the failure of the Tower Amendment, and the subsequent regulation of intercollegiate athletics in the 1975 Regulations, the NCAA filed suit against the Office of Civil Rights in 1978. In *NCAA v. Califano,* the NCAA claimed that the Department of Health, Education, and Welfare had exceeded its regulatory authority by issuing the 1975 Regulations.

In 1984, the Supreme Court rendered Title IX inapplicable to athletics programs. In *Grove City College v. Bell,* the Court held that only programs that specifically received federal funds must be Title IX compliant. Prior to this decision, it was assumed that if an educational institution received federal funding, all programs run by that institution must comply with Title IX. In this decision, the Supreme Court narrowed the scope of Title IX regulation by mandating that the specific program must receive federal funding, not just the overall institution. For the next four years, most athletics programs ignored Title IX, and some schools eliminated girls programs that had been added. In 1988, Congress overruled the Supreme Court decision (and a veto by President Ronald Reagan) by passing the Civil Rights Restoration Act. The Civil Rights Restoration Act established that Title IX should be interpreted through the institution-wide, rather than the program-specific, approach. All educational programs, including athletics, were required to be Title IX compliant of any program within the institution received federal funding.

In 1992, the Supreme Court made it much more attractive for an individual to file a Title IX lawsuit by allowing compensatory damages to be paid. In *Franklin v. Gwinnett County Public Schools,* the Supreme Court definitively addressed a conflict among the Circuits by unanimously holding that compensatory damages can be awarded when intentional discrimination is established. Prior to this decision, an individual could receive declaratory judgment—a declaration by the Court of the rights of the plaintiff and the institution—or an injunction that would force the institution to stop discriminatory practices. Money was awarded only to cover attorney fees. This case established that all available remedies, including compensatory and punitive damages, could be awarded when intentional discrimination is established.

For four years, from 1993 to 1997, the case of *Cohen v. Brown University,* held the attention of university presidents and athletics administrators. In 1991, Brown University cut four athletics teams in an attempt to decrease its athletics budget. In a class action suit, female athletes received a preliminary injunction reinstating the women's teams. The case continued through two appeals with the First Circuit clearly outlining the requirements for Title IX compliance in their decision. Although Brown University offered one of the broadest athletics programs in the country, the court found non-compliance. The decision reinforced the 1975 Regulations, and emphasized the Three-Prong Test of the 1979 Policy Interpretation as the standard for determining compliance. Although the NCAA, athletics conferences and individual institutions lobbied for the Supreme Court to review the case, the Supreme Court denied certiorari because there were no conflicting decisions among the Circuit Courts.

During this time period, Congress strengthened their resolve to eliminate sex discrimination in athletics. In 1995, the Equity in Athletics Disclosure Act was passed, requiring schools to provide data about participation rates and funding of their male and female athletics programs. The Act requires institutions to file reports with the Office of Civil Rights and to have the reports available on campus to those who inquire from the general public.

Although the courts, like institutions, have paid the most attention to the proportionality requirement of the Three-Prong Test, litigation in the late 1990s validated the second and third prong of the test in proving compliance with Title IX. In *Pederson v. Louisiana State University,* the District Court judge downplayed the strict proportionality standard and focused on whether LSU complied with the second or third prongs of the test. Unfortunately for LSU, the court held that the university did not produce any credible evidence to establish the interest and abilities of its student population, nor did it show a history of expansion of athletics opportunities for female athletes. However, in 1998, the court held in *Boucher v. Syracuse University* that Syracuse was in compliance with Title IX by proving a history of continuing expansion of opportunities of the underrepresented sex.

Although much of the significant litigation concerns colleges and universities, Title IX also applies to scholastic sports. School districts have been under attack by community groups and individual plaintiffs, and most have settled their claims with promises and plans to create equitable facilities and policies for male and female high school athletes. One of the most notable cases is *Communities for Equity v. Michigan High School Athletic Association*. A class action suit was filed against the Michigan High School Athletic Association (MHSAA) claiming discrimination against female student-athletes because girls' sports seasons were scheduled at less advantageous times of the academic year than boys' sports. In Michigan high schools, the girls' sports of basketball, volleyball, tennis, soccer, Lower Peninsula golf, and Lower Peninsula swimming were scheduled during non-traditional seasons, while the boys' sports competed during the traditional season. The MHSAA rationalized this treatment by citing lack of facilities and qualified coaches for male and female athletes to both compete during traditional seasons. The federal district court held that the current NSHAA sports scheduling system violated the female student-athletes' equal protection rights as well as Title IX and enjoined the MHSAA from continuing its current scheduling system. The MHSAA was ordered to create a plan that would equitably distribute the benefits and burdens between male and female athletes. Although the MHSAA plan that was approved by the court still remained inequitable—girls had fewer sports to choose from in each athletics season and there were fewer post-season tournaments for girls—the court denied the plaintiffs' motion for reconsideration and ordered the MSHAA to implement its plan.

Coinciding with the 30th Anniversary of Title IX, and fulfilling the campaign promises of President George W. Bush to eliminate Affirmative Action and racial quotas, the Secretary of Education, Rod Paige, created a commission to investigate whether Title IX is fair to both boys and girls. Called the Commission on Opportunity in Athletics, a panel of 15 men and women, primarily representing the interests of major NCAA Division I athletics programs, was assembled to hear testimony on whether Title IX created opportunity for men and women. Fact-finding was directed by the staff of the US Department of Education through four Town Hall meetings across the United States. The Commission then filed a final report on February 28, 2003, with several recommendations. Unhappy with what they perceived as a politically-tainted process and the Majority Report, Commissioners Julie Foudy and Donna de Varona filed a Minority Report voicing their concerns and providing additional information regarding participation and opportunities for both boys and girls under Title IX that had been ignored by the Majority Report. Secretary Paige accepted both reports, and publicly declared that the US Department of Education would not act on any recommendation that did not have unanimous support. The Department of Education continues to enforce Title IX based on the 1975 Regulations and 1979 Policy Interpretation.

The *Mercer v. Duke University* (2002) case addressed the seldom-discussed "contact sports exemption" included in the Title IX Regulations. Heather Sue Mercer was a high school kicker that tried out as a walk-on for the Duke football team. Although Duke had a liberal walk-on policy (essentially, no one was ever cut), Mercer was required to "try-out" for the team. She served as a team manager for the fall 1994 season, attended practices, practiced kicking, participated in fitness training and participated in spring training through spring 1997. After kicking the winning field goal in a spring intra-squad scrimmage, Mercer was told that she was on the team. However, after intense media coverage among other events, Mercer was told by the coaching staff that she had "no right" to be on the team and to leave.

After this abrupt removal from the team, Mercer filed a discrimination suit in 1997 against Duke University under Title IX. Technically, the coaching staff was correct in informing Mercer that she had no legal right to participate on a varsity football team. Title IX acknowledges that there are physical differences between men and women and allows sex-segregated teams. The contact sport exemption allows schools to prevent a person of one sex from participating on a team of the opposite sex in a contact sport. The trial court dismissed the case because Title IX did not grant Mercer the right to participate in a male-only contact sport, but the Fourth Circuit held that where a university permits a member of the opposite sex to try out for a single sex team in a contact sport, the university is subject to Title IX and cannot subsequently discriminate against the athlete on the basis of her sex. Although the decision was a "win" for Mercer, some schools have chosen to limit their risk under Title IX by instituting policies that forbid opposite sex athletes from trying out for any single-sex contact sport team. This policy may be effective for private schools, but public schools will still have to address equal protection claims if their policies are not substantially related to an important educational purpose.

Title IX and Reverse Discrimination

Title IX is often the cited scapegoat for schools that choose to eliminate men's sports rather than reallocate current funding or seek additional funding sources. Schools that claim to have cut men's teams to comply with Title IX have often been the target of litigation claiming reverse discrimination.

One of the most recent cases making the reverse discrimination claim is *Miami University Wrestling Club, et al., v. Miami University, et al.* In 1994, the University conducted a self-study which found that although females made up more than half of the student population, only 29% of student-athletes were women. To address this inequity, four women's varsity athletics teams were added. In reviewing their progress in 1997, the University found that the female proportion of the student body had increased to 55%, while female student-athletes were still only at 42% of the athlete population. Further inquiry noted that there was substantial female interest in equestrian, crew, golf, lacrosse and water polo, so the University could not claim compliance with the second or third prongs of the Three-Prong Test. The University further determined that they lacked funds to create additional women's teams, so they chose to eliminate men's varsity golf, soccer, tennis and wrestling. Male student-athletes from these teams sued the University in 1999 claiming that the elimination of these programs violated the Equal Protection Clause and Title IX. The federal district court granted the University's motion to dismiss, and the Sixth Circuit upheld the decision.

Every claim of reverse discrimination has ultimately been unsuccessful (see *Kelley v. Board of Trustees, Univ. of Illinois; Chalenor v. Univ.of N.D.; Neal v. California State Univ. at Bakersfield; Harper v. Board of Regents; Boulahanis v. Board of Regents of Illinois State Univ.*) Title IX is civil rights legislation that was enacted to redress past discrimination. It does not protect the over-represented sex. Although cutting men's teams does not provide opportunity for women, it is a legal prerogative of an institution to make the decision to do so in order to achieve proportionality and therefore Title IX compliance. Although adding more women's sports would be a preferred practice, not all schools are able to reallocate current funds or find additional funding to support additional sports. Consider the following example: a school has boys' lacrosse and hockey, but no girls' teams, although there is considerable interest. The school chooses to eliminate boys hockey and reallocate those funds to create a girls lacrosse team. The male hockey players are understandably upset, but so are the female hockey players who are interested and will never have a team. The girls that are now able to play varsity lacrosse have an opportunity that is fairer than the initial situation. Resources for boys' sports have historically been available because girls were denied the opportunity to utilize these resources. When schools cannot or chose not to reallocate current funding to support equitable boys and girls programs, eliminating boys program is a legal alternative.

Organizations have also filed lawsuits claiming that Title IX discriminates against men. In 2002, the National Wrestling Coaches Association (NWCA) and other affiliated organizations filed suit against the US Department of Education claiming that Title IX regulations and interpretations unlawfully authorized intentional discrimination (*National Wrestling Coaches Association v. U.S. Department of Education*, 2003). The lawsuit claimed that the Three Part Test intentionally discriminates against men because men are more interested in sport than women, but are afforded fewer athletic opportunities than women based on their interest. Several procedural claims were also advanced that the rules were not properly developed or authorized. The lawsuit was dismissed in a 119-page decision providing a detailed and comprehensive review of the statutory and regulatory framework of Title IX, including the cases that have defined Title IX. The NWCA claim that men are more interested in sport than women is constitutionally impermissible. More recently, the advocacy group Equity in Athletics, Inc. filed a lawsuit in response to James Madison University's decision to eliminate 7 men's and 3 women's varsity athletics teams against the U.S. Department of Education, claiming that the Three-Prong Test violated equal protection, (*Equity in Athletics, Inc. v. Department of Education*, 2011). The case was dismissed, and an appeal to the Supreme Court was denied.

Additional Causes of Action under Title IX

In addition to protecting against sex discrimination in providing opportunities and treatment of student-athletes, several additional causes of action are recognized under Title IX that should be fully considered in risk management planning. Sexual harassment is discrimination based on sex, and is therefore prohibited. Schools must have policies in place to educate students and employees about sexual harassment, and establish procedures for reporting, investigating, addressing and preventing incidence of sexual harassment. Similarly, acts of sexual violence are extreme acts of sexual harassment, and schools may be liable for acts of peer sexual assault or rape, particularly when the perpetrator is a recruited student-athlete with known aggressive tendencies (see *Simpson v. Univ. of Colorado*, 2007; *Williams v. Bd. of Regents of Univ. Sys. Of Ga.*, 2007). Sexual orientation discrimination is also a potential sexual harassment claim if the unwanted behavior is related to a failure to conform to gender stereotypes (*Pratt v. Indian River Cent. Sch. Dist.*, 2011). Pregnancy is perhaps the ultimate sex-related condition, and discrimination against student-athletes who are pregnant is also prohibited by the Title IX Regulations (34 C.F.R. § 106.40(b)). Under Title IX, pregnant athletes need to be treated like any other athlete with a temporary medical condition—they can't be kicked off the team, prevented from dressing for games, or prevented from traveling to games, *unless* that is the same way that other athletes who are medically unable to play are treated. Finally, schools cannot retaliate against students or employees who complain about inequities (*Jackson v. Birmingham Board of Education*, 2005).

In My Opinion

Common sense dictates that athletics directors should operate under principles of fairness, and obey the spirit as well as the letter of the law. In 1991, the NCAA Gender Equity Task force developed a statement that illustrates this concept of fairness: "an athletics program is gender equitable when either the men's or women's sports program would be pleased to accept as its own the overall program of the other gender."

Athletics programs should be periodically reviewed to determine if male and female athletes are being treated fairly. Title IX risk management guidelines are published by several organizations, including the Women's Sports Foundation, National Association of Girls and Women in Sports, and the National Women's Law Center. Institutions can create their own assessment instrument based on the 1975 Regulations, paying particular attention to the "laundry list." Schools should also keep records to assist with evaluation of their athletics programs relative to all three portions of the Three-Prong Test outlined in the 1979 Policy Interpretation to show compliance with the law. Likewise, schools should utilize an accounting system that makes it simple to access figures for EADA reports. Above all, every effort should be made to preserve athletics opportunities for all athletes through efficient fiscal management and fair operational policies.

References

Legislation

Civil Rights Restoration Act, 20 U.S.C. s. 1687 (1988).

Policy Interpretation of Title IX, 44 Fed. Reg. 71,413 (1979).

Regulations to Interpret Title IX, 34 C.F.R. Part 106 (1975).

Title IX of the Education Amendments, 20 U.S.C. s. 1681–1688 (1972).

Cases

Boucher v. Syracuse University, 164 F. 3d 113 (2d Cir. 1998).

Boulahanis v. Board of Regents of Illinois State Univ., 198 F.3d 633 (7th Cir. 1999).

Canon v. University of Chicago, 441 U.S. 677 (1979).

Chalenor v. Univ.of N.D., 142 F. Supp. 2d 1154 (Dist. N.D. 2000).

Cohen v. Brown University, 991 F.2d 888 (1st Cir. 1993); 101 F.3d. 155 (1st Cir. 1996); 520 U.S. 1186 (1997).

Communities for Equity v. Michigan High School Athletic Association, 2003 U.S. Dist. 2872 (W.D. Mich. 2003).

Equity In Athletics, Inc. v. Dep't of Educ., 639 F.3d 91(3d Cir Mar. 8, 2011).

Franklin v. Gwinnett County Public Schools, 112 S. Ct. 1028 (1992).

Grove City College v. Bell, 465 U.S. 555 (1984).

Harper v. Board of Regents, 35 F. Supp. 2d 1118 (Dist. Ill. 1999).

Jackson v. Birmingham Board of Education, 544 U.S. 167 (2005).

Kelley v. Board of Trustees, Univ. of Illinois, 35 F. 3d 265 (7th Cir. 1994).

Mercer v. Duke University, 181 F. supp. 2d 525 (D. NC 2001); 50 Fed. Appx. 643 (4th Cir. 2002).

Miami University Wrestling Club, et al., v. Miami University, et al., 302 F.3d 608 (6th Cir. 2002).

NCAA v. Califano, 444 F. Supp. 425 (D. Kan. 1978) rev'd & remanded, 622 F. 2d 1362 (10th Cir. 1980).

National Wrestling Coaches Association v. US Department of Education, Civ. No. 02-0072 EGS.

Neal v. California State Univ. at Bakersfield, 198 F. 3d 763 (9th Cir. 1999).

Pederson v. Louisiana State University, 912 F. Supp. 892 (M.D.La. 1996); 213 F. 3d 858.

Pratt v. Indian River Cent. Sch. Dist., 2011 U.S. Dist. LEXIS 32596.

Simpson v. Univ. of Colorado, 2007 U.S. App. LEXIS 21478 (10th Cir. 2007).

Williams v. Bd. of Regents of Univ. Sys. Of Ga., 477 F.3d 1282 (11th Cir. 2007).

Chapter 29

Accommodating Individuals with Disabilities in Regular Sport Programs

The Department of Justice has indicated that changes in sport rules must be made to accommodate otherwise qualified individuals with disabilities.

Julian U. Stein

The Americans with Disabilities Act (ADA) "establishes a clear and comprehensive federal prohibition of discrimination against persons with disabilities in private sector employment and ensures equal access for persons with disabilities to public accommodations, public services, transportation, and telecommunications" (National Easter Seal Society). ADA prohibits discrimination against otherwise qualified individuals with disabilities in all programs and activities, including physical education, recreation, and sport—for example, an individual with a disability can be cut from a team because of insufficient ability, but not because of a disability.

Otherwise qualified individuals with disabilities cannot be denied benefits of, excluded from, or discriminated against because of their disability. Whenever and wherever possible, otherwise qualified individuals with disabilities must be included in and integrated into regular programs and activities, not relegated to special or segregated programs and activities, unless not otherwise qualified for regular programs and activities. Program sponsors are expected to make necessary accommodations that are readily accessible and readily available so otherwise qualified individuals with disabilities can participate and compete—separate but equal is not good enough! (Stein 1993).

Public Accommodations

A major section of the ADA deals with *places of public accommodation*. Of the twelve areas included as places of public accommodation, ten deal directly with or have implications for recreation, physical activities, and/or sport. Public accommodations include places of lodging, places serving food or drink, places of exhibition or entertainment, places of public gathering, sales or rental establishments, stations specified for public transportation, places of displays or collections, places of recreation, places of education, social center establishments, and places of exercise or recreation (Stein 1993).

The Department of Justice, the federal agency responsible for enforcing sections of ADA related to public accommodations, has indicated sport playing rules are included under ADA (Personal telephone call with Department of Justice Staff via its hotline). However, rule changes can neither alter the basic nature, structure, or integrity of a sport, give individuals with disabilities unfair advantages, nor place non-disabled participants at a disadvantage. Changes should be designed so sport rules themselves are not discriminatory, but instead provide otherwise qualified individuals with disabilities opportunities to participate and compete actively in the sport.

People with Disabilities Defined

Discrimination affects all categories of people with disabilities, including:

- Individuals with mobility impairments, sensory conditions, mental retardation, and other physical and mental impairments—typical and traditional categorical disabilities.

- Individuals who have hidden disabilities, such as cancer, diabetes, epilepsy, heart disease, or mental illness, including people with HIV.

- Individuals who have a history of disability but are no longer disabled, such as a person who was mis-classified as being mentally retarded, or an individual who has been rehabilitated from a mental illness, emotional condition, or physical disability.

- Individuals who do not have a disability, but who are treated or perceived by others as having a disability (Scott 1990).

Definitions of people with disabilities found in ADA are identical to definitions in Section 504 of the Rehabilitation Act of 1973. This means of identifying individuals with disabilities has been known and utilized for well over thirty years.

Sport Rules Discriminate

In addition to ADA, legal responsibilities (Individuals with Disabilities Education Act [IDEA], Section 504 of the Rehabilitation Act of 1973, Amateur Sport Act of 1978), and ethical values require every consideration be given to including individuals with disabilities in *all* school programs and community activities to the maximum extent possible. Sport at all levels, field/play/sport days, youth, club, recreation, intramural/extramural, interscholastic, intercollegiate are important activities in both educational and community programs.

Playing rules in many sports blatantly discriminate against individuals with various disabilities, not only prohibiting them from participating, but excluding many from opportunities even to try out for teams;[1] coaches in wheelchairs, on crutches, or with walkers are often barred from playing fields (Associated Press 1992)!

---

1. For example, prior to rule changes in 1976, stimulated by provisions of Section 504 of the Rehabilitation Act of 1973, individuals with any kind of prosthetic device (hand, arm, foot, leg) were by rule barred from interscholastic football. In addition, during this same period, accommodations to enable individuals with disabilities to participate could not be found in rule books of any sport at any level.

Rule Changes during the 1970s

During the mid-1970s, stimulated by provisions of Section 504 of the Rehabilitation Act of 1973, rules of several interscholastic sports were modified to enable athletes with disabilities to participate and compete right along with non-disabled classmates, teammates, and opponents. *Basic principles governing such modifications were to make necessary accommodations so playing rules were not discriminatory, while at the same time not giving unfair advantages to participants with disabilities and placing non-disabled competitors at disadvantages* (Stein 1995).

Representative of such rule changes by the National Federation of State High School Associations for interscholastic sport[2] included (Stein 1995):

FOOTBALL: an Individual with Either an Arm or Leg Prosthesis May Participate. However, Such Prosthetic Devices must Be Approved by the Individual's State High School Athletic/activities Association.

Teams consisting of deaf players are permitted to use a sideline drum for keying offensive plays.

WRESTLING: an Individual with Limb Amputations May Wrestle with or Without a Prosthetic Device. However, If an Individual Is to Wrestle While Wearing a Prosthetic Device, Weigh-in Has to Be While Wearing the Prosthesis.

It is illegal for a sighted wrestler to move behind a wrestler who is blind without maintaining contact before and during the move to the rear. Nothing in the change requires wrestlers to *lock* in the standing position.

SOCCER: an Individual May Participate While Wearing an Arm or Leg Prosthesis.

TRACK/CROSS COUNTRY: a Runner Who Is Blind May Compete in Track Events (Middle Distance and Distance) and Cross Country with a Sighted Guide (With or Without a *tether*). Nothing in this Accommodation Requires the Sighted Guide to Be a Teammate, or Even a Student in School. All Rules Governing Guide Runners in Specific Competitions for the Blind and Partially Sighted (United States Association of Blind Athletes, International Blind Sport Association) must Be Strictly Adhered To, and Meet Directors Notified in Advance That a Runner Who Is Blind with a Guide Is to Compete in the Meet.

Progress and Needs in the 21st Century

Similar reviews and changes of various sport rules are still necessary and urgently needed to enable individuals with disabilities to compete in regular sport programs and activities. The same principles as followed in the mid-1970s must guide and govern reviews and changes in the 2000s, and into the 21st century: *make necessary accommodations so playing rules are not discriminatory, while at the same time not giving unfair advantages to participants with disabilities and placing non-disabled competitors at disadvantages (Stein, 2012)*. Recommended changes should be placed in appropriate sections in each sport rule book, with interpretations and applications placed in respective sport casebooks. In

---

2. Similar changes and accommodations were not made by organizations responsible for intercollegiate sport, or by National Governing Bodies or other sport administrative groups for specific sport at national or international levels.

addition, publicity and promotion about these changes and the added opportunities in sport for individuals with disabilities must be communicated by all appropriate sport governing bodies and administrative units.

The National Collegiate Athletic Association (NCAA) included the following *Physically Challenged Guidelines* statement in its 1995–96 and 1996–97 track and field rule books under *Points of Emphasis*:

> Guidelines may be secured from Margaret Simmons, secretary-rules editor of the NCAA Men's and Women's Track and Field Committee, Murray State University, Murray, Kentucky 42071(Simmons 1995, 1996).

These guidelines are ones found later in this chapter.

Progress for track and field rule accommodations has not moved forward to this same degree in the National Federation of State High School Associations. It should be noted regarding the National Federation that "Each state association is the governing body for competition regarding high school athletics in their respective state. Therefore, we do not require that rule proposals come through the state associations or a member of the rules committee" (Kovaleski 1996). While several states (i.e., Minnesota, Louisiana, Iowa, New Jersey, Washington) have special non-scoring track and field events for athletes with disabilities (mostly for athletes competing in wheelchairs), none at this point have incorporated rule changes to accommodate athletes with disabilities in scoring events in regular meets. Pressure must be exerted on individual state associations to bring about such changes and make it possible for athletes with disabilities to compete and score in regular track and field meets.

Competition rules for USA Track & Field contain a note that starting procedures "may be modified to accommodate the hearing impaired" (Hersh 1995). In addition, a special section, *Adaptations to USA Track & Field Rules of Competition for Individuals With Disabilities*,"contains adaptations to USA Track & Field rules for the four national disabled sport organizations[3] recognized by USA Track & Field as conducting programs in the sport for individuals with disabilities." However, these are adaptations for meets involving athletes with these specific disabilities, not ways to include and integrate them into regular meets. While this is an important step, next steps must be taken so athletes with disabilities can compete against non-disabled athletes, and score in regular meets.

In addition to integrating individuals with disabilities into regular track and field meets, opportunities must be provided for events in which individuals with specific disabilities compete against others with similar disabilities, much in ways done over the years in the United States Olympic Festivals (Mushett and Cooper 1986). These could be introduced as demonstration or exhibition non-scoring events as currently done in the five states previously mentioned. However, every effort must be made to make these scoring events as quickly as possible. This approach can also lead to including more and different events for individuals with various disabilities (i.e., electric wheelchair slalom for individuals with severe and multiple conditions). Functional classifications (Lindstrom 1985), as opposed to conventional medical categorization, need to be given careful consideration, especially when involving individuals with different disabilities.

Various kinds of relays involving individuals with disabilities need to be given consideration. Relay teams could consist of those with the same disability, individuals with different disabilities, and/or athletes with and without disabilities — after all, *medley relays* simply mean *mixed relays*! Relay teams might also consist of more than the traditional

---

3. United States Cerebral Palsy Athletic Association, National Wheelchair Athletic Association (now Wheelchair Sport, U.S.A.), Special Olympics, and United States Association of Blind Athletes.

four. Thought must also be given to other *new* events with which greater numbers of athletes with disabilities can be involved. Innovation, creativity, and resourcefulness are important parts of this exciting evolutionary process (although some might consider it revolutionary).

The National Federation of State High School Associations has made accommodations for athletes with disabilities in swimming. "If a disabled athlete does not gain an advantage over an 'able' athlete, the accommodation is legal" (True 1996). "The swimming and diving rules accommodate handicapped more than any of the other sport I work with because it is relatively easy to do without giving them an unfair advantage, endangering them or other competitors, etc." (True 1995). More of this philosophy and approach is needed in other sport, and by other governing bodies at all levels: local, regional, national, and international.

Several national governing bodies (NGBs) have taken bold steps forward in behalf of individuals with disabilities. U.S. Ski, governing body for skiing, not only has developed a continuum from basic instruction to coaching and preparation for elite competitions, but supports the U.S. Disabled Ski Team in exactly the same ways it supports the U.S. Ski Team. The American Racquetball Association has incorporated sub-structures for those with disabilities as integral parts of its operations. Several NGBs have recognized disabled sport organizations as affiliates of their groups. More of this type of activity is sorely needed by other NGBs and sport governing organizations.

Some Recommended Rule Accommodations

Representative of some recommended sport rule changes include the following:

Track and Field

Starting Races — positioning the starter's gun in races in which a deaf or hard of hearing runner competes.

- Place the starter's gun in a *down (rather than in an up) position with the starter's gun arm extended down and away from the body (same relative position as always, but down rather than up). This enables a deaf/hard of hearing runner to turn his/her head only slightly to see the gun and react to its flash. The changed position in no way affects other runners in the heat, section, or final race. Electronic timing devices are triggered with the firing of the gun, regardless of its position. Timers can be alerted in these races to look for the gun in the down position, rather than in the up position, so timing will be unaffected. Assistant starters must be alerted to the lane or starting position of a deaf/hard of hearing competitor.*

- *Each deaf/hard of hearing competitor must identify him/herself to the clerk of the course when checking in for heat, section, and/or final race. The clerk is responsible for seeing that starter, head timer, and head judge are all notified of any race involving a deaf/hard of hearing competitor.*

- *Starters may have to adjust their positions according to the starting pattern of the race (i.e., lanes, waterfall, staggered lanes, boxes/alleys) in relation to the starting position of the deaf/hard of hearing competitor.*

- *Consider using a .45 caliber gun when deaf/hard of hearing competitors are in heats, sections, or final races (many deaf/hard of hearing competitors can respond/react to the greater concussion from a .45 caliber gun).*

- *Consider synchronizing a special strobe light or flashing device with the starter's gun when a deaf runner is identified for a particular track event.*

Sprints

- Allow a blind/partially-sighted sprinter/runner in lane events with a guide runner (note—this requires two lanes, one for the runner and one for the guide). Guide runners are already permitted in middle distance and distance events and cross country at the interscholastic level, in most marathons, and road races regardless of sponsors.

Track Events

- Consider permitting runners who are blind/partially-sighted to be given directions from a coach through some type of telecommunication system (especially in events conducted around the oval).
- Spell out in rule books and casebooks official procedures for marathons and road races for competitors in wheelchairs, on crutches, or with walkers.

Shot/Discus

- Allow a coach/aide into the circle to orient a blind/partially-sighted athlete for the put/throw, after which the coach/aide must leave the circle and follow all regular coaching rules.
- Permit a sound device of some type (i.e., caller, portable radio) in the middle of the fair sector as an aid for blind/partially-sighted athletes (permit in the javelin also).
- Allow athletes in wheelchairs to compete from their wheelchairs: (a) if tie downs are available, the individual in the wheelchair should take all efforts (trials or finals) at one time when in the circle; (b) if tie downs are not available, a coach/aide be permitted to hold the wheelchair and the put/throw be either (1) in regular/official rotation, or (2) all at one time as in (a) above.

Javelin

- Allow a coach/aide onto the runway to orient a blind/partially-sighted athlete for the throw.
- Allow the coach to call to a blind/partially-sighted athlete during the run-up to insure they are running straight and in the middle of the runway.
- Allow individuals in wheelchairs to compete from their wheelchairs as outlined above for shot/discus events.

Long Jump/Triple Jump

- Allow a coach/aide during the approach to call to a blind/partially-sighted athlete from the far end of the pit (behind and away from the runway) to insure they are running straight, and to indicate when the athlete is to initiate the jump.
- Measure the distance of a blind jumper from his/her takeoff point (rather than the edge of the takeoff board nearer to the landing pit), provided takeoff is within twenty-four inches of the edge of the takeoff board nearer to the landing pit.

High Jump

- Allow a blind/partially-sighted jumper to place a colored piece of cloth at whatever place desired along the bar.

Pentathlon/Heptathlon/Decathlon

- Allow blind/partially-sighted athletes the same accommodations as for the individual track and field events.

Swimming

- Allow coaches/aides at each end of the pool to indicate to a blind/partially-sighted swimmer when to initiate his/her turn by using a *tactile end of the lane indicator* (as simple as a tennis ball attached to the end of a seven foot pole).

- Allow a signal be given to a blind/partially-sighted swimmer in a relay when the previous swimmer touches the finish pad (i.e., sighted individual touching and releasing the touch of an ankle of the blind/partially sighted swimmer).

- Have position of starter's gun down (rather than up) when there is an identified deaf/hard of hearing swimmer in an event, regardless of distance or stroke (see recommendations for starting track events).

- Have a person stand at the starting blocks with a hand on a deaf/hard of hearing swimmer's ankle, removing it when the starting device goes off.

- Use a strobe light connected to the starting device for deaf/hard of hearing swimmers.

- Permit a swimmer with a disability to start in the water, rather than diving from the starting blocks.

Tennis/Racquetball

- Allow individuals in wheelchairs to participate in both singles and doubles competitions. In doubles, all regular tennis/racquetball rules apply. In singles, determine whether one or two bounces are permitted for the player in a wheelchair.

Bowling

- Allow a blind/partially-sighted competitor to use a (a) bowling rail, or (b) some other means for orienting him/herself to the lane, approach area, and foul line. Allow teammates, coaches, or aides to give information to the competitor as to (a) pins fallen, and (b) pins remaining up. Encourage use of electronic scoring devices that enable blind/partially-sighted bowlers to participate independently.

- Allow competitors in wheelchairs to use (a) bowling ramps, (b) special spring handle bowling balls, (c) pushers, or (d) other approved and accepted devices.

- Allow competitors with identified physical disabilities who do not use wheelchairs (i.e., cerebral palsy, les autres, amputations, arthritis, muscular dystrophy, multiple sclerosis) to use (a) special spring handle bowling balls, (b) pushers, or (c) other approved and accepted devices.

Archery

- Allow athletes in wheelchairs to participate following all regular rules.

- Permit a sound device (i.e., portable radio) to be placed in a position of choice behind the target for a blind/partially-sighted competitor. Permit a coach or aide to provide necessary orientation information regarding the target to the competitor.

Concluding Comments

Review rules for other sports, i.e., badminton, baseball/softball, canoeing, crew, equestrian activities, judo, riflery, soccer, volleyball, skiing (both downhill and cross country), in addition to most team sports, to determine what accommodations (if any, some sports need no accommodations, only encouraging coaches to seek, recruit, and involve those with disabilities in their sport) are necessary to enable individuals with disabilities to participate without placing non-disabled participants at any disadvantages, creating an undue hardship on program sponsors, or in any way changing the basic nature or integrity of the sport.

Incorporate into *all* rule books statements encouraging program administrators, meet directors, organizing committees, coaches, and others involved in the sport to seek and include participants with disabilities. In those sports where no accommodations are required, be sure this fact is included in appropriate statements in each rule book and casebook. A brief note about accommodations that have been included should also be mentioned. Rule reviewers must also be alert to ways in which certain rules discriminate against coaches (i.e., what can and cannot be taken into a coach's box in baseball and softball, wheelchairs in team areas in football).

All rule committees, including youth sport, National Federation of State High School Associations (NFSHSA), National Collegiate Athletic Association, National Association of Intercollegiate Athletics, Junior College Athletic Association, national governing bodies (NGBs), and international federations,should continually review their rules to make sure they do not unduly, unfairly, and illegally discriminate against individuals with disabilities.

All rules committees should annually review their rules to insure that they are not discriminatory, and find new ways to include participants with disabilities in their sport.

Official rules for specific sport should be obtained from appropriate *Disabled Sport Organizations (DSOs)* (i.e., United States Association of Blind Athletes, Wheelchair Sport, U.S.A., United States Cerebral Palsy Athletic Association, United States Deaf Athletic Association, Disabled Sport USA, Special Olympics, United States Dwarf Athletic Association, and/or through the Committee on Sport for the Disabled [United States Olympic Committee]) to review how these organizations accommodate disabilities in their programs. NGBs and DSOs must also work more closely together by communicating, cooperating, coordinating, complementing, and supplementing each other's efforts, while understanding and respecting each other's uniqueness. Practical accommodations successful in one sport can provide impetus for similar accommodations in other sports.

In My Opinion

Sport should bring out the best in each individual competitor and provide opportunities to test oneself against others. Individuals with disabilities have these same drives and desires to establish goals that are important to the individual, and then work hard to attain these goals. Various accommodations are already legion in sport, e.g., kicking tees and special kicking shoes in football, different size racquets in tennis, skis of different lengths, bats and gloves of various sizes and materials in baseball and softball, choices of which fourteen clubs to carry in golf, different shoes for different events in track and field, *ad infinitum*. Rules accommodations for individuals with disabilities are simply extensions of procedures already in effect in sport. In no way are these accommodations to give competitors with disabilities unfair advantages over non-disabled opponents, place non-disabled competitors at any disadvantages, or change the nature or integrity of a sport. They are designed to provide opportunities for those with disabilities to participate and compete on equitable bases with non-disabled athletes.

However, rule changes in and of themselves will not automatically increase numbers of individuals with disabilities participating in any sport. Coupled with rule changes must be sincere efforts on the part of all involved in sport at every level, youth to elite, to promote and publicize how these changes increase opportunities of individuals with disabilities to participate and compete. Leaders in sport programs, especially coaches, must encourage, recruit, and involve those with disabilities on their teams.

The Department of Justice has indicated that changes in sport rules must be made to accommodate otherwise qualified individuals with disabilities, accommodations that are readily accessible and readily available. At the same time, the courts have ruled, and justifiably so, that an individual who used a crutch could not play soccer because use of the crutch, in *kicking* the ball, changed the nature of the game (Soccer League Sued 1996). Although the legal mandate is there and abundantly clear, the nature of sport itself and espoused philosophies of sport leaders make it even clearer that ethical responsibilities dictate such accommodations so individuals with disabilities can attain their inherent right to participate and compete in the sport of their choice.

References

Associated Press. 1992. "Paraplegic Can Coach." *Oak Ridger* July 9, p. 10.

Hersh, R.M. (Ed.). 1995. *Competition Rules.* Indianapolis, IN: USA Track & Field.

Kovaleski, F. 1996. Personal communication, May 28.

Lindstrom, H. 1985. "An Integrated Classification System." *Palaestra* vol. 1, no. 2, Winter.

Mushett, M. and M.A. Cooper. 1986. "Disabled Athlete Participation in the U.S. Olympic Festival." *Palaestra* vol. 3, no. 1, Fall.

National Easter Seal Society. [n.d.] *Awareness is the First Step Brochures: The Americans with Disabilities Act-Tips for Disability Awareness.* Chicago, IL: National Easter Seal Society.

Scott, Kimberly (Ed.) 1990. *The Americans with Disabilities Act: An Analysis.* Silver Spring, MD: Business Publishers, Inc.

Simmons, M. 1995. Personal communication, December 15.

Simmons, M. 1996. Personal communication, June 18.

"Soccer League Sued To Let Boy On Crutches Play Soccer." 1996. *From The Gym To The Jury* vol. 7, no. 5, The Center for Sport Law and Risk Management, Inc.

Stein, J.U. 1993. "The Americans with Disabilities Act: Implications for Recreation and Leisure." In *Leisure Opportunities for Individuals with Disabilities: Legal Issues.* Reston, VA: American Alliance for Health, Physical Education, Recreation, and Dance.

Stein, J.U. 1995. "Dealing with Disabilities." *From The Gym To The Jury* vol. 6, no. 6, The Center for Sport Law and Risk Management, Inc.

Stein, J.U. 2012. Risk Management in Sport, Third Edition.

True, S.S. 1995. Personal communication, November 7.

True, S.S. 1996. Personal communication, May 28.

U.S. Department of Justice. 1990. *Americans with Disabilities Act Requirements Fact Sheet.* Washington, DC: U.S. Department of Justice, Civil Rights Division, Coordination and Review Section. (Available in braille, large print, audiotape, electronic file on computer disk, and electronic bulletin board.)

Chapter 30

Aquatics and the Law

Most Americans are unaware of the high level of risk involved in aquatic activities.

Annie Clement

Americans enjoy water and aquatic participation; however, most Americans are unaware of the high level of risk involved in aquatic activities. A recent Sporting Goods Manufacturing Association Sport Marketing Survey found that over seventeen million people reported swimming in 2010. Canoeing was reported in the same amount for about ten and one half million people while sailing accounted for nearly four million. Over fifty-five million people engaged in some form of fishing with seven and three quarter million jet skiers, six and one half million kayakers, three million scuba divers, and nine million participated in snorkeling activities. The new sport of stand-up paddling, first reported in 2011, claimed over a million people. Participation was reported as engaging in a sport between one and forty-nine times over the past year (SGMA, 2011, 15–16, 28–29).

Kendra Kozen (2011), in *Aquatics International,* stated that "Americans' ability to swim remains distressingly low ... states are showing record numbers of incidents; over 1,500 were lost to drowning between May 1 and August 26 of 2011" (Kozen, 2011, 11). "Children under 15 years account for 23% of all drowning" (Injury Research Agenda, 2009, 57). Drowning was the fifth leading cause of death in the United States in 2009, with 3,700 deaths from swimming, playing in the water, or falling into the water. The figures did not include floods or boat-related fatal incidents (Injury Facts, 2011). Of the drowning deaths, 2,681 were male and 762 were female. Six hundred children, ages birth to four years drowned, two hundred and fifty persons ages five to fourteen drowned, six hundred and fifty ages fifteen to twenty-four died, and eight hundred and fifty drowned in each of the age brackets, twenty-five to forty-four, and forty-five to sixty-four. A much smaller group died in the older populations; two hundred twenty in the sixty-five to seventy-four age group, and two hundred and eighty among those seventy-five or older (Injury Facts, 2011, 9).

"Drowning was also the fifth leading cause of unintentional injury death in 2007, with 168 fatalities for one-year-olds. Drowning was the second leading cause of injury death for children ages 1–5, 8, 10, and 13–15 in 2007. Of the 3,443 deaths in 2007, 2,681 were male and 762 were female" (Injury Facts, 2011, 14). Most people drown in the months of June, July, and August. States with the highest drowning rates among children, 0–19 for 2000 through 2005, were Arkansas with 3.9 per 100,000, and Mississippi at 2.9 and Florida at 2.7 per 100,000 (Borse, 2008, 54). North Dakota, Vermont, South Dakota, Rhode Island, and the District of Columbia were the lowest.

The rate of injury in sport, in general, among males is 26 per 1,000 males; female injuries are 11 per 1,000 females (Injury Facts, 2011, 24). The CDC Childhood Injury Report found the injury rate for 1- to 4-year-olds, in general, was 3.0 per 100,000, the highest for all ages between one and nineteen years of age (Borse, 2008, 53).

Headfirst Entry Injuries

Headfirst entry into unknown or misunderstood water conditions accounts for a few drowning deaths and many severe spinal and neurological injuries that do not result in death. The 2010 Report from the National Spinal Cord Injury Statistical Center identified a total of 1,723 persons who survived a spinal cord incident; no spinal cord death reports were available. Among the injuries, 1,587 were male and 135 were female. Diving ranked fourth behind auto accidents, falls, and gunshot wounds in spinal cord injury rates (38). "Each year more than 7,000 young Americans experience a diving accident ... 90% of diving related accidents occur in water less than six feet deep" (Kraus Back and Neck Institute, 2011). Among the accidents were head first entries into shallow above ground and in ground pools; flips and back dives from boards; shallow water entries into lakes and rivers; and rip tides. Kraus also reported that 90% occurred in private residential pools.

Clement and Otto's (2007) investigation of headfirst entry into water court decisions from 1990 to June 2005 was an effort to understand the frequency and magnitude of litigation in aquatic injuries. All court decisions (247) rendered between 1990 and June 2005 were obtained from LEXIS/NEXIS Universe (http:110-web-lexis-nexis.com.wncln.org/universe/). A database was created to address a range of topics. Six states, New York, Illinois, Michigan, Ohio, California, and Louisiana, constituted nearly half of the cases that had gone to a court of appeals. The male/female ratio was 83% to 17%. Thirty-nine percent of the injuries occurred in a home or residential pool. Twenty-seven percent of the females succeeded with their complaints while the courts found for only twenty percent of the males. Immunity, the fact that you cannot sue the government, became a factor in situations where the pool was owned by a municipality or the government. For example, in *Fisher v. United States Corp of Engineers* (1994), Fisher broke his neck diving into shallow water. The court dismissed the case on immunity even though the injury was severe (Clement & Otto, 2007, 119).

Legal Theories

Negligence, premise liability, and product liability are the primary legal theories involved in aquatics. An understanding of each of these legal theories will assist professionals in tailoring the risk management program to their individual needs. "Primary factors to consider in ascertaining whether the person's conduct lacks reasonable care are the foreseeable likelihood that the person's conduct will result in harm, the foreseeable severity of any harm that may ensue, and the burden of precautions to eliminate or reduce the risk of harm" (Restatement Third, Torts: Liability for Physical and Emotional Harm, Section 3).

Negligence

Negligence is doing something a reasonable person would not be expected to do or failing to do something that a reasonable person would be expected to do. For negligence to be found, the following elements must exist: duty, breach of duty, factual cause, scope of liability (foreseeability), and damages. The legal duty is the standard of the profession and the industry. Aquatic standards are created by state and federal statutes, local ordinances, and various certificates held by aquatic professionals. Standards are also created by coach-athlete, instructor-learner, therapist-client, employer-employee, and principal-agent relationships. Once the legal duty is established, proof must be provided by the injured person to the court that the professional failed to meet their legal duty or standard of care. When proof has been provided, the court must determine that the breach of the professional's duty was the cause of the victim's injury and that the breach was foreseeable. Further, the victim has to have sustained substantial damage.

There are three basic standards of care: a reasonable person, special relationships, and a professional standard. A reasonable person is what an ordinary person would do while a special relationship is the expectation of a parent for a child, or a teacher for a student. In aquatics, the reasonable person and the special relationship person who cannot swim or could not rescue a person are not expected to attempt the feat! Parents have died in their attempt to rescue a child. The third, a professional standard, is the role of a lifeguard or swimming instructor. They would be expected to possess the knowledge and skills essential to teach and to rescue a person under their care. Should a swimming instructor not hold a current lifeguard certification, a lifeguard should be provided while that person is teaching and be responsible for the safety of members of the class. Today, most pools employ both a lifeguard and a swimming instructor for the same time period. This enables the instructor to focus complete attention on each student as they are acquiring skills.

Defenses to a court action in negligence are contributory negligence and assumption of risk. Contributory negligence occurs when a person engages in an activity that creates all or a portion of the damage sustained. For example, it exists when a person old enough to make decisions jumps into deep water knowing they cannot swim. A beginner who removes her or his required life jacket has contributed to his or her damages in an accident situation. Assumption of risk is the willingness to assume risks that are inherent in the sport. In order to assume the risk, the participant must be aware of, understand, and appreciate the risks involved in a particular sport. An adult may sign an agreement (contract) to assume all risks of engaging in an activity. Only adults are permitted to enter into contracts; therefore, minors are not allowed to sign away their rights. Warnings and risk information is to be provided to enable participants and, when appropriate, their parents or guardians, to know and appreciate the risks.

Premise Liability

Premise liability is the duty of the owner and person in possession of land to those entering their land. This liability has an impact on those managing thousands of people in wave parks as well as the home owner who invited the neighbor for a swim. A party injured on the property of another is classified in one of three ways: trespasser, licensee, or invitee. Trespassers are owed the lowest, or zero duty: invitees have the greatest protection. Licensees are given reasonable care.

Trespasser

A trespasser is a person who goes onto someone's land without permission and without the knowledge of the possessor. The owner or possessor has no duty of care to the trespasser. Owners of land have no duty to inspect the premises, to make the property safe, to warn of dangers, or to use reasonable care for trespassers. If an owner or possessor of land becomes aware that someone frequently enters the property the owner/possessor's duties change. States differ on the standard of care extended to known trespassers; some hold the owner to a reasonable case standard, others hold the owner to a licensee standard.

Licensee

A licensee is a person who is on the land with expressed or implied permission for no economic benefit. The difference between a trespasser and a licensee is that the owner has consented to the presence of the licensee on the land. A social guest is a licensee. Duties to the licensee are to keep the property in a reasonably safe condition and to warn or protect persons entering the land from harms of which the possessor of the land is aware. There is no duty to inspect, discover dangerous conditions, or make the land safe.

Invitee

An invitee is a person who has either expressly or impliedly been invited onto the land of another for an economic benefit to the person in possession of the land or one who enters land open to the public. A paid patron of a wave pool is an invitee. Duties to the invitee include keeping the premises in a reasonably safe condition and when dangerous conditions exist, providing warnings of such conditions. The possessor of land has a duty to inspect for unknown dangers and to prevent harm from being caused by active operations. The possessor of land is not only responsible for reasonable care and adequate warnings to an invitee about known dangers, but also about those conditions of which the invitee should have been aware.

Natural Conditions

The owner of property retained in its natural condition does not have a duty to prevent injury to persons who might be injured by the natural conditions of the land. Natural conditions are found in the wilderness. They include lakes, trees, rocks, etc. Person-made or artificial conditions such as fences, swimming pools, lakes, beaches, groomed camp sites, and buildings require the owner to assume a duty of reasonable care to prevent injuries to persons entering the property. When the owner or occupier of natural land alters or changes the natural land, and the change in the natural land is the reason for the injury, they assume the higher duty of the owner or occupier of artificial land.

Intentional Torts

An intentional tort means that the act was intended. Harm may or may not have been intended. Battery is the intentional tort most often associated with aquatic incidents. Battery is an intentionally harmful or offensive contact with another person, without the person's consent. The physical contact must be intentional; however, there does not have to be intent to injure, and injury or damage does not have to occur. Continuous, intentional tagging and pushing in a water polo game or engaging in locker room pranks can, given the right circumstances, become battery. Throwing swimming team members into a pool or sailing crews into a lake or ocean in celebration of success is a battery. Numerous batteries, seldom recognized as such, exist in the traditional rituals of recreational and competitive sport. In addition to batteries occurring within the competitive arena, there are batteries occurring as a result of athletes injuring spectators. Hazing is treated as a battery.

One does not commit a battery if the other person consented to the act. Consent, however, is difficult to assess. For example, does competing in and winning a swimming meet give consent to a fellow team members to toss one into the water in celebration of the success?

Product Liability

Product liability is the liability of the manufacturers, retailers, and sellers of defective products, in this case, defective equipment and/or chemicals. The defect may be a manufacturing defect, a design defect, or inadequate instructions or warnings when foreseeable risks of harm or injury could have been reduced or avoided (Restatement of the Law, Third, Torts, Product Liability, 1998, Section 2). A manufacturer's defect may exist in only a few of the products while a design defect will exist in all products. Owners and agencies leasing equipment may be sued under product liability in certain circumstances. Employees are to protect the agencies for which they work against the purchase and installation of faulty products, know the agencies' rights when products fail, and be effective in passing manufacturer's warnings to appropriate audiences. Under the Consumer Product Safety Commission regulations a person harmed by a product may bring a case against the manufacturer in federal court. When a product is recalled, the agency is to follow the instructions provided on the recall. Failure to do so may result in the agency assuming liability for the identified risk or injury.

Contributory negligence, assumption of risk, misuse, and the Uniform Commercial Code disclaimers are defenses to product liability. A combination of state and federal laws govern product liability.

The Occupational Safety and Health Act (OSHA)

The Occupational Safety and Health Act (OSHA), a Department of Labor standard effective in 1992 and updated in 2001, mandates a written safety and health program that identifies, evaluates, documents, and corrects worksite hazards; a safety committee; and a system for investigating hazards. Hazardous chemicals and confined spaces are areas of OSHA uniquely related to aquatic activities; blood borne pathogens must be considered by all agencies, including aquatic agencies, providing emergency medical care. Hazardous chemicals are used in swimming pool water control and in cleaning decks. Confined spaces are areas having limited or restricted means of entry or exit, large enough for an employee to enter and perform assigned work. OSHA's requirement for fitness club pools notes that chlorine is bleach and that a maximum of only one part per million should be used in a working environment. Chlorine vapors should not be inhaled or come in contact with eyes, skin, or clothing. Should it come in contact with eyes or skin, the area is to be flushed immediately. In light of this advice, a shower should be located close to the area where chemicals are stored and used. Signs and symbols indicating chemicals and other potentially hazardous products need to be posted and brought to the attention of all. Blood borne pathogens are pathogenic microorganisms that are present in human blood and can cause disease in humans. These pathogens include but are not limited to hepatitis

B (HBV) and human immunodeficiency virus (HIV) (29 CFR 1910.1030). A system for protecting first responders against these health hazards is to be devised and implemented.

Confined spaces include underground vaults, tanks, storage bins, pits and diked areas, vessels, and silos. The regulation requires that the atmosphere in the space be tested for oxygen level, flammable gases and vapors, and toxic air contaminants, such as hydrogen sulfide and carbon monoxide, before an employee enters the space. The use of a buddy system is recommended for persons entering confined spaces to check meters and other equipment in the aquatic environment.

Electricity is also monitored by OSHA. A single circuit breaker is to be installed within ten feet of the inside walls of the pool. The circuit breaker for a pool pump motor must be within five feet of the pump (Miles, 2010).

Risk Management System

Risk management is a system to identify, evaluate, and control loss to personal and real property, clients and students, employees and the public. It will make the program as safe as possible and the business efficient. The first step in risk management is the identification of all risks. Once the risks are identified, a professional must evaluate each risk. The evaluation is based on the probability of the occurrence of a particular risk, the severity of injuries or death if it occurs, and the magnitude or numbers of people that will be involved. Any incident with a high probability of risk or a high level of severity or one that will involve many people is treated as a high risk. Even though only one factor has a high probability of occurring, the occurrence will have a major impact on the business. One death can have a serious effect on a business; many people sustaining even minimal damage can be a public relations disaster.

Once the evaluation is complete, control becomes the priority. Control involves four choices: eliminating the high risk venture; modifying the high risk venture so that it is safer; retaining the high risk venture and transferring the risk through insurance or contract; or retaining the high risk venture and assuming the responsibility.

The aquatic professional has a number of unique areas for examination in the risk management program. The following is provided to assist the professional in tailoring a program to meet the needs of their facility. Model areas will include local, state, and federal regulations and industry standards; facilities and equipment; staff and supervision; and instruction.

Local, State, and Federal Regulations and Industry Standards

Pools, water slides, lakes, streams, swimming, diving, boating, personal water craft, and camping are among the areas addressed in local, state, and federal laws, codes, and regulations. The laws, codes, and regulations are under health, safety, bathing, waste disposal, water pollution, medical emergency, weather, fire, crime, swimming pools, electrical, OSHA, and Environment Protection. Laws, codes, and regulations affecting an agency should be posted, made available to employees whose jobs are affected, retained and updated yearly, and enforced. Employee education is a must in this area; employees need to know the law, be able to interpret the law to the public, and enforce the law. The

National Swimming Pool Foundation, Aquatic Risk Management (2009) provides a comprehensive list of federal regulatory agencies and professional organizations' aquatic standards (30).

Instructor and pool operator certificates dictate many of the standards required in the aquatic industry. Aquatics areas, in comparison to other physical activity areas, are known for having and maintaining standards. Should professionals be required to defend their teaching or management in a court of law, professionals will be forced to contrast the standards in operation on the day of the incident with accepted aquatic standards. Should an agency choose to ignore accepted standards, it should note the decision in their plans and give the reasons for the decision.

Facilities and Equipment

Facilities and equipment have been the major sources of litigation in aquatics over past years and as a result of the litigation, plans must be specific and must be followed. In addition to routine facility inventories, inspection for cleanliness, adherence to the Americans with Disabilities Act (ADA), and other general routines, the aquatic facility operator must consider the following items specific to swimming pools.

1. Pool bottom is clearly visible; a coin can be seen on the bottom. No water within the pool is cloudy.

2. Pool pumps, filters, chemical feeders, and heaters are in working order.

3. Safety equipment, including external defibrillators (AEDs), rescue tubes, reaching poles, and spine boards meet recommended standards, and are checked routinely.

4. Water quality testing meets up to date standards with a consistent pattern for assessing and reporting compliance.

5. Water depth markings are obvious and meet or exceed code. "Hopper bottom" pools are appropriately marked so that patrons understand the unique risks associated with that pool design.

6. Headfirst entries into the water are controlled, and locations for such entries marked. If possible, use of the word "headfirst" rather than "diving" in signage. The word diving is often misunderstood by the public.

7. Speed swimming racing blocks meet contemporary standards, are used only under supervision, and covered by sleeves when not in use.

8. Emergency buttons or phones are accessible to lifeguards and professionals.

9. Pools meet humidity and ventilation standards established by the American College of Sports Medicine (ACSM). Signs of failure of these standards are stained and falling ceiling tiles and walls.

10. Lifeguard chairs and equipment are in good working order and ready for use. All equipment meets industry standards.

11. Pool decks are clean and neat. They are disinfected routinely.

12. Pool ladders and stairs are designed to prevent entrapment.

13. Pool ceiling height is adequate for diving, and placement of diving boards.

14. Water temperature is between 78 and 84 degrees.

15. Life guard chairs and stations permit full pool visibility.

16. Pool meets all codes. For example, emergency lighting system enables patrons to find pool exit ladders, move to locker room, dress, exit locker room, and exit buildings. Lights are near ladders in the swimming pool.

17. Suction drain covers are secure in place.

18. Ground fault circuit interrupters are located in pools and locker rooms.

19. Swimming pool designs that create hazards are identified and remediated. The following are examples of some of the hazards found in aquatic environments:

    A. Pools are too shallow for intended use.

    B. Sharp edges, inadequate lighting and objects, such as drinking fountains and bleachers, protruding into walk spaces.

    C. Slippery floors. They may be caused by design flaws or improper pool maintenance.

20. A system for opening and closing the pool each day is used, recorded, and retained.

21. Entire building, including locker rooms and swimming pool, is monitored hourly by a person who has current first aid and CPR credentials.

22. Manufacturer's warnings and instructions are posted in conspicuous places and on equipment.

23. Staff are trained in the use of equipment; manufacturer's warranties are honored.

24. Changes in laws are implemented. For example, the new ADA primary access code effective March 15, 2011 has been implemented.

Staff

Staff includes lifeguards, instructors, coaches, and those who would be involved in an incident or disaster situation.

1. An employee handbook exists and covers employee and participants rights and responsibilities.

2. All certifications, including lifeguarding, first aid, cardiopulmonary resuscitation (CPR) for the professional rescuer, pool operator, and others are up-to-date at all times.

3. Staff orientation and in-service training is provided for new employees and repeated periodically for the entire staff.

4. Employees are expected to maintain personal physical skills adequate to perform in an emergency situation.

Supervision

Supervision is the identification and carrying out of the safety and program plans.

1. Rules, essential to aquatics, are taken from the agency's policies and procedures. The rules are posted and explained.

2. Signage meets codes and is easy to read and understand.

3. A detailed supervision plan exists. It covers location and duties of guards, para-professionals, pool operators, and other staff. Breaks and rest periods are identified.

Even though a specific protocol of supervision has been selected, i.e., American Red Cross, YMCA, Jeffrey Ellis, or the National Swimming Pool Foundation, the protocol is re-enforced in the written documents.

4. A pool scanning system is established and followed. The responsibilities of each employee are contained in his/her job description.

5. A system for crowd control exists and is in writing.

6. Penalties for violation of rules have been established and are sufficient to deter participants from further bad behavior.

7. Horseplay is not tolerated.

Instruction

1. Continuous education and updating of information is provided for lifeguards, instructors, and coaches.

2. Instructional content is used only by those qualified to use such content. In most cases, knowledge of physiology and biomechanics is essential to successful interpretation of instructional materials. All persons teaching headfirst entry to water (diving) must fully understand the physics of the human body.

3. Instructional content is selected with the capacity of the client in mind. Learners are pre-tested.

4. All instruction, including course outlines, curricular plans, lessons, learning sequences, routines, and learner's advancement is retained and could be presented to a court of law.

5. When safety and skill progression information is essential, all class members can verify that such information was presented.

6. Records document participant's achievement and demonstrate that students are ready for advanced skills.

7. All instruction includes warm-up, matched partners in contact situations, and safety equipment if necessary.

8. Instruction meets the test of peer scrutiny.

Emergency Action Plan

An emergency action plan is a must for an aquatic environment. The plan is to be in writing, known to all who will be part of an emergency, practiced often, evaluated, and updated continuously. Emergency planning is not an area where one can make a choice; it is a must! Injuries that require emergency medical care at the scene of the incident and those that require medical attention at a later date are the subject of the emergency action plan. A successful plan is based on research, planning, training, and follow-up.

Research

Professionals are to identify all possible injuries, accidents, and unforeseen emergencies such as riots or terrorism that could occur in their aquatic environment. Valuable information can be gathered from recent accident reports from the existing program and from three or four similar programs. Confer with authorities in the local area as to potential threats of terror, riots, utility disruptions, and others. Considerable information on aquatic incidents exist in the literature. Remain up-to-date on incidents involving aquatics across the nation and potential threats from the local environment.

Planning

The plan is created in response to the findings of the research. The plan is put in writing. It identifies the first and second responders and their duties. The process to be used in making the decision to obtain emergency medical care is created. Immediate and temporary care is to be provided by staff competent in emergency care (first aid, use of defibrillators, et al.). The same employees are to be skilled in recognizing injuries needing emergency medical attention and are able to provide quality victim assessment to emergency responders. The system for obtaining emergency medical assistance has been discussed and rehearsed with emergency medical authorities. Emergency numbers and advice are contained in cell phones or other communication devices readily available. Lifeguard stands are often the location for such devices. Again, the system for reporting has been rehearsed. During rehearsals specific time frames, including traffic at various times of the day or night, have been estimated so that professionals can anticipate the time period between identification of the incident and the arrival of professional help.

Learning the System

All employees who participate in the emergency action system must know the plan, have adequate practice to be sure they can carry out the plan, and practice periodically to ensure retention of skills. Practices are to include all potential types of emergencies that can be envisioned. First aid, rescue, and other emergency equipment and supplies are appropriately prepared for use, checked often, and carefully repacked after each use. Personnel know how to use equipment. Emergency medical personnel have been consulted in planning and, if possible, have participated in practice.

The plan is rehearsed periodically. All new employees learn and practice the system before assuming their jobs. Monitoring, including trial accidents, are used to be sure employees are ready for an incident. Records are maintained of all staff instruction and practice.

Follow-Up

All seriously injured staff and participants are monitored immediately after the injury. A planned follow-up is used. One administrator is asked to stay in touch with an injured staff member to be sure the staff member is familiar with workers compensation requirements and successfully returns to full-time work. Another person is asked to continue to contact an injured participant. A means of working with the media has been designed and is carried out. The entire emergency system is known by all, rehearsed often, and monitored for flaws. Accident reports are the standard reports used by the agency for all accidents. They are created as soon as possible following the incident. Top administrators and staff media persons are notified by a designated professional at about the same time that the emergency medical people are summoned. Today, the media often works closely with the emergency personnel and is on the scene as soon as the emergency personnel arrive; thus agency professional need to be prepared to make or not make statements to the media in a very short period of time. This enables an administrator to be prepared. A comprehensive incident follow-up, including all persons present at the time of the incident, is conducted as soon as possible following the incident.

References

Blood Borne Pathogens Standard, 29 CFR 1910.1030.

Borse, N. et al. (2008). CDC childhood injury report: Patterns of unintentional injuries among 0–19 year olds in the United States, 2000–2006, Atlanta, GA: United States Department of Health and Human Services, Division of Unintentional Injury Prevention.

Clement, A. & Grady, J. (2012). *Law in sport: Cases and concepts.* Morgantown, WV: Fitness Information Technology.

Clement, A. & Otto, K. A. (Winter, 2007). Aquatic incident court decisions: The plaintiffs odds. *17 J. Legal Aspects of Sport 107.*

Fisher v. United States Corps of Engineers, 31 F. 3d 683 (8th Cir. 1994).

Injury Facts. (2011). Itasca, IL: National Safety Council.

Injury Research Agenda, 2009–2018. (2009). Atlanta, GA: Center for Disease Control.

Kozen, K. (2011). New swimming lessons. *Aquatics International,* 11.

Kraus Back and Neck Institute (2011). *Diving and spinal cord injuries.* http://www.spinehealth.com/blog/index.php/2011/02/21/diving-spinal-cord-injury/.

Miles, B. (2010). OSHA requirements for Fitness Club Pools. Retrieved 11/5/2011. From http://www.ehow.com/list_7297376_osha-reguirements-fitness-pools.html.

National Spinal Cord Injury Statistical Center (2010). Annual report for the spinal cord injury model system, Birmingham, Alabama.

National Swimming Pool Foundation. (2009). *Aquatic risk management.* Colorado, Springs, CO: National Swimming Pool Foundation.

Restatement Third, Torts: Liability for physical and Emotional Harm. (2010). St. Paul, MN: American Law Institute.

Restatement of the Law, Third, Torts, Product Liability. (1998). St. Paul, MN: American Law Institute.

Sporting Goods Manufacturing Association (SGMA) (2011). Sport, fitness & Recreation topline participation report. Jupiter, FL: SGAA Research/Sport Marketing Survey USA.

Chapter 31

Expert Witnessing: Definition of an Expert

The expert, in accepting a case, has a professional obligation to see the case through to its finality.

Tom Bowler

Many professionals may think of themselves as experts within their chosen field, however the Federal Rules of Evidence, more specifically Rule 702, actually defines an expert (Babitsky, et al., 2006). One can be considered an expert within their field if they have specific skills. Knowledge is another element by which one may be considered an expert. The person's education may qualify a professional as an expert. Experience within a chosen endeavor may also qualify someone. Lastly, a person's training may endorse an individual as an expert. Rule 702 allows the professional to have only one element from the five listed to be considered an expert. An individual need not have all five elements or more than one. Certainly, it is very helpful to the retaining attorney if the expert does possess more than one element. This makes the expert more credible to the retaining attorney, as well as to the opposing attorney and to the jurors.

Types of Experts

There are basically two types of experts who are retained by attorneys. One is called a "consulting" expert. The other is a "testifying" expert. The consulting expert's role is exactly what the name implies. The expert will consult, advise, and research the case and pass along judgment on various opinions within the litigation matter. More likely than not, their name is not disclosed to the opposing side as a consulting expert. Experts within this category may feel uncomfortable about testifying, hence their role is limited to only advising the retaining attorney. On the other hand, most attorneys, in retaining an expert, will want consultation, research, review of the case, inspections and testimony in the form of the expert's deposition or the expert's testimony at trial. Therefore, most would be looking for a testifying expert and would not want to invest in someone who is hesitant in giving their opinions in deposition or trial. Many professionals are very well versed in their fields, but do not enjoy the stress that comes with testifying.

Percentage of Plaintiff vs. Defendant Cases

The true balance of cases for an expert between plaintiff and defendant cases will be difficult to achieve. When an expert advertises on the internet, their name is available to plaintiff and defendant attorneys. However, if an expert witness wants to "stack the deck" they may do so by advertising in only plaintiff-driven legal journals, if their choice is to do mostly plaintiff cases. The confident expert will accept cases which are within their area of expertise, can be supported and where they feel a comfort level with the attorney. Within deposition testimony of the expert, one usual question posed by the opposing counsel will be "What percentage of your cases are plaintiff versus defendant?" If the expert only chooses to do one side, then it would appear to the opposing attorney that they are biased and not open to other opinions. Balance is key. Fifty percent for each side is usually unattainable for an expert. For example, an excellent balance may be seventy (70) percent of the expert's cases for the plaintiff and thirty (30) percent for the defendant. The telephone contacts, internet contacts and word of mouth contacts will come randomly. The expert who turns down a case just because they do not enjoy working the "other side of the aisle" is doing themselves an injustice.

The Initial Telephone Call

When the initial telephone call comes in for the expert, the expert needs to have some type of intake notes to jot down the specifics of the case. The following items should be part of the expert's notes for the initial call: date, time, name of client, telephone number, fax number, e-mail address, how initial contact was made (i.e. telephone contact, e-mail, brokerage firm, formal letter, fax or telephone voice mail). The recreational expert will need to refer to the type of case venue (i.e. outdoor playground, gymnasium, indoor playground, field, health/fitness center). The details of the case should be jotted down for future reference and placed in a pending file. Lastly, the status of the telephone call with the attorney should be listed on the in-take notes. In other words, will the attorney be interviewing other potential experts? Will the attorney be calling you in one week? Did the attorney request your fee schedule and curriculum vitae?

The expert, in accepting a case, has a professional obligation to see the case through to its finality. Some attorneys will be very demanding and some attorneys will be unprofessional. When an attorney oversteps their bounds, it may be time to abort the case. A micro-managing attorney is difficult to deal with from the standpoint of the expert.

Credentials of an Expert

The credentials of the expert are extremely important to the retaining attorney. All too often, an expert is retained after one initial telephone call without checking references with other attorneys! When we hire a plumber for a toilet repair or a professional roofer to shingle our homes, sometimes more details and references are checked than when an attorney retains an expert! The curriculum vitae of the expert needs to be extensive and enumerate: degrees, certificates/licenses, professional associations, professional lectures, written professional works, etc. The concept of the one to two page curriculum vitae may be adequate for a job interview, however it simply does not do justice to an entire career.

Attorneys want detail. Therefore, include as much as you can. One word of advice, do not put down your litigation work on the curriculum vitae. For example, don't list all your testimony and attendance at expert witness symposiums. If the retaining attorney or opposing attorney wants your history of testimony, this is usually requested when you are subpoenaed for your deposition. It is wise to keep a running list of all testimony which you have given. However, to co-mingle your professional work with your litigation work on your curriculum vitae is a mistake. It will appear that you are just a "hired gun," working for profit.

Credibility of an Expert

When another attorney recommends you, this is by far the best credibility you can achieve. Word of mouth endorsements are very favorable for the expert. This is the best and most inexpensive advertising you can ever receive. The credibility of an expert will be enhanced through attorneys' listserv internet sites. When an attorney finds an expert who is honest, fair, articulate, and who attends to details along with being punctual for an assignment, attorneys will send this message through their networking systems. Therefore, it is very important to always treat each assignment with the utmost respect for the profession.

The credibility of an expert can be diminished by stepping outside one's comfort zone. If the expert takes on an assignment without any skill, knowledge, education, experience or training within the area, it is a recipe for disaster. The reputation of the expert will be ruined through the network system of attorneys. It is far better to "stay within one's comfort level" for an assignment.

The credibility of the expert can be maintained by having a fee agreement that is fair, firm and consistent. Unless it is stipulated within the fee agreement, rates should not fluctuate in the middle of a case. The retaining attorney will be upset if the rates are inflated without due notice for such an increase. It is best to have a clause within the agreement that the rates will hold for one year from the time of retention.

Lastly, the expert's own professional authorship of articles, chapter(s) in books, and PowerPoint lectures must be consistent with the expert's testimony. Certainly, by saying one thing within testimony only to have it quoted back in a contradictory passage within an article is most detrimental to the credibility of the expert.

Retention of an Expert

The expert is retained in a variety of ways. There are a number of brokerage firms which deal exclusively with expert witnesses from various professionals fields. Basically, the brokerage firm is a third party, which will match the attorney's request for an expert within that field. There is no charge to the expert, however a surcharge is placed upon the expert's base fees and passed along to the attorney. A surcharge is applied to the expert's fee schedule and travel schedule. Acting as a third party, they will handle all financial arrangements and billing. The expert will only bill the brokerage firm. As one can envision, this is a much slower process for the expert than realizing a payment immediately. The disadvantage of the brokerage firm for the average sole proprietor attorney is it may be cost prohibitive. The advantage of the brokerage firm is the expert is in their databank and was used previously and has a track record.

Colleagues within the field of litigation come from various professional backgrounds. It is not too uncommon for experts within the same field to recommend other colleagues. This occurs for several reasons. There may be a conflict of interest between parties resulting in recommending someone else. It might be the expert contacted has limited experience within that field and has opted to recommend another colleague with far more experience. It may be as simple as the expert having a full case load and being unable to take on any additional cases. Attorneys will recommend experts to other attorneys when they have had a good experience with a case.

Bar associations are excellent organizations in which the expert witness can network. Giving pro bono lectures is an excellent way to make oneself known to the profession. The newer concept of internet webinars has been gaining in popularity. Webinars can function in a variety of different ways. The lecturer can be at a central studio with a PowerPoint presentation and this can be presented electronically over the internet. Or, it can be as simple as the expert preparing a PowerPoint in advance with a registered audience and delivering the presentation on a specific day and time over the internet. The audience will never see the presenter in this fashion. The expert would deliver the presentation via a telephone hook-up, which may last one hour. Questions and answers would be interspersed in this type of interactive presentation. The advantage of this type of presentation is the presenter never leaves his work station. Another advantage is the audience does not have to travel to a conference to hear the speaker. Realistically, the telephone audience can virtually be from coast to coast. The disadvantage for a seasoned presenter is the fact you never see the audience and have face to face communication. This can be troublesome for some speakers.

The expert may want to advertise on their own in a variety of other places. Hard copy journals, websites, and expert witness internet sites are various additional ways beyond brokerage firms. Each of these comes with a fee assessed on a yearly basis. The Sport & Recreation Law Association is another excellent source for expert witnesses in a variety of disciplines.

Fee Schedules of an Expert

Experts within the general fields of recreation, physical education, athletics, and sports will need to research the fee continuum to ascertain a fee pricing schedule. The key to not overpricing oneself is to ask the question, "What is reasonable?" Certainly, commanding a fee which is too high will prevent an attorney from hiring you. Conversely, if you command a very low fee, the attorney will know your experience is at question. Again, the key is balance and knowing the market. An attorney who is operating as a sole proprietor in Maine, for example, will have a completely different budget for a case than a multiple principal firm in New York City. Sometimes the gravity of the case will dictate the budget and hiring the expert(s). Certainly, a death case in Maine versus New York City may command the exact same need for expert(s) and warrant the same budget.

The savvy expert will want to request a non-refundable retainer from the retaining attorney. This will cover the initial phases of reading some of the discovery items within the case. The reason for the requested "non-refundable" retainer is to make certain the expert's name isn't being used as a wedge just to settle the case quickly, without ever being officially retained. Without a non-refundable retainer, the attorney can request return of his check or the balance of the check. Experts can request a "naming fee" from the retaining attorney, as another separate part of their fee schedule.

Presently, in today's market (and the market does fluctuate with the economy), experts within the general field of recreation will be demanding somewhere between $100.00 and $325.00 per hour. Many attorneys may question the expert's knowledge within the field with a rate so low as $100.00. Novice experts will unknowingly rank themselves low, since they do not know the "going rate" within the field. At the high end, $325.00 per hour would represent the expert's fee coupled with the surcharge by a brokerage firm.

Fees can be based upon total educational degrees and total experience. Someone with a Ph.D. will command a higher rate than someone with just a bachelor's degree. This is obvious. Someone with forty years experience within the profession will command more than someone with just part-time experience over a ten year period. One needs to factor in all these variables.

The engagement letter or fee schedule letter is critical for the expert to place in writing all fees to be assessed. Usually, this is shared immediately after an initial conversation with the potential retaining attorney. There must be some thought that goes into this letter, prior to sending it off to the attorney. The hourly fee must be spelled out as to what it covers. The hourly fee for testimony must be spelled out as well. Travel arrangements to the site need to be mentioned (i.e. flight, rental car, tolls, fuel, hourly fee on the road etc.). Lodging and food arrangements need to be mentioned within this letter. If the expert needs to fly to the incident site or deposition, in addition to the cost of the flight, travel time on the airplane needs to be addressed with the attorney. This can either be a flat fee or hourly fee. Compensation is justified for time going to the airport, flying and then going to the site or deposition.

Some cases may be on the expert's shelf for literally years. It is incumbent upon the expert to have a caveat within the engagement letter stating the prices will hold for one year. It is unreasonable to assume a case that came on seven years ago will have the same rate applied. Payment within a thirty day period should be stated within the engagement letter. It is always a good policy to have the engagement letter signed by both parties agreeing to the terms.

Collecting your fees from the attorney may be an adventure! As with any business, certain clients will pay on time and others will not. Ideally, the secret is to always replenish your retainer fee once the hours are depleted. In this fashion, you are never waiting for your money. However, this isn't always feasible, since the retainer will be expended for much of the initial work on the case. Billing hourly from that point forward sometimes can make more sense. Some attorneys, for a "small" case or a case whose merits they do not know, are reluctant to pay the entire retainer up front. This can be handled by requesting an hour or two of hourly fees just to handle the immediate need of reviewing the case. The attorney is more than willing to handle it in this fashion, since it will not deplete their budget on an unknown case.

When the bill is in excess of thirty days, another sixty day notice should be sent to the attorney. When ninety days has gone by, a final notice should be presented to the attorney. If no response is made, it may be wise to indicate to the attorney that the appropriate grievance committee within their bar association will be contacted. This is usually the type of incentive needed to force the attorney to pay. Needless to say, your association with this attorney will be seriously affected in the future.

Local Expert vs. National Expert

The use of the local expert over the national recognized expert has its advantages, as well as disadvantages. The local expert may be better equipped to know the locale, customs of the community, state laws, local ordinances and political nuances of the community. The national expert will have to study the community and get to know the state and/or local laws which may pertain to the case. For example, if it is a board of education case, the national expert would have to know how various state agencies may oversee, interface with, or evaluate the district.

Admittedly, the national expert will be more recognized, and perhaps valued, by the litigation team. The old saying "no one is a prophet in his own land" holds true here regarding the local expert. The old definition of an expert is one who has traveled at least fifty miles from their home! However, there can also be a backlash effect by using an outside resource. The stereotype of the "city slicker" expert coming into a small sleepy town will be scrutinized by the local community. The acceptance of the national expert at a trial may not be so warm a welcome as one would think!

Standard of Care

The standard of care is based upon any given number of standards within the field. One encompassing definition of a "standard" is:

> A standard is something established for use as a rule or basis of comparison in measuring or judging capacity. A standard applies to some measure, principle, model etc., with which things of the same class are compared in order to determine their quantity, value, or quality. A standard has a set of criteria used to test or measure the excellence, fitness, or correctness of something (Sawyer, 2009).

Experts need to know the existing industry standards to be totally knowledgeable regarding their chosen case. The retained expert can't feign their ignorance regarding the existence of a specific standard. If the expert does, this is paramount to committing professional suicide. One needs to know when the standard is updated in order that the appropriate standard is cited within a case. Additionally, the standard cited can't post date the day of the incident. If it does, the admissibility may come into question. Careful research into the published date needs to be ascertained. When the date has been obtained, the expert will need to weigh the reasonableness of its implementation. For example, if the standard was published on the first of June, would it be reasonable to assume the agency/owner could implement the standard on the first of September? The expert will need to weigh how accessible the standard was for the owner/operator. One will need to take into account how fast the standard was disseminated.

Generally speaking, it would be reasonable to assume most agencies may not be able to implement new existing standards immediately. Therefore, six (6) months to one (1) year might be a reasonable time frame for coming into compliance with any new existing standard. Again this is situational, depending on the standard and how well it was disseminated. In our electronic age, documents can be downloaded from the internet. Therefore, documents are available to the general public. For example, the U. S. Consumer Product Safety Commission makes their voluntary guidelines for playground equipment available to the public on their website. It would be reasonable to assume an elementary school principal looking into playground safety for their school would be knowledgeable about the contents of the *Public Playground Safety Handbook* (U. S. Consumer Product Safety Commission, 2010).

The expert will need to know a variety of standards, depending on their area of expertise. Certainly, position statements, rule books, facility books, medical protocol, teaching methodologies, and government related documents will all have relevance to the recreational/athletic expert. Treatises, books, and documents will need to be checked as to their validity. The author's background will need to be investigated to ascertain if the author has expertise within that chosen field. For example, a prominent health/fitness document published in 2007 has included a small section devoted to playground equipment. Unfortunately, the authors cited a source from 1988. The playground industry has exploded since 1988. The citation is outdated and would give the owner/operator of an agency the incorrect information. The informed expert would not rely on this outdated resource or even bring it to a deposition, unless it directly related to a case involving old, outdated equipment.

Reference to "authoritative" textbooks is the slippery slope question within a deposition or trial. If the opposing attorney questions whether a textbook is "authoritative," it may be answered in two ways. One can say it is "authoritative," thus relying on every word within the document as being upheld. This is dangerous, since any passage in the entire book could be called into question and be presented to the deponent. Or, the deponent might say the text they just brought for an exhibit is NOT "authoritative," thus contradicting what they just said. The proper answer for such a question would be the textbook is "authoritative" on the issue involved within this litigation matter. The deponent might say that the treatise is very helpful within this case, however, I don't necessarily agree with the author's view throughout the entire book (Babitisky & Mangraviti, 2008).

Referencing various professional associations will assist the expert in the litigation matter. There are a number of associations which publish journals, position statements, professional literature, standards, and guidelines. The following list points out some professional organizations the expert within the sports litigation field may use for their case:

- American Alliance for Health, Physical Education, Recreation & Dance
- American College of Sports Medicine
- American Society for Testing & Materials International
- National Association for Sport and Physical Education (AAHPERD)
- National Collegiate Athletic Association
- National Federation of State High School Associations
- National Program for Playground Safety
- National Recreation & Park Association
- National Strength and Conditioning Association
- U.S. Consumer Product Safety Commission

Certainly, the above listing is not all inclusive, however most experts within the areas of athletics, physical education, recreation, and playgrounds would be familiar with their existence.

Discovery Techniques for the Sport/Recreation Expert

The site inspection is key for the expert witness in gaining actual knowledge of the case. Public property can be inspected, providing no local ordinances preclude trespassers on the property. The expert should ascertain from the retaining attorney the circumstances for such an inspection. If the expert is going to a public domain, they should check if there is fencing surrounding the venue or locked gates which would prevent an inspection. Private schools, public restaurants, daycare centers, health/fitness clubs, and private businesses will need a court motion for inspection from the plaintiff expert's side. Local ordinances on some public education sites will prevent trespassers from accessing the property.

Photographs and videotapes of the incident scene do not really replace the actual site inspection. The expert will need to be armed with some basic "tools of the trade" in order to do a complete inspection. The following basic items should be in the expert's tool kit for a sufficient on-site inspection:

- Digital camera (at least two)
- Compass (for directionality)
- Measuring tapes (25', 100', 150' & 300')
- 5 lbs. wt. (to hold the tape down at zero feet!)
- Folding ruler (6')
- Measuring surveyor's rod (8')
- Walking wheel for measuring
- Tent number sign or orange cones with sleeve numbers for identification
- Protractor or electronic level for angles
- Contour gauge
- Stopwatch (situational for some cases)
- Number hand counter (situational for some cases)

The inspection of playgrounds will require some specialty tools, such as a torso probe, a head Probe, and protrusion gauges. These are available through the National Recreation and Park Association.

A *thorough* inspection will take usually two to three hours for any court, field, or playground. When it comes to measurements and photographs, one cannot take too many. The saying "you only get one bite from the apple" applies to inspections. It is better to have too many measurements and photographs than not enough. If the site is two thousand miles away from the expert's home, it is better not to miss a crucial measurement, since it can't be redone. Therefore, it is critical to take several measurements of the gymnasium for example, if the case involves a buffer zone related problem of the end line of the court. The address of the site, type of venue, (e. g. football field, soccer field, playground, health/fitness facility etc.), the temperature, the time of day, the weather conditions (if outdoors), the manufacturer's name (e.g. soccer goal), the type of surfacing (e.g. carpet, synthetic flooring, wooden floor, grass, etc.), and signage within immediate area need to be recorded on intake form notes.

The inspection notes should be as complete as possible upon leaving the site. Any additional thoughts afterwards should be noted with the date on the inspection sheets, indicating any changes. Photographs should be downloaded to the computer immediately from the camera to insure the photographs will not be lost, and a backup disk should be used.

Interviews (plaintiff driven) are very helpful for the expert in establishing what took place within an incident. However, the expert will need to clear access for the interview with the retaining attorney. Some attorneys want little or no contact between the expert and their client. The interview may contradict what has already been stated within deposition testimony by the witness. Hence, the attorney's concern for no contact. If the attorney agrees to their client being interviewed, it may be handled in two ways. The attorney can be present so they will know what took place. The second option would be the attorney is not present and the expert interviews the client in person, or over the telephone. The attorney may want to conference in for such an interview of their client.

The expert's "incident report" form (plaintiff driven) for the interview should include the following standard items: name of the client, date of birth, age now, address, parents' names, telephone number, dominant hand, regularly wears eyeglasses or contact lenses, weight now, weight at time of incident, height now, height at time of incident, names of persons in charge at time of injury, location of injury (e.g. behind school, football field, etc.), address of location of incident, date of incident, time of day, weather on date of incident, approximate temperature on date of incident, and a narrative of how the incident occurred. The incident report form should also detail: the body part(s) injured, what first aid was immediately given, who administered the first aid, knowledge of this first responder's training (if known), knowledge of whether the person was ever moved, what clothing and footwear the client was wearing, where the client went for medical treatment, what rules were given to the client, whether the rules written or verbally given, and the status of the body part today. This incident report form should be shared with the retaining attorney prior to filling it out with the client.

The discovery process will present a number of items to the expert. Depositions will allow the expert to read sworn testimony about the cast of people with direct or indirect knowledge of the incident. Within some large cases, there may be as many as twenty (20) depositions or more to read. Within typically smaller cases, there will only be three (3) to six (6) depositions to read. Interrogatory responses are sworn answers to questions involving the case. They are helpful in noting formal responses to questions involving the litigation matter.

The incident form (i.e., accident form) is very helpful in noting the date and time of the incident. It will also indicate the person in charge of the activity. A short detailed description of how the incident took place will also be included. The incident form is a key piece of evidence within the discovery process.

The medical records of the injured party are important to the plaintiff expert. It is incumbent upon the expert to request the medical records of the injured party. The sports and recreation expert is not trained in the medical field, however it will make the expert more credible when testimony is given. It is not necessary to read the entire medical history of the client. The immediate first aid given, the immediate ambulance report, and hospitalization and physical therapy reports would be important to review in preparation for testimony.

Written Reports by the Expert

The written report by the expert is crucial to the outcome of the case. Certainly, a well written report may hasten the case to settlement without ever going to trial. Within the report, the expert should state the known facts regarding the case. The format of the report will vary depending upon the expert. However, the following items should be included within any basic report: executive summary, background of the expert, material reviewed, date of inspection and findings, tools employed during the inspection, opinions stated numerically within paragraph formation, compensation for the case, photographs, and summary (Babitsky & Mangraviti, 2002).

The expert needs to remember the "magic" words attorneys will be looking for in summarizing the report. For example, when stating the compensation the attorney is paying the expert, one should use a phrase, "I am being paid for my time and not my opinions within this matter." This will alleviate the expert looking like a "hired gun."

In the closing statements, most attorneys will be looking for the catch phrase, "…. with a reasonable degree of professional certainty I am opining …" This should be part of every expert's closing. Also, key catch phrases such as, "the treadmill injury was caused 'significantly and substantially' by XYZ Fitness employees and their agents" is jargon that can be used within the written report.

It must be remembered the complaint filed is not fact. It is the allegations of how an injury took place. Therefore, it should not be relied upon solely as to how the injury occurred. In writing a report, it would be unwise to rely heavily upon the filed complaint.

The background of the expert should be briefly stated within the report. It is not necessary to lay out the entire scope and work of the expert. The expert should always include within the report their latest curriculum vitae along with copies of any certifications and/or licenses. The curriculum vitae should *NOT* allude to any litigation work for attorneys. Therefore, references to cases consulted, listing of testimony and listing of the total case load over the last few years would not be appropriate to include. Professionally, the attorney would only be interested in your educational background and work-related experience as it relates to their case. If the attorney desires a complete listing of testimony (depositions and trials), they may request it. This is a separate listing divorced from the curriculum vitae and can be updated periodically as testimony is completed. The inclusion of testimony and expert witness work within a curriculum vitae makes the document less than professional.

Photographs are vital to the report and should be included for the attorney. This can be done in a variety of ways. Hard copy photographs can be included at the rear of the report with an accompanying key indicating the significance of each photograph. The expert may choose to only include selective photographs to characterize certain elements of the case. The expert should include an entire CD Rom of the photographs taken at the site within the report. In this fashion, the retaining attorney will have a copy of the photographs taken on the inspection day.

Professionalism is the key in writing a report for an attorney. Derogatory comments towards the opposing expert are not warranted. Quoting passages correctly and with the appropriate dates are incumbent upon the expert. Utilizing the correct standard with the date and year as it applies to the case is extremely important. The report should be presented to the attorney in a bound cover folder.

The length of the report will be based upon the case and its many facets. Some cases are simple and can be covered in a very short report. On the other hand, some cases are multi-faceted. Some attorneys will demand a short one or two page report. Others will want the opinions expressed in detail, since this report may act within their state as the disclosure of the expert. If a particular opinion is not stated within the report, the expert will be excluded from stating it at trial in those states that use the expert's report as their disclosure.

Challenging the other expert's report needs to be based upon total professionalism. Finding other written articles or books by the opposing expert is an excellent way to attack the other expert's credibility, if previous opinions are found in conflict with their report. By indicating one "respectfully disagrees," the tone will be set for the expert writing the report which discredits the opposing expert. It is unwise to directly attack their character within the report.

Many experts will network, as noted previously within this chapter. It is unwise to discuss the case with another colleague who you may be opposing at trial. It is best to keep all conversations with the opposing expert to topics unrelated to the case.

Lastly, a written report should never be rendered until the retaining attorney requests it. This is of utmost importance, since materials may have to be shared with the opposing side. By writing an unsolicited report, the expert may show the retaining attorney's "hand" prematurely.

Testimony

Testimony takes the form of depositions and trial testimony. It is well founded in many personal injury cases that matters within the domains of physical education, athletics, recreation, and playgrounds get settled prior to trial. The percentage of cases is extremely low, which actually go to trial. For the plaintiff, it is foolhardy to press for a trial if a reasonable demand and offer have been made. If the plaintiff is greedy and is seeking more of a monetary award, they could potentially wind up with nothing, if the jury does not find in their favor. In some states with tort reform, there are caps or ceilings on the monetary amount one can seek in a case against municipalities. For example, in one state, the maximum award for a fracture or even death is only $100,000! This seriously limits the plaintiff's bargaining power.

In preparing for testimony, the expert needs to study, much the same as studying for a final exam in college. The date of the incident, the client's birthday, the deposition testimony, the complaint, medical facts surrounding the case, the opposing expert's report, and the expert's own report need to be reviewed so they can be recalled easily. The expert's file needs to be broken down alphabetically into sub-category files in order for them to be able to pull out the appropriate file when questioned at deposition. At trial, the expert's file can be with the expert on the witness stand. The file should be organized into categories. The following categories represent some typical sub-files the expert may want to generate: accident report, advertising of opposing attorney, billing, checklist for litigation, communications, complaint, curriculum vitae of the expert, deposition transcripts, deposition exhibits, inspection, interrogatories, medical records, personal notes, production requests, testimony previously given, and travel arrangements.

It is crucial to the expert's file to have a form to check off to summarize the documents within the case as they are received. For lack of a better term, this sheet may be called "Checklist for Litigation." On this form, the documents are checked off as they are received. It is an easy way to determine what outstanding documents are still needed within the case. For example, perhaps the paralegal may have forgotten to send out the interrogatories to the expert. By seeing this category not checked off, the expert may want to be in touch with the paralegal to secure these documents. This will assist the expert in getting ready for testimony. Once all the sub-files are within the folder, the expert really needs to review each and every file prior to testimony. All depositions should be read again. The expert's report is critical with regard to the opinions being offered within the matter. Certainly, this needs to be read a couple of times in order for the expert to be very familiar with its contents.

The expert will need to meet with the retaining attorney prior to the deposition to go over testimony and any questions the expert may have. With seasoned experts, some attorneys may think this is superfluous. However, it is still needed by seasoned veterans in the field!

Any physical evidence needs to be prepared ahead of time. This may involve various props for exhibits. One caution regarding exhibits. They need to work! Therefore, you must try out any working exhibit to make certain it will not fail at the time of testimony. For example, in a case involving gymnastics, the simulation of uneven parallel bars was needed. Obviously, for a courtroom, it would be too cumbersome to actually bring in uneven bars. The injured youngster was doing a "lat" pull-down with a bungee type cord from one of the bars. PVC pipe with the appropriate "T"'s and elbows were used to simulate the uneven parallel bars. However, PVC will bend when it is pulled down. Therefore, the exhibit could fail, if the PVC pipe broke at trial. The expert reinforced the PVC pipe by placing wooden dowels inside of the pipe. This gave the exhibit more stability. The entire exhibit could be broken down and placed in a duffle bag for easy transport. At the time for the demonstration at the trial, it worked well without any difficulties. Had the expert not reinforced the PVC pipe, it may have cracked upon the demonstration to the jury. This would have left a very embarrassed expert in front of the judge and jury, not to mention a chagrined retaining attorney. The expert should always check ahead with the retaining attorney to make certain an exhibit is warranted and needed.

Depositions are important from the standpoint of the expert stating all their opinions. Depositions can be scheduled at mutually agreeable times for the deponent, retaining attorney and deposing attorney. With regard to deposition testimony, it is imperative to allow yourself enough time to travel to the offices where the deposition is taking place. More likely than not, it will be held within the offices of the requesting attorney. Your entire file needs to be brought to the deposition along with any other requests. Schedule "A" will enumerate all the items the deposing attorney will expect the expert to bring. This will be the entire file, including any treatises, documents, books, position statements, and rule books the expert relied upon in arriving at their opinion. Also, the expert may be asked within Schedule "A" to produce a complete listing of previous testimony along with: reference to the case, attorneys involved, addresses of the attorneys, and date of the testimony. An updated version of the expert's curriculum vitae will be requested as well.

The deposition is usually taken in a conference room at the opposing attorney's office. This room can be small, cramped, and most uncomfortable. It can be just the opposite (i.e. large, roomy, and most comfortable, with captain's chairs). The expert will sit at the discretion of the court reporter and opposing attorney. If given a choice of seats, the expert should try to sit where glare from any windows will not be an issue.

In some situations, the deposition may take place at a hotel, if the parties are flying in from various parts of the country. Again, selecting a seat without glare will be important to the expert from the standpoint of being comfortable.

After being sworn in by the court reporter, the expert must bear in mind, it is perfectly acceptable to refer to any sub-file or reference within the file. The expert must take their time in attempting to locate the correct document without getting flustered. Usually, any exhibit will be marked by the court reporter. It is always wise to state the exhibit number when referring to a specific exhibit. Most depositions within a typical sports/recreation case will take two hours on average. However, some may run longer. Therefore, it is imperative to take breaks periodically after each hour. Just to move around or go outside the deposition room is important in keeping fresh and keeping one's focus. One word of caution here—do not speak to anyone about the case, including the retaining attorney. Any conversation during a break may be fair game for the deposing attorney to question the expert upon, when the deposition resumes. Therefore, idle talk about the weather, sports, or the news would be more appropriate.

After the conclusion of the deposition, there may be items the deposing attorney will want copies of for their files. This is handled in three ways. The deposing attorney may retain the materials and send them back to the expert. The retaining attorney may copy them for the deposing attorney. The last option is the expert will copy their own materials. The expert should not leave the deposition without knowing the financial arrangements for copying the file. Also, if certain copies are desired in color this should be stipulated. The best solution is requesting the deposing attorney reduce to writing exactly what needs to be copied. In that fashion, there is no mistake or quarrel about the billing later on in the process.

Trial testimony is not as flexible as deposition testimony. The trial is scheduled on the court calendar well in advance. At the same time, the expert is made known of the trial date well in advance. Therefore, appropriate travel arrangements need to be made as the trial approaches. Trial testimony may entail flying or traveling to the site the evening beforehand. Again, the expert will need to arrange for their flight, lodging, and rental car. If plans shift and an additional day is required for the expert's testimony, the expert will need to shuffle their plans with the airline, hotel, and rental car agency. Therefore, the life of an expert witness cannot be rigid! The expert needs to be flexible.

With regard to grooming and dressing for a testimony (deposition or trial), business casual dress is *not* acceptable. Men and women need to dress in suits. Conservative suits would be the best choice. Men need to wear white shirts. Personal grooming needs attention. The opposing attorney will judge the expert by their appearance.

After the deposition is completed it is best to pack all your materials and leave the office. The expert should not be discussing the case within earshot of the deposing attorney. No comments should be made to any parties still left within the room concerning the case.

Videotaped depositions may occur under certain circumstances. The videographer will be opposite the expert and will be recording the expert's every move, as well as the expert's audio. Therefore, it is extremely important to remain calm and divorce the camera from one's testimony. By focusing on the opposing attorney's questions and looking at the opposing attorney will help to alleviate the pressures of the camera staring at the expert. The expert needs to articulate clearly and annunciate their words. Grooming is crucial with this type of deposition!

With trial testimony, it is best to leave the courtroom after the expert delivers their testimony. By staying within the courtroom, it will give the jurors the feeling the expert has a vested interest within the case. This would not be a positive image to present to the jury. Any conversation concerning the expert's testimony can be discussed at a later point in time. It is also imperative at the trial lunch breaks to avoid any contact with jurors, who may be dining in the court's common cafeteria. Certainly, the judge could declare a mistrial if you were seen speaking to the jurors.

In My Opinion

Is the role of the expert to win the case? Obviously, the expert has been retained for their expertise. However, the *ultimate role of the expert is in educating* the jury to the case by interpreting the facts for them. Within the role of a recreational expert, this person has the unique position to educate the jury by virtue of their background. By reducing questions to simple answers without talking over the heads of the jury, or by talking beneath them, the expert is in a very persuasive role. The expert should not be an advocate for the side they have been retained for in the case. The jury will sense if the expert is over reaching to prove their position and might be turned off by such a gesture. Staying with the facts, stating them calmly, and controlling emotions is the name of the game. It is the attorney's role to prevail in the case.

Case Study

In applying the above principles to an actual case, the fictional title to protect the actual parties involved will be referenced "*Jane Doe, et al. v. ABC Gymnastics, d/b/a Olympic Tumblers, et al.*" Briefly, Jane Doe was enrolled in a pre-school program at ABC Gymnastics. At the time of her trip and fall incident, she was three (3) years and four (4) months old. The case was placed into suit with the plaintiff attorney filing the complaint. The plaintiff attorney retained the recreational expert by sending the expert a non-refundable retainer. The plaintiff attorney's recreational expert had access to the following discovery items: the Department of Children and Families case worker's report, the incident report, interrogatories, witnesses' statements, and notes/ photographs from a two (2) hour personal inspection of the facility. The expert also interviewed Jane Doe's mother over the telephone.

Jane Doe was running up a wedge (ramp) mat to access a higher level and to ultimately access a trampoline. While doing so, she tripped on the depression of the wedge mat, where it met the firmer stacked mats. In tripping, she lost her balance and fell against an unpadded wall and struck her head, which left a scar with a depression. In doing the inspection, the expert measured the distance from the trip area to the wall as three (3) feet, nine (9) inches. It was *foreseeable* that a young child running towards an unpadded wall could trip and fall. Lack of appropriate supervision was cited as well by the expert.

Upon inspection of the facility, it was so noted three (3) walls were padded and the incident wall was not padded. Thus, the owner/operator set up a double standard of care within their own gymnasium. The expert filed a written report at the request of the retaining plaintiff attorney. The written report cited the materials reviewed along with the expert's opinions. Within five months of the expert's inspection, the expert's deposition was taken. The expert cited the American Society for Testing & Materials International's F 2440-04 (i.e. Standard Specification for Indoor Wall/Feature Padding) which was published in 2004. The expert also cited a well known physical education book on safety within his report. Portions of this book would be considered "authoritative" within the industry. It was noted the incident occurred on January 09, 2008. Therefore, the expert cited the appropriate standard by referencing a treatise, which was in effect at the time of the incident.

The case was scheduled for trial approximately six (6) months after the expert's deposition. As with the majority of personal injury cases relating to recreation/athletics, the plaintiff attorney's paralegal communicated to the expert that the case had settled. Therefore, the expert's testimony at trial was not needed.

References

Babitsky, S., Mangraviti, J. J., & Babitsky, A. (2006). *The A–Z guide to expert witnessing.* Falmouth, MA: SEAK, Inc.

Babitsky, S., & Mangraviti, J. J. (2008). *The biggest mistakes expert witnesses make and how to avoid them.* Falmouth, MA: SEAK, Inc. Babitsky, S., & Mangraviti, J. J. (2002). Writing and defending your expert report. The step-by-step guide with models. Falmouth, MA: SEAK, Inc.

Sawyer, T. H. (2009). Equipment and facility design standards. In T. H. Sawyer (Ed.), *Facility planning and design for health, physical activity, recreation, and sport.* (12th ed., p. 427). Champaign, Illinois: Sagamore Publishing.

U.S. Consumer Product Safety Commission. (2010). *Public playground safety handbook.* Bethesda, MD: U.S. Consumer Product Safety Commission.

Chapter 32

Cheerleading and the Law: A Statistical Report

Cheerleading should be conducted within the limits of safety.

Frederick O. Mueller

The association of injuries and cheerleading is something that has taken place within the last 30 years. As a comparison, football injury data collection began in the late 1800s. Cheerleading actually began around the same time as American football, with young men leading the cheers and school songs at sporting events. According to A. B. Frederick, cheerleading has gone through three distinct periods (Frederick 1990). In the pre-World War II era, cheerleading was a student-organized activity which consisted of yelling cheers and simple tumbling. After World War II, cheerleading spread rapidly across the country, and equipment like the miniature trampoline began to be used in gymnastics maneuvers, which increased the possibility of accidents. During the last period, from approximately 1975 to the present, when the numbers of participants has grown to hundreds of thousands, stunts have become increasingly complex, competitions have been organized for a national championship, and summer training camps have become popular. It has been during this last period that cheerleading also became associated with injuries, both catastrophic and minor.

The Consumer Product Safety Commission (CPSC) reported an estimated 4,954 hospital emergency room visits in 1980 caused by cheerleading injuries (CPSC 1995). By 1986 that number had increased to 6,911 and was continuing to grow. The 1995 CPSC data showed an estimate of 16,982 cheerleading injuries that involved an individual going to a hospital emergency room. The 2002 CPSC injury data for cheerleading shows 24,675 emergency room injuries. The 2009 CPSC data show 31,455 emergency room visits for cheerleading injuries. There is no doubt that the number of participants has also increased during this time; but the problem is that the number of cheerleaders was not known in the early years, and that participation figures have been collected at the high school level only within the last ten years. The latest participation numbers from the National Federation of State High School Associations (NFHS 2010), which calls the activity **competitive spirit**, show the following:

	Boys	Girls	Total
Competitive Spirit	2,746	123,644	126,390

These numbers are for competitive spirit only, and do not include participation numbers for drill, pom-pom, or sideline cheerleading. These numbers do not include a wide variety of other cheerleading groups, which could increase these numbers dramatically.

Table 1. High School Cheerleading Direct Catastrophic Injuries, 1982–83 to 2009–10

Year	Fatalities	Disability	Serious
1982–1983	0	0	0
1983–1984	0	0	0
1984–1985	0	2	0
1985–1986	0	1	0
1986–1987	0	0	1
1987–1988	0	2	1
1988–1989	0	0	1
1989–1990	0	1	1
1990–1991	0	1	1
1991–1992	1	1	0
1992–1993	0	0	1
1993–1994	0	0	2
1994–1995	0	2	2
1995–1996	0	0	1
1996–1997	0	1	1
1997–1998	0	1	0
1998–1999	0	0	5
1999–2000	0	0	4
2000–2001	0	1	1
2001–2002	0	4	3
2002–2003	0	2	2
2003–2004	0	3	3
2004–2005	0	0	4
2005–2006	1	0	10
2006–2007	0	0	3
2007–2008	0	3	0
2008–2009	0	1	1
2009–2010	0	2	0
Total	2	28	48

National Center for Catastrophic Sports Injury Research

The National Center for Catastrophic Sports Injury Research began collecting cheerleading data when a number of cases were reported at the college level in 1982–1983. Following are the results of 28 years of data collection.

Direct Cheerleading Fatalities (1982–83 to 2009–10)

There have been three cheerleading direct fatalities during the twenty-eight year period from 1982–2010 (see Tables 1 and 2). High school cheerleading accounted for two fatal injuries and college cheerleading accounted for one. One of the high school fatalities involved a high school cheerleader who died a week after the accident in which she fell from a double-level cheerleading stunt during practice and struck her head on the gym

Table 2. College Cheerleading Direct Catastrophic Injuries, 1982–83 to 2009–10

Year	Fatalities	Disability	Serious
1982–1983	0	1	1
1983–1984	0	1	2
1984–1985	0	1	0
1985–1986	1	1	0
1986–1987	0	0	1
1987–1988	0	0	0
1988–1989	0	0	0
1989–1990	0	0	1
1990–1991	0	0	0
1991–1992	0	0	1
1992–1993	0	0	0
1993–1994	0	0	2
1994–1995	0	1	1
1995–1996	0	0	0
1996–1997	0	1	1
1997–1998	0	0	1
1998–1999	0	1	0
1999–2000	0	0	1
2000–2001	0	1	0
2001–2002	0	1	2
2002–2003	0	0	0
2003–2004	0	2	0
2004–2005	0	0	0
2005–2006	0	0	1
2006–2007	0	0	3
2007–2008	0	0	2
2008–2009	0	0	2
2009–2010	0	0	1
Total	1	11	23

floor. She suffered massive head injuries. The second high school cheerleader was a flyer and was not caught by her teammates and suffered a ruptured spleen. The college cheerleader also died from injuries suffered during a cheerleading stunt. Her injuries included multiple skull fractures and massive brain damage. The athlete fell from the top level of a pyramid-type stunt and struck her head on the gym floor. The direct fatality injury rate, if one used the estimates provided (approximately 130,000 high school cheerleaders and 10,000 college cheerleaders per year) would be 0.06 per 100,000 participants at the high school level and 0.4 per 100,000 participants at the college level.

Disability Injuries in Cheerleading (1982–83 to 2009–10)

There have been 28 permanent disability injuries at the high school level for the twenty-eight year period mentioned above. A majority of the injuries happened when the athlete fell from a pyramid stunt or when she/he was dropped during a basket catch or dropped during another activity that involved being caught during a cheerleading stunt. Following are a sample of the cases involving high school cheerleading:

1) A high school cheerleader was injured during a practice after falling from the top of a pyramid. She struck her head and neck on a hard surface and was partially paralyzed.

2) A high school cheerleader was attempting to complete a back flip off the shoulders of another cheerleader. She landed on her head and neck, fractured a cervical vertebra, and was diagnosed as quadriplegic.

3) A high school cheerleader fell from a pyramid in practice. She was six feet off the floor when she fell and was not using spotters. Her injuries included a fractured collarbone, a damaged ear drum, and a basal skull fracture. She has suffered a partial hearing loss and has to wear special glasses for reading.

4) A high school cheerleader was tossed into the air by two of her teammates and was supposed to flip backwards and land feet first on the shoulders of two other cheerleaders. She fell on a hard surface during the stunt and was paralyzed from the waist down.

5) A high school cheerleader fractured a cervical vertebra during practice. She was doing a series of back flips during a tumbling run, slipped on the wet grass, and landed on her neck. She is a quadriplegic.

6) A high school cheerleader was injured during a stunt when a fellow cheerleader fell on her head. She has had permanent medical problems since the accident.

Disability injury rates for high school cheerleading are 0.77 per 100,000 participants. This rate is very low, but there are concerns that there should not be any catastrophic injuries in cheerleading.

Disability injuries at the college level numbered 11 from 1982–2010. The etiology of college injuries is no different than that of the high school injuries — a cheerleader falling from a pyramid stunt and striking a hard surface or being dropped during another stunt. Following are sample cases involving college disability injuries:

1) A cheerleader was injured while cheering at a basketball game when he performed a dive from a mini-trampoline over several cheerleaders into a forward roll. He fractured and dislocated several cervical vertebrae and had permanent paralysis.

2) A college cheerleader fractured her skull in practice after falling from the top level of a three-high pyramid. She struck her head on the wood floor in the gym. She was in critical condition for a period of time, but was released from the hospital and is involved in occupational therapy. She has permanent disabilities.

3) A cheerleader was paralyzed after a fall in practice. He was attempting a front flip from a mini-trampoline. He dislocated several cervical vertebrae and is now a quadriplegic.

4) A college cheerleader was paralyzed after attempting a double flip during a basket toss. At the present time she is a quadriplegic.

The disability injury rate at the college level is 3.93 per 100,000 participants (participation numbers are estimated since participation numbers are not collected at the college level). When compared to other college sports this rate is fairly high.

Table 3. Cheerleading Injuries Consumer Product Safety Commission by Age and Sex, Calendar Year 2009

Age	Male	Female	Total
5–14	245	15,398	15,643
15–24	593	14,825	15,418
25–44	15	372	387
Other	0	7	7
Total	853	30,602	31,455

Serious Injuries in Cheerleading (1982–83 to 2009–10)

From 1982 through 2010 there were 48 serious high school cheerleading injuries with recovery. The etiology is exactly the same as the disability injuries and in most cases can be prevented. The serious injury rate is 1.32 per 100,000 participants in high school cheerleading. There were also 23 serious injuries in college cheerleading during the same time period. The case of the college cheerleader who suffered a head injury during practice is a good example of how many of the serious injuries could have been disability injuries or fatalities if there had not been proper medical care or medical facilities available to the individual. The cheerleader was thrown into the air, but was not caught by her teammates and struck her head on the gym floor. She was in critical condition, was downgraded to serious and is expected to recover. The serious injury rate is 8.21 per 100,000 participants for college cheerleading and this rate is high when compared with other college sports.

Consumer Product Safety Commission Data

As previously mentioned in this chapter, the Consumer Product Safety Commission collects injury data on product-related injuries and sport is one of those areas in the data collection. The CPSC's most recent figures on cheerleading revealed an estimate of 31,455 injuries in 2009. These estimates were calculated using data from a sample of hospitals which are statistically representative of institutions with emergency treatment departments located within the United States and its territories.

As shown in Table 3, females are injured at much greater numbers than males, but if one looks at participation numbers there are many more female cheerleaders. This table also shows that there is not much of a difference between the 5- to 14-year-old and the 15- to 24-year-old age groups. It is not surprising that the numbers are low for the 25- to 44-year-old age group since participation levels are very low for this group. It is impossible to estimate injury rates since the number of participants is unknown, and it is not known how many of these participants were high school or college cheerleaders.

Table 4 shows the types of injuries that cheerleaders are receiving, and it is not surprising that sprains and strains lead the list, followed by contusions/abrasions and fractures. This would be true for most sports, and cheerleading is a sport. What may be surprising is the percentage of fractures, dislocations, lacerations, and concussions (19.2%).

Table 4. Cheerleading Injuries Consumer Product Safety Commission by Injury Type, Calendar Year 2009

Injury Type	Frequency	Percentage
Sprain-Strain	12,773	40.6
Fracture	3,915	12.4
Contusion-Abrasion	5,596	17.8
Internal Injury	2,707	8.6
Laceration	736	2.3
Dislocation	535	1.7
Concussion	888	2.8
Dental Injury	52	0.2
Hematoma	15	0.1
Other	4,238	13.5
Total	31,455	100.0

In most athletic injury studies, the knee and ankle are the body parts most injured, but as shown in Table 5 the head-neck-face lead the list in the CPSC data with 26.3%, followed by the arms-wrist-hand-fingers (25.6%). The head-neck-face are at the top of the list since many of the stunts performed involve either tumbling or catching or throwing a partner. Falling from pyramids or shoulders onto a hard surface or onto another athlete accounts for most of these injuries.

A high percentage of these injuries are not severe, as shown in Table 6. Ninety-eight percent of the injured participants were treated and released, with only 0.6% being hospitalized.

Table 7 reveals the fact the cheerleading injuries are happening most during the football season and the winter basketball season. The months of June, July, and August involve the cheerleaders preparing for the football season and participating in camps. Preparation during the summer months is as intense for the cheerleading squad as it is for the football team.

The incidence of catastrophic injuries in sports at the high school and college levels is low, but even one is too many. Permanent paralysis, brain damage, and death should not be associated with teenagers and young adults participating in high school and college

Table 5. Cheerleading Injuries Consumer Product Safety Commission by Body Part, Calendar Year 2009

Body Part	Frequency	Percentage
Arms, Wrist, Hand, Fingers	8,055	25.6
Head, Neck, Face	8,282	26.3
Knee, Ankle	6,449	20.5
Upper Trunk, Shoulders	3,302	10.5
Lower Trunk	1,703	5.4
Lower Leg, Foot, Toes	2,279	7.2
Upper Leg	266	0.8
Other	1,119	3.6
Total	31,455	100.0

Table 6. Cheerleading Injuries Consumer Product Safety Commission by Disposition, Calendar Year 2009

Disposition	Frequency	Percentage
Treated & Released	30,847	98.1
Hospitalized	197	0.6
Held for Observation	97	0.3
Transfer	146	0.5
Other	168	0.5
Total	31,455	100.0

athletics. One catastrophic injury is not only devastating to the injured athlete, but also to the athlete's family, school, and community.

Injury Prevention

With proper medical care and safety precautions, a number of these injuries can be prevented. It is possible to reduce the number of catastrophic injuries with a good data collection system, the implementation of participation rules, proper medical care, and good coaching. Following are a number of recommendations for injury prevention.

Pre-Participation Exams

A mandatory medical examination and a medical history should be taken before allowing a cheerleader to participate. The National Collegiate Athletic Association (NCAA) recommends a comprehensive medical examination when an athlete first enters a college athletic program and an annual health history update with use of referral exams when warranted. This initial evaluation should include a comprehensive health history, an immunization history as defined by the current Centers for Disease Control (CDC) guidelines, and a relevant physical exam, part of which should include an orthopedic evaluation. High schools should follow the recommendations set by their state high school athletic associations. If there are no set recommendations, the National Federation of State High School Associations in Indianapolis, IN, should be contacted. If the physician or coach has any questions about the readiness of the athlete, the athlete should not be allowed to participate. Both high school and college medical exams should include information on sickle cell trait and safety recommendations for athletes with sickle cell trait should be followed.

Table 7. Cheerleading Injuries Consumer Product Safety Commission by Month, Calendar Year 2009

Months	Frequency	Percentage
December, January, February	7,774	24.7
March, April, May	4,666	14.8
June, July, August	5,862	18.6
September, October, November	13,153	41.8
Total	31,455	100.0

Proper Conditioning

All personnel concerned with training cheerleaders should emphasize proper, gradual, and complete physical conditioning. Adequate conditioning would include cardiovascular conditioning, muscular strength, muscular endurance, and flexibility.

Medical Care

Medical coverage of both practice and game situations is important. Certified athletic trainers can provide good medical coverage, but a physician should be on call for practices and possibly present at games. A physician on-site is preferred, but if this is not possible, written emergency procedures should be prepared in advance. Emergency plans for a possible catastrophic injury should be written and distributed to all personnel involved with the program. Personnel will include, but not be limited to, the head coach, assistant coaches, managers, athletic trainers, and physicians. Cheerleaders should also be made aware of emergency procedures. If everyone understands his/her responsibility in the event of a catastrophic injury, the chances of permanent disability or death may be reduced.

When a cheerleader has experienced or shown signs of head trauma (loss of consciousness, visual disturbances, headache, inability to walk correctly, obvious disorientation, memory loss) she/he should receive immediate medical attention and should not be allowed to practice or cheer without permission from the proper medical authorities. A new NFHS concussion rule for the 2010–2011 sport seasons will apply to all sports and states the following:

> "Any player who exhibits signs, symptoms or behaviors consistent with a concussion (such as loss of consciousness, headache, dizziness, confusion, or balance problems) shall be immediately removed from the contest or practice and shall not return to play until cleared by an appropriate health-care professional. An athlete with a concussion shall not be allowed to continue play in a game or practice the same day and may not return to play in subsequent days without being cleared by a medical professional."

After medical clearance, return to play should follow a step-wise protocol with provisions for delayed return to play based upon return of any signs or symptoms. The NFHS also has suggested guidelines for concussion management on their web site (www.nfhs.org). There is also a concussion course available through the NFHS Coach Certification at nfhslearn.com. Cheerleading coaches and athletes should be aware of these rules.

Each institution should strive to have a team athletic trainer who is a regular member of the faculty and is adequately prepared and qualified. Trainers certified by the National Athletic Trainers Association (NATA) are preferred. Coaches should never be involved in making medical decisions concerning their cheerleaders and only medical personnel should decide when she/he returns to cheer after an injury or illness.

Proper Training of Coaches

Hiring coaches with the ability and expertise to teach the fundamental skills of cheerleading is most important. Competent coaching in cheerleading is a major cause of concern. High schools are having a difficult time employing coaches who are full-time faculty members and in many cases have to hire part-time coaches. This is not a problem if these coaches know the fundamental skills of the sport and have the ability to teach these skills to the participants. Improper teaching of sport skills can be a direct cause of injuries—both catastrophic and otherwise. Cheerleaders should be trained by qualified coaches with training in gymnastics. This person should also be trained in the proper methods for spotting and other safety procedures. Coaches should supervise all practice sessions in a safe facility and should also keep up-to-date on new safety procedures and safety equipment. The days of hiring coaches with no knowledge of cheerleading skills should end. In addition, cheerleading coaches should place an emphasis on providing excellent facilities and securing the safest and best equipment possible.

Cheerleaders should receive proper training and instruction before attempting gymnastic-type stunts and should not attempt stunts they are not capable of completing. A qualification system demonstrating mastery of stunts in progression is recommended. Mini-trampolines and flips off pyramids and shoulders are prohibited and should never be attempted. Pyramid and partner stunts higher than shoulder level should not be performed without mats and spotters.

In My Opinion

Finally, there should be continued research concerning safety in cheerleading. There is no excuse for the number of participants being injured. Cheerleading should be conducted within the limits of safety. The American Association of Cheerleading Coaches and Advisors' Safety Certification Program has been implemented and a great number of coaches have participated. Every attempt should be made to have all cheerleading coaches go through a certification program. At the present time the National Cheer Safety Foundation is the leader in cheerleading safety and their coaches certification program is one of the best in the country. The NCSF also has an excellent emergency plan on their web site that can be downloaded.

According to the National Federation of State High School Associations (NFHS), the primary purpose of spirit groups (cheerleaders, pom squads, dance/drill teams, flag corps) is to serve as support groups for the interscholastic athletic programs within the school. However, spirit groups have also evolved to include competition as athletes. These participants must condition, practice, and warm up the same as other athletes in preparation for a performance. The NFHS states that competition should be a secondary consideration for spirit groups.

A rule book for spirit groups is published by the NFHS and includes information on both legal and illegal stunts (2011–2012 Spirit Rules Book). All of the rules were and are adopted to enhance the safety of the participants. Copies of the spirit group rules book are available from the NFHS office at PO Box 690, Indianapolis, IN 46206.

References

Consumer Product Safety Commission, National Injury Information Clearinghouse. 2009. Washington, DC.

Frederick, A.B. Educational and Safety Materials for Cheerleading. *AACCA Cheerleading Safety Manual*. Tennessee: UCA Publications.

George, G.S. 1985. *USGF Gymnastics Safety Manual*. Indianapolis, IN: The USGF Publications Department.

National Center for Catastrophic Sports Injury Research. 2011. 28th Annual Report 1982–83 to 2009–2010. Chapel Hill, NC: University of North Carolina at Chapel Hill.

National Collegiate Athletic Association. 2009. 2009–10 NCAA Sports Medicine Handbook. Twentieth Edition. Indianapolis, IN.

National Federation of State High School Associations. 2011. *National Federation Rules Book—Spirit 2011–2012.* Indianapolis, IN.

Chapter 33

Expecting the Unexpected: Preparation and Leadership in Emergencies

Everyone can help maintain safety and order at your facility by being aware, at all times, of any possible sources of danger.

Herb Appenzeller,
Todd Seidler & David Scott

An earthquake hits during a World Series game. A college football stadium is filled with 70,000 fans when a tornado warning suddenly sounds. Halfway through the finals for the district volleyball championship, an anonymous caller phones in a bomb threat. A patron working out in a fitness center collapses from an apparent heart attack. Emergencies like these, and countless others, can and do occur. Just what are the legal responsibilities of facility managers and program directors to foresee and prepare for such incidents? The courts have clearly stated that we each have a legal duty to act as a reasonable and prudent professional. The implementation of an overall risk management plan is now the standard expected of reasonable and prudent professional facility managers and program directors. One essential part of an overall risk management program is to prepare for the occurrence of emergencies by developing a formalized and structured Emergency Action Plan (EAP). In recent years, properly planning for emergencies has become expected and is now the accepted "standard of care."

An emergency action plan should also include a crisis communication plan for managing public relations during and after an emergency. Organizations have a responsibility to their internal and external publics to provide timely and accurate information during times of crisis. Elements of an effective crisis communication plan will be discussed in more detail in Section 4 below.

One of the major concepts that we must be concerned with is that of foreseeability. Basically, foreseeability asks the question "should you have known that there was a reasonable possibility of a given emergency occurring?" Is it reasonable to believe that an earthquake might possibly occur in Southern California? If the answer is yes, then it is also reasonable to expect facility managers in Southern California to plan to properly respond to an earthquake when their facility is full of patrons. Is it foreseeable that a severe thunderstorm may develop during a high school baseball game in Oklahoma in May? If it is, then it is also reasonable to expect a high school athletic director to develop a standardized procedure and train the coaches how to react when such a situation arises.

In order to develop an EAP we must ask ourselves many "what if ..." questions. What if one of my wrestlers has a severe neck injury during practice? What is the proper response to such a situation? A mistake commonly made is to think that "I'll know what to do when the situation arises." In fact, most people do not know the proper way to react to emergency situations. The correct reaction must be thought out in advance and staff must be trained to respond quickly and correctly.

An EAP is a highly individualized plan that is rarely identical from one facility to the next. Differences in location, staffing, clientele, programs offered, and layout of the facility, as well as foreseeable problems, all impact the structure of the EAP.

The first step in developing an EAP is to determine who will do it. An Emergency Action Planning Team can consist of as few as one person to as many as necessary. Usually, the larger the organization, the larger the planning team.

Once the EAP team has been established, the primary task is to identify as many potential risks or emergency situations as possible. These should include any possible occurrence, from major catastrophes to minor incidents. At this point, it is important to consider all situations as long as there is a potential for injuries to occur.

Once a list of potential emergencies has been established, it must then be prioritized. Three primary factors must be considered when prioritizing potential problem situations. First we must decide how many people are likely to be affected by a given situation. Is it likely to affect one or two people or thousands? The more people possibly affected, the higher this incident will fall on the priority list. If a set of bleachers collapses, it is likely to produce injuries to a great many people, while hockey pucks flying into the crowd will probably not injure more than a few.

The second factor to consider when prioritizing possible emergency situations is the severity of the injuries that are likely to occur. The greater the possibility of severe injuries or death, the higher the priority of that situation. In this part of the prioritization phase, a loose railing preventing someone from falling off of a walkway 15 feet above the floor would receive a higher priority than a six-inch deep pothole in the parking lot.

The third consideration is how likely the incident is to occur. The higher the probability of occurrence, the higher the priority it is given. It is much more likely for a high school basketball player to sprain an ankle during practice than it is for one of them to have a heart attack. This does not necessarily mean that it is more important to plan to respond to a sprained ankle than a heart attack. All three factors must be considered together. Using the best professional judgment of the committee, each of the identified dangers should be ranked in order of the probability of a loss occurring. Once this list has been established, it is then time to look at the first one and make some decisions on the proper way to prepare for and respond to it if it should occur. As an appropriate emergency response to each possible danger is determined, the next one on the list can then be addressed.

In addition to the above factors, several other questions may be asked in order to determine other effects an incident may have on an organization. These questions vary from one organization to the next and should be determined by the EAP Team. Examples include: does the situation have the potential of escalating in intensity; will the situation affect the public image of the organization; and will the potential situation affect profits in any way? (Sobkowski 1992).

The primary purpose of an emergency plan and evacuation procedures is to define responsibilities and educate all persons connected with the facility on proper protocol for any type of an emergency. The safety of the patrons and employees is a major concern. An organized and comprehensive emergency plan is essential in saving lives and property.

It is the responsibility of facilities to have an updated emergency plan and evacuation procedure. It is also its responsibility to orient and drill all personnel employed at the facility to familiarize themselves with these programs. This reduces injury, loss of life, and property damage. Only a well thought out emergency plan that assigns responsibilities to trained members of a team can assure the most effective response.

Everyone can help maintain safety and order at a facility by being aware, at all times, of any possible sources of danger. Once identified, they should be immediately reported to a supervisor.

The Basics

Each individual facility must develop an EAP that is specific to that unique situation. Large spectator facilities, such as arenas and stadiums, may require the most complex EAP due to the need to be able to quickly evacuate large groups of people and also simply because of the size of the facility. Whether it is an arena, a high school gym, a private health club, or a community baseball complex, the required response to emergencies may vary greatly. It may be appropriate to consult outside agencies when developing an EAP. Planning in conjunction with local EMS, Police, Fire, and other agencies can only improve the plan and can also improve their response to a call for help. Some basic information is necessary to act as a foundation for the EAP. The following lists are not meant to be complete. They are only meant to act as a starting point for the person beginning to develop or improve an EAP. The following factors should be considered and used if appropriate.

1. The location of all gas meters, sprinklers, main valve areas, fire extinguishers, and main electrical panels should be identified and designated by signage in hallways.
2. Chain of command.
3. Roster of key personnel.
4. List of phone numbers readily available for anyone it may be necessary to contact in an emergency. Examples include the following:
   - Principal
   - Key Staff
   - Cleaning Supervisor
   - Athletic Director
   - Fire Department
   - Chief Administrator
   - Police Department
   - Highway Patrol
   - Emergency Rescue
   - Team Doctor
   - Hospitals

- Gas Company
- Electric Company
- Water Department
- Elevator Company
- Glass Contractor
- Locksmith Contractor
- Tenants
- City, County, or State Officials (whichever is appropriate)
- Corporate Staff

5. Engineering plans including locations of:
   - gas, power, and water lines
   - cut-off valves
   - switches
   - alarm systems
   - back-up power
   - exits
   - communication systems
   - elevator overrides

6. Facility drawings of every level
7. Exterior traffic patterns
8. Vicinity maps
9. Location of nearest:
   - hospitals
   - fire stations
   - police stations

Specific Emergencies

Since it is not practical or possible to give examples of all emergency situations for every type of facility, the following section will present a few examples for study. This list is by no means exhaustive. All information and procedures must be evaluated for appropriateness and customized for each situation. It is then essential to inventory, evaluate, and update these procedures at least on a yearly basis.

What to do in case of:

Medical Emergencies

The degree to which you provide medical services may be dictated by the promoter, the nature of the event and past experience at your facility. When the promoter fails to recognize the importance of adequate medical provisions, it is up to you to make a case and insist that there is adequate medical coverage. For further information on medical emergencies, see Chapter 18 Emergency Medical Preparedness.

The number of medical stations and medical personnel available depends on the size of the facility and the nature of the event.

1. Medical stations should be:
   - readily accessible to the public
   - well stocked
   - neat and clean

2. Medical personnel should be:
   - trained and professional
   - courteous and helpful

3. All medical emergencies should be:
   - stabilized and treated as well as possible
   - reported and documented

One medical emergency that should always be prepared for is Sudden Cardiac Arrest (SCA). According to Dr. Barry Maron, Director of the Hypertrophic Cardiomyopathy Center at the Minneapolis Heart Institute Foundation (Epstein, 2007), "Hypertrophic cardiomyopathy is the most common cause of sudden death in young athletes." Training all coaches, teachers, and staff members in CPR and AED use is an inexpensive and effective method of ensuring a proper response during a cardiac emergency. Automated External Defibrillators (AED) should be accessible at all times and events. A well-designed AED maintenance program will ensure that each AED is in good working condition, batteries charged and kept in locations that are easy to find. The National Athletic Trainers Association has an excellent consensus statement regarding emergency preparedness and SCA management. It can be located at http://www.nata.org/sites/default/files/sudden-cardiac-arrest-consensus-statement.pdf.

Fire

1. In the event of a fire, inform the Director of Operations immediately. The Director of Operations should then report to the scene.

2. If an audible alarm is sounded, inform patrons to keep calm and wait for further instructions.

3. The Director of Operations should decide the magnitude of the fire and the course of action taken for a serious, life-threatening fire:
   - Call Fire Department, give information as to magnitude of the fire and the location of the facility.
   - Begin evacuation procedures.
   - Notify chief administrator.
   - Cordon off the dangerous part of the facility.
   - Check sprinkler system (if appropriate).
   - Have maintenance use in-house equipment to control fire from spreading.

- If flames are part of a chemical fire, notify the Fire Department immediately.
- Appoint someone to wait for the Fire Department and direct them to the location of the fire.
  - Maintain constant communication with chief administrator.
  - Upon order of chief administrator, assist in evacuation.
  - After fire is extinguished, Director of Operations should survey scene and report damages to the chief administrator.
  - Director of Operations should file an evaluation of Fire Department, facility personnel, police, and any other group present during the incident.

Bomb Threat

One of the leading facility mangers in the United States said that he never took bomb threats too seriously until the Oklahoma City bombing disaster in 1995. Because of the enormity of the catastrophic injuries and the devastation of the federal building, his attention is now directed at such threats as never before.

A nationally-televised basketball game between the University of New Mexico and the University of Texas El Paso was delayed when two bomb threats were called in during the first half. The standing-room-only crowd of 19,000 had to be evacuated from University Arena (Appenzeller and Baron, 1991). Due to good planning and preparation for just such an occurrence, the arena was evacuated in less than nine minutes. No bomb was found, the crowd was readmitted, and the game was resumed about 90 minutes later.

Most bomb threats do not involve the planting of a bomb. However, it is important to treat every bomb threat as if one had been planted.

It can be very helpful to make up an information sheet in advance to be used by the person receiving a bomb threat. This allows the receiver to concentrate on what the caller is saying rather than trying to think of what to do or say (see Form A). If a bomb threat is received by telephone, the person receiving it should:

1. Treat the call seriously.
2. Remain calm and courteous.
3. Listen carefully to what the person is saying.
4. Pretend to have difficulty hearing in order to keep person talking and on the line.
5. Quietly attract the attention of someone else to listen in, if possible.
6. Try to be attentive for voice identifying characteristics and background sound.
7. Fill out the questions on a prepared information sheet while talking to the caller (see Form A).

The information sheet should incorporate the following items and the person receiving the call must try to obtain as much information as possible:

1. Where is the bomb?
2. What's your name?
3. When did you (or others) put the bomb in the facility?
4. Why did you (they) put bomb in the facility?

Form A. Bomb Threat Instructions & Checklist

If you receive a bomb threat:

1. Stay calm and NO RADIOS.

2. Stay on the phone and be polite and patient.

3. Listen carefully and get the following information:

    a. date: _____ time: _____ a.m./p.m.

    b. When will the bomb go off? _____ a.m./p.m.

    c. Where is the bomb right now? Bldg: _____ Floor: _____ Area: _____

    d. What does the bomb look like?

    e. Why are you doing this?

    f. Who are you?

    g. Caller's statement:

    h. Circle any that apply:

Caller	Voice	Speech	Language	Accent
male	loud	fast	obscene	local
female	soft	slow	course	regional
adult	rough	distinct	normal	foreign:
juvenile	educated	blurred	educated	_____
high	slurred			
low	stutter			

Manner		Background Sounds	
calm	deliberate	factory	party
angry	hysterical	traffic	quiet
rational	aggravated	music	voices
disturbed	humorous	office	other:
coherent	incoherent		_____

    i. Other information:

NOTIFY DIRECTOR OF OPERATIONS, POLICE, AND SECURITY

Name: _____   _____

        (officer taking call)   (receiving phone)

---

5. Why type of bomb is it?

6. When is the bomb set to explode?

7. Remember what the person's voice sounds like:

- old or young

- any distinctive background noises

- was person nervous or calm

- was person drunk or sober

- does person call back more than once

The key is to *get as much information as possible.*

Once the caller hangs up, the person receiving the call should relax a moment and reflect on what was just heard. The receiver should then notify only those people who were predetermined as necessary to be informed on such an occasion. This list should always be located with the information sheet (Form A) so that the person receiving the call will always know who to inform.

1. Director of Operations
2. Police
3. Security

The operator should *not tell anyone else* about the call. The Director of Operations and Security should report directly to the chief administrator's office without telling anyone else about the call.

Once the Director of Operations, chief administrator, and local police are informed, form a search team and set up a Control Center to conduct a preliminary search for the facility.

Remember:

1. Treat the bomb threat seriously.
2. Bombs are usually placed in inconspicuous locations where they are not likely to be seen.
3. Almost any object can conceal a bomb, so look for items out of place and unattended.
4. Never touch a suspicious package when searching for a bomb.
5. Most bombs are placed away from "people" areas.

Instruct the search team not to touch any suspicious objects and to report them immediately to the Control Center. The Director of Operations, chief administrator, and local police should decide together if evacuation is necessary. If any event is in progress, the tenant or promoter should be part of the process.

If evacuation is necessary, follow the predetermined evacuation procedures. Remain calm and proceed in an orderly fashion. More people may be injured by panic than if the bomb actually goes off.

Evacuation Procedures

The primary goal of the evacuation procedure is to provide an orderly and safe departure from the facility in the event of any emergency situation that potentially creates a threat to lives or property.

The most complicated evacuation procedures usually involve large spectator facilities. The following procedure is for such a facility and will have to be adapted for other situations.

1. Once it has been decided to evacuate, make an announcement advising everyone to move to their nearest exit, and to remain calm and proceed in an orderly manner. The announcement should be written in advance and the public address announcer should always have it available. The house sound system should have a battery back up so that announcements are possible during power failures.
2. After making the announcement, all employees on duty should perform their assigned responsibilities as previously trained and drilled.
3. All security, police, ushers, ticket takers, and any other available employees should assist patrons in an orderly evacuation from the facility. This should be

done by way of the nearest exit to their seat, towards the parking lot areas, and away from danger.

4. Utilize all available exits in any form of evacuation.

5. Establish a central area for all lost children, guests, and injured persons.

6. All personnel connected with the facility should assist in the evacuation process and keep everyone calm and orderly while moving the crowd at quick pace. Staff should not rush people and should report any injuries or problems.

7. All service employees and concessionaires should secure cash drawers, lock the stands, check all heating equipment to be sure it is turned off, and leave the facility by the nearest exit. All merchandise and money should be locked in the stand.

8. Designated security should report to the Medical Station to assist in the evacuation of any person under their supervision. The person in charge should supervise the evacuation of patrons and report to the Director of Operations when evacuation is complete.

9. Depending on the number of patrons with limited mobility or in wheelchairs in attendance, a specified number of ushers and security guards should be responsible for assisting these patrons in evacuation. If there are problems with evacuation, the Director of Operations and the chief administrator should be notified immediately.

10. Once patrons are evacuated, security and police should check the seating areas, concourses, and restrooms to ensure the facility is empty. Once a comprehensive check is completed, police should report to the chief administrator.

11. If re-entry into the facility is desired, the Director of Operations should notify security and police.

12. If there is an emergency that merits cancellation or postponement of an event, notify the patrons outside by bullhorns regarding dispersal and when and where refunds will be handled.

13. A press information post should be set up outside of the facility so that all media people can be informed of the situation without directly interfering. One person from the facility should be designated to be a liaison to the media and feed them information that is factual and correct. All other staff members should be instructed not to speak to the media and refer all questions to the media spokesperson.

Tornadoes and Hurricanes

Tornadoes are the most violent atmospheric phenomenon on the planet. Winds of 200–300 mph can occur with the most violent tornadoes. Flying glass and debris pose the greatest danger when a building is struck by a tornado. Therefore, it is vitally important that all employees, visitors, and participants move to an area away from windows and exterior doors when a tornado is expected. When a tornado is sighted or reported to be in the vicinity of the facility, an announcement will be made over the public address and all employees, visitors, and participants should follow those directions until the "all clear" signal has been given.

As with tornadoes, the principal danger of hurricanes is from flying glass and debris. Compared to tornadoes, hurricanes move very slowly. Time is available to plan for their arrival, and in all likelihood the facility will be closed as the hurricane passes over the area. Any employees stationed at the facility during a hurricane should remain alert for any dangerous conditions and stay in constant communication with weather officials and the facility manager.

An issue of disaster preparedness that can become especially challenging with tornadoes and hurricanes is the potential loss of critical organizational information and records (both paper based and electronic) that can occur in these emergencies. A recent example is the May 2011 EF-5 tornado that struck the Joplin, Missouri area and particularly the St. John's Regional Medical Center and its associated data center. According to Ericson (2011), once the medical emergency needs were addressed and survivors cared for, attention became focused on the medical records and documents critical to ongoing operations. As Ericson described, fortunately the St. John's medical facility had migrated the majority of patient data and other critical hospital registration, scheduling, and record-keeping information to off-site data centers in St. Louis and Washington, Missouri only weeks before the disaster. The onsite data center was largely destroyed in the tornado, however, because most of the current and recent historical data had been migrated to an off-site center, hospital management and technicians were not faced with the immediate loss of mission critical information in this disaster. This crisis situation points out the need for all organizations to carefully evaluate their information management plans, including back-up processes and off-site data storage.

Floods

When a flood is recognized, the Director of Operations and the chief administrator should be notified and should report to the scene immediately. The primary danger attributable to localized flooding is electrocution. Electrical equipment that has been flooded with water is a shock hazard. Occupants should evacuate an area as soon as flooding becomes evident. Building Services should be notified immediately and the occupants should remain well away from the flooded area until they have been instructed it is safe to return.

Civil Disruption

Sport programs and sporting events must be prepared to face challenging boycotts, protests, take-overs of facilities, and other disruptive behavior. Administrators who are unaware of the legal aspects of disruption are vulnerable to the actions of the protestors. During the Vietnam War and Desert Storm, protests were common. A Big Ten basketball game between Northwestern and Minnesota was delayed when a group protesting the American flag on the players' uniforms took over Center Court. After the National Anthem they dispersed and the game proceeded without further incident.

In another incident, over 150 students left the stands to join a black female at mid-court to demonstrate against the president of Rutgers University. The president had said that "Minorities don't have the genetic background to do well on college entrance exams." At the time of the protest, Rutgers was leading 31–29 and the sellout crowd was disappointed when the game was canceled because of the potential for injuries in the tension-filled arena.

A wild celebration can cause safety problems that can escalate into an emergency situation. Colorado State University fans stormed the field to tear down the goal posts after their team rallied to defeat Wyoming in an exciting football game. The rowdy fans injured nine people in a post-game melee.

What can facility managers do in response to such behavior? The courts have consistently held that institutions and facilities can set reasonable rules to protect their patrons and these rules need to be followed. Courts have also ruled that disruptive action by protestors causes them to lose their constitutional rights (Appenzeller 1993). To combat disruptive behavior, schools often develop a policy designed to settle disputes. These schools require at least one administrator to be present at every sports contest subject to disruptive action. If demonstrators attempt to disrupt an event, the administrator can acknowledge that a problem exists and invite the demonstrators to meet with him/her off the court. If they refuse to leave, the administrator can summon security or police to escort them out. Having a pre-approved policy such as this is reassuring to the administrator. Setting such policies prior to disruptive outbursts is a sound risk management strategy.

If a situation such as described above is foreseeable, that is if it has happened before or there is some indication that it will happen, facility managers have a duty to plan for it. If a civil disturbance takes place many facilities notify security immediately. Security should follow the planned procedures which will probably include the following:

1. Attempt to end the disturbance.

2. Investigate and document the case.

3. Report and document any injuries that occur.

Civil disturbance, a common occurrence at many events, requires that security be well informed and trained on how to handle and document any incident that occurs.

Power Outage

Before a power outage occurs, emergency lighting should be inspected for adequacy and condition. Is there any other safety equipment that might be inoperable with a loss of power? If so, how can it be compensated for? If a power outage occurs:

1. Notify the Director of Operations, the chief administrator and the local power company immediately and have them report to the scene.

2. Inform patrons about the situation and keep them calm.

3. Call in maintenance and engineers immediately to attempt to alleviate the situation.

4. Evacuate if necessary.

Hazardous Material

Is the facility located near a hazardous material storage area, railroad tracks, or a highway where such material may be transported? If it is suspected that hazardous material has spilled:

1. Notify the Director of Operations and the chief administrator immediately and have them report to the scene.

2. Determine if local emergency response units should be called.

3. Cordon off the dangerous area.

4. Attempt to correct the problem by in-house maintenance or an outside agency.

5. Evacuate if necessary.

It is important to train and drill all employees on their responsibilities for any emergencies. Well prepared employees ensure that any emergency will be handled in a safe, efficient, and competent manner.

Lightning

In 2008, lightning struck the field during a middle school football game in Georgia. Twelve people were hospitalized, including one adult in critical condition (AP, 2008).

Ten football players from Pahokee High School in Florida were injured by lightning as they headed off the practice field to the locker room. The boys sued the Palm Beach School Board alleging that the coaches knew the storm was impending, but refused to safeguard the students by canceling practice. According to the lawsuits, "the coaches waited too late to move the players to the gymnasium to prevent injury from the thunderstorm" (Appenzeller and Baron 2007).

According to the National Oceanic and Atmospheric Administration, about 70 people are killed by lightning in the United States each year and another 400 are injured (NOAA, 2004). The National Athletic Trainers' Association (NATA) has published a position paper on lightning entitled "Lightning Safety for Athletics and Recreation." It is an excellent resource and may be downloaded at: http://www.nata.org/publications/otherpub/lightning.pdf. It provides an exceptional guide for developing a comprehensive, proactive lightning safety policy or emergency action plan for lightning. Other excellent resources include the National Lightning Safety Institute (http://www.lightningsafety.com/) and the NCAA's report on Lightning Safety available at: www.ncaa.org/library/sports_sciences/sports_med_handbook/2003-04/1d.pdf.

Robert Rennell, assistant golf professional at Richland Country Club in Nashville, Tennessee, reported that an appeals court in Tennessee recently held a club liable when a player was struck by lightning. The court held that the club was negligent for:

1. Failure to post signs warning of the hazards of lightning;

2. Failure to provide lightning-proof shelters;

3. Lack of a policy to clear the course during thunderstorms.

Airborne Research Associates, a meteorological research firm warned that "half of the people killed or injured by lightning each year in the United States are on golf courses." The report noted that "most are not struck directly, but are in the immediate vicinity since lightning can induce currents in nearly grounded objects." This poses a very real threat and impacts the liability factor of golf courses (Airborne Research Association 1995).

The National Summary of Lightning reported that 85 were killed in 1995 in the United States by lightning while 510 were injured in the same year (*Angel v. Hison* 1995). The report lists the places of occurrence as follows:

1. Golf Courses

2. Open fields, ball fields, etc.

3. Under trees

4. Boating, fishing, and water-related activities

5. Near tractors, heavy road equipment

6. At telephones

7. Various other unknown locations (*Angel and Hison* 1995).

Procedure for Severe Weather Detection

"Thunderstorms constitute the major source of severe weather," according to researchers at Airborne Research Associates in Weston, Massachusetts. Other disturbances include "accompanying strong wind gusts, microbursts, tornadoes, hail, heavy rainfall (flooding) as well as lightning."

The National Weather Service advises that when thunder is heard, lightning is present—despite not being visible to the human eye. Therefore, the National Weather Bureau advises reasonable procedures that would dictate a policy that people seek shelter as soon as thunder is heard and not wait for the appearance of lightning. An excellent resource for information on lightning safety is the NOAA website http://www.lightningsafety.noaa.gov/.

In an effort to prevent injuries from severe weather, the University of Oklahoma developed "severe weather procedures" through its Department of Public Safety. The Athletic Department purchased a Lightning Director to "determine when outdoor practice and/or competition should be suspended." The detector alerts school officials when "severe weather or lightning is detected within 30 miles of Norman." A watch condition would follow and campus police would notify athletic department personnel who would then notify coaches, staff, and student-athletes of the threatening conditions (Webb, 1997). If lightning is detected within eight miles of the campus, a warning is declared and all outdoor activities such as intramurals, athletic practice or competition, and other campus activities will cease until lightning has cleared the area. The weather detector was purchased for less than $200 and offers protection to the participants at the university.

Technology is improving rapidly. As of 2003, the NCAA provides an online lightning detection system to all rounds of competition for spring championship events.

Many Professional Golfers Association (PGA) Tournaments now utilize lightning detectors to alert patrons and golfers of approaching severe weather. Lights are activated on the leader boards to warn spectators of severe weather. Spectators are then instructed where to go or how to respond.

A plan must already be in place before the thunder is heard. All too often, people wait until lightning is very close before deciding to seek shelter. The National Collegiate Athletic Association (NCAA) recommends in their Guideline 1d, Lightning Safety (2003), many tips, including the following:

As a minimum, NSSL (National Severe Storms Laboratory) staff strongly recommend that by the time (an observer) obtains a flash-to-bang count of **30** seconds (equivalent to six miles), all individuals should have left the athletics site and reached a safe structure or location. Athletics events may need to be terminated (p. 2).

Other tips regarding lightning safety include:

If Outdoors: Avoid water. Avoid all metal objects including electric wires, fences, golf clubs, machinery, motors, power tools, etc. *Unsafe places* include golf carts, tents, open-sided rain shelters, small boats, or underneath isolated trees. Avoid high ground and open spaces. Where possible, find shelter in a building or in a fully enclosed vehicle such as a car, truck, or van with the windows completely shut. If no shelter is available and lightning is striking nearby, you should:

1. Avoid direct contact with other people.

2. Remove all metal objects from your person.

3. Crouch down, with feet together and hands on knees.

If Indoors: Avoid water. Stay away from open doors and windows. Hang up the telephone and take off headsets. Lightning may strike electric and phone lines and induce shocks. Turn off and stay away from appliances, computers, power tools, TV sets, etc. Remain inside until the storm has passed.

If a nearby person is injured from lightning, give first aid procedures if you are qualified to do so. An injured person does not carry an electrical charge and can be handled safely. Call 911 or send for help immediately.

Documentation

It is extremely important to document everything that is done to prepare for and respond to emergencies. If an emergency situation were to result in injuries and a subsequent lawsuit, the more that can be shown in court that the organization did its best to prevent and was prepared to respond to the emergency, the better the chances are of successfully defending itself in court. "If it wasn't written down ... it didn't happen" is a good guide to follow when planning for emergencies. It is not a good strategy to base a legal defense on one person's word against another when proper documentation is relatively simple and effective. In addition to the written EAP itself, a few examples of different methods of documenting emergency preparation are listed below.

1. Records of all meetings related to EAPs.

2. Records of all training.

3. Accident/incident report forms.

4. Copies of communications with staff regarding emergencies and EAPs.

5. Post-incident follow-up reports.

Crisis Leadership, Communications and Public Relations

"The most influential variable in regulating the anxiety of any work group is the presence of a clear-thinking leader. Leadership regulates the anxiety of any group—the family, a company, the nation."

"A hallmark of an exceptional leader is the ability to spend time thinking about a crisis problem. Good leaders have the presence not to get taken out of action by their anxiety."

John Engels, Leadership Coaching Incorporated (in Weiss (2002), Crisis leadership)

Emergencies, such as those described in this chapter, can create challenging leadership, communications, and public relations problems for organizations. Often, emergencies result in crisis situations that disrupt normal operations and lead to confusion. These situations also heighten the emotional state of everyone involved. As a result, it is imperative that organizational leaders understand their critical roles in crisis situations and that a crisis communication plan be in place to adequately inform internal and external publics so as to ultimately protect the organization's integrity and reputation.

From an organizational leadership perspective, it is thought by many that truly effective leadership becomes most apparent during times of organizational crisis. Crisis situations create changes in the nature of decision-making that can be stressful to even the most seasoned leaders (Muffett-Willett and Kruse, 2008). These authors point out that the "ability of a leader to adapt to a changing and complex environment is a key foundation of crisis leadership" (p. 255). Additionally, Muffett-Willett and Kruse (p. 255) suggest the following about crisis situations and decision-making:

- Crisis decisions are made under close scrutiny
- Increased levels of stress exist in crisis situations
- Protocols are typically not well established
- There are severe threats to organizational viability
- Crisis situations create complex and non-routine decision environments

Thus, in times of crisis, leaders have the challenge and opportunity as well as the professional responsibility to: (a) effectively communicate with multiple constituents, (b) provide clear guidance and direction, (c) be visible, (d) make difficult but informed decisions, and (e) demonstrate exceptional care and concern for those affected by a crisis.

A widely recognized example suggested to be indicative of highly effective leadership and crisis communications was that of New York City Mayor Rudy Giuliani in the hours and days following the September 11, 2001, terrorist attack on the World Trade Center. In this deeply disturbing and globally exposed crisis situation, Giuliani was eminently available, made himself publicly visible in person and appeared regularly on television. He was calm when communicating with the media, was up-to-date on what was happening, and was well informed of what emergency response plans and actions were in progress. The message that he sent to the public was one of caring, concern, and control, which increased the public's confidence in his leadership.

During and after emergencies, many important communication decisions must be made. Because of this, there are some simple foundational guidelines that should be initially considered in a crisis communication plan. Two elements that are essential for effective crisis communications are: (a) honest communication and disclosure of only information known to be completely accurate at the time and (b) reassuring internal staff, media, and external constituents that everything possible is being done to minimize the impacts of the emergency.

In emergency situations, the media will want information rapidly and will serve as the primary outlet for organizations to communicate with their external publics. While it may not be possible to totally prevent emergency situations from happening, individuals responsible for crisis communications must effectively manage interactions with the media, be available for press conferences as appropriate, and continue to keep media personnel updated throughout the existing crisis as well as post-crisis period.

A widely accepted first step in crisis communication is to organize a pre-crisis communication team and identify a single spokesperson for the organization. It is good practice during emergencies to require that all outside inquiries be directed to this designated spokesperson. The crisis team should minimally include the chief administrator of the organization, the public relations department, a facility manager and/or building supervisor, various department or unit heads, the organization's legal counsel, and any others whose knowledge and technical skills will be necessary for communications in an emergency situation. This team should meet initially to develop a crisis communication plan and meet at least annually thereafter to review and update the plan as needed. The spokesperson selected to communicate during and after an emergency is often the chief administrator or the director of public relations. What is most important is that the individual selected should be one who has extensive knowledge of the organization as well as the ability to: a) speak effectively on camera and with reporters, b) project confidence, c) avoid antagonizing the media, d) demonstrate professional dignity and, e) remain calm and rational in stressful situations (Clawson-Freeo, 2004; Connaughton, 2003).

Regarding internal and external communication during an emergency, it is essential that the crisis communication team first meet in a pre-determined location to activate the plan. Key personnel of the various departments should be briefed as soon as possible and made aware that their emergency communication plans need to be set in motion. It should be evident that organizations without a well organized and accessible pre-crisis communication plan will immediately encounter problems communicating effectively. It is critical that internal publics be provided with information that is truthful and accurate. Staff should be reminded of their responsibility to direct all media inquiries to the designated spokesperson. It is also important that no individual other than the authorized spokesperson be allowed to publicly reveal any names of victims, speculate on casualties and/or identify possible perpetrators in an emergency situation. In addition, Clawson-Freeo (2004) recommends that coordination occur between your organization's spokesperson and the spokespeople of other involved parties (e.g., health officials, police, or fire).

Regarding external communications during a crisis, it is imperative that the organization establish credibility and demonstrate that everything possible is being done to provide for the safety and well-being of all involved. Since the various print, radio, television, and internet media are the primary outlets for corresponding with the broad external public, effectively communicating with the media is essential. While there are volumes of information written to provide guidance on this topic, the following detailed points are suggested as a foundation for communicating with the media during a crisis.

- Have an accurate and up-to-date list of media contacts and their phone numbers available at all times. The list should include all press and electronic media organizations in your area. It is also good to have a card or personal electronic device with key media contact information that is kept by two or more individuals on the crisis team in case access cannot be gained to offices, computers, and files.

- Contact key media with basic information such as phone numbers to call, email addresses, meeting places, and initial news conference time and location.

- Treat media representatives with respect but do not allow them to interfere with the organization's ability to effectively implement emergency procedures.

- Develop a pre-designed "template" for a news release that can be easily completed and presented by the crisis spokesperson without lengthy planning.

- Never talk "off the record" with media representatives and always avoid speculation when unsure of any component of the crisis situation or crisis response.

- Always demonstrate concern and respect for the individuals affected by the crisis.

- Offer praise and support for all entities assisting in the crisis.

- Continue to keep the media informed in the post-crisis period so as to maintain contact with your external publics.

Effectively accommodating and communicating with the media during and after an emergency situation will greatly strengthen your organization's opportunity to gain credibility and confidence with external publics. As a result, it is recommended that a crisis communication plan be integrated with the EAP and overall risk management plan for an organization.

Post-Incident Follow-Up

After any incident related to an emergency situation, an analysis of the incident and the organization's response to it is important. It is unusual when an EAP prepares for everything that occurs during an emergency. By conducting an in-depth follow-up of the incident, much information can be gathered that can then be used to improve the EAP for the future. Interviews with the victims, first responders, staff, EMS, police, and others involved may elicit new information that can provide insight into the incident. This information should then be used when evaluating the EAP and the way it was carried out. It is important to note that EAPs are not stagnant documents. They must be continually analyzed and updated by an organization so that they provide the best possible preparation for emergencies.

In Our Opinion

Planning for emergency situations is an essential part of an effective risk management program that is overlooked by many organizations. Whether it's preparing to handle a few minor injuries or a major catastrophe, emergency planning is essential to protect patrons, staff, and others against injuries caused by foreseeable events. As with most risk management plans, an EAP must be customized for each individual situation. Simply copying one from a book or another facility can be a good start, but is usually not adequate. Since every situation is different, care must be given to making the EAP the best that it can be. Once the EAP has been developed, it is necessary to train the staff to respond correctly and then to practice carrying out the plan. Only through training and practice can staff members be expected to react appropriately when faced with a real emergency situation. After each practice session as well as after real emergencies, a debriefing of all staff should take place. This will help to identify problems with the EAP and lead to constant improvement. Updating and improving all risk management plans is a never-ending process. An organization must not fall into the trap of complacency by developing a plan and then sticking it on the shelf somewhere. You can never prepare too well when people's health and safety are at stake.

References

Airborne Research Association. (1995). Weston, Massachusetts.

Appenzeller, H. and R. Baron. (1991). *From The Gym To The Jury* vol. 2, no. 4, Greensboro, NC.

Appenzeller, H. and R. Baron. (1996). *From The Gym To The Jury* vol. 7, no. 2, Greensboro, NC.

Appenzeller, H. and R. Baron. (2007). *From The Gym To The Jury* vol. 18, no. 4, Greensboro, NC.

Appenzeller, H. (2003). *Managing Sports and Risk Management Strategies.* Durham, NC: Carolina Academic Press.

Associated Press. (2008). Lightning strikes during football game; 12 hospitalized.

Bonanno, D. & Dougherty, N. (2001). Emergency action plans. In *Safety notebook.* 3, (pp. 1–3) Reston, VA: American Association for Active Lifestyles and Fitness.

Clawson-Freeo, S.K. (2004). Crisis communication plan: A PR blue print. Retrieved March 14, 2004, from http://www3. niu.edu/newsplace/crisis.html.

Connaughton, D. (2003). Crisis management. In Cotton, D.J. & Wolohan, J.T. (Eds.), *Law for recreation and sport managers.* (pp. 341–351).

Epstein, D. (2007). Following the Trail of Broken Hearts. *SI.com.* Retrieved from http://si.printthis.clickability.com/pt/cpt?action=cpt&title=SI.com+-...007%2Fmore%2F12%2F04%2Fbroken.hearts1210%2Findex.html&partnerID=2356

Ericson, J. (2011). Data disasters only partly about scale. *Information Management Online.* Retrieved February 18, 2012 from http://www.information-management.com.

Lightning Safety. Retrieved February 20, 2012 from http://www.lightningsafety.noaa.gov/.

Muffett-Willett, S.L., & Kruse, S.D. (2008). Crisis leadership: Past research and future directions. *Journal of Business Continuity & Emergency Planning, 3,* (3), 248–258.

National Collegiate Athletic Association. (2003). Guideline 1d—Lightning safety. www.ncaa.org/library/sports_sciences/sports_med_handbook/2003-04/1d.pdf.

National Summary of Lightning. 1997. Asheville, NC: National Climatic Data Center.

Sobkowski, A. (1992). "Damage Control When A Crisis Hits." *Executive Female* vol. 15, pp. 67–68.

Stoldt, G.C., Miller, L.K., Ayres, T.D. & Comfort, P.G. (2000). Crisis management planning: A necessity for sport managers. *International Journal of Sport Management, 4,* 253–266. Dubuque, IA: Kendall-Hunt.

Webb, J. 1995. "Policies and Procedures for Severe Weather." *University of Oklahoma, Athletic Department,* Norman, OK.

Weiss, R.P. (2002). Lead on! Crisis leadership. *Training and Development (March, 2002).*

WFMY-TV. (1997). "Lightning Safety Tips." Greensboro, NC.

Part VII

Risk Management Forms, Checklists and Surveys

A yearly audit is recommended, however, Risk Management Committee or administrative personnel should develop a policy decision that addresses this issue.

Gary Rushing

Chapter 34

Necessary Medical Protocols for College Athletics

"Every college and university that has a sports program will have emergency procedures in place and follow medical protocols which best meets their needs."

Gary Rizza

Colleges and universities are responsible for the health care and safety of their student-athletes. The NCAA provides guidelines and recommendations to consider when developing protocols emphasizing health and a safety. These general guidelines are not intended to supersede the medical judgment of the sports medicine staff but can, however, provide them a foundation to design protocols ensuring effective care in the event of injuries.

Guilford College requires all student-athletes participating in intercollegiate sports to provide and complete important medical history, waivers, and athletic insurance forms. All medical documents are conveniently available on the school's website. Additional, information on concussions and sickle cell trait in athletes is also available. Every college and university that has an intercollegiate sports program will have emergency procedures in place and follow medical protocols which best meets their needs. Guilford College uses the following forms for their student-athletes:

Athletic Forms for Student-Athletes

The following is a list of forms required from each student-athlete.

1) Parent insurance letter explains primary and secondary (athletic) insurance benefits, coverage and costs.

2) Athletic physical forms consist of questions pertaining to medical history and related health issues. This will be completed and signed by the team physician. Each student-athlete entering Guilford College is required to have a physical by our team physician.

3) Sickle Cell Trait information and verification sheet provides valuable information about Sickle Cell Trait in athletes. Sickle Cell Screening is mandatory for each student-athlete participating in intercollegiate sports at Guilford College. (See Figure 1.)

4) NCAA Shared Responsibility for Sport Safety waiver emphasizes the potential risk of serious head and neck injuries when wearing a football or lacrosse helmet. (See Figure 2.)

5) Participation Waiver warns each student-athlete of the possible dangers of participation in contact sports. (See Figure 3.)

6) HIPPA authorization form involving an athlete's medical information. (See Figure 4.)

7) Drug/Banned Substance Awareness, Education and Screening Policy.

8) Concussion Awareness information sheet can assist student-athletes in identifying signs and symptoms of concussions. This concussion awareness form also has prevention tips and stresses the importance of seeking proper medical attention. (See Figure 5.)

Figure 1. Sickle Cell Trait Verification Form

Guilford College Sports Medicine Sickle Cell Trait Verification

The NCAA has requested that its member institutions verify Sickle Cell Trait status on all athletes. Sickle cell trait is not a disease, but rather a genetic predisposition to a sickle shaping of the oxygen-carrying red blood cells. Although there are no requirements that limit participation in sports by student-athletes who have the sickle cell trait, the NCAA recommends athletic departments identify each athlete's status. People at high risk for having sickle cell trait are those whose ancestors come from Africa, South or Central America, Caribbean, Mediterranean countries, India, and Saudi Arabia. All student-athletes at Guilford College will be required to provide documentation demonstrating the presence or absence of sickle cell trait. Typically, this test is performed on all newborns in the United States; however, those records may be difficult to access. Please have your healthcare provider complete this form by either doing a sickle cell trait test or documenting the test you had performed at an earlier time.

You will be unable to complete as an athlete until this form and all other forms are completed and turned into the athletic training staff. For questions or more information, please contact Gary Rizza, Med, ATC, LAT, Head Athletic Trainer.

Thank you for your attention to this matter.

To be completed by healthcare provider

Athlete's Name:_____ Date of Birth: _____

Sickle Cell Trait Positive Sickle Cell Trait Negative Date of Sickle Cell Testing: _____

Contradictions to Activity: _____

Examiner Name: _____ (MD, NP, DO, PA)

Address: _____

City: _____ State: _____ Zip: _____

Telephone Number for Consultations: _____

Examiner Signature: _____ Date: _____

Figure 2. NCAA Shared Responsibility for Sport Safety Waiver

GUILFORD COLLEGE
NCAA SHARED RESPONSIBILITY FOR SPORT SAFETY

The NCAA Committee on Competitive Safeguards and Medical Aspects of Sports encourages coaches of collision sports to discuss the following information with their teams at the onset of the season, to put it on each player's locker for emphasis and then to remind them of the essentials periodically during the season:

1.) Serious head and neck injuries leading to death, permanent brain damage or quadriplegia (extensive paralysis from injury to the spinal cord at the neck level) occur each year in athletics. The toll is relatively small (less than one fatality for every 100,000 players and an estimated two to three non-fatal severe brain and spinal cord injuries for every 100,000 players), but persistent. (They cannot be completely prevented due to the tremendous forces occasionally encountered with collisions, but can be minimized by manufacturer, coach and player compliance with accepted safety standards.)

2.) The NOCSAE seal on a helmet indicates that a manufacturer has complied with the best available engineering standards for head protection. By keeping a proper fit, by not modifying its design, and by reporting to the coach or athletic trainer any need for its maintenance, the athlete is also complying with the purpose of the NOCSAE standard.

3.) The rules against intentional butting, ramming or spearing the opponent with the helmeted head are there to protect the helmeted person much more than the opponent being hit. The athlete who does not comply with these rules is the candidate for catastrophic injury. For example, no helmet can offer protection to the neck, and quadriplegia now occurs more frequently than brain damage. The helmet cannot always protect you from injuries that may result from slashing or any other kind of direct contact that may occur during play, nor can a helmet protect you from a blow from an opponent that was intentional or accidental. The typical scenario of this catastrophic injury in football/lacrosse involves lowering one's head while making a tackle/contact. The momentum of the body tries to bend the neck after the helmeted head is stopped by the impact, and the cervical spine cannot be splinted as well by the neck's musculature with the head lowered as with the preferred "face up, eyes forward, neck bulled" position.

4.) Because of the impact forces in football/lacrosse, even the "face up" position is no guarantee against head or neck injury. Further, the intent to make contact "face up" is no guarantee that this position can be maintained at the moment of impact. Consequently, the teaching of playing techniques that keep the helmeted head from receiving the brunt of the impact are now required by rule and by coaching ethics. Coaching techniques teach athletes to maintain or regain the "face up" positioning during the course of a play, must be respected by the athletes. A **WARNING LABEL** has been placed with each helmet to remind the user of the **RISK** and to **WARN** him against dangerous conduct. This label should **ALWAYS** appear on the outside of the helmet and it reads as follows:

FOOTBALL WARNING

DO NOT use this helmet to butt, ram, or spear an opposing player. This is in violation of the football rules and can result in severe head, brain, or neck injuries, paralysis, or death to you and possible injury to your opponent. There is a risk these injuries may occur as a result of accidental contact without intent to butt, ram, or spear. No helmet can prevent all such injuries.

LACROSSE WARNING

Lacrosse is a contact sport played with sticks and a hard ball moving at high speed. This means you can be injured while playing the sport. To reduce the risk of injury, you must exercise common sense and obey the rules at all times. For example, do not use this helmet to butt, ram, or spear another player. This can severely injure you.

Even when you play lacrosse according to the rules, you expose yourself to serious injury. THIS HELMET WILL NOT PROTECT YOU AGAINST ALL INJURIES; AMONG OTHERS, NECK AND HEAD INJURIES.

Alteration of the helmet can increase your chance of injury. This helmet should not be worn if cracked or otherwise damaged. Use this helmet for FIELD LACROSSE ONLY. Athletes, it is strongly encouraged that you adhere to these suggestions and rules, as no one can afford to suffer the consequences! Inspect your helmet on a daily basis for any defects or irregularities. Report any problem with your helmet to your coach PRIOR to beginning practice.

To assure that both the parent and the athlete have read and understand this notice, please sign and return this form to the address below.

Athlete Name (Printed): _____

Sport: _____

Athlete Signature: _____

Date: ____/_____/_____

Parent/Guardian Signature: _____

Date: ____/_____/_____

Return Both Pages To: Gary Rizza, MEd, ATC, LATC
Head Athletic Trainer
Guilford College
5800 West Friendly Ave.
Greensboro, NC 27410

**GUILFORD COLLEGE
SPORTS MEDICINE DEPARTMENT
SHARED RESPONSIBILITY FOR SPORTS SAFETY**

WARNING: PARTICIPATION IN INTERCOLLEGIATE ATHLETICS INVOLVES THE INHERENT RISK OF INJURY, THE SEVERITY OF WHICH MAY RANGE FROM MINOR TO CATASTROPHIC, OR FROM TEMPORARY IMPAIRMENT TO PERMANENT DISABILITY, INCLUDING PARALYSIS OR DEATH.

Minor to severe injuries can occur in athletics. However minor or severe an injury, each student-athlete must report all injuries to the athletic trainer for evaluation and possible referral to a physician. Failure to comply will place the outcome of the injury as the responsibility of the student-athlete.

Preventative taping and protective equipment is available to athletes as needed in each sport. However, protective equipment and taping will not prevent all injuries from occurring. To maximize the effectiveness of protective equipment, inspect it daily and make sure that it is properly fitted and worn during all practices and games.

Since participation in sports requires an acceptance of the risk of injury by the student-athlete, he or she rightfully assumes that reasonable precaution will be taken to minimize the risks of serious injury. The student-athletes, having this informed awareness of the risks, share the responsibility for minimizing those risks. STUDENT-ATHLETES MUST COMPLY WITH ALL SAFETY GUIDELINES, REPORT ALL PHYSICAL PROBLEMS TO THE APPROPRIATE MEDICAL PERSONNEL OR COACH, ADHERE TO SOUND CONDITIONING PROGRAMS AND INSPECT THEIR EQUIPMENT DAILY.

Having read the above statement, I am aware of the inherent risks of injury involved in athletic participation. Finally, I understand that in accepting the risks associated with athletic participation, I will also share the responsibility of minimizing those risks. I certify that I am physically fit to participate in the sport of

_____.

Athlete's Name (please print)

Athlete's Signature

Guardian's Name, if under 18 (please print)

Guardian's Signature

Figure 3. Participation Waiver

GUILFORD COLLEGE ATHLETICS
PARTICIPATION WAIVER

Waiver and Release of Liability for the Sport(s) of _____ to be completed by the Student-Athlete.

Because of the dangers of participating in the herein-specified sport, I recognize the importance of following the coach's instructions regarding playing techniques, training, rules of the sport, and other team rules and to obey such instructions.

In consideration of the benefits for growth and development to be derived from participating in intercollegiate sports and of Guilford College permitting me to practice, play or try out for Guilford College's _____ team, and to engage in all activities related to the team, including practicing, playing and travel, I hereby voluntarily assume all risks associated with participation and agree to exonerate and save harmless Guilford College, their agencies, trustees, servants and employees, the athletic staff of Guilford College, the physicians, athletic trainers and all other practitioners of the healing arts treating me, from any and all liability, claims, causes of action or demands of any kind and nature whatsoever which may arise by or in connection with my participation in any activities related to the Guilford College _____ program.

I am aware that playing or practicing in any sport can be a dangerous activity involving MANY RISKS OR INJURY. I understand that the dangers and risks of playing or practicing in the above sport include, but are not limited to, death, serious neck and spinal injuries which may result in complete or partial paralysis or brain damage, serious injury to virtually all bones, joints, ligaments, muscles, tendons, and other aspects of the muscular-skeletal system and serious injury or impairment to other aspects of my body, general health and well-being. It is also understood that the dangers and risks of playing or practicing the sport of _____ may result not only in serious injury, but also in serious impairment of my future abilities to earn a living and to engage in social and recreational activities.

The terms hereof shall serve as a release and assumption of risk for my heirs, estate, executor, administrator, assignees and all members of my family. I hereby agree to submit any disputes that may arise between myself and Guilford College, its agents, servants and employees, the athletic staff of Guilford College, the physicians, athletic trainers and other practitioners of the healing arts treating me, and all their agents, trustees, servants and employees, in connection with my activities at Guilford College, to binding arbitration before three arbitrators, in accordance with the Rules of the American Arbitration Association.

(For contact or collision sports, all sports except golf, volleyball and tennis):

I specifically acknowledge that _____ (indicate sport) is a VIOLENT CONTACT sport, involving even a greater risk of injury than other sports.

Student Athlete

Date

Student Athlete's Parent

Date

Figure 4. HIPPA Release

GUILFORD COLLEGE
RELEASE OF ATHLETIC HEALTHCARE INFORMATION

I, _____ (print name), hereby grant permission and request that the Guilford College Athletic Training Department release and discuss what they deem necessary for my safety, any information relating to my health care to the coaching staff, athletic administration, sports information office, and parents/guardians. This shall include injury/illness evaluation and diagnosis, treatment/rehabilitation plans and progress, availability and extent of my athletic participation and information related to referrals and possible surgical interventions. I understand that my injury/illness information is protected by federal regulations under either the Health Information Portability and Accountability Act (HIPPA) or the Family Educational Rights and Privacy Act of 1974 (the Buckley Amendment) and may not be disclosed without either my authorization under HIPPA or my consent under the Buckley Amendment. I understand that my signing of this authorization/release is voluntary and that my institution will not condition any health care treatment or payment, enrollment in a health plan or receipt of any benefits (if applicable) on whether I provide consent or authorization requested for this disclosure. I also understand that I am not required to sign this authorization/consent in order to be eligible for participation in NCAA or conference athletics. I do understand that failure to sign this consent/release will terminate my privilege to participate in varsity athletics at Guilford College.

I, also permit the medical providers for Guilford College Athletic Department, Guilford College Student Health Services, the Guilford College Athletic Training Department and sports information director to discuss all aspects of my injuries/illnesses with each other, as they deem necessary for my safety and health care as well as to share all medical documentations. Documentation can include but is not limited to medical notes, diagnostic and radiological test results and operative notes. Communications shall include injury/illness evaluation and diagnosis, treatment/rehabilitation plans and progress, availability and extent of my athletic participation and information related to referrals and possible surgical interventions.

This release remains valid for 380 days unless revoked by me in writing.

Printed Name: _____ Sport: _____

Signature: _____ Date: _____/_____/_____

Return form to: Gary Rizza, Head Athletic Trainer, Guilford College, 5800 West Friendly Ave., Greensboro NC 27410

Figure 5. Concussion Awareness Information Sheet

CONCUSSION

A fact sheet for student-athletes

What is a concussion?

A concussion is a brain injury that:

- Is caused by a blow to the head or body.
    - From contact with another player, hitting a hard surface such as the ground, ice or floor or being hit by a piece of equipment such as a bat, lacrosse stick or field hockey ball.
- Can change the way your brain normally works.
- Can range from mild to severe.
- Presents itself differently for each athlete.
- Can occur during practice or competition in ANY sport.
- **Can happen even if you do not lose consciousness.**

How can I prevent a concussion?

Basic steps you can take to protect yourself from concussion:

- Do not initiate contact with your head or helmet. You can still get a concussion if you are wearing a helmet.
- Avoid striking an opponent in the head. Undercutting, flying elbows, stepping on a head, checking an unprotected opponent, and sticks to the head all cause concussions.
- Follow your athletics department's rules for safety and the rules of the sport.

- Practice good sportsmanship at all times.
- Practice and perfect the skills of the sport.

It's better to miss one game than the whole season.

When in doubt, get checked out.

For more information and resources, visit www.NCAA.org/health-safety and www.CDC.gov/Concussion.

What are the symptoms of a concussion?

You can't see a concussion, but you might notice some of the symptoms right away. Other symptoms can show up hours or days after the injury.

Concussion symptoms include:

- Amnesia.
- Confusion.
- Headache.
- Loss of consciousness.
- Balance problems or dizziness.
- Double or fuzzy vision.
- Sensitivity to light or noise.
- Nausea (feeling that you might vomit).
- Feeling sluggish, foggy or groggy.
- Feeling unusually irritable.
- Concentration or memory problems (forgetting game plays, facts, meeting times).
- Slowed reaction time.

Exercise or activities that involve a lot of concentration, such as studying, working on the computer, or playing video games may cause concussion symptoms (such as headache or tiredness) to reappear or get worse.

What should I do if I think I have a concussion?

Don't hide it. Tell your athletic trainer and coach. Never ignore a blow to the head. Also, tell your athletic trainer and coach if one of your teammates might have a concussion. Sports have injury timeouts and player substitutions so that you can get checked out.

Report it. Do not return to participation in a game, practice or other activity with symptoms. The sooner you get checked out, the sooner you may be able to return to play.

Get checked out. Your team physician, athletic trainer or health care professional can tell you if you have had a concussion and when you are cleared to return to play. A concussion can affect your ability to perform everyday activities, your reaction time, balance, sleep and classroom performance.

Take time to recover. If you have had a concussion, your brain needs time to heal. While your brain is still healing, you are much more likely to have a repeat concussion. In rare cases, repeat concussions can cause permanent brain damage, and even death. Severe brain injury can change your whole life.

Reference to any commercial entity or product or service on this page should not be construed as an endorsement by the Government of the company or its products or services.

Emergency Management Plan

The Emergency Management Plan provides guidelines outlining steps taken on campus in the event of an emergency. These guidelines include the activation of EMS and phone numbers for local hospitals, physicians, and athletic training staff. Enclosed in the

Figure 6. Guilford Concussion Management Plan

Obtain Baseline Testing: Symptom checklist and ImPact Testing data obtained for athletes in high-risk sports for concussions at the beginning of the season (football, soccer, lacrosse, basketball, baseball and softball) or with pertinent medical history of concussion

Concussion Identified and Assessed: Physical examination and assessment of concussion symptoms by medical staff (athletic trainer, physician assistant and/or physician: if a physician is not immediately available, athlete should be referred to physician for evaluation within 24 hours of injury if possible, if not emergent; if emergent, an athlete should be transported to closest emergency department); athlete held from all physical activity; given concussion information home instruction sheet; notify parent/guardian of concussion; Athlete repeats baseline testing with Symptoms checklist, and ImPact (within 24 hours of injury if possible)

Concussion Management: Athlete held from all physical activity; re-assess athlete daily by medical staff; administer symptom checklist daily until completely asymptomatic; notify academic advisor (consideration of academic modifications/restrictions)

Athlete Asymptomatic: athlete repeats baseline testing with Symptoms checklist, SCAT, and ImPact (unless directed otherwise by physician)

Test Results Return to Baseline: Perform exertional testing; re-evaluation by physician for return to play	**Test Results NOT Returned to baseline:** When medically cleared by physician, repeat test battery

When medically cleared by physician, repeat exertional testing; re-evaluation by physician for return to play decision

emergency management plan are policies involving inclement weather, lightning safety, prevention of heat illness, head injuries and even heart attacks. In addition, directions to all sport venues to provide easy access for emergency vehicles. The following is a list of necessary components which are important in any emergency management plan:

All coaches on staff are re-certified each year in CPR/AED,

Certified athletic trainers attend all practices and games,

There is access to a team medical physician,

There is an AED located at each sport venue,

The plan includes a Concussion Management Plan (See Figure 6).

Chapter 35

Safe Facilities: Conducting a Facility Risk Review

One of the most effective methods of managing risks associated with facilities is the facility risk review.

Todd L. Seidler

Introduction

Managers of sport, physical activity and recreation programs have a number of legal duties that they are expected to carry out. Among these are an obligation to take precautions to ensure reasonably safe programs and facilities for all participants, spectators and staff. The responsibility of a facility manager to ensure the safety of the patrons is usually referred to as premises liability. According to Page (1988), premises liability comprises "one of the largest subcategories within the broad spectrum of tort law." This chapter will focus on one of the most effective methods of ensuring facility safety: conducting a facility risk review.

It is important to note that throughout this chapter it is necessary to keep in mind that everyone who enters the facility has a right to expect that the facility will be reasonably safe. This includes participants, spectators and visitors as well as staff that work within the facility. When doing a risk analysis, facility managers must not lapse into thinking that participant safety is more important than the safety of others. A safe facility for all is essential and expected.

Legal Duty

The legal duty owed to participants and spectators by managers of facilities is generally determined by the status of the visitors. Sharp, Moorman and Claussen (2010) state, "… the scope of the duty varies depending upon whether the person is on the property with permission or without permission. The duty also varies depending upon whether a person who is there with permission brings an economic benefit to the property owner."

When determining the status of visitors, they are generally divided into four categories: invitees, licensees, trespassers and recreational users. Those designated as invitees receive the most protection, licensees receive moderate protection, and trespassers and recreational users only minimal legal protection. Usually, the vast majority of participants and spectators in sport and recreation facilities are considered to be invitees. This designation has the most stringent safety expectations and, therefore, this chapter will focus on the legal duty owed to invitees. It is expected that managers of facilities will provide a reasonably safe environment and at least carry out the following five duties.

1) Keep the premises in safe repair.

2) Inspect the premises to discover obvious and hidden hazards.

3) Remove the hazards or warn of their presence.

4) Anticipate foreseeable uses and activities by invitees and take reasonable precautions to protect the invitee from foreseeable dangers.

5) Conduct operations on the premises with reasonable care for the safety of all.

When determining standards of conduct, facility managers are held to the standard of that of a reasonably prudent and careful facility manager. If someone is injured in a facility and initiates a lawsuit claiming that the injury was caused by a situation that the facility manager should not have allowed to exist, the court will partially base it's findings of liability on the concept of foreseeability. Was it foreseeable that the situation in question was likely to cause an injury? If the court determines that a reasonably prudent facility manager would have recognized it as a potential danger and acted to reduce or eliminate the hazard, the chances of being found liable for the injury are greatly enhanced. However, if it is determined that a reasonably prudent facility manager probably would not have identified the situation as likely to cause an injury, the likelihood of liability is greatly reduced. It is the legal duty of facility managers and program directors to address or treat all foreseeable risks in one way or another.

Critical to the determination of foreseeability is the concept of notice. There are two types of notice: actual and constructive. Actual notice occurs when a facility has direct information regarding a defect or hazard on the premises. This may come about by any number of means such as inspection, reporting of the hazard by a user, or from someone actually being injured. It is especially important to remedy a situation where actual notice occurs by way of a previous injury. It may be hard to justify not repairing a known hazard that later causes an injury but it can be especially difficult to justify not fixing a hazard that has already been responsible for a previous injury. If a person were injured by a given hazard, it then becomes highly foreseeable that someone else may also be injured by it.

A good example of foreseeability and actual notice occurred in a recreation center with a 25 yard long pool that is equipped with a portable aluminum handicapped access ramp. The ramp is left in the pool on a permanent basis in order to make the pool accessible to those with disabilities. One day, a young man swam under the ramp and accidentally brushed the underside with his arm. He came in contact with a very sharp piece of aluminum that cut him severely enough that he had to immediately go to the hospital and get stitches in his arm. Later, he reported the incident to the manager of the recreation center. The manager said "Oh, you're number ten. The tenth person to get cut on that ramp." The recreation center had at least nine people previously injured on the ramp and still had not done anything to fix the hazard. With nine people injured on a particular piece of equipment, was it highly foreseeable that it might harm someone else unless it is repaired? Situations like this with multiple previous injuries are extremely foreseeable to cause further injuries and must be fixed as soon as possible. The greater the foreseeability, the higher the likelihood of the court finding liability for negligence or even gross negligence. Once again, actual notice occurs when a facility has direct information regarding a defect or hazard on the premises.

Constructive notice, however, occurs when management should have known of a hazard and would have known if proper inspection procedures had been carried out. Facility managers are legally responsible to regularly inspect the premises to discover obvious and hidden hazards. Facility managers are held accountable for both actual and constructive notice.

Once facility staff members learn of a hazardous condition, the courts will allow a reasonable time in which to repair or compensate for it. This time period is determined by a jury and based on several factors such as the severity and likelihood of possible injuries, as well as the ease and expense of the repair. For example, a loose railing on the end of the bleachers in a spectator facility would probably be expected to be repaired prior to the next event. Because of the probability and severity of the potential injuries, such a hazard should be corrected before the next time it is used. However, in a situation where the danger is less imminent and the seriousness of the potential injury is lower, a longer time might be allowed for repair. It is important to understand that whenever a recognized hazard cannot be immediately fixed or removed, it is necessary to warn patrons of the hazard and possibly to rope it off until proper treatment can occur. It is the facility manager's responsibility to determine the best method of reducing the likelihood of injuries. The bottom line is, once actual or constructive notice is established, it is expected that appropriate steps will quickly be taken to remedy the situation.

The Basis for Hazards

Safety problems in facilities can usually be traced to two primary causes. These are:

1) Poor Facility Planning and Design

2) Poor Management

Poor design can typically be attributed to a failure of the planning and design team before the facility was constructed. It is not uncommon for a sport, physical education or recreation facility to be designed by an architect who has little or no experience in that type of building. For those without the proper background and understanding of the unique properties of sport and recreation facilities, many opportunities for mistakes exist which may lead to increased problems related to safety, operations and staffing. Design problems commonly seen in activity facilities include inadequate buffer zones around courts, planning pedestrian traffic flow through activity areas, a lack of proper storage space, and the use of improper building materials, such as putting a slippery floor surface in the shower room. An all-too-common example of how a safety problem may be designed into the facility is as follows. An architect designing a gym doesn't know how much clear space should be provided beyond the lines of a basketball court. He or she may go to the high school basketball rules book and find the guideline "Minimum of 3 feet. Preferably 10 feet of unobstructed space outside." With every extra foot of space in the gym adding to the construction cost, the architect may decide that providing three feet is enough. Unfortunately, a vast majority of risk management experts believe that a three foot buffer zone is totally inadequate and presents a dangerous condition for the players.

The author has also seen many facilities that have been built with major design flaws such as a gym that was constructed with no locker rooms, a varsity football field only 80 yards long, a competitive swimming pool that is only three feet deep under the starting blocks (which cannot be used in that depth), and a gym with standard glass windows on the walls at both ends of the basketball court. It is essential that these facilities be planned and designed by professionals with activity-related knowledge and experience. Often the safety problems related to design are difficult, expensive or impossible to fix once the facility has been built. On the other hand, just because a facility was constructed with a safety problem built in does not mean that there isn't anything that can be done about it. Good management can often alleviate or at least lessen safety problems that are the result of poor planning.

Safety problems attributed to poor management are also of great concern. It has been estimated that negligent maintenance is the most common allegation of the cause of injuries in facility-related claims. Management practices that promote facility safety include performing a facility risk review, developing a safety checklist and applying it through periodic inspections, establishing a good preventive maintenance program and educating staff about safety and risk management. A properly-managed facility will inspect, identify and properly treat hazards as they are discovered.

Facility Risk Review

One of the most effective methods of managing the risks associated with facilities is the facility risk review. This is typically performed by an inspection team and begins with a review of the entire facility. The first step of conducting a facility risk review is to determine who will be a part of the inspection team. The size of the team is usually proportional to the size of the facility and the organization managing it. This team may consist of one person, such as with a small school gym, up to a dozen or more in the case of a major college athletic department or a large multi-purpose arena. For large facilities, it is beneficial to have representatives from different areas of specialization included for the initial inspection. The director of security will notice potential hazards that are different than a P.E. teacher, the head custodian or the director of parking and traffic control. It is usually beneficial to include users of the facility, such as a coach, student, parent, or fan, on the inspection team. In order to do a thorough inspection, input must be gathered from many points of view.

It can also be very beneficial to invite someone from outside the organization who is not familiar with the facility to come and inspect, thereby providing a fresh point of view. Often, someone who works in a facility everyday becomes used to the way things are and may not notice a potential hazard simply because they have seen it too many times. It is surprising the seriousness of some hazards that have been overlooked until a "fresh set of eyes" finally spotted the problem. It can be very helpful for managers from two different organizations to trade off and each inspect the other's facilities. The facility risk review is broken down into three major parts.

1) Initial Inspection
2) Risk Treatment
3) Periodic Inspection

Initial Inspection

Once the inspection team has been established, the primary task is to conduct the initial inspection. This begins by trying to identify as many potential risks or hazards as possible. Any hazard that may cause an injury, from minor incidents to major catastrophes, must be identified and written down. At this point, it is important to consider all situations as long as there is a potential for injury to occur. The initial inspection should include all areas inside (gyms, locker rooms, hallways, lobbies, pools, etc.) and outside (playfields, sidewalks, parking lots, fences, etc.) of the building as well as other areas that may be associated with it. Each inspector should tour the entire facility and look for potential hazards. Taking notes, they should consider every possible activity that may take place in the facility and try to imagine how different circumstances might affect safety. For example, in a high school gym, each should try to imagine everything a student approaching the building for a physical education class might do. From entering the door, walking down the hallway to the locker room and changing clothes, to participating in physical education class, showering and changing and leaving the building for the next class. What potential hazards might students come in contact with? What different activities might they encounter throughout the school year? As these potential hazards are identified, they should be written down for further evaluation later. Then the next scenario should be evaluated. What about the gym during an athletic event when it is filled with spectators? It is likely that new and different hazards will be identified in the different scenarios. Whenever possible, performing the inspections during actual events is most effective. Also, repeating inspections at different times may help to identify problems that are unique to a certain time of day or night. A college athletic department employee was performing a facility risk review and went out during the afternoon to inspect the track for potential hazards. At that time they thought they had identified all of the uses and hazards associated with the track. The inspection team later went back at ten o'clock at night and found that many people exercised at night and that there were no lights on or leading up to the track. Security lights were installed shortly thereafter, thereby reducing the hazards of the formerly unknown situation.

Once a list of potential hazards has been identified, it must then be prioritized. This priority list will establish the order in which the hazards will be addressed. Three primary factors must be considered when prioritizing potential problem situations. First, how many people are likely to be affected by a potential hazard. Is it likely to involve one or two people, or fifty or thousands? The more people possibly affected, the higher this incident will move up on the priority list. If a set of bleachers collapses, it is likely to produce injuries to a great many people while a loose bottom step on a seldom used set of bleachers will probably not injure more than a few.

The second factor to consider when prioritizing possibly hazardous situations is the severity of the injuries that are likely to occur. The greater the possibility of severe injuries or death, the higher the priority. As an example of this part of the prioritization phase, a loose railing designed to prevent someone from falling off of a walkway 15 feet above the floor would receive a higher priority than a six-inch deep pothole in the parking lot.

The third factor to consider is the likelihood that an incident will occur. The higher the probability of occurrence, the higher the priority given. It is much more likely that someone will slip on a wet spot in the gym than will get hit by a falling ceiling panel.

Finally, considering all three factors together, and using the best professional judgment of the committee, each of the identified dangers should be ranked in order of priority. Once this list has been established, it is then time to start at the top, or most hazardous, and determine the best method of addressing each. As each hazard is dealt with, the next one on the list can then be dealt with. This does not mean that items with a lower priority on the list must wait until the ones before have been treated. If an item cannot be treated immediately, do not wait to go to the next hazard on the list and deal with it. Many situations can be quickly and easily treated and removed from the priority list while others may take some time.

Risk Treatment

Once the potential risks in the facility have been identified and prioritized, it is time to treat those risks so that they are eliminated or at least made as safe as possible. The decision on the best method for treating the risks will rely on the best professional judgment of the facility risk management committee. There are two primary methods used to treat or deal with facility hazards. These are:

1) Eliminate it.

    This means to repair or fix the problem so that it is no longer a hazard. If there is a broken board on the bleachers, replace the board and inspect the rest to determine whether other boards are ready to break. The hazard is eliminated.

2) Reduce it and compensate for it.

    If a hazard cannot be totally eliminated, every effort should be made to reduce it. This means to make it as safe as possible and then determine other methods of reducing the risk even further. This may include warning of the situation or changing the rules slightly to reduce the hazard as much as possible.

With some hazards it will be obvious how to best remedy the situation. If there is a wet spot on the gym floor, dry it immediately and determine its source. If it was a one-time accident, no more concern is necessary. If, however, it was caused by something that is likely to happen again, such as a leaky drinking fountain, it should be fixed as soon as possible. If it will take some time before the required repairs can be made, it may be necessary to warn patrons of the hazard and rope it off until it can be properly addressed.

Some hazards, however, will not be so easy to fix. If it is determined that it is not feasible to repair or eliminate the hazard, it will be necessary to determine another way to compensate for it in order to reduce it as much as possible. An example would be if a gym were built with inadequate buffer zones, the space between the end lines of the basketball court and the wall. A mistake commonly made by facility managers is thinking that there is nothing that can be done with a safety zone that is too small. Although it is unrealistic to move the walls further away, there are almost always other ways to compensate and reduce the risk as much as possible. In this situation, it is prudent to mount appropriate wall pads on the wall in order to reduce the severity of injuries of those that may lose control while going out-of-bounds. When compensating for a hazard, it is also important to place signs warning of the remaining hazard so that all participants are well aware of the differences between this situation and a normal one. If they are aware of the risks associated with the facility, it is then up to them to decide if they want to assume those risks and participate anyway.

Periodic Inspections

The next step is to develop a checklist with which to perform periodic facility inspections on a regular, on-going basis. This checklist should be developed for each facility and customized for that particular situation. All too often, facility managers will borrow a checklist from another facility, put their name and logo on it, and use it for their building. This is not an effective practice. Every facility and situation is unique. Therefore, every checklist should be customized for each given situation. It can be very helpful to look at checklists from other facilities and borrow ideas from them, but make sure that each item is appropriate.

It is important to keep the checklist relatively simple. If it is so long and complex that it becomes a major operation to perform, it probably won't be performed correctly, if at all. On the other hand, make sure that all items of importance are included.

Next, an inspection schedule should be established. The frequency of inspections depends upon the type of facility and programs involved. In a spectator facility, it may be appropriate to perform an inspection immediately prior to each event. In an activity facility it might be effective to establish a regular schedule for inspection, such as on a bi-weekly basis. The risk review committee must determine what is appropriate for the individual situation.

In some organizations it may be appropriate to develop two or even several checklists. It may be that a daily checklist should be developed to help perform a quick check of areas to identify factors that can easily change on short notice. This might include checking access doors, looking for water on the floor of an activity area, seeing that the stairs are clear of debris, or making sure there are no children in the weight room. Another, more detailed, in-depth checklist can then be used on a less frequent basis. This list could prompt the inspector to check for things such as loose bolts and frayed cables on the weight machines, or bent and broken rims on the basketball courts. Again, professional judgment will best determine the frequency and detail of the inspections.

Including the following items on a checklist is necessary for it to be as effective as possible.

Name of the organization

Inspector's name (printed)

Date of inspection

Location of inspection (if needed)

Inspector's signature

What problems were discovered

Word questions so that "No" answer means something is wrong

If a problem is found, what action is recommended.

An example of a partial checklist appears on the following page.

Especially in larger facilities, it may be advantageous to have an additional sheet attached that prompts the inspector to report all items that require action. By including this one page action report when an inspection discovers problems that need to be addressed, it is less likely that an item will be overlooked. If the facility manager has to look at each item on every page of a multiple page inspection report in order to discover those that require action, there is more chance that some will be overlooked. Procedures must then be established so that once a hazard has been identified, it will be treated as quickly as possible.

Figure 1. ABC Health Club

Safety Inspection Checklist

Inspector's Name _____Paul Edwards_____   Date _____3/7/11_____

Location of Inspection _____Fitness Pool_____

Inspector's Signature _____

Instructions for Inspector:
1. Inspect and complete all items.
2. Include comments on all "NO" responses.
3. Fill-out and submit Action Report on completion of inspection.

#	POOL DECK	YES	NO	COMMENTS
1.	Deck clear of obstacles and debris	✓		
2.	All equipment properly stored	✓		
3.	Emergency procedures clearly posted	✓		
4.	Clear of standing water		✓	Drain in N.E. corner backed-up
5.	Deck drains secure and unbroken	✓		
6.	Ground fault circuit interrupters (GFCI) have been installed on all electrical outlets	✓		
7.	All pool ladders, guard chairs, railings and other equipment is tightly secured.		✓	Ladder in deep end loose
8.	Decks are clean, disinfected and algae-free	✓		
9.	Emergency telephone located on pool deck	✓		
10.	Emergency phone numbers and directions to facility are posted by the phone	✓		
11.	Pool rules and warning signs posted.	✓		
12.	Starting blocks removed or covered to prevent use	✓		
13.	Rescue equipment, including ring buoys, extension poles and shepherd's crooks, in good repair and in proper place		✓	Extension pole missing
14.	Ingress and egress points opened or locked as appropriate	✓		
15.	Bleachers secure and in good repair	✓		
16.	Back board, rigid cervical collar and head immobilizer in good repair & available	✓		

Safety Rules

Another method of reducing the risks associated with facility hazards is to establish rules concerning safety. Safety rules must be considered carefully. It is important to make sure that all rules are appropriate and necessary. Once safety rules have been de-

Figure 2. ABC Fitness Club

Inspection Checklist

Action Report

Item #	Problem	Recommendation
P 4	Drain in N.E. corner backed up	Report to maintenance immediately
P 7	Ladder in deep end loose	Report to maintenance immediately
P 13	Extension pole missing	Contact pool manager & replace it

Inspector's Name   Date

Inspector's Signature

termined, they must be posted in plain sight and in locations that are appropriate to the given hazard. Some examples include "No Running" in locker rooms, "No Diving" or "No Glass Containers" in pool areas or "Protective Eyewear Required" in racquetball courts. Safety rules must be clear, obvious and direct in order to be effective. Once safety rules have been established, it is essential that they be strictly enforced. It is hard to justify making rules to protect patrons' safety and then allowing them to disobey the rules. The facility manager is entitled to assume that patrons will obey the rules.

Establish a Preventative Maintenance Program

An effective facility manager does not put off maintenance until something breaks or becomes a problem. Proper maintenance should take place before problems or failure occur. It is important to know, understand and follow manufacturer's recommendations for maintaining and repairing equipment. Most equipment manufacturers will provide printed guidelines for preventive maintenance and repair. These guidelines should be kept on file, followed and documented upon completion. A system for developing and maintaining good written records of all preventive maintenance and repair work performed is essential (see Documentation). A common problem in weight training facilities is a lack of preventive maintenance of the equipment. Most manufacturers of weight machines provide preventive maintenance schedules, which outline cleaning, lubrication, testing and replacement intervals for each piece. Many also provide specific procedures for repairing and replacing parts. It is important to follow these guidelines and procedures and then document it upon completion.

Train Staff

Another essential step in making a facility as safe as possible is to train staff members to become risk managers. They must understand the importance of risk management and know that safety is a top priority of the organization. Establishing a "climate of safety" goes a long way in providing safe facilities and programs. Each staff person should be instructed on the kinds of hazards they are likely to encounter while performing his/her daily duties and to actively look for potentially hazardous conditions. They must also be taught the process of reporting such conditions and following up to ensure they are dealt with properly. This process allows for several sets of eyes to be continually looking for hazards instead of one person, and only during the periodic inspections. In order for the staff to truly help recognize hazards, it is important for the facility manager to follow up on their comments in a timely manner. If a staff person reports a few hazards and nothing ever gets done about them, they will probably quickly become discouraged and give up. Concern for safety should become core value of the organization.

Documentation

An organized, thorough, consistent method of documenting facility safety efforts is an integral part of any risk management program. If litigation over an injury occurs, the court will want to see evidence of what the facility did to ensure the safety of the participants, spectators and staff. Keeping good records is essential if one has to demonstrate in court that safety inspections were done or what preventive maintenance was performed. The facility manager may have done a great job of inspection and maintenance but if there is no documentation to show it, why should the court take the manager's word for it? The old adage, "If it wasn't written down, it didn't happen" is a great one to apply to a risk management program. It is important to keep copies of all periodic inspection reports, accident reports, preventive maintenance programs, repair work orders, staff training, etc. It is necessary to document and save everything done that relates to safety.

If an injury does occur, the facility manager must be especially diligent in regards to documentation related to the incident. Thorough documentation as part of a good overall risk management program is one of the best defenses in court. How long should these records be saved? The statute of limitations, i.e., the length of time an injured individual has in which to initiate a lawsuit, varies from state to state. Usually it is between three and five years but can be as little as one year and even longer than five. Especially in the case of an injury to a minor, the time can be much longer. It is important for each facility manager to find out what the statute of limitations is in his/her state and maintain all records at least until it expires. Facility managers are expected to keep and be able to produce all records associated with an incident, even if it occurred several years ago.

It is also very helpful to develop a good system for organizing and cataloging all such documents. It is not a good idea to throw them into boxes and stick them in the basement somewhere. If it were necessary to find a checklist performed the third week of October, four years ago, how hard would it be?

Common Hazards

Although there are innumerable different hazards possible in sport and recreation facilities, some are more common than others. This section is a sample of some that occur more commonly than most.

Indoors

1) Inadequate buffer zones and wall padding around courts.
2) Improper storage of equipment.
3) Traffic patterns routed through activity areas.
4) Improper building materials.
5) Weight machines not properly maintained.
6) High risk areas or equipment left unsupervised.
7) Poor control of access.
8) Improper maintenance of facilities and equipment
9) Non-safety glass in activity areas.
10) Slick floors in locker/shower rooms or activity areas.

Outdoors

1) Overlapping fields.
2) Improper storage of equipment.
3) Playing surface abnormalities.
4) Baseball team benches exposed to batted balls
5) Improper surface material on playground
6) Soccer goals not anchored or stored properly
7) Slippery pool decks
8) No warning track on baseball field
9) Unsafe bleachers
10) Improper fences for activity

In My Opinion

Providing reasonably safe facilities is one of the primary legal duties expected of managers of sport, physical activity and recreation programs. In order to do this, managers must truly believe that the safety of patrons, spectators and staff is a top priority. A good facility risk management program can usually be achieved through effort and, for the most part, without great expense. Most hazards, once identified, take little time or money to repair, remove or compensate for when facility managers use their imagination. The key is caring enough to recognize potential hazards and deal with them before they become a problem.

References

Ammon, R. (2010). Risk management process. *Law for Recreation and Sport Managers.* (5th ed.). Champaign, IL: Kendall/Hunt Publishing Co.

Appenzeller, H. (2003). Equipment and facilities. *Managing sports and risk management strategies.* Durham, NC: Carolina Academic Press.

Appenzeller, T. (2000). *Youth sport and the law.* Durham, NC: Carolina Academic Press.

Berg, R. (1994). Unsafe. *Athletic Business, 18*(4), 43–46.

Borkowski, R.P. (1997). Checking out checklists. *Athletic Management, IX* (1), 18.

Brown, M. (2003). Risk identification and reduction. *Law for Recreation and Sport Managers.* (3rd ed.). Champaign, IL: Kendall/Hunt Publishing Co.

Dougherty, N., & Seidler, T. (2007). Viewpoints: Injuries in the buffer zone: A serious risk management problem. *Journal of Physical Education Recreation and Dance, 78*(2), 4–7.

Hart, J. (1990). Locker room liability. *Strategies, 3* (3), 33–34.

Maloy, B.P. (1993). Legal obligations related to facilities. *Journal of Physical Education, Recreation, and Dance, 64* (2), 28–30, 68.

Page, J.A. (1988). *The law of premises liability.* Cincinnati: Anderson Publishing Co.

Seidler, T. (2009). Planning facilities for safety and risk management. *Facilities planning for health, fitness, physical activity, recreation and sport.* (12th ed.). Champaign, IL: Sagamore Publishing.

Seidler, T. (2006). Planning and designing safe facilities. *Journal of Physical Education Recreation and Dance, 77*(5), 32–37, 44.

Sharp, L., Moorman, A. & Claussen, C. (2010). *Sport Law: A managerial approach.* (2nd ed.). Scottsdale, AZ: Holcomb Hathaway Publishers.

van der Smissen, B. (1990). *Liability and Risk Management for Public and Private Enterprises.* Cincinnati: Anderson Pub. Co.

Chapter 36

A Safety and Risk Management Audit for Secondary School Athletic Programs

The purpose of this instrument is to enable school personnel to identify safety and legal liability problems relative to the operation of their school's athletics program.

Gary Rushing

This instrument contains 187 objective statements that represent established standards and practices against which a secondary school's athletic program may be compared. The standards/practices are grouped into seven categories, with each category representing a major aspect of the operation of an athletic program. The categories are insurance (15), facilities and equipment (39), supervision (34), instruction (20), student rights (21), medical care (37), travel/transportation (21). The categorical grouping is significant in that it enables the evaluator to see more specifically where problems exist.

The purpose of this instrument is to enable school personnel to identify safety and legal liability problems relative to the operation of their school's athletics program. The audit should produce corrective action in the areas identified as being out of compliance with the standard. As corrective action occurs, participant safety will improve while reducing the likelihood of a lawsuit.

Who Should Use the Self-Appraisal?

Only one knowledgeable and conscientious person is needed to adequately perform the audit. However, the ideal method of assessing a program is to have a number of people (preferably a risk management committee), perform the evaluation and compare the scoring. This method provides a variety of viewpoints and produces a more accurate profile of the program. One of the benefits of this assessment is that it provides the evaluators with an increased awareness of the safety and legal liability aspects of the program. For this reason, those most directly involved with the operation of the program should be selected as evaluators. The ideal evaluators would be to a risk management team composed of people who are most familiar with all aspects of the program.

The following are examples of possible evaluators :

Superintendent

Principal

Assistant principals

Athletic director/activity directors

Head coaches

Assistant coaches

Directions for the Evaluator

The evaluator should consider each statement carefully and determine the extent to which the athletic program conforms to the standard or practice listed. Answer each item based on personal judgment; however, if the evaluator lacks familiarity with an item, that item should be investigated in order to make an accurate rating.

If a school completely conforms to a standard the evaluator should mark a "C" (conforms) in the appropriate box. If the school does not *fully* comply with a standard, the evaluator should mark "NCA" (needs corrective action). Should an evaluator believe that an item does not apply to the evaluated program an "N/A" (does not apply).

NCA: NEEDS CORRECTIVE ACTION

C: CONFORMS COMPLETELY TO STANDARD

N/A: DOES NOT APPLY — this practice does not have application to this program

EVALUATOR PERSONAL DATA SHEET

Position Held:

Years of Experience in Position:

Number of Years Employed by the School:

INSURANCE STANDARDS AND PRACTICES	Date Checked	Conforms Completely or Needs Corrective Action	Action Taken & Date
1 Insurance coverage for accident and general liability is purchased by the school or is available to all persons involved in the athletic program, including athletes, employees, volunteers, and school boards.			
2 There is a person or group of persons delegated to explore insurance policies, and after developing a set of criteria, to purchase the best possible coverage.			
3 Catastrophic lifetime medical liability plans are available to your athletes.			
4 Dental injury benefits are included in the school athletic insurance coverage.			
5 Administrators have a clear understanding of what claims the insurance company will and will not pay.			
6 The school insists that all athletes are enrolled in some form of athletic insurance program.			

7	The school has a liability policy, which has generous excess medical, rehabilitation, and work loss benefits. It also provides lifetime benefits for permanent athletic injury.			
8	The school has a comprehensive plan for insurance to protect itself.			
9	The school has a comprehensive plan for insurance to protect its personnel (all coaches, administrators, and trainees, etc.).			
10	The school seeks good advice from qualified persons (broker, lawyer, agent, etc.) concerning its insurance needs.			
11	Athletic personnel know the difference between liability and accident insurance coverages.			
12	The policy limits of the athletic insurance are kept current and are adequate.			
13	Athletic insurance coverage includes protection for non-students (general public) in the use of facilities.			
14	All employees (coaches, etc.) are aware that they should have adequate insurance to cover them while transporting students in the course of their employment.			
15	Each coach has personal liability insurance that provides adequate coverage when coaching.			

FACILITIES AND EQUIPMENT STANDARDS AND PRACTICES	Date Checked	Conforms Completely or Needs Corrective Action	Action Taken & Date
1	All equipment used in athletic activities is regularly and systematically inspected and complete repair on faulty equipment is done prior to any use.			
2	There are clear, written policies for identifying and correcting potential hazards within the athletic environment.			
3	The line of responsibility for inspection and repair of equipment is clearly defined so that a specific person or department is responsible for its duty of periodic inspection.			
4	Accurate records are kept of all equipment and facility inspections. The records include the inspector's name, the date of the inspection, the condition of the equipment and facilities, and the recommendations for repair.			
5	Facilities and equipment inspectors use a simple objective checklist of everything that needs to be inspected and the frequency with which inspection is needed.			
6	Supervisors insure that inspections are done and that the recommended repairs are done properly and as soon as possible.			
7	Coaches are requested to check equipment and facilities before each usage.			

8	During equipment inspection, special attention is given ropes, ladders, lockers, and bleachers.
9	Hard walls, radiators, slick floors, glass windows, fire extinguishers, etc. are considered when evaluating the safety of the practice and playing areas.
10	Faculty and coaches are required to report unsafe facilities or equipment both verbally and in writing (retaining a copy).
11	The highest quality equipment is issued to all participants, including varsity, junior varsity, and freshman level.
12	There are qualified personnel who know how to fit equipment and supervise the fitting of the protective equipment to ensure everyone has a proper fit.
13	All athletic equipment and facilities are within the guidelines of federal statutes, building codes, and executive orders.
14	If the school uses facilities other than its own, such as city or county parks and recreation facilities, a written agreement that indemnifies for injuries is drawn up indicating who is responsible for maintenance and repairs of equipment, facilities, and grounds.
15	All catalogs and instructions furnished by the manufacturers of sports equipment for installing, fitting, and maintaining equipment are followed and kept for reference.
16	Appropriately designed and safe areas of play are provided and these areas are carefully and continuously maintained.
17	Athletic facilities and buildings are designed for the safety of spectators as well as the athletes.
18	Safety rules for use of athletic facilities are posted. The rules orient students, staff, and spectators to potential dangers in activities, facilities, and personal conduct. These rules are strictly enforced.
19	Safety rules include the regulation of vehicular traffic on or near all playing fields and other areas which athletes and spectators use.
20	All athletic apparatus are safely secured when not in use under supervision—either put away, locked, roped off, or covered with mats.
21	All passage facilities are safe and there is a safe system of pedestrian traffic within the athletic plant.
22	During assemblies and sport events athletic facility doors are locked from the inside, according to Fire Ordinances.
23	A safe limit in the number of spectators has been determined for each area and the limit strictly followed.
24	Adequate fire extinguishers are available in every area and all staff members are trained in the methods of correct operation.

25 Potential risks are explained to athletes in such a way that they know, understand, and appreciate the potential risks involved in the use of equipment.

26 Athletic trainers or team physicians work with the coaches in selecting protective equipment.

27 Sufficient athletic equipment is purchased to ensure immediate replacement in case of damage or wear in hazardous activities.

28 Equipment is purchased on the basis of established criteria, which ensures the selection of safe equipment.

29 There are established regulations for the use of school facilities by outside groups with regard to safety, accident prevention, and insurance coverage.

30 All sports equipment is inventoried at the conclusion of each athletic season, and the replacement of defective equipment is made to ensure no unsafe equipment is issued at the start of the next season.

31 The manufacturer's engineers or other highly-qualified personnel inspect bleachers and grandstands periodically.

32 Swimming pools and shower rooms are maintained in a hygienic and safe condition. Procedures to control fungal infections, rules of behavior for students and athletes, cleaning procedures, and control of temperature of shower water are included.

33 When, and if, serious injuries occur, items of evidence associated with the injury, such as pieces of equipment, are preserved.

34 Only reputable reconditioning equipment companies with high standards are used for reconditioning of equipment. For example, NOCSAE STAMP of approval should apply to reconditioned helmets.

35 Inspection of facilities and equipment is done with disabled athletes and spectators in mind in order to remove obstacles and provide them with adequate access and opportunity to participate.

36 The school has a written policy for crowd management, which includes maintenance and inspection of bleachers, aisle space, and exit space, as well as location of fire extinguishers.

37 Athletic administrators anticipate potentially dangerous situations involving spectators and take preventative steps to reduce those risks.

38 Care is taken to ensure that movable bleachers cannot tip over.

39 Padding and other protective devices are used around playing areas to prevent injuries from sharp objects, poles, sprinklers, holes, etc.

SUPERVISION STANDARDS AND PRACTICES	Date Checked	Conforms Completely or Needs Corrective Action	Action Taken & Date
1 High-risk activities are eliminated from the total program when qualified instructors and coaches are not available.			
2 All athletic contests involving physical contact are scheduled on the basis of equitable competition with regard to size, skill, and other controlling factors.			
3 The school has a clear anti-hazing policy and all coaches and athletes are trained in how to handle hazing issues.			
4 All coaches are under the direct supervision of an athletic director, whose position holds a minimum qualification of an advanced professional degree in an area that includes study in coaching, competency areas such as first aid, and the care and prevention of athletic injuries.			
5 Activities are never placed in the control of non-qualified personnel for any reason.			
6 The selection of athletic personnel is done on the basis of the best-qualified person and not inbreeding or hiring someone who is "on-board" already.			
7 Each coaching position has a job description for selecting qualified personnel, which includes a listing of safety procedures to be followed in the specific activities. Knowledge, skills, and understanding required of the jobholder are also specified.			
8 Rules and policies concerned with athletic safety have been established and are enforced. These policies are printed, posted, and/or distributed to students and faculty.			
9 Meetings are held to orient athletes to the safety and health requirements of athletic participation.			
10 Only referees who are competent and have passed both written and practical examinations are hired for officiating.			
11 There is a written policy of assigning an adequate number of supervisory personnel for groups engaged in athletic activities. The number of supervisors is determined by the nature and size of the group and the type of activity involved.			
12 There is a written and strictly-enforced policy that prohibits having unsupervised athletic practice sessions or leaving athletes unsupervised during practice sessions.			
13 An attorney is consulted whenever there is uncertainty regarding the legality of planned actions, such as contracts over $500, fund-raising contests, and lotteries.			
14 All coaches and/or administrators attend seminars and workshops that deal with tort liability and the prevention of injuries.			
15 All coaches are administratively evaluated on how well they follow the school's safety and participation policies.			

16   Records are kept of all safety and liability seminars which are attended by coaches and athletic administrators.

17   Administrators provide leadership in the development and implementation of sound policies, procedures, and safety regulation. This includes posting safety regulations in proper places; a standardized system of emergency care in the case of accidents; and a standard procedure of reporting accidents.

18   All coaches and other athletic personnel adhere to all the guidelines and procedures of the athletic department.

19   There are administrative policies and guidelines stating how fans, cheerleaders, and announcers should behave during games and how they could be disciplined for unruly behavior.

20   There is an effort on the part of school officials to keep parents/guardians and the general public informed of the safety precautions that are undertaken to prevent accidents and to provide a safe environment.

21   The school's administration lends complete support and provides high priority to the school's safety program.

22   A safety audit is conducted periodically to check for possible safety and/or legal problems within the athletic program.

23   There is a written policy concerning use of equipment and hours during which fields can be used.

24   Records are kept concerning objective and fair evaluation of all of your personnel, including their background and training.

25   There are written policies and guidelines setting forth how practices are to be conducted and who is responsible for them. These guidelines include use of volunteer workers, coaches, and teachers.

26   The school utilizes contracts extensively, including contracts concerning employees, team doctors, concessionaires, common carriers, insurance coverage, and game officials, as well as leases of your premises to outside groups and summer camps.

27   Athletic personnel participate in and stay current with information reports from the injury-reporting systems and the equipment involved in injuries.

28   Coaches know and understand the rules of the athletic association to which the school belongs.

29   Special supervision is provided for less qualified and less experienced coaches until they become more experienced.

30   School supervisors understand that if they assign unqualified personnel to conduct an activity, they may be held liable.

31   The following documents from parents are kept on file: 1. Agreement to Participate consent forms signed by parents/guardians and students. 2. Written permission from

parents allowing their children to return from athletic trips with friends or relatives rather than returning on the school-provided carrier. 3. Written permission from a physician allowing an athlete to return to practice and competition. Limits on the type and amount of activity are specified. 4. Written permission from parents allowing a medical doctor to treat their child if injured in practice or a game.

32	The school conducts an annual analysis of accident data and trends in athletic injury prevention.	
33	There are special emergency procedures for fire and other disaster emergencies. The coaching staff is aware of these procedures.	
34	There is an established philosophy, which includes objectives and policies related to the school's sport safety program, and interpretation of this philosophy is presented to faculty, administrators, service personnel, students, and parents/guardians.	

INSTRUCTION STANDARDS AND PRACTICES	Date Checked	Conforms Completely/ Needs Corrective Action	Action Taken & Date
1 All coaches have either majored or minored in physical education, or they have completed a coaching minor, or have completed a systematic in-service program recommended by the state or an institution of higher education.			
2 In-service programs are conducted to train athletic personnel in tort liability and first aid procedures.			
3 Athletic coaches do not assign athletes activities that are beyond their ability and capacity. Size, skill level, age, maturity, and physical condition are taken into consideration.			
4 Special care and training is provided athletes in gymnastics, tumbling, and other activities in which dangerous equipment is used.			
5 All coaches follow a written policy which requires them to teach sports skills starting with simple skills, and gradually progress to more sophisticated advanced skills.			
6 All coaches involved with teaching gymnastics or wrestling are properly trained and qualified for specialized work.			
7 The school uses Agreements to Participate, rather than waiver forms, as means of assuring that parents/guardians recognize the students' intent to participate in a sport and to inform them of the risks involved in participating in that sport.			
8 Athletes and their parents are provided written and verbal warning of the possible dangers inherent to each sports activity. The warnings are clear and understandable. The written warning is signed by the athlete and parents and is			

kept on file. An audio recording is made of the verbal
warning and the date noted.

9	Posters are placed around athletic facilities providing warnings of the risks involved in certain sports activities.			
10	Players are well instructed prior to allowing them to perform in an athletic activity.			
11	Coaches and administrators for safety improvement and as a matter of public policy analyze all coaching methods; coaches are encouraged not to allow the use of tactics and techniques that increase hazards on the playing field.			
12	Coaches stress safety in the performance of techniques taught to athletes.			
13	Prospective players are given directions to follow and activities to perform for preseason conditioning.			
14	Coaches never use drills or techniques that are disapproved by professional associations or respected leaders in the field.			
15	All of the coaches keep current on changes in equipment and skill techniques that will improve the safety and performance of the sports activity.			
16	All of the coaches use a proper systematic and sequential coaching method of teaching and conditioning in order to prepare athletes for competition.			
17	All of the coaches understand tort liabilities (negligence) as they relate to providing proper instruction and supervision.			
18	All of the coaches are required or strongly encouraged to attend coaching clinics in order to stay current in the best coaching techniques.			
19	Rules and regulations of games are strictly enforced in practice sessions as well as in games in order to reduce the risk of injury and keep players from developing bad habits.			
20	School administrators do checks and periodic evaluations to ensure that coaches are instructing properly.			

MEDICAL STANDARDS AND PRACTICES	Checked Date	Conforms Completely/ Needs Corrective Action	Action Taken & Date
1	All staff, volunteers, and visiting team coaches are provided with printed instructions on emergency care procedures.			
2	Coaches conduct a preseason conditioning program at least three weeks prior to the first contest and they encourage players to improve their physical condition between seasons.			
3	Local anesthetics are never used to enable an injured player to continue participation.			
4	There is a policy which prohibits the return of any seriously injured athlete to competition or practice			

	without the permission of a certified athletic trainer or physician.
5	Coaches are required to become knowledgeable about the health and medical histories of the athletes under their care.
6	Coaches are knowledgeable in the following areas and are able to apply this knowledge: 1.Routine first aid. 2. Care of simple and common athletic trauma. 3. Cardiopulmonary resuscitation. 4. Water safety (swim coaches only).
7	Emergency care drills are scheduled and conducted during which all employees are provided the opportunity to practice specific emergency care procedures.
8	All coaches obtain medical advice and approval for any medically-related treatment beyond first aid.
9	Accurate and up-to-date medical records are kept on each athlete. The information is used to provide appropriate medical treatment.
10	Coaches and athletic trainers have a written policy on how to conduct first aid and emergency care. The policy specifies the limits to which they can go in treating athletic injuries.
11	Procedures for handling emergencies include calling a nurse or doctor immediately and notifying parents.
12	First responders to injuries (coaches, athletic trainers, etc.) use cellular phones or radio devices to expedite emergency communication.
13	There is a well-equipped training room which is adequately supervised.
14	Proper clearance is obtained when dispensing pharmaceuticals of any kind.
15	Pharmaceuticals are kept under lock and key.
16	Comprehensive pre-participation medical exams by a qualified health care provider are required of student-athletes prior to participation.
17	There is a uniform procedure for reporting, recording, and investigating all accidents within the program.
18	All accidents requiring medical attention are reported to the athletic director the following morning, at the latest. Serious injuries are reported as soon as possible.
19	Head coaches or athletic trainers are responsible for filling out proper accident forms the following school day, at the latest. These reports are kept on file for future reference.
20	Coaches or athletic trainers are required to make a follow-up call to parents on all injured players.
21	Each athletic team has a first aid kit available at all times. The kit contains adequate and proper first aid supplies.
22	A complete inventory of first aid and emergency medical supplies is assembled and maintained and these supplies

are accessible.

23	There is a qualified person (doctor, athletic trainer, or paraprofessional) immediately available at all practices and contests that is designated to render emergency care to a seriously injured athlete.
24	There is planned access to a medical facility—including a plan for communication and transportation between the athletic site and medical facility—for prompt medical services when needed (away sites included).
25	Emergency medical transportation is available at all contact sport events.
26	Ongoing in-service programs are provided to the coaches of every sport on how to manage specific sport injuries.
27	An athlete is not permitted, under penalty of dismissal from the squad, to insert himself/herself back into the contest after an injury.
28	Coaches or athletic trainers are required to withdraw obviously injured players from the contest.
29	Injured athletes are treated immediately.
30	Special procedures have been adopted for handling suspected spinal cord injuries.
31	Coaches and trainers are encouraged as a matter of public policy to err on the side of conservatism when predicting the seriousness of an injury.
32	Recommendations by coaches concerning the gaining and losing of weight are done in a prudent manner.
33	There is a policy which recommends or requires updating first aid and emergency medical care credentials for all coaches.
34	Coaches are aware of the state's laws and their legal ramifications in case of injury to one of their athletes resulting in a lawsuit.
35	The school has an athletic trainer who is certified by the National Athletic Trainer's Association.
36	There is a written agreement between the team (athletic) physician and the school which identifies each party's responsibility in the event of alleged negligence.
37	Athletic trainers and other athletic personnel know and follow state laws governing the use of modalities, such as whirlpool and Ultrasound, and only qualified personnel are allowed to operate these therapeutic devices.

STUDENT RIGHTS/STANDARDS AND PRACTICES	Date	Conforms Completely/ Needs Corrective Action	Action Taken
1 Rules and practices are examined regularly to determine if they serve a justifiable public interest.			
2 All initial decisions and rulings, which are appealed, are provided full consideration, taking all factors of the individual's position into account.			
3 Administrators and coaches understand the mandates of the federal laws regarding handicap and sex discrimination.			
4 Periodic review is made of the current status of laws and judicial decisions concerning students' rights.			
5 School officials voluntarily initiate programs that are in compliance with the law rather than await a judicial mandate.			
6 Administrators and coaches permit athletes with disabilities to participate in sports according to current laws, such as Public law 94-142, Section 504 of the Rehabilitation Act, Individuals With Disabilities Education Act, and Americans with Disabilities Act.			
7 The welfare of the individual is the basis of all decisions and is the paramount goal in the operation of the educational program.			
8 Adequate notice of charges is given to student athletes who have violated rules.			
9 Student-athletes who may have violated rules are given adequate time to prepare answers to the charges and provide evidence in his or her behalf.			
10 Student-athletes who may have violated rules are given a hearing to consider the evidence for or against them.			
11 Student-athletes who may have violated rules are given fair and impartial decisions and the decisions are put in writing.			
12 Rules are published and announced in advance.			
13 When rule violations occur, there is a prepared plan to deal with the problem.			
14 Seminars and workshops are provided to faculty to improve legal knowledge and to keep them abreast of changes in the law involving student rights.			
15 Due process is provided to student-athletes and students are made aware of the procedures available should they be accused of a rule violation.			
16 A staff member is assigned to handle due process procedures for rule violations.			

17 Rules are constructed so as to avoid rendering students ineligible due to circumstances beyond their personal control.

18 Clear policies and practices concerning rules and regulations are published and students and coaches are aware of them.

19 All training rules, eligibility rules, and rules of conduct are reasonable and fair. They are specific and not vague or too broad and are rationally related to the school's interest, demonstrating function as a means to such ends as preventing unfair competition, injury, or excessive pressure on young people.

20 Rules relative to conduct and eligibility are published, distributed, and thoroughly explained to athletic participants (student trainers, cheerleaders, etc.) prior to beginning the sport season.

21 Any written information concerning the student-athlete's character or ability is open and accessible to the athlete.

TRANSPORTATION STANDARDS AND PRACTICES	Date Checked	Conforms Completely/ Needs Corrective Action	Action Taken & Date
1 Transportation plans are canceled if school personnel are unable to be thoroughly convinced of the personal and prudent reliability of drivers, means of transportation, and adequacy of insurance coverage.			
2 The school has high standards required of all its drivers who are involved in athletic transportation.			
3 When transportation is provided to an athletic event, parents, volunteers, and athletes are never used to transport participants.			
4 Drivers used for transporting athletes are required to satisfactorily complete an appropriate driver education program.			
5 There are rules and regulations governing student-athlete conduct on transportation vehicles and drivers have the authority to enforce such rules.			
6 There is a continuing training program for school bus drivers transporting student-athletes.			
7 Age, experience, attitude, and emotional stability, as well as knowledge and skill, are used as criteria for selecting bus drivers.			
8 The school's driver instruction program includes the following: 1. Policies and procedures. 2. Traffic accident problems. 3. Human consideration in driving. 4. Natural laws and their relationship to driving. 5. A job description for the school bus driver. 6. Responding to emergency driving situations and providing first aid to injured			

passengers. 7. Proper care and maintenance of the school bus. 8. Record keeping and required reporting.

9	Drivers are trained in traffic, including a variety of situations requiring the application of defensive driving techniques.
10	Athletic team members are required to go to contests as a team and return as a team (in the same vehicle, if possible).
11	There is a written policy forbidding overcrowding of cars and other vehicles.
12	If a number of vehicles are necessary for transporting athletes, the vehicles travel in a caravan and the car drivers are given complete instructions, which include speed, route, and meeting place. Whenever possible, the coach travels in the lead vehicle.
13	The kind and amount of insurance is checked prior to the trip.
14	Coaches and other drivers understand whether or not they are adequately covered by insurance.
15	Vehicles are thoroughly checked before use.
16	School officials have adopted safe rules and policies for all travel of athletic teams.
17	School officials use commercial vehicles when appropriate and competent adult drivers at all times.
18	Coaches are rarely, if ever, utilized as drivers to transport their own athletes to and from competitive sites.
19	Athletic personnel are aware of state laws pertaining to inspection requirements, proper licensure, age requirements, and other details, and adhere to them.
20	School-owned motor vehicles or approved commercial carriers are used for transporting athletes to contests.
21	Athletic staff members understand the liabilities involved in allowing their athletes to drive their own vehicles to athletic contests.

PROFILE OF SAFETY AND LEGAL ASPECTS OF A SCHOOL ATHLETIC PROGRAM

This section can be used to provide an overall rating of the areas above (Poor, Fair, Good) and/or it can be useful for notes related to each section.

SCHOOL'S overall rating in each section = POOR   FAIR   GOOD

AREA/SECTION

1. Insurance

2. Facilities & Equipment

3. Supervision

4. Instruction

5. Medical

6. Student Rights

7. Transportation

Interpretation of scores:

a. A score rating of **Poor** or **Fair** indicates need for concern. This area is highly vulnerable to safety and legal problems. It should be investigated thoroughly and corrective measures taken.

b. A score rating in the **Good** column indicates a sound area and should provide a sense of well-being; however, failure to comply with any of the standards listed could have serious consequences. A school should strive for complete compliance in all standards.

Footnote:

The above audit profile is only meant to be guide or tool to identify safety and legal problems in the most vulnerable areas of concern. An exact rating of a school's vulnerability to a lawsuit or other legal problems is impossible to determine. No amount of precaution is going to prevent the possibility of a lawsuit; however, if the above standards and practices are diligently pursued the chances of a lawsuit are greatly decreased and the consequences, should one occur, diminished.

Audit Frequency: A yearly audit is recommended; however, a Risk Management Committee or administrative personnel should develop a policy decision that addresses this issue.

Chapter 37

Athletic Department Drug/Banned Substance Awareness, Education, and Screening Policy

"The most important part of this program is the ongoing educational effort through which students may become thorougly infiromed about abuse of drugs/banned substances."

Robert Casmus

Program Purpose

The purpose of the drug/banned substance education, screening, and counseling program:

1. Help persons avoid improper involvement with drugs/banned substances by insuring that they are well informed about drugs/banned substances and abuse.

2. Detect possible drug/substance abuse through a screening program based on periodic testing designed to reveal the use of drugs/banned substances.

3. Assist in the rehabilitation of persons found to be misusing drugs/substances.

4. Disassociate from our athletic programs any person who is found to be engaged in chronic, improper use of drugs/banned substances and/or who does not respond to rehabilitation efforts.

Prohibited Drugs/Banned Substances

A student, during the period of either their membership on or affiliation with an intercollegiate athletic team, may not use the drugs/banned substances specified in **Appendix A** (NCAA list of banned substances and unprescribed drugs) found at the end of this document. Any use of these or other unprescribed substances is expressly prohibited, whether such use occurs before, during, or after the student-athlete's competitive season.

Any student-athlete who has a medical condition for which the use of a prescribed drug is authorized, must ask a physician to provide a statement of such authorization to the Head Athletic Trainer at Catawba College.

Educational Activities

The most important part of this program is the ongoing educational effort through which students may become thoroughly informed about the abuse of drugs/banned substances. All Catawba college student-athletes will participate in educational seminars (2 per semester). The seminars will involve educational videos and/or various professionals who will educate the members of the Catawba College Athletic Department regarding drug abuse/substance misuse and related problems confronting administrators, coaches, student-athletes, cheerleaders, managers, and athletic training students.

Voluntary Admission and Request for Counseling

Any athlete may come forward at any time and seek help by contacting their head coach, athletic trainer, or athletic director. In such cases, the athlete will go through the steps listed in **Section F-1** concerning the consequences of impermissible drug/substance use.

Screening Program

By subscribing to this education, screening, and counseling program, a participating student agrees to submit to tests to reveal the use of any drugs/substances listed in **Appendix A**. No such test will be administered without the student first having signed an individual consent form.

The basic test to be used for drug/substance screening is a urinalysis. However, other types of tests from time to time may be utilized to determine the presence of drugs/substances listed in **Appendix A**. Except as otherwise provided herein, the standards for determining "non-negative" tests will be those prescribed by the manufacturers of the tests. The testing based on urinalysis will be implemented as follows:

1. **When the test will be administered**

    a. Unannounced, random testing. All student-athletes, student managers, cheerleaders, student coaches, and athletic training students will be subject to periodic, unannounced random testing. The selection of individuals will be made through a random drawing of names from the team roster (augmented to include cheerleaders, student managers, student coaches, and athletic training students) by the Athletic Director or Head Athletic Trainer. Student-athlete or student notification of selection shall come from the Head Athletic Trainer as to the date on which testing will take place. The notification procedure shall occur at any time prior to the scheduled testing. Such notification shall be accomplished by the delivery of a copy of a signed statement, **Appendix B**, to the student as one who was duly selected, at random, to be tested on the date specified. The notification shall also include the time and location of the test. The student is required to sign and submit to the Certified Athletic Trainer or delegate the form and acknowledge the time specified for conducting the test.

b. Coaches may request the screening of a student or student-athlete when reasonable concern merits such a request.

2. **Consequences of failure to participate in or cooperate with testing**

a. If the student or student-athlete declines to execute the required individual consent form, eligibility to participate in intercollegiate athletics will be suspended.

b. If the student or student-athlete fails to appear at the designated time and place for testing, he/she will be suspended from athletic participation for 30 days during their active season. This action will be treated as a "non-negative" drug test result. The student or student-athlete will be **eligible** for reinstatement following the completion of urinalysis and service of their 30 day suspension. These procedures will be subject to the actions and sanctions prescribed in **Section H.**

c. If the student or student-athlete fails within a reasonable period of time (not to exceed one hour from the time scheduled for collection of the specimen) to produce the required urine specimen, eligibility to participate in intercollegiate athletics will suspended until the subsequent testing day or until the student produces the required specimen, whichever is the lesser period of time. The period of suspension may be extended indefinitely upon failure to produce the required specimen on subsequently rescheduled testing dates. The procedures prescribed in **Section H** apply to any such suspension exceeding one week.

d. Any student or student-athlete refusing to sign the memoranda regarding notification of random selection shall be suspended from all athletic participation.

3. **Administration of drug screening program (Subject to change as conditions and needs merit)** See **Appendix C**

a. The student or student-athlete will report to the Abernethy Gym athletic training room, Hayes field house training room, or otherwise specified location at the designated time in shorts and a t-shirt with a current photo ID card (Catawba College ID or driver's license). A jacket and sweatpants may be worn if the weather necessitates.

b. The Certified Athletic Trainer will select a sealed and approved drug screen test kit each with its own lot number, expiration date, and laboratory chain of custody test form.

c. One kit is prepared for each athlete to be tested.

d. The athlete's information is entered on the laboratory chain of custody test form.

e. The student or student-athlete watches the process to ensure accuracy and integrity of the test.

f. The Certified Athletic Trainer or certified drug screen staff member takes the student or student-athlete, laboratory chain of custody test form, and specimen bottle to the collection area.

g. The specimen collection area must be sealed and only one student or student-athlete will be present at a time. Prior to specimen collection, the student or student-athlete will be visually inspected to check for hidden or secreted tampering materials. Any and all pockets will be emptied prior to collection of the urine specimen.

h. The student or student-athlete will enter the specimen collection room (private restroom) to produce the acceptable level/amount of urine at a specific concentration needed for testing. **Please note that the collection of a urine specimen for drug/banned substance testing is a "witnessed" procedure.** When the urine collection process is complete, the specimen will be checked by the staff member for temperature. The temperature check is done in full view of the athlete. The urine specimen is also checked for Specific Gravity (concentration) via a urine dipstick or other device. A specimen that is found to be too dilute is discarded and a new sample must be produced and collected. The urine specimen is also given a "Quick Check/Screen" to detect substance abuse as per the MedTox protocol.

i. The urine specimen bottle is sealed per the testing protocol.

j. As the student or student-athlete watches, the staff member checks the number of the testing kit against the number on the laboratory chain of custody testing form, places the laboratory chain of custody testing form and the sealed urine specimen bottle in a plastic bag and seals it.

k. The specimen is signed over to a courier service.

l. "Non-negative" tests are confirmed by gas chromatography/mass spectrometry by a contracted professional laboratory service to confirm the non-negative "Quick Check/Screen" result.

4. **Notification of results**

a. The Head Athletic Trainer will receive the results and correlate the number with the screened student or student-athlete.

b. Notification of "non-negative" results are communicated as needed to the following:

1. Athletic Director

2. Head Athletic Trainer

3. Head Coach

4. Parents

5. Team Physician

6. Dean of Students

Consequences of Impermissible Drug/Banned Substance Use

When there has been a reliable determination of improper drug use, through verified "non-negative" test results, the student or student-athlete will be subject to the following requirements:

1. **Voluntary admission and request for counseling**

    a. Confidential meeting to evaluate the nature and extent of drug involvement. The student or student-athlete will be required to meet privately with the Head Athletic Trainer, Athletic Director, Head Coach, and Catawba College counselor to ascertain the facts about the nature, history, and extent of the problem. In eliciting information from the student or student-athlete, responses are to be oral and are not given under oath, and are to be revealed only to college officials, persons authorized by the student or student-athlete, and the parents of the student if he/she is a minor or is a dependent student as defined in section 152 of the Internal Revenue Code of 1954 (viz., essentially one who is financially dependent on the support of his or her parents, which would include most undergraduate students). No other persons or agencies will be given information except in response to a valid subpoena or court order.

    b. Counseling or rehabilitation. The nature and extent of institutional counseling and medical intervention that may be required as a condition to continued athletic eligibility, service as a cheerleader, student coach, student manager, or athletic training student will depend on the nature of the individual's drug/substance involvement. As a minimum, the student or student-athlete will be required to complete an individual education and counseling seminar program developed by the college counselor.

    c. The student or student-athlete may be subject to weekly testing as long as is deemed appropriate by either the Athletic Director or Head Athletic Trainer for the balance of the intercollegiate athletic season. Follow-up testing for non-negative test results will allow adequate time for the drug/substance to be removed from the system. The student or student-athlete will not be permitted to participate in post-season play or activities until they retest with a "negative" result.

2. **First "Non-Negative" Test Result**

    a. Notification via a conference call with the Director of Athletics, Head Coach, and Head Athletics Trainer. The student or student-athlete's parents will be informed of the known facts concerning drug/banned substance abuse and the conditions to be imposed by the institution in response to those facts.

    b. Following a meeting with the head coach, the student or student-athlete is informed of a retest to be performed following the half-life of the drug for which they tested "non-negative." The date is noted in the meeting and failure to retest constitutes up to a semester suspension.

    c. The student or student-athlete will be suspended from participation in intercollegiate activities for 30 consecutive days; any suspension may be imposed only in accordance with the procedures specified in **Section E**. The Athletic Director will set the beginning date of the thirty (30) day suspension at his discretion so as to ensure this suspension impacts upon the student or student-athlete's participation in his/her respective sport or activity.

d.   Appropriate medical and psychological monitoring and counseling will be supplied to the student or student-athlete for the duration of any period of suspension and thereafter as long as the Athletic Director, college counselor, and Head Athletic Trainer deem appropriate.

e.   During the period of suspension, and at any time following reinstatement, the student may be subject to frequent testing for as long as is deemed appropriate by either the Athletic Director or Head Athletic Trainer. Follow-up testing for non-negative test results will allow adequate time for drug/banned substances to be removed from the system. If the test results are again "non-negative," the student or student-athlete will be treated as a second "non-negative" offender.

f.   **The student or student-athlete's refusal to take the required actions listed above will be treated as a second "non-negative" offense.**

3.   Second "Non-Negative" Test Result

a.   Notification via a conference call with the Director of Athletics, Head Coach, and Head Athletics Trainer. The student or student-athlete's parents will be informed of the known facts concerning drug/banned substance abuse and the conditions to be imposed by the institution in response to those facts.

b.   Permanent cancellation of eligibility and varsity athletic participation for all student-athletes, student coaches, student managers, cheerleaders, and athletic training students.

c.   The Dean of Students shall also be notified and may at their discretion pursuer sanctions along the Catawba College Code of Discipline.

d.   Discontinuance of athletic aid or scholarship aid.

e.   Any such cancellation may be imposed only in accordance with the procedures specified in **Section H**. Prior to being barred from participation in intercollegiate athletics or activities, and the discontinuance of athletic or scholarship aid, the student or student-athlete shall be given the opportunity to meet with the Athletic Director to be heard on the matter of imposition of the sanction upon them.

Confidentiality of Information Concerning Drug/Banned Substance Use

Any information concerning a student's or student athlete's alleged or confirmed improper use of drugs/banned substances, solicited or received pursuant to implementation of this program, shall be restricted to institutional personnel responsible for the administration of the program, and to parents of minors or dependent students. No other release of such information will be made without the student's or student-athlete's written consent, unless in response to appropriate judicial process. The institution cannot guarantee that law enforcement or prosecutorial authorities will not gain access to information in the possession of the institution, since a valid subpoena or other enabling court order might be issued to compel disclosure; the institution, however, will not voluntarily disclose such information in the absence of a court order.

Violation of the Code of Student Conduct or Team Rules

The Catawba College's Code of Student Conduct states the following:

"Catawba College reserves the right to require the withdrawal from the college of any student at any time for unsatisfactory conduct. Furthermore, any student who by his or her actions is judged to be mentally unbalanced or thought to be of possible harm to himself/herself or others shall be subject to withdrawal. Students are referred to the Catawba student handbook, the Tom Tom, for a de-lineation of Catawba College regulations in the various areas of campus life."

Head coaches have established rules concerning the use of drugs/banned substances and alcohol by their team's members. This drug screening and education program is not intended to replace these team rules. A student or student-athlete may be determined by a head coach or supervising college faculty/staff member to have violated team rules related to the use of drugs/banned substances and alcohol on the basis of evidence acquired outside of the drug screening program. Results of drug screening tests performed under this program can be used in determining or confirming a student's or student-athlete's violation of team rules.

Improper Provision of Drugs by Institutional Personnel

No official, employee, or agent of Catawba College may supply to any student or student-athlete any drug/banned substance or alcohol that may endanger a student or student-athlete or affect his or her ability or athletic performance, or otherwise encourage or induce any student or student-athlete to improperly use drugs/banned substances and alcohol, except as specific drugs that may be prescribed by qualified medical personnel for the treatment of individuals. Any person who has information about a possible violation of this policy should report such information promptly to the Dean of Students, who shall have full authority to investigate the allegation and to report the results of any investigation to the President, for appropriate disciplinary proceedings against anyone who is charged with having violated this policy.

Appeal to "Non-Negative" Test Results

Upon notification that their drug test was reported non-negative, the student or student-athlete may request that the urine specimen be re-tested to rule out laboratory testing error. This notification of appeal must be done within 24 hours of receipt of the "non-negative" test result. The re-testing of the urine specimen will be conducted at the expense of the student or student-athlete and paid for in advance of the actual re-testing process. During this time of appeal, the student or student-athlete will not be permitted to participate in intercollegiate varsity athletic activity until results are known of the re-tested urine specimen. In the event that the specimen re-tests as "negative" for drug/banned substance abuse, the student or student-athlete may return to full athletic activity participation. In the event the specimen still re-tests "non-negative" for drug/banned substance abuse, the sanctions and procedures previously discussed in **Section F** shall be instituted.

Catawba College Athletic Alcohol Consumption Statement

The following guidelines shall exist:

1. Alcohol involved police offense during the season or while school is in session, e.g., DWI/DUI, drunk and disorderly conducted, contributing to the delinquency of a minor, or unlawful purchase or possession of alcohol,

    Action: Suspended until all legal actions and or penalties have been officially documented. A guilty plea, admission of guilt, or guilty verdict shall be treated as a "non-negative" drug test result.

2. Drinking on any athletic trip, to include vans/busses to or from games.

    First Offense: Treated as a "non-negative" drug test result.

    Second Offense: Treated as a second "non-negative" drug test result.

3. Major Campus Violation of Catawba College Drug and Alcohol Policy, e.g., Underage possession or consumption, or drunk and disorderly conduct.

    First Offense: Treated as a "non-negative" drug test result.

    Second Offense: Treated as a second "non-negative" drug test result.

Students and Student-athletes should be aware of the campus policies as written in the Tom Tom. The Dean of Students, at their discretion, can also pursue sanctions per the Catawba College Code of Discipline.

**Catawba College Athletic Department Statement of Informed Consent:
Drug/Banned Substance Awareness, Education, and Screening Policy**

I certify that I have read the statement of Catawba College's Drug/Banned Substance Awareness, Education, and Screening Policy and fully understand the program and agree freely, voluntarily, and knowingly to participate in the program during my entire intercollegiate career at Catawba College.

Specifically, I agree to:

1. Submit a urine sample for drug testing when I am requested to do so in accordance with the Catawba College Athletic Department Drug/Banned Substance Awareness, Education and Screening Policy.

2. Abide by the sanctions imposed.

3. Cooperate in the drug education, counseling, and rehabilitation programs required.

I authorize the notification of my parent/parents, legal guardians, or spouse, of any "non-negative" drug/banned substance test results. I further authorize the confidential release of test results to other individuals, including Catawba College officials, as provided in the statement of the program.

Student/Student-Athlete Name (Print): _____

Student/Student-Athlete Signature: _____

Date: _____/_____/_____

Parent/Legal Guardian Signature (If a minor): _____

Date: _____/_____/_____

Appendix A: NCAA and/or Catawba College Drug/Banned Substance Classifications

NCAA BANNED & PROHIBITED SUBSTANCES

DRUG CLASS	NCAA STATUS
Alcohol	PROHIBITED in Riflery
Anabolic Steroids	PROHIBITED
Beta2 Agonists (ex. asthma medicine)	PROHIBITED or RESTRICTED
Beta Blockers	PROHIBITED in Riflery
Corticosteroids (ex. prednisone)	ALLOWED
Dietary Supplements (ex. creatine)	*WARNING*
Diuretics	PROHIBITED
Local Anesthetics	RESTRICTED
Masking Agents	PROHIBITED
Peptide Hormones (ex. growth hormone)	PROHIBITED
Stimulants (ex. ephedrine)	PROHIBITED (except pseudoephedrine)
Street Drugs (ex. marijuana)	PROHIBITED

PROHIBITED: drug class may not be used.

RESTRICTED: drug class may be used under special circumstances defined by the NCAA.

ALLOWED: category may be used, assuming the use is legal, appropriate, or medically justified.

1. Local anesthetics
2. Asthma- or exercise-induced bronchospasm and corticosteroids

DIETARY SUPPLEMENT WARNING—Products sold as over-the-counter dietary supplements might contain NCAA banned substances. NO one can guarantee the purity of a dietary supplement. You are solely responsible for what you consume. If you use any, you use them at your own risk!

If you have any questions about NCAA banned substances, contact:

- If you have questions about dietary supplements, the Resource Exchange Center, REC, website uses the following username and password:

Username—NCAA II   Password—NCAA2

Resource Exchange Center (REC)
www.drugfreesport.com/rec
877-202-0769

THE REC does not provide dietary supplement recommendations or medical advice!

Appendix B: Drug Screening Notification

To: _____

From: Director of Intercollegiate Athletics

Re: Mandatory Drug Screening

Date: _____

Your name has been selected for drug/banned substance testing/screening. You are to report to the _____ @ _____ am pm on ____/____/____.

You will be required to produce a urine specimen of adequate amount, temperature, and concentration.

Failure to produce urine will result in immediate suspension from your team until a proper urine sample is submitted. Failure to appear at the designated time will constitute a withdrawal of your consent to be tested and will result in an immediate 30-day suspension from intercollegiate athletic activity. This will be treated as a "non-negative" drug/banned substance test result with the appropriate sanctions imposed.

Athlete's Signature: _____ Date: _____

Witness Signature: _____ Date: _____

Appendix C: Administration of the Drug/Banned Substance Screening Program/Test

a.   The student or student-athlete will report to the Abernethy Gym athletic training room, Hayes field house training room, or otherwise specified location at the designated time in shorts and a t-shirt with a current photo ID card (Catawba College ID or driver's license). A jacket and sweatpants may be worn if the weather necessitates.

b. The Certified Athletic Trainer will select a sealed and approved drug screen test kit, each with its own lot number, expiration date, and laboratory chain of custody test form.

c. One kit is prepared for each athlete to be tested.

d. The athlete's information is entered on the laboratory chain of custody test form.

e. The student or student-athlete watches the process to ensure accuracy and integrity of the test.

f. The Certified Athletic Trainer or certified drug screen staff member takes the student or student-athlete, laboratory chain of custody test form, and specimen bottle to the collection area.

g. The specimen collection area must be sealed and only one student or student-athlete will be present at a time. Prior to specimen collection, the student or student-athlete will be visually inspected to check for hidden or secreted tampering materials. Any and all pockets will be emptied prior to collection of the urine specimen.

h. The student or student-athlete will enter the specimen collection room (private restroom) to produce the acceptable level/amount of urine at a specific concentration needed for testing. **Please note that the collection of a urine specimen for drug/banned substance testing is a "witnessed" procedure.** When the urine collection process is complete, the specimen will be checked by the staff member for temperature. The temperature check is done in full view of the athlete. The urine specimen is also checked for Specific Gravity (concentration) via a urine dip stick or other device. A specimen that is found to be too dilute is discarded and a new sample must be produced and collected. The urine specimen is also given a "Quick Check/Screen" to detect substance abuse as per the MedTox protocol.

i. The urine specimen bottle is sealed per the testing protocol.

j. As the student or student-athlete watches, the staff member checks the number of the testing kit against the number on the laboratory chain of custody testing form, places the laboratory chain of custody testing form and the sealed urine specimen bottle in a plastic bag and seals it.

k. The specimen is signed over to a courier service.

l. "Non-negative" tests are confirmed by gas chromatography/mass spectrometry by a contracted professional laboratory service to confirm the non-negative "Quick Check/Screen" result.

Part VIII

Trends in Risk Management

Both sport and law have grown in proportion to the growth of our society. It was inevitable that the two would eventually collide.

Anonymous

Chapter 38

New Approach to Resolve Disputes

Dispute resolution techniques are more business and consumer friendly.

Gil B. Fried

Sport administrators continue to embrace new means to resolve disputes. Alternative dispute resolution involves different techniques designed to avoid the court room and reach a speedy, equitable, and less expensive resolution to a dispute. Techniques that can be utilized in alternative dispute resolution include: arbitration (where an independent party or parties hear a dispute and render a decision), mediation (where a mediator helps the parties negotiate a settlement), private judging (where a private judge conducts a trial and then renders a verdict), and a mini-trial (where a slimmed down trial is performed in front of neutral experts who help the parties understand strengths and weaknesses in each side's case as a means to help the parties settle the dispute). A recent survey by the American Bar Association concluded that 77% of potential litigants are willing to try mediation while 64% of potential litigants are willing to try arbitration to resolve disputes (Reuben 1995). More and more attorneys and their clients are resorting to alternative means for resolving disputes. Litigants seem more willing to trade the cost, complexity, formality, and inconvenience of the courtroom for the ease, simplicity, convenience, timeliness, and cost savings offered by alternative dispute resolution techniques.

The athletic, sport, and recreation industries have faced countless challenges concerning player eligibility, the interpretation of governing rules, and the application of these rules. Individuals who have been affected by the application or interpretation of a sport organization's governing rule often feel that the only means of having an impartial analysis of the rules is to litigate. Temporary restraining orders and injunctions have reduced numerous competitions to a war of wills, and an expensive one at that. Local judges often try of help the hometown heroes against a national bureaucracy. Others claim that the governing rules should be more flexible as, "it is just a game and let the kid play." However, without strictly enforced rules, everyone would want to push the boundaries to help the hometown team win.

While some of these claims against governing rules or their application are valid claims, most cases lead to a verdict in favor of the sport organization. Sport organizations will traditionally prevail as long as the rules are reasonable, designed to further a legitimate objective (level playing field), and are enforced uniformly.

Several cases highlight the need for an effective "out" to avoid costly and wasteful litigation. A pinnacle case epitomizing this need occurred in Illinois. Due to a rule interpretation, the Illinois High School Association (IHSA) refused to allow a favored wrestling team the opportunity to compete in the 1995 state championship (Scorecard 1995). With the support of all other competing states, the team decided to go to court. The IHSA, in turn, canceled the wrestling championship. Money, time, effort, and a year's worth of hard work by dedicated athletes throughout the state were wasted on a matter that probably could have been settled by a neutral, level-headed, third party.

Another case suitable for arbitration involved two teams that were banned from a Little League tournament. Little League rules prohibited the teams from participating in a charity game as the game could provide the two teams with an edge in preparation. The two teams sued and a judge reinstated the teams into the Little League tournament. One team went on to win two games before it was disqualified again for allegedly using some players from beyond league boundaries. While Little League ended up winning through finally disqualifying the team, the League lost some very valuable public relations points, as this case was the focus of a *USA Today* article on legal problems in youth sport playoffs (Mihoces 1995).

The question is not whether we need a means to resolve these disputes. Rather, the question is how to start implementing an alternative dispute resolution system. The key to creating a path towards alternative dispute resolution lies in contract law. Contracts are now regularly written with arbitration clauses. An arbitration clause requires all disputes stemming from the contract to be brought to arbitration, mediation, or some other forum rather than the courts. Parties to the contract, by agreeing to accept the contractual terms, specifically agree that arbitration (or mediation) will be the exclusive remedy for resolving any dispute. In fact, the National Association of Security Dealers (NASD) and the New York Stock Exchange (NYSE) have such clauses in all their client and employment contracts. Both organizations also have their own arbitration programs utilizing unbiased arbitrators from within and outside the investment community.

For sport organizations, especially facilities, it is very easy to include a clause in all rental, concession, employment, or membership contracts that any dispute will be brought to arbitration or mediation. Most parties to a contract are willing to accept such provisions as long as they do not waive any significant rights. Further, courts are willing to uphold such contractual provisions as long as all the terms are clearly set fourth in the contract. Thus, the court will allow a federal discrimination case to proceed in arbitration, rather than through the federal court system, if the contract specifically indicated that the potential employee agreed to bring all federal discrimination claims to arbitration. To pass judicial scrutiny, all arbitration clauses should be as specific as possible. Specific mention should be made concerning such issues as what laws could be used in arbitration, whether the arbitrator can decide a case using equitable principles, and who has to pay the arbitration expenses.

There are several organizations that can help resolve disputes through providing arbitrators or mediators. The American Arbitration Association (AAA) is the oldest provider of arbitration service. The AAA even has a sport arbitration panel. However, the primary focus of AAA's sport arbitration work revolves around Olympic eligibility disputes. The International Olympic Committee established an independent group called the International Court for the Arbitration of Sport (ICAS) to resolve Olympic disputes and disputes involving national sport governing bodies. In fact, the 1996 Olympics saw the deployment of 12 ICAS arbitrators to resolve disputes on the spot (Browning 1996). After the 2004 Olympic games, the ICAS was called into action when a dispute arose around the scoring of a Korean gymnast's routine. The ICA, on October 21, 2004, upheld the gold medal for American gymnast Paul Hamm. Korea asked Hamm to return his gold medal, which he refused to do. The matter was heard by the ICAS and at the time of this book going to press there has not been a final decision. All Olympic athletes had to sign a contract agreeing not to go to court and to only use arbitration for resolving any disputes. A new organization entitled Athletic Dispute Resolution Service (ADRS) has been founded by several nationally known sport law experts specifically to resolve disputes facing youth, nonprofit, and interscholastic sport organizations. However, the same principles easily apply to health clubs, equipment rental businesses, and sporting goods manufacturers and/or sellers. A revolutionary aspect of ADRS's service includes a 24-hour arbitration service which prevents disruptions during tournaments or championships, and all arbitrators are specially trained in sport law.

No matter which service is used, it is imperative that all sport organizations review their contract and governing rules to determine if it is feasible to add arbitration rules or requirements. By embracing change, sport organizations can also embrace the concept that they might be able to resolve disputes more quickly, with less animus, and for less money.

Risk Management: The ECT Approach

Numerous legal topics have been discussed throughout this text concerning different legal issues or strategies which might benefit the reader and sport organizations. This chapter provided the authors with the opportunity to pull out our crystal ball and provide some insight as to what several sport law professionals feel are major concerns confronting the sport industry. Besides providing a brief snapshot of various concerns, the authors felt they would be remiss in their obligation to provide educational services if they did not provide some useful hints which the reader could employ to hopefully avoid many of the issues discussed throughout this text.

Risk management is the process by which an individual can identify potential legal concerns and develop effective procedures or tactics to minimize or eliminate those concerns. A useful tool is called the "front headlines test." Ask all your associates to examine their actions prior to undertaking any activity to determine how such activity would look if it was reported on the front page of a major newspaper. While saving someone's life would look great on the front page, sexually harassing a subordinate employee or not providing reasonable accommodations to a patron with disabilities would destroy an organization's image.

The ECT approach is one strategy to help implement a risk management system. The ECT approach is appropriately named because every element of it ends with the letters ECT.

RflECT—A facility manager needs to determine why he/she is interested in implementing a risk management program. Is the purpose to save money, reduce insurance obligation, and/or possibly run a safer facility? Another concern in the refLECT stage is to rank potential concerns in order of magnitude and impact. For example, an earthquake is not a major concern on the East Coast, but could be one of the bigger concerns on the West Coast.

DeflECT—A facility can possibly improve the risk management efforts by deflECTing liability onto others. This can be accomplished through: purchasing insurance that will pay attorney fees and any damages if a claim is filed, inserting clauses in rental contracts that require the renter to have insurance, assume liability, and hold the facility harmless from any claims, and have participants (possibly parents) sign a waiver that they understand the risk of participating in the activity and will not sue the facility if they are injured while participating in the activity.

DetECT—A facility manager needs to learn how to identify potential concerns or to retain individuals that are knowledgeable in risk management. For example, the National Fire Protection Association requires larger facilities to conduct annual life safety inspections. Such inspections are designed to identify numerous potential concerns that can create a dangerous environment.

InspECT—It is not enough to identify risks and dangerous conditions; someone has to physically examine the facility and its policies to see if there is a hazard or if any area needs to be repaired or blocked from use.

CorrECT—Once an area or concern has been identified as hazardous, someone has to repair the hazard. This might require completing a work order or other means of communicating the needed repair to the appropriate individuals.

Re-InspECT—Just because a work order has been completed does not mean the repairs or required actions were undertaken, or were undertaken correctly to resolve the hazard. Thus, the area needs to be re-inspECTed to make sure it is safe.

RefIECT—After a set time such as a year, or an event, the entire risk management process needs to be re-evaluated to determined if it was effective and what steps can be taken to make it more effective in the future (Fried 1999).

In My Opinion

The law is always in a state of flux. The same legal concerns that affect countless businesses also influence sport organizations. Courts and legislatures are grappling with trying to make the legal system more user friendly, while at the same time trying to protect both plaintiffs and defendants. The primary "hot topics" we feel will produce the greatest amount of litigation in the next decade continue to be negligence and employment law concerns. Furthermore, more business- and consumer-friendly dispute resolution and risk management techniques will be developed and implemented to help avoid and resolve liability issues.

References

Browning, Lolita. 1996. "Olympics '96. Is there An Arbitrator In The House?" *Texas Lawyer* July 22.

Mihoces, Gary. 1995. "Lawsuits Overshadow Youth League Playoff." *USA Today* August 17.

Reuben, Richard. 1995. "The Lawyer Turned Peacemaker." *ABA Journal* August.

Scorecard. 1995. "Illegal Hold." *Sport Illustrated* March 6.

Chapter 39

Trends and Issues in Risk Management for Recreational Sport Programs

No longer will risk management planning be viewed as a necessary evil, rather it will be considered a management priority.

Sarah J. Young

Sport is of major importance in American society. Not only is it important from a business perspective, with an emphasis upon professional sport and collegiate sport, but sport is extremely significant in its contributions to society from a recreational perspective. Recreational sport programs provide opportunities for a diverse spectrum of participation in a variety of settings reaching unprecedented levels.

Risk is inherent in any sport and without it sport would lack the challenge that attracts many participants. However, from a liability perspective, risk is viewed as something to be eliminated. For managers of recreational sport programs, the task becomes a balancing act of providing an environment where sport programs and activities can take place safely yet are exciting, challenging and risky enough to attract participant interest. While management of risk is a top priority for most recreational sport managers today, the question of what is the appropriate balance of risk still remains.

The likelihood that an administrator will be a defendant in a sport-related lawsuit has increased over the last three decades. Appenzeller (2004) indicates that sport-related litigation has become a multimillion dollar industry. Litigation has become so common to the administrator of recreational sport programs that risk management and a fundamental knowledge of liability and the law have become an essential part of the professional preparation for the 21st century administrator. Traditionally, administrators of recreational sport programs have been reactive to liability claims and risk hazards. Yet, instead of being reactive to liability and risk management problems facing recreational sport programs it behooves administrators to play more of a preventive role in confronting liability and risk management trends and issues. Therefore, it is certainly to the advantage of the administrator to stay abreast of current trends in liability and risk management in order to understand the implications and plan for the future in recreational sports.

In light of litigation in recreational sport over the past three decades, an appropriate question to ask is: What does the future hold in terms of liability and risk management for administrators of recreation and sport programs? Over a decade ago, Huber (1990) speculated that current societal trends in litigation would continue as "newly established legal principles are deployed to open up fresh areas of litigation" (p. 9). Judicial decisions concerning liability are indeed helpful in indicating precedence, but equally important is the contribution of research to the problem of anticipating what the future holds. In a review of the literature, a study by Young (1998) used forecasting methodology to determine the key liability and risk management trends in the delivery of recreational sport programs in public, private and commercial settings through the year 2020. A review of that study and its results follows.

Key Liability and Risk Management Trends Study

The focus of the study was upon recreational sport settings in North America. Since there is such a diversity in the types of recreational sport settings, operational definitions were developed for each of these settings based upon a review of the literature. Settings labeled as commercial were defined as providing recreational sport experiences for profit with examples including fitness clubs, family-fun centers and resorts. Public settings were characterized as government agencies providing recreational sport services to meet people's leisure needs without regard to ability to pay, occupational status, or any other distinction which restricts recreational sport to special groups (Russell, 2002). Examples of the public setting included municipal recreational sport programs, recreational sport programs at public colleges and universities, and military recreation programs. Finally, private settings were defined as organizations providing recreational sport experiences for their members (Edginton, Jordan, DeGraaf & Edginton, 1998). Examples of private settings included private clubs, recreational sport programs at private colleges and universities, and non-profit organizations.

The research method employed was the Delphi technique, which is based upon the collective opinion of knowledgeable experts, and is frequently used as a forecasting method. Because the Delphi relies upon knowledgeable experts, a panel was comprised of recreational sport administrators representing the commercial, private and public settings along with scholars who had studied liability and risk management in recreational sport settings. A group of 69 experts representing 32 states and Canada agreed to serve as the panel for this study. Through a series of three Delphi rounds administered via a website, the panel of experts obtained consensus on 11 key trends they perceived would greatly impact the delivery of recreational sport into the 21st century. Table 1 contains a list of the trends resulting from the study.

Trend Implications

The emergence of key trends from the study was significant and noteworthy from a research perspective. Yet without a discussion of the implications of the trends, this study is of little value to professionals in the field as well as recreation and sport management students preparing for careers in recreational sport. It is also important to note that while the study focused on recreational sport settings in public, private and commercial settings, the results and implications of the study also apply to other sport settings. Facility managers

**Table 1. Top Rated Trends Impacting the Delivery of
Recreational Sport Through 2020**

1. Liability issues will continue to manifest as problems requiring sound risk management plans.

2. Sport managers must continue to educate themselves in risk management in an attempt to provide safer programs.

3. Risk management will continue to be a key element in the design of recreational sport facilities.

4. There will be an increase in the number of people with disabilities participating in recreational sport programs.

5. Professional preparation in liability and risk management will become more important for students pursuing careers in sport management.

6. Risk management planning will take on increased importance to recreational sport programs.

7. More recreational sport programs/agencies will develop comprehensive risk management plans.

8. There will be an increased demand for employee certification in specialized activity programs (i.e., aerobic leaders, aquatics personnel, etc.).

9. Sport equipment manufacturers and recreational sport managers will continue to provide safer and more protective equipment so that individuals do not suffer as much risk of injury from potential defects in products.

10. There will be an increase in willingness of participants to engage in litigation to resolve issues related to participation in recreational sport.

11. There will be increased demand for the requirement of safety equipment to be worn by recreational sport participants.

of professional sport arenas and stadia, college and high school athletic directors and varsity-level coaches can all find value in the results of this study. Therefore, what follows is a discussion of the implications of each trend.

1. Liability issues will continue to manifest as problems requiring sound risk management plans.

The future implication of this trend is fairly straightforward in that it underscores the importance of a risk management plan. As immunity has eroded and continues to disappear as a defense to negligence, the only way for recreational sport agencies to deal with liability is through sound risk management. Recreational sport programs must have a risk management plan in place which is not only functional, but also updated on a regular basis. Implementation of these risk management plans cannot be the exclusive responsibility of the administrator, or even of a designated risk manager, but of all staff members in the organization. This trend also implies the importance of recreational sport practitioners being proactive rather than reactive in regard to risk management. A future issue which spins off of this trend is the changing standard of care. What is currently considered a safe or accepted practice may not be considered as such by the year 2020. The implication of this issue is that risk management plans cannot be static, but must evolve with the parallel changes in society. As a result, administrators must be ready to devote time and resources to continuous updating of these plans. Another issue that evolved from this was an increased cost of programs as a result of the agency resources being spent on the development of comprehensive risk management plans which makes it more costly for individuals to participate in programs.

2. Education in risk management strategies will continue to be in demand by sport managers seeking to provide safer programs.

Education in risk management strategies currently is a part of the training for recreational sport managers; however, to avoid litigation and provide a safe environment which encourages participation, this type of education will become a requirement, not only in the form of preparing new professionals for the field but as continuing education for practitioners currently in the field. Knowledge and practice in risk management strategies will not only be the expectation for those individuals serving in administrative roles, but will become a criterion for the selection of administrators and managers in the future. Another implication is the requirement of a risk management certification process for practitioners in recreational sport. Colleges and universities providing the training for sport managers will need to offer a comprehensive risk management curriculum. The curriculum must be a balance between theoretical and practical application but it also is up-to-date and aligned with current realities. While more training and certification will be available, it will still be at the discretion of each practitioner to use sound and reasonable judgment in making program decisions.

Educational and specialized certification requirements will inevitably increase for recreational sport manager positions. This could result in the industry being viewed more favorably by consumers as well as result in the achievement of higher safety standards. An issue that could evolve from the additional training and certifications, however, may be an increased standard of care that creates a greater responsibility or burden for the recreational sport manager. If practitioners become a part of a risk management team within their organization or agency, the team concept will provide a diversity of perspectives in approaching and working for solutions that are sensible and effective. Another issue that evolved from this trend was who the facilitators of this on-going educational process should be. Professional organizations may come to play a role in providing training for instructors and facilitators of risk management workshops and seminars.

3. Risk management will continue to be a key element in the design of new recreational sport facilities.

A future implication of this trend is the necessity of state-of-the-art recreational sport facilities. Because of the vast knowledge of risk management and facility design gained over the past 20 years, administrators will continue to be more aware of faulty designs. Another implication of this trend is the involvement of more than just architects in the plans for a new facility. Program and maintenance staff as well as risk management personnel should review facility designs before they become final. Administrators can use accident data and accident investigation reports to assist in making facilities safer. While facilities more likely will be safer as a result of implementing these strategies, they could also be more expensive. As accessibility issues take a more prominent role in the design of new facilities, it is important for the recreational sport administrator to choose his/her architect carefully.

4. There will be an increase in the number of people with disabilities participating in recreational sport programs.

This trend is almost certain to occur and the underlying theme is a manageable situation in regard to risk management issues. Some future implications of this trend are special training for programmers to be better equipped to meet the needs of this group, specialized or modified equipment and a lower ratio of supervisors to participants. The challenge of this trend occurs not in the risk management plan, but in providing programming that can accommodate the diversity of participants with disabilities. The Americans with Disabilities Act has paved the way for this trend to come to fruition and it will continue to be further defined by case law.

5. Professional preparation in liability and risk management will become more important for students pursuing careers in sport management.

Professional preparation in liability and risk management is important now but in the future it should become a well-established part of the training of new recreational sport managers. As students prepare for their first full-time, professional position in recreational sport management, they must understand and be ready to assume liability for their programs. Some of the implications of this trend deal with college curricula in recreational sport management. Existing college curricula must change in the future to reflect this needed training and must train students to engage in proactive and preventive risk management planning. Besides a solid grounding in risk management, additional specialized courses in business law, contracts, torts and labor law will be required rather than available only as elective courses. As this type of professional preparation becomes the norm, a "ripple-effect" will be the revision of job descriptions to reflect the higher standard of proof of education and/or experience in risk management. Employers will view training and education in liability and risk management as essential and those candidates without it may not find jobs.

There will be a necessity for collaboration between educators and practitioners in recreational sport management. Such a collaborative effort would assist both educators and practitioners to stay in tune with current liability and risk management issues. One issue that could evolve from this trend is the increased time and money that students may have to spend in order to obtain adequate training in this area. Another issue that evolved was the background, experience and credentials of the individual(s) instructing the students in these courses. While individuals with law degrees and experience in practicing law bring technical knowledge about the law into the classroom, educators with training in sport programming and a good understanding of liability and risk management may provide even more adequate preparation for students without losing sight of the value of sport participation.

6. Risk management planning will take on increased importance to recreational sport programs.

A risk management plan will become a selling point for recreational sport programs, both for employees who work in the program and participants in the program. No longer will risk management planning be viewed as a necessary evil, rather it will be considered a management priority. More comprehensive risk management training for employees will become the standard of the industry, along with risk orientation programs for participants. There will be a greater awareness by the recreational sport manager of the issues which have created claims against the agency. This awareness will guide the actions of the agency in the future related to facility design, programs and staff training. A further implication of this trend will be that future risk management planning will force the administrator to be more proactive in facing and accepting liability. Planning followed by implementation and practice of safety procedures will become the industry standard. An additional implication of increased risk management planning and prevention that was mentioned by the panel of experts was that play could become so regulated that the leisure satisfaction of participants may be reduced to the point that some participants will discontinue their participation.

7. More recreational sport programs/agencies will develop comprehensive risk management plans.

Practitioners already have recognized the importance that risk management plays in the program's existence and that through the development of a comprehensive risk management plan, their programs and participants will benefit. The implications of developing a comprehensive risk management plan are enhanced staff training, hiring of staff to develop such a plan and developing plans that are realistic. Enhanced staff training will involve employees developing foresight and becoming more proactive in preventing hazardous situations rather than only being reactive to problems. Agencies may find themselves hiring risk managers or consultants to develop comprehensive risk plans and to periodically update them. Another future implication was that some programs or agencies could likely be put out of business for lack of planning, or for not fully implementing a plan. An issue which could evolve from this trend is that through the development of comprehensive risk management plans the corresponding tasks to implement the plan may become so idealistic that they become counter-productive to the provision of safe, fun recreational sport programs.

8. There will be an increased demand for employee certification in specialized activity programs (i.e., aerobics leaders, aquatics personnel, etc.).

As recreational sport participation becomes more diverse, specialized certification will be imminent. For some states this could be state licensure for professionals wishing to work in a particular state. Another implication is the possibility of certification demanding increased salaries or dictating additional pay scales. The primary issues of this trend deal with the entire certification process. A further implication is the quality and value of certifications being developed, encompassing the questions: Who should certify? How is certification updated? Who establishes the standards? What are the minimum qualifications for certification and how far beyond the minimum qualifications should professionals be required to go? An implication might be the establishment of an accrediting agency which determines the value of the certification as well as its administration. Certification may even be replaced in the future with professional development programs which require employees to attend continuing education programs or refresher courses. In turn this could mean an increase in costs of the program which is usually passed along to the participant. Because of the number of questions, it is clear that more study of the certification issue is needed.

9. Sport equipment manufacturers and recreational sport managers will continue to provide safer and more protective equipment so that individuals do not suffer injuries from potential defects in products.

While providing for the safety of participants is a top priority, the primary implication of this trend is that equipment will become more expensive. The money versus safety issue is directly related to this implication in that safety may be sacrificed because it becomes cost prohibitive. Product research and development must continue on the part of the manufacturers with input from recreational sport managers playing an increasingly important role. Another implication for the manufacturer is the provision of clear instructions and visible warnings on products. An implication for the recreational sport manager is staying current with product research and design to make the best possible decisions in purchasing safety equipment. Additionally, recreational sport managers must maintain the equipment according to manufacturers' recommendations. Managers will also have to deal with the issue of how to require the use of equipment by participants. Should there be mandatory requirements before a participant is allowed to play? This question brings up an additional issue of whether safety equipment really protect the user, or does it give the participant a false sense of security? The future will more than likely call for a combination of safety equipment and rule modifications to improve safety and reduce liability.

10. There will be an increase in willingness of participants to engage in litigation to resolve issues related to participation in recreational sport.

While the consensus of the panel of experts was that this trend serves simply as a reflection of society in the United States, recreational sport seems to be an especially attractive target for litigation. Recreation and sport managers will need to be educated in the operational aspects of lawsuits. For example, administrators and managers need to learn how to be good witnesses and how to prepare records that can serve as strong supportive documentation in a court of law. Administrators of recreational sport programs will need to emphasize loss exposures and prevention in their risk management plans, understand legal defense principles, and seek training in accident investigation. Budgets for recreational sport programs will have to accommodate a category or line item for attorney fees and court costs. Another implication of this trend could be the continued elimination of some recreational sport activities because of their risky nature. An implication that counters this trend is that the courts will begin to limit awards and hold individuals more accountable for their own actions. As participants learn more about the legal requirement of shared responsibility they may not be so eager to engage in litigation because they are less likely to win their case. An issue that could evolve from this trend is that alternative dispute strategies will be implemented more frequently to resolve situations that arise. This alternative to litigation may lessen the impact of this trend upon the delivery of recreational sport programs.

11. There will be increased demand for the requirement of safety equipment to be worn by recreational sport participants.

Although this trend is similar to a previously mentioned one, the focus is upon enforcement of the policy. The biggest challenge for the recreational sport manager will be upon policing and enforcing the use of mandatory safety equipment once the policies have been implemented to require such equipment. While the implication of this trend is that the wearing of safety equipment must become the norm and not simply a recommendation by the sport manager, another implication is that some individuals may drop out of sport rather than be mandated to wear or use such protective equipment. The key issues that evolve from this trend are the participants' freedom to choose how they will participate as well as in what type of risk-taking activity they choose. While this trend is consumer-driven, the recreational sport manager will have to undertake a public awareness campaign to sell the idea to participants. As participants become more educated in how certain pieces of equipment help them avoid injury, there will be a greater demand for such equipment. Another implication for the recreational sport manager regarding safety equipment programs is the cost of purchasing equipment. As the cost of equipment increases this cost will be passed along to the consumer, forcing user fees to increase. A final implication of this trend is the inspection and maintenance of equipment by the recreational sport agency. Managers will have to be more accountable in their maintenance and replacement procedures for protective equipment.

Summary

A theme that was by far most apparent in the discussion of implications for all the top-rated trends as well as for many of the trends that did not rate as high on the impact scale was the emphasis upon risk management planning. The implementation of appropriate and adequate risk management plans for recreational sport programs was viewed by the panel of experts as the key factor in being able to manage the challenges created by a litigious society. Insurance carriers for recreational sport agencies and programs will demand that providers demonstrate proof of adequate risk management. This emphasis upon risk management led to several other sub-themes echoed by the jury. Risk management should not be the job of just one staff person, but should play a role in the job descriptions of every staff member working for a recreational sport program—even volunteers! Yet, while it was acknowledged that everyone should be attuned to risk management, there is a greater likelihood that more agencies will look for risk management specialists or consultants to develop plans, monitor their implementation and regularly update those plans. The emphasis upon adequate risk management also promotes a proactive approach to facing the challenges created by liability. In order to be effective risk managers, recreational sport professionals must be proactive rather than reactive.

Another theme which served as a common denominator for almost all of the top-rated trends was the importance of education in risk management. Preparation of the new professional entering the field and continuing education for practitioners currently in the field was viewed as paramount to the success of a recreational sport program in providing the safest programs possible. Because judicial decisions are made almost everyday which can affect the delivery of a recreational sport program, any type of education or training program in risk management must be current with the most recent precedence as well as aligned with realistic expectations. A by-product of the educational theme was the role of professional organizations in facilitating continuing education in risk management. Professional organizations affiliated with recreational sport programs in different settings seem to be the natural place for professionals to seek the additional education and training that they need to stay current in liability and risk management issues.

A final theme that emerged from the implications discussion was the development of standards and related certification. As the industry raises the standard of care to fit societal needs and attitudes, there were several issues that evolved. This theme raised many concerns and questions from the jury: Who should be responsible for developing the standards? Will there be a universal standard of care for all recreational sport activities, or should the diversity of programs dictate the number and level of standards? Who should police and enforce compliance to the standard? The answers to these questions are not simple, nor is the development of an appropriate standard of care. Yet, this may be the opportunity for professional organizations closely related to recreational sport to work at finding answers to these questions. If the standard of care does change in the coming years, and the demand for certification, both in specialized areas and in risk management, does become a requirement for employment, then the door is open for professional organizations to fill the gap in terms of training and certification.

References

Appenzeller, H. (2004). *Managing sport and risk management strategies, 2nd edition.* Durham, NC: Carolina Academic Press.

Edginton, C. R., Jordan, D. J., DeGraaf, D. G., & Edginton, S. R. (1998). *Leisure and life satisfaction.* Boston, MA: WCB McGraw-Hill.

Huber, P. W. (1990). *Liability The Revolution and Its Consequences.* New York: Basic Books, Inc. Publishers.

Russell, R. V. (2002). *Pastimes: The context of contemporary leisure.* Madison, WI: Brown and Benchmark Publishers.

Young, S. J. (1998). Perceived liability and risk management trends and issues impacting the delivery of recreational sport programs into the 21st century. (Doctoral dissertation, Indiana University, 1998). *Dissertation Abstracts International, 60*(02), 548A.

About the Authors

Herb Appenzeller, EdD, Editor, was an athletics director for 40 years on the secondary, junior college and senior college level. He has edited or authored 22 books in sport management, risk management and sport law. He is a member of eight sport halls of fame and the recipient of numerous national honors and recognitions. He is co-editor of the sport law newsletter *From The Gym To The Jury*. He conducts risk reviews of college and university sport programs and venues on a national basis. He has made presentations on a state and national level on risk management in sport and serves as a consultant to sport programs. Herb Appenzeller retired from Guilford College after 37 years as the Jefferson-Pilot Professor of Sport Management Emeritus. For the next four years he was adjunct professor in the graduate sport administration at the University of North Carolina at Chapel Hill and for three years he was Executive-in-Residence in the sport management graduate program at Appalachian State University. He received the 2004 NASPE award for outstanding achievement in sport management.

Elizabeth Appenzeller is in her third year as the head cheerleading coach at Coastal Carolina University. Her 2010 All-Girl team finished 17th at UCA Nationals and her 2011 Small Co-Ed team finished 4th at NCA Nationals.

Appenzeller came to Coastal Carolina after being the assistant cheerleading coach at Wingate University in Wingate, N.C. While at Wingate, she helped facilitate practices, tryouts and tumbling lessons. She was the head cheerleading coach and spirit liaison at Greensboro College in Greensboro, N.C., from 2006–2008. Appenzeller not only managed the cheerleading team and mascots at Greensboro, but also organized fundraising and community service opportunities, managed the budget, created football and basketball game scripts and coordinated promotional activities as well as game day and halftime entertainment. Prior to Greensboro College, she was the assistant coach at High Point University in High Point, N.C., from 2005–2006, where she managed mascot appearances, created a recruiting database and helped facilitate practices and tryouts.

Appenzeller also worked at the Sport Management Group in Greensboro, N.C., starting in 2005 and was the cheerleading director at the Spears Family YMCA in Greensboro. She is certified by the Certified American Association of Cheerleaders, Coaches and Advisors (AACCA), the Certified National Council for Spirit Safety and Education (NCSSE) and holds a Cheer Ltd. National Cheer Judges Certification.

Appenzeller has a bachelor's degree in history and criminal justice from Guilford College in Greensboro, N.C. She has a master's of science in sport studies from High Point. Appenzeller was a cheerleader at Guilford as well as being on the women's tennis and women's soccer teams. She also is the co-author of *Cheerleading and the Law: Risk Management Strategies for Cheerleading*.

Thomas Appenzeller, EdD, is Professor of Sport Management at Catawba College. The former Assistant Athletic Director at Chowan College and Athletic Director at

Riverheads High School, Appenzeller received his EdD from the University of North Carolina, Greensboro, his master's degree from the University of Massachusetts in sport management and in history education from the University of North Carolina, Greensboro. An alumnus of Presbyterian College in Clinton, South Carolina, Appenzeller has coached football on the college level for 17 years and was a high school teacher, coach, and administrator on the interscholastic level for 12 years. Tom is the author of *Youth Sport and the Law.*

T. Ross Bailey, MEd, AT,C, LAT, now in his 26th year as the Head Athletic Trainer at Texas Christian University, is responsible for coordinating the athletic health care, injury recognition, and rehabilitation needs of Horned Frog student-athletes. He also directs the CAAHEP (AMA) approved Athletic Training Curriculum major in the Department of Kinesiology—the athletic training program is among the top programs in the country. He is certified by NATA and licensed by the State of Texas. He received both his BS and MEd degrees from Texas Christian University. He is the former chairman of the District Six-SWATA College and University Athletic Trainers Committee and is an associate in the Justin Sports Medicine Program. He now sits on NATA's Entry Level Education Committee and the Administrative Services Committee of the Texas Board of Athletic Training.

Richard T. Ball is a trial lawyer who specializes in sports injury matters. Now retired from the full-time practice of law, he serves as a consultant and educator in the field of sports risk management. Ball has written numerous publications and produced several videos pertaining to sports injury prevention and risk management issues, and teaches university graduate courses on such subjects.

Martin E. Block, PhD, is an Associate Professor with the Kinesiology Program in the Curry School of Education at the University of Virginia. His specialty is adapted physical education, and he serves as Director of the Masters Program in Adapted Physical Education at the University of Virginia. Dr. Block has published over 50 articles and conducted over 100 presentations in the area of adapted physical education. He also has authored or co-authored several chapters in books, and he is perhaps best known as the author of the popular text: "A teacher's guide to including students with disabilities in general physical education." Dr. Block served as Chair of the Adapted Physical Activity Council and Motor Development Academy within the American Alliance of Health, Physical Education, Recreation and Dance (AAHPERD). He currently serves on the editorial boards of *Adapted Physical Activity Quarterly, Mental Retardation and Teaching Elementary Physical Education.*

Tom Bowler has been involved in over 310 cases in the last 19 years through acting as an expert witness on behalf of either the plaintiff party or defendant party. He has testified at trials in New York State, Connecticut, Massachusetts and Maryland. Tom received his BS degree in physical education from the University of Connecticut in 1966. His master's degree (MEd) was earned at Springfield College in 1973 in physical education. Tom has a Certificate of Advanced Graduate Studies (CAGS30 credits) from the University of Connecticut in 1981, in the administration and supervision of special education. At Eastern Connecticut State University, Tom has been an adjunct, as well as director of intramurals and recreation. Tom was also an adjunct at Central Connecticut State University, teaching a course in "the application of tort law to physical activity." He taught a graduate course at Central entitled, "Sport, Physical Education, Athletics and the Law". He is certified by two nationally recognized playground agencies. He earned his Certified Playground Safety Inspector (CPSI) from the National Recreation and Park Association. Also, he earned his S.A.F.E. certification from the National Program for Playground Safety.

Robert J. Casmus has been head athletic trainer and instructor at Catawba College since 1990. He oversees the athletic health care and the athletic drug testing and education program of the Catawba athletes. A native of Sinking Spring, PA, Casmus earned a master's degree in exercise and sports science from the University of Arizona in 1985. During that time, he worked as head athletic trainer at Palo Verde High School. He earned a bachelor's degree in health education from Temple University in 1983 and during his time in the Pennsylvania area, he worked as an athletic trainer for St. John Neumann High School, and as a summer intern for the Philadelphia Eagles. In addition, Casmus completed the Advanced Athletic Training Program at West Chester University in 1983 and is a certified EMT in the state of North Carolina. Prior to his current position, Casmus was the head athletic trainer at Chowan College (1985–1990). He also volunteered at the 1987 Pan American Games and was an intern at the U.S. Olympic Training Center in 1988. He served on the athletic training staff for the 1990 Olympic Sports Festival in Minneapolis, MN. Casmus was the head athletic trainer for the United Football League exhibition game in Taipei, Taiwan in July of 1994. He served as a test site administrator for the BOC and is currently on the Board of Certification's examination development committee. Bob served two terms as the District III Representative to the NATA Public Relations Committee from 1998–2005. Bob completed his second and final term as the District III representative to the NATA Research and Education Foundation Board of Directors in June 2011. He also served two terms as the District III representative to the NATA College & University Athletic Trainers Committee. Currently, Casmus is the District III representative to the NATA Honors & Awards Committee and serves on the NATA Hall of Fame Committee. At the NATA National Convention in June 2005, Casmus received the Athletic Training Service Award from the NATA and the Dan Libera Service Award from the Board of Certification. Bob was named the North Carolina College & University Athletic Trainer of the Year in 2003 and in 2008. In 2007, he was named the NCAA Division II College and University Athletic Trainer of the Year by the NATA. Bob was appointed to the North Carolina Board of Athletic Trainer Examiners which oversees the licensure and practice act for certified athletic trainers in North Carolina. Bob also serves as a member of the Catawba College Community Emergency Response Team (CERT) and is a member of the Emergency Response Committee.

Annie Clement, PhD, JD, is Associate Professor of Sport Administration at the University of New Mexico. Dr. Clement is currently best known for her texts, *Law in Sport and Physical Activity, Legal Responsibility in Aquatics* and *Teaching Physical Activity*. One additional book, twenty book chapters, seventy articles, and over one hundred and fifty presentations are among her achievements. In-depth study of risk management, aquatics, intellectual property, antitrust, equal pay, and gender equity are a few of the areas in which her research and writing have been continuous. Annie holds a bachelor's degree from Minnesota, Duluth and a master's degree from Minnesota, Minneapolis. Her doctorate is from the University of Iowa and her juris doctorate from Cleveland State University. She also studied at Cambridge University and the University of Oslo. Unique honors for Dr. Clement include the Fellow of the American Bar Foundation (ABA), a distinction given to only one third of one percent of the ABA membership, the Nonprofit Lawyers Award, distinguished speaker at ten different universities, President of the National Association for Sport and Physical Education, President, Ohio Teacher Educators, the American Alliance for Health, Physical Education and Recreation Honor Award, Merit Award (Aquatic Council) and the Joy of Effort Award (NASPE). Also, she was a recipient of the Ohio (OAHPERD) Honor Award, Tsunami Spirit Award from the Aquatic Therapy and Rehab Institute, the Susan B. Anthony Award from Ohio NOW, and Honor Award from the Council for National Cooperation in Aquatics.

Michael Clopton is the former Administrative Assistant to the Head Coach (football) at the University of Oklahoma. A former Sooner quarterback, Clopton has been with the university's athletic department since his graduation in 1985. Starting in the business office, he was named travel coordinator in 1987, assistant business manager in 1991, and moved to the football office with the arrival of Coach Blake. He has written numerous articles for *Athletic Business,* and he is currently working in business.

Craig Eilbacher, EdD, ATC, LAT is an Assistant Professor and Program Coordinator of Sports Medicine Education in the Sport Studies Department at Guilford College. He received his MS in education from the University of Akron and his undergraduate degree in physical education from the University of North Carolina at Wilmington. Dr. Eilbacher worked as a graduate assistant in the Physical Education Department and also worked as a graduate athletic trainer for the Athletic Department at the University of Akron. He served as the head athletic trainer at Central Davidson High school for five years while teaching anatomy and physiology, sports medicine, biology, and physical education. He was also the assistant men's varsity basketball coach.

Currently, at Guilford College, Eilbacher teaches sports medicine courses including physical exam and assessment, therapeutic rehabilitation and modalities, health and wellness, and emergency procedures in sports medicine. When needed, Eilbacher also assists the athletic training staff in providing coverage for Guilford College athletics.

Eilbacher completed his EdD at the University of North Carolina at Greensboro in Kinesiology, where his research focus examined the perceived knowledge and behaviors of first responders for North Carolina high school football. He continues to play an active role in shaping the type of medical care being provided for high school athletes. Additionally, he is currently working with a local sports medicine physician (Dr. Bert Fields) on a statewide project to implement the use of automated external defibrillators in all public/private high schools and middle schools. He is actively engaged in the athletic training profession by serving as one of two college/university representatives on the North Carolina Athletic Trainers' Board of Directors.

Gil B. Fried is Professor and chairman, Department of Management and Sport Management, College of Business and Interdisciplinary Programs at the University of New Haven. Fried is a specialist in sport law, finance, and facility management. He received his masters in sport management and his law degree from The Ohio State University. He has written several books on sport risk management and sport finance. He lectures nationally on preventing sexual abuse in youth sport, ADA compliance, financial risk management, risk management, and sports violence. He has handled a large number of sport injury cases and has worked as an expert witness in various cases, from stadium stampedes to four ball cases. He also serves on several board of directors of sport-related businesses and organizations. Besides his teaching, he coordinates the graduate program in Management of Sports Industries and the internships for the School of Business. He has an active consulting practice named Gil Fried & Associates, LLC and one of his major clients is OR&L Facility Management, where he serves as Director of Risk Management for several million square feet of public assembly facility space (government, office, and school facilities). In 2011 Fried received the Betty van der Smissen Leadership Award from SRLA.

Paul L. Gaskill, EdD, is Director and Professor in the Recreation Management Program in the Department of Health, Leisure and Exercise Science at Appalachian State University. He earned his BS in recreation administration from The Pennsylvania State University, MS in recreation administration from The University of North Carolina at Chapel Hill, and his EdD in higher education administration from The University of North Carolina at Greensboro. Gaskill has taught at Elon University for eight years and at Appalachian State University for eighteen years. He has authored numerous publications on recreation and sport administration and is currently editor of the *Introduction to Leisure Services in North Carolina* text.

J. Jason Halsey received his BA degree from the University of North Carolina at Chapel Hill, and his MA degree from Appalachian State University. He is a member of the Sport and Recreation Law Association (SRLA), the Sport Marketing Research Institute, the National Intramural-Recreational Sports Association, and the North American Society for Sport Management. Jason is currently the Director of Sport Clubs and the Risk Management Chair for the Department of Campus Recreation at the University of North Carolina at Chapel Hill. He also served as the Assistant Director of Intramurals and Club Sports at the University of Northern Colorado and holds a MA in sport administration from Appalachian State University.

David Harlowe graduated from Guilford College (Greensboro, NC) with a BS in sport management. He is president of the Sport Management Group with experience within the athletic and fitness industries. He was an intercollegiate athlete, coached on the college level, and was a Strength and Conditioning Coach for a minor league hockey team. David has worked in the front office of a minor league baseball team and has been a fitness facility owner. He has become one of the industry's leading experts in risk management and the many fields that make up sport management. He has personally performed over 1,500 risk reviews on fitness and athletic facilities nationwide. David is currently writing a bi-monthly article on fitness and recreation safety for *Fitness Management* magazine.

Terrill Johnson Harris is a partner with the law firm of Smith Moore, L.L.P. in Greensboro, North Carolina. She practices primarily in the areas of general litigation, health care, and administrative law. She has handled litigation in state and federal courts at the trial and appellate levels. She received her B.A, magna cum laude, with honors in politics, from Wake Forest University and was a member of Phi Beta Kappa. She received her JD, with honors, from Duke University School of Law, where she was a member of the *Duke Law Journal*.

Jerald D. Hawkins is Professor Emeritus and former Monica Martin Stranch Endowed Professor of Exercise Studies and Director of Sports Medicine at Lander University in Greenwood, South Carolina. A Fellow of the American College of Sports Medicine, Dr. Hawkins is a certified athletic trainer with broad expertise in exercise science and sports medicine. He has served on the sports medicine staff at numerous national and international sports events including the 1990 Goodwill Games, World Junior Luge Championships, and U.S. Olympic Festivals. The author of five books and numerous book chapters and articles, Dr. Hawkins is an active writer, speaker, and consultant in the areas of wellness, exercise science, legal issues in sport, and sports medicine.

David LaVetter, PhD, is currently Associate Professor and Director of the B.S. Sport Management and M.S. Sport Administration programs at Arkansas State University, Jonesboro, AR. Previous to his pursuits as an academician, LaVetter spent 12 years employed in intercollegiate athletics as a basketball coach and administrator (NCAA Divisions I and II, and junior college). His administrative responsibilities in college athletics included marketing, game operations, development, and academic services/compliance. His specialized research of transportation policy and practice in amateur sport organizations has appeared in *Athletic Business, Athletic Management, Community College Journal of Research & Practice, Journal of Sport Administration & Supervision*, and *NCAA News*. His research has also been presented at national and international conferences:

AAHPERD, SRLA, Athletic Business, EASM, NASSM, and CSRI. Over the last 10 years, Dr. LaVetter has taught courses in Legal Issues in Sport, Risk Management in Sport, Facility & Event Management, and Ethical Issues in Sport. He earned the Higher Educator of the Year (2007) from ArkAHPERD. He has served on boards for *Journal of Youth Sport*, Southern AAHPERD, and Sport & Recreational Law Association. Additionally, he has served as legal counsel for school transportation liability cases. LaVetter holds a PhD in sport administration from the University of New Mexico, an MS in educational leadership from University of Nevada-Las Vegas, and a BS in social sciences at the University of Utah, where he participated as a football athlete.

Leonard K. Lucenko is professor emeritus of Montclair State University where he has been the Coordinator of Recreation Professions Program. He is a former coach of soccer and track at the University. Dr. Lucenko has been part of the playground safety and risk management effort as a Certified Playground Safety Inspector of the NRPA and NPPS, member of ASTM, and other playground organizations. He has presented playground safety programs at the National Elementary School Principals Association, Sport and Recreation Law Association, and the New Jersey Recreation and Park Association.

David R. Maraghy is a sports attorney with more than 25 years in the sports industry. He oriented and managed golf events around the world, such as the 1995 Hyundai Motor Golf Classic in Seoul, Korea. He founded the VCU Sports Center at Virginia Commonwealth University, a graduate program offering the Master's Degree in Sports Leadership. He served as Director of the program until he founded Sports Management International, LLC (SMI), a Richmond, Virginia-based company in professional sports management and marketing firm specializing in golf. Corporate clients include Kiawah Island Resort, world famous Ocean Course, the PGA Tour and Virginia Tourism Corporation. Maraghy is currently teaching at the Elon University Law School.

Kenny Morgan received his BA from the University of North Carolina at Chapel Hill and a MA in sport management from Appalachian State University. He is currently the Account Manager for the Charlotte Bobcats and the Charlotte Bobcats Arena for Show Pros Entertainment Services of Charlotte. He held the same position for the Carolina Panthers and Bank of America Stadium from 2003 to 2005. In addition to his work with the NFL and the NBA, Morgan has been a part of management teams associated with the 2005 Greater New York Billy Graham Crusade, the PGA's Wachovia Championship and Greater Greensboro Open, multiple ACC and NCAA Men's Basketball Tournaments, Division I and IAA college football and over 200 concerts and special events. He has previously authored a chapter in *Managing Sports* (2004).

John Miller received his doctorate at the University of New Mexico in Sport Administration. He is currently the Associate Dean of the College of Health and Human Services at Troy University in Troy, Alabama. He has more than 40 publications in sport management in peer-reviewed academic journals, 20 book chapters, more than 100 presentations at national and international conferences, and serves on six editorial review boards of nationally recognized sport management journals. He has also served as President of the Sport and Recreation Law Association and chair of the Safety and Risk Management Council. He has recently been selected as the Editor for the *Journal of Legal Aspects of Sport*.

Frederick O. Mueller is a Professor of Exercise and Sport Science at the University of North Carolina at Chapel Hill. He is also the Director of the National Center for Catastrophic Sports Injury Research and the Research Director for the National Operating Committee on Standards for Athletic Equipment. The National Center collects catastrophic (death and permanent disability) sports injury data for high schools and colleges on a national level.

Barbara Osborne, JD is an Associate Professor and teaches undergraduate and graduate courses in the department of Exercise and Sport Science at the University of North Carolina at Chapel Hill. Osborne coordinated the graduate specialization in sport administration from 2001–2008. She is currently coordinator of the undergraduate program and co-directs the dual degree program in law and sport administration. Osborne advises graduate students and directs independent study and honors research. Her research focuses on legal and women's issues in intercollegiate athletics. Osborne is also adjunct professor at the School of Law, where she teaches a sports law course. She is faculty advisor for the Sport and Entertainment Law Society student organization and directs independent study as well as identifying sports-related externship experiences. Prior to her appointment at UNC, she worked for 14 years as an administrator in intercollegiate athletics. Osborne has an undergraduate degree in communications from the University of Wisconsin-Parkside, a master's degree in sport administration from Boston University, a law degree from Boston College and is licensed to practice law in Massachusetts and North Carolina. She also has experience as a competitive athlete, coach, public relations coordinator, television sports commentator, publisher, and sports information director. Osborne's current research focuses on women's leadership in intercollegiate athletics and legal issues in college sport.

Gary Rizza, MEd, ATC, LAT, has been Head Athletic Trainer at Guilford College since 2009. Before coming to Guilford College, Gary was Director of Sports Medicine Outreach for Therasport in Eden, NC from 1990–2009, providing medical coverage for local high schools and providing marketing and public relations services. He also served as head athletic trainer for McMichael High School and for Rockingham Community College's baseball and basketball teams. Gary spent six years as assistant athletic and instructor at Massachusetts Institute of Technology where he worked with 37 varsity sport teams, and served as football's Head Athletic Trainer. In addition, Gary worked as the clinical supervisor for athletic training student from neighboring Northeastern University and coordinated MIT's health and fitness center. Gary received his bachelor's degree in physical education with athletic training /business and industry in 1982 from Boston State College and 1989 received a master's degree in human movement from Boston University. Gary was selected to travel abroad and teach in Australia. While in Australia, Gary worked with an Australian Rules Football Team. He has participated as an athletic trainer in a variety of international competitions, including the 1990 Goodwill games and the 1984 Olympic Soccer Tournament. Gary has also completed short assignments with the national football league's New York Giants, the United States Olympic Training Center, United States Luge Association and the 2010 United States Figure Skating Championships, held in Greensboro, NC.

Gary Rushing, EdD is Department Chair of the Human Performance Department at Minnesota State University, Mankato. He teaches both undergraduate and graduate courses in Sport Law, as well as Facility Design/Management, Principles of Sport Management, and Leadership/Management of Sport. Rushing is a member of the North American Society of Sport Management (NASSM), American Alliance for Health, Physical Education, Recreation and Dance (AAHPERD), Minnesota Alliance of Health Physical Education Recreation and Dance MAHPERD, and the Sport and Recreation Law Association (SRLA). Rushing taught at the high school (8 years) and college levels (20 years) and coached at the high school (8 years) and college (13 years) levels. He has been both a head coach and an assistant football coach and head and assistant wrestling coach. Dr. Rushing's primary research area is Sport Law and he is published in several law reporters and coaching journals. He has book chapters in the following: *Sport Law for Sport Managers, Athletic Protective Equipment, and Successful Sport Management*

John Sadler is president of Sadler & Company, Inc., which specializes in insuring sports and recreation organizations in all 50 states. The client base includes over 5,000 local organizations and many national, regional, and state organizations. Sadler graduated Magna Cum Laude from the University Of South Carolina in 1983 with degrees in insurance and finance. Sadler also graduated from the University Of South Carolina School Of Law in 1986 and is licensed by the South Carolina Bar. In addition, he holds the Certified Insurance Counselor professional designation. Sadler is the risk manager for over 15 national sports organizations; is the risk management and sports insurance faculty member for the Academy For Youth Sports Administrators (AYSA), which is a division of the National Alliance for Youth Sports (NAYS); and sits on the Medical and Safety Advisory Committee of USA Baseball.

David Scott, EdD, is an Associate Professor of Sport Administration at the University of New Mexico and Associate Dean for Research and Information Management in the College of Education. He earned his bachelor's degree from Texas A&M University, a master's from Midwestern State University and a doctorate from the University of Northern Colorado.

He was a teacher and coach in both public schools and college for 17 years prior to assuming a faculty role at the University of New Mexico. Currently, he teaches undergraduate courses in fitness management and graduate courses in Sport Administration. His primary teaching and research focus is in the area of sport organizational behavior, with emphasis on leadership and organizational culture. He also has interest in leadership as it relates to crisis management. Dr. Scott enjoys consulting and conducting workshops dealing with various aspects of management training for coaches and sport administrators.

Todd L. Seidler is currently Professor and coordinator of the graduate program in Sport Administration at the University of New Mexico, one of only a few programs that offer both the Master's and Doctorate in Sport Administration. He received his bachelor's degree in physical education from San Diego State University and then taught and coached in high school. He then went to graduate school and earned his master's and PhD in sports administration from the University of New Mexico. Prior to returning to UNM, Dr. Seidler spent six years the coordinator of the graduate Sports Administration Program at Wayne State University and then coordinated the undergraduate Sport Management Program at Guilford College. He is Past President of the Society for the Study of Legal Aspects of Sport and Physical Activity (SSLASPA), contributing editor to *From The Gym To The Jury* newsletter, past chair of the Sport Management Council and of the Council on Facilities and Equipment within AAHPHERD.

Julian Stein is Adjunct Professor in Physical Education at the University of Tennessee, Knoxville. Between 1966 and 1981, Stein served as Director of the Project on Recreation and Fitness for the Mentally Retarded, and Executive Director and National Consultant for the Unit on Programs for the Handicapped/Physical Education and Recreation for the Handicapped, Information and Research Utilization Center of the American Alliance for Health, Physical Education, Recreation, and Dance. He also served two years as Chair of the AAHPER (D) Task Force on Recreation and Fitness for the Mentally Retarded. Stein has conducted over 1,000 national and international programs focusing on various aspects of physical education, recreation, and sport for persons with disabilities. He has written extensively on this subject besides serving as Editor for the Journal of the International Council for Health, Physical Education, Recreation, Sport, and Dance and

Associate Editor of *Palaestra: Forum of Sport, Physical Education, and Recreation for the Disabled*. Stein has been involved in legislation development relating directly to physical education, recreation, and sport for persons with disabilities and was responsible for the addition of aquatics in the definition of physical education in P.L. 94-142—The Education for All Handicapped Children Act.

Travis Teague has served in many capacities related to teaching and research in higher education. He is the former program coordinator of the Motorsport Management Program at Winston-Salem State University. He is now the Dean of the School of Sport Sciences at Wingate University. He has served in leadership positions with the Society of Manufacturing Engineers, including being the chair of the National Motor Sports Education Advisory Committee. Teague also served as the President of the Sport Management Association of the North Carolina Alliance for Athletics, Health, Physical Education, Recreation and Dance. His primary areas of research and scholarly activity focus upon workforce development and diversity within motor sport as well as crowd dynamics and risk management.

Richard A. Weintraub, MD, FACC, is a graduate of Boston University and Georgetown School of Medicine. He is actively engaged in the private practice of clinical and interventional cardiology in Greensboro, North Carolina. Dr. Weintraub has a special interest in and has published many papers on the subject of acute intervention in mycardial infarction. He has special interests in Coronary, peripheral vascular diseases, electrophysiology, interventions and cardiac device implantation. He is Board Certified in Internal Medicine, Cardiology, Peripheral Vascular Disease, Cardiac Device implantation, and Coronary CT angiography.

Weintraub holds fellowships in multiple medical societies, including the American College of Physicians; American College of Cardiology; American College of Chest Physicians; Society of Coronary Angiography and Interventions; Society of Vascular Medicine; and Society of Angiology. He is an author and co-author of numerous scientific medical articles and text book chapters (including "Sudden Death in Competitive Athletes").

Michael J. Welch, PhD, currently serves as manager of the Emergency Preparedness and Chronic Disease Programs for the Richmond City Department of Public Health. He serves on the Board of Directors of the Hayes E. Willis Health Center and is Chair of the Richmond City Fitness Commission. He has held previous positions at Guilford College as the Associate Professor and Coordinator of Sports Medicine and Associate Professor and Director of Sports Medicine at the United States Military Academy at West Point.

Sarah J. Young, PhD, is an Associate Professor with the Department of Recreation, Park, and Tourism Studies at Indiana University. She earned her BS degree in recreation and park administration from Illinois State University, and earned both her PhD in leisure behavior with a minor in law, and her MS in recreational sport administration from Indiana University. Prior to becoming a full-time faculty member, she worked as Assistant Director of Intramural Sports for nine years with the Division of Recreational Sports at Indiana University. Dr. Young teaches courses in legal aspects of sport and recreation. Her research interests, which are published in a variety of journals, encompass sport management issues, legal and risk management issues in recreation and sport, sport and health issues, and scholarship of teaching.

Index